D0824580

SOMETHING ABOUT THE AUTHOR

SOMETHING ABOUT THE AUTHOR

Facts and Pictures about Authors and Illustrators of Books for Young People

ANNE COMMIRE

VOLUME 23

GALE RESEARCH COMPANY
BOOK TOWER
DETROIT, MICHIGAN
48226

Editor: Anne Commire

Associate Editors: Agnes Garrett, Helga P. McCue

Assistant Editors: Dianne H. Anderson, Susette A. Balogh, Kathryn T. Floch, Mary F. Glahn, D. Jayne Higo, Linda Shedd, Susan L. Stetler, Victoria H. Welling

Consultant: Adele Sarkissian

Sketchwriters: Rosemary DeAngelis Bridges, Mark Eisman, Barbara G. Farnan

Research Assistant: Kathleen Betsko

Editorial Assistants: Lisa Bryon, Susan Pfanner, Elisa Ann Sawchuk

Production Supervisor: Nancy Nagy

Cover Design: Arthur Chartow

Special acknowledgment is due to the members of the *Contemporary Authors* staff who assisted in the preparation of this volume.

Library of Congress Catalog Card Number 72-27107

ISBN 0-8103-0086-9
ISSN 0276-816X

Table of Contents

Introduction ix **Acknowledgments** xiii

Forthcoming Authors xi **Illustrations Index** 241

Author Index 253

A

Vincent Arthur Alexander 1925-1980
Obituary Notice 1

Allyn Allen
see Irmengarde Eberle
Obituary Notice 68

Althea
see Althea Braithwaite 11

Anita
see Anita Daniel 65

Phillip H. Ault 1914- 1

B

Jeannie Baker 1950- 3

Laura Stockton Voorhees Banks 1908(?)-1980
Obituary Notice 5

John Keith Bassett
see Lawrence A. Keating 107

Stewart Taft Beach 1899- 5

Dorothy Potter Benedict 1889-1979
Obituary Notice 5

Laura Benet 1884-1979
Obituary Notice 6

Crosby Bonsall 1921- 6

James Cloyd Bowman 1880-1961 7

Helen Boylston 1895- 8

Virginia Bradley 1912- 11

Althea Braithwaite 1940- 11

Robin F. Brancato 1936- 14

Carl T. Brandhorst 1898- 16

Robbie Branscum 1937- 17

Michael Braude 1936- 18

Grace N. Brett 1900-1975 19

Raymond Briggs 1934- 19

Ruth Brindze 1903- 22

Lynn Bronson
see Evelyn Sibley Lampman
Obituary Notice 115

Jerome Brooks 1931- 23

Edward G. E. L. Bulwer-Lytton
see Baron Lytton,
Edward G. E. L. Bulwer-Lytton 125

Janet Burroway 1936- 24

Maurice Burton 1898- 27

C

Rachel Carson 1907-1964 28

Phyllis Ann Carter
see Irmengarde Eberle
Obituary Notice 68

Pisistratus Caxton
see Baron Lytton,
Edward G. E. L. Bulwer-Lytton 125

Mary Challans 1905- 33

Elizabeth Cleaver 1939- 34

Mary Louise Clifford 1926- 36

Jean Poindexter Colby 1909- 37

Robert Coles 1929- 38

Jane Collier
see Zena Collier 41

Zena Collier 1926- 41

Antonio J. Colorado 1903- 42

Henry Steele Commager 1902- 43

Hilda Conkling 1910- 45

Robert Leslie Conly 1918(?)-1973 45

Gordon Cooper 1932- 47

Paul W. Copeland 48

Sabra Lee Corbin
see Gladys Malvern 133

Dorothy Corey 49

Jean Gay Cornell 1920- 50

Samuel James Cornish 1935- 51
Adeline Corrigan 1909- 53
David F. Costello 1904- 53
Jonathan Cott 1942- 55
Donald William Cox 1921- 56
John Ernest Craig 1921- 58
Bill Crofut
see William E. Crofut III 59
William E. Crofut III 1934- 59
Anne Eliot Crompton 1930- 61
Alexander L. Crosby 1906-1980
Obituary Notice 62
Cathy Cunningham
see Chet Cunningham 63
Chet Cunningham 1928- 63
Daniel Curley 1918- 63
Patricia Curtis 1921- 64

D

Anita Daniel 1893(?)-1978 65
Louis Darling, Jr. 1916-1970
Obituary Notice 66
Rosamond Dauer 1934- 66
Rosalie Davidson 1921- 67
Esther M. Douty 1911-1978
Obituary Notice 68
Roger Duvoisin 1904-1980
Obituary Notice 68

E

Irmengarde Eberle 1898-1979
Obituary Notice 68
Edith Berven Eckblad 1923- 68

F

Anne Irvin Faulkner 1906- 70
Nancy Faulkner
see Anne Irvin Faulkner 70
Winifred Finlay 1910- 71
Genevieve Foster 1893-1979
Obituary Notice 73
Marian Curtis Foster 1909-1978 73
Fontaine Talbot Fox, Jr. 1884-1964
Obituary Notice 75

G

Ellen Galinsky 1942- 75
John A. Garraty 1920- 76
Adele Geras 1944- 76
Gail Gibbons 1944- 77
Virginia Kirkus Glick 1893-1980
Obituary Notice 78
Philip Goldstein 1910- 79
Gloria Gonzalez 1940- 80
Samuel Griswold Goodrich 1793-1860 82
Sirak Goryan
see William Saroyan 210
Hardie Gramatky 1907-1979
Obituary Notice 89
Ellin Greene 1927- 89
Nigel Grimshaw 1925- 91
Elizabeth Gundrey 1924- 91

H

Donald Hall 1928- 92
Elizabeth Hamilton 1906- 94
Lynn Haney 1941- 95
Janet Harris 1932-1979
Obituary Notice 97
Ellen Hartley 1915- 97
William B. Hartley 1913- 98
Jimmy Hatlo 1898-1963
Obituary Notice 100
Wally Herbert
see Walter William Herbert 101
Walter William Herbert 1934- 101
Grete Janus Hertz 1915- 102
A. T. Hopkins
see Annette Turngren
Obituary Notice 233
Katharine Hull 1921-1977 103
Jane Andrews Hyndman 1912-1978
Obituary Notice 103

J

Grete Janus
see Grete Janus Hertz 102
D. William Johnson 1945- 103

K

Jonah Kalb 1926- 105

Lucy Kavaler 1930- 106

Lawrence A. Keating 1903-1966 107

Bettyann Kevles 1938- 107

Alexander Key 1904-1979
Obituary Notice 108

Marian King 108

Virginia Kirkus
see Virginia Kirkus Glick
Obituary Notice 78

J. C. Kocsis
see James Paul 161

Theodora Koob 1918- 110

Joseph Krumgold 1908-1980
Obituary Notice 111

L

Saul Lambert 1928- 111

Albert Lamorisse 1922-1970 112

Evelyn Sibley Lampman 1907-1980
Obituary Notice 115

Jerome E. Leavitt 1916- 115

Thomas B. Leekley 1910- 117

Alfred Leutscher 1913- 117

Norman Lloyd 1909-1980
Obituary Notice 118

Christopher Logue 1926- 119

Maud Hart Lovelace 1892-1980
Obituary Notice 120

Lois Lowry 1937- 120

Harriett M. Luger 1914- 122

Richard B. Lyttle 1927- 123

Baron Lytton, Edward G. E. L.
Bulwer-Lytton 1803-1873 125

M

Alistair MacLean 1923- 131

Gladys Malvern (?)-1962 133

Mariana
see Marian Curtis Foster 73

Margaret L. Marks 1911(?)-1980
Obituary Notice 134

Robert McEwen 1926-1980
Obituary Notice 134

Emilie Warren McLeod 1926- 135

Marion Meade 1934- 136

Charles T. Meadow 1929- 136

Hilary Milton 1920- 137

Jane Belk Moncure 139

Ruth Moore 142

S. E. Moore 142

John Morressy 1930- 143

Marietta D. Moskin 1928- 144

Donald Myrus 1927- 147

N

Mary Carroll Nelson 1929- 147

Crosby Newell
see Crosby Bonsall 6

James R. Newton 1935- 149

Charles Nordhoff 1887-1947 150

O

Robert C. O'Brien
see Robert Leslie Conly 45

F. D. Ommanney 1903-1980 159

P

Norvin Pallas 1918- 160

Peter Parley
see Samuel Griswold Goodrich 82

James Paul 1936- 161

Mervyn Peake 1911-1968 162

Arthur Pendennis, Esquire
see William Makepeace Thackeray 223

Jean Piaget 1896-1980
Obituary Notice 166

Edgar Allan Poe 1809-1849 167

Katherine Anne Porter 1890-1980
Obituary Notice 192

Christine Price 1928-1980
Obituary Notice 192

R

Elaine Raphael 1933- 192

John J. Reiss 193

Mary Renault
see Mary Challans 33

Seymour Resnick 1920- 193

Felix Riesenberg, Jr. 1913-1962....................194

Ray Robinson 1920-....................194

Norman Rockwell 1894-1978....................195

W. G. Rogers 1896-1978....................208

S

William Saroyan 1908-....................210

Miroslav Sasek 1916-1980
Obituary Notice 218

Malcolm Saville 1901- 218

John Anthony Scott 1916-....................219

Tony Scott
see John Anthony Scott 219

Sheila Turner Seed 1937(?)-1979
Obituary Notice 220

Katherine B. Shippen 1892-1980
Obituary Notice 221

Zena Shumsky
see Zena Collier 41

Ikey Solomons, Esquire, Jr.
see William Makepeace Thackeray 223

George Rippey Stewart 1895-1980
Obituary Notice 221

Ian Stuart
see Alistair MacLean....................131

T

Miyuki Tanobe 1937-....................222

William Makepeace Thackeray 1811-1863....................223

H. C. Thomas
see Lawrence A. Keating....................107

Michael Angelo Titmarsh
see William Makepeace Thackeray 223

Michel Tournier 1924- 232

Sheila R. Turner
see Sheila Turner Seed
Obituary Notice 220

Annette Turngren 1902(?)-1980
Obituary Notice 233

V

Count Palmiro Vicarion
see Christopher Logue....................119

Vahrah von Klopp
see Gladys Malvern 133

W

Bruce Wannamaker
see Jane Belk Moncure 139

Mary Hays Weik 1898(?)-1979
Obituary Notice 233

Rudolph Wendelin 1910-....................233

Robert Westall 1929- 235

Opal Wheeler 1898-....................236

Arch Whitehouse
see Arthur George Whitehouse
Obituary Notice 238

Arthur George Whitehouse 1895-1979
Obituary Notice 238

Lee Wyndham
see Jane Andrews Hyndman
Obituary Notice 103

Introduction

Beginning with Volume 15, the time span covered by *Something about the Author* was broadened to include major children's writers who died before 1961, which was the former cut-off point for writers covered in this series. This change will make *SATA* even more helpful to its many thousands of student and professional users.

Authors who did not come within the scope of *SATA* have formerly been included in *Yesterday's Authors of Books for Children,* of which Gale has published two volumes.

It has been pointed out by users, however, that it is inconvenient to have a body of related materials broken up by an arbitrary criterion such as the date of a person's death. Also, some libraries are not able to afford both series, and are therefore denied access to material on some of the most important writers in the juvenile field.

It has been decided, therefore, to discontinue the *YABC* series, and to include in *SATA* at least the most outstanding among the older writers who had been selected for listing in *YABC*. Volumes 1 and 2 of *YABC* will be kept in print, and the listings in those two volumes will be included in the cumulative *SATA* index.

A Partial List of Authors and Illustrators Who Will Appear in Forthcoming Volumes of *Something about the Author*

Adrian, Mary
Ahlberg, Allan
Ahlberg, Janet
Ainsworth, William H.
Allard, Harry
Allen, Agnes B.
Allen, Jack
Anastasio, Dina
Ashley, Bernard
Atwater, Richard
Ayme, Marcel
Bach, Alice H.
Baldwin, James
Ballantyne, Robert M.
Baskin, Leonard
Becker, May Lamberton
Beim, Jerrold
Beim, Lorraine
Bell, Robert S. W.
Bennett, Jay
Bernheim, Evelyne
Binzen, Bill
Blos, Joan W.
Blyton, Enid
Boase, Wendy
Boegehold, Betty
Bolognese, Don
Boning, Richard A.
Bowden, Joan C.
Brady, Lillian
Brewton, Sara W.
Bright, Robert
Broger, Achim
Bronin, Andrew
Bronson, Wilfrid
Brookins, Dana
Brooks, Charlotte K.
Bruna, Dick
Brunhoff, Jean de
Brunhoff, Laurent De
Burchard, Marshall
Burgess, Gelett
Burke, David
Burkert, Nancy Ekholm
Burstein, Chaya
Butler, Hal
Carey, M. V.
Carigiet, Alois
Carrick, Malcolm
Carroll, Ruth R.
Chandler, Caroline Augusta
Chesterton, G. K.
Choate, Judith
Christopher, John
Clarke, Joan B.
Clements, Bruce
Cohen, Joel H.
Cohen, Miriam
Cole, Joanna
Collodi, Carlo
Cooper, Elizabeth Keyser
Cox, Palmer
Craik, Dinah M.
Crews, Donald
Dabcovich, Lydia
Danziger, Paula
Dasent, Sir George Webbe
D'Aulnoy, Marie-Catherine
DeGoscinny, Rene
Delessert, Etienne
Disney, Walt
Ditmars, Raymond
Donovan, John
Doty, Jean Slaughter
Dumas, Philippe
Eaton, Jeanette
Eckert, Allan W.
Elwood, Roger
Erickson, Russell E.
Ernst, Kathryn F.
Erwin, Betty K.
Etter, Les
Everett-Green, Evelyn
Falkner, John Meade
Falls, C. B.
Farber, Norma
Farmer, Penelope
Fischer, Hans Erich
Forest, Antonia
Freeman, Barbara C.
Freschet, Berniece
Fujikawa, Gyo
Gackenbach, Dick
Gans, Roma
Gardam, Jane
Gardner, John C.
Gatty, Margaret
Gauch, Patricia L.
Gault, Clare
Gault, Frank
Gelman, Rita G.
Gemme, Leila Boyle
Giovanni, Nikki
Goble, Dorothy
Goble, Paul
Gorey, Edward St. John
Gould, Chester
Grabianski, Janusz
Gregor, Arthur S.
Gregorian, Joyce
Gridley, Marion E.
Gross, Ruth B.
Gruelle, Johnny
Gutman, Bill
Gwynne, Fred
Halacy, Daniel S., Jr.
Haley, Gail E.
Hale, Lucretia P.
Hayes, Geoffrey R.
Hazen, Barbara S.
Heide, Florence Parry
Hentoff, Nat
Henty, George Alfred
Hicks, Clifford B.
Highwater, Jamake
Hirshberg, Albert S.
Hood, Thomas
Housman, Laurence
Hughes, Ted
Hunt, Clara Whitehill
Ingelow, Jean
Isadora, Rachel
Jacobs, Joseph
Jacques, Robin
Jameson, Cynthia
Jeschke, Susan
Jewell, Nancy
Johnston, Norma
Jones, Hettie
Judson, Clara Ingram
Kahl, Virginia
Kahn, Joan
Kalan, Robert
Kantrowitz, Mildred

Kasuya, Masahiro
Keith, Eros
Kemp, Gene
Kent, Jack
Kerr, Judith
Kessler, Ethel
Ketcham, Hank
Klein, Aaron E.
Knotts, Howard
Koehn, Ilse
Kotzwinkle, William
Kraske, Robert
Leach, Maria
Leckie, Robert
Levoy, Myron
Levy, Elizabeth
Lewis, Naomi
Lines, Kathleen
Little, Mary E.
Livermore, Elaine
Longsworth, Polly
Lubin, Leonard
Macaulay, David
MacDonald, George
MacGregor, Ellen
MacKinstry, Elizabeth A.
Manley, Deborah
Marryat, Frederick
Mazer, Norma Fox
McKee, David
McKillip, Patricia A.
McNaught, Harry
McPhail, David
Mendoza, George
Milgrom, Harry
Miller, Edna
Mohn, Peter Burnet
Molesworth, Maria L.
Molloy, Anne S.
Momaday, N. Scott
Moore, Lilian
Moore, Patrick
Morgenroth, Barbara
Murphy, Shirley Rousseau
Myers, Elisabeth P.
Myers, Walter Dean
Nordhoff, Charles
Nordlicht, Lillian
Oakley, Graham
O'Brien, Robert C.
O'Hanlon, Jacklyn
Orr, Frank
Orton, Helen Fuller
Overbeck, Cynthia
Packard, Edward
Pearson, Susan
Perkins, Lucy Fitch
Perrault, Charles
Peterson, Jeanne Whitehouse
Plotz, Helen
Pogany, Willy
Pope, Elizabeth M.
Porter, Eleanor Hodgman
Poulsson, Emilie
Prather, Ray
Pursell, Margaret S.
Pursell, Thomas F.
Pyle, Katharine
Rae, Gwynedd
Raynor, Dorka
Rees, David
Reid, Mayne
Reynolds, Marjorie
Ribbons, Ian
Richler, Mordecai
Roberts, Elizabeth Madox
Rock, Gail
Rockwell, Anne
Rockwell, Harlow
Rose, Elizabeth
Rose, Gerald
Ross, Diana
Ross, Frank, Jr.
Ross, Wilda
Roy, Cal
Ruskin, John
Sabin, Francene
Sabin, Louis
Salten, Felix
Schellie, Don
Schick, Alice
Schneider, Leo
Schoonover, Frank
Seaman, Augusta
Sendak, Jack
Sewall, Helen
Sewall, Marcia
Sewell, Anna
Shapiro, Milton J.
Shearer, John
Silverstein, Shel
Simon, Hilda
Smith, Doris Buchanan
Steiner, Charlotte
Stevens, Leonard A.
Stevenson, James
Stong, Phil
Sutton, Felix
Tallon, Robert
Taylor, Ann
Taylor, Jane
Taylor, Mark
Tenniel, Sir John
Todd, Ruthven
Tomalin, Ruth
Tomes, Margot
Tourneur, Dina K.
Tripp, Wallace
Tunis, John R.
Turska, Krystyna
Van Iterson, S. R.
Varga, Judy
Villiard, Paul
Waber, Bernard
Wagner, Jenny
Walters, Hugh
Watson, Nancy D.
Watts, Franklin
Welber, Robert
Welles, Winifred
Wellman, Alice
Wild, Jocelyn
Wild, Robin
Wilde, Oscar
Willard, Nancy
William-Ellis, Amabel
Wilson, Gahan
Windsor, Patricia
Winn, Marie
Winterfeld, Henry
Wolde, Gunilla
Wolf, Bernard
Wolitzer, Hilma
Wong, Herbert H.
Wood, Phyllis Anderson
Wyss, Johann David
Yeoman, John
Yonge, Charlotte M.
Zei, Alki
Zollinger, Gulielma

In the interest of making *Something about the Author* as responsive as possible to the needs of its readers, the editor welcomes your suggestions for additional authors and illustrators to be included in the series.

GRATEFUL ACKNOWLEDGMENT

is made to the following publishers, authors, and artists, for their kind permission to reproduce copyrighted material.

ACADEMY EDITIONS. Photographs from *Mervyn Peake* by Maeve Gilmore and Shelagh Johnson. Copyright © 1974 by Maeve Gilmore and Academy Editions./ Illustration by Mervyn Peake from *Alice's Adventures in Wonderland* [*and*] *Through the Looking-Glass* by Lewis Carroll. All reprinted by permission of Academy Editions.

ATHENEUM PUBLISHERS. Illustration by Zena Bernstein from *Mrs. Frisby and the Rats of NIMH* by Robert C. O'Brien. Copyright © 1971 by Robert C. O'Brien./ Illustration by Susan Crofut from *The Moon on the One Hand: Poetry in Song* by William Crofut. Copyright © 1975 by William Crofut. Both reprinted by permission of Atheneum Publishers.

AUGSBURG PUBLISHING HOUSE. Illustration by Jim Roberts from *Soft as the Wind* by Edith Eckblad. Copyright © 1974 by Augsburg Publishing House. Reprinted by permission of Augsburg Publishing House.

BEAUFORT BOOKS. Jacket illustration by Robert Chronister from *The Brats and Mr. Jack* by Hilary Milton. Copyright © 1980 by Hilary Milton. Reprinted by permission of Beaufort Books.

BRADBURY PRESS, INC. Illustration by John J. Reiss from *Shapes* by John J. Reiss. Copyright © 1974 by John J. Reiss. Reprinted by permission of Bradbury Press, Inc.

BROWN & BIGELOW. Illustrations by Norman Rockwell from the archives of the publishers Brown & Bigelow. Reprinted by permission of Brown & Bigelow.

CAMBRIDGE UNIVERSITY PRESS. Illustration by Edward Ardizzone from *The Newcomes* by William Makepeace Thackeray. Reprinted by permission of Cambridge University Press.

CHATTO & WINDUS LTD. Illustration by Mervyn Peake from *The Hunting of the Snark* by Lewis Carroll. Reprinted by permission of Chatto & Windus Ltd.

CHILD'S WORLD, INC. Illustration by Franz Altschuler from *Barbara's Pony, Buttercup* by Jane Belk Moncure. Copyright © 1977 by Child's World, Inc. Reprinted by permission of Child's World, Inc.

WILLIAM COLLINS SONS & CO. LTD. Painting by Wally Herbert from *Eskimos* by Wally Herbert. Copyright © 1976 by the International Library. Copyright © 1976 by William Collins, Sons and Co. Reprinted by permission of William Collins Sons & Co. Ltd.

CONCORDIA PUBLISHING HOUSE. Illustration by Rudolph Wendelin from *The City That Forgot About Christmas* by Mary Warren. Copyright © 1968 by Concordia Publishing House. Reprinted by permission of Concordia Publishing House.

COWARD, McCANN AND GEOGHEGAN, INC. Illustration by Raymond Briggs from *Father Christmas* by Raymond Briggs. Text and illustrations copyright © 1973 by Raymond Briggs./ Illustration by Raymond Briggs from *Jim and the Beanstalk* by Raymond Briggs. Copyright © 1973 by Raymond Briggs./ Illustration by Richard Lebenson from *Waiting for Mama* by Marietta Moskin. Text copyright © 1975 by Marietta Moskin. Illustrations copyright © 1975 by Richard Lebenson. All reprinted by permission of Coward, McCann and Geoghegan, Inc.

DELL PUBLISHING CO., INC. Illustration by J. C. Kocsis from *Edge of Two Worlds* by Weyman Jones. Text copyright © 1968 by Weyman Jones. Illustrations copyright © 1968 by J. C. Kocsis. Reprinted by permission of Dell Publishing Co., Inc.

ANDRE DEUTSCH LTD. Illustration by Jeannie Baker from *Grandfather* by Jeannie Baker. Copyright © 1977 by Jeannie Baker./ Illustration by David McPhail from *The Bear's Bicycle* by Emilie Warren McLeod. Text copyright © 1975 by Emilie Warren McLeod. Illustrations copyright © 1975 by David McPhail. Both reprinted by permission of Andre Deutsch Ltd.

THE DIAL PRESS. Sidelight excerpts from *Days of Life and Death and Escape to the Moon* by William Saroyan. Reprinted by permission of The Dial Press.

DINOSAUR PUBLICATIONS LTD. Illustration by Althea from *Desmond and the Monsters* by Althea. Copyright © 1975 by Althea Braithwaite. Reprinted by permission of Dinosaur Publications Ltd.

DODD, MEAD & CO. Illustration from *"All Aboard!": The Story of Passenger Trains in America* by Phil Ault. Copyright © 1976 by Phillip H. Ault./ Illustration by William Makepeace Thackeray from *Vanity Fair* by William Makepeace Thackeray. Both reprinted by permission of Dodd, Mead & Co.

DOUBLEDAY & CO., INC. Photograph taken during the filming of the movie "The Red Balloon" from *The Red Balloon* by Albert Lamorisse. Copyright © 1956 by A. Lamorisse./ Sidelight excerpts from *Complete Stories and Poems of Edgar Allan Poe.*/ Sidelight excerpts from *Norman Rockwell, My Adventures as an Illustrator* by Norman Rockwell./ Illustration by Suzanne Verrier from *The Tooth and My Father* by William Saroyan. Copyright © 1974 by William Saroyan. All reprinted by permission of Doubleday & Co., Inc.

ELSEVIER-DUTTON PUBLISHING CO., INC. Jacket illustration by Troy Howell from *The Big Dipper Marathon* by Jerome Brooks. Copyright © 1979 by Jerome Brooks./ Illustration by Philip Gough from *An Hour in the Morning* by Gordon Cooper. Copyright © 1971 by Gordon Cooper./ Photograph by Miriam Austerman from *Watching the Wild Apes* by Bettyann Kevles. Copyright © 1976 by Bettyann Holtzmann Kevles./ Illustration by Henry J. Gillette from *Paganini, Master of Strings* by Opal Wheeler. Copyright 1950 by Opal Wheeler. All reprinted by permission of Elsevier-Dutton Publishing Co., Inc.

FOUR WINDS PRESS. Illustration by Judith Gwyn Brown from *Secret Island* by S. E. Moore. Text copyright © 1977 by S. E. Moore. Illustrations copyright © 1977 by Scholastic Magazines, Inc. Reprinted by permission of Four Winds Press (a division of Scholastic Magazine, Inc.).

GARRARD PUBLISHING COMPANY. Illustration by Victor Mays from *Louis Armstrong, Ambassador Satchmo* by Jean Gay Cornell. Copyright © 1972 by Jean Gay Cornell. Reprinted by permission of Garrard Publishing Company.

GOLDEN GATE JUNIOR BOOKS. Illustration by Bernard Garbutt from *Dinosaurs: The Terrible Lizards* by Rosalie Davidson. Text copyright © 1969 by Rosalie Davidson. Illustrations copyright © 1969 by Bernard Garbutt. Reprinted by permission of Golden Gate Junior Books (a division of Childrens Press).

GREENWILLOW BOOKS. Illustration by Byron Barton from *Bullfrog Grows Up* by Rosamond Dauer. Text copyright © 1976 by Rosamond Dauer. Illustrations copyright © 1976 by Byron Barton. Reprinted by permission of Greenwillow Books (a division of William Morrow & Co., Inc.)

HAMISH HAMILTON LTD. Illustration by Raymond Briggs from *Father Christmas* by Raymond Briggs. Copyright © 1973 by Raymond Briggs./ Illustration by Raymond Briggs from *Jim and the Beanstalk* by Raymond Briggs. Copyright © 1973 by Raymond Briggs./ Illustration by Doreen Caldwell from *Tea at Mrs. Manderby's* by Adele Geras. Text copyright © 1976 by Adele Geras. Illustrations copyright © 1976 by Doreen Caldwell. All reprinted by permission of Hamish Hamilton Ltd.

HAMMOND, INC. Photograph from *America's Explorers of Space* by Donald W. Cox. Copyright © 1967, 1969 by Hammond, Inc. Reprinted by permission of Hammond, Inc.

HARCOURT BRACE JOVANOVICH, INC. Illustration by Carl Owens from *Your Hand in Mine* by Sam Cornish. Copyright © 1970 by Harcourt Brace Jovanovich, Inc./ Illustration by Don Freeman from *The Human Comedy* by William Saroyan. Copyright 1943, © 1971 by William Saroyan./ Illustration by Don Freeman from *My Name Is Aram* by William Saroyan. Copyright 1937, 1938, 1939, 1940 by William Saroyan./ Sidelight excerpts from *Not Dying* by William Saroyan. All reprinted by permission of Harcourt Brace Jovanovich, Inc.

HARPER & ROW, PUBLISHERS, INC. Illustration by Crosby Bonsall from *The Day I Had to Play with My Sister* by Crosby Bonsall. Copyright © 1972 by Crosby Bonsall./ Illustration by C. Walter Hodges from *The Lion in the Gateway* by Mary Renault. Copyright © 1964 by Mary Renault./ Photograph from *Theodore Roosevelt, The Strenuous Life* by John A. Garraty.

Copyright © 1967 by American Heritage Publishing Co., Inc./ Frontispiece from *Faery Lands of the South Seas* by James Norman Hall and Charles Bernard Nordhoff. Copyright 1921 by Harper & Brothers. All reprinted by permission of Harper & Row, Publishers, Inc.

GEORGE G. HARRAP & CO. LTD. Illustration by Winifred Finlay from *Danger at Black Dyke* by Winifred Finlay. Copyright © 1968 by Winifred Finlay. Reprinted by permission of George G. Harrap & Co. Ltd.

HARVARD UNIVERSITY PRESS. Sidelight excerpts from *The Letters of Edgar Allan Poe: Volumes I and II* edited by John Ward Ostrom. Copyright 1948 by the President and Fellows of Harvard College./ Sidelight excerpts from *The Letters of William Makepeace Thackeray, Volume II* by Gordon Ray. All reprinted by permission of Harvard University Press.

HARVEY HOUSE, PUBLISHERS. Illustration by Anne Marie Jauss from *Selections from Spanish Poetry* by Seymour Resnick. Text copyright © 1962 by Seymour Resnick. Illustrations copyright © 1962 by Anne Marie Jauss. Reprinted by permission of Harvey House, Publishers.

HASTINGS HOUSE, PUBLISHERS, INC. Photograph by Barbara Cooney from *Lexington and Concord, 1775: What Really Happened* by Jean Poindexter Colby. Text copyright © 1975 by Jean Poindexter Colby. Photographs copyright © 1975 by Barbara Cooney. Reprinted by permission of Hastings House, Publishers, Inc.

HERITAGE CLUB. Illustration by Norman Rockwell from *The Adventures of Tom Sawyer* by Mark Twain. Reprinted by permission of Heritage Club (a division of MBI Books Division).

HERITAGE PRESS. Illustration by Fletcher Martin from *Mutiny on the Bounty* by Charles Nordhoff and James Norman Hall. Copyright 1932 by Charles Nordhoff and James Norman Hall. Copyright 1940 by Little, Brown & Co. Special contents of this edition copyright 1947 by The George Macy Companies, Inc./ Illustrations by Norman Rockwell from *The Adventures of Huckleberry Finn* by Mark Twain. Text copyright 1884 by Samuel L. Clemens. Copyright 1896 and 1899 by Harper & Bros. Copyright 1912 by Clara Gabrilowitch. Copyright 1923 by the Mark Twain Company. Special contents of this edition copyright 1940 by Heritage Press./ Illustration by Edward Ardizzone from *The Newcomes* by William Makepeace Thackeray. All reprinted by permission of Heritage Press (a division of MBI Books Division).

HODDER & STOUGHTON LTD. Illustration by Edmund Dulac from *The Bells, and Other Poems* by Edgar Allan Poe. Copyright by the Estate of Edmund Dulac. Reprinted by permission of Hodder & Stoughton Ltd.

HOLIDAY HOUSE, INC. Jacket illustration by Paul Frame from *The Rain-Cloud Pony* by Anne Eliot Crompton. Reprinted by permission of Holiday House, Inc.

HOLT, RINEHART & WINSTON. Illustration by Vernon Wooten from *Second Son* by Nancy Faulkner. Copyright © 1969 by Colonial Williamsburg, Inc. Reprinted by permission of Holt, Rinehart & Winston.

HOME & VAN THAL LTD. Sidelight excerpts from *Bulwer-Lytton* by The Earl of Lytton, K. G. Copyright 1948 by Home & Van Thal Ltd. Reprinted by permission of Home & Van Thal Ltd.

THE HORN BOOK, INC. Sidelight excerpts from *Newbery and Caldecott Medal Books: 1966-1975,* edited by Lee Kingman. Copyright © 1972 by The Horn Book, Inc. Reprinted by permission of The Horn Book, Inc.

HOUGHTON MIFFLIN COMPANY. Pictures by John Vernon Lord from *The Giant Jam Sandwich,* story by John Vernon Lord. Verses by Janet Burroway. Copyright © 1972 by John Vernon Lord./ Illustrations by Lois and Louis Darling from *Silent Spring* by Rachel Carson. Copyright © 1962 by Rachel L. Carson./ Illustration by Sandy Kossin from *The Goof That Won the Pennant* by Jonah Kalb. Copyright © 1976 by Jonah Kalb./ Illustration by Jenni Oliver from *A Summer to Die* by Lois Lowry. Copyright © 1977 by Lois Lowry./ Sidelight excerpts from *The Life of Edgar Allan Poe* by George E. Woodberry./ Sidelight excerpts from *The House of Life: Rachel Carson at Work* by Paul Brooks. All reprinted by permission of Houghton Mifflin Company.

ALFRED A. KNOPF, INC. Jacket illustration by Richard Cuffari from *Something Left to Lose* by Robin F. Brancato. Copyright © 1976 by Robin Brancato./ Illustration from *Gaucho* by Gloria Gonzalez. Copyright © 1977 by Gloria Gonzalez./ Illustration by David Stone Martin from *Friday and Robinson* by Michel Tournier. Translated by Ralph Manheim. English translation copyright © 1972 by Aldus Books Ltd. Illustrations copyright © 1972 by Alfred A. Knopf, Inc. All reprinted by permission of Alfred A. Knopf, Inc.

LANTERN PRESS, INC. Illustration from *Wonders of Parasites* by Philip Goldstein. Copyright © 1969 by Philip Goldstein. Reprinted by permission of Lantern Press, Inc.

J. B. LIPPINCOTT COMPANY. Photograph by Paul W. Copeland from *The Land and People of Syria* by Paul W. Copeland. Copyright © 1964 by Paul W. Copeland./ Photograph by David F. Costello from *The World of the Prairie Dog* by David F. Costello. Copyright © 1970 by David F. Costello./ Illustration by Leonard Vosburgh from *Benjy Brant: Dragooning with the Swamp Fox* by Theodora Koob. Copyright © 1965 by Theodora Koob. All reprinted by permission of J. B. Lippincott Company.

LIPPINCOTT & CROWELL, PUBLISHERS. Illustration by Donna Diamond from *Ann's Spring* by Daniel Curley. Text copyright © 1977 by Daniel Curley. Illustrations copyright © 1977 by Donna Diamond./ Illustration by Charles Robinson from *The March of the Lemmings* by James R. Newton. Text copyright © 1976 by James R. Newton. Illustrations copyright © 1976 by Charles Robinson./ Illustration by Richard Cuffari from *The Dangers of Noise* by Lucy Kavaler. Copyright © 1978 by Lucy Kavaler./ Jacket illustration by Nicholas Gaetano from *Gertrude Stein Is Gertrude Stein Is Gertrude Stein: Her Life and Work* by W.G. Rogers. Copyright © 1973 by W.G. Rogers./ Illustration by Trevor Stubley from *Bisha of Burundi* by Mary Louise Clifford. Copyright © 1973 by Mary Louise Clifford. All reprinted by permission of Lippincott & Crowell, Publishers.

LITTLE, BROWN & CO. Illustration by Forrest W. Orr from *Sue Barton, Student Nurse* by Helen Dore Boylston. Copyright 1936 by Helen Dore Boylston./ Illustration by Norman Rockwell from *Dead End School* by Robert Coles. Text copyright © 1968 by Robert Coles. Illustrations copyright © 1968 by Norman Rockwell./ Illustration by D. William Johnson from *The Willow Flute: A North Country Tale* by D. William Johnson. Copyright © 1975 by D. William Johnson./ Illustration by N.C. Wyeth from "Men Against the Sea," in *The Bounty Trilogy* by Charles Nordhoff and James Norman Hall. Copyright 1932, 1933, 1934, 1936 by Charles Nordhoff and James Norman Hall. Copyright 1940 by Little, Brown & Co.; copyright renewed 1960, 1961, 1962./ Illustration by A. Vimnèra from *Falcons of France* by Charles Nordhoff and James Norman Hall. Copyright 1929 by Little, Brown & Co./ Sidelight excerpts from *My Island Home* by James Hall. Copyright 1952 by James Norman Hall. All reprinted by permission of Little, Brown & Co.

LOTHROP, LEE & SHEPARD BOOKS. Illustration by Michael Eagle from *The Ugliest Boy* by Robbie Branscum. Text copyright © 1978 by Robbie Branscum. Illustrations copyright © 1978 by Michael Eagle./ Illustration by Mariana from *Miss Flora McFlimsey's May Day* by Mariana. Copyright © 1969 by Marian Foster Curtiss./ Illustration by Barbara Cooney from *Midsummer Magic* by Ellin Greene. Copyright © 1977 by Ellin Greene. All reprinted by permission of Lothrop, Lee & Shepard Books (a division of William Morrow & Co., Inc.).

MACDONALD EDUCATIONAL LTD. Illustration by Patricia Leander and Malcolm McGregor from *The Life of Birds* by Maurice Burton. Adapted by Louis M. Moyle. Copyright © 1975 by Macdonald Educational Ltd. Reprinted by permission of Macdonald Educational Ltd.

MACMILLAN, INC. Illustration by William Steinel from *A Man's Work* by Donald Myrus. Text copyright © 1965 by Donald Myrus. Illustrations copyright © 1965 by Macmillan, Inc. Reprinted by permission of Macmillan, Inc.

MACMILLAN LTD. Sidelight excerpts from *The Life of Edward Bulwer, Volumes I and II* by The Earl of Lytton. Reprinted by permission of Macmillan Ltd.

McGRAW-HILL, INC. Illustration by Deborah Fulford from *Frogs, Toads & Newts* by F. D. Ommanney. Text copyright © 1973 by F. D. Ommanney. Illustrations copyright © 1973 by Deborah Fulford./ Sidelight excerpts from *Thackeray—The Uses of Adversity—1811-1846* by Gordon Ray. Copyright © 1955 by McGraw-Hill, Inc./ Sidelight excerpts from *Thackeray—The Age of Wisdom—1847-1863* by Gordon Ray. Copyright © 1958 by McGraw-Hill, Inc. All reprinted by permission of McGraw-Hill, Inc.

JULIAN MESSNER. Illustration by Susanne Suba from *Dancing Star: The Story of Anna Pavlova* by Gladys Malvern. Copyright 1942 by Gladys Malvern; copyright renewed © 1969 by George F. McKendry, executor. Reprinted by permission of Julian Messner.

W. W. NORTON & CO., INC. Sidelight excerpts from *Chance Meetings* by William Saroyan. Reprinted by permission of W. W. Norton & Co., Inc.

OXFORD UNIVERSITY PRESS, INC. Illustration by Elizabeth Cleaver from *The Loon's Necklace,* retold by William Toye. Copyright © 1977 by Oxford University Press./ Illustration by Philip Gough from *An Hour in the Morning* by Gordon Cooper. Copyright © 1971 by Gordon Cooper. Both reprinted by permission of Oxford University Press, Inc.

PENMAEN PRESS LTD. Wood engravings by Helen Siegl from *An Act or Two of Foolish Kindness* by William Saroyan. Text copyright © 1977 by William Saroyan. Illustrations copyright © 1977 by Helen Siegl. Reprinted by permission of Penmaen Press Ltd.

S. G. PHILLIPS, INC. Illustration by Winifred Finlay from *Danger at Black Dyke* by Winifred Finlay. Copyright © 1968 by Winifred Finlay. Reprinted by permission of S. G. Phillips, Inc.

PRAEGER PUBLISHERS. Sidelight excerpts from *Places Where I've Done Time* by William Saroyan. Reprinted by permission of Praeger Publishers.

PRENTICE-HALL, INC. Illustration by Gail Gibbons from *Salvador and Mister Sam: A Guide to Parakeet Care* by Gail Gibbons. Copyright © 1975 by Gail Gibbons. Reprinted by permission of Prentice-Hall, Inc.

G.P. PUTNAM'S SONS. Photograph by Bruce Curtis from *Perfect Balance: The Training of an Elite Gymnast* by Lynn Haney. Text copyright © 1979 by Lynn Haney. Illustrations copyright © 1979 by Bruce Curtis./ Sidelight excerpts from *American Literature: Readings and Critiques* by R. W. Stallman and Arthur Waldhorn. Copyright © 1961 by G.P. Putnam's Sons./ Sidelight excerpts from *Edgar A. Poe: A Psychopathic Study* by John W. Robertson. Copyright 1923 by G.P. Putnam's Sons. All reprinted by permission of G.P. Putnam's Sons.

RANDOM HOUSE, INC. Illustration by Paula Hutchison from *Clara Barton, Founder of the American Red Cross* by Helen Dore Boylston. Copyright 1955 by Helen Dore Boylston./ Photograph by Erica Anderson from *The Story of Albert Schweitzer* by Anita Daniel. Copyright © 1957 by Anita Daniel./ Illustration by Saul Lambert from *Mystery and More Mystery* by Robert Arthur. Copyright 1936, 1939, 1948, 1951, 1952, © 1957, 1958, 1960, 1964, 1966 by Robert Arthur; copyright renewed © 1964 by Robert Arthur. Copyright 1940 by Popular Publications, Inc./ Illustration by Gil Walker from *Lawrence of Arabia* by Alistair MacLean. Copyright © 1962 by Alistair MacLean./ Illustration by Fritz Eichenberg from *Tales of Edgar Allan Poe* by Edgar Allan Poe. Copyright 1944 and renewed © 1972 by Random House. All reprinted by permission of Random House, Inc.

SCHOCKEN BOOKS, INC. Illustration by Mervyn Peake from *Alice's Adventures in Wonderland [and] Through the Looking-Glass* by Lewis Carroll./ Illustration by Mervyn Peake from "The Three Spinners" in *Household Tales* by the Brothers Grimm. Text adaptation copyright © 1973 by Methuen Children's Books Ltd. Illustrations copyright 1946 under the Berne Convention by Mervyn Peake. Copyright © 1973 by Maeve Peake./ Illustration by Mervyn Peake. Copyright © 1973 by Maeve Peake./ Illustration by Mervyn Peake from *Treasure Island* by Robert Louis Stevenson. Copyright © 1976 by Methuen Children's Books Ltd. Illustrations copyright 1949 by Maeve Peake. All reprinted by permission of Schocken Books, Inc.

SCHOLASTIC-TAB PUBLICATIONS LTD. Illustration by Alan Daniel from *The Wormburners* by John Craig. Copyright © 1975 by John Craig. Illustrations copyright © 1975 by Scholastic-TAB Publications Ltd. Reprinted by permission of Scholastic-TAB Publications Ltd.

CHARLES SCRIBNER'S SONS. Illustration by F. C. Yohn from *The Last Days of Pompeii* by Edward Bulwer Lytton. Copyright 1926 by Charles Scribner's Sons. Reprinted by permission of Charles Scribner's Sons.

SHEED ANDREWS AND McMEEL INC. Sidelight excerpts from *A Rockwell Portrait* by Donald Walton. Copyright © 1978 by Donald Walton. Reprinted by permission of Sheed Andrews and McMeel, Inc.

STERLING PUBLISHING CO., INC. Drawing by Joyce Behr from *Calculator Puzzles, Tricks & Games* by Norvin Pallas. Copyright © 1976 by Sterling Publishing Co., Inc. Reprinted by permission of Sterling Publishing Co., Inc.

THEOSOPHICAL PUBLISHING HOUSE. Photograph from the "Cottingley Photographs" from *Beyond the Looking Glass,* edited by Jonathan Cott. Reprinted by permission of Theosophical Publishing House.

TRIDENT PRESS. Sidelight excerpts from *Here Comes, There Goes You Know Who* by William Saroyan. Reprinted by permission of Trident Press.

TUDOR PUBLISHING. Illustrations by Harry Clarke from *Tales of Mystery & Imagination* by Edgar Allan Poe. Reprinted by permission of Tudor Publishing.

TUNDRA BOOKS. Illustration by Miyuki Tanobe from *québec je t'aime: i love you* by Miyuki Tanobe. Copyright © 1976 by Miyuki Tanobe. Reprinted by permission of Tundra Books.

VANGUARD PRESS, INC. Illustration by Robert Bruce from *The Story of Gold* by Ruth Brindze. Copyright © by Ruth Brindze./ Illustration by Yeffe Kimball from *The World of Manabozho: Tales of the Chippewa Indians* by Thomas B. Leekley. Copyright © 1965 by Thomas B. Leekley. Both reprinted by permission of Vanguard Press, Inc.

THE VIKING PRESS. Illustration by Barbara Cooney from *Ox-Cart Man* by Donald Hall. Text copyright © 1979 by Donald Hall. Illustrations copyright © 1979 by Barbara Cooney Porter./ Illustration by Wayne Anderson from *Ratsmagic* by Christopher Logue. Text copyright © 1976 by Jonathan Cape Ltd. Illustrations copyright © 1976 by Wayne Anderson./ Illustration by Diane de Groat from *Chasing Trouble* by Harriett Luger. Text copyright © 1976 by Harriett Mandelay Luger. Illustrations copyright © 1976 by Viking Penguin, Inc./ Illustration and design by Don Bolognese and Elaine Raphael from *Letters to Horseface* by F. N. Monjo. Text copyright © 1975 by Ferdinand Monjo and Louise L. Monjo. Illustrations copyright © 1975 by Don Bolognese and Elaine Raphael. All reprinted by permission of The Viking Press.

WALKER & COMPANY. Illustration by Stanley Skardinski from *The Drought On Ziax II* by John Morressy. Text copyright © 1978 by John Morressy. Illustrations copyright © 1978 by Stanley Skardinski. Reprinted by permission of Walker & Company.

WATSON-GUPTILL PUBLICATIONS. Sidelight excerpts from *Norman Rockwell, Illustrator* by Arthur L. Guptill. Copyright 1946 by Watson-Guptill Publications. Reprinted by permission of Watson-Guptill Publications.

FRANKLIN WATTS, INC. Illustration by Leonard Everett Fisher from *The First Book of American History* by Henry Steele Commager. Copyright © 1957 by Franklin Watts, Inc./ Illustrations by Bette J. Davis from *The First Book of Caves* by Elizabeth Hamilton. Copyright © 1956 by Franklin Watts, Inc./ Painting by Wally Herbert from *Eskimos* by Wally Herbert. Copyright © 1976 by the International Library. Copyright © 1976 by William Collins, Sons and Co. Ltd./ Illustration by Rick Schreiter from *The Murders in the Rue Morgue* by Edgar Allan Poe. Illustrations copyright © 1966 by Franklin Watts, Inc. All reprinted by permission of Franklin Watts, Inc.

WEATHERVANE BOOKS. Illustration by Arthur Rackham from *Tales of Mystery & Imagination* by Edgar Allan Poe. Copyright MCMXXXV by George G. Harrap & Co. Ltd. Reprinted by permission of Weathervane Books.

GEORGE WEIDENFELD & NICOLSON LTD. Sidelight excerpts from *The Extraordinary Mr. Poe* by Wolf Mankowitz. Copyright © 1978 by Wolf Mankowitz. Reprinted by permission of George Weidenfeld & Nicolson Ltd.

ALBERT WHITMAN & COMPANY. Illustration by Laura Bannon from *Pecos Bill: The Greatest Cowboy of All Time* by James Cloyd Bowman. Copyright 1937, © 1964 by Albert Whitman & Company./ Illustration by Robert Kresin from *That Willy and Wally* by Grace Neff Brett. Copyright © 1964 by Albert Whitman & Company./ Illustration by Lois Axeman from *Tomorrow You Can* by Dorothy Corey. Text copyright © 1977 by Dorothy Corey. Illustrations copyright © 1977 by Lois Axeman./ Illustration by Rainey Bennett from *Holiday Ring: Festival Stories and Poems* by Adeline Corrigan. Copyright © 1975 by Albert Whitman & Company. All reprinted by permission of Albert Whitman & Company.

WINDMILL BOOKS, INC. Illustration by Norman Rockwell from *Norman Rockwell's Hometown* by Thomas Rockwell. Text copyright © 1970 by Thomas Rockwell. Illustrations copyright 1948, 1949, 1950, 1952, 1955, © 1956, 1957, 1959, 1960, 1962, 1963 by Brown & Bigelow. Reprinted by permission of Windmill Books, Inc.

WORLD'S WORK LTD. Illustration by Crosby Bonsall from *The Day I Had to Play With My Sister* by Crosby Bonsall. Copyright © 1972 by Crosby Bonsall./ Illustration by Byron Barton from *Bullfrog Grows Up* by Rosamond Dauer. Text copyright © 1976 by Rosamond Dauer. Illustrations copyright © 1976 by Byron Barton. Both reprinted by permission of World's Work Ltd. (a division of William Heinemann Ltd.).

Photographs by Erica Anderson from *The Story of Albert Schweitzer* by Anita Daniel. Copyright © 1957 by Anita Daniel. Reprinted by permission of Erica Anderson./ Sidelight excerpts from *In Search of Paradise* by Paul Briand, Jr. Reprinted by permission of Paul Briand, Jr./ Photograph from *The First Book of Puerto Rico* by Antonio J. Colorado. Copyright © 1965, 1972, 1978 by Franklin Watts, Inc. Reprinted by permission of Commonwealth of Puerto Rico Tourism Development Co./ Photograph by Tom McHugh from *Animal Doctors: What It's Like to Be a Veterinarian and How to Become One* by Patricia Curtis. Copyright © 1977 by Patricia Curtis. Reprinted by permission of Tom McHugh, Photo Researchers, Inc./ Photograph from *The Alligator: King of the Wilderness* by William and Ellen Hartley. Copyright © 1977 by William and Ellen Hartley. Reprinted by permission of *The Miami Herald.*/ Illustration by Mervyn Peake from *The Hunting of the Snark* by Lewis Carroll. Reprinted by permission of Maurice Michael./ Illustration by Mervyn Peake from "The Three Spinners" in *Household Tales* by the Brothers Grimm. Text adaptation copyright © 1973 by Methuen Children's Books Ltd. Illustrations copyright 1946 under the Berne Convention by Mervyn Peake. Copyright © 1973 by Maeve Peake. Reprinted by permission of Maurice Michael./ Illustration by Mervyn Peake from *Treasure Island* by Robert Louis Stevenson.

Copyright © 1976 by Methuen Children's Books Ltd. Illustrations copyright 1949 by Maeve Peake. Reprinted by permission of Maurice Michael./ Sidelight excerpts from *Not Dying* by William Saroyan. Reprinted by permission of Laurence Pollinger Ltd./ Photograph by Charles Pratt from *The Sense of Wonder* by Rachel Carson. Text copyright © 1956 by Rachel L. Carson. Photograph copyright © 1965 by Charles Pratt. Reprinted by permission of Charles Pratt./ Paintings from *Norman Rockwell's America* by Christopher Finch. Text and reproductions of works of art copyright © 1975 by Harry N. Abrams. Reprinted by permission of Joan Raines./ Sidelight excerpts from *The Bicycle Rider in Beverly Hills* by William Saroyan. Reprinted by permission of William Saroyan./ Sidelight excerpts from *Sons Come and Go, Mothers Hang in Forever* by William Saroyan. Reprinted by permission of William Saroyan./ Illustration by Henry Koerner from *Tracy's Tiger* by William Saroyan. Copyright 1951 by William Saroyan. Reprinted by permission of William Saroyan.

Appreciation also to the Performing Arts Research Center of the New York Public Library at Lincoln Center for permission to reprint the following theater stills: "Hello Out There," "My Heart's in the Highlands," and "The Time of Your Life."

PHOTOGRAPH CREDITS

Althea Braithwaite: Michael Alcott St. Ives; Robin F. Brancato: Jay G. Branch; Robbie Branscum: Nancy Edwards; Carl T. Brandhorst: Sample's Portrait Studio; Mary Challans: Philip DeVos; Robert Coles: © 1975 Peter Jones; Henry Commager: ABC photo; Adeline Corrigan: Clifford Norton Studio; Winifred Finlay: Eric Ager; Gail Gibbons: Jack Kendrick; Nigel Grimshaw: Duncan; Marian King: Bill Snead; Theodora Koob: Andrews Photographers; Alistair MacLean: Geodfrey Argent; Marion Meade: John Potyé; Charles T. Meadow: I. George Bilyk; Hilary Milton: Ken Ives Studio; Donald Myrus: Bill Owens; William Saroyan: Jim Marshall; Malcolm Saville: Richard Mewton; John Anthony Scott: Arthur Hartog; Michel Tournier: Jacques Robert.

SOMETHING ABOUT THE AUTHOR

ALEXANDER, Vincent Arthur 1925-1980

OBITUARY NOTICE: Born November 4, 1925, in Wyckoff, N.J.; died after a long illness, May 22, 1980, in Boston, Mass. Editor best known for his work for Holt, Rinehart & Winston, Inc., on publications involving mathematics and science. In 1969 Alexander was named editor-in-chief of the school department; he became a vice-president in 1972. *For More Information See: Who's Who in America,* 40th edition, Marquis, 1978. *Obituaries: Publishers Weekly,* June 27, 1980; *Contemporary Authors,* Volume 101-104, Gale, 1981.

AULT, Phillip H. 1914-
(Phil Ault)

PERSONAL: Born April 26, 1914, in Maywood, Ill.; son of Frank W. and Bernda A. (Halliday) Ault; married Karoline Byberg, June 5, 1943; children: Frank, Ingrid, Bruce. *Education:* DePauw University, A.B., 1935. *Home:* 2614 Terrace Dr., Santa Maria, Calif. 93455.

CAREER: LaGrange Citizen, LaGrange, Ill., reporter, 1935-37; United Press International, corresponding editor in Chicago, Ill., New York, N.Y., Iceland, North Africa, and London, England, 1938-48, bureau chief, London, 1944-45; *Times-Mirror Co.,* Los Angeles, Calif., assistant managing editor, director of editorial page, 1948; *Mirror-News,* Los Angeles, editorial page editor, 1948-57; Associated Desert Newspapers, executive editor, 1958-68; *South Bend Tribune,* South Bend, Ill., associate editor, 1968-79, contributing ed-

PHILLIP H. AULT

A drawing titled, "The Modern Ship of the Plains," in *Harper's Weekly,* 1886. ■ (From *"All Aboard!": The Story of Passenger Trains in America* by Phil Ault.)

itor, 1979—. *Member:* Sigma Nu. *Awards, honors:* Commonwealth Club of California Literature Award, children's book category, 1959, for *This Is the Desert;* Western Writers of America Spur Award, best western juvenile category, 1976, for *"All Aboard!": The Story of Passenger Trains in America.*

WRITINGS—Juvenile; under name Phil Ault: *This Is the Desert: The Story of America's Arid Region* (illustrated by Leonard Everett Fisher), Dodd, 1959; *News Around the Clock* (illustrated by Frank Nicholas), Dodd, 1960; *Wonders of the Mosquito World,* Dodd, 1970; *These Are the Great Lakes,* Dodd, 1972; *Wires West: The Story of the Talking Wires,* Dodd, 1974; *"All Aboard!": The Story of Passenger Trains in America* (Junior Literary Guild selection), Dodd, 1976; *By the Seat of Their Pants: The Story of Early Aviation* (Junior Literary Guild selection), Dodd, 1978.

Adult; under name Phillip H. Ault: (With John A. Parris, Jr., Ned Russell, and Leo Disher) *Springboard to Berlin,* Crowell, 1943; (with Edwin Emery) *Reporting the News,* Dodd, 1959; *How to Live in California: A Guide to Work, Leisure, and Retirement There and in the Southwest,* Dodd, 1961; (compiler and editor) *The Home Book of Western Humor,* Dodd, 1967; (with Edwin Emery and Warren K. Agee) *Introduction to Mass Communications,* 2nd edition, Dodd, 1965, instructor's manual, 4th edition, 1973, 6th edition, Harper, 1979.

SIDELIGHTS: "Among my first memories as a small boy after World War I was riding in a slow local train drawn by a steam locomotive to visit my grandparents in Indiana. . . . I revisited their little farm town and found all signs of the railroad gone—trains, station, even the tracks themselves.

"I remember especially the 'grown-up' thrill I had the first time I made the train trip back to Chicago at night in a sleeping car. I rode in an upper berth, behind the green curtains that formed a cloth tunnel down the center of the Pullman. For an eight-year-old boy it was a fascinating experience.

"When I realized in talking with young men and women . . . that they never could have such an experience because old-style railroading has vanished, I thought that they should at least have the opportunity to know what it was like. That is how *'All Aboard!'* was born. The book was created from my own memories and the accumulated lore of railroading that has grown up during the last 140 years."

Ault entered college intending to major in English and write for a living, a decision he has never regretted. "Turning desire into reality wasn't easy when I graduated in the

Depression year of 1935. No employers visited campuses to recruit graduates in those hard times. I found a part-time job on my hometown weekly newspaper, starting at ten dollars a week. In 1937 I quit and with money I had scraped together made a 2,500-mile bicycle trip through Europe. After my return, I went to work for the United Press in Chicago.

"It was in the UP [United Press] office that I first had contact with Morse telegraph operators. Their ability to 'talk' to each other in dots and dashes intrigued me. That probably was the origin of *Wires West.* Those Morse operators were a dying breed, and I am glad that I had the opportunity to see them at work."

Ault's ten years with the United Press were stimulating, strenuous, and occasionally dangerous. "I moved to the New York foreign desk in 1940. Three months before Pearl Harbor I was assigned to Reykjavik, Iceland. I traveled there in the first convoy to be escorted by American warships.

"Something else happened to me on that trip. Also aboard was a nurse in the Norwegian Naval Air Force who was being sent to the Norwegian hospital in Reykjavik. Later in the war we were married in Scotland by the High Sheriff of Edinburgh. In the meantime I had gone on the invasion of North Africa and covered that entire military campaign. Our first child was born in London during the bombing and spent many of his early days in an underground shelter. By then I had become manager of the United Press London Bureau."

Since World War II Ault has been editorial director of the Los Angeles *Mirror-News* and executive editor of the Associated Desert Newspapers of California. He is contributing editor of the South Bend, Indiana, *Tribune.*

Ault has focused his writings on nonfiction books. A newsman himself, Ault has published informational books on the mass media, reporters, and press associations. He has also researched and written books about such things as mosquitoes, the Great Lakes, and passenger trains in America. Although his books are primarily factual, critics comment on the "life" Ault incorporates into his writing.

How beautiful is youth! how bright it gleams
With its illusions, aspirations, dreams!
Book of Beginnings, Story without End,
Each maid a heroine, and each man a friend!

—Henry Wadsworth Longfellow

And he who gives a child a treat
Makes joy-bells ring in Heaven's street,
And he who gives a child a home,
Builds palaces in Kingdom come.

—John Masefield

Better to be driven out from among men than to be disliked of children.

—Richard Henry Dana

JEANNIE BAKER

BAKER, Jeannie 1950-

PERSONAL: Born November 2, 1950, in England; daughter of Bernard Victor (a welder) and Barbara Joan (a tracer; maiden name, Weir) Baker. *Education:* Attended Croydon College of Art, 1967-69; Brighton College of Art, B.S., (with honors), 1979. *Politics:* Left. *Home and office:* 42 Cross St., Double Bay, Sydney, N.S.W. 2028, Australia.

CAREER: Free-lance artist and illustrator, 1972—. *Exhibitions*—One-man shows: Brettenham House, Waterloo Bridge, London, 1975; Gallery One, Hobart, Australia, 1977; Bonython Gallery, Adelaide, Australia, 1980; Crafts Council of Australia Gallery, Sydney, 1980; Newcastle Regional Art Gallery, N.S.W., 1980.

Group shows: Royal Academy Summer Exhibition, 1974, 1975; Portal Gallery, London, 1975; Crafts Council of Australia Gallery, Sydney, Australia, 1977-79; Hogarth Gallery, Sydney, 1978; Robin Gibson Gallery, Sydney, 1979; Interiors State Gallery of N.S.W., Sydney, 1981.

Permanent collections: The Australian National Gallery; The State Gallery of Queensland; Droomkeen Museum of Chil-

I noticed he had cotton wool stuffed in his ears. It makes him deaf so I had to shout. ■ (From *Grandfather* by Jeannie Baker. Illustrated by the author.)

dren's Literature, Riddall, Victoria, Australia. *Awards, honors:* Visual arts grants from Australia Council, 1977-78, 1978-79.

WRITINGS—Self-illustrated children's books: *Grandfather,* Dutton, 1977, revised edition, 1980; *Grandmother,* Dutton, 1978, revised edition, 1980; *Millicent,* Dutton, 1980.

Illustrator: Elaine Moss, *Polar,* Deutsch, 1975, Dutton, 1979. Contributor of illustrations to magazines, including *Nova, Observer, New Scientist,* and *The Times.*

WORK IN PROGRESS: A counting and natural history book for young children entitled, *One Hungry Spider.*

SIDELIGHTS: "I am inspired by my surroundings, and I feel the occasional need for personal new adventures into my surroundings to nurture my creative growth.

"I am fascinated by eccentrics (especially old people), wild overgrown places and houses and textures—the crumbling erosion of decay.

"I call my art work 'relief collage.' It is very painstaking and detailed. I use such natural materials as stone, veneer, paint peeled from old doors and windowsills, and plaster from old walls. I collect grass and leaves. For hair on my characters I use real hair. If they are to wear woollen jumpers, I knit them myself.

"As the pictures are relief, when they are photographed for reproduction, shadows will be cast, often in strange places, giving the reproduction a slightly three-dimensional effect.

"My writing is mainly for children. I communicate personal feelings and images through a mixture of writing and pictures."

FOR MORE INFORMATION SEE: Painter and Craftsman, October, 1975; *Hobart Mercury,* January 28, 1976; *Pol,* June, 1976, June, 1980; *The Age*, October 14, 1976; *Craft Australia,* 1976, 1980; *Saturday Evening Mercury,* February 12, 1977; *Vogue Living,* June, 1980; *Artists and Galleries of Australia and New Zealand,* Lansdonne Editions, 1980.

BANKS, Laura Stockton Voorhees 1908(?)-1980

OBITUARY NOTICE: Born about 1908 in Washington, D.C.; died after a stroke, June 18, 1980, in Arlington, Va. Researcher, editor, and author of historical novels for children, including *Washington Adventures.* Banks assisted Allan Nevins on his 1933 biography of Grover Cleveland by doing research on the former president. From 1972 to 1975 she was editor of the *Review of the American Historical Association. Obituaries: Washington Post,* June 27, 1980; *Contemporary Authors,* Volume 101-104, Gale, 1981.

BEACH, Stewart Taft 1899-

PERSONAL: Born December 17, 1899, in Pontiac, Michigan. *Education:* Graduated from the University of Michigan.

CAREER: Author, editor. Reporter, Pontiac (Michigan) *Daily Press,* 1916; managing editor, *House Beautiful,* 1934-1939; executive editor, *This Week,* starting in 1947. Has written a wide variety of books, ranging from how to write short stories, to history and travel, to children's books to plays.

WRITINGS—For children: *Racing Start,* Little, Brown, 1941; *Good Morning, Sun's Up!* (illustrated by Yutaka Sugita; first published by Shiko-Sha, Japan, 1968), Scroll Press, 1970.

Other: *Short-Story Technique,* Houghton, 1929; (with Philip Wood) *Time Calls for the Jasper* (three-act play), 1935, reissued as *Lend Me Your Ears,* Samuel French, 1937; (editor) *This Week's Short-Short Stories,* Random House, 1953; (editor; introduction by Alfred Hitchcock) *This Week's Stories of Mystery and Suspense,* Random House, 1957; *Samuel Adams: The Fateful Years, 1764-1776* (history), Dodd, 1965; *New England in Color* (travel; photographs by Samuel Chamberlain), Hastings House, 1969; *Lexington and Concord in Color* (travel; photographs by S. Chamberlain), Hastings House, 1970.

SIDELIGHTS: Beach's wide-ranging interests are reflected in the variety of his writings. Regarding his book, *Short-Story Technique,* the *Boston Evening Transcript* wrote this critique: "It would be difficult for a solitary beginner to lay his hands and spend his time on a more concise and clear-headed technical guide and text. So entirely is the book written with the serious beginning student in mind, that there are carefully listed and assorted questions at the end of each chapter."

STEWART TAFT BEACH

A book very much different from this guide, *Samuel Adams: The Fateful Years, 1764-1776,* also received favorable reviews. The *New York Times Book Review* is of the opinion that although, "Mr. Beach's reluctance to read greater significance into the context of Adam's revolutionary years and to extract more from the uniqueness of his role makes for a narrative and a portrait that seems so thin as to lack plausibility. On the other hand, this is a conscientious work, painstakingly careful and sound in its references. . . . Mr. Beach's book deserves high marks for its restraint, its respect for its subject and its tone of reasoned reappraisal."

FOR MORE INFORMATION SEE: Boston Evening Transcript, August 3, 1929; "He Read His Own Book," *Saturday Evening Post,* October 25, 1947; W. J. Burke and Will D. Howe, *American Authors and Books,* revised, Crown, 1962; Martha E. Ward and Dorothy A. Marquardt, *Authors of Books for Young People,* Scarecrow, 1964; *New York Times Book Review,* May 1, 1966.

BENEDICT, Dorothy Potter 1889-1979

OBITUARY NOTICE—See sketch in *SATA* Volume 11: Born April 15, 1889, in Chicago, Ill.; died December 4, 1979, in Washington, D.C. During World War I Benedict was an American Red Cross worker in France. During World War II she served as a translator and secretary for the U.S. Air Service and later worked as speech writer for the U.S. Air Force. She was the author of three children's books, *Pagan the Black, Fabulous,* and *Bandoleer,* and also contributed short stories and articles to magazines. *For More Information See: Contemporary Authors, Permanent Series,* Volume 1, Gale, 1975. *Obituaries: Washington Post,* December 9, 1979; *Contemporary Authors,* Volume 93-96, Gale, 1980.

BENET, Laura 1884-1979

OBITUARY NOTICE—See sketch in *SATA* Volume 3: Born June 13, 1884, in Brooklyn, N.Y.; died February 17, 1979, in New York, N.Y. Social worker, newspaper editor, poet, and author. After her retirement from social work, Benet worked for several New York newspapers, including the *New York Evening Post*. In addition to writing children's books, such as *The Hidden Valley*, and novels and literary biographies about such persons as Dickinson, Shelley, Poe, and Thackeray, Benet was also the author of two books on her brothers, Stephen Vincent and William Rose Benet. She wrote numerous volumes of poetry, including *Bridge of a Single Hair*, published in 1974. *For More Information See: Junior Book of Authors*, Wilson, 1951; *Authors of Books for Young People*, 2nd edition, Scarecrow, 1971; *Who's Who of American Women*, 8th edition, Marquis, 1973; *Contemporary Authors*, Volume 9-12, revised, Gale, 1974. *Obituaries: New York Times*, February 19, 1979; *AB Bookman's Weekly*, March 26, 1979; *Contemporary Authors*, Volume 85-88, Gale, 1980.

BONSALL, Crosby (Barbara Newell) 1921- (Crosby Newell)

PERSONAL: Born January 2, 1921, in New York City; married George Bonsall. *Education:* Attended American School of Design and New York University School of Architecture, New York City. *Home:* New York, N.Y.

CROSBY BONSALL

(From *The Day I Had to Play with My Sister* by Crosby Bonsall. Illustrated by the author.)

CAREER: Author and illustrator. Began working in small advertising agencies after college: a doodle developed into a rag doll, bringing her recognition as a creator, writer and illustrator of doll characters for children. *Awards, honors: I'll Show You Cats*, illustrated by Ylla (pseudonym of Camilla Koffler), was named as one of *New York Times* best illustrated children's books of the year, 1964.

WRITINGS—Under name Crosby Newell: (With George Bonsall) *What Are You Looking At?*, Treasure Books, 1954; (with G. Bonsall) *The Helpful Friends*, Wonder Books, 1955; *The Surprise Party* (self-illustrated), Wonder Books, 1955; *Captain Kangaroo's Book* (illustrated by Evan Jeffrey), Grosset, 1958; *Polar Bear Brothers* (illustrated by Ylla), Harper, 1960; *Kippy the Koala* (illustrated by George Leavens), Harper, 1960; *Hurry up, Slowpoke* (self-illustrated), Grosset, 1961.

Under name Crosby Bonsall; all published by Harper, except as noted: *Listen, Listen!* (illustrated by Ylla), 1961; *Tell Me Some More* (illustrated by Fritz Siebel), 1961; *Look Who's Talking* (illustrated by Ylla), 1962; *Who's a Pest?* (self-illustrated), 1962; *The Case of the Hungry Stranger* (self-illustrated), 1963, Spanish edition, translated by Pura Belpré as

El Caso del Forastero Hambriento, 1969; *What Spot?* (self-illustrated), 1963; *I'll Show You Cats* (illustrated by Ylla), 1964; *It's Mine!* (self-illustrated), 1964; *The Case of the Cat's Meow* (self-illustrated), 1965; *The Case of the Dumb Bells* (self-illustrated), 1966; *Here's Jellybean Reilly* (illustrated by Ylla), 1966; *Whose Eye Am I?* (illustrated by Ylla), 1968; *The Case of the Scaredy Cats*, 1971; *The Day I Had to Play with My Sister* (self-illustrated), 1972; *Mine's the Best* (self-illustrated; *Horn Book* Honor List), 1973; *Piggle* (self-illustrated), 1973; *And I Mean It, Stanley*, 1974; *Twelve Bells for Santa*, (self-illustrated), 1977; *Good-bye Summer*, Greenwillow, 1979.

Illustrator; Under name Crosby Newell: George Bonsall, *The Really Truly Treasure Hunt*, Treasure Books, 1954; George Bonsall, *The Big Joke*, Wonder Books, 1955.

Under name Crosby Bonsall: Joan L. Nodset, *Go Away, Dog*, Harper, 1963; Phil Ressner, *August Explains*, Harper, 1963; Joan Kahn, *Seesaw*, Harper, 1964; Ralph Underwood, editor, *Ask Me Another Riddle*, Grosset, 1964; Oscar Weigle, editor, *Great Big Joke and Riddle Book*, Grosset, 1970.

SIDELIGHTS: As a child growing up in Long Island, Bonsall spent summers making paper dolls. In school she took an active interest in school papers until she enrolled at The American School of Design where she specialized in commercial art.

Bonsall's early career was spent in small advertising agencies. Her entry into children's literature resulted from a doodle on her drawing board in the advertising agency in which she was a partner. A doll manufacturer who saw the doodle bought the rights to manufacture the doll. Bonsall created a family of dolls which were used as characters in her first book.

Since then, Bonsall has illustrated several books as well as writing and illustrating her own books for children. Her belief that children might enjoy some very simple mystery stories started "The Case of the . . ." series which has been so popular with younger children.

Bonsall's illustrations are primarily done in black-and-white and two colors. A *Horn Book* reviewer said of the author's *Tell Me Some More*, ". . . [the book] is highly original and full of fun." "An overly farcical prolongation of the story must be forgiven," wrote a *Saturday Review* critic, "for the real sense of the wonder of reading that is contained in this one brief book about it."

Bonsall wrote, as well as illustrated, *The Case of the Cat's Meow*. The *New York Times Book Review* observed of this book, "Mrs. Bonsall's deceptively simple style conceals a wealth of artistry, skillful characterization, suspense and humor rarely found in children's books. . . . The drawings, as delightful as the text, are an extra dividend."

Bonsall's works are included in The Kerlan Collection at the University of Minnesota.

FOR MORE INFORMATION SEE: Horn Book, August, 1965, April, 1979, June, 1979; Lee Kingman and others, compilers, *Illustrators of Children's Books: 1957-1966*, Horn Book, 1968; Doris de Montreville, editor, *Third Book of Junior Authors*, H. W. Wilson, 1972.

JAMES CLOYD BOWMAN

BOWMAN, James Cloyd 1880-1961

PERSONAL: Born January 18, 1880, in Leipsic, Ohio; died September 27, 1961, in Chapel Hill, North Carolina; son of Martin Van Buren and Anne (Hull) Bowman; married Mabel Edna Fessenden, June 19, 1911; children: Jeanne Claire. *Education:* Ohio Northern University, B.S., 1905, B. Litt., 1908; Harvard University, A.M., 1910. *Politics:* Republican. *Religion:* Presbyterian. *Home:* Marquette, Michigan.

CAREER: Iowa State College (now Iowa State University of Science and Technology), Ames, professor of English, 1910-21; Northern State Teachers College (now Northern Michigan University), Marquette, chairman of English department, 1921-30; author. *Member:* Modern Language Association of America, National Council of Teachers of English, Midwest Authors Association, Eugene Field Society, Phi Kappa Phi, Rotary International. *Awards, honors:* Litt. D., Ohio Northern University, 1923; runner-up for the John Newbery Award, 1938, for *Pecos Bill: The Greatest Cowboy of All Time*.

WRITINGS—Juvenile: *The Knight of the Chinese Dragon*, Pfeifer Press, 1913; *The Adventures of Paul Bunyan*, Century, 1927; *Pecos Bill: The Greatest Cowboy of All Time* (illustrated by Laura Bannon) Whitman, 1937, reprinted, 1972; *Mystery Mountain* (illustrated by Lucille Wallower), Whitman, 1940; *Winabojo: Master of Life* (illustrated by L. Wallower), Whitman, 1941; *John Henry: The Rambling Black Ulysses* (illustrated by Roy La Grone), Whitman, 1942; *Mike Fink: Snapping Turtle of the O-hi-o-o, Snag of the Mas-sa-sip* (illustrated by Leonard Everett Fisher), Little, Brown, 1957.

"A man can't be expected to waste his entire lifetime catching a single horse or cow." ■ (From *Pecos Bill: The Greatest Cowboy of All Time* by James Cloyd Bowman. Illustrated by Laura Bannon.)

With Margery Bianco; all juvenile: *Tales from a Finnish Tupa* (stories from a translation by Aili Kolehmainen; illustrated by Laura Bannon), Whitman, 1936 (reissued in England as *Tales from a Finnish Fireside,* Chatto & Windus, 1975); *Seven Silly Wise Men* (excerpts from *Tales from a Finnish Tupa;* illustrated by John Faulkner), Whitman, 1965; *Who Was Tricked?* (translation by A. Kolehmainen; illustrated by J. Faulkner), Whitman, 1966.

Other writings; *Into the Depths,* University Press, (Valparaiso, Ind.), 1905; *The Gift of White Roses,* 3rd revised edition, Pilgrim Press, 1914; (editor with Louis I. Bredvold, and others) *Essays for College English,* Heath, 1915; (editor) *Essays for College English,* 2nd series, Heath, 1918; (editor) *The Promise of Country Life* (short stories), Heath, 1916; *On the Des Moines,* Cornhill, 1921; (with J. Lawrence Eason) *Composition and Selected Essays for Normal Schools and Colleges,* Harcourt, 1923; (editor) *Contemporary American Criticism,* Holt, 1926.

SIDELIGHTS: An appreciation for nature developed naturally in James Cloyd Bowman, who grew up in the rural village of Leipsic, Ohio. As a child, he enjoyed roaming the woods and listening to frontier legends told to him by his mother, whose family had emigrated from New York. Bowman's love for both nature and folklore grew throughout his adult life as he came into contact with a wider variety of peoples and legends.

Bowman attended Ohio Northern University in the nearby town of Ada, Ohio. Later, while doing graduate research at Harvard, his interest in folklore developed into a desire to retell legends in books for young people.

Bowman chose to write about folk heroes from many walks of American life, as well as from foreign countries. His books grew out of library research and interviews with people of different regions and races. Bowman was fascinated by better known American heroes such as Paul Bunyan and Pecos Bill, as well as by the folk heroes of American minorities. His interest in the cultures of American Indians and black Americans lead him to write *Winabojo: Master of Life* and *John Henry: Rambling Black Ulysses.*

Bowman collaborated with Margery Bianco in the writing of three books of Finnish folklore. In 1969, Educational Enrichment Materials, Inc., created a filmstrip for elementary school audiences based on *Who Was Tricked?*. Bowman's greatest satisfaction was in the retelling of folklore and his greatest passion was to see that all children were given the chance to enjoy it.

FOR MORE INFORMATION SEE: Kunitz & Haycraft, editors, *Junior Book of Authors,* second edition, H. W. Wilson, 1951; Martha E. Ward and Dorothy A. Marquardt, *Authors of Books for Young People,* second edition, Scarecrow Press, 1971. *Obituary: New York Times,* September 28, 1961.

BOYLSTON, Helen (Dore) 1895-

PERSONAL: Born April 4, 1895, in Portsmouth, New Hampshire; daughter of Joseph and Fannie Dore (Wright) Boylston. *Education:* Graduated from the nursing school at Massachusetts General Hospital, Boston, 1915. *Home:* Trumbull, Connecticut.

CAREER: Nurse and author. Following graduation from nursing school, she enlisted in the Harvard Medical Unit, serving with the British Expeditionary Force during World War I, 1915-19; joined the Red Cross after the war, doing reconstruction work in Europe for a year and a half. Returned to Massachusetts General Hospital, teaching nose and throat anesthesia for two years; also worked for a while as a psychiatric nurse.

WRITINGS: Sister: The War Diary of a Nurse, I. Washburn, 1927; *Sue Barton, Student Nurse* (illustrated by Forrest W. Orr), Little, Brown, 1936; *Sue Barton, Senior Nurse* (illustrated by F. W. Orr), Little, Brown, 1937; *Sue Barton, Visiting Nurse* (illustrated by Orr), Little, Brown, 1938; *Sue Barton, Rural Nurse* (illustrated by Orr), Little, Brown, 1939; *Sue Barton, Superintendent of Nurses* (illustrated by Orr), Little, Brown, 1940; *Carol Goes Backstage* (illustrated by Frederick E. Wallace), Little, Brown, 1941; *Carol Plays Summer Stock* (illustrated by Major Felton), Little, Brown, 1942; *Carol Goes on the Stage* (illustrated by F. E. Wallace), J. Lane, 1943; *Carol on Broadway* (illustrated by M. Felton), Little, Brown, 1944; *Carol on Tour* (illustrated by Felton), Little, Brown, 1946; *Sue Barton, Neighborhood Nurse,* Little, Brown, 1949; *Sue Barton, Staff Nurse,* Little, Brown, 1952; *Clara Barton, Founder of the American Red Cross* (illustrated by Paula Hutchison), Random House, 1955.

Contributor to magazines including *Atlantic Monthly, Harper's, Forum, Country Gentlemen, McCall's,* and *Liberty.*

SIDELIGHTS: **April 4, 1895.** Born in Portsmouth, New Hampshire, Boylston's childhood was a happy one, lively and unstrained. She was educated in the Portsmouth Public Schools where she was an average student. ". . . I went fishing down in the Maine woods with Dad. I remember the smell of the hot pine-needles and dry leaves and burnt underbrush; the great broad lake, blue and motionless in the summer heat; the dry buzz of insects; and the nights, the beautiful lonely nights, when the lake was full of stars and the woods lay heavy with blackness along the shores, and there was no sound except the far-off call of a loon, or the sad, questioning '*Quosh?*' of a lonely heron sweeping through the night. And then the nights when the wind was up, and I lay awake listening to the crackle and snap of branches overhead. . . . Day after day of peace and good comradeship. Long hours of fishing by lonely streams. Days that I spent by myself paddling over the lake, now landing to pick berries, now lying in the bottom of the canoe, letting it drift. Rainy days, spent standing knee-deep in Dead Brook trying to catch my supper, or in camp reading, while the rain pattered and dripped and there was only a white throat singing on the ridgepole to keep me company. How far away and long ago it seems!. . ." [Helen Dore Boylston, *"Sister:" The War Diary of a Nurse,* Ives Washington, 1927.[1]]

1915. Fulfilled a childhood ambition to become a nurse and graduated from nursing school in Boston. During World War I Boylston enlisted in the Harvard Medical Unit, where she served as a nurse overseas with the British Expeditionary Force.

HELEN BOYLSTON

Sue was a dark fleeing shadow down the corridor in the opposite direction. ■ (From *Sue Barton, Student Nurse* by Helen Dore Boylston. Illustrated by Forrest W. Orr.)

May, 1918. "The war news is excellent. We've checked them all along the line, and in many places have recaptured lost ground. How little that means—and how much! Today a ditch is full of Germans, and tomorrow it is full of Englishmen. Neither side really wants the silly muddy ditch, yet they kill each other persistently, wearily, ferociously, patiently, in order to gain possession of it. And whoever wins, it has won—nothing. It's so futile. But after all, I don't know that it's any more futile than the struggles of everyday life. It's only more intensified. How ridiculous human beings are! It's well for the war that everybody doesn't feel as I do, or they would, every one, sit down comfortable, saying, 'What th' hell,' and the war would stop because nobody would take the trouble to continue it.

"I don't know why we aren't busier here. It must be that the men have all been killed."[1]

November 11, 1918. "In ten minutes the war will be over. Hostilities are to cease at eleven o'clock, and it is ten minutes to eleven now. It's incredible that one can measure peace in actual units of time. I lay awake all last night, thinking.

While the Senate was deliberating [the Geneva Treaty], the Mississippi River overflowed its banks down its entire length, causing great loss of life and property. ■ (From *Clara Barton, Founder of the American Red Cross* by Helen Dore Boylston. Illustrated by Paula Hutchison.)

"What are we all to do now? How can we go home to civilian life, to the never ending, never varying routine?

"And the Twenty-second General Hospital, that vital living thing, saturated with the heights and depths of human emotion, will become a slowly fading memory of days when we really lived.

"There go the bells! And the Drums! And the Sirens! And the bagpipes! And cheering that swells louder and louder! The war is over—and I never felt so sick in my life. Everything is over.

"But it shan't be! I *won't* stop living!"[1]

1919-1921. Joined the Red Cross in Europe, where she lived in Albania, Italy, Germany, and other countries.

1921-1923. Returned to the United States and worked at the Massachusetts General Hospital. ". . .I was the slightly astonished possessor of a job, taken for one year. I was to have charge of the Nose and Throat Department of the Out-Patient. I was to teach etherizing, and I was to come July first. The 'one year' scared me a little. I wondered if I'd be able to stick it.

". . . It still seems miraculous to me to have everything in the world to work with. I have worked so long with nothing at all. I can hardly understand the complaints of the other head nurses about equipment. It seems so amazing to me to have more than one of anything. I suppose in a little while I'll forget and grumble too. One always does." [Helen Dore Boylston, "Everyday Life," *Atlantic,* November, 1925.[2]]

1929. Worked as a psychiatric nurse in New York City until she found that she could earn her living by writing. Her stories and articles appeared in a wide variety of magazines.

1936. Began her series of vocational novels for girls based on the nursing profession. "The Victorians were far more hard-boiled than we are in their attitude toward the young. They eliminated sex, true enough, but a run-through of the works of Louisa M. Alcott will reveal everything from drunkenness to death. It is doubtful if any book for children written today would include so harrowing a scene as the death of Beth in *Little Women,* or, for that matter, the scene in *Rose in Bloom* in which Cousin Charlie turns up roaring and passes out cold.

"We are not complaining. Nobody, we are convinced, was ever corrupted by *Rose in Bloom,* but it does give us pause—to ask what *should* be left out of books for young people. We think we have two answers, at least. Defeat and despair are not proper topics for pre-adolescents; and as for the teenagers, if they must encounter unredeemed tragedy in their reading, let us hope that they will not be able to identify themselves with it." [Helen Dore Boylston and Jane Cobb, "New Books for Children," *Atlantic,* December, 1950.[3]]

Boylston's books are still very much in demand today as they were forty years ago. The author lives quietly in a nursing home, St. Joseph's Manor, in Trumbull, Connecticut.

Sue Barton, Neighborhood Nurse, one of Boylston's later books in the "Sue Barton" series, was described by a *New York Times* reviewer as ". . . an easy, natural story with a satisfying background for those girls who like domestic settings."

HOBBIES AND OTHER INTERESTS: Photography.

FOR MORE INFORMATION SEE: "Helen Dore Boylston," *Current Biography,* H. W. Wilson, 1942; (for children) Stanley J. Kunitz and Howard Haycraft, editors, *Junior Book of Authors,* second revised edition, H. W. Wilson, 1951; Brian Doyle, editor, *Who's Who of Children's Literature,* Schocken Books, 1968.

The hills are dearest which our childish feet
Have climbed the earliest; and the streams most sweet
Are those at which our young lips drank.
—John Greenleaf Whittier

VIRGINIA BRADLEY

BRADLEY, Virginia 1912-

PERSONAL: Born December 2, 1912, in Omaha, Neb.; daughter of Stephen (a lawyer) and Anne (a secretary; maiden name, Healy) Jonas; married Gerald Bradley (a business executive), June 8, 1940; children: Stephen, Michael, Betty (Mrs. Alfred Ramsey), Patricia (Mrs. James Curtis). *Education:* University of Nebraska, B.F.A., 1933. *Home:* 425 15th St., Santa Monica, Calif. 90402.

CAREER: Omaha World Herald, Omaha, Neb., member of classified advertising staff, 1937-38; workshop director of Los Angeles Schools, adult division, 1963-78. Southern California Woman's Press Club, 1974—, and Santa Monica Emeritus College, 1975—. *Member:* Society of Children's Book Writers, American Film Teachers Association, P.E.N., Southern California Educational Theatre Association, Santa Monica Writers Club (president, 1954-55).

WRITINGS: Is There an Actor in the House? Dramatic Material from Pantomime to Play (juvenile), Dodd, 1975; *Stage Eight* (young adult; eight one-act plays), Dodd, 1977; *Bend to the Willow* (young adult novel), Dodd, 1979. Contributor to *Yankee, Young Miss, McCall's, Girltalk, Southland, Scouting, Western Family,* and religious journals.

WORK IN PROGRESS: A book of holiday plays; another young adult novel as yet untitled.

SIDELIGHTS: "Always a dreamer I lived in a world of 'let's pretend' throughout my childhood. Many a summer afternoon my friends and I strung a blanket over a couple of poles in the backyard and put on a show for the neighborhood.

"This interest in drama, along with my love for the magic of words, took me to the theater arts and creative writing departments at college. Then, during my single life, I taught English and journalism and even had a brief stint with a repertory company. Finally, with marriage and a family, I turned to writing plays for Cub Scouts, Brownies and school functions. Since I was inept at handicraft (the glue would never stick for me) the young people who joined my troops provided the entertainment. Many of the skits and sketches in my first book came from those performances.

"Plays are not my only interest. I am a story teller, and my novel, *Bend to the Willow,* is set in the 'olden days' of 1935 in a small Nebraska town. Because I am from the midwest I remember how it was on the prairie."

FOR MORE INFORMATION SEE: Ms. Magazine, December, 1978.

BRAITHWAITE, Althea 1940-
(Althea)

PERSONAL: Born June 20, 1940, in Pinner, Middlesex, England; daughter of Francis Joseph (in Royal Air Force) and Rosemary (Harris) Braithwaite; married Mike Graham-Cameron, December 1, 1966 (divorced, 1975); married Edward Parker (an engineer), June 28, 1979; children: (first marriage) Duncan Charles. *Education:* Attended Felixstowe College, 1951-56. *Religion:* "Humanist." *Home and office:* Beechcroft House, Over, Cambridge CB4 5NE, England.

CAREER: Polyhedron Printers, Ltd., Cambridge, England, director and chairman, 1964-79; Dinosaur Publications, Cam-

ALTHEA BRAITHWAITE

bridge, managing editor, director and chairman, 1966—. Illustrator of postcards and designer of books and painting books. *Member:* Society of Authors, Society of Illustrators. *Awards, honors:* British Toymakers Guild awards for thirty of her books; Young Publishers Award for contribution to children's books.

WRITINGS—All juvenile: *Victoria and the Flowerbed Children,* Dinosaur, 1971; *Victoria and the Balloon Keeper,* Dinosaur, 1971; *All About Squirrels and Moles and Things,* Dinosaur, 1971; *All About Guns and Armour and Things,* Dinosaur, 1972; *Night,* Souvenir Press, 1972; *Water,* Souvenir Press, 1972; *Going on Wheels,* Souvenir Press, 1972; *All About Poppies and Bluebells and Things,* Dinosaur, 1973; *Going to the Doctor,* Dinosaur, 1973, Merrimack Book Service, 1978; *Making a Road,* Dinosaur, 1973, Merrimack Book Service, 1978; *The New Baby,* Souvenir Press, 1973; *Whirling Windmills,* Colourmaster International, 1973, Merrimack Book Service, 1978; *Life in a Castle,* Colourmaster International, 1973, Merrimack Book Service, 1978; *Signposts of the Sea,* Colourmaster International, 1973; *Man in the Sky,* Colourmaster International, 1973, Merrimack Book Service, 1978; *Making a Car,* Dinosaur, 1974; *Building a House,* Dinosaur, 1974; *How Life Began,* Dinosaur, 1974, Merrimack Book Service, 1978; *Going Into Hospital,* Dinosaur, 1974, Merrimack Book Service, 1978; *Visiting the Dentist,* Dinosaur, 1974, Merrimack Book Service, 1978; *Man Flies On,* Colourmaster International, 1974, Merrimack Book Service, 1978; *Iron Roads,* Colourmaster International, 1974; *Inland Waterways,* Colourmaster International, 1974; *Bridges,* Colourmaster International, 1974.

Fighting Fires, Dinosaur, 1975; *Going on a Train,* Dinosaur, 1975; *Starting School,* Dinosaur, 1975; *Hospitals,* Dinosaur, 1975; Merrimack Book Service, 1978; *Cars,* Dinosaur, 1975; *Zoos,* Dinosaur, 1975, Merrimack Book Service, 1978; *Farms*, Dinosaur, 1975, Merrimack Book Service, 1978; *Life in the Garden,* Dinosaur, 1975; *Life in Ponds and Streams,* Dinosaur, 1975; *Life in Hedges and Verges,* Dinosaur, 1975; *Life on the Seashore,* Dinosaur, 1975; *Exploring Breckland,* Dinosaur, 1975; *Exploring the Broads,* Dinosaur, 1975; *The Gingerbread Men,* Dinosaur, 1975; *A Baby in the Family,* Dinosaur, 1975, Merrimack Book Service, 1978.

David and His Sister Carol, Dinosaur, 1976, Merrimack Book Service, 1978; *Where Does Food Come From?,* Dinosaur, 1976, Merrimack Book Service, 1978; *I Go to Playschool,* Souvenir Press, 1976; *Moving House,* Souvenir Press, 1976; *Castle Life,* Dinosaur, 1977; *Flying in an Aeroplane,* Dinosaur, 1977; *Having an Eye Test,* Dinosaur, 1977; *Thomas Telford: Man of Iron,* Dinosaur, 1977; *Bath from Roman Times,* Dinosaur, 1977; *The Great Family: Bernardo's,* Dinosaur, 1977; *I Go to Hospital,* Souvenir Press, 1977; *Machines in the Home,* Penguin, 1977; *My Babysitter,* Dinosaur,

Sometimes Desmond walked through the town. ■(From *Desmond and the Monsters* by Althea. Illustrated by the author.)

1978; *My Childminder,* Dinosaur, 1979; *About Bees and Honey,* Dinosaur, 1979; *A Visit to the Factory,* Dinosaur, 1979; *Moth and Butterfly Collection,* Dinosaur, 1979; *Machines on a Farm,* Dinosaur, 1979; *Making a Book,* Dinosaur, 1980; *Visiting a Museum,* Dinosaur, 1980; *Caterpillars to Butterflies,* Dinosaur, 1980.

Self-illustrated juveniles: *Cuthbert and Bimbo,* Dinosaur, 1967, Merrimack Book Service, 1978; *Desmond,* Dinosaur, 1967; *Benjamin,* Dinosaur, 1967; *Jeremy Mouse,* Dinosaur, 1968, Merrimack Book Service, 1978; *Peter Pig,* Dinosaur, 1968, Merrimack Book Service, 1978; *Desmond the Dinosaur,* Dinosaur, 1968; *Desmond Goes to Scotland,* Dinosaur, 1968; *George and the Baby,* Dinosaur, 1968, Merrimack Book Service, 1978; *Desmond and the Fire,* Dinosaur, 1969; *Desmond the Dusty Dinosaur,* Dinosaur, 1969; *Desmond Meets a Stranger,* Dinosaur, 1971; *The Gingerbread Band,* Dinosaur, 1971; *Smith the Lonely Hedgehog,* Dinosaur, 1971; *Smith and Matilda,* Dinosaur, 1971; *Desmond at the Carnival,* Dinosaur, 1971; *Tugby Is Given an Umbrella*, Dinosaur, 1971; *Round and Round,* Souvenir Press, 1971; *All About Creatures on Islands and Things,* Dinosaur, 1972; *All About Pines and Oaks and Things,* Dinosaur, 1972; *All About Snails and Ladybirds and Things,* Dinosaur, 1972; *Up and Down,* Souvenir Press, 1972.

All About Cuckoos and Robins and Things, Dinosaur, 1973; *All About Voles and Sticklebacks and Things,* Dinosaur, 1973; *The First National Trust Painting Book,* Dinosaur, 1973; *The Second National Trust Painting Book,* Dinosaur, 1973; *High in the Sky,* Souvenir Press, 1973; *The First Country Book,* Dinosaur, 1974; *Althea's First Picture Book,* Dinosaur, 1974; *Desmond Goes to New York,* Dinosaur, 1975; *The Third National Trust Painting Book,* Dinosaur, 1975; *The Fourth National Trust Painting Book,* Dinosaur, 1975; *The Second Country Book,* Dinosaur, 1975; *Desmond and the Monsters,* Dinosaur, 1975; *A Visit to Canterbury Cathedral,* Cathedral Gifts, 1975; *Desmond and the Stranger,* Dinosaur, 1976; *Day by Day Diary,* Dinosaur, 1977; *Desmond Goes Boating,* Dinosaur, 1977; *Colours and Cars,* Souvenir Press, 1977; *Desmond and the Fancy Press Party,* Dinosaur, 1979; *Desmond the Dinosaur Story Book,* Dinosaur, 1979; *The Big Desmond Story Book,* Dinosaur, 1980; *Animals at Your Feet,* Dinosaur, 1980; *Jeremy Mouse and Cat,* Dinosaur, 1980; *Address Book,* Dinosaur, 1980; *Frogs,* Longmans, 1980; *Birds,* Longmans, Green, 1980; *A Flower,* Longmans,

1980; *The Butterfly,* Longmans, Green, 1980; *Wearing Many Hats,* Dinosaur, 1980.

Also designer and illustrator of cards, mobiles, friezes, and games for children.

SIDELIGHTS: "I think that books are of great importance to children in explaining what new situations will be like and in helping them to cope with their own emotions and feelings. Later, books can be a marvelous escape as we begin to need fantasy and use our imagination.

"Besides writing for children I visit schools and bookshops to read and talk to children and try to inspire their own creativity. My husband and I are hoping to start a mobile bookshop for people who do not usually go to bookshops."

Braithwaite has shown a talent for drawing, painting, and photography since childhood. The daughter of Lady Earle and the late Air Marshal F. St. J. Braithwaite, she was educated at Felixstowe College and spent much of her childhood on the Suffolk coast. She published her first children's books under the Dinosaur imprint in 1968, and the success of these, both in Britain and throughout the world, led the company to expand into offering editorial services to other publishers.

Souvenir Press commissioned Dinosaur Publications to produce a series of pre-school starter books shortly after the company's foundation. The Brightstart Books now include nineteen titles, all offering information in a happy and reassuring way, on subjects ranging from natural history to things the child sees around him and activities that can cause anxiety in small children, such as going to hospital or night time.

Many Dinosaur publications have won awards for their high standard, including fifty-three British Toymakers Guild Awards, five special recommendations from the English Speaking Union, twenty-nine Design Centre selections and ten British Council selections.

Braithwaite and her small son live in a sleepy Cambridgeshire village where she and her team of designers work in a warren of stables and outbuildings.

HOBBIES AND OTHER INTERESTS: "I am interested in natural history and photography."

FOR MORE INFORMATION SEE: Times Literary Supplement, December 6, 1974; *Junior Bookshelf,* February, 1975, April, 1977; *New Statesman,* May 20, 1977; *Growing Point,* December, 1977.

BRANCATO, Robin F(idler) 1936-

PERSONAL: Born March 19, 1936, in Reading, Pa.; daughter of W. Robert and Margretta (Neuroth) Fidler; married John J. Brancato (a teacher), December 17, 1960; children: Christopher Jay, Gregory Robert. *Education:* University of Pennsylvania, B.A., 1958; City College of City University of New York, M.A., 1976. *Residence:* Teaneck, N.J.

CAREER: John Wiley & Sons, New York, N.Y., copy editor, 1959-61; Hackensack High School, Hackensack, N.J., teacher of English, journalism, and creative writing, 1967—.

WRITINGS: Don't Sit Under the Apple Tree, Knopf, 1975; *Something Left to Lose,* Knopf, 1976; *Winning,* Knopf, 1977; *Blinded by the Light,* Knopf, 1978; *Come Alive at 505*, Knopf, 1980.

SIDELIGHTS: "As a young reader I preferred realism in fiction: a family of orphans surviving by their wits in a boxcar home; the pale, scrawny city girl adapting slowly to life in rural Vermont; square-jawed athletes (and, occasionally but too rarely, a female athlete of rounder features) winning points for prowess and character. I was always poring through the fiction, between the unicorns and the time machines, for the book that could show me literally what I was and what I might become.

"Now, as an adult, I'm trying to write the kind of books I've always liked to read. In my first two novels I explored remembered personal experiences—early pleasures and triumphs, fears and defeats. In my second two novels—for those elusive, exotic readers who have come to be called young adults—I have gone beyond personal experience in an attempt to combine research and observation with the art of fiction.

"The gradual disappearance of certain taboos today has given writers an exciting, widening choice of subject matter and language. But the pitfalls have widened, too. Along with the freedom to 'write about anything,' comes the responsibility to avoid poor taste, sensationalism, trendiness.

"Setting out to write realistic fiction is something I have done more consciously than I have set out to write specifically for young people. I like to think that I write *about* young people but not exclusively *for* them. Down with distinctions . . . well-written stories that happen to be about the young can and should be read without apology by adults. If I have, so far, written primarily about young people, it is probably because in my life adolescence is inescapable. My sons are in

ROBIN F. BRANCATO

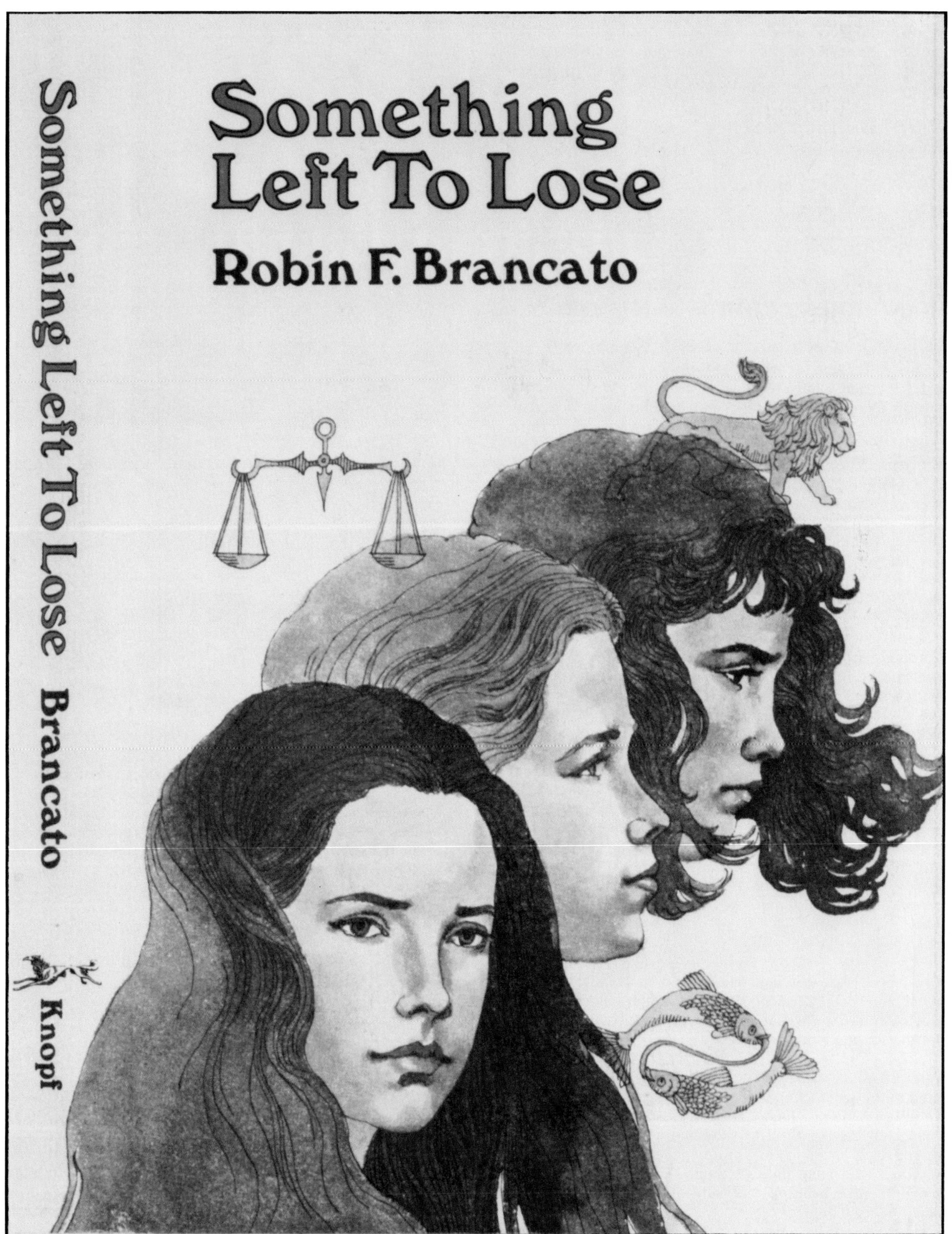

(From *Something Left to Lose* by Robin F. Brancato. Jacket illustrated by Richard Cuffari.)

their teens. I taught for many years in a public high school. My own childhood and teenage years stand out in sharper focus for me, most of the time, than more recent stages of my life. Finally, I like young people enormously. I hope I convey that, above all, in my books."

Brancato lives in Teaneck, New Jersey with her husband John and their two sons.

FOR MORE INFORMATION SEE: Horn Book, August, 1976.

BRANDHORST, Carl T(heodore) 1898-

PERSONAL: Born August 24, 1898, in Lincoln, Neb.; son of Charles William (a farmer) and Alwina (Backhaus) Brandhorst; married Louise Koeneke, June 28, 1922; children: Dorothy (Mrs. William Johnstone), Adeline (Mrs. E. P. Costello), Olivia (Mrs. Joseph Ishikawa), L. Carl, Ellen (Mrs. Edward Wiesehan), Charlotte (Mrs. D. W. Rohren), Curt W., Mark T. *Education:* Concordia Teachers College, Seward, Neb., diploma, 1917; Fort Hays Kansas State College, summer study, 1932-41, B.S. in Ed., 1939, M.S., 1941; University of Nebraska, summer study, 1943-60, Ph.D., 1961. *Politics:* Democrat. *Religion:* Lutheran. *Home:* 55 Pearl, Seward, Neb. 68434.

CAREER: Teacher in private schools, 1917-38; Concordia Teachers College, Seward, Neb., associate professor, 1938-57, professor of biology and chairman of department, 1957-65; retired, 1972. San Fernando Valley State College, visiting associate professor and researcher, 1962-63. Associate editor, *Issues in Christian Education,* Concordia Teachers College. Lutheran Church-Missouri Synod, former member of television commission and former chairman of audiovisual board. *Member:* American Association for the Advancement of Science, National Association of Biology Teachers, Entomological Society of America, Nebraska Academy of Science (past president), Kansas Academy of Science, Sigma Xi, Phi Kappa Phi, Kansas Entomological Society.

WRITINGS: (With Robert Sylwester) *Tale of Whitefoot* (juvenile), Simon & Schuster, 1968. Also author of a *Brief History of Concordia's Teachers College* and contributor to scientific publications.

WORK IN PROGRESS: Jewels in the Grass, a children's book on water; research on plant galls of southwestern desert areas; *Nature and the Bible,* a book for high school students, which emphasizes the basic harmony existing between nature and the written word of God.

SIDELIGHTS: "Since earliest childhood I have been interested in the wildflowers, birds, butterflies, and mammals of the prairie among which I grew up in Oklahoma Territory. I can still feel the thrill of watching a caterpillar that had hanged itself on a stem of a prairie grass. It hung there wriggling and squirming until its outer skin dropped off and it swung there a beautiful chrysalis from which a butterfly would later emerge.

"The wonders of nature have always fascinated me. The delicate petals of the purple sheep-sorrel, the water strider running on the surface of a pond, the powdery scales of the butterfly's wings, the beautiful colors of the coral snake, the community life of the prairie-dog town—all were to be investigated by my brother, Art and me.

Suddenly out of nowhere came a flash of brown and white. The grasshopper was brushed rudely from his leaf, and he found himself in the paws of a little creature with shining black eyes.... ▪(From *The Tale of Whitefoot* by Carl T. Brandhorst and Robert Sylwester. Illustrated by Grambs Miller.)

"We had our own names for the creatures we met—but what were their real names? There was no library and very few books of reference anywhere to be found. Even at college very little information was to be found about the flora and fauna of our part of the country. Some of the 'old timers' who had spent their lives on the prairie could tell us many things about plants and animals but they also had their own names for the various creatures. And often we found their stories to be untrue. For example, an old trailhand told me that if I took a hair from a horse's tail and put it in a bottle of water for a week it would turn into a snake. I tried it and it didn't work. Later I found what appeared to be a horse hair swimming in the water of a buffalo wallow, I fished it out and it curled itself into a knot. Then I wasn't sure. The dearth of material available to elementary school children of the prairie states continues even today.

CARL T. BRANDHORST

"Later, I became a teacher in a rural school in Kansas, where I endeavored to teach the individuals of the coming generation how to enjoy the wonders of nature. What fun we had in our junior Audubon Society when on Friday afternoons we gave reports of our observations or as we took hikes through the wooded ravines or the open prairie. The state of Kansas issued a series of books about the fauna and flora which were very helpful for the teachers but they were still not suitable for the grades. Nebraska issued none at all for many years.

"It is this dearth of materials suitable for elementary children that has caused me to write. I do not enjoy writing, but I see the need for some guidance for the elementary schools. E. Laurence Palmer of Cornell did a good deal of work of the nature needed and his writings were very helpful to me, as also were some of the writings of John Burroughs, John Muir, and Ernest Seton. But I feel if I can induce the elementary school child to go out into nature and to observe nature in action, I shall be happy."

BRANSCUM, Robbie 1937-

PERSONAL: Born June 17, 1937, in Arkansas; daughter of Donnie H. (a farmer) and Blanch (Balitine) Tilley; married Duane Branscum (divorced, 1969); married Lesli J. Carrico, July 15, 1975; children: Deborah. *Home:* 2175 Pacific Dr., Bakersfield, Calif. 93305.

CAREER: Author.

WRITINGS—All juvenile: *Me and Jim Luke,* Doubleday, 1971; *Johnny May,* Doubleday, 1975; *The Three Wars of Billy Joe Treat,* McGraw, 1975; *Toby, Granny and George,* Doubleday, 1976; *The Saving of P.S.,* Doubleday, 1977; *Three Buckets of Daylight,* Lothrop, 1978; *To the Tune of a Hickory Stick,* Doubleday, 1978; *The Ugliest Boy,* Lothrop, 1978; *For Love of Jody,* Lothrop, 1978; *Toby Alone,* Doubleday, 1978; *Toby and Johnny Joe,* Doubleday, 1978.

SIDELIGHTS: "I sometimes resent being raised a hundred years before my time. Yet in many ways I am glad, since it gives me a chance to write about a way of life that our children and their children will only be able to read about.

"I was born on a farm somewhere on the outskirts of Big Flat, Arkansas. No winds howled, no thunder crashed, no

ROBBIE BRANSCUM

(From *The Ugliest Boy* by Robbie Branscum. Illustrated by Michael Eagle.)

lightning sizzled. In fact, it was a hot June night and it was a matter of whether the doctor or the night bugs got to me first.

"My dad died when I was four years old, and we five children were sent deep and far, back into the hills to a small dirt farm to live with our grandparents. We didn't have inside toilets or electricity. The whole family was used to taking a bath in the same tub of sun-warmed water. I reckon we couldn't have gotten much poorer, but there was so much work to do and so many things to see and to explore that we didn't know we were poor. Our days were filled with activities such as gathering corn, potatoes and pumpkins, making shirts and dresses out of flour sacks, hunting rabbits with a forked stick, sneaking off to the old forbidden baptizing hole to go swimming, telling ghost stories and visiting kinfolk.

"From the time I was very young, words fascinated me. Every new one I heard, I repeated over and over to myself. It always seems to me that I was like a walking tape recorder, remembering all and forgetting nothing. Our house was papered in newspapers (as all the other folks' homes around there were). I read every room in the house, standing on chairs to read the ceiling and sometimes standing on my head where the papers had been pasted upside down.

"I went to a small, one-room schoolhouse at a time when the eighth grade was as high as a person aimed. I can remember the mental hunger for books; a book was something to cherish, to be read again and again. My first whole book was the biggest joy I had . . . that and my discovery of a whole house of books called a library.

"I was married at fifteen to a boy not much older, both of us too young to make a marriage work. I have a daughter who, like me, enjoys reading and writing.

"One of the reasons I like children and write about them is because they are honest. Since I couldn't share the wonders of the world with everyone, I started living in my mind, making up fantasies like children do and writing them down."

Branscum now makes her home in Bakersfield, California. A prolific writer, she still manages to find time to read, raise her own vegetables and cook up a storm. Branscum continues to dream of "a small barn, a creek, a moon as big as a summer sky, the far off bay of hounds, running fox and coon and my Arkansas hills that never quite leave one's blood.

"I love the things of childhood—slow moving rivers, woods, fields and fishing poles, tall tales and mystery, long summer days and slipping away from the adult world into the world of children where the lines are boldly drawn."

FOR MORE INFORMATION SEE: Horn Book, August, 1975, October, 1976, December, 1978.

BRAUDE, Michael 1936-

PERSONAL: Born March 6, 1936, in Chicago, Ill.; son of Sheldon and Nan (Resnik) Braude; married Linda Miller (a teacher), August 20, 1961. *Education:* University of Missouri, B.S., 1957; Columbia University, M.S., 1958. *Politics:* Independent. *Religion:* Jewish. *Home:* 5319 Mission Woods Ter., Shawnee Mission, Kan. 66205. *Office:* American Bank and Trust Co., 1 West Armour Blvd., Kansas City, Mo. 64111.

CAREER: Commerce Bank of Kansas City, Kansas City, Mo., 1962—, vice-president, 1966-74; American Bank and Trust Co., Kansas City, Mo., executive vice-president, 1974—. Lecturer in business administration at Kansas City Extension Center, University of Kansas, and Evening Division, Rockhurst College. A vice-president, Kansas City Philharmonic Orchestra. *Member:* Kansas City Chamber of Commerce, Kansas City Advertising and Sales Executives Club, Beta Gamma Sigma, Alpha Pi Zeta, Omicron Delta Kappa.

WRITINGS—Children's books: *Shelby Goes to Wall Street,* Denison, 1965; *Danny Graham—Banker,* Denison, 1966; *Bruce Learns About Life Insurance,* Denison, 1967; *Andy Learns About Advertising,* Denison, 1967; *Peter Enters the Jet Age,* Denison, 1967; *Chad Learns About Naval Aviation,* Denison, 1968; *Jeff Learns About the F.B.I.,* Denison, 1968;

Ray Visits the Air Force Academy, Denison, 1968; *Ronald Learns About College Teaching,* Denison, 1968; *Tim Learns About Mutual Funds,* Denison, 1969; *Richard Learns About Railroading,* Denison, 1969; *Managing Your Money: A Guide to Personal Finance,* Management Center of Cambridge (Mass.), 1969; *Larry Learns About Computers,* Denison, 1969; *A Man and His Money: A Primer on Personal Money Management,* Denison, 1971.

BRETT, Grace N(eff) 1900-1975

PERSONAL: Born February 11, 1900, in Chicago, Ill., died December 27, 1975, in Clearwater, Fla.; daughter of George Gottlob (a teacher) and Sophia (Bach) Neff; married Gilbert James Brett (a writer, editor, and radio moderator), July 15, 1942. *Education:* University of Illinois, B.A.; postgraduate work at Northwestern University, New School of Social Research, and Columbia University. *Home:* 1566 Grove St., Clearwater, Fla. 33515.

CAREER: Writer; lecturer on books, art, and related subjects. *Member:* Children's Reading Round Table, Society of Midland Authors, Matrix, Chicago Women's Literary Club, Theta Sigma Phi, Alpha Delta Kappa (honorary), Women in Communications, Society of Midland Authors, National League of American Pen Women.

WRITINGS: Squiffy the Skunk, Rand McNally, 1953; *The Runaway,* Follett, 1958; *That Willy and Wally,* A. Whitman, 1964; *The Picture Story and Biography of Tom Paine,* Follett, 1965; *Hatsy Catsy: The Cat That Loved Hats,* Denison, 1969. Contributor of articles to *American People's Encyclopedia, Chicago Tribune,* and trade journals.

HOBBIES AND OTHER INTERESTS: Photography, gardening, house furnishings, and fashion designing.

FOR MORE INFORMATION SEE: Christian Science Monitor, March 10, 1943; *Ladies' Home Journal,* October, 1943; *Chicago Tribune,* March 29, 1953; *Milwaukee Journal,* November 13, 1958.

"From now on, no more high rides. Even if you didn't fly off the track, think of what all those drops and jerks around curves do to your nervous system." ■ (From *That Willy and Wally* by Grace Neff Brett. Illustrated by Robert Kresin.)

RAYMOND BRIGGS

BRIGGS, Raymond (Redvers) 1934-

PERSONAL: Born January 18, 1934, in London, England; married Jean Taprell Clark (a painter; deceased), 1963. *Education:* Attended Wimbledon School of Art and Slade School of Fine Art. *Home:* Sussex, England.

CAREER: Illustrator and author. Became interested in becoming a cartoonist at the age of fifteen; started as a free-lance illustrator while still in school; began writing and illustrating children's books, 1957; part-time teacher, Brighton College of Art, 1961—. *Military service:* Served in the British Army for two years. *Member:* Society of Industrial Artists, Dairy Farmer's Association. *Awards, honors:* Kate Greenaway Medal, runner-up, 1964, for *Fee Fi Fo Fum,* and winner, 1966, 1974, for *Mother Goose Treasury,* and *Father Christmas,* respectively; Lewis Carroll Shelf award, 1979, Premio Critici in Erba from Bologna Book Fair, 1979, Boston *Globe-Horn Book* Award, 1979, Kate Greenaway Medal, runner-up, and Dutch Silver Pen Award, all for *The Snowman.*

WRITINGS—All self-illustrated: *Midnight Adventure,* Hamish Hamilton, 1961; *The Strange House,* Hamish Hamilton, 1961; *Ring-a-Ring o' Roses,* Coward, 1962; *Sledges to the Rescue,* Hamish Hamilton, 1963; (editor) *The White Land,* Coward, 1963; (editor) *Fee Fi Fo Fum,* Coward, 1964; (editor) *The Mother Goose Treasury* (*Horn Book* Honor List), Coward, 1966; *Jim and the Beanstalk,* Coward, 1970; *Father Christmas* (ALA Notable Book), Coward, 1973; *Father Christmas Goes on Holiday,* Coward, 1975; *Fungus the Bogeyman,* Hamish Hamilton, 1977; *The Snowman* (*Horn Book* Honor List), Random House, 1978; *Gentleman Jim,* Hamish Hamilton, 1980.

. . . And he explained about glasses while the Giant listened carefully. ■ (From *Jim and the Beanstalk* by Raymond Briggs. Illustrated by the author.)

Illustrator: (With others) Julian Sorell Huxley, *Wonderful World of Life,* Doubleday, 1958; Ruth Manning-Sanders, *Peter and the Piskies,* Oxford University Press, 1958, Roy, 1966; Alfred Leo Duggan, *Look at Castles,* Hamish Hamilton, 1960, published in America as *The Castle Book,* Pantheon, 1961; A. L. Duggan, *Arches and Spires,* Hamish Hamilton, 1961, Pantheon, 1962; Jacynth Hope-Simpson, editor, *Hamish Hamilton Book of Myths and Legends,* Hamish Hamilton, 1964; William Mayne, *Whistling Rufus,* Hamish Hamilton, 1964, Dutton, 1965; R. Manning-Sanders, editor, *Hamish Hamilton Book of Magical Beasts,* Hamish Hamilton, 1965, published in America as *A Book of Magical Beasts,* Thomas Nelson, 1970.

James Aldridge, *The Flying 19,* Hamish Hamilton, 1966; Bruce Carter (pseudonym of Richard Alexander Hough), *Jimmy Murphy and the White Duesenberg,* Coward, 1968; B. Carter, *Nuvolari and the Alfa Romeo,* Coward, 1968; Nicholas Fisk, *Lindbergh: The Lone Flier,* Coward, 1968; N. Fisk, *Richthofen: The Red Baron,* Coward, 1968; W. Mayne, editor, *The Hamish Hamilton Book of Giants,* Hamish Hamilton, 1968, published in America as *William Mayne's Book of Giants,* Dutton, 1969; Michael Brown, *Shackelton's Epic Voyage,* Coward, 1969; Elfrida Vipont (Brown) Foulds, *The Elephant and the Bad Baby,* Coward, 1969; Showell Styles, *First up Everest,* Coward, 1969; James Reeves, *Christmas Book,* Dutton, 1970; Ian Serraillier, *The Tale of Three Landlubbers,* Hamish Hamilton, 1970, Coward, 1971; Virginia Haviland, editor, *The Fairy Tale Treasury,* Coward, 1972; Ruth Manning-Sanders, editor, *Festivals,* Heinemann, 1972, Dutton, 1973.

SIDELIGHTS: As a child, Briggs wanted to be an artist. By the age of fifteen he had enrolled in the Wimbledon School of Art with the intention of becoming a cartoonist. "When I told my parents I wanted to study art, they agreed at once. Though they were working-class people, they weren't fussed that I didn't want to learn a useful trade." [Arnold W. Ehrlich, editor, *Publishers Weekly,* November 5, 1973.[1]]

After two years in the British Army, Briggs enrolled at the Slade School of Fine Art. Because he had always wanted to illustrate as well as paint, Briggs began making the rounds to publishing companies. Discovering that virtually all book illustrations were children's books, he began what became his career—illustrating for children. "Fact is, my publishers got hold of my stuff and they decided it would attract children. I don't work with or near children; don't know much about them, really. I just write and draw to please myself and feel it ought to please others."[1]

The 897 illustrations that he created for *The Mother Goose Treasury* were given the Kate Greenaway award for 1966. These drawings established Briggs' reputation as one of the finest modern illustrators.

Briggs created a sequel to *Jack and the Beanstalk. Jim and the Beanstalk* portrays a giant too old to digest children, and in need of glasses, new teeth, and a toupee. *Commonweal* called it "a hilarious, modern sequel to the famous tale . . . with wonderful pictures," while the *New York Times Book Review* described it as "a gigantic delight."

Briggs' colored illustrations of Showell Styles' *First Up Everest* were called ". . . as much picture as text," by the *Times Literary Supplement.*

When Briggs is not writing or painting he teaches part-time at a local art school. He enjoys vegetable gardening and is especially concerned with keeping England from becoming too urbanized. "Alistair Cooke has warned us British that we are making the same mistake as Americans. We go about widening roads, tearing down old buildings and trees . . . this sort of destruction only leads to more. The more roads, the more cars, it's never ending. We must leave our trees and our wilderness as they are. They can't be replaced once they're gone."[1]

HOBBIES AND OTHER INTERESTS: Reading, gardening, growing fruit, and modern jazz.

FOR MORE INFORMATION SEE: Brian Doyle, *The Who's Who of Children's Literature,* Shocken Books, 1968; Lee Kingman and others, compilers, *Illustrators of Children's Books: 1957-1966,* Horn Book, 1968; Lee Bennett Hopkins, *Books Are by People,* Citation, 1969; *Horn Book,* February, 1971, August, 1974, October, 1974, June, 1979, October, 1979, February, 1980; Doris de Montreville, editor, *Third Book of Junior Authors,* H. W. Wilson, 1972; *New York Times Book Review,* October 8, 1972, December 7, 1975; *Publishers Weekly,* November 5, 1973, February 3, 1975; *Library Journal,* September 15, 1974; Margery Fisher, *Who's Who in Children's Books,* Holt, 1975.

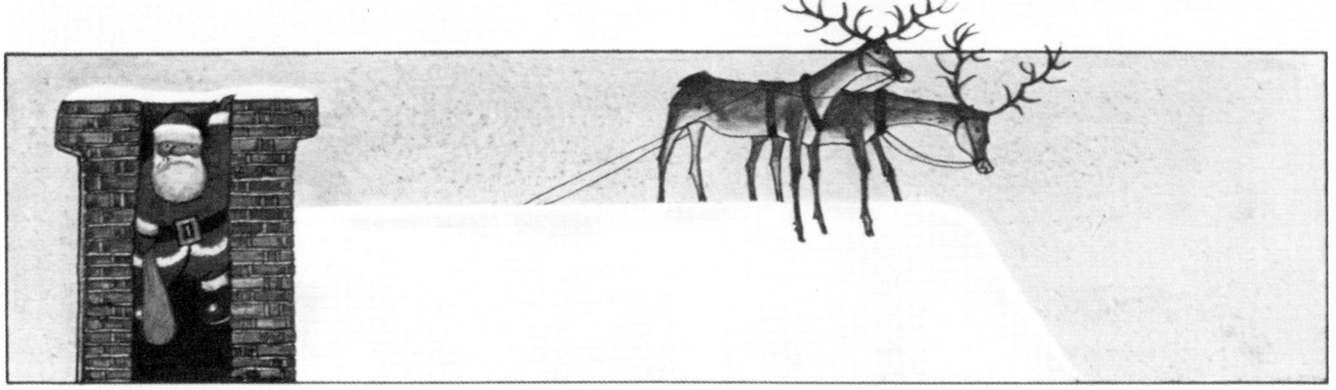

(From *Father Christmas* by Raymond Briggs. Illustrated by the author.)

RUTH BRINDZE

BRINDZE, Ruth 1903-

PERSONAL: Born in 1903, in New York City; married Albert W. Fribourg (a lawyer). *Education:* Graduated from Columbia University. *Home:* Mt. Vernon, N.Y.

CAREER: Author. Worked on newspaper staffs before writing magazine articles and books. *Awards, honors: The Gulf Stream* won a first prize in the *New York Herald Tribune* Children's Book Festival, 1945; *Look How Many People Wear Glasses: The Magic of Lenses* was chosen an outstanding science book for children, 1975, by the committee of science educators, the National Teachers Association, and the Children's Book Council, and received honorable mention at the 5th annual Children's Science Books awards from the New York Academy of Sciences.

WRITINGS: How to Spend Money: Everybody's Practical Guide to Buying, Vanguard, 1935, another edition published as *How to Spend Money: How to Get Your Money's Worth,* Garden City Publishing, 1938; *Not to be Broadcast: The Truth about the Radio,* Vanguard, 1937, reprinted, Da Capo Press, 1974; *Johnny Get Your Money's Worth* (illustrated by Emery I. Gondor), Vanguard, 1938; *Seamanship Below Deck,* Harcourt, 1939, new edition, 1947; *Daily Bread and Other Foods* (illustrated by Harry Daugherty), Row, Peterson, 1941; *Stretching Your Dollar in Wartime,* Vanguard, 1942; *You Can Help Your Country Win* (illustrated by E. I. Gondor), Vanguard, 1943; *The Gulf Stream* (illustrated by Helene Carter; Junior Literary Guild selection), Vanguard, 1945; *Boating Is Fun* (illustrated by Kurt Wiese), Dodd, 1949; *The Story of Our Calendar* (illustrated by H. Carter), Vanguard, 1949. *The Story of the Totem Pole* (illustrated by Yeffe Kimball), Vanguard, 1951; *The Story of Gold* (illustrated by Robert Bruce), Vanguard, 1955; *The Experts' Book of Boating* (illustrated by Fred Wellbrock), Prentice-Hall, 1959; *All About Undersea Exploration,* Random House, 1960; *The Story of the Trade Winds* (illustrated by Hilda Simon), Vanguard, 1960; *All about Sailing the Seven Seas,* Random House, 1962; *All about Courts and the Law* (illustrated by Leonard Slonevsky), Random House, 1964; *The Rise and Fall of the Seas: The Story of the Tides* (illustrated by Felix Cooper), Harcourt, 1964; *Investing Money: The Facts about Stocks and Bonds,* Harcourt, 1968; *The Sea: The Story of the Rich Underwater World,* Harcourt, 1971; *Charting the Oceans,* Vanguard, 1973; *Hurricanes: Monster Storms from the Sea,* Atheneum, 1973; *Look How Many People Wear Glasses: The Magic of Lenses,* Atheneum, 1975.

Also author of the booklet, *How To Get the Most for Your Money,* Home Institute, 1938.

SIDELIGHTS: "As long as I can remember, I have been writing about the things that interest me. When I was going to school in New York City, where I was born, the assignment I liked best was the writing of themes. Long before I was ready for college, I knew that writing was what I wanted to do, but at that time I was thinking of working as a newspaper reporter. At college, therefore, I took special courses in journalism and studied at the Columbia School of Journalism. During summer vacations I worked on real newspapers. It was hard work, but lots of fun.

"After a while I wrote a book, and then another, and another. My first books were written for grownups, but then I wrote one for boys and girls called *Johnny Get Your Money's Worth* which describes how to make a good buy in sporting equipment, clothing, and many other things. Soon after World War II started, I wrote another book called *You Can Help Your Country Win* to tell boys and girls how to take care of the things they have and how to do their part on the home front. . . .

"I spend every weekday working at my desk in a New York City office, but I like the country much better than I do the city, and I like the water even better than I do the country. After that, my hobby is meteorology. Part of each year we live on our sailboat, and all our vacations are spent cruising along the coast. During the rest of the year I live in a suburb of New York in a house that looks like a woodland camp. In the living room we have an enormous stone fireplace, and all around the room there are shelves filled with books that go right up to the ceiling."

Brindze's own curiosity led her to write many of her books for children. *Horn Book* called *All about Undersea Exploration,* "gripping stories of man's ventures into the dark, mysterious, crushing pressures of the oceanic abyss." *Library Journal* commented that "the unique content here is the chapter on oceanographer's discoveries, goals, and tools. . . ."

Reviews of *The Story of the Trade Winds* were mixed. *New York Herald Tribune* said the ". . . text is a satisfactory mingling of exposition with anecdote," while *Saturday Review* said, "the factual material is important and clearly pre-

But neither Captain Drake nor the English people thought there was anything wrong or dishonorable about his plundering. He had been commissioned by the queen as a privateer, which meant that, according to English law, he was authorized to conduct a private war against the Spanish and to attack their treasure ships. ■ (From *The Story of Gold* by Ruth Brindze. Illustrated by Robert Bruce.)

sented, but the effect of the volume is marred by the fictionalized approach to historical events."

Investing Money: The Facts about Stocks and Bonds was described by *Young Readers Review* as doing ". . . a fairly good job of surveying the major portion of the stock market investment picture for the general small investor. . . . Though there is some unevenness in the presentation and some inadequacies, it is a good introductory book, and does mention some items that are often completely ignored in other treatments. . . ."

HOBBIES AND OTHER INTERESTS: Reading, writing, cooking, gardening, and sailing.

FOR MORE INFORMATION SEE: Muriel Fuller, editor, *More Junior Authors,* H. W. Wilson, 1963; *Horn Book,* February, 1976.

BROOKS, Jerome 1931-

PERSONAL: Born July 17, 1931, in Chicago, Ill.; son of Samuel and Rose (Malina) Brooks; married Marilyn Glaser, May 27, 1956 (divorced November 22, 1970); children: Eliot Mitchell, Elise Beth. *Education:* Roosevelt University, B.A., 1953; George Washington University, M.A., 1957. *Home:* 2338 Prairie, Evanston, Ill. 60201. *Office:* Department of English, Richard J. Daley College, 7500 South Pulaski, Chicago, Ill. 60652.

CAREER: Chicago City College, Chicago, Ill., Fenger Campus, instructor in English, 1958-60, Bogan Campus, assistant professor of English and chairman of department, 1960-65, acting dean of faculty, 1969, Crane Campus (now Malcolm X College), administrative assistant and assistant dean for curriculum, 1965-67, Urban Education Center, dean, and director of projects Co-op and Success, 1967-69; Richard J.

Daley College, Chicago, Ill., professor of English, 1970—. *Military service:* U.S. Army, 1953-55.

WRITINGS: Uncle Mike's Boy, Harper, 1973; *The Testing of Charlie Hammelman,* Dutton, 1977; *The Big Dipper Marathon,* Dutton, 1979; *Make Me a Hero,* Dutton, 1980.

WORK IN PROGRESS: "I am currently working on a book for juveniles, tentatively entitled *A Mask on the Mountain,* which wants to be a fantasy based on an actual nightmare I had. . . ."

SIDELIGHTS: "I knew I wanted to write when I was in my teens, but when my first novel, *The Sound of a Driven Leaf,* was rejected by several publishers in 1960, I decided that, to support my family, I'd give up writing and devote my life to teaching, which I did until 1970, when untoward circumstances returned me to my old love.

"*Uncle Mike's Boy* began as a short story, which I never dreamed of publishing but which I sent to a trusted friend for critiquing. That friend gave the story, unread, to a senior editor at Harper & Row. The next thing I knew that editor liked it so much, she asked me to expand it into a novel for young adults. That first story, as indeed is true of the subsequent ones I've written, sprang from experiences in my life.

"Usually, I'm haunted by an intense climactic event. When that's ready to be born, I must find ways of leading up to and away from it in order to shape what I hope will be a memorable novel. While I don't set out writing for young adults, the haunting memories I write about tend to come from that period of my own life."

When the three get beyond The Big Dipper, he halts abruptly. With a voice that's trembling, he says to BC and Clarissa, "I'm sorry. I'm sorry I got you two into trouble." ■ (From *The Big Dipper Marathon* by Jerome Brooks. Jacket illustrated by Troy Howell.)

JEROME BROOKS

BURROWAY, Janet (Gay) 1936-

PERSONAL: Born September 21, 1936, in Tucson, Ariz.; daughter of Paul M. (a tool and die worker) and Alma (Milner) Burroway; married Walter Eysselinck, March 18, 1961 (divorced, 1973); married William Dean Humphries (a writer and illustrator), February 10, 1978; children: (first marriage) Timothy Alan, Tobyn Alexander. *Education:* Attended University of Arizona, 1954-55; Barnard College, B.A., 1958; Cambridge University, B.A., 1960, M.A., 1965; additional study at Yale School of Drama, 1960-61. *Politics:* Liberal. *Home:* 240 DeSoto St., Tallahassee, Fla. 32303.

CAREER: During her school years, worked for Young Men's Hebrew Association, *New Yorker,* and for UNICEF in Paris, France; supply teacher in Binghamton, N.Y., 1961-63; director of classical music program for schools in upstate New York, 1963; University of Sussex, Brighton, England, School of English and American Studies, 1965-70, began as assistant lecturer, became lecturer; University of Illinois at Champaign-Urbana, Urbana, special assistant to the writing laboratory, 1971; Florida State University, Tallahassee, associate professor of English literature and creative writing, 1971-74, professor, 1975—. *Awards, honors:* National Endowment for the Arts Creative Writing fellowship, 1966; *The Buzzards* received a Pulitzer prize nomination, 1970; AMOCO award for excellence in teaching, 1974, from Florida State University.

WRITINGS: Descend Again (novel), Faber, 1960; *But to the Season* (poems), Keele University Press, 1961; *The Dancer from the Dance* (novel), Faber, 1965, Little, Brown, 1967; *Eyes* (novel), Little, Brown, 1966; *The Buzzards* (novel), Little, Brown, 1969; *The Truck on the Track* (juvenile; Junior Literary Guild selection), J. Cape, 1970, Bobbs-Merrill, 1971; (with John V. Lord) *The Giant Jam Sandwich* (juvenile), J. Cape, 1972, Houghton, 1973; *Raw Silk* (novel), Little, Brown, 1977. *Material Goods* (poems), University Presses of Florida, 1980.

Plays: "The Fantasy Level" and "The Beauty Operators," produced in Brighton, England, 1968, and by Thames Television Ltd. in London, 1970; "Hoddinott Veiling," produced by ATV Network Ltd., London, 1970.

WORK IN PROGRESS: A sixth novel, *Opening Nights,* about a grant-funded Georgian theater; a children's book, *Camille and the Battum Bomb,* about a "plucky and fussy chameleon mother who prevents a nuclear test;" a textbook in fiction writing, tentatively titled *Narrative Techniques,* Little, Brown, 1982.

SIDELIGHTS: "I was born in Phoenix, Arizona in 1936, lived there until at eighteen I went to New York (I saw it as 'escaping to'—a view since somewhat modified) as a *Mademoiselle* magazine guest editor, and stayed to take a degree in English at Barnard College (1958). At Barnard I worked part time at the YMHA Poetry Center (mainly making coffee and onion dip for the Younger Poets' series, but also reading manuscripts for the Center's Poetry Award), made costumes for the Columbia Players, spent a summer as a *New Yorker* receptionist, took every writing course in sight (Auden, Rolfe Humphries, Louise Bogan, George Plimpton, Hortense Calisher; probably a dozen altogether). I wrote, won a number of writing prizes there, and settled into writing as the major of my childhood ambitions (the others were acting and fashion design.) *The Atlantis* published a poem and through Howard Teichmann's efforts my first play was produced at Barnard, with professional male actors and undergraduate Barnard women; and Janet Roberts of the then-MCA agency took me on as a playwright. Through her I came into contact with Phyllis Jackson and, in England, Elaine Greene, who have nursed my fiction through twenty lean and fat years, mostly lean.

"In 1958-60 I was at Cambridge University, England on a Marshall Scholarship where I took a second B.A. with first class honors in English, and where Faber and Faber published my first novel, *Descend Again,* and Keele University my first and only volume of poems, *But to the Season.*

"What *can* we *do?*" And they said, "Good question!" But nobody had a good suggestion.
▪(From *The Giant Jam Sandwich,* story and pictures by John Vernon Lord. Verses by Janet Burroway.)

JANET BURROWAY

"In 1960 I came back to Yale Drama School where I did a year under John Gassner as an NBC fellow in playwrighting. I married there, and my husband and I spent two years in Binghamton, N.Y., two in Belgium, and seven more in England. During these years I wrote three more novels, all published by Faber and Faber in London and Little, Brown in America: *The Dancer from the Dance, Eyes,* and *The Buzzards.* The last was nominated for a Pulitzer prize in 1970.

"I also designed and executed costumes for the Belgian National Theatre and the Gardner Center for the Arts in Sussex, taught at the University of Sussex, under my Cambridge supervisor David Daiches, and wrote for British television. My television play 'Hoddinott Veiling,' produced by ATV, went to the Monte Carlo Festival in 1970. My two sons were born in 1964 (Timothy Alan) and 1966 (Tobyn Alexander).

"In 1971 I returned to America, first for a semester teaching at the writing lab at the University of Illinois, then to Florida State University, where I was an associate professor of writing and literature. I was divorced in 1973.

"In addition to the novels, I have published two children's books, *The Truck on the Track* and *The Giant Jam Sandwich,* both here and in England, have reviewed fiction for the *New Statesman* in England, and have published various poems, stories and articles, most recently in *Story Quarterly* and *Ms.* magazine. In 1974 I was awarded the AMOCO Award for excellence in teaching at FSU, a National Endowment for the Arts creative writing fellowship which freed me from teaching until January, 1977. This was an urgently needed blessing, as teaching absorbed more and more of the kind of energy and concentration that I needed to write.

"For a period of years I thought teaching a danger to my writing because it might make me more introspective, contrived and academic. Now I fear it for a reason very nearly the opposite. I like it. My students are so alive, the gratification of exchange and feedback so immediate, that it makes the lonely hours at the typewriter more austere by comparison. When I have an idea for a book, it's likely to be three or five years before anyone else sees it. When I have one in class, if it's any good there's someone there to say, 'I see!' Tallahassee is a bad place to get to anywhere else from, a good place to raise children, animals, suntans and ideas. Tim, Toby, my second husband and I live in a rambling 1925 brick house with green shutters and a picket fence, a very English-looking house except that it is fronted by palms and magnolias, surrounded with azaleas. Which operates pretty well for me as a synthesis of my Arizona-to-England-and-back life.

"In 1977 I was promoted to full professor at Florida State. In February of 1978 I married William Dean Humphries, who is a writer and illustrator, and is illustrating my current children's book, *Camille and the Battum Bomb.* His illustrations are brilliantly colored and absolutely meticulous—every scale of the chameleon's skin defined—and are a delight, I think. Camille is a mother chameleon living in the White Sands of New Mexico, fuss-budget protector of her forty children, and because *everything* in her world is white, she's lost the ability to change color. Then one day she overhears Professor Dimthwistle and General Pugnat planning to conduct an underground test of the Battum Bomb right next to her burrow! She has to learn how to change colors again (to her children's delight) in order to foul up the plans and prevent the test.

"John Lord and I used to like to say that *The Truck on the Track* was a primer in labor relations, and *The Giant Jam Sandwich* was a child's first lesson in ecology. If that's so, then I guess *Camille and the Battum Bomb* is both a feminist tract and anti-nuke. You see that I'm absolutely unashamed about being a moralist, although the children's books I like best tend to be violent or wry—*Strewelpeter, Where the Wild Things Are, Where the Sidewalk Ends* and nearly all of Seuss. One thing that I felt very strongly when my children were of an age to be read to (they do their own now), was that although the first and most important readership of children's books is children, it's also very important that the parents enjoy them, because if they do, they'll read more. I was conscious that if my toddlers brought me Enid Blyton, I was always much too busy with dinner to stop and read to them; whereas if they brought me *I Had Trouble in Getting to Solla Sollew,* I would discover that the potatoes could cook themselves.

"When I was a child, I never had a notion of writing for children. I wanted to get into the adult world as quickly as possible, and writing was one of the ways I thrust myself there. It was when [my sons] were about two and five that children's books began to delight me, and I wrote *The Truck on the Track* deliberately for them. *They* liked nothing better than trucks and trains, and *I* liked nothing better than playing around with sounds, and so when the phrase 'the truck stuck on the track' popped into my mind, I thought maybe I could write a book to please all three of us. Though most of my writing is now for adults, I do still find great pleasure in trying to write for children, who are in many ways the most demanding audience. They'll brook no nonsense when it comes to plot, and they're better in touch with the delight of the senses, both shape and sound, than older more sophisticated readers. Apart from "Camille," I've one as yet unpublished children's book in verse, *Wings and Fins and Wheels and Feet,* which really needs to meet its publisher!"

FOR MORE INFORMATION SEE: Newsweek, April 4, 1977.

BURTON, Maurice 1898-

PERSONAL: Born March 28, 1898, in London, England; son of William Francis and Jane Burton; married Margaret Rosalie Maclean, 1928; children: Richard Francis, Jane Mary, Robert Wellesley. *Education:* University of London, D.Sc., 1934. *Home:* Weston House, Albury, Guildford, Surrey GU5 9AE, England.

CAREER: Latymer Foundation, Hammersmith, London, England, biology master, 1924-27; British Museum of Natural History, London, 1927-58, began as assistant keeper, became deputy keeper in zoology department; free-lance writer, 1928—. *Member:* Royal Society of Arts (fellow), Zoological Society (fellow).

MAURICE BURTON

(From *The Life of Birds* by Maurice Burton. Adapted by Louis M. Moyle. Illustrated by Patricia Leander and Malcolm McGregor.)

WRITINGS—Juveniles: *Animals and Their Behaviour,* Arnold, 1950; *The Elephant,* Gawthorn Press, 1951; *The Ox,* Gawthorn Press, 1951; *The Reindeer,* Gawthorn Press, 1951; *The Camel,* Gawthorn Press, 1951; *The Ass,* Gawthorn Press, 1951; *The Sheep,* Gawthorn Press, 1951; *When Dumb Animals Talk,* Hutchinson, 1955; *The True Book about Animals,* Muller, 1956; *Animal Families,* Routledge & Kegan Paul, 1958; *British Mammals,* Oxford University Press, 1958; *Life in the Deep,* Roy, 1958; *The True Book about the Seas,* Muller, 1959.

(Editor and contributor) *The Wonder Book of Animals,* Ward Lock, 1960; *In Their Element: The Story of Water Mammals,* Abelard, 1960; *Mammals of the Countryside,* Wheaton, 1960; *Wild Animals and Birds of the World,* Longacre Press, 1960; *Birds and Beasts of Field and Jungle,* Odhams, 1960; *The True Book about Prehistoric Animals,* Muller, 1961, 2nd edition published as *Prehistoric Animals,* International Publications Service, 1974, Transatlantic, 1975; *The True Book about Deserts,* Muller, 1961, 2nd edition published as *Deserts,* International Publications Service, 1974, Transatlantic, 1975; *More Mammals of the Countryside,* Wheaton, 1961; *Water Creatures,* Longacre Press, 1961; *Baby Animals,* Longacre Press, 1961; *Birds,* Gawthorn Press, 1961; *Mammals,* Gawthorn Press, 1961; (with E. W. Groves) *The Wonder Book of Nature,* Ward Lock, 1961; *Reptiles and Amphibians of the World,* Longacre Press, 1962, 2nd edition,

1971; *Birds of Britain,* Odhams, 1962, 2nd edition, 1971; *Mammals of Great Britain,* Odhams, 1962; *The True Book of the Seashore,* Muller, 1963; (with W. B. Shepherd) *The Wonder Book of Our Earth,* Ward Lock, 1963; *Young Animals,* Hamlyn, 1964; *The Zoo Book,* Bancroft, 1966; (editor) *Animal World in Colour,* Volume 1: *Artists and Entertainers,* Volume 2: *Explorers and Wanderers,* Volume 3: *Animal Eccentrics,* Volume 4: *Animal Oddities,* Volume 5: *Builders and Breakers,* Volume 6: *Comrades and Companions,* Volume 7: *Hunters: Mammals,* Volume 8: *Hunters: Birds, Fish, and Amphibians,* Volume 9: *Hunters: Reptiles, Insects, and Invertebrates,* Volume 10: *Animal Specialists,* Volume 11: *Unusual Feeders,* Volume 12: *Sleep and Hibernation,* Odhams, 1966, Children's Press, 1969; *Animals,* Oxford University Press, 1966, F. Watts, 1968; *The Animal World: Birds, Fish, Reptiles [and] Insects,* F. Watts, 1968; *The Sea's Inhabitants,* Golden Press, 1968; *More Animals,* F. Watts, 1968; *Animal Partnerships,* Warne, 1969; *Animals of Australia,* Abelard, 1969.

Maurice Burton's Book of Nature, Purnell, 1971, 4th edition, 1974; *The Life of Birds,* edited by Angela Littler, Macdonald, 1972, Golden Press, 1974; *The Life of Fishes,* edited by Littler, Macdonald, 1972, Golden Press, 1974; *The Life of Insects,* Macdonald, 1972, Golden Press, 1974; (with Robert Burton) *The Life of Meat Eaters,* Macdonald, 1973, Golden Press, 1974; *The Life of Reptiles and Amphibians,* Golden Press, 1974; *First Encyclopedia of Animals,* Purnell, 1974. Also author and editor of numerous adult natural science books. (For complete listing see *Contemporary Authors* Vol. 65-68.)

SIDELIGHTS: Burton's books have been translated into Dutch, Portuguese, Japanese, Spanish, Italian, French, German, Swedish, Finnish, Norwegian, Hindustani, and Icelandic.

HOBBIES AND OTHER INTERESTS: Gardening.

FOR MORE INFORMATION SEE: Observer, February 8, 1970; *Library Journal,* July, 1970, September, 1970; *Horn Book,* April, 1974.

RACHEL CARSON

CARSON, Rachel (Louise) 1907-1964

PERSONAL: Born May 27, 1907, in Springfield, Pa.; died April 14, 1964 in Silver Spring, Maryland; daughter of Robert Warden and Maria Frazier (McLean) Carson. *Education:* Pennsylvania College for Women, A.B., 1929; Johns Hopkins University, A.M., 1932; additional graduate study at the Marine Biological Laboratory, Woods Hole, Mass. *Religion:* Presbyterian. *Residence:* Silver Spring, Md.

CAREER: University of Maryland, College Park, member of the zoology staff, 1931-36; Johns Hopkins University, Baltimore, Md., instructor at summer school, 1930-36; U.S. Bureau of Fisheries (now the Fish and Wildlife Service), Washington, D.C., aquatic biologist, beginning, 1936, editor-in-chief, 1949-52; resigned, July, 1952, to devote entire time to writing. *Member:* Royal Society of Literature (fellow), National Institute of Arts and Letters, Audubon Society (director in Washington, D.C.), Society of Women Geographers, American Ornithologists' Union.

AWARDS, HONORS: Eugene Saxton Memorial fellowship, 1949; George Westinghouse Science Writing award, 1950; National Book Award, 1951, for *The Sea Around Us;* Guggenheim fellowship, 1951-52; John Burroughs medal, 1952; Henry G. Bryant Gold Medal, 1952; Page-One award, 1952; Frances K. Hutchinson medal, 1952; Limited Editions Club, silver jubilee medal, 1954; National Council of Women in the U.S., book award, 1956; American Association of University Women, achievement award, 1956; Animal Welfare Institute, Schweitzer medal, 1962; Women's National Book Association Constance Lindsay Skinner award, 1963; New England Outdoor Writers Association award, 1963; National Wildlife Federation, Conservationist of the Year award, 1963; Einstein College of Medicine, achievement award, 1963; New York Zoological Society, gold medal; special citations from the Garden Club of America, the Pennsylvania Federation of Women's Clubs, and the Izaak Walton League of America, 1963; D.Litt., Pennsylvania College for Women, 1952, Drexel Institute of Technology, 1952, Smith College, 1953; D.Sc., Oberlin College, 1952.

WRITINGS: Under the Sea-Wind: A Naturalist's Picture of Ocean Life (illustrated by Howard French), Simon & Schuster, 1941, new edition, Oxford University Press, 1952, reissued, Panther Books, 1965; *Food from the Sea: Fish and Shellfish of New England,* U.S. Government Printing Office, 1943; *Food from Home Waters: Fishes of the Middle West,* U.S. Department of the Interior, Fish and Wildlife Service,

1943; *Fish and Shellfish of the South Atlantic and Gulf Coasts,* U.S. Government Printing Office, 1944; *Fish and Shellfish of the Middle Atlantic Coast,* U.S. Government Printing Office, 1945; *The Sea Around Us* (illustrated by Katherine L. Howe), Oxford University Press, 1951, revised edition, 1961, revised edition, Watts, 1966; *The Edge of the Sea* (illustrated by Bob Hines), Houghton, 1955, reissued, New American Library, 1971; *Silent Spring* (ALA Best Young Adult Book; illustrated by Lois and Louis Darling), Houghton, 1962, reissued, Fawcett, 1975; *The Sense of Wonder* (originally appeared in *Woman's Home Companion* under the title, "Help Your Child to Wonder"), Harper, 1965; *Life Under the Sea* (selection from *The Sea Around Us*), Golden Press, 1968; *The Rocky Coast* (first appeared as a chapter entitled "The Rocky Shores" in *The Edge of the Sea*), Macmillan, 1971.

SIDELIGHTS: Carson combined her interest in nature and her desire to write into a very successful career. She acquired her love of nature from her mother, who introduced her to the marvels of the outdoors and its creatures. As early as age ten, her writing ability was manifested in contributions to the *St. Nicholas Magazine.* "As a very small child I was fascinated by the ocean, although I had never seen it. I dreamed of it and longed to see it, and I read all the sea literature I could find. In college I drifted naturally enough into biology and soon came to specialize in marine zoology. I spent several summers at the Marine Biological Laboratory at Woods Hole, Massachusetts, where I was almost literally surrounded by the ocean. There I could see the racing tidal currents pouring through the 'Hole' or watch the waves breaking at Nobska Point after a storm, and there I first became really aware of the unseen ocean currents, for masses of drifting sargassum weed would come in from the distant Gulf Stream after a storm, and tropical creatures like the beautiful Portuguese man-of-war were carried in from the warm rivers offshore.

"At Woods Hole, too, I first had an introduction to a large library specializing in the field that so fascinated me. It was immensely exciting to discover the rich but greatly scattered information about the sea that was contained in both old and new books, and in the bewildering variety of scientific journals that the excellent library of the Marine Biological Laboratory contains. I used to spend long hours searching for the answers to questions that filled my mind. At that time

I should ask that her gift to each child in the world be a sense of wonder so indestructible that it would last throughout life, as an unfailing antidote against the boredom and disenchantment of later years, the sterile preoccupation with things that are artificial, the alienation from the sources of our strength. ■ (From *The Sense of Wonder* by Rachel Carson. Photograph by Charles Pratt.)

I had not the slightest idea that one day my own book about the sea would stand on the shelves of that same library, but I am sure that the genesis of *The Sea Around Us* belongs to that first year at Woods Hole, when I began storing away facts about the sea—facts discovered in scientific literature or by personal observation and experience. . . ." [Paul Brooks, *The House of Life: Rachel Carson at Work*, Houghton, 1972.[1]]

One of Carson's most memorable books, *The Sea Around Us*, required a vast amount of research and two years to write. A *Christian Science Monitor* critic commented, "Rachel Carson has achieved that rare, all but unique phenomenon—a literary work about the sea that is comparable with the best, yet offends neither the natural scientist nor the poet." "Rare indeed," added *Saturday Review of Literature*, "is the individual who can present a comprehensive and well-balanced picture of such a complex entity as the sea in an easy and fluent style and in terms anyone can understand. Rachel Carson is such an individual. Many books have been written on the sea, most of them by scholars with a very detailed knowledge of some aspect of oceanography, but with a limited knowledge of popular presentation. Miss Carson's book is different." Observed *Nation*: "Scientifically, *The Sea Around Us* has its shortcomings, but it would be hard to find a style, a sensitivity, a balancing of detail more perfectly suited for the evoking of the sea." Several chapters of the book originally appeared in the *New Yorker* in the summer of 1951, under the title, "Profile of the Sea." A chapter entitled "Birth of an Island" was published earlier in the *Yale Review*, and won for its author the George Westinghouse Foundation award, given for outstanding scientific writing in a periodical. By October, 1951, sales of the book—338,000 hardcover copies—had carried it to a ninth printing, and to first place on nonfiction best-seller lists. A documentary film of the book was made by RKO, which won an Academy Award for best documentary of feature length in 1952.

Like most writers, Carson required seclusion when she wrote. Her first drafts were usually in longhand and went through numerous revisions before publication. "Writing is a lonely occupation at best. Of course there are stimulating and even happy associations with friends and colleagues, but during the actual work of creation the writer cuts himself off from all others and confronts his subject alone. He moves into a realm where he has never been before—perhaps where no one has ever been. It is a lonely place, and even a little frightening. . . .

"No writer can stand still. He continues to create or he perishes. Each task completed carries its own obligation to go on to something new.

"The writer must never attempt to impose himself upon his subject. He must not try to mold it according to what he believes his readers or editors want to read. His initial task is to come to know his subject intimately, to understand its every aspect, to let it fill his mind. Then at some turning point the subject takes command and the true act of creation begins. . . . The discipline of the writer is to learn to be still and listen to what his subject has to tell him.

"Given the initial talent . . . writing is largely a matter of application and hard work, of writing and rewriting endlessly until you are satisfied that you have said what you want to say as clearly and simply as possible. For me, that usually means many, many revisions. If you write what you yourself

As man proceeds toward his announced goal of the conquest of nature, he has written a depressing record of destruction, directed not only against the earth he inhabits but against the life that shares it with him. ▪ (From *Silent Spring* by Rachel Carson. Illustrated by Lois and Louis Darling.)

The contamination of our world is not alone a matter of mass spraying. ■ (From *Silent Spring* by Rachel Carson. Illustrated by Lois and Louis Darling.)

sincerely think and feel and are interested in, the chances are very high that you will interest other people as well.''[1]

Silent Spring was probably Rachel Carson's most influential, as well as most controversial book. The work, which sold over 500,000 hardcover copies, is an indictment of farmers for the use of poisonous chemical fertilizers, and points out the potentially dangerous effects of these on animals, birds, and humans. Called by *Christian Century,* ''a shocking and frightening book,'' it was further critiqued by the *Christian Science Monitor* which noted, ''. . . Miss Carson has undeniably sketched a one-sided picture. But her distortion is akin to that of the painter who exaggerates to focus attention on essentials. It is not the half-truth of the propagandist.'' Added *Saturday Review:* ''It is a devastating, heavily documented, relentless attack upon human carelessness, greed, and irresponsibility. . . . If her present book does not possess the beauty of *The Sea Around Us,* it is because she has courageously chosen, at the height of her powers, to educate us upon a sad, an unpleasant, an unbeautiful topic, and one of our own making. . . .'' Intense public concern created over the book caused President John F. Kennedy to announce a federal investigation into the problem. The report of the President's Science Advisory Committee, issued in May, 1963, agreed with the basic premise of *Silent Spring,* warning against the indiscriminate use of pesticides and urging stricter controls and more research.

When Carson wrote *Silent Spring* she never expected it to be as controversial as it became. ''The beauty of the living world I was trying to save has always been uppermost in my mind—that, and anger at the senseless, brutish things that were being done. I have felt bound by a solemn obligation to do what I could—if I didn't at least try I could never again be happy in nature. But now I can believe I have at least helped a little. It would be unrealistic to believe one book could bring a complete change."[1]

Although suffering from cancer, Carson continued to work on her book, *The Sense of Wonder,* during the last year of her life. "A large part of my life has been concerned with some of the beauties and mysteries of this earth about us, and with the even greater mysteries of the life that inhabits it. No one can dwell long among such subjects without thinking rather deep thoughts, without asking himself searching and often unanswerable questions, and without achieving a certain philosophy.

"There is one quality that characterizes all of us who deal with the sciences of the earth and its life—we are never bored. We can't be. There is always something new to be investigated. Every mystery solved brings us to the threshold of a greater one.

"The pleasures, the values of contact with the natural world are not reserved for the scientists. They are available to anyone who will place himself under the influence of a lonely mountain top—or the sea—or the stillness of a forest; or who will stop to think about so small a thing as the mystery of a growing seed.

"I am not afraid of being thought a sentimentalist when I say that I believe natural beauty has a necessary place in the spiritual development of any individual or any society. I believe that whenever we destroy beauty, or whenever we substitute something man-made and artificial for a natural feature of the earth, we have retarded some part of man's spiritual growth. . . .

"We see the destructive trend on a national scale in proposals to invade the national parks with commercial schemes such as the building of power dams. The parks were placed in trust for all the people, to preserve for them just such recreational and spiritual values as I have mentioned. Is it the right of this, our generation, in its selfish materialism, to destroy these things because we are blinded by the dollar sign? Beauty—and all the values that derive from beauty—are not measured and evaluated in terms of the dollar.

"Years ago I discovered in the writings of the British naturalist Richard Jefferies a few lines that so impressed themselves upon my mind that I have never forgotten them.

"'The exceeding beauty of the earth, in her splendor of life, yields a new thought with every petal. The hours when the mind is absorbed by beauty are the only hours when we really live. All else is illusion, or mere endurance.'

"Those lines are, in a way, a statement of the creed I have lived by . . . I have had the privilege of receiving many letters from people who, like myself, have been steadied and reassured by contemplating the long history of the earth and sea, and the deeper meanings of the world of nature. . . . In contemplating 'the exceeding beauty of the earth' these people have found calmness and courage. For there is symbolic as well as actual beauty in the migration of birds; in the ebb and flow of the tides; in the folded bud ready for the spring. There is something infinitely healing in these repeated refrains of nature—the assurance that dawn comes after night, and spring after the winter.

"Mankind has gone very far into an artificial world of his own creation. . . . But I believe that the more clearly we can focus our attention on the wonders and realities of the universe about us, the less taste we shall have for destruction."[1]

On April 14, 1964 Carson succumbed to cancer in Silver Spring, Maryland before completing her book, *The Sense of Wonder.* "For all at last return to the sea—to Oceanus, the ocean river, like the ever-flowing stream of time, the beginning and the end."[1]

FOR MORE INFORMATION SEE: Scientific Book Club Review, October, 1941; *Books,* December 14, 1941; *Saturday Review of Literature,* December 27, 1941, July 7, 1951; *Christian Science Monitor,* July 5, 1951, November 10, 1955, September 27, 1962; *Nation,* August 4, 1951; *Time,* November 7, 1955; *Saturday Review,* December 5, 1955, September 29, 1962; "Gentle Storm Center," *Life,* October 12, 1962; *Christian Century,* December 19, 1962; S. L. Udall, "Legacy of Rachel Carson," *Saturday Review,* May 16, 1964; *Publishers Weekly,* June 19, 1967; M. E. Mason, "Time of Singing: Hero Story," *Instructor,* May, 1968; Philip Sterling, *Sea and Earth: The Life of Rachel Carson,* Crowell, 1970; Frank Graham, Jr., *Since Silent Spring,* Houghton, 1970; S. A. Briggs, "Remembering Rachel Carson," *American Forests,* July, 1970; Paul Brooks, *House of Life: Rachel Carson at Work,* Houghton, 1972; Adela Rogers St. Johns, *Some Are Born Great,* Doubleday, 1974; Elizabeth Anticaglia, *Twelve American Women,* Nelson-Hall, 1975.

For children: Henry Gilfond, *Heroines of America,* Fleet Press, 1970; Donald W. Cox, *Pioneers of Ecology,* Hammond, 1971; Robert Elliot, *Banners of Courage,* Platt, 1972; Jean L. Latham, *Rachel Carson Who Loved the Sea,* Garrard, 1973; C. B. Squire, *Heroes of Conservation,* Fleet Press, 1974; Ruth A. Coates, *Great American Naturalists,* Lerner, 1974.

Filmstrips: "Heroes of Ecology," in "Heroes and Heroines Read-Aloud Series," Miller-Brody Productions.

Obituaries: *New York Times,* April 15, 1964; *Oil, Paint, and Drug Report,* April 20, 1964; *Illustrated London News,* April 25, 1964; *Publishers Weekly,* April 27, 1964; *Gleanings,* July, 1964; *Current Biography Yearbook,* 1964.

The greatest poem every known
Is one all poets have outgrown:
The poetry, innate, untold,
Of being only four years old.

—Christopher Morley

'Tis well to give honor and glory to Age,
With its lessons of wisdom and truth;
Yet who would not go back to the fanciful page,
And the fairy tale read but in youth?

—Eliza Cook

CHALLANS, Mary 1905-
(Mary Renault)

PERSONAL: Born September 4, 1905, in London, England; emigrated to South Africa in 1948; daughter of Frank (a doctor) and Mary (Baxter) Challans. *Education:* Attended St. Hugh's College, Oxford University; Radcliffe Infirmary, Oxford University, S.R.N., 1936. *Politics:* Progressive. *Address:* "Delos," Glen Beach, Camps Bay, Cape Town 8001, South Africa.

CAREER: Held minor jobs before becoming a full-time novelist, 1939—. *Wartime service:* Served as a nurse during World War II. *Member:* P.E.N. Club of South Africa (past president), Royal Society of Literature (fellow). *Awards, honors:* MGM award, 1946, for *Return to Night;* National Association of Independent Schools Award, 1963; Silver Pen Award, 1971.

WRITINGS—All under pseudonym Mary Renault; novels: *Promise of Love,* Morrow, 1939, reissued, Queens House, 1976 (published in England as *Purposes of Love,* Longmans, Green, 1939); *Kind Are Her Answers,* Morrow, 1940, reissued, Queens House, 1976; *The Friendly Young Ladies,* Longmans, Green, 1944, published in America as *The Middle Mist,* Morrow, 1945, reissued, Queens House, 1976; *Return to Night,* Morrow, 1947, reissued, Queens House, 1976; *North Face,* Morrow, 1948, reissued, Queens House, 1976; *The Charioteer,* Longmans, Green, 1953, reissued, Bantam, 1974; *The Last of the Wine,* Pantheon, 1956, reissued, Random House, 1975; *The King Must Die,* Pantheon, 1958, reissued, Bantam, 1974; *The Bull from the Sea,* Pantheon, 1962, reprinted, Vintage Books, 1975; *The Mask of Apollo,* Pantheon, 1966, reissued, Bantam, 1974; *Fire from Heaven,* Pantheon, 1969, reissued, Vintage Books, 1977; *The Persian Boy,* Pantheon, 1972.

Other: *The Lion in the Gateway* (juvenile; illustrated by C. Walter Hodges), Harper, 1964; *The Nature of Alexander,* Pantheon, 1975.

SIDELIGHTS: Challans decided as early as age eight that she wanted to be a writer. Her novels draw on her experiences as a nurse during the war, as well as on ancient and mythological subjects.

Written under the pseudonym Mary Renault, her first novel was *Promises of Love.* A *Books* critic observed, "With a fluid technique rare in a first novel, Miss Renault tells a story of emotional and psychological development which is engrossing because of, rather than in spite of, its familiarity. . . . The writing is excellent, the portrayal of the principal characters convincing and moving, the description of life in an English hospital interesting, the narrative swift and dramatic."

Return to Night was described as "an expert, vivid novel," by *New Yorker.* "Miss Renault sets forth the characters of three extremely complex people with a penetrating lucidity and a certain moderate reasonableness, making this not just an impassioned love story but a novel of considerable depth." *Return to Night* was selected as the winner of the MGM prize in 1946, with $150,000 going to the author. The book was never made into a film, but the publicity it received as the winner of the largest financial award in the field of literature made Mary Renault's name well known to the American reading public.

MARY CHALLANS

Following the end of World War II, Challans traveled extensively in France, Italy, Africa, Greece, and the Aegean Islands. She was most impressed with Greece, and it became the setting for many of her historical novels. The first of these novels, *The Last of the Wine,* takes place during the Third Peloponnesian War. "To read *The Last of the Wine,*" wrote a critic in the *New York Herald Tribune Book Review,* "is to walk for a while in the shadow of the Acropolis with Plato and his friends." Observed the London *Times Literary Supplement:* "*The Last of the Wine* is a superb historical novel. The writing is Attic in quality, unforced, clear, delicate. The characterization is uniformly successful and, most difficult of all, the atmosphere of Athens is realized in masterly fashion. Miss Renault is not only obviously familiar with the principal sources. She has disciplined her imagination so that the reader ceases to question the authenticity of her fiction." The *New York Times* added, "This canvas is rich in battles by land and sea, in the starvation of siege and the disaster of defeat . . . and in sensitively poised emotional bonds between both men and women, and man and man. Renault moves through all aspects of Athenian relationships with disarming candor and flawless taste."

In a review of *The King Must Die,* a *Commonweal* reviewer wrote, "Miss Renault's episodes are described often with a beguiling use of indirection, assumption, offhand reference to details that make the scenes startlingly immediate. . . . Miss Renault has a vigorous sense of the life and variety of the cities and personalities of the era, and renders them without a trace of effort or monotony. The language in which she

They brought . . . some fire from the sacred hearth at home, keeping it tended all through the long sea voyage in a sheltered lamp. When they had settled in their new home, they kindled their own sacred hearth-fire from it. ■ (From *The Lion in the Gateway* by Mary Renault. Illustrated by C. Walter Hodges.)

has Theseus tell his story is not elaborate, but it has elegance and pace. . . .'' Added the *New York Herald Tribune Book Review:* ''Miss Renault's historical novels are excellent. They hold their own as artistically wrought and moving stories and they are rich in the adult entertainment which is the special province of historical fiction. They are particularly welcome because they illuminate uncharted but essential passages and epochs in the formative stages of our civilization. . . . Her narrative is not, nor does it claim to be, history; but it is a well-considered suggestion of how things may have happened, and for the personality and culture with which she deals we have nothing more plausible. . . .'' ''As intrinsic parts of the setting promiscuity and homosexuality do not detract from the excellence of the work,'' noted *Booklist.*

FOR MORE INFORMATION SEE: Times Literary Supplement, February 25, 1939, June 29, 1956; *Books,* March 12, 1939; *New York Times,* March 12, 1939, April 20, 1947; *New Yorker,* April 19, 1947; *New York Herald Tribune Book Review,* October 14, 1956, July 13, 1958; *Booklist,* June 15, 1958; *Commonweal,* August 1, 1958; *Current Biography,* H. W. Wilson, 1959; *Horn Book,* October, 1964, April 1970; Peter Wolfe, *Mary Renault,* Twayne, 1969; Bernard F. Dick, *The Hellenism of Mary Renault,* Southern Illinois Press, 1972; John Wakeman, editor, *World Authors, 1950-1970,* H. W. Wilson, 1975; *Contemporary Literary Criticism,* Volume 3, Gale, 1975.

CLEAVER, Elizabeth (Mrazik) 1939-

PERSONAL: Born November 19, 1939, in Montreal, Quebec. *Education:* Attended Sir George Williams University, the College of Sárospatak, Hungary, School of Art and Design, Montreal Museum of Fine Arts, Ecole des Beaux Arts, Montreal; Concordia University, M.A., 1980.

CAREER: Full-time illustrator of children's books since 1968. *Member:* Royal Canadian Academy of Arts. *Awards and honors:* Amelia Frances Howard-Gibbon medal for outstanding illustration from the Canadian Association of Children's Librarians for *The Wind Has Wings; Poems from Canada* and honor book citations for *How Summer Came to Canada* and *The Mountain Goats of Temlaham,* all 1971; runner-up for the Hans Christian Andersen Award from International Board on Books for Young People, 1972; Best Book of the Year for Children, medal from Canadian Association of Children's Librarians, 1974, for *The Miraculous Hind;* Amelia Frances Howard-Gibbon medal from the Canadian Association of Children's Librarians for *The Loon's Necklace,* 1978; recipient of several Canada Council art bursaries for research and travel.

WRITINGS—All self-illustrated and retold by the author: *The Miraculous Hind: A Hungarian Legend,* Holt (Toronto), 1973, French translation by Irene E. Aubrey, published as *La Biche Miraculeuse, une Legende Hongroise,* Holt, 1973; *Petrouchka,* Atheneum, 1980.

Illustrator: Mary Alice Downie and Barbara Robertson, *The Wind Has Wings: Poems from Canada* (Notable Canadian Children's Book), Oxford University Press (Toronto), 1968; William Toye, reteller, *How Summer Came to Canada,* Walck, 1969; William Toye, reteller, *The Mountain Goats of Temlaham* (Notable Canadian Children's Book), Walck, 1969; Cyrus Macmillan, reteller, *Canadian Wonder Tales,* Bodley Head, 1974; Luko Paljetak, *Love and Kisses Heart Book,* Melville (Montreal), 1975; Mary Alice Downie, adapter, *The Witch of the North: Folk Tales of Northern Canada,* Oberon, 1975; William Toye, *The Loon's Necklace,* Oxford University Press (Toronto), 1977; William Toye, *The Fire Stealer,* Oxford University, Press (Toronto), 1979.

SIDELIGHTS: Cleaver has brought recognition to Canada as a recipient of both national and international awards. Her illustrations for *The Wind Has Wings,* a collection of Canadian poetry, were awarded the first Amelia Frances Howard-Gibbon medal and she has represented Canada at numerous international competitions and exhibitions.

Her philosophy about work is simple: ''I am deeply committed and have a strong sense of responsibility. Through my work—books, prints (words and images) I have a meaning to life. I love the book form. There is a saying that a picture is worth a thousand words. But before it can have value we have to put these thousand words into it. We have to invent them, live them and love them. Two of the most important elements are the spirit and love we put into our work. At the moment I am most interested in worded images where words are a part of the structural element of my work." [Irma McDonough, *Profiles*, Canadian Library Association, 1975.]

Through the medium of torn paper collage, Cleaver has been able to successfully reflect the moods and roots of various cultures. From her own country, Cleaver has been inspired by the art and artifacts of Canadian Indians and Eskimos. In 1971, at the invitation of the Canadian National Film Board, Cleaver created the filmstrip "The Miraculous Hind," based on a Hungarian tale. She extensively researched Hungarian culture in order to reproduce native art and dress. Due to the fact that Cleaver spent her teen years in Hungary, "The Miraculous Hind" has special significance for her and she personally wrote the text for the book version of the tale.

Cleaver received her early art education at the gimnazium [gymnasium] in Sárospatak, Hungary where, in the seventeenth century, Comenius created the *Orbis Pictus*, the first picture book used in schools. She received further grounding in art and art history at Canadian institutions as well as through extensive travel funded by Canada Council grants.

An important adjunct to Cleaver's traditional education is the time she spends in historical research and in observation of peoples of various cultures. As a result of her stay with Canadian Eskimo children in 1972, Cleaver began using shadow puppetry to reenact Eskimo legends. Cleaver designed shadow puppets for Montreal's Centaur Theater, and has since taught courses in puppetry for both adults and children.

Cleaver was chosen to do illustrations for Young Canada's Book Week in 1969 and her work has become part of permanent collections at the McGill University rare book department, and Toronto Public Library.

FOR MORE INFORMATION SEE: Horn Book, August, 1972; *In Review*, Winter, 1972, Winter, 1974; *Bookbird*, Number 1, 1973; Irma McDonough, *Profiles*, Canadian Library Association, 1975; Doris de Montreville and Elizabeth D. Crawford, editors, *Fourth Book of Junior Authors & Illustrators*, H. W. Wilson Co., 1978; Lee Kingman and others, compilers, *Illustrators of Children's Books: 1967-1976*, Horn Book, 1978; *Publishers Weekly*, February 19, 1979.

ELIZABETH CLEAVER

. . . Another song reached his ears. Heard from afar, it was sad and lonely. But the old man smiled because he knew it as the song of Loon. ■ (From *The Loon's Necklace,* retold by William Toye. Illustrated by Elizabeth Cleaver.)

CLIFFORD, Mary Louise (Beneway) 1926-

PERSONAL: Born August 15, 1926, in Ontario, N.Y.; daughter of Frank W. (a fruit grower) and Helen (Teats) Beneway; married Robert L. Clifford (retired United Nations economic advisor), July 14, 1951; children: Christopher, Joan Candace. *Education:* Cornell University, A.B., 1948; College of William and Mary, M.A., 1978. *Politics:* Republican. *Religion:* Episcopalian. *Home:* 109 Shellbank Dr., Williamsburg, Va. 23185.

CAREER: United States Foreign Service, American legation, Beirut, Lebanon, 1949-51; National Center for State Courts, Williamsburg, Va., research associate, 1977—. *Member:* Phi Beta Kappa.

WRITINGS—All for young people: *The Land and People of Afghanistan,* Lippincott, 1962, revised edition, 1973; *The Land and People of Malaysia,* Lippincott, 1968; *The Land and People of Liberia,* Lippincott, 1971; *Bisha of Burundi* (fiction), Crowell, 1973; *The Land and People of Sierra Leone,* Lippincott, 1974; *Salah of Sierra Leone* (fiction), Crowell, 1975; *The Land and People of the Arabian Peninsula,* Lippincott, 1977.

Also author of *The Noble and Noble African Studies Program* (social studies program for high school students), Noble and Noble, 1971. Contributor of articles on social problems and economic development to professional journals and newspapers.

WORK IN PROGRESS: Book on the Virginia Indians in the period between 1560 and 1622, from the Indian point of view, and a teachers' and librarians' guide on how to write social studies materials for grades 1-6.

FOR MORE INFORMATION SEE: Horn Book, February, 1963, June 6, 1973, February, 1976; *Publishers Weekly,* February 28, 1977.

Bisha heard their leader begin chanting the rhythm of the dance and the first sound of their feet stamping in perfect unison on the bare dirt, but she had no desire to push back into the crowd in order to watch them. ■ (From *Bisha of Burundi* by Mary Louise Clifford. Illustrated by Trevor Stubley.)

COLBY, Jean Poindexter 1909-

PERSONAL: Born July 26, 1909, in Pine Orchard, Conn.; daughter of Charles Edward and Lena (Von Steinhopf) Poindexter; married Fletcher Colby, 1932; children: Antonia (Mrs. Robert Shoham), Peter Fletcher, Jean. *Education:* Wellesley College, B.A., 1928. *Religion:* Episcopalian. *Home:* 27 Chestnut St., Brookline, Mass. 02146.

CAREER: Houghton Mifflin Co., Boston, Mass., editor, 1945-50; Pellegrini & Cudahy, New York, editor, 1950-52; Farrar, Straus & Cudahy, New York, editor, 1952-56; Hastings House, Inc., New York, editor, 1956-70; The Manuscript Service, Brookline, Mass., founder and editor, 1960—. Founder and editor, *Junior Reviewers* and *The Catalog of the Best Books for Children. Member:* The Country Club (Brookline).

WRITINGS: Peter Paints U.S.A., Houghton, 1948; *The Children's Book Field,* Pellegrini & Cudahy, 1952; *Jim the Cat,* Little, Brown, 1957; *Jenny,* Hastings House, 1957; *The Elegant Eleanor,* Hastings House, 1958; *Dixie of Dover,* Little, Brown, 1958; *Tear Down to Build Up,* Hastings House, 1960; *Writing, Illustrating and Editing Children's Books,* Hastings House, 1966; *Plimouth Plantation, Then and Now,* Hastings House, 1970; *Building Wrecking,* Hastings House, 1970, revised edition, 1972; *Mystic Seaport: The Age of Sail,* Hastings House, 1970; *Lexington and Concord, 1775: What Really Happened,* Hastings House, 1975.

WORK IN PROGRESS: "*Your Game of Golf, and How It Came to Be,* is a history of golf told against the social and economic background of the countries where it was played. In other words what *was* happening at the same time. It emphasizes the times rather than the players. It includes the development of the courses, the clubs, and the equipment as well as the tournaments."

SIDELIGHTS: "I would say that I have always felt very close to children. I was the last of five children, born over a long stretch of years, so that I was nearer to some of my nieces and nephews and their friends than to my own brothers and sister.

"In my writing I reflect my own background as most authors do. I am very fond of sports and of history, and in Wellesley I majored in zoology and also took chemistry and physics, so you could say I am interested in about everything!

"My parents loved the outdoors and I do too. One of my greatest loves is to go fishing with my granddaughter and grandson, and don't think we come home empty-handed, either!

"I had many pets, and two of my most cherished possessions are two male Dalmations, gifts of Wesley Dennis, the late artist so beloved by children for his horse and dog paintings.

"It is a full life I lead and I love it and I share it as much as I can with young friends, and with my own three children."

FOR MORE INFORMATION SEE: Horn Book, January-December, 1948, June, 1975.

(From *Lexington and Concord, 1775: What Really Happened* by Jean Poindexter Colby. Photograph by Barbara Cooney.)

JEAN POINDEXTER COLBY

COLES, Robert (Martin) 1929-

PERSONAL: Born October 12, 1929, in Boston, Mass.; son of Philip Winston (an engineer) and Sandra (Young) Coles; married Jane Hallowell (a teacher), July 4, 1960; children: Robert Emmet, Daniel Agee, Michael Hallowell. *Education:* Harvard University, A.B., 1950; Columbia University, College of Physicians and Surgeons, M.D., 1954. *Politics:* Independent. *Religion:* Episcopalian. *Home address:* Carr Rd., Concord, Mass. 01742. *Office:* Harvard University Health Services, 75 Mt. Auburn St., Cambridge, Mass. 02138.

CAREER: University of Chicago clinics, Chicago, Ill., intern, 1954-55; Massachusetts General Hospital, Boston, resident in psychiatry, 1955-56; McLean Hospital, Belmont, Mass., resident in psychiatry, 1956-57; Judge Baker Guidance Center—Children's Hospital, Roxbury, Mass., resident in child psychiatry, 1957-58, fellow in child psychiatry, 1960-61; Massachusetts General Hospital, Boston, member of psychiatric staff, 1960-62; Harvard University, Cambridge, Mass., clinical assistant in psychiatry at Medical School, 1960-62, research psychiatrist in Health Services, 1963—, lecturer in general education, 1966—. Member of alcoholism clinic staff, Massachusetts General Hospital, 1957-58; supervisor in children's unit, Metropolitan State Hospital (Boston), 1957-58; psychiatric consultant, Lancaster Industrial School for Girls (Lancaster, Mass.), 1960-62; research psychiatrist, Southern Regional Council (Atlanta, Ga.), 1961-63. Consultant to Ford Foundation, Southern Regional Council, and Appalachian Volunteers. Member of board of trustees,

The next thing we were at the school and my mother was calling my name. There were a lot of other women with her, about a dozen. She was holding a sign on a long stick and the minister stood beside her. ■(From *Dead End School* by Robert Coles. Illustrated by Norman Rockwell.)

Robert F. Kennedy Memorial; member of board: Field Foundation, Institute of Current World Affairs, Reading is Fundamental, American Freedom from Hunger Foundation, National Rural Housing Coalition, and Twentieth Century Fund; member of National Sharecroppers Fund and National Advisory Committee on Farm Labor. *Military service:* U.S. Air Force, 1958-60; chief of neuropsychiatric service, Keesler Air Force Base, Biloxi, Miss.

MEMBER: American Psychiatric Association, American Orthopsychiatric Association, Group for the Advancement of Psychiatry, American Academy of Arts and Sciences (fellow), Phi Beta Kappa, Harvard Club (New York and Boston). *Awards, honors:* Atlantic Grant, 1965, in support of work on *Children of Crisis;* National Educational Television award, 1966, for individual contribution to outstanding programming; Family Life Book Award from Child Study Association of America, Ralph Waldo Emerson Award from Phi Beta Kappa, Anisfield-Wolf Award in Race Relations from *Saturday Review,* Four Freedoms Award from B'nai B'rith, and *Parents' Magazine* Medal, all in 1968, all for *Children of Crisis;* Hofheimer Prize for Research from American Psychiatric Association, 1968; Pulitzer Prize, 1973, for Volumes II and III of *Children of Crisis;* McAlpin Award from National Association of Mental Health, 1973.

WRITINGS: Children of Crisis, Atlantic-Little, Brown, Volume I, *A Study in Courage and Fear,* 1967, Volume II, *Migrants, Sharecroppers, Mountaineers,* 1971, Volume III, *The South Goes North,* 1971, Volume IV, *Eskimos, Chicano, Indians,* 1978, Volume V, *Privileged Ones: The Well Off and the Rich in America,* 1978; *Dead End School* (juvenile; illustrated by Norman Rockwell), Atlantic-Little, Brown, 1968; *Still Hungry in America* (introduction by Edward M. Kennedy), World Publishing, 1969; *The Grass Pipe* (juvenile), Little, Brown, 1969; *The Image Is You,* edited by Donald Erceg, Houghton, 1969; (with M. W. Piers) *The Wages of Neglect,* Quadrangle, 1969.

Uprooted Children: The Early Lives of Migrant Farmers (Horace Mann lecture, 1969), University of Pittsburg Press, 1970; (with Joseph H. Brenner and Dermot Meagher) *Drugs and Youth: Medical, Psychiatric, and Legal Facts* (ALA Best Young Adult Book), Liveright, 1970; *Erik H. Erikson: The Growth of His Work,* Little, Brown, 1970; *Teachers and the Children of Poverty,* The Potomac Institute, 1970; *The Middle Americans* (photographs by Jon Erikson), Atlantic-Little, Brown, 1971; (with Daniel Berrigan) *The Geography of Faith* (conversations between Berrigan and Coles), Beacon Press, 1971; *Saving Face* (juvenile), Atlantic-Little, Brown, 1972; (editor with Jerome Kagan) *Twelve to Sixteen: Early Adolescence* (essays), Norton, 1972; *Farewell to the South,* Atlantic-Little, Brown, 1972; *Riding Free* (juvenile), Atlantic-Little, Brown, 1973; *A Spectacle Unto the World,* Viking, 1973; *The Old Ones of New Mexico,* University of New Mexico Press, 1973; *The Buses Roll,* Norton, 1974; *Irony in the Mind's Life: Essays on Novels by James Agee, Elizabeth Bowen, and George Eliot,* University of Virginia Press, 1974; *The Darkness and the Light* (juvenile), Aperture, 1974.

The Mind's Fate, Atlantic-Little, Brown, 1975; *Headsparks* (juvenile), Atlantic-Little, Brown, 1975; *William Carlos Williams: The Knack of Survival in America,* Rutgers University Press, 1975; *A Festering Sweetness* (poetry), University of Pittsburgh Press, 1978; (with Jane Hallowell Coles) *Women of Crisis* (Radcliff biography series) Delacorte, Volume I, *Lives of Struggle and Hope,* 1978, Volume II, *Lives of Work and Dreams,* 1980; *The Last and First Eskimos,* New York

ROBERT COLES

Graphic Society, 1978; *Walter Percy: An American Search,* Atlantic-Little, Brown, 1978; *Flannery O'Connor's South,* Louisiana State University Press, 1980.

Contributor: Charles Rolo, editor, *Psychiatry in American Life,* Little, Brown, 1963; Erik H. Erikson, editor, *Youth: Change and Challenge,* Basic Books, 1963; Talcott Parsons and Kenneth Clark, editors, *The Negro American,* Houghton, 1966; Jules Masserman, editor, *Science and Psychoanalysis,* Volume IX, Grune, 1966; James L. Sundquist, *On Fighting Poverty,* Basic Books, 1969; Philip Kelley and Ronald Hudson, editors, *Diary by E.B.B.: The Unpublished Diary of Elizabeth Barrett Browning, 1831-1832,* Ohio University Press, 1969; John H. Fandberg, editor, *Introduction to the Behavioral Sciences,* Holt, 1969; Urie Bronfenbrenner, *Influences on Human Development,* Dryden Press, 1972; John and Erna Perry, *The Social Webb,* Canfield Press, 1973; Jean Stouse, editor, *Women in Analysis,* Viking, 1974; John Raines, editor, *Conspiracy,* Harper, 1974; *The Infant at Risk,* Intercontinental Medical Books, 1974; *The Americans: 1976,* Heath, 1976; *Things Appalachian,* Morris Harvey College Press, 1976; E. Janis and W. MacNeil, editors, *Photography Within the Humanities,* Addison House, 1977.

Author of introduction: Barbara Field Bensiger, *The Prison of My Mind,* Walker & Co., 1969; *What Is a City?: A Multi-Media Guide on Urban Living,* Boston Public Library, 1969; *A Letter to a Teacher,* Random House, 1970; Anthony Dunbar, *Our Land, Too,* Pantheon, 1971; George Mitchell, *Blow My Blues Away,* Louisiana State University Press, 1971;

Dwayne Wells, *The Chickenbone Special,* Harcourt, 1971; Robert Liebert, *Radical and Militant Youth,* Praeger, 1971; Harry Caudill, *My Land is Dying,* Dutton, 1971; Maisie Ward, *The Tragi-Comedy of Pen Browning,* Sheed and Ward, 1972; Colman McCarthy, *Disturbers of the Peace,* Houghton, 1973; Francoise Dolto, *Dominique: Analysis of an Adolescent,* Dutton, 1973; Drew Davis, *On the Other Side of Anger,* John Knox Press, 1975; Bryan Wolley and Ford Reid, *We Be Here When the Morning Comes,* University of Kentucky Press, 1975; Christine Chapman, *America's Runaways,* Morrow, 1975; *The Students Themselves,* Schenkman, 1975; Dorothy Gallagher, *Hannah's Daughters,* Crowell, 1976; E. P. Cohen and R. S. Gainer, *Art: Another Language for Learning,* Citation, 1976; Jonathan Sher, *Education in Rural America,* Westview, 1977.

Author of afterword, George Tice, *Artie Van Blarcum,* Addison House, 1977.

Contributor to periodicals and professional journals, including *Atlantic Monthly, New Yorker, New Republic, New York Review of Books, Book Week, Partisan Review, Harper's, Saturday Review, Massachusetts Review, New York Times Book Review, Yale Review, American Journal of Psychiatry, Daedalus, Dissent, Appalachian Review, Harvard Educational Review, Contemporary Psychoanalysis, Commonweal,* and many others. Contributing editor, *New Republic,* 1966—; member of editorial board, *American Scholar,* 1968—, *Contemporary Psychoanalysis,* 1969-70, and *Child Psychiatry and Human Development,* 1969—.

SIDELIGHTS: "I have wanted to bring to the attention of readers something about the lives of their fellow Americans—especially those poor and humble people many of us, relatively well off, aren't likely to know. I write because I want to find out what I have seen and heard; and because I want to share what I have come to observe with others."

Coles lived in the South and began *Children of Crisis* during the early years of school integration. Robert Belenky called it "an important social document about the personal correlates of political change in the American South." Edgar Friedenburg noted: "Robert Coles is well known both as a psychiatrist of exceptional range and humaneness and as a 'participant observer' in the civil rights movement. In this book, he brings his training and experience to bear on the individuals, of all ages and mixed motives, whom he came to know through his work in the South. . . . He shares with Capote the virtue—essential to the humanist these days but nevertheless rather chilling—of being able to treat the destroyer and his victims with equal respect and full compassion. . . . Cole's writing is so forthright and unobtrusive that the reader may not notice how much his work owes to its methodological sophistication. . . . Apart from the absorbing content of the book, it is a delight to see data handled with such canny simplicity . . . it is a nearly perfect example . . . of deft and humane application of psychology to the understanding of man in a social situation." The committee recommending *Children of Crisis* for the Ralph Waldo Emerson Award commented: "These case studies, presented with a meticulous concern for significant detail and with a compassionate understanding of man at his noblest and his vilest, add a psychiatric and psychoanalytical dimension to the usual social, economic, and political analyses of one of the, perhaps *the,* crucial issues of our society. . . ."

Coles, who spent seven years with migrant workers as they followed the bean, cucumber, potato and apple crops north from Florida, has explained: "For over a decade now I have tried as a psychiatrist to study the range of attitudes held by white and black people in the rural South, in Appalachia and in our Northern metropolitan areas. I have not handed out questionnaires or asked anyone to say 'yes' or 'no' or 'maybe' to anything. Rather, I have gone to certain homes week after week, until it has come to pass that I have known certain families for many years. Nor have those men and women and children been 'patients' or 'special' in any particular way. They have been Mr. George Wallace's average man on the street." Walker Percy has described Coles as "that rarest of creatures, the social scientist who keeps his theory and his ideological spectacles in his pocket and spends his time listening to people and trying to understand them. Like Freud he is humble before the facts. . . . He treads a narrow path between theorizing and novelizing and emerges as what in fact he is: physician, and a wise and gentle one. He is doctor to the worst of our ills."

HOBBIES AND OTHER INTERESTS: Tennis, skiing.

COLLIER, Zena 1926-
(Jane Collier, Zena Shumsky)

PERSONAL: Born January 21, 1926, in London, England; married Lou Shumsky (a photographer), May 3, 1945 (divorced, 1967); married Thomas M. Hampson, 1969; children: (first marriage) Jeffrey A., Paul E. *Religion:* Jewish. *Home:* 83 Berkeley St., Rochester, N.Y. 14607. *Agent:* Curtis Brown Ltd., 575 Madison Ave., New York, N.Y. 10022.

ZENA COLLIER

CAREER: Free-lance writer.

WRITINGS—Juvenile fiction: (under pseudonym Jane Collier) *The Year of the Dream,* Funk, 1962; (with Lou Shumsky, under name Zena Shumsky) *First Flight,* Funk, 1962; (with Lou Shumsky, under name Zena Shumsky) *Shutterbug,* Funk, 1963; (under pseudonym Jane Collier) *A Tangled Web,* Funk, 1967.

Juvenile nonfiction; under name Zena Collier: *Seven for the People: Public Interest Groups at Work,* Messner, 1979. Contributor (under name Zena Collier) of short stories to *McCall's, Woman's Day, Canadian Home Journal, University of Kansas City Review, Literary Review, University Review, Prairie Schooner, Southwest Review, Alfred Hitchcock's Mystery Magazine,* and other publications. Also author of articles for *Family Circle, Money, Publishers Weekly, Ford Times, Upstate,* and other publications.

WORK IN PROGRESS: An adult novel.

SIDELIGHTS: "I was born in London, educated there, and lived there until my marriage to an American during World War II, after which I came to live in the United States."

Bound for the major leagues? ■ (From *The First Book of Puerto Rico* by Antonio J. Colorado. Photograph courtesy of the Commonwealth of Puerto Rico Tourism Development Co.)

COLORADO (CAPELLA), Antonio J(ulio) 1903-

PERSONAL: Born February 13, 1903, in San Juan, Puerto Rico; son of Rafael Colorado D'Assoy (a photographer) and Lorenza Capella; married Isabel Laguna Matienzo (a social worker), 1940; children: Antonio, Isabelita, Rafael. *Education:* University of Puerto Rico, B.A., 1932; Clark University, M.A., 1933; Universidad Central, Madrid, Spain, Ph.D., 1934. *Politics:* Popular Democratic Party. *Religion:* Roman Catholic. *Home:* 821 Vesta St., Rio Piedras, Puerto Rico 00923.

ANTONIO J. COLORADO

CAREER: U.S. Department of State, writer, 1942-43; University of Puerto Rico, dean of social science, 1943-46, director of University Press, 1946-48; Department of Education of Puerto Rico, director of department press, 1948-55; Labor Relations Board of Puerto Rico, president, 1962—. Metropolitan Bus Authority, Puerto Rico, board of directors. *Member:* Academia Puertorriqueña de la Lengua Española (secretary), Academia de Artes y Ciencias (Puerto Rico), Ateneo Puertorriqueño.

WRITINGS—Under name Antonio J. Colorado: (Collaborator) *New World Guides to Latin America Republics,* Duell, Sloan & Pearce, 1943; *Puerto Rico y Tu,* Prentice-Hall, 1948; (with Lidio Cruz Monclova) *Noticia y Pulso del Movimiento Político Puertorriqueño,* 1955; *Luis Palés Matos, el Hombre y el Poeta,* Rodadero, 1964; *The First Book of Puerto Rico,* Watts, 1964, third edition, 1978; *Puerto Rico: la Tierra y Otros Ensayos,* Editorial Cordillera, 1972. Editor, *Diario de Puerto Rico,* 1948-50.

Translations: *Historia de los Estados Unidos,* Ginn & Co., 1953; *La Canción Verde,* Troutman, 1956; *Nuestro Mundo a Traves de las Edades,* Prentice-Hall, 1959; *America de Todos,* Rand McNally, 1963; *El Arbol de la Violeta,* Troutman, 1964.

WORK IN PROGRESS: Campãnas Politicas y Ensayos.

SIDELIGHTS: "I began to write early in my life. My father had a fairly good library for that time. There I became interested in books. I admired the great Spanish classics. I also read history and politics and began sending articles to the press mostly on politics. I became a journalist and wrote hundreds of editorials and feature articles. Soon after entering the University of Puerto Rico, I was appointed captain of a debating team which went through the States and Canada debating with the great American and Canadian universities. It was a great experience!

"As a teacher I believe that education begins really in the lower grades, and that children can grasp the essentials of politics, economics and sociology if they are taught with emotion and sincerity.

"I am a lover of nature: trees, flowers, rivers, sky and clouds. The sea has a special appeal to me: it is a demonstration of the grandeur of the Creator.

"We have a garden at home, which my wife tenders with love. There are orchids, ferns of all kinds and some fruit-bearing trees. There is a swimming pool where my grandchildren and youngsters from the neighborhood come to swim and play in the crystalline water.

"I truly believe that life is worth living if one has friends and treats his neighbors as one would like to be treated."

Colorado Capella is interested in journalism, labor relations, political science and sociology. He has travelled through central and northern South America, Spain, France, Dominican Republic, Caribbean Islands, Cuba, United States and Canada and is competent in English.

COMMAGER, Henry Steele 1902-

PERSONAL: Born October 25, 1902, in Pittsburgh, Pa.; son of James Williams and Anna Elizabeth (Dan) Commager; married Evan Carroll, July 3, 1928; children: Henry Steele, Nellie Thomas McColl, Elisabeth Carroll. *Education:* University of Chicago, Ph.B., 1923, M.A., 1924, Ph.D., 1928; attended University of Copenhagen, Cambridge University, M.A.; Oxford University, M.A. *Politics:* Independent Democrat. *Home:* 405 South Pleasant St., Amherst, Mass. 01002. *Office:* Amherst College, Amherst, Mass. 01002.

CAREER: New York University, New York, N.Y., instructor in history, 1926-29, assistant professor, 1929-30, associate professor, 1930-31, professor, 1931-38; Columbia University, New York, N.Y., professor of American history, 1939-56, adjunct professor, 1956-59, Sperenza Lecturer, 1960; Amherst College, Amherst, Mass., Smith Professor of History, 1956-72, Simpson Lecturer, 1972—. Pitt Professor of American History, Cambridge University, 1941, 1947-48; Bacon Lecturer, Boston University, 1943; Richards Lecturer, University of Virginia, 1944; Harmsworth Professor of American History, Oxford University, 1952-53; Gottesman Lecturer, Uppsala University, 1953; Ziskind Professor, Brandeis University, 1955; Commonwealth Lecturer, University of London, 1963; Harris Lecturer, Northwestern University, 1964. Visiting professor or lecturer at Duke University, Harvard University, University of Chicago, and University of California, 1926-38, University of Copenhagen, 1956, University of Jerusalem, 1958, University of Mexico, 1965, New York University, and Massachusetts Institute of Technology, 1975; lecturer for the Department of State at universities in Germany, 1954, Israel and Italy, 1955, Trinidad, 1959, Italy, spring, 1960, Chile, 1963, Mexico, 1964, and Japan, 1975. Member of War Department Commission on History of the War; traveled to Britain for War Department, Office of War Information, summer, 1943, and to France and Belgium, 1945. *Military service:* Served with U.S. Army Information and Education Division, 1945.

HENRY STEELE COMMAGER

MEMBER: American Academy of Arts and Letters, American Scandinavian Society (fellow and trustee), American Antiquarian Society, Massachusetts Historical Society, Phi Beta Kappa, Century Association, St. Botolph's (Boston), Savile Club (London), American Friends of Cambridge University (trustee). *Awards, honors:* Herbert B. Adams Award of the American Historical Association, 1929; Guggenheim fellowship, 1960-61; decorated Knight, Order of Dannebrog. Honorary degrees from numerous colleges and universities including: Litt.D., Washington College (Maryland), 1958, Ohio Wesleyan University, 1958, Monmouth College, 1959, Cambridge University, 1962; D.C.L., Alfred University; Ed.D., Rhode Island College; LL.D., Brandeis University, 1960, Michigan State University, 1960, Franklin and Marshall College, 1962; L.H.D., University of Hartford, 1962, Uni-

Another tiny colony, a little village named after Plymouth in England, was established by the Pilgrims on the cold sandy shores north of Cape Cod. ■ (From *The First Book of American History* by Henry Steele Commager. Illustrated by Leonard Everett Fisher.)

versity of Puget Sound, 1963. Aspen Institute, honorable trustee.

WRITINGS—Juvenile: (With Lynd Ward) *America's Robert E. Lee,* Houghton, 1951; *Chestnut Squirrel,* Houghton, 1952; *First Book of American History,* Watts, 1957; *Great Declaration,* Bobbs-Merrill, 1958; *A Picture History of the United States of America,* Watts, 1958; *Great Proclamation,* Bobbs-Merrill, 1960; *Great Constitution,* Bobbs-Merrill, 1961; *Crusaders for Freedom,* Doubleday, 1962.

Other: *The Literature of the Pioneer West,* [Saint Paul], 1927; (with Samuel Eliot Morison) *The Growth of the American Republic,* Oxford University Press, 1931, 7th edition, 1962; *Our Nation's Development,* Harper, 1934; *Theodore Parker,* Little, Brown, 1936, reissued with a new introduction, Beacon Press, 1960; (with Eugene Campbell Barker) *Our Nation,* Row, Peterson, 1941; (with Allan Nevins) *America: The Story of a Free People,* Little, Brown, 1942, reissued in paperback as *The Pocket History of the United States,* Pocket Books, 1943, revised edition, 1956; *Majority Rule and Minority Rights,* Oxford University Press, 1943; (with Samuel Eliot Nevins) *A Short History of the United States,* Modern Library, 1945, 5th edition, 1966; *The American Mind: An Interpretation of American Thought and Character Since the 1880's,* Yale University Press, 1950; (with others) *Civil Liberties Under Attack,* University of Pennsylvania Press, 1951; (contributor) Courtlandt Canby, editor, *The World of History,* New American Library, 1954; (with Geoffrey Brunn) *Europe and America Since 1492,* Houghton, 1954; *Freedom, Loyalty, Dissent,* Oxford University Press, 1954; *Federal Centralization and the Press,* University of Minnesota, 1956. (With Robert W. McEwen and Brand Blanshard) *Education in a Free Society,* University of Pittsburgh Press, 1961; *The Nature and the Study of History,* C. E. Merrill, 1965; *The Role of Scholarship in an Age of Science,* Laramie, 1965; *Freedom and Order: A Commentary on the American Political Scene,* Braziller, 1966; *The Study of History,* C. E. Merrill, 1966; (with Elmo Giordonetti) *Was America a Mistake?: An Eighteenth Century Controversy,* Harper, 1967; *The Search for a Usable Past, and Other Essays in Historiography,* Knopf, 1967; *The Commonwealth of Learning,* Harper, 1968; *The Defeat of America,* Simon & Schuster, 1974; *Britain Through American Eyes,* McGraw, 1974; *Jefferson, Nationalism, and the Enlightenment,* Braziller, 1974; *The Empire of Reason,* Doubleday, 1977; *Tocqueville Redivivus,* Oxford University Press, 1980.

Also editor of numerous historical anthologies and consulting editor of the *Encyclopedia of American History.* Contributor to *Book Week, New York Times Book Review, New Republic, Saturday Review, New York Review of Books, American Scholar,* and other publications.

WORK IN PROGRESS: Editing "The Rise of the American Nation," a projected fifty-volume series.

FOR MORE INFORMATION SEE: Christian Science Monitor, April 6, 1936; *Saturday Review (of Literature),* April 1, 1944, January 5, 1946, January 28, 1967; *New York Herald Tribune Book Review,* May 30, 1954; *Christian Century,* October 24, 1962; *New York Times Book Review,* October 23, 1966, June 25, 1967; *New Republic,* May, 1967; *New Statesman,* June 2, 1967; Harold Hyman and Leonard Levy, editors, *Freedom and Reform: Essays in Honor of H. S. Commager* (includes a biography), Harper, 1967.

Hilda Conkling, age 10. The year her first book of poetry was published.

CONKLING, Hilda 1910-

PERSONAL: Born October 8, 1910, in Catskill-on-Hudson, N.Y.; daughter of Roscoe Platt and Grace Hazard (a poet; maiden name, Walcott) Conkling.

CAREER: Poet.

WRITINGS—Poems: *Poems by a Little Girl,* F. A. Stokes, 1920; *Shoes of the Wind,* F. A. Stokes, 1922, CORE Collection, 1976; *Silverhorn* (selections from *Poems by a Little Girl* and *Shoes of the Wind*), F. A. Stokes, 1924; *Summer-Day Song* (selections from *Poems by a Little Girl*), L. W. Singer, 1969.

SIDELIGHTS: At the age of four, Conkling began "talking" her poems to her mother, a professor of English at Smith College, who wrote them down and had them published in 1920.

FOR MORE INFORMATION SEE: J. C. McAlpine, "Life in Reverse?" *Elementary English,* December, 1972.

Children are the keys of Paradise.

—Richard Henry Stoddard

CONLY, Robert Leslie 1918(?)-1973 (Robert C. O'Brien)

PERSONAL: Born about 1918; died of a heart attack on March 5, 1973 in Washington, D.C.

CAREER: Author and editor. Began writing career, 1943; worked as editor, *National Geographic Magazine;* staff writer, *Newsweek;* rewrite man, *Washington Times Herald;* news editor, *Pathfinder. Awards, honors:* Lewis Carroll Shelf Award, 1972, Newbery Medal, 1972, National Book Award, runner-up, 1972, Mark Twain Award, 1973, Pacific Northwest Library Association Young Readers' Choice Award, 1974, William Allan White Children's Book Award, 1974, all for *Mrs. Frisby and the Rats of NIMH;* Jane Addams Children's Book Award, 1976, Mystery Writers of America, best juvenile novel, 1977, both for *Z for Zachariah.*

WRITINGS—Under pseudonym Robert C. O'Brien; all published by Atheneum: *The Silver Crown* (illustrated by Dale Payson), 1968; *Mrs. Frisby and the Rats of NIMH* (ALA Notable Book; *Horn Book* honor list; illustrated by Zena Bernstein), 1971; *A Report from Group 17* (ALA Best Young Adult Book), 1972; *Z for Zachariah* (*Horn Book* honor list; ALA Best Young Adult Book), 1975.

SIDELIGHTS: Conly began creating imaginary worlds at a very young age, but it wasn't until he was in his late forties that he decided to share his storytelling talents with the public. In his Newbery Award acceptance speech, the author revealed how he came to write *Mrs. Frisby and the Rats of NIMH.* "I regret to say that if there was ever a precise answer to that question, it is lost. I have searched my memory and my files to try to find out how and when the idea first came

ROBERT LESLIE CONLY

Beside the entrance way, looking at her with dark, unblinking eyes, stood the biggest rat she had ever seen. ■ (From *Mrs. Frisby and the Rats of NIMH* by Robert C. O'Brien. Illustrated by Zena Bernstein.)

to me. My files show that I began writing the book in November, 1967, and that by March, 1968, I had finished only two chapters and was debating whether or not to continue. (I was, at the time, also working on another book.) But I have no recollection at all of Mrs. Frisby's initial appearance in my thoughts. I think that may be true of many works of fiction. They are rather like plants. You put a seed under ground. You come back a few days later and find a small green stalk growing. But how often do you actually see the stalk emerge?

"I do know some of the thinking and reading I had done before I wrote about Mrs. Frisby, and I know that these must have been connected with her sudden appearance. I had been, and still am, concerned over the seeming tendency of the human race to exterminate itself—as who is not? I have wondered: If we should vanish from the earth, who might survive us? What kind of civilization might follow ours? I had read in a scientific journal that scorpions were good candidates for survival, since they are resistant to radioactivity. I read the same about cockroaches. But I was unable to imagine a cockroach or a scorpion civilization.

"By coincidence, I had been reading a book by Loren Eiseley called *The Immense Journey*. There was in it a chapter about prairie dogs. It discussed the evidence paleontologists have found that the prairie dogs' ancestors drove our ancestors, the ancestors of the simian primates, out of the prairies and into the woods. In short, the prairie dogs were, millions of years ago, ahead of us in the race toward dominance. While we were still in the trees, they were building little villages. And prairie dogs, as we know, are not dogs at all, but rodents.

"Dr. Eiseley's essay reminded me in turn of another essay—one by Clarence Day called 'This Simian World.' It was required reading when I was in college. That was a long time ago; but, as I recall, it begins by pointing out that many of the things people do—for example, talking a lot and gathering in large groups—are traceable to their simian ancestry. (Monkeys do these things, too.) Then the essay goes on to speculate on what the world would be like if people were descended not from monkeys but from, say, dogs or cats. I remember that Clarence Day thought a cat civilization would be much less gregarious than ours: Cats walk by themselves. Also, a cat culture would be more musical than ours, with a lot of singing.

"Still thinking about survival, I began to speculate: Rats are tough, highly adaptable to a changing environment, and enormously prolific. Maybe, if people should eliminate one another by means of war or pollution, rats would be the survivors. Or if not the only survivors perhaps the most intelligent.

"What, then, would a rat civilization be like? This, of course, is not precisely what *Mrs. Frisby* is about. In the book there is no war, and the human race has not been exterminated. But it was this *kind* of speculation that led to the birth of *Mrs. Frisby and the Rats of NIMH*.

"I suppose it's a rather grim idea to serve as background for a children's book. But once I got it started, the rats took charge, and they turned out to be much saner and pleasanter than we are.

"To the much more general question—Why do I write books for children?—the honest answer is not very enlightening. I write them because a story idea pops up in my mind; and that really is the way it feels, to me at least. And since I am in the writing business, when I get a story idea I write it down before I forget it. It isn't always for children, of course, but those are the stories I most like to write, because children like a straightforward, honest plot—the way God meant plots to be—with a beginning, a middle, and an end: a problem, an attempt to solve it, and at the end a success or a failure.

"I would prefer to rephrase the question. Why is it *good* to write books for children? The answer to that is easy: because it is good for children to read books.

"The problems in a book can be much more horrendous than any we would willingly face in real life, and the solutions can be more ingenious. In fact, the characters are quite capable now and then of coming up with solutions better than those the author had planned; unfortunately, they can also develop unexpected new problems of their own. These they toss to the writer to work out.

"When a child (or an adult) reads a book, I think his mind is getting pretty much the same kind of exercise it gets when it deals with real-life problems, though perhaps less intensely. It is certainly not turned off or lulled. If you watch a child reading—or better, recall your own reading as a child—how often did you put the book down for a minute and wonder: How is the hero going to get out of *this* mess? And try to figure out ways, hoping he would turn right at the next corner, because that's the way the bad guys went.

"Did I mention bad guys? Did I say Long John Silver? Long John is a liar; he is unctuous, greedy, tricky; he is a thief. Then why do we like him better than anybody else in the book? The mind learns that it is not easy to separate good from bad; they become deviously intertwined. From books it learns that not all doors are simply open or shut, and that even rats can become heroes.

"And the lovely thing about a book is that when you finish wondering about these things and pick the book up again, the story is still there, right where you left it. You can't do that with movies or television.

"Not that I am against movies or television when the programs are reasonably good. There are thousands of children who would never read a book anyway—there always were, long before electronics—and a television program can let them know who Romeo and Juliet were, or at least what it's like to go to the moon. And I don't think the medium weans many real readers away from books.

"My own children, who are omnivorous and voracious readers, tend to watch television in spurts which may last an afternoon or two. Then they get tired of it, and I see them back with a book again. They got the reading habit early, and now I think they are hooked for life." [Lee Kingman, editor, *Newbery and Caldecott Medal Books: 1966-1975,* Horn Book, 1975.[1]]

HOBBIES AND OTHER INTERESTS: Music, gardening, and furniture making.

FOR MORE INFORMATION SEE: Publishers Weekly, February 5, 1973; Lee Kingman, editor, *Newbery and Caldecott Medal Books: 1966-1975,* Horn Book, 1975; *Horn Book,* December, 1976. Obituaries: *New York Times,* March 8, 1973; *Publishers Weekly,* March 12, 1973; *Library Journal,* March 15, 1973; *Time,* March 19, 1973.

"Well," said Mrs. Linden, "would you like to come and live at Penrose Farm?" ■ (From *An Hour in the Morning* by Gordon Cooper. Illustrated by Philip Gough.)

COOPER, Gordon 1932-

PERSONAL: Born March 27, 1932, in Melksham, Wiltshire, England; son of Jack (a trellis dispatcher) and Emma (a cook; maiden name, Hale) Cooper. *Education:* Attended schools in England. *Politics:* None. *Religion;* Anglican. *Home:* 6 Beanacre Re., Melksham, Wiltshire, England.

CAREER: Clerk for two commercial companies, 1948-67; government service clerk, 1967—.

WRITINGS—All children's novels: *An Hour in the Morning,* Oxford University Press, 1971, Dutton, 1974; *A Time in a City,* Oxford University Press, 1972, Dutton, 1975; *A Second Springtime* (Junior Literary Guild selection in United States), Oxford University Press, 1973, Elsevier-Nelson, 1975; *Hester's Summer,* Oxford University Press, 1974; *A Certain Courage,* Oxford University Press, 1975.

WORK IN PROGRESS: Research on the effects on the countryside of the dissolution of the monasteries by Henry VIII.

SIDELIGHTS: "Soon after learning to read I thought how wonderful books were and I always hoped that one day I would be able to offer something to a publishing house. In primary school we were always encouraged to write. I remember that we were given pictures and told to write a story about the people in them. In the senior school magazines which appeared in each term, in addition to the reports of the school's activities, there were pages where short stories, articles and poems by the pupils were printed. I often submitted short stories to the editor, but none of my work ever achieved print, simply because other people's contributions were better. I saw my first Shakespearean play when I was twelve—a matinee performance of 'Twelfth Night' and it made a great impression on me. Over the years I have seen other productions of the play, but I can still remember the costumes and groupings of the performance. I used this experience in one of the chapters of my second book.

"I have written poems for my own pleasure, and on one occasion I wrote a few lines entitled 'Country Girl' after I had been looking at an old brown photograph of a group of girls standing outside a village school with their teacher in 1914. The reason we possessed the photograph was that one of the girls wearing a long white pinafore was my mother. Having written the poem I then went on to write my first book, *An Hour in the Morning,* and in many ways Kate Bassett, the heroine, is how I imagined my mother might have been at that age. She did many of the things that Kate did. She passed the Labour examination, left school when she was twelve, and then went to work as a general maid in a farmhouse. I was very pleased to be able to dedicate the book to her.

"A local weekly newspaper has a 'March of Time' column in which are reprinted news items of twenty-five, fifty, seventy-five and one hundred years ago. On one occasion there was a short paragraph which was originally printed in an issue of 1870, stating that six orphan girls had appeared before the local magistrates in order to obtain the necessary certificates which would enable them to emigrate to Canada under a special welfare scheme to be adopted by early settlers. I remembered that child emigration had been touched on in a history lesson at school and it was because of the paragraph I began writing *A Second Springtime. A Certain Courage* describes the war years of 1939-1945 as I remembered them.

"I've always been interested in the past—in old buildings, furniture, and especially old china. Some of the pieces of china in my own very modest collection appear in the books. Real-life circumstances and settings play an important part in my writing. To create the background I need, I find I use streets, buildings, rooms and furniture from many sources, seen by that 'inward eye' referred to by William Wordsworth in his poem 'Daffodils.' I try to read as widely as possible, because an awareness of other people's writing seems to sharpen my judgement when applied to any work I may have in progress. I set aside a certain length of time each evening for writing my stories. Sometimes the work goes well—sometimes it doesn't, but I find it essential to have a set period for working. The same discipline is needed in keeping a diary. I usually write the end of the story first. Sometimes it has been the final chapter, but very often it is just a few short paragraphs. When, after a great many revisions and rewritings a manuscript is finally completed, I feel a sense of great thanksgiving. I find, too, that I have a deep admiration for the people whose lives I have tried to describe."

HOBBIES AND OTHER INTERESTS: Theater; collecting old china.

FOR MORE INFORMATION SEE: Christian Science Monitor, May 1, 1974; *Horn Book,* August, 1974, August, 1975, October, 1975.

GORDON COOPER

Young village girls dressed for a party. ■ (From *The Land and People of Syria* by Paul W. Copeland. Photograph courtesy of Paul W. Copeland.)

COPELAND, Paul W.

PERSONAL: Born in New York. *Education:* Graduated from Whitman College; University of Washington, M.A.

CAREER: Children's author, teacher. Has taught English at the American University, Beirut, Lebanon, high school in Seattle, Washington and in Aleppo, Syria, 1952. *Awards, honors:* Smith Mundt grant from the U.S. Department of State, 1952.

WRITINGS—All for children; all published by Lippincott: *The Land and People of Syria,* 1964, revised edition, 1972; *The Land and People of Jordan,* 1965, revised edition, 1972; *The Land and People of Libya,* 1967, revised edition, 1972.

SIDELIGHTS: Having lived and taught in the Middle East, Copeland wrote his books from an informed position. However, critics are divided on how successful this type of book is for children. In reviewing *The Land and People of Jordan, Best Sellers'* opinion of the book was that it was, "Informative and heavy and boring. . . . Perhaps the editors expect the miraculous of the author when they order the geography, the history, past and present political set-ups, the culture and just about everything of a land and its people to be sandwiched into a mere 160 pages."

On the other hand, a *Book Week* reviewer felt that *The Land and People of Syria,* "is simple enough for a child of eleven to get an excellent idea of the nation and its people, yet so comprehensive that we wish we had read it before we visited the country."

FOR MORE INFORMATION SEE: Book Week, July 19, 1964; *Best Sellers,* June 15, 1965; Martha E. Ward and D. A. Marquardt, *Authors of Books for Young People,* Scarecrow Press, 1967.

COREY, Dorothy

PERSONAL: Born in Rush Lake, Saskatchewan, Canada; married Edward Corey (an engineer); children: Richard, Jan Khouri (Mrs. Jan Sebastian). *Education:* Attended school in Nebraska. *Home:* 16654 Parthenia St., Sepulveda, Calif. 91343.

CAREER: Writer. Active in a cooperative nursery school, Parent/Teacher Association; leader in Girl Scouts of America. *Member:* Society of Children's Book Writers (charter member).

WRITINGS—All children's books: *You Go Away,* A. Whitman, 1975; *No Company Was Coming to Samuel's House* (bilingual), Blaine Ethridge, 1976; *Tomorrow You Can,* A. Whitman, 1977; *Pepe's Private Christmas,* Parents' Magazine Press, 1978; *Everybody Takes Turns,* A. Whitman, 1979; *We All Share,* A. Whitman, 1980. Contributor of short stories to *Humpty Dumpty.*

(From *Tomorrow You Can* by Dorothy Corey. Illustrated by Lois Axeman.)

DOROTHY COREY

WORK IN PROGRESS: More concept stories for very young children; miscellaneous fiction; an autobiographical easy-to-read story of life in Canada; *You Can Depend on Santa.*

SIDELIGHTS: "I made my first sale when I was ten years old. A large garage in Omaha was having a slogan contest. I entered and won fourth prize—a generous two hundred fifty dollars worth of parts and labor at the garage!

"I wrote many extra-curricular skits during the seventh and eighth grades and I sometimes think I did my best writing in the eighth grade.

"I didn't write again, until, as a teen-ager I published some verse and Rebecca Caudill encouraged me to continue my writing.

"I taught briefly at Spencer, Idaho and wrote an account of my year there. *Reader's Digest* had shown interest in condensing it but I felt I would have to change all names. I sent my only copy home and my mother, who would keep a slip five years old because it still had some wear in it, threw it out because 'it was only a bunch of old papers.' It was my only copy.

"I felt that participating in and observing nursery schools was the most educational thing I had ever done. When you go to college you have done term papers before, you've dissected before, and you have encountered Shakespeare before.

"When I read to my first child I decided to write for children. I made a brief start. Then I moved to the country and had so much outdoor work and another child that I didn't get back to juvenile manuscripts for many years.

"In the meantime I fell into the clutches of the local Parent Teacher Association and I spent years preparing skits and programs for them (they always needed one more) when I could have had books of my own. After all, memories are not very permanent.

"I wish I could say that I was imaginative enough to make up plots and situations, but all my manuscripts, published and unpublished, grew out of things that really happened. My child left the door open for Santa Claus so I wrote *Pepe's Private Christmas*. My niece received a bike with one wheel so I wrote *You Can Depend on Santa*. I looked into my two year old daughter's mouth one day and was horrified to find a large, brown spot. A cavity at two! So I rushed her to a children's dentist where the cavity turned out to be walnut skin from a piece of nut she had been eating. I wrote a book, "Robby and the Cavity" [unpublished] about that.

"My concept books grow from my own experiences and the suggestions of a panel of nursery school teachers I am fortunate to have as friends. A bilingual teacher told me there was no material about a Spanish Thanksgiving. Everything was American turkey and her pupils could not relate to it. So I wrote the bilingual *No Company Was Coming to Samuel's House*.

"In nursery school we used to tell the children that 'maybe tomorrow' they would be able to go down the slide and do all kinds of grown-up things, so I wrote *Tomorrow You Can*. *You Go Away* was inspired by seeing Glo Coalson's "On Mother's Lap," but it drew upon many departures. Nursery school teachers have found *You Go Away* especially useful.

"With PTA at last behind me, I hope to use my time for more children's books."

HOBBIES AND OTHER INTERESTS: Music.

One day the band marched in a parade that passed through Louis' old neighborhood. Now his mother was able to see him in his uniform. She visited him often, but she had never seen the band parading. ▪ (From *Louis Armstrong: Ambassador Satchmo* by Jean Gay Cornell. Illustrated by Victor Mays.)

CORNELL, Jean Gay 1920-

PERSONAL: Born August 17, 1920, in Streator, Ill.; daughter of John Charles (a certified public accountant) and Florence (Dixon) Werckman; married Francis G. Cornell, June 14, 1968 (divorced March 26, 1973); children: (first marriage) Steven C. Howard, David G. Howard. *Education:* Beloit College, student, 1938-40; University of Illinois, B.A., 1942. *Politics:* Republican. *Religion:* Episcopalian. *Home:* Amberlands Apt. 5-L, Croton-on-Hudson, N.Y. 10520.

CAREER: Spencer Press, Campaign, Ill., executive assistant to managing editor, 1953-62; University of Illinois, College of Electrical Engineering, Champaign, head of publications department, 1964-66; Garrard Publishing, Scarsdale, N.Y., head of production department, 1966-68; Educational Research Services, White Plains, N.Y., vice-president, 1968-72; free-lance writer, 1972-75; *Reader's Digest,* associate editor, condensed books copy desk, 1975—.

WRITINGS: (Editor with A. Atwood) *Sports Alive,* Spencer Press, 1960; *Louis Armstrong: Ambassador Satchmo,* Garrard, 1972; *Mahalia Jackson: Queen of Gospel Song,* Garrard, 1974; *Ralph Bunche: Champion of Peace,* Garrard, 1976. Also author of numerous articles.

WORK IN PROGRESS: Suspense novel, as yet untitled.

SIDELIGHTS: "Something I remember most vividly from childhood is my father playing the piano. He could play any kind of music—classical, ballads, jazz—by ear or from written music. He had only eight piano lessons in his life, but music came to him naturally. I adored listening to him play, especially jazz, but unfortunately I didn't inherit his talent. From those early years, I date my love of music.

"That is why I chose Louis Armstrong as the subject of my first children's book. For many years I was a writer-editor for publishing companies, where I wrote articles on assigned subjects. But being able to *choose* what you are going to write makes the job easier and more fun.

"Since the three books I have had published are biographies, the most careful research was necessary. Having worked for a company which published encyclopedias, I was familiar with research methods. A course in library science in college was also of great help. In fact, I find researching the most enjoyable part of doing a book. The harder tasks are organizing the material one has gathered and getting it put down on paper.

"If you are able to get the facts from the subjects themselves, this is the best way of researching a book. This wasn't possible for me, and I never met any of the people I wrote about. Mr. Armstrong was the only one of the three who was alive at the time I wrote my book. Through his agent, I was able to pass on my manuscript to him for his approval or corrections. He had the manuscript when he suddenly died, and it was a great sorrow to me that I was never able to meet him.

"I find writing a very good form of discipline, and it is only possible for me to accomplish anything by setting up regular hours for writing—and then I let nothing interfere with those hours. I do all my writing on an electric typewriter, since I can in that way capture the end of a thought before it slips away. I do, however, keep many memo pads in handy places to jot down a phrase or an idea while it is still fresh.

"I have started to block out and outline a novel I have had in mind for some time. It will be a new kind of writing for me, since I have become used to thinking in terms of fourth-grade vocabularies. I must say that one of the rewards of my children's books has been the many letters I have received from children saying they liked my books. I've answered them all with love and gratitude."

SAMUEL JAMES CORNISH

CORNISH, Samuel James 1935-
(Sam Cornish)

PERSONAL: Born December 22, 1935, in Baltimore, Md.; married Florella Orowan. *Education:* Goddard College in Vermont. *Home address:* 50 Monastery Rd. #1, Brighton, Mass. 02135. *Office:* Education Development Center, Newton, Mass.

CAREER: Former editor of *Chicory* magazine for the Enoch Pratt Library, Baltimore, Md., and of *Mimeo*, a poetry magazine; Education Development Center, Open Education Follow Through Project, Newton, Mass., staff adviser and consultant on children's writing, 1973—. *Military service:* 1958-60. *Awards, honors:* National Endowment for the Arts grant, 1967.

WRITINGS—Juveniles: *Your Hand in Mine*, Harcourt, 1971; *Grandmother's Pictures*, Bradbury Press, 1975; *Walking the Streets With Mississippi John Hurt*, Bradbury Press, in press. Also author of *Harriet Tubman*, published by Third World Press.

Verse: *In This Corner*, Fleming McCallister Press, 1961; *People Under the Window*, Sacco Publishers, 1962; *Generations*, Beanbag Press, 1964, Beacon Press, 1968, 1971; *Angles*, Beanbag Press, 1965; *Winters*, San Souci Press, 1968; (editor, with Lucian Dixon), *Chicory* (poetry and prose collection), Associated Press, 1968; *Streets*, Third World Press, 1973; *Sam's World*, Decatur Press, 1977.

Work is represented in anthologies, including among others: *Black Fire*, edited by LeRoi Jones and Larry Neal, Morrow, 1968; *Smith Poets*, edited by Harry Smith, Horizon Press, 1969; *New Black Poetry*, edited by Clarence Major, International Publishers, 1969; *American Literary Anthology 3*, edited by George Plimpton and Peter Ardery, Viking, 1970; *Natural Process*, edited by Ted Wilentz and Tom Weatherly, Hill & Wang, 1972; *One Hundred Years of Black Poetry*, Harper, 1972; *A Penguin Anthology of Indian, African, and Afro-American Poetry*, Penguin, 1973; *New Voices in American Poetry*, edited by David Alan Evans, Winthrop, 1973. Contributor of poems and reviews to *Ann Arbor Review*, *Poetry Review*, *Journal of Black Poetry*, *Essence*, *Boston Review of the Arts*, and Boston newspapers.

SIDELIGHTS: "Most of my major themes are of urban life, the Negro predicament here in the cities, and my own family. I try to use a minimum of words to express the intended thought or feeling, with the effect of being starkly frank at times. Main verse form is unrhymed, free.

"My most recent interests in relation to my writing have been the examination of historical materials, both fictional and non-fictional, that relate to the black American community during the 18th and 19th centuries, and the ways in which the cultural heritage of black people in America developed, concurrent with, and in spite of, other social values and trends (for example, slavery, the Civil War, Reconstruction and black migration, etc.)."

Sam was a small brown boy who spent most of his time alone. ■(From *Your Hand in Mine* by Sam Cornish. Illustrated by Carl Owens.)

CORRIGAN, (Helen) Adeline 1909-

PERSONAL: Born May 31, 1909, in Cleveland, Ohio; daughter of Patrick James and Norah (Walsh) Corrigan. *Education:* Notre Dame College, South Euclid, Ohio, B.A., 1930; Western Reserve University (now Case Western Reserve University), M.S.L.S., 1931. *Home:* 3716 Lytle Rd., Shaker Heights, Ohio 44122.

CAREER: Cleveland Public Library, Cleveland, Ohio, children's librarian, 1931-48, assistant supervisor of Work with Children, 1949-53, supervisor, 1954-65, assistant to director of library and head of branch libraries, extension and bookmobile services, 1965-72; writer, 1972—. Lecturer at Case Western Reserve University, 1947-72. *Member:* Delta Kappa Gamma.

WRITINGS—Juvenile: (Editor and author of introduction) *Holiday Ring: Festival Stories and Poems,* A. Whitman, 1975. Contributor of articles and reviews to library journals. Member of editorial advisory board of *Highlights for Children.* Consultant to H. W. Wilson Co.

WORK IN PROGRESS: Editing an anthology of prose and poetry for children.

ADELINE CORRIGAN

(From *Holiday Ring: Festival Stories and Poems* by Adeline Corrigan. Illustrated by Rainey Bennett.)

SIDELIGHTS: "I enjoy music and dance, travel, nature and the outdoor world. I have had the collecting spirit, from music-boxes to Belleek porcelain and Lalique crystal, and the Cinderella legend in literature. No hobby has brought me more pleasure than bringing young readers and books together. In introducing books to children, I have used story, poetry, puppets, films, and recordings."

COSTELLO, David F(rancis) 1904-

PERSONAL: Born September 1, 1904, in Nebraska; son of Thomas (manager of a grain elevator business) and Mary L. (Mallory) Costello; married Cecilia C. Waldkirch, June 12, 1929; children: Barbara M. (Mrs. Barbara M. McDougle), David K., Donald R. *Education:* Peru State Teachers College (now Peru State College), Peru, Neb., A.B., 1925; University of Chicago, M.S., 1926, Ph.D., 1934. *Home and office:* 4965 Hogan Dr., Fort Collins, Colo. 80525.

CAREER: Marquette University, Milwaukee, Wis., instructor in botany, 1926-32; U.S. Forest Service, Rocky Mountain Forest and Range Experimental Station, Fort Collins, Colo., forest ecologist, 1934-37, chief of Division of Range Research, 1937-53; U.S. Forest Service, Pacific North West and Range Experimental Station, Portland, Ore., chief of Division of Range, Wildlife Habitat, and Recreation Research, 1953-64. Special lecturer, Colorado Agricultural and

Mechanical College (now Colorado State University), 1942-53; guest professor, State College of Washington (now Washington State University), 1957; guest speaker, University College of North Wales, 1962; consultant on environmental preservation and management, 1975—. President, Welfare Bureau, Inc., Fort Collins, 1938-48.

MEMBER: American Association for the Advancement of Science (fellow), Ecological Society of America, Outdoor Photographers League (life member), Authors League of America, American Institute of Biological Sciences, Sigma Xi. *Awards, honors:* Citation of American Society of Range Management for distinguished service in range research and ecology, 1970.

WRITINGS: Range Ecology, U.S. Department of Agriculture Forest Service, 1939; *The World of the Porcupine,* Lippincott, 1966; *The World of the Ant,* Lippincott, 1968; *The Prairie World,* Crowell, 1969, 1975; *The World of the Prairie Dog,* Lippincott, 1970; *The World of the Gull,* Lippincott, 1971; *The Desert World,* Crowell, 1972; *The Mountain World,* Crowell, 1975; *The Seashore World,* Crowell, 1980. Contributor of more than 150 articles to popular periodicals, including *True, Sports Illustrated, Outdoor Life,* and *Farm Journal,* and about the same number of technical articles on ecology, range management, and recreation research to professional journals.

WORK IN PROGRESS: A book entitled *The Moon Was Ten Feet Wide.*

SIDELIGHTS: "I grew up, as an only child, on our farm in southeastern Nebraska where the prairie met the wooded hills on the Missouri River bluffs. From earliest boyhood I knew the birds, mammals, insects and plants of the grasslands, forests and fields. I did not know their proper names until later when I studied botany, zoology, and ecology in college and in graduate school at the University of Chicago.

"Since I was alone on our farm my observation of nature was my youthful entertainment. The things I saw were the beginning of my writing career since I treasured each memory of the outdoors. I still remember, after more than fifty years, the wonders I saw as a barefoot boy—wonders that have haunted me through a lifetime.

"I also experienced tragedies which have become a part of my writing. I had two fox terrier dogs which were my constant companions. They scared up rabbits, helped me kill rats in our barn, and warned of tramps who came to our door from the railroad that ran through our farm. Then they killed some of my father's fine hogs while we were away from home and he immediately killed them with his shotgun. I also witnessed the tragedy of natural things as my father broke the virgin sod of the prairie and destroyed beautiful flowering plants and grasses that had waved over the hills for 10,000 years. The plowing attracted the little Franklin gulls that followed the plow in search of insects and worms. It also destroyed the habitats of mice, bumblebee homes, and ground nesting birds.

"My father also cut much of our oak-hickory forest to make available more land for cultivation and to sell cord wood to fuel the stoves in the little town a mile north of our farm. He also used tile to drain the prairie marsh where muskrats, mink, blackbirds and a multitude of other creatures lived. He straightened the creek in our pasture where all the oxbows and deep fishing holes with catfish, buffalo fish, minnows, and turtles lived.

"I do not blame my father for doing these things since times were hard and money was difficult to get. He was a good man, honest as Abe Lincoln, and respected by all who knew him. But all these things were symbols of a vanishing paradise, symbols of a present worldwide destruction of our planet by man who now exists in almost incomprehensible numbers.

"My mother was a strong woman who loved nature, including birds, rocks, and many forms of wildlife. Once I found a huge snapping turtle in a pond. When I suggested turtle soup, she took my father's revolver, held the muzzle above the turtle's head, and shot him in the water. When she pulled the trigger the explosion covered us from head to toe with water and slimy mud. The turtle was stunned and we opened it with an axe after it died. And we had turtle soup.

"I described the incident for *Lone Scout* magazine—my first literary attempt, but my article was rejected. Then I tried poetry. It did not sell. My writing career began when I was teaching botany at Marquette University. For a $50 prize I answered a contest in the old *Liberty* magazine. The question was, 'What would you do if two armed men stopped you while driving with a young woman? Fight or let them take her.' I listed seven reasons why I'd let them take her, including the 'law of self preservation.' Also, if I were dead then she still would have no protection. My fan mail included comments about being a live coward, a dead hero, and about a dozen proposals for marriage. I won the contest and my writing career was launched.

DAVID F. COSTELLO

Young prairie dog with dirt on its fur after digging. ■ (From *The World of the Prairie Dog* by David F. Costello. Photograph by the author.)

"Most of my early articles were about fox and coon hunting. My farmer friends always kept a number of dogs that were experts in trailing. Even if we did not catch anything we enjoyed the hound 'music' as it echoed up and down the wooded hills and valleys. My stories were mostly character studies of the hunters.

"As I became more experienced in article writing, I contributed to many national magazines with pieces on subjects that ranged from party games, the weather, conservation of natural resources, childhood and adult recreation, and medical procedures useful to the general public. Finally I began writing books.

"As I once told a newspaper reporter, 'Writing a book is ten years of looking, remembering, and putting pieces of paper into drawers and three months of writing.' It also involves photography and library research to make sure that technical information is right. But my impelling motive always has been to help readers see the natural world more clearly and to appreciate the relationships between living things and their natural environment.

"As I became better known, magazine editors used me as an expert rewrite man. They would send me articles by other authors with the chronology all wrong or the scientific and statistical information all wrong. A short note from the editor would say, 'Take the hogwash out of this.' Sometimes they paid me as much as the author received for the article. So, I ended up being both an author and an editor."

COTT, Jonathan 1942-

PERSONAL: Born December 24, 1942, in New York, N.Y.; son of Ted (a television executive) and Jean (an artist; maiden name Cahan) Cott. *Education:* Columbia University, B.A., 1964; University of California, Berkeley, M.A., 1966. *Home:* 247 East 33rd St., New York, N.Y. 10016. *Office: Rolling Stone* magazine, 745 Fifth Ave., New York, N.Y. 10022.

CAREER: Fulbright fellow at University of Essex, England, 1967-69; Granada Television, London, England, production deviser, 1969-70; *Rolling Stone,* San Francisco, Calif., associate editor, 1970-71, contributing editor, 1971-75; Stonehill Publishing Co., New York, N.Y., executive editor, 1974-76; *Rolling Stone* magazine, New York, N.Y., associate editor, 1976—. Producer of contemporary music programs, WNYC-radio, New York, 1960-62, and KPFA-radio, Berkeley, 1965-67. *Awards, honors:* Woodrow Wilson fellowship, 1964; Fulbright fellowship, 1967-69; Ingram Merrill Foundation grant, 1972.

WRITINGS: He Dreams What Is Going On Inside His Head: Ten Years of Writing (film reviews, poems, essays), Straight Arrow, 1973; *Stockhausen: Conversations with the Composer,* Simon & Schuster, 1973; (editor and author of introduction; juvenile) *Beyond the Looking Glass: An Anthology of Victorian Fairy Tales, Novels, Stories, and Poems,* Stonehill, 1974; (editor) *The Roses Race Around Her Name: Poems from Fathers to Daughters,* Stonehill, 1975; *City of Earthly Love* (poems), Stonehill, 1975; *Forever Young,* Random House, 1978; (general editor) *Masterworks of Children's Literature: 1550-1900,* five volumes, Stonehill and Chelsea House, 1981.

Contributor: Richard Kostelanetz, editor, *On Contemporary Literature,* Avon, 1964; Richard Kostelanetz, editor, *New American Arts,* Horizon Press, 1965; *Young American Writing,* St. Martin's, 1972.

Poetry represented in anthologies: *Young American Poets,* edited by Paul Carroll, Follett, 1968; *A Cinch-Amazing Works from the Columbia Review,* edited by Leslie Gottesman and others, Columbia University Press, 1969; *The World Anthology,* edited by Anne Waldmar, Bobbs-Merrill, 1969; *Another World,* edited by Anne Waldmar, Bobbs-Merrill, 1971; *In Youth,* edited by Richard Kostelanetz, Ballantine, 1972.

JONATHAN COTT

(From *Beyond the Looking Glass* edited by Jonathan Cott. Photograph courtesy of Cottingley Photographs.)

Contributor of poetry to magazines, including *American Poetry Review, Paris Review,* and *The World,* and articles to *New York Times, Ramparts, Sunday Ramparts, Rolling Stone, American Review,* and *Radio Times* (London).

WORK IN PROGRESS: "A book on several creators of children's literature."

Children, you are very little,
And your bones are very brittle;
If you would grow great and stately,
You must try to walk sedately.
—Robert Louis Stevenson

There is no frigate like a book to take us lands away,
Nor any coursers like a page of prancing poetry.
—Emily Dickinson

COX, Donald William 1921-

PERSONAL: Born April 16, 1921, in Rutherford, N.J.; son of Henry John (life insurance) and Mabel (Doremus) Cox; married Jane Marshall (city planner), December 16, 1961; children: Donalee, Heather. *Education:* Montclair State College, B.A., 1942; Columbia University, M.A., 1947, Ed.D., 1948; National Training Labs in Group Development, Bethel, Me., certificate. *Politics:* Democrat. *Religion:* Unitarian Universalist. *Home:* 1237 Lombard St., Philadelphia, Pa.

CAREER: University of Florida, Gainesville, assistant professor of education, 1948-52; Air Command and Staff College, Air University, Montgomery, Ala., professor, 1952-57; Martin Co., Baltimore, Md., manager of public relations, Project Vanguard, 1957-58; Franklin Institute, Philadelphia, Pa., senior lecturer for NASA Space Science Program, 1961-62; freelance author, lecturer, and consultant, 1963-65; Philadelphia (Pa.) School District of Joseph Priestley Science Center, 1965—. New York University, visiting professor, 1961. Consumers Cooperative of Rutherford, N.J., president, 1947. Co-chairman of Educational Action Coalition (EAC), Philadelphia Schools, 1973-74; co-chairman of Citizens Committee Against the Pay Grab, 1975. *Military service:* U.S. Army Air Forces, weather observer and forecaster, 1942-45, became sergeant. *Member:* American Association of University Professors, National Education Association, Philadelphia Federation of Teachers, Directors of Philadelphia SANE World (board member), Phi Delta Kappa.

WRITINGS: Spacepower, Winston, 1958; *Man in the Universe* (children's book), Winston, 1959; *Rocketry Through the Ages* (children's book), Winston, 1959; *Stations in Space* (children's book), Holt, Rinehart & Winston, 1960; *You in the Universe* (children's book) Winston, 1960; *The Space Race,* Chilton, 1962; *America's New Policymakers,* Chilton, 1964; *Islands in Space,* Chilton, 1964; *The Perils of Peace,* Chilton, 1965; *Explorers of the Ocean Depths* (children's book), Hammond, 1968; *Pioneers in American Ecology* (children's book), Hammond, 1969; *America's Explorers of Space* (children's book), Hammond, 1969; *The City as a Schoolhouse* (children's book), Judson Press, 1972. Contributor to magazines.

WORK IN PROGRESS: A biography of Senator Everett Dirksen; an anthology of space poetry; other books on education, oceanography, and a joint Soviet-American man to Mars program.

HOBBIES AND OTHER INTERESTS: Oil painting, swimming, and mountain climbing.

Secured to spacecraft by a golden umbilical line, Maj. White maneuvers freely in space. ■(From *America's Explorers of Space* by Donald W. Cox. Photograph courtesy of NASA.)

DONALD WILLIAM COX

CRAIG, John Ernest 1921-

PERSONAL: Born July 2, 1921, in Peterborough, Ontario; son of Fred D. and Dorothy Mae (Fenwick) Craig; married Frances Patten Morrison, June 1, 1945; children: David, Catherine, John and Paul (twins). *Education:* University of Manitoba (King Fellow), B.A., 1951; University of Toronto, M.A. *Agent:* McClelland and Stewart Ltd., 25 Hollinger Rd., Toronto, Ont. M4B 3G2, Canada.

CAREER: Canadian Facts Co. Ltd., Toronto, market researcher, 1952-69; ORC International Ltd., Toronto, market researcher, 1969-71; full time writer, 1972—. *Military service:* Royal Canadian Naval Volunteer Reserve, 1941-45.

WRITINGS—Juvenile; all fiction except as indicated: *Wagons West* (illustrated by Stanley Wyatt), Dent, 1955, Dodd, 1956; *The Long Return* (illustrated by Robert Doremus), Bobbs-Merrill, 1959; *By the Sound of Her Whistle* (nonfiction; illustrated by Fred Craig), Peter Martin Associates, 1966; *No Word for Good-bye* (illustrated by Harri Aalto), Peter Martin Associates, 1969, Coward, 1971; *Zach,* Coward, 1972; *Who Wants to be Alone?,* Scholastic, 1975; *The Clearing,* Longman (Canada), 1975; *Wormburners* (illustrated by Alan Daniel), Scholastic, 1976; (with wife, Frances) *Track and Field* (nonfiction), Watts, 1979.

Adult—Fiction: *The Pro,* Peter Martin Associates, 1968, published in the United States as *Power Play,* Dodd, 1973; *If You Want to See Your Wife Again,* Putnam, 1971; *In Council Rooms Apart,* Putnam, 1971; *Superdude,* Warner Paperback, 1974; *All G.O.D.'s Children,* Morrow, 1975; *Close Doesn't Count,* Macmillan of Canada, 1975.

Non-fiction: *How Far Back Can You Get?,* Doubleday, 1974; (with David Steen) *Canada's Olympic Chances,* Simon & Schuster of Canada, 1976; *The Noronic Is Burning,* General Publishing, 1976; *Some of My Best Friends are Fishermen,* McClelland and Stewart, 1976; *Simcoe County: The Recent Past* (illustrated by Margot Anderson), Corporation of the County of Simcoe (Midhurst, Ont.), 1977; *The Years of Agony, 1910-1920,* Natural Science of Canada, 1977; *Chappie and Me* (autobiographical novel), Dodd, 1979.

Has also written for television series "Adventures in Rainbow Country," 1970-71, and "Starlost," 1973.

SIDELIGHTS: Craig is an author whose work covers a variety of topics for a variety of audiences. In genre, Craig's books range from suspense to autobiography, fiction to nonfiction. His settings run the gamut from the Canadian woods to the world of professional hockey with his characters ranging from multi-millionaires to disadvantaged minority children.

JOHN ERNEST CRAIG

"Anybody can quit," he'd insist. "That's easy. It's hanging in there that makes winners out of losers." ■ (From *The Wormburners* by John Craig. Illustrated by Alan Daniel.)

Craig was raised in Peterborough, Ontario, and much of his fiction is rooted in Canada. Many of Craig's characters are faced with the challenge of leaving the Ontario woods and grow as a result of their leave-taking. Zach Kenebec, an Indian boy in *Zach*, for example, sets out to look for others of his tribe only to realize that the bonds of friendship go deeper than those of race or origin.

The plight of Canadian Indians is a subject Craig handles with special sensitivity. Through the experiences of Indian youths, the problems of leaving familiar surroundings as well as those of race relations and the struggle for personal identity are dealt with in *The Long Return, No Word for Good-bye, Zach,* and *Who Wants to be Alone?* These are problems Craig experienced himself as he reveals in his autobiographical novel, *Chappie and Me,* the story of a white boy who tours the country with an all-black baseball team.

Craig's love of his native land and his boyhood memories have also inspired much of his non-fiction. Books like *By the Sound of Her Whistle* and *The Noronic Is Burning* stem from his early exposure to Canadian steamboats. Craig has also written histories of Canadian localities and two books dealing with the sports world.

FOR MORE INFORMATION SEE: Irma McDonough, *Profiles,* Canadian Library Association, 1975.

CROFUT, William E. III 1934-
(Bill Crofut)

PERSONAL: Born December 14, 1934, in Cleveland, Ohio; son of William E., Jr. (a businessman) and Grace (Benfield) Crofut; married Emily Holran, June 21, 1958; married second wife, Susan Plehn, March 17, 1962; children: (second marriage) Erika, Andrea, Catherine. *Education:* Allegheny College, B.A., 1958. *Home:* New Hartford Rd., Sandisfield, Mass. 01255.

CAREER: Concert folk and jazz musician, New York, N.Y., 1960—. Has made concert tours for the U.S. State Department, visiting more than twenty-nine countries in the last fifteen years. President of Crofut Productions, Sandisfield, Mass. Teacher of music at Wesleyan University, Middletown, Conn. *Military service:* U.S. Army, 1958-60. *Awards, honors:* Presidential citation and Department of Defense citation, 1965, for work in cultural exchange.

WRITINGS: Troubador: A Different Battlefield, preface by Robert F. Kennedy, Dutton, 1968; *The Moon on the One Hand: Poetry in Song* (illustrated by wife, Susie Crofut), Atheneum, 1975. Compiler with Pham Duy and Steve Addiss of Vietnamese music for a research record; has recorded, with Steve Addiss, "Addiss and Crofut" and "Eastern Ferris

WILLIAM E. CROFUT III

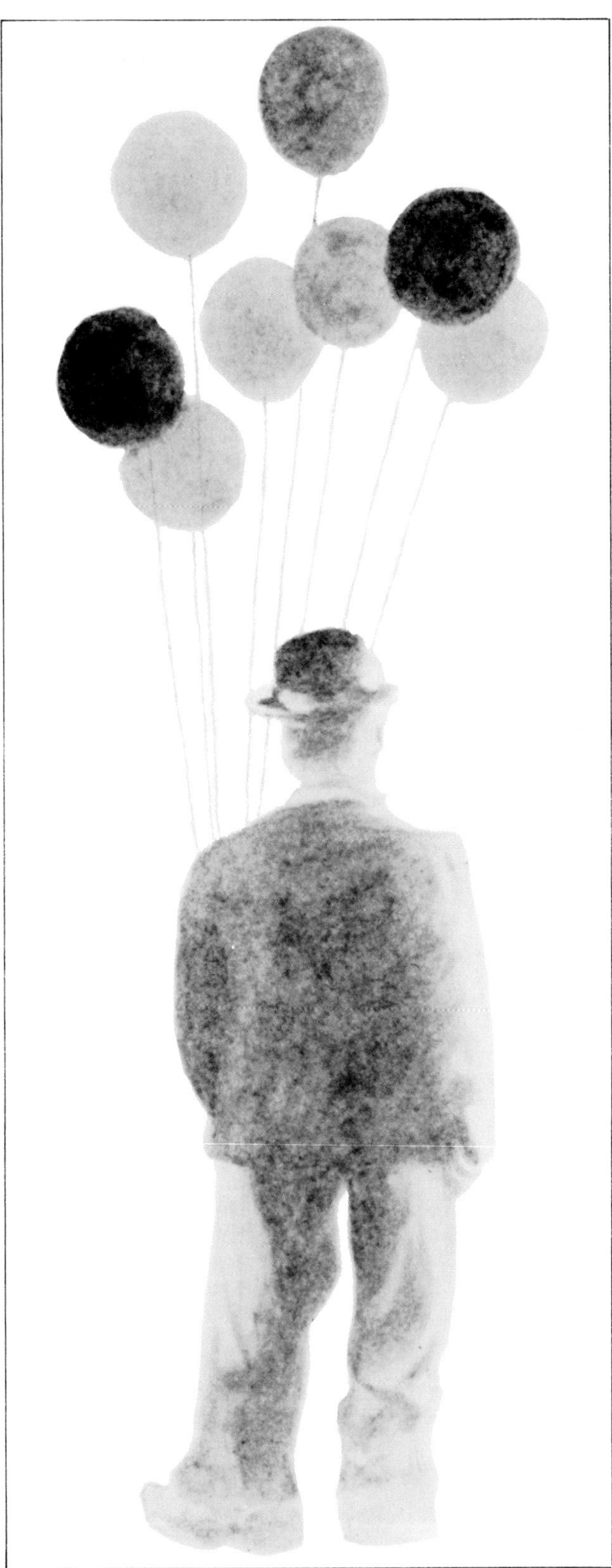

(From *The Moon on the One Hand: Poetry in Song* by William Crofut. Illustrated by Susan Crofut.)

Wheel'' for Columbia Records, with Kenneth Cooper, ''Folk and Baroque'' and with Benjamin Luxou, ''English and American Folk Songs.'' Contributor to newspapers.

CROMPTON, Anne Eliot 1930-

PERSONAL: Born April 6, 1930, in Northampton, Mass.; daughter of Samuel A. (a professor) and Ethel (a writer; maiden name, Cook) Eliot; married Willard Crompton (a woodworker), November 24, 1951; children: Carrie, Joseph, Nancy, Catherine, Samuel. *Education:* Kenwood Academy, student, 1943-48; Newton College, student, 1948-49. *Politics:* ''Quite liberal most of the time.'' *Religion:* Catholic. *Residence:* Chesterfield, Mass.

WRITINGS: *The Sorcerer,* Atlantic-Little, Brown, 1971; *Deer Country,* Atlantic-Little, Brown, 1973; *The Winter Wife* (juvenile), Atlantic-Little, Brown, 1975; *The Rain-Cloud Pony* (juvenile), Holiday House, 1977; *A Woman's Place* (young adult), Atlantic-Little, Brown, 1978; *The Lifting Stone* (juvenile), Holiday House, 1978; *Queen of Swords,* Methuen, 1980; *The Ice Trail,* Methuen, 1980.

SIDELIGHTS: ''When I was a child I fully expected to grow up and write books, as most of the grownups I knew did. As soon as I learned how to write words I began to write stories, and illustrate them. In my teens I tried to market my short stories, without much success. Fortunately I knew this game, from watching my relatives play it. I knew that a story sale was a very rare jackpot, so I did not get too discouraged.

''I married at twenty, and spent the next fifteen years raising a family. Then I went back to writing.

''In winter I write for three hours a day beside a wood stove. I write long books in winter, picture books in summer. I write about what I love. The world is wonderful, every second we

ANNE ELIOT CROMPTON

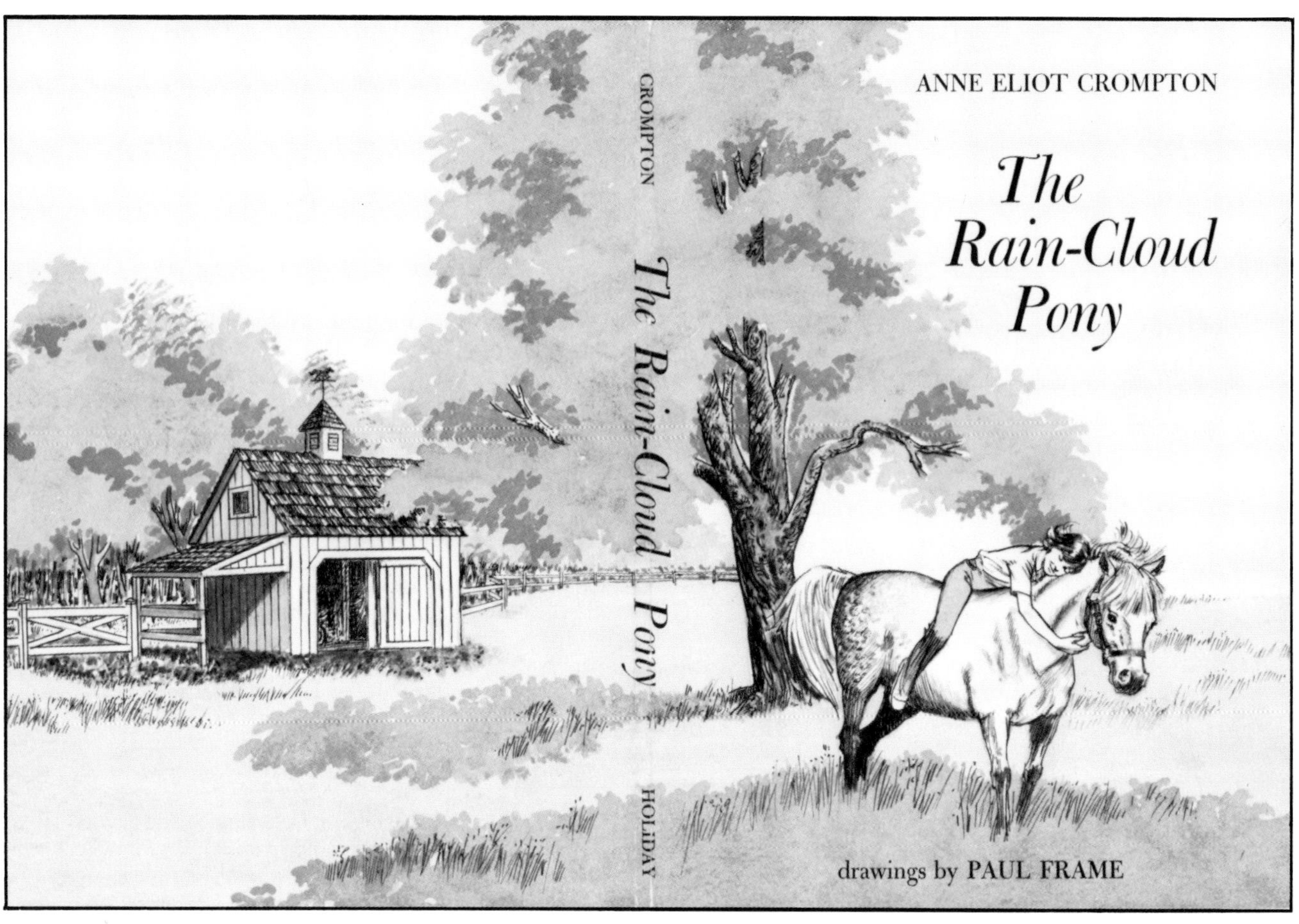

(From *The Rain-Cloud Pony* by Anne Eliot Crompton. Jacket illustrated by Paul Frame.)

breathe is wonderful—but it's easy to forget that. You have to keep your eyes wide open, watching the world, to see its wonder. I hope my stories remind people to keep watching.

"All my stories are true. I take a real scene and scramble in real events from some place else, and parts of real people. One person's temper with another person's humor and a third person's looks make a new character.

"I love the worlds I put together almost as much as the real world.

"In my writing I try to put the beautiful, fantastic real world of nature before the reader and say; 'Look at this! This is to love!' "

HOBBIES AND OTHER INTERESTS: Ecology, piano, gardening.

FOR MORE INFORMATION SEE: Horn Book, August, 1975, April, 1979.

CROSBY, Alexander L. 1906-1980

OBITUARY NOTICE—See sketch in *SATA* Volume 2: Born June 10, 1906, in Catonsville, Md.; died January 31, 1980, in Quakertown, Pa. Journalist, editor, and writer. Crosby was an editorial writer for the *Staten Island Advance* from 1929 to 1934, when he was fired for trying to organize a chapter of the American Newspaper Guild. After his dismissal he held jobs as editor of the *Paterson Press,* assistant New Jersey Supervisor of the Federal Writers Project, news editor of the Federated Press, and executive director of the National Housing Conference. In 1944 he became a free-lance writer of children's books and pamphlets. Crosby and his wife, Nancy Larrick, have published a number of books for children, including *The Rio Grande* and *Steamboat Up the Colorado. For More Information See: Authors of Books for Young People,* 2nd edition, Scarecrow, 1971; *More Books by More People,* Citation Press, 1974; *Contemporary Authors,* Volume 29-32, revised, Gale, 1978. *Obituaries: Contemporary Authors,* Volume 93-96, Gale, 1980; *New York Times,* February 1, 1980; *School Library Journal,* April, 1980

Children, you are very little,
And your bones are very brittle;
If you would grow great and stately,
You must try to walk sedately.

—Robert Louis Stevenson

CUNNINGHAM, Chet 1928-
(Cathy Cunningham)

PERSONAL: Born December 9, 1928, in Shelby, Neb.; son of Merle Burritt and Hazel (Zedicher) Cunningham; married Rose Marie Wilhoit, January 18, 1953; children: Gregory, Scott, Christine. *Education:* Pacific University, B.A., 1950; Columbia University, M.S., 1954. *Home and office:* 8431 Beaver Lake Dr., San Diego, Calif. 92119.

CAREER: News-Times, Forest Grove, Ore., city editor, 1954-55; Jam Handy, Detroit, Mich., writer of educational and church films, and sales training materials, 1955-59; Convair, San Diego, Calif., writer in motion picture section, 1959-60; Cunningham Press, San Diego, Calif., publisher and writer, 1960—. Free-lance writer, 1960—. Chairman of San Diego Writers Workshop, 1962—. *Military service:* U.S. Army, 1950-52; became sergeant.

WRITINGS—Juvenile nonfiction: *Your Wheels,* Putnam, 1973; *Your Bike,* Putnam, 1977; *Your First Car,* Putnam, 1980.

Juvenile fiction: *Dead Start Scramble,* Scholastic, 1973, reissued, 1976; *Baja Bike,* Putnam, 1974; *Locked Storeroom Mystery,* Scholastic, 1976; *Narc One Going Down,* Scholastic, 1977; *Apprentice to a Burglary,* Scholastic, 1978.

Other: *Bushwackers at Circle K.,* Avalon, 1969; *Killer's Range,* Avalon, 1970; *Gold Wagon,* Pinnacle, 1972; *Bloody Gold,* Pinnacle, 1972; *Northwest Contract,* Pinnacle, 1973; *Bloody Boston,* Pinnacle, 1973; *Blood on the Strip,* Pinnacle, 1973; (under pseudonym Cathy Cunningham) *Demons of Highpoint House,* Popular Library, 1973; *Fatal Friday,* Venice Publishing, 1973; *Die of Gold,* Pinnacle, 1973; *Hijacking Manhattan,* Pinnacle, 1974; *Terror in Tokyo,* Pinnacle, 1974; *Hellbomb Flight,* Pinnacle, 1974; *Mankill Sport,* Pinnacle, 1975; *Deep Sea Shootout,* Pinnacle, 1976; *The Patriots,* Tower Publications, 1977; *Seeds of Rebellion,* Tower Publications, 1977; *The Freedom Fighters,* Tower Publications, 1977; *The Gold and the Glory,* Tower Publications, 1978; *The Power and the Prize,* Tower Publications, 1978; *The Poker Club,* Condor Books, 1978; *Countdown to Terror,* Pinnacle, 1978; *High Disaster,* Pinnacle, 1978; *Cryogenic Nightmare,* Pinnacle, 1978; *Rainbow Saga,* Tower Publications, 1979; *This Splendid Land,* Tower Publications, 1979; *Radiation Wipeout,* Pinnacle, 1979; *Mexican Brown Death,* Pinnacle, 1979; *Skyhigh Betrayers,* Pinnacle, 1980; *Software Devastation,* Pinnacle, 1980.

Author of monthly column "Truck Talk," appearing in numerous trade magazines, 1956—; author of ghost-written column, "Your Car," appearing in a number of weekly and daily newspapers, 1959—.

WORK IN PROGRESS: Several novels.

CURLEY, Daniel 1918-

PERSONAL: Born October 4, 1918, in East Bridgewater, Mass. *Agent:* John Schaffner, 425 East 51st St., New York, N.Y. 10022.

CAREER: Writer. Associate, University of Illinois Center for Advanced Study, 1968. *Awards, honors:* Guggenheim fellowship in fiction, 1958; National Council on the Arts award, for *In the Hands of Our Enemies.*

"Why aren't you in school, children?" he said as an afterthought. Mr. Modzelewski was a member of the school board and liked to see every seat filled everyday. ■ (From *Ann's Spring* by Daniel Curley. Illustrated by Donna Diamond.)

WRITINGS: That Marriage Bed of Procrustes (stories), Beacon Press, 1957; *How Many Angels?* (novel), Beacon Press, 1958; *A Stone Man, Yes* (novel), Viking, 1964; *In the Hands of Our Enemies* (stories), University of Illinois Press, 1979; *Love in the Winter* (stories), University of Illinois Press, 1976; *Ann's Spring* (juvenile), Crowell, 1977; *Billy Beg and the Bull* (juvenile), Crowell, 1978; *Hilarion* (juvenile), Houghton, 1979. Also author of several plays produced on college campuses. Contributor of short stories, poetry, and criticism to *Kenyon Review, Epoch, Modern Fiction Studies,* other literary periodicals. Member of editorial board, *Accent,* 1955-60.

WORK IN PROGRESS: "I'm working on an indescribable novel and on a children's book about a boy who fears his mother has become allergic to him and goes to live in a barn with cows and cats."

DANIEL CURLEY

SIDELIGHTS: "I once had four little girls and wanted in the worst way to write books for them, but nothing ever happened. Now that I no longer have any little girls I find I am writing the books I should have written for them then. *Billy Beg and the Bull* is an old story I used to tell them—my mother read it to me when I was little. So there is at least that much of a connection. *Hilarion* started out as a dream. I dreamed what is the first chapter of the book: four men are sitting around in a room and someone comes up the stairs. When they open the door, all they can see is an enormous vest, filling the door from side to side. A voice announces the name 'Hilarion.' From that point on all I had to do was explain who the four men were and who Hilarion was. In the dream I knew he was magic, so I had that much to go on. It was really very interesting explaining everything to myself, and I hope readers will find it interesting too."

FOR MORE INFORMATION SEE: Publishers Weekly, February 28, 1977; *Horn Book,* June, 1978.

CURTIS, Patricia 1921-

PERSONAL: Born July 31, 1921, in Orange, N.J.; daughter of Harry A. (a chemical engineer) and Irene (Hall) Curtis; married William Palitz, 1948 (deceased); children: Wendy, Stephen. *Education:* University of Missouri, B.A., 1942. *Agent:* McIntosh & Otis, Inc., 475 Fifth Ave., New York, N.Y. 10017.

CAREER: Fawcett Publications, New York, N.Y., editor, 1959-61; *House and Garden,* New York, N.Y., assistant managing editor, 1961-66; Cowles Book Co., New York, N.Y., senior editor, 1967-68; *This Week* (magazine), New York, N.Y., copy editor, 1969; *Family Circle,* New York, N.Y., copy director, 1970-79. *Member:* American Society of Magazine Editors.

WRITINGS: The Breakfast and Brunch Book, Winter House, 1972; *Animal Doctors: What It's Like to Be a Veterinarian and How to Become One* (juvenile), Delacorte, 1977; (editor) Barbara and Gideon Seaman, *Women and the Crisis in Sex Hormones,* Rawson Associates, 1977; *Animal Rights,* Four Winds, 1980; *The Indoor Cat,* Doubleday, 1981; *Cindy, a Hearing Ear Dog,* Dutton, 1981. Contributor to *College Management* and to popular magazines, including *Family Circle, House and Garden, Cue, Pageant, Working Woman, Ladies' Home Journal, The New York Times Magazine, Good Housekeeping, Cosmopolitan,* and *Smithsonian.*

WORK IN PROGRESS: Book on animals and the handicapped, to be published in 1981 or 1982 by Four Winds Press. Also a book on a dog for Elsevier-Dutton.

SIDELIGHTS: "I have had a rich career as an editor in magazine and book publishing, especially in the women's magazine field. My main current interests are animals, animal welfare and feminism. I especially like to write for young readers. Many of my books are for teenagers."

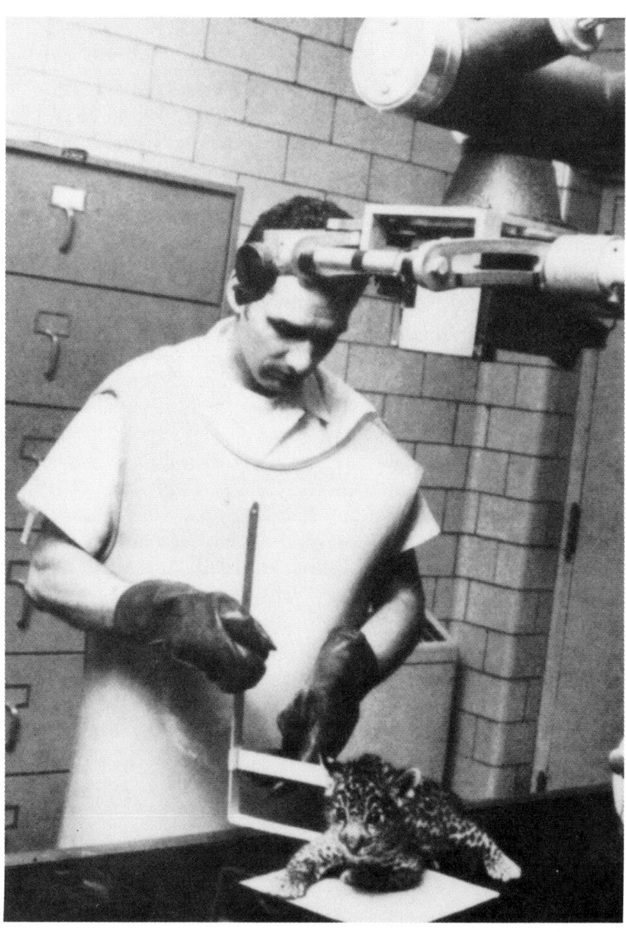

A jaguar kitten, pride and joy of a large zoo, has had a fall and seems to have hurt her leg. An animal technologist is taking X-rays of the little animal's leg. ▪ (From *Animal Doctors: What It's Like to Be a Veterinarian and How to Become One* by Patricia Curtis. Photograph by Tom McHugh.)

PATRICIA CURTIS

DANIEL, Anita 1893(?)-1978 (Anita)

PERSONAL: Born about 1893 in Lassy, Rumania; naturalized citizen of the United States; died June 17, 1978 in New York City. *Education:* Attended schools in France. *Home:* New York, N.Y.

CAREER: Free-lance writer. Contributed articles to various U.S. newspapers and magazines including *Christian Science Monitor* and *New York Times Magazine;* served as the New York correspondent for *Nationalzeitung* and other Swiss publications; author of several books on travel.

WRITINGS: I Am Going to Switzerland (illustrated by J. Marianne Moll), Coward, 1952, revised edition, Birkhauser (Basel, Switzerland), 1968; *I Am Going to Italy* (illustrated by Moll), Coward, 1955, revised edition, Birkhauser, 1964; *Ein Bisschen Liebe,* Birkhauser, 1957; *The Story of Albert Schweitzer* (juvenile; illustrated by Erica Anderson and W. T. Mars), Random House, 1957; *You'll Love New York,* Birkhauser, 1964.

Under pseudonym Anita: *Ich Reise Nach New York: Kleine Gebrauchsanweisung für die Grosse Stadt,* Birkhauser, circa 1952; *Ich Reise Nach Paris,* Birkhauser, 1959; *Ferien in USA: Kleine Hinweise für die Grosse Reise,* Birkhauser, 1962; *Sehnsucht Nach Der Ferne,* Birkhauser, 1965; *Ich Reise Nach London,* Birkhauser, 1967; *Ich Reise Nach Mexico,* Birkhauser, 1968; *Gedanken Über Dies und Jenes,* Birkhauser, 1971.

SIDELIGHTS: Daniel made a career of her love for travel. She wrote in German as well as English, several travel guides about various places, such as, Italy, Switzerland, Mexico, Paris, and New York City.

In the course of her travels, Daniel had the opportunity to interview many prominent individuals including the late Albert Schweitzer about whom she wrote a biography for children. In a critique of this work, entitled *The Story of Albert Schweitzer,* the *New York Times* commented: "Anita Daniel knows Albert Schweitzer personally, and she has made her story of his life a warm and realistic book. . . . The author has succeeded in making his life as thrilling and dramatic to young people as that of any explorer or military hero."

FOR MORE INFORMATION SEE: New York Times, November 17, 1957; Martha E. Ward and Dorothy E. Marquardt, editors, *Authors of Books for Young People,* Scarecrow, 1967.

Dr. Schweitzer with Jean-Baptiste, one of his pet antelopes. ■ (From *The Story of Albert Schweitzer* by Anita Daniel. Photograph by Erica Anderson.)

DARLING, Louis, Jr. 1916-1970

OBITUARY NOTICE—See sketch in *SATA* Volume 3: Born April 26, 1916, in Stamford, Conn.; died of cancer, January 21, 1970, in Norwich, Conn. Artist, illustrator, and author of children's books. Darling illustrated more than sixty books, including Rachel Carson's *Silent Spring* and Beverly Cleary's "Henry Huggins" series. Many of his books were written in collaboration with his wife, Lois Darling. Among them are *Before and After Dinosaurs* and *A Place in the Sun*. In 1966 he received the John Burroughs Medal for *The Gull's Way*. *For More Information See: Illustrators of Children's Books,* Horn Book, 1957; *More Junior Authors,* Wilson, 1963; *Contemporary Authors,* Volume 5-8, revised, Gale, 1969; *Authors of Books for Young People,* 2nd edition, Scarecrow, 1971. *Obituaries: New York Times,* January 24, 1970; *AB Bookman's Weekly,* February 16, 1970; *Publishers Weekly,* February 23, 1970; *Contemporary Authors,* Volume 89-92, Gale, 1980.

DAUER, Rosamond 1934-

PERSONAL: Born June 29, 1934, in New York, N.Y.; daughter of R. Sterling Mueller (a surgeon) and Edith Louise (a businesswoman; maiden name, Welleck) Greenman; children: (first marriage) Christian John, Matthew John. *Education:* Middlebury College, B.A., 1956; Columbia University, M.A., 1957. *Home and office:* 90 Olmstead Lane, Ridgefield, Conn. 06877. *Agent:* A. Watkins, Inc., 77 Park Ave., New York, N.Y. 10016.

"I am off to find a very big lake," he said. "I will start my *own* family." ■ (From *Bullfrog Grows Up* by Rosamond Dauer. Illustrated by Byron Barton.)

ROSAMOND DAUER

CAREER: Colby-Sawyer College, New London, N.H., member of staff in English department, 1957-61; *Encyclopedia Americana,* New York, N.Y., editor, 1961-62; Staten Island Institute of Arts and Sciences, Staten Island, N.Y., curator of education, 1962-63; poet and writer, 1963—. Vice-president of Staten Island Council on the Arts, 1973-75.

WRITINGS—For children: *Bullfrog Grows Up,* Greenwillow Books, 1976; *Mrs. Piggery Snout,* Harper, 1977; *Bullfrog Builds a House,* Greenwillow Books, 1977; *My Friend, Jasper Jones,* Parents' Magazine Press, 1977; *Bullfrog and Gertrude Go Camping,* Greenwillow Books, 1980; *The 300 Pound Cat,* Holt, in press. Contributor of poems to national periodicals.

SIDELIGHTS: "When I was in the fourth grade I decided to read every book in the library. I never did, of course. This was partly due to the fact that I was captivated by the pleasures of writing. It was equally true that I decided to skip the library books devoted to mathematics, animal husbandry, and ticks. Since then, I have been haunted by the possibility that I have missed something I could be using today. In another five years I might even buy a book titled, *Tap Dancing for Ticks*.

"I have written serious stories and poetry. A long time ago I wrote a play. It was terrible. I enjoy writing humorous stories and that is what I do with most of my time.

"I write for everyone I have ever met and for myself. I like to pick up information, sort through what I have found, and somehow create something new, funny, and true.

"Working and dreaming are important to me."

FOR MORE INFORMATION SEE: Horn Book, June, 1976.

DAVIDSON, Rosalie 1921-

PERSONAL: Born July 25, 1921, in Paoli, Ind.; daughter of Roger Carl and Annabel (McIntosh) Davidson. *Education:* University of Louisville, student, 1939-41; University of Denver, B.A., 1948, M.A., 1950; University of California, San Diego, graduate study, 1970. *Home:* 6315 Connie Dr., San Diego, Calif. 92115. *Office:* San Diego Unified Schools, Grant School, 1425 Washington Pl., San Diego, Calif. 92103.

CAREER: Seagram's Distillery, Louisville, Ky., in quality laboratory, 1941-43; public school teacher in Denver, Colo., 1948-50; Grant School, San Diego, Calif., first grade teacher, 1950—. *Military service:* U.S. Navy, Women Accepted for Volunteer Emergency Service (WAVES), chief storekeeper, 1943-46. *Member:* National Science Association, Society of Children's Book Writers, National Education Association, California Teachers Association, San Diego Teachers Association. *Awards, honors:* Honorable mention in "articles" category in the *Writer's Digest* contest, 1980.

WRITINGS—For children: *Dinosaurs: The Terrible Lizards,* Golden Gate, 1969; *When the Dinosaurs Disappeared,* Golden Gate, 1973. Contributor to *Grade Teacher, Instructor.*

WORK IN PROGRESS: Tidepool Animals; Sea Dragons of Long Ago; Warm-Blooded Dinosaurs; a book on nutrition.

SIDELIGHTS: "I grew up in a small town in Southern Indiana. My cousins and I used to wander over the hills looking for plant and animal fossils in the many limestone quarries. We also found Indian relics, geodes, bird nests, etc.

"My uncle, A. C. McIntosh, was a botanist (who knew lots about paleontology) at the South Dakota School of Mines in Rapid City. I would save all my finds until he came home to visit my grandparents with whom I lived. Then he would help me classify my collections. I adored my uncle and some of his love for nature rubbed off on me.

"When I began teaching primary children I was horrified to find that many of them didn't really know much about, or had ever *seen,* the plants and animals living around them. I worked out a program by which I taught reading, spelling and writing to first grade children by using information about the animals and plants that live in their immediate environment. They wrote their own books. I attempted to make their environment interesting and exciting enough so that they would build life-long hobbies and a caring attitude towards plants and animals as they learned to read and write.

"My school children and I have written many books. My favorite is a dinosaur cookbook—because we like to cook and we like dinosaurs, so we read about the dinosaurs while our food is cooking—the children love it, but I guess it's too way out for publishers. I have had no luck selling the idea! In fact, my school children continue to be enchanted with several of my manuscripts, but I can't meet up with an enchanted publisher these days!

"The most fun about being an 'author' is getting called by teachers and librarians who want me to come and talk about writing and about dinosaurs and early mammals. I really love to get out and meet other teachers and other children. It's also great fun to receive letters from children who have read my books, though I can't really send them *dinosaurs,* much as I'd like to do so! It's surprising how many requests I get for them!

"I continue to teach first, second and third grades with an emphasis on science and nature. Children need much "hands on" exposure to animals and plants. They need realities and friendships and caring and LOVE . . . and love for and interest in plants and animals fulfills some of these needs."

HOBBIES AND OTHER INTERESTS: Collecting books on Western Americana and natural history, bicycling, horses, swimming, selling used books by mail (using the *Antiquarian Bookman* as a guide).

ROSALIE DAVIDSON

(From *Dinosaurs: The Terrible Lizards* by Rosalie Davidson. Illustrated by Bernard Garbutt.)

DOUTY, Esther M(orris) 1911-1978

OBITUARY NOTICE—See sketch in *SATA* Volume 8: Born March 24, 1911, in Mount Vernon, N.Y.; died of cancer, December 13, 1978, in Washington, D.C. Educator, social worker, and author. Best known for her biographies for children, Douty was director of the workshop in junior biography of the Writers' Conference at Georgetown University. Her writings include *Story of Stephen Foster, Mr. Jefferson's Washington,* and *Charlotte Forten: Free Black Teacher. For More Information See: Contemporary Authors,* Volume 5-8, revised, Gale, 1969. *Obituaries: Washington Post,* December 16, 1978; *Contemporary Authors,* Volume 85-88, Gale, 1980.

DUVOISIN, Roger (Antoine) 1904-1980

OBITUARY NOTICE—See sketch in *SATA* Volume 2: Born August 28, 1904, in Geneva, Switzerland; died of a heart attack, June 30, 1980, in Morristown, N.J. Author of more than forty books and illustrator of more than one hundred forty books for children. Duvoisin was perhaps best known as the illustrator of the "Happy Lion" series, written by his wife, Louise Fatio. In 1956 the series won the first children's book award given in the Republic of West Germany. Duvoisin created many popular animal characters in books like *Veronica, Petunia, Donkey-Donkey,* and *Hector-Penguin.* He was also noted for his translation and illustration of medieval European folk tales, such as *The Crocodile in the Tree* and *Chanticleer: The Real Story of the Famous Rooster.* His numerous awards and prizes include the 1948 Caldecott Medal for *White Snow, Bright Snow.* Duvoisin's work was chosen four times for the New York Times Best Illustrated Children's Books of the Year and seventeen times for the American Institute of Graphic Arts Fifty Best Books of the Year. *For More Information See: Illustrators of Children's Books,* Horn Book, 1957; *Who's Who in Graphic Art,* Amstutz & Herzog Graphis, 1962; *Books Are by People: Interviews with 104 Authors and Illustrators of Books for Young Children,* Citation Press, 1969; *Famous Authors and Illustrators for Young People,* Dodd, 1973; *Who's Who in American Art,* Bowker, 1973; *Contemporary Authors,* Volume 13-16, revised, Gale, 1975. *Obituaries: Publishers Weekly,* July 25, 1980; *Contemporary Authors,* revised, Volume 101-104, Gale, 1981.

EBERLE, Irmengarde 1898-1979 (Allyn Allen, Phyllis Ann Carter)

OBITUARY NOTICE—See sketch in *SATA* Volume 2: Born November 11, 1898, in San Antonio, Tex.; died February 27, 1979. Editor and author of children's books. Eberle was a fabric designer and magazine editor before she became a full-time writer in 1937. She was the author of sixty-three children's and young adult books, including nature stories, biography, and fiction. Her writings include *A Good House for a Mouse, Come Be My Friend,* and *Hop, Skip, and Fly. For More Information See: Current Biography,* Wilson, 1946; *Authors of Books for Young People,* 2nd edition, Scarecrow, 1971; *Who's Who in America,* 40th edition, Marquis, 1978. *Obituaries: Publishers Weekly,* April 2, 1979; *Contemporary Authors,* Volume 85-89, Gale, 1980.

ECKBLAD, Edith Berven 1923-

PERSONAL: Born April 14, 1923, in Baltic, S.D.; daughter of Leander G. (a teacher) and Louise (Simonson) Berven; married Marshall D. Eckblad (a company president), June 9, 1943; children: Mark, Jonathan, James, Nancy, Peter. *Education:* Wheaton College, Wheaton, Ill., student, 1941-42. *Home:* 5224 Spring St., Racine, Wis. 53406.

CAREER: Free-lance writer. Gateway Institute, Racine, Wis., creative writing instructor, 1972-78. Guest lecturer at Parkside Capsule College & Arts Festival (University of Wisconsin), Concordia College (Milwaukee) Writers Conference, and at The Chicago Reading Round Table. *Member:* National League of American Pen Women (past president of Lake Shore branch), Racine Writers (co-chairman), Council for Wisconsin Writers (past board member), Wisconsin Regional Writers Association, Racine and National Federation of Women's Club. *Awards, honors:* Midwest Writers' Conference award for juvenile nonfiction; Council for Wisconsin Writers Juvenile Picture Book award (shared), 1975.

WRITINGS: Just Marty, W. Frederick, 1947; *Living with Jesus,* Augsburg, 1955; *Something for Jesus,* Augsburg, 1959; *Danny's Straw Hat,* Augsburg, 1962; *Kindness Is a Lot of Things,* C. R. Gibson, 1966; *A Smile Is to Give,* Rand McNally, 1969; *Danny's Orange Christmas Camel,* Augsburg, 1970; *Soft as the Wind,* Augsburg, 1974; *Walking on

(From *Soft as the Wind* by Edith Eckblad. Illustrated by Jim Roberts.)

the Water, C. R. Gibson, 1974; *Qu'est-Ce Qui Est Doux?*, Editions du Cerf [Paris], 1976. Contributor of verse, short stories, and features to religious and family-type magazines.

WORK IN PROGRESS: Several whimsical, fantasy-type, juvenile picture books; inspirational material for adults and young adults.

SIDELIGHTS: "My early childhood was a happy time filled with delightful experiences, all of which I draw upon in writing for children. Born on my grandparents' farm in eastern South Dakota in the lush and lovely Sioux Valley, I enjoyed all of the love and attention a first grandchild normally receives! There was much hustle and bustle, coming and going, picnics, ice cream socials, band concerts, and the eagerly anticipated morning and afternoon coffee-times so common to rural areas.

"Then shortly before my third birthday my father and mother moved to Madison, Wisconsin, where my father was a student at the university. This was an extremely traumatic experience for me. I can still hear the wail of the train whistle as we left Sioux Falls and my beloved Mammy and Baba (my own names for grandma and grandpa). It is as vivid to me as if it were yesterday!

"Madison was, as is, a very unique city. (I now have a son teaching at the university.) Beautifully situated on three lakes, Madison is a vibrant city, stimulating to live in—a city open to new and creative ideas. As a child I remember my pleasure in visiting the campus, watching boat races, chasing the balloon man, and buying *huge* caramel apples from a vendor! My parents also supplied stability, and very importantly, spiritual values which later on gave a sense of direction to my life.

"But I looked forward with anticipation to summers spent in South Dakota. Fortunately, every summer until I became a teenager was spent on that farm. How I loved the animals! Today it is difficult for me to resist stopping to pat a horse when I see one near a fence. There is nothing so deliciously soft as the feel of a horse's velvety nose!

"South Dakota days were filled with sunshine and night skies looked as if someone had flung gold-dust from one end of heaven to the other. *Never* have I seen stars so bright! My love of nature and the out-of-doors stems from this period.

"Both parents read to me at an early age and even before entering school I was creating my own 'books' with paper, cardboard, metal clasps, and alphabet stamp pad, and magazine illustrations.

"In second grade something wonderful happened! A kind lady gave money so that each second and third grade student could order a book of his own choosing. I ordered *Bunny Brown and Sister Sue* by Laura Lee Hope. I shall never forget the sense of wonder, the *smell* and *feel* of that *special* book. (I remember thinking, 'I should like to grow up to write books.')

"One day years later my son Mark said to me as we browsed in a bookstore, 'Mom, don't you love the smell of a bookstore!' I understood just what he meant. My daughter and four sons have provided me with much material—and my

EDITH BERVEN ECKBLAD

husband with much understanding and encouragement. (In *Danny's Orange Christmas Camel* Danny's father gave him a rabbit punch—my own boys were always doing this to one another. The disappointment my own children felt at not participating in a birthday party or program at church or school provided the basis for the plot.)

"In *Soft as the Wind* I drew upon my farm background. One of the joys of my life was when I was told that a Paris publisher was bringing out a French edition of this book! To see an idea that has formed in your mind take shape in an attractively illustrated book is the reward an author receives for hard work, sometimes lonely work, discipline, and times of disappointment!

"You must love words if you want to write. Enter essay contests. (Winning one at fourteen provided me with unbelievable motivation to continue writing.) Be aware of people around you! Notice what they say and do. Observe situations, nature, animals—and use your imagination! Plan your own life and activities. Study hard, love life, and read, read, read. Then write!"

HOBBIES AND OTHER INTERESTS: Foreign travel, family entertaining, books, music, the out-of-doors, gourmet cooking, growing herbs, golf, bicycling, knitting, interior decorating, and "of course, my six grandchildren."

When I am grown to man's estate
I shall be very proud and great,
And tell the other girls and boys
Not to meddle with my toys.
—Robert Louis Stevenson

FAULKNER, Anne Irvin 1906-
(Nancy Faulkner)

PERSONAL: Born January 8, 1906, in Lynchburg, Va.; daughter of John Adams (business executive) and Marianne Tucker (Clark) Faulkner. *Education:* Wellesley College, B.A., 1928; Cornell University, M.A., 1933. *Politics:* Independent. *Religion:* Episcopalian. *Home:* 942 Rosser Lane, Charlottesville, Va. 22903.

CAREER: Sweet Briar College, Sweet Briar, Va., history instructor, 1929-31, academic secretary, 1937-42; Salem Academy, Winston-Salem, N.C., history instructor, 1935-36; University of Virginia, Charlottesville, director of bureau of school and community drama, 1942-44; National Recreation Association, New York, N.Y., editor, 1944-47; Chandler Records, New York, vice-president, 1947-57; Walker & Co., New York, editorial consultant, 1961-62. Author of children's books. *Member:* Authors League.

WRITINGS—All under name Nancy Faulkner; all published by Doubleday, except as noted: *Rebel Drums,* 1952; *The West Is on Your Left Hand,* 1953; *Side Saddle for Dandy* (Junior Literary Guild selection), 1954; *Pirate Quest* (Junior Literary Guild selection), 1955; *Undecided Heart* (Junior Literary Guild selection), 1957; *Sword of the Winds,* 1957;

. . . The stranger was talking on and the more he talked the more angry he sounded. ■ (From *Second Son* by Nancy Faulkner. Illustrated by Vernon Wooten.)

ANNE IRVIN FAULKNER

The Yellow Hat, 1958; *Tomahawk Shadow* (Junior Literary Guild selection), 1959; *Mystery at Long Barrow House* (Junior Literary Guild selection), 1960; *Small Clown,* 1960; *The Sacred Jewel* (Junior Literary Guild selection), 1961; *A Stage for Rom* (Junior Literary Guild selection), 1962; *Traitor Queen* (Junior Literary Guild selection), 1963; *Knight Besieged,* 1964; *The Secret of the Simple Code* (Junior Literary Guild selection), 1965; *Journey Into Danger,* 1966; *Mystery of the Limping Stranger,* 1967; *Small Clown and Tiger,* 1968; *Second Son,* Colonial Williamsburg, 1969; *Great Reckoning,* Dutton, 1970; *The Witch With the Long Sharp Nose,* Dutton, 1972.

Adult books: *Witch's Brew,* Curtis, 1973; *Jade Box,* Popular, 1974; *Summer of the Fireship,* Popular, 1976; *Savannah,* Popular, 1978.

SIDELIGHTS: "I was born in what was then a sleepy little southern town (Lynchburg, Virginia) where life was a leisurely thing and there was ample time for reading. No doubt because I was a 'constant reader' I wanted, from the time when my memory runs not to the contrary, to be a writer. I remember one summer project when I was about twelve. A friend and I decided we'd write a ghost story. We labored for a few days but, as I recall, never finished our stint because we came, literally, to blows over the working out of the plot!

"I had the normal life of a youngster growing up in a town like mine in the first quarter of the twentieth century. Each season had it's delights—many of which I'm sure no youngster of today would enjoy, or indeed, believe—roller skating on sidewalks outside our homes; playing a thing called piggy-wiggy stickball; riding our sleds, belly-buster-wise, down the middle of streets practically free of motor traffic; putting on plays in my family's drawing room, plays which we found in the *Ladies' Home Journal*; watching for the postman to grab the latest copy of *St. Nicholas.*

"I had hoped to learn the writer's craft when I went to college, but my hopes took a severe beating when, in my sophomore year, my professor (and a stupid woman she was!) called me to her office and said I'd best give up all notions of becoming an author because my vocabulary was too big! I was too shy to argue and too unsure of myself to question her advice so it was years before I wrote my first book. By that time I'd learned what the professor meant; that I, being in love with language, always chose the long, 'dictionary' word, when a more commonplace one would say the thing as well or better.

"What led me to my first effort at writing fiction was job in radio which brought me into contact with the writers of books for young people. All of those authors spoke of the agonies of writing and I wondered since most of them were not financially dependent on their royalties, why they continued to write. So, I decided I'd try my hands at a book for young people. The result was *Rebel Drums.*

"I write for anyone who will read. Many of my books for young readers have been read and, I'm told, enjoyed by adults. The only people I *don't* write for are those whose interests are either pornographic or sweetly sentimental.

"It's almost impossible for me to say where I get my material. Ideas come from reading, from travel, from chance conversations, from the odd looks of a stranger passing in the street, from an old house. I do not consciously draw on my own life, although, of course, I'm sure my subconscious is at work in that department. I usually do my actual writing in the morning for, perhaps, three hours at a time; but it is, I'm sure, true that when I'm working on a book, the book is always with me, 'even in my dreams.'"

FINLAY, Winifred 1910-

PERSONAL: Born April 27, 1910, in Newcastle-upon-Tyne, Northumberland, England; married Evan Finlay (a college lecturer, now retired), July, 1935; children: Gillian Finlay Hancock. *Education:* Kings College, Newcastle-upon-Tyne, England, M.A., 1933. *Home:* The Old House, Walgrave, Northampton, England.

CAREER: Schoolmistress at Newcastle, England, 1933-35, Stratford-on-Avon, England, 1941-44, and Leeds, England, 1945-48; writer. Former lecturer on books to school children and librarians. *Member:* Society of Authors. *Awards, honors:* Edgar Allan Poe special award, Mystery Writers of America, 1969, for *Danger at Black Dyke.*

WRITINGS—All published by Harrap, except as indicated: *The Witch of Redesdale,* 1951; *Peril in Lakeland,* 1953; *Peril in the Pennines,* 1953; *Cotswold Holiday,* 1954; *Lost Silver of Langdon,* 1955; *Storm Over Cheviot,* 1955; *Judith in Hanover,* 1955; *Canal Holiday,* 1957; *The Cruise of the Susan,* 1958; *The Lost Emeralds of Black Howes,* 1961; *The Castle and the Cave,* 1961; *Alison in Provence,* 1963; *Mystery in the Middle Marches,* 1965; *Castle for Four,* 1966; *Adventure in Prague,* 1967; *Danger at Black Dyke,* S. G. Phillips, 1968; *Folk Tales from the North,* Kaye & Ward, 1968, F. Watts,

Bud paused, trying to go over in his mind all that had happened in the last few days, wondering how much he could tell these boys who were his protectors, and how much he must suppress for his own sake as well as for theirs. ■ (From *Danger at Black Dyke* by Winifred Finlay. Illustrated by the author.)

1969; *The Cry of the Peacock,* 1969; *Summer of the Golden Stag,* 1969; *Folk Tales from Moor and Mountain,* Kaye & Ward, 1969, Roy, 1970; *Singing Stones,* 1970; *Cap O'rushes,* Harvey House, 1974; *Beadbonny Ash,* Nelson, 1973, 1975; *Tattercoats and Other Folk Tales,* Harvey House, 1975, 1977; (with daughter, Gillian Hancock) *Ghosts, Ghouls, and Spectres,* Kaye & Ward, 1976; (with Gillian Hancock) *Treasure Hunters,* Kaye & Ward, 1977; *Spies and Secret Agents,* Kaye & Ward, 1977; (with Gillian Hancock) *Clever and Courageous Dogs,* Kaye & Ward, 1978; *Tales from the Hebrides and Highlands,* Kaye & Ward, 1978; (with Gillian Hancock) *Famous Flights of Airships and Balloons,* Kaye & Ward, 1979; *Tales of Sorcery and Witchcraft,* Kaye & Ward, 1980.

WORK IN PROGRESS: Tales of Fantasy and Fear, for Kaye & Ward; *Children in Peril,* for Kaye & Ward.

SIDELIGHTS: "I have read books and written stories ever since I can remember, and still possess a fairy tale I wrote when I was seven. I first wrote professionally for my own daughter during World War II, when there was a shortage of books for children. My early books were adventure stories for boys and girls of ten plus. Gradually, I suppose as my daughter grew older, I concentrated on novels for teenage girls, trying to bring out the way in which the action and the need to make decisions led to the development of character and understanding.

"All these books have authentic backgrounds—somewhere in England, Scotland, France, Germany or Czechoslovakia . . . . With only a vague idea of my characters and plot I revisited the particular area in which I was interested and made notes on anything which stimulated my imagination—topography, architecture, history, archaeology, folktales and legends. I invariably learned a great deal when talking to local people who were knowledgeable about some particular aspect of the place in which they lived.

"When I returned home it was to months of sheer hard work, of elation and despair, of writing and rewriting. I was never satisfied. Each time I finished a book I hoped the next would be better.

"A few years ago a pneumonectomy followed by complications meant I had to come to terms with severe disabilities, including being unable to walk or travel.

"The notes on legends, folktales, ballads and ghost stories which I had amassed, now stood me in good stead and I began to retell old tales, drawing chiefly on areas I knew when a child—Northumberland and the northern counties, the English-Scottish border country, the North of Scotland and the Highlands and Islands.

"Of course I still require reference books. Here the county library is invaluable. Any book I need is put on the library van which comes to the village once a fortnight. Any book the library does not stock is obtained quickly from another county, or relevant pages are photocopied and sent to me.

"Now I am writing for young children, including my own grandchildren. My daughter collaborated with me on several books, and my husband has read everything I have written and helped me enormously. When I was young I was taught to have a healthy respect for the English language, and because I feel very strongly that only the best is good enough for children, I have always tried to maintain high literary standards."

HOBBIES AND OTHER INTERESTS: Reading.

FOR MORE INFORMATION SEE: Books and Bookmen, December, 1963, September, 1968; *Best Sellers,* December 1, 1968; *Times Literary Supplement,* June 26, 1969; *Book World,* August 17, 1969.

WINIFRED FINLAY

FOSTER, Genevieve (Stump) 1893-1979

OBITUARY NOTICE—See sketch in *SATA* Volume 2: Born April 13, 1893, in Oswego, N.Y.; died August 30, 1979, in Westport, Conn. Commercial artist, illustrator, and author of children's books. Foster wrote nineteen children's books, and was best known for her technique of choosing historical figures and weaving a story around their perception of events around them. Her first book was *George Washington's World.* Three of her books were Newbery Honor Books and her work has been translated into fifteen languages. *For More Information See: Junior Book of Authors,* Wilson, 1951; *Illustrators of Children's Books,* Horn Book, 1957; *Contemporary Authors,* Volume 5-6, revised, Gale, 1969; *More Books by More People,* Citation, 1974; *Writers Directory, 1980-82,* St. Martin's, 1979. *Obituaries: New York Times,* September 1, 1979; *Publishers Weekly,* September 17, 1979; *AB Bookman's Weekly,* October 8, 1979; *School Library Journal,* November, 1979; *Contemporary Authors,* Volume 89-92, Gale, 1980.

FOSTER, Marian Curtis 1909-1978 (Mariana)

PERSONAL: Born in 1909, in Cleveland, Ohio; died October 27, 1978, in Southampton, N.Y. *Education:* Attended Sophie Newcomb College, Art Students League, New York City; and Grande Chaumiere, Paris, France. *Residence:* New York City and Long Island, N.Y.

CAREER: Author and illustrator of books for children. *Exhibitions*—Permanent collections: Mariana Room, Hockessin Elementary School, Wilmington, Delaware; University of Mississippi; Phineas T. Barnum Museum, Bridgeport, Conn.

WRITINGS—Under pseudonym Mariana; all self-illustrated; *The Journey of Bangwell Putt,* F.A.R. Gallery, 1945, reprinted, Lothrop, 1965; *Miss Flora McFlimsey's Christmas Eve,* Lothrop, 1949; *Miss Flora McFlimsey's Easter Bonnet,* Lothrop, 1951; *Miss Flora McFlimsey and the Baby New Year,* Lothrop, 1951; *Miss Flora McFlimsey's Birthday,* Lothrop, 1952; *Hotspur,* Lothrop, 1953; *Miss Flora McFlimsey and Little Laughing Water,* Lothrop, 1954; *Doki, the Lonely Papoose* (a Junior Literary Guild selection), Lothrop, 1955; *Miss Flora McFlimsey and the Little Red School House,* Lothrop, 1957; *Miss Flora McFlimsey's Valentine,* Lothrop, 1962; *Miss Flora McFlimsey's May Day,* Lothrop, 1969; *Miss Flora McFlimsey's Halloween,* Lothrop, 1972.

Illustrator: Elizabeth Gordon. *Happy Home Children,* P. F. Volland, 1924; Rhoda Berman, *When You Were a Little Baby,* Lothrop, 1954; Betty Peckinpah, *Coco Is Coming,* Lothrop, 1956; Jean Y. Jaszi, *Everybody Has Two Eyes,* Lothrop, 1956; Janice, pseudonym of Janice Brustlein, *Little Bear's Pancake Party,* Lothrop, 1960; Janice, *Little Bear's Christmas,* Lothrop, 1964; Janice M. Udry, *Danny's Pig,* Lothrop, 1965; Janice, *Little Bear's Thanksgiving,* Lothrop, 1967; Janice, *Little Bear Marches in the St. Patrick's Day Parade,* Lothrop, 1967; Janice, *Little Bear Learns to Read the Cookbook,* Lothrop, 1969; Janice, *Little Bear's New Year's Party,* Lothrop, 1973.

SIDELIGHTS: "The house where I lived as a child was an old fashioned Victorian one. It was in what had once started

MARIAN CURTIS FOSTER

to be a suburb, but for some reason the idea of the suburb had been given up and everything allowed to go back to it's natural wildness.

"In front of the house was what had been intended to be a small park with a deep hollow in the center. Broomstraw, which came to our waists, grew in it and persimmon trees and tall poplars. Jack rabbits lived there and in the summer we picked blackberries and on frosty mornings we found ripe persimmons on the ground among the leaves.

"In our backyard my sister and I had a playhouse. It was a tall wooden box in which the piano had come. It stood between two fig trees. One had little purple figs on it and the other big green figs. We had doll chairs and sofas in it and a little black stove. Among other dolls was one called Wilhimena. She was a large rag doll which had belonged to my mother when she was a little girl. Wilhimena had shoe-button eyes and we were supposed to treat her with great respect.

"Two cats were also constant visitors, Mrs. Rorer (named for mother's cookbook) and Lieutenant Bromby, though why he was called that I have forgotten.

"There was Dion, too, a black and white setter. Dion had belonged to a French family before he had come to us, and we were very proud of him because as we told people, he understood French.

"There was a much grander playhouse than our piano box in the neighborhood. It was a real little house with doors and windows and you could walk around inside it.

"In this doll house as we called it, was a rather strange plaything. The father of the little girl who owned it had known a judge who had once sent some men to jail for making counterfeit money, and had taken away their tools. He gave one of these to the father of our little friend as a curiosity and it had found its way out to their doll house.

"It looked like a small waffle iron, and with it we made quarters of red clay. We dried these in the sun and played store with them.

"Some day I [would like to] write a mystery story and call it 'Three Little Girls,' or 'The Counterfeiters in the Doll-House.' The mystery will be that they bought more fun with their mud quarters than they could have with real silver ones. But perhaps that isn't a mystery after all."

As a child, Foster opted for drawing lessons over piano lessons, considering the former the lesser of the two evils. Her interest in dolls began in childhood. She had a doll house in the yard big enough for a child to walk in, and numerous dolls. During the Depression, she worked on the American Index Project of the W.P.A., making drawings of early Americana at museums. The old toys and dolls in the museums fascinated her the most. In a book, *Child Life in Colonial Days,* she found a picture of a rag doll named Bangwell Putt who became the basis for *The Journey of Bangwell Putt.* At the New York Historical Society, she came upon an old doll named for the heroine of the nineteenth-century poem, *Miss Flora McFlimsey of Madison Square.* This doll became the heroine in the series of books by Marian Curtis Foster, all written under the pseudonym of Mariana.

The drawings she did for her books were usually watercolor and gouache, with black-and-white put in with a Chinese ink stick. Many of her original drawings are housed in the special Mariana Room of the Hockessin Elementary School Library in Wilmington, Delaware.

Mariana's works are included in the Kerlan Collection at the University of Minnesota.

Three times Miss Flora McFlimsey filled her apron with flowers and carried them back to Mrs. Cotton Tail. ■ (From *Miss Flora McFlimsey's May Day* by Mariana. Illustrated by the author.)

FOR MORE INFORMATION SEE: *Chicago Tribune,* March 18, 1951; *Life,* September 22, 1952; *New York Times,* January 24, 1954; B. M. Miller and others, compilers, *Illustrators of Children's Books, 1946-1956,* Horn Book, 1958; *New York Times Book Review,* November 14, 1965; *Horn Book,* December, 1965; Lee Kingman and others, compilers, *Illustrators of Children's Books: 1957-1966,* Horn Book, 1968; Doris de Montreville and Donna Hill, *Third Book of Junior Authors,* H. W. Wilson, 1972.

FOX, Fontaine Talbot, Jr. 1884-1964

OBITUARY NOTICE: Born June 4, 1884, in Louisville, Ky.; died August 9, 1964, in Greenwich, Conn. Cartoonist and author. Creator of the cartoon strip "The Toonerville Trolley That Meets All the Trains," Fox was a cartoonist at the *Louisville Herald, Louisville Times,* and the *Chicago Evening Post* before 1915, when he began working independently. The Toonerville trolley comic strip, a caricature of the people and habits of the rural community in which Fox grew up, featured such characters as Powerful Katrinka, Skipper, and Aunt Eppie Hogg. The Toonerville trolley eventually came to be a part of the language, symbolizing dilapidated public transportation. Fox, whose comic strips were featured by more than two hundred fifty newspapers, was also the author of several books, including *Fontaine Fox's Funny Folks, Fontaine Fox's Cartoons,* and *The Toonerville Trolley. For More Information See: Who Was Who in America,* 4th edition, Marquis, 1968; *National Cyclopaedia of American Biography,* Volumes 1-51, reprinted edition, University Microfilms, 1971. *Obituaries: New York Times,* August 10, 1964; *Contemporary Authors,* Volume 89-92, Gale, 1980.

GALINSKY, Ellen 1942-

PERSONAL: Born April 24, 1942, in Pittsburgh, Pa.; daughter of Melvin H. (a businessman) and Leora (a businesswoman; maiden name, Osgood) May; married Norman Galinsky (an artist), August 15, 1965; children: Philip Andrew, Lara Elizabeth. *Education:* Vassar College, A.B., 1964; Bank Street College of Education, M.S.Ed., 1970. *Home address:* Lawrence Lane, Palisades, N.Y. 10964. *Agent:* Virginia Barber, 44 Greenwich Ave., New York, N.Y. 10011. *Office:* Bank Street College of Education, 610 West 112th St., New York, N.Y. 10025.

CAREER: Teacher in private elementary school in New York, N.Y., 1964-68; Bank Street College of Education, New York, N.Y., faculty member, 1964—, Program Development Institute at Bank Street College, educator, writer, and photographer, 1980—. Founder and coordinator of Family Center at Bank Street. *Member:* Authors Guild of Authors League of America.

WRITINGS: Catbird (juvenile; with own photographs), Coward, 1971; *Beginnings* (non-fiction), Houghton, 1976; (with William H. Hooks) *The New Extended Family* (non-fiction; with own photographs), Houghton, 1977; *The Baby Cardinal* (juvenile; with own photographs; Junior Literary Guild selection), Putnam, 1977. *Between Generations: The Six Stages of Parenthood* (non–fiction), Times Books, 1980.

Contributing photographer: Betty Miles, *Around and Around: Love,* Knopf, 1975; *Women See Woman,* Crowell, 1976.

ELLEN GALINSKY

Contributor to magazines, including *Parents' Magazine* and *Redbook.*

SIDELIGHTS: "I have wanted to write children's books for as long as I remember. I was one of those children who disappeared into the pages of a book, reappearing in the story. I lived in its time and place, experienced what the character experienced.

"I also grew up in West Virginia where story-telling was an art as well as a form of social recreation. It was the way that the young were instructed in the ways of the world and the way the older people made sense of their lives.

"Then, too, I worked on a school project that added to my interest in writing. We interviewed the oldest people about what our hometown was like when they were children and how it had changed. We compiled these recollections into a book. I realized that without writing these stories down, their history would have been lost.

"One other school experience was significant. I wrote to the author and illustrator, Lois Lenski, and suggested that she write a book about West Virginia. That book was published the year I entered college.

"At Vassar College I majored in child development and then moved onto Bank Street College [of Education] an institution known for its group of children's book writers.

"Now, I have begun to achieve what I wanted to—I am writing for children and adults—which means that I have an opportunity to pursue my own questions in depth and then communicate what I've learned.

"I now have two children, Philip and Lara. They both make books—often write or tell the stories and draw pictures to go with them."

On a 1905 trip to his beloved West, the President of the United States relaxes amid simple pleasures: a sunny doorway, comfortable old clothes, a book in his hand, a dog on his knee. ■ (From *Theodore Roosevelt, The Strenuous Life* by John A. Garraty. Photograph courtesy of The Theodore Roosevelt Association.)

GARRATY, John A. 1920-

PERSONAL: Born July 4, 1920, in Brooklyn, N.Y.; married Joan Perkins, 1945 (divorced, 1964); married Gail Kernan, 1965; children: Katharine, John A., Jr., Sarah. *Education:* Columbia University, Ph.D., 1948. *Home:* Robertson Dr., Sag Harbor, N.Y. 11963. *Office:* Columbia University, New York, N.Y. 10027.

CAREER: Michigan State University, East Lansing, instructor to professor, 1947-59; Columbia University, New York, N.Y., professor of history, 1959—. *Military service:* U.S. Navy, 1942-45; became petty officer, first class. *Member:* American Historical Association, Organization of American Historians, Society of American Historians (secretary-treasurer, 1959-63; vice-president, 1963-69; president, 1969-71), American Association of University Professors.

WRITINGS: *Silas Wright,* Columbia University Press, 1949; *Henry Cabot Lodge,* Knopf, 1953; *Woodrow Wilson,* Knopf, 1956; *Nature of Biography,* Knopf, 1957; *Right Hand Man,* Harper, 1960; (editor) *Quarrels That Have Shaped the Constitution,* Harper, 1964; *The American Nation,* Harper, 1966; *Theodore Roosevelt, The Strenuous Life* (juvenile), American Heritage, 1967; *The New Commonwealth,* Harper; 1968; *American History,* Harper, 1970; *The Columbia History of the World,* Harper, 1972; *Encyclopedia of American Biography,* Harper, 1974; *Unemployment in History,* Harper, 1978. Also editor of *Dictionary of American Biography,* Scribner.

GERAS, Adele (Daphne) 1944-

PERSONAL: Surname rhymes with "terrace"; born March 15, 1944, in Jerusalem, Palestine; daughter of Laurence David (a lawyer) and Leah (Hamburger) Weston; married Norman Geras (a lecturer), August 7, 1967; children: Sophie, Jenny. *Education:* Attended St. Hilda's College, Oxford, 1963-66. *Religion:* Jewish. *Residence:* Manchester, England.

Hannah sat on a chair with a tapestry seat which made her legs itch. If only she could have worn her jeans. ■ (From *Tea at Mrs. Manderby's* by Adele Geras. Illustrated by Doreen Caldwell.)

CAREER: Writer, 1976—.

WRITINGS—For children: *Tea at Mrs. Manderby's,* Hamish Hamilton, 1976; *Apricots at Midnight and Other Stories From a Patchwork Quilt,* Hamish Hamilton, 1977; *Beyond the Cross-stitch Mountains,* Hamish Hamilton, 1977; *The Girls in the Velvet Frame,* Hamish Hamilton, 1978, Atheneum, 1979; *Ritchie's Pastry Rabbit,* Hodder & Stoughton, 1980. Contributor to *Cricket.*

WORK IN PROGRESS: A Thousand Yards of Sea for Hodder & Stoughton, and *Other Echoes,* a novel set in North Borneo in 1953.

SIDELIGHTS: "I write because I enjoy it. I write about places and things that have been important to me in one way or another. I lived in many countries as a child and have traveled quite widely.

"I write very quickly once I get started, but hate getting started—it's like diving from a high board into cold water—terrifying in prospect, but terrific when you've taken the plunge. My advice to writers is to read all the time and learn to type. It takes me almost as long to copy a novel out neatly for the typist as it does to write it."

HOBBIES AND OTHER INTERESTS: "I enjoy the movies more than anything and read an enormous amount of everything, but my great love is thrillers and detective stories. I am very lazy, and like sleeping in the afternoons."

GIBBONS, Gail 1944-

PERSONAL: Born August 1, 1944, in Oak Park, Ill.; daughter of Harry George (a tool and die designer) and Grace (Johnson) Ortmann; married Glenn Gibbons, June 25, 1966 (died May 20, 1972); married Kent Ancliffe (a builder), March 23, 1976; children: (stepchildren) Rebecca, Eric. *Education:* University of Illinois, B.F.A., 1967. *Home address:* Corinth, Vt. 05039. *Agent:* Florence Alexander, 50 East 42nd St., New York, N.Y. 10017. *Office:* 114 West 16th St., #4E, New York, N.Y. 10011.

CAREER: WCIA-Television, Champaign, Ill., artist, 1967-69; Bob Howe Agency, Chicago, Ill., staff artist, 1969-70; WNBC-Television, House of Animation, New York, N.Y., staff artist, 1970-76; free-lance writer, 1976—. Makes graphic slides, distributed by United Press International, for use on television news programs.

WRITINGS—Self-illustrated children's books: *Willy and His Wheel Wagon* (Junior Literary Guild selection), Prentice-Hall, 1975; *Salvador and Mister Sam: A Guide to Parakeet Care,* Prentice-Hall, 1976; *Things to Make and Do for Halloween,* F. Watts, 1976; *Things to Make and Do For Columbus Day,* F. Watts, 1977; *Things to Make and Do for Your Birthday,* F. Watts, 1978; *The Missing Maple Syrup Sap Mystery,* Warne, 1979; *Clocks and How They Grow,* Crowell, 1979; *The Too Great Bread Bake Dood,* Warne, 1980; *Locks and Keys,* Crowell, 1980.

Illustrator: Jane Yolen, *Rounds About Rounds,* F. Watts, 1977; Judith Enderle, *Good Junk,* Dandelion Press, 1979; Catharine Chase, *Hot & Cold,* Dandelion Press, 1979; Catharine Chase, *The Mouse in My House,* Dandelion Press, 1979; Catharine Chase, *My Balloon,* Dandelion Press, 1979;

GAIL GIBBONS

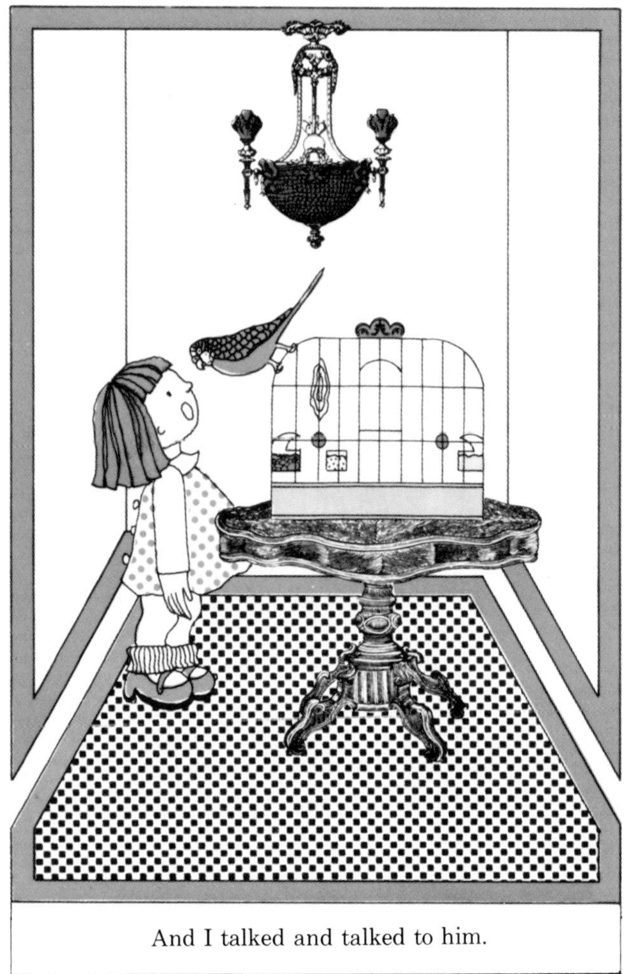

And I talked and talked to him.

(From *Salvador and Mister Sam: A Guide to Parakeet Care* by Gail Gibbons. Illustrated by the author.)

Catharine Chase, *Pete, the Wet Pet,* Dandelion Press, 1979; Catharine Chase, *The Mouse at the Show,* Dandelion Press, 1980.

WORK IN PROGRESS: The Tail of Morris Mouse, for children.

SIDELIGHTS: Gail Gibbons spent her childhood in the Illinois towns of Oak Park, Palos Heights, and Blue Island. Her early interest in drawing was encouraged by several of her teachers. In 1967 she received her B.F.A. degree in graphic design from the University of Illinois. "While I was studying at the university I had an illustrating instructor who took a particular interest in the writing and illustrating of children's books. I believe he was the individual who opened up my interest in the area of books for children."

After college, Gibbons worked as a television graphic artist for WCIA-TV in Champaign, Illinois. There she was involved in many areas of art productions: on-air graphics, animation, and printed promotional material. She next did some free-lance work in animation for NBC in Chicago. In 1970 she moved to New York with her husband, Glenn Allen Gibbons, whom she had married while at the university.

In New York, Gibbons worked for NBC-TV's local news program; and she began illustrating for children when she was assigned to do the graphics for a network children's program called *Take a Giant Step.*

In 1972, Gibbons' first husband was killed in an accident. "A few months later I decided to reduce my work load to put my life back into some kind of order. I started working on John Chancellor's nightly news show on NBC, and I began getting involved in my art work again, on a free-lance basis. I still had a strong interest in the illustrating being done in children's books, so I contacted Florence Alexander, a children's book representative in New York. She encouraged me to try both writing and illustrating and also expressed to me the need for a book that would teach the rudiments of basic set theory to children. At that point I started *Willy and His Wheel Wagon,* doing research in the area of new math. Then the idea of using sets of wheels to explain set theory began to develop. *Willy and His Wheel Wagon* is the first book I have ever written and illustrated, and I have enjoyed it thoroughly.

"My two stepchildren, Backy and Eric, give me a lot of insight as to what children enjoy. They are always coming up with stimulating ideas. As of late, the area we live in, Corinth, Vermont, has played an important role in my most recent writings. We live in a rural farm area where maple sugaring is done and other home spun activities take place. The *Missing Maple Syrup Sap Mystery* book is written from the country life influence."

GLICK, Virginia Kirkus 1893-1980 (Virginia Kirkus)

OBITUARY NOTICE: Born December 7, 1893, in Meadville, Pa.; died September 10, 1980, in Danbury, Conn. Editor, critic, businesswoman, and author. Virginia Kirkus headed the children's department at Harper & Brothers publishing company from 1926 to 1932. She later established a prepublication book reporting service, *Kirkus Reviews,* to fill the void that she felt existed between publishers and bookshops. The immensely successful service aided booksellers in deciding which books to order. Her writings include *A House for the Weekends* and *The First Book of Gardening. For More Information See: Current Biography,* Wilson, 1941, 1954; *Contemporary Authors Permanent Series,* Volume 2, Gale, 1978. *Obituaries: New York Times,* September 11, 1980; *Newsweek,* September 22, 1980; *Publishers Weekly,* September 26, 1980; *Contemporary Authors,* Volume 101-104, Gale, 1981.

How pleasant is Saturday night,
When I've tried all the week to be good.
Not spoken a word that is bad,
And obliged every one that I could.

—Nancy Dennis Sproat

GOLDSTEIN, Philip 1910-

PERSONAL: Born May 3, 1910, in New York, N.Y.; son of Harry (in needle trades) and Sarah (Wolinsky) Goldstein; married Margaret Garber, March 26, 1939; children: Joel, Richard, Vida. *Education:* City College (now City College of the City University of New York), B.A., 1930, M.S. (education), 1937; New Mexico Highlands University, M.S. (natural science), 1961. *Politics:* Democrat. *Religion:* Jewish. *Home and office:* 9470 Poinciana Pl., #310, Ft. Lauderdale, Fla. 33324.

CAREER: High school teacher of biology in public schools of New York, N.Y., 1931-68, and chairman of department of biology at Abraham Lincoln High School, 1949-68. Lecturer in biology, City College (now City College of the City University of New York), 1942-48; assistant examiner for New York City Board of Examiners, 1949-68; lecturer in methods of teaching science, Brooklyn College of the City University of New York, 1962-64. *Member:* National Association of Science Writers, National Association of Biology Teachers (charter member), National Association of Science Teachers, New York Association of Biology Teachers.

WRITINGS: *Genetics Is Easy,* Garlan, 1947, 4th edition, Lantern Press, 1967; *Practical Biology Workbook,* Van Nostrand, 1949; *How to Do an Experiment,* Harcourt, 1957; *Teacher's Manual to Accompany Exploring Biology,* Harcourt, 1961; (with others) *Biological Investigations for Secondary School Students,* Volumes I and II, Doubleday, 1963; *Triumphs of Biology,* Doubleday, 1965; (with Alvin Nason) *Biology: Introduction to Life* (teacher's manual with Gabrielle Edwards), Addison Wesley, 1969; *Wonders of Parasites,* Lantern Press, 1969; (with Jerome Metzner) *Experiments with Microscopic Animals,* Doubleday, 1971; *Animals and Plants That Trap,* Holiday House, 1974; (with Margaret Goldstein) *How Parasites Live,* Holiday House, 1976.

Series of books: "Wonders of Life," Doubleday, Volume V: *Animal Tissues: How Cells Worm Together,* Volume VI: *The Skin: A Jack of All Trades,* Volume VII: *The Matter of Digestion,* Volume VIII: *Blood and Circulation,* Volume IX: *Behavior: Responding to the Environment,* Volume X: *The Nervous System: Sensation, Communication, Response,* Volume XI: *The Hormones: Chemical Control of Coordination,* Volume XII; *Respiration: The Release of Energy* (Goldstein was not associated with earlier volumes), 1963-64.

"Textfolders in Biology," National Teaching Aids, Number 67: *The Digestive System,* Number 68: *The Circulatory System,* Number 69: *The Central Nervous System,* Number 70: *The Reflex Arc,* Number 71: *The Endocrine System,* Number 72: *The Respiratory System,* Number 73: *Smoking and Health,* Number 74: *Parasitism: A Way of Life,* Number 75: *Animal Parasites of Man,* Number 76: *The Hydra,* Number 77: *Roots of a Flowering Plant,* Number 78: *Stem of a Flowering Plant,* Number 79: *Leaf of a Flowering Plant,* Number 80: *Flower of a Flowering Plant,* Number 81: *Non-Green Plants and Heterotrophic Nutrition,* Number 82: *Green Plants and Autotrophic Nutrition,* Number 83: *Chromosomes and Genes in Action,* Number 84: *Life Cycle of the Fern,* Number 85: *Life Cycle of Aurelia,* Number 86: *Life Cycle of Obelia,* Number 87: *Life Cycle of Marchantia,* Volume 88: *Life Cycle of Moss,* Number 89: *Air Pollution and Human Health,* Number 90: *Air Pollution and Plant Health,* Number 91: *Measurement Under the Microscope,* Number 94: *Venereal Disease,* Number 97: *Viruses,* Number 99: *The Senses,*

PHILIP GOLDSTEIN

Number 201: *Algae,* Number 202: *Protozoa,* Number 204: *Body Defenses Against Infection,* 1964-78.

"The Inquirers," National Teaching Aids, Number 1: *Anthony Van Leeuwenhoek,* Number II: *Louis Pasteur,* Number III: *Andreas Vesalius,* IV: *Lazzaro Spallanzani,* Number V: *Charles Darwin,* Number VI: *Joseph Lister,* Number VII: *William Harvey,* Number VIII: *Edward Jenner,* Number IX: *Robert Koch,* 1964-66.

Also author of *Genetics Made Easy* (a kit for the teaching of genetics in high school with a teacher's guide), Lantern Press, 1978. Contributor to *World Book Encyclopedia* and *Grolier's Book of Popular Science.* Contributor to professional journals, including *Science Education, Science Perspectives, High Points, American Biology Teacher, Teaching Biologist,* and *New York State State Conservationist.* Associate editor, *American Biology Teacher* and *Teaching Biologist.*

WORK IN PROGRESS: A series of folios.

SIDELIGHTS: "When I was a youngster it never occurred to me that some day I might write books. You see, I was an underprivileged kid, growing up in a ghetto slum on the lower east side of New York. Of course, I never knew I was underprivileged because in those days nobody bothered to tell me. I thought that this was the normal way of life.

"My parents had both arrived as immigrants from Russia with little to their names except their bare hands. Their first

Even though he looks so cheerful, happy, and healthy, a barefoot boy walking through the warm fields of our southern states is an ideal candidate for hookworm infection. ■ (From *Wonders of Parasites* by Philip Goldstein.)

American work experience was gained in the sweat shops of the clothing industry. They slaved away all their lives trying to make ends meet. But they always stressed to their children that learning and education were the greatest things in life. Despite hardships and deprivations they managed to send all their children through college and on to professional careers. We can thank the *FREE TUITION AT THE CITY COLLEGES* that made this possible. My older brother became an electrical engineer, my younger brother a doctor, and my sister and I became school teachers.

"I was a teacher of biology, and my first assignment was to a high school on the lower east side where I had grown up. During the years that followed I advanced through the system, ending up as chairman of the biology department in one of the large New York City high schools. But early in my career I found that most printed textbooks were unsatisfactory. Pupils failed to find them exciting or understandable. So I began to prepare my own materials in mimeographed form. That was my first entry into the writing field. I discovered that I had a knack for explaining complex biological concepts in terms that pupils could comprehend . . . and this without sacrificing the accuracy of scientific fact.

"My first experience in writing for pay came about in a strange way. I was familiar with a slick paper magazine that served the brewing industry all over the world. This magazine catered to two diverse classes of readers—the scientists and the practical brewers who had no scientific background. I don't know where I got the courage, but I went to the editor and offered to write an article to explain the fundamentals of genetics to the brewers. 'No,' he said. 'That's impossible! It can't be done!' But I persisted, pointing out that for many years I had been explaining the fundamentals of genetics to high school pupils. If I could do this for reluctant pupils, I should be able to do it for practical brewers who are anxious to have the information.

"'Well,' said the editor, probably to get rid of me, 'If you want to try, go ahead. No commitment, you understand . . . .' I wrote the article and sent it off. Much to my amazement I received a check in the mail. My article was printed with color illustrations, and it received fine reviews from brewing establishments all over the world. This decided me. If I could explain the fundamentals of genetics to brewers, I could certainly do the same for high school students. And so *Genetics Is Easy* was born. It became an instant success. I am happy to say it was used not only in high school classes but in freshman college classes as well.

"One of my own favorites is my book entitled *How to Do an Experiment*. Somewhere along the line of my teaching career I had created a brand new course for bright students. In this course each pupil carried through an individual experimental project. Unfortunately there wasn't a single book available to guide pupils in this type of work. It behooved me to develop my own book which could lead them through the entire process, from the selection of a problem to the presentation of the final results. *How to Do an Experiment* turned out to be one of my most successful books because it filled a niche that had been empty for a long time.

"In still another book I used my three young children as vehicles for developing the concept of parasitism. Conversations among the children introduced the various ideas, and cousins were brought into the discussion to help analyze the concepts. All the children whose names appeared in the book considered it a great tribute.

"Yes, in my day I have authored many books. Most of these were intended for the high school level. However, I also did some things on the elementary level. I feel that the wonders of life should make inspirational reading for children. So my last two books have been pointed at the junior reader, for general enjoyment rather than as textbooks. This is the area in which I hope to concentrate my efforts in the future."

FOR MORE INFORMATION SEE: Publishers Weekly, February 23, 1976; *Horn Book,* October, 1976.

GONZALEZ, Gloria 1940-

PERSONAL: Born January 10, 1940, in New York, N.Y.; daughter of Angel and Mary (Cabrera) Gonzalez; children: Arleen, Kelly, Troy. *Education:* Studied playwrighting at the New School with Harold Callen and Jean-Claude van Itallie, playwrighting and directing with Lee Strasberg, and acting with Anthony Mannino. *Address:* 5907 Blvd. E. Apt. A7, West New York, N.J. 07093. *Agent:* Robert Freedman, Brandt & Brandt, Dramatic Dept., 1501 Broadway, New York, N.Y. 10036.

CAREER: Investigative reporter for various New Jersey daily newspapers; free-lance writer; now full-time playwright. *Member:* Dramatists Guild, Authors League of America, Drama Desk. *Awards, honors:* First prize in Jacksonville University College of Fine Arts national playwriting contest, 1975, for "Curtains"; finalist for Stanley Drama Award, 1975; Webster Groves Russell B. Sharp Annual Playwriting Award, 1976, for "Lights."

WRITINGS—Juveniles: *The Glad Man,* Knopf, 1975; *Gaucho,* Knopf, 1977.

Published plays: *Moving On!* (all one-acts; includes "Moving On!," first produced in New York City at Playbox Theatre, October, 1972; "Cuba: Economy Class!"; and "The New America"), Samuel French, 1971; *Curtains* (produced in New York City at Hudson Guild Theatre, October, 1975), published by Dramatists Play Service.

Unpublished plays: (With Edna Schappert) "Celebrate Me," first produced in New York City at Playbox Theatre, April, 1971; "Love Is a Tuna Casserole," produced by New York Theatre Ensemble, September, 1971; "Waiting Room," produced in New York City at Theatre at Noon, January, 1974; "A Sanctuary in the City," produced in Altadena, Calif., at Theatre Americana, March, 1975; "Let's Hear It for Miss America," produced in St. Petersburg, Fla., at Country Dinner Playhouse, August, 1976; "Lights," produced in St. Louis, August, 1976.

Television drama: "Gaucho," first broadcast on Columbia Broadcasting System, Inc. (CBS television), June 2, 1970; broadcast on American Broadcasting System, Inc. (ABC television) as an "After School Special," 1978.

Also author of play, *Checkmate of a Queen,* published by Performance Publishing.

Plays included in anthologies, *One-Act Plays for Our Times,* edited by Frances Griffith and others, Popular Library, 1973; and *Best Short Plays of 1976,* edited by Stanley Richards, Dodd, 1976. Contributor of articles to *New York Times* and

(From *Gaucho* by Gloria Gonzalez.)

GLORIA GONZALEZ

New York Daily News; regular contributor to *Dramatists Quarterly.*

WORK IN PROGRESS: A mystery novel; feature film for NBC television tentatively titled "Every Wednesday"; two comedy sitcom pilots for CBS television.

SIDELIGHTS: "Despite the inherent pain, frustrations and anguish—the theatre, for me, remains the only arena worth writing for. I require the excitement and challenge of an instant reaction from a friendly or hostile audience as opposed to book reviews months, even a year after the book is written.

"I always like to encourage new writers especially among children. That is the age, I believe, when one decides to pursue such an endeavor. The child who scribbles a poem today or merely jots down his or her thoughts—is tomorrow's novelist or dramatist. Keep at it!"

FOR MORE INFORMATION SEE: Horn Book, April, 1978.

Books are keys to wisdom's treasure;
Books are gates to lands of pleasure;
Books are paths that upward lead;
Books are friends. Come let us read.

—Emilie Poulsson

PETER PARLEY'S

BOOK OF FABLES.

ILLUSTRATED BY

NUMEROUS ENGRAVINGS.

HARTFORD:

SILAS ANDRUS AND SON.

1852.

(Title page from *Peter Parley's Book of Fables.*)

GOODRICH, Samuel Griswold 1793-1860 (Peter Parley)

PERSONAL: Born August 19, 1793, in Ridgefield, Conn.; died May 9, 1860, in New York City; buried in Southbury, Conn.; son of Samuel (a Congregational minister) and Elizabeth (Ely) Goodrich; married Adeline Gratia Bradley, February 2, 1818 (died, 1822); married Mary Boott, January 2, 1826; children: (second marriage) Frank Boott, Emily. *Education:* Attended local schools. *Home:* Southbury, Conn.

CAREER: Publisher, editor, and author of books for children. Bookseller and publisher, Hartford, Conn., 1818-22; editor and publisher of *The Token,* a gift-book magazine, 1826-42; established *Parley's Magazine,* for children, 1833; founder and editor of *Merry's Museum,* 1841-50. Elected to the Massachusetts legislature, 1837; U.S. Consul at Paris, 1851-53. *Military service:* Served for six months in the War of 1812. *Member:* Friendly Club. *Awards, honors:* Honorary M.A., Williams College, 1836; honorary M.A., Yale University, 1848.

WRITINGS: (Editor) *Cabinet of Curiosities, Natural, Artificial, and Historical,* [Hartford, Conn.], 1822; *Outlines of Chronology, Ancient and Modern,* Richardson & Lord, 1828; *Stories about Captain John Smith, of Virginia,* H. & F. J. Huntington, 1829; *A System of School Geography,* Collins & Hannay, 1830; *A System of Universal Geography, Popular and Scientific, Comprising a Physical, Political, and Statistical Account of the World, and Its Various Divisions,* Roffe & Young, 1832; *A Book of Quadrupeds, for Youth,* P. Hill, 1832; *A Book of Mythology, for Youth,* Richardson & Lord, 1832; *The Outcast, and Other Poems,* Shattuck & Williams, 1836; *The First Reader for Schools,* Broaders, 1839; *The Second Reader for Schools,* Morton & Griswold, 1839; *The Third Reader for the Use of Schools,* Broaders, 1839; *The Fourth Reader for the Use of Schools,* Broaders, 1839.

A Pictorial Geography of the World, Tanner & Disturnell, 1840; *The Common-School Primer,* Morton & Griswold, 1841; *The Young American; or, Book of Government and Law, showing Their History, Nature, and Necessity,* W. Robinson, 1842; *A Pictorial Natural History, Embracing a View of the Mineral, Vegetable, and Animal Kingdoms,* J. Munroe, 1842; *A Pictorial History of America, Embracing Both the Northern and Southern Portions of the New World,* E. Strong, 1844; *A Pictorial History of England,* Sorin & Ball, 1845; *A National Geography, for Schools,* Huntington & Savage, 1845; *A Pictorial History of Greece, Ancient and Modern,* Sorin & Ball, 1847; *Ancient History, from the Creation to the Fall of Rome, A.D. 476,* Morton & Griswold, 1847; *The History of New England,* D. Ticknor, 1847; *Modern History, from the Fall of Rome, A.D. 476, to the Present Time,* Morton & Griswold, 1848; *A History of All Nations, from the Earliest Periods to the Present Time; or, Universal History, in Which the History of Every Nation, Ancient and Modern, is Separately Given,* Wilkins, Carter, 1849-51.

A Primer of Geography, Huntington & Savage, 1850; *A History of Asia and Oceanica,* Morton & Griswold, 1850; *A Comprehensive Geography and History, Ancient and Modern,* Huntington & Savage, 1850; *Sketches from a Student's Window,* D. Ticknor, 1851; *Poems,* Putnam, 1851; *Winter Wreath of Summer Flowers,* Appleton, 1855; *The World as It Is, and as It Has Been; or, A Comprehensive Geography and History, Ancient and Modern,* J. H. Colton, 1855; *A Pictorial History of France,* E. H. Butler, 1855; *A Pictorial History of Ancient Rome,* E. H. Butler, 1855; (editor) *A Gem Book of British Poetry,* E. H. Butler, 1855; *Recollections of a Lifetime; or, Men and Things I Have Seen* (autobiography), Miller, Orton, 1856, reprinted, Gale, 1967; *Goodrich's Fifth School Reader,* Morton & Griswold, 1857; *Goodrich's Sixth School Reader,* W. Flemming, 1858; *Illustrated Natural History of the Animal Kingdom,* Derby & Jackson, 1859; *The American Child's Pictorial History of the United States,* E. H. Butler, 1861.

Under pseudonym Peter Parley: *The Tales of Peter Parley about America,* Carter & Hendee, 1827, reprinted, Dover, 1974; *The Tales of Peter Parley about Europe,* Carter & Hendee, 1828; *Peter Parley's Method of Telling about Geography to Children,* H. & F. J. Huntington, 1829; *Peter Parley's Winter-Evening Tales,* C. Thomas, 1829; *The Tales of Peter Parley about Africa,* Gray & Bowen, 1830; *Peter Parley's Tales about the Sun, Moon, and Stars,* C. Thomas, 1830; *Peter Parley's Story of the Pleasure Boat,* Carter & Hendee, 1830; *Peter Parley's Juvenile Tales,* 1830, revised edition, H. S. & J. Applegate, 1851; *Peter Parley's Tales of the Sea,* Gray & Bowen, 1831; *Peter Parley's Tales about the Islands in the Pacific Ocean,* Gray & Bowen, 1831; *Peter Parley's Tales about the World,* 1831; *The Child's Book of American Geography,* Waitt & Dow, 1831; *Peter Parley's Tales about Animals,* 1831; *The First Book of History: For Children and Youth,* Collins & Hannay, 1831; *The Second Book of History: For Children and Youth,* Collins & Hannay, 1831; *The Second Book of History, including the Modern History of Europe, Africa, and Asia,* Carter, Hendee, 1832; *Popular Biography,* Leavitt & Allen, 1832; *Peter Parley's*

Tales about the State and City of New York, Pendleton & Hill, 1832; *Peter Parley's Tales about Great Britain, including England, Wales, Scotland, and Ireland,* J. Jewett, 1832; *Peter Parley's Tales about South America,* J. Jewett, 1832; *Peter Parley's Tales about Ancient and Modern Greece,* Collins & Hannay, 1832; *Peter Parley's Method of Telling about the History of the World to Children,* F. J. Huntington, 1832; *Peter Parley's Book of Curiosities, Natural, and Artificial,* Collins & Hannay, 1832.

Peter Parley's Tales about Ancient Rome, with Some Account of Modern Italy, Carter, Hendee, 1833; *Peter Parley's Story of the Umbrella and the Tiger,* Allen & Ticknor, 1833; *Peter Parley's Tales about Asia,* Desilver, Jr. & Thomas, 1833; *Peter Parley's Method of Teaching Arithmetic to Children,* Carter & Hendee, 1833; *Peter Parley's Story of the Orphans,* Allen & Ticknor, 1833; *Peter Parley's Story of the Little Wanderers,* Allen & Ticknor, 1833; *Peter Parley's Story of the Two Friends; or, Harry and His Dog,* Allen & Ticknor, 1833; *Peter Parley's Story of Alice Gray; or, The Young Dreamer,* Allen & Ticknor, 1833; *Peter Parley's Story of the Freshet; or, The Morning Walk,* Allen & Ticknor, 1833; *Peter Parley's Story of the Little Gardener,* Allen & Ticknor, 1833; *Peter Parley's Story of Robert Seaboy, the Bird Robber,* Allen & Ticknor, 1833; *The Third Book of History, containing Ancient History in Connection with Ancient Geography,* Carter, Hendee, 1834; *Peter Parley's Short Stories for Long Nights,* W. D. Ticknor, 1834; *Parley's Picture Book,* 1834; (editor) *Peter Parley's Book of Bible Stories: For Children and Youth,* Lilly, Wait, 1834; *The Every Day Book, for Youth,* Carter, Hendee, 1834; *Peter Parley's Primer,* T. T. Ash, 1835; (editor) *The Parent's Present,* Light & Horton, 1835.

Peter Parley's Tales of Animals, Containing Descriptions of Three Hundred Quadrupeds, Birds, Fishes, Reptiles, and Insects, Morton & Smith, 1836; *Peter Parley's Dictionary of Astronomy,* F. Hunt, 1836; *Peter Parley's Dictionary of the Animal Kingdom,* F. Hunt, 1836; (editor) *Peter Parley's Book of Fables,* White, Dwier, 1836; *Peter Parley's Book of Anecdotes,* 1836; *Peter Parley's Bible Dictionary,* F. Hunt, 1836; *Peter Parley's Universal History on the Basis of Geography,* American Stationers' Co., 1837; *Peter Parley's Method of Telling about the Geography of the Bible,* American Stationers' Co., 1837; *Peter Parley's Book of the United States, Geographical, Political, and Historical,* C. J. Hendee, 1837; *Peter Parley's Almanac for Old and Young,* Otis, Broaders, 1837; *Tales about Greece,* T. Tegg, 1838; *Peter Parley's Common School History,* American Stationers' Co., 1838; *Fireside Education,* S. Colman, 1838.

Peter Parley's Wonders of the Earth, Sea, and Sky, S. Colman, 1840; *Peter Parley's Farewell,* S. Colman, 1840; *The Story of Captain Riley, and His Adventures in Africa,* H. F. Anners, 1841; *A Tale of Adventure; or, The Siberian Sable Hunter,* Wiley & Putnam, 1843; *Make the Best of It; or, Cheerful Cherry, and Other Tales,* Wiley & Putnam, 1843; *Curiosities of Human Nature,* Bradbury, Soden, 1843; *Lives of Celebrated American Indians,* Bradbury, Soden, 1843; *Famous Men of Ancient Times,* Bradbury, Soden, 1843; *Famous Men of Modern Times,* Bradbury, Soden, 1843; *Wit Bought; or, The Life and Adventures of Robert Merry,* Wiley & Putnam, 1844; *Peter Parley's Little Leaves for Little Readers,* J. Munroe, 1844; *The Manners, Customs, and Antiquities of the Indians of North and South America,* Bradbury, Soden, 1844; *Lives of Celebrated Women,* Bradbury, Soden, 1844; *Lives of Benefactors,* Bradbury, Soden, 1844; *Lights and Shadows of European History,* Bradbury, Soden, 1844; *Fairy Land, and Other Sketches for Youth,* J. Munroe, 1844; *Lights and Shadows of African History,* Bradbury, Soden, 1844; *Lights and Shadows of American History,* Bradbury, Soden, 1844; *A Glance at the Physical Sciences; or, The Wonders of Nature, in Earth, Air, and Sky,* Bradbury, Soden, 1844; *History of the Indians of North and South America,* Bradbury, Soden, 1844; *What to Do and How to Do It; or, Morals and Manners,* 1844; *Lights and Shadows of Asiatic History,* Bradbury, Soden, 1844.

The Wonders of Geology, Bradbury, Soden, 1845; *The World and Its Inhabitants,* Bradbury, Soden, 1845; *A Tale of the Revolution, and Other Sketches,* Sorin & Ball, 1845; *Illustrative Anecdotes of the Animal Kingdom,* Bradbury, Soden, 1845; *Enterprise, Industry, and Art of Man, as Displayed in Fishing, Hunting, Commerce, Navigation, Mining, Agriculture, and Manufactures,* Bradbury, Soden, 1845; *A Glance at Philosophy, Mental, Moral, and Social,* Bradbury, Soden, 1845; *Manners and Customs of the Principal Nations of the Globe,* Bradbury, Soden, 1845; *Literature, Ancient and Modern, with Specimens,* Bradbury, Soden, 1845; *A Home in the Sea; or, The Adventures of Philip Brusque,* Sorin & Ball, 1845; *Dick Boldhero; or, The Wonders of South America,* 1846; *Tales of Sea and Land,* Sorin & Ball, 1846; *Truth-Finder; or, Inquisitive Jack,* 1846; *Right Is Might, and Other Sketches,* Sorin & Ball, 1846; *North America; or, The United States and the Adjacent Countries,* Morton & Griswold, 1847; *History of South America and the West Indies,* Morton & Griswold, 1848; *Peter Parley's Illustrations of Commerce,* H. H. Hawley, 1849; *Peter Parley's Illustrations of the Vegetable Kingdom,* H. H. Hawley, 1849.

Take Care of No. 1; or, The Adventures of Jacob Karl, 1850; *A History of Africa,* Morton & Griswold, 1850; *A Primer of History, for Beginners at Home and School,* H. W. Derby, 1851; *Peter Parley's First Book of Spelling and Reading,* B. B. Mussey, 1852; *Parley's Present for All Seasons,* Appleton, 1853; *The Wanderers by Sea and Land, with Other Tales,* Appleton, 1855; *The Balloon Travels of Robert Merry and His Young Friends over Various Countries in Europe,* J. C. Derby, 1855; *Parley's Panorama; or, Curiosities of Nature and Art, History and Biography,* M. R. Barnitz, 1855; *Faggots for the Fireside; or, Fact and Fancy,* Appleton, 1855; *The Travels, Voyages, and Adventures of Gilbert Go-Ahead, in Foreign Parts,* J. C. Derby, 1856; (editor) *Peter Parley's Kaleidoscope; or, Parlor Pleasure Book, consisting of Gleanings from Many Fields of the Curious, the Beautiful, and the Wonderful,* M. R. Barnitz, 1857; *Parley's Adventures of Billy Bump, All the Way from Sundown to California,* 1857; *Parley's Balloon Travels of Robert Merry and His Young Friends in the Holy Land and Other Parts of Asia,* 1857.

SIDELIGHTS: ". . . In this town [Ridgefield, Connecticut], in an antiquated and rather dilapidated house of shingles and clapboards, I was born on the **19th of August, 1793.**

"My father, Samuel Goodrich, was minister of the First Congregational Church of that place, there being then, no other religious society and no other clergyman in the town, except at Ridgebury—the remote northern section, which was a separate parish. . . . My mother was a daughter of John Ely, a physician of Saybrook, whose name figures not unworthily in the annals of the revolutionary war.

"I was the sixth child of a family of ten children, two of whom died in infancy, and eight of whom lived to be married and settled in life. . . . My father's annual salary for the first twenty-five years, and during his ministry at Ridgefield, averaged £120, old currency—that is, about four hundred dollars a year: the last twenty-five years, during which he was settled at Berlin, near Hartford, his stipend was about five hundred dollars a year. He was wholly without patrimony . . . my mother had not even the ordinary outfit, as they began their married life. Yet they so brought up their family of eight children, that they all attained respectable positions in life, and at my father's death, he left an estate of four thousand dollars. These facts throw light upon the simple annals of a country clergyman in Connecticut, half a century ago; they also bear testimony to the thrifty energy and wise frugality of my parents, and especially of my mother, who was the guardian deity of the household.

"My memory goes distinctly back to the year 1797, when I was four years old. At that time a great event happened—great in the near and narrow horizon of childhood: we removed from the Old House to the New House! This latter, situated on a road tending westward and branching from the main street, my father had just built; and it then appeared to be quite a stately mansion and very beautiful, inasmuch as it was painted red behind and white in front—most of the dwellings thereabouts being of the dun complexion which pine-boards and chestnut-shingles assume, from exposure to the weather. Long after—having been absent twenty years—I revisited this my early home, and found it shrunk into a very small and ordinary two-story dwelling, wholly divested of its paint, and scarcely thirty feet square.

"One thing . . . I remember: I was barefoot; and as we went up the lane which diverged from the main road to the house, we passed over a patch of earth, blackened by cinders, where my feet were hurt by pieces of melted glass and metal. I inquired what this meant, and was told that here a house was burned down by the British troops . . .—and then in full retreat—as a signal to the ships that awaited them on the Sound where they had landed, and where they intended to embark.

"This detail may seem trifling, but it is not without significance. It was the custom in those days for boys to go barefoot in the mild season. I recollect few things in life more delightful than, in the spring, to cast away my shoes and stockings, and have a glorious scamper over the fields. Many a time, contrary to the express injunctions of my mother, have I stolen this bliss, and many a time have I been punished by a severe cold for my imprudence, if not my disobedience. Yet the bliss then seemed a compensation for the retribution. In these exercises I felt as if stepping on air—as if leaping aloft on wings. I was so impressed with the exultant emotions thus experienced, that I repeated them a thousand times in happy dreams, especially in my younger days. Even now, these visions sometimes come to me in sleep, though with a lurking consciousness that they are but a mockery of the past—sad monitors of the change which time has wrought upon me.

"As to the black patch in the lane, that too had its meaning. The story of a house burned down by a foreign army, seized upon my imagination. Every time I passed the place, I ruminated upon it, and put a hundred questions as to how and when it happened. I was soon master of the whole story, and of other similar events which had occurred all over the country. I was thus initiated into the spirit of that day, and which has never wholly subsided in our country, inasmuch as the war of the Revolution was alike unjust in its origin, and cruel as to the manner in which it was waged. It was, moreover, fought on our own soil, thus making the whole people share, personally, in its miseries. There was scarcely a family in Connecticut whom it did not visit, either immediately or remotely, with the shadows of mourning and desolation. The British nation, to whom this conflict was a foreign war, are slow to comprehend the depth and universality of the popular dislike of England, here in America.

"I was about six years old when I first went to school. My teacher was Aunt Delight, that is, Delight Benedict, a maiden lady of fifty, short and bent, of sallow complexion and solemn aspect. I remember the first day with perfect distinctness. I went alone—for I was familiar with the road, it being that which passed by our old house. I carried a little basket, with bread and butter within, for my dinner, the same being covered over with a white cloth. When I had proceeded about half way, I lifted the cover, and debated whether I would not eat my dinner, then. I believe it was a sense of duty only that prevented my doing so, for in those happy days, I always had a keen appetite. Bread and butter were then infinitely superior to *pâté de foie gras* now; but still, thanks to my training, I had also a conscience. As my mother had given me the food for dinner, I did not think it right to convert it into lunch, even though I was strongly tempted.

"The school being organized, we were all seated upon benches, made of what were called *slabs*—that is, boards having the exterior or rounded part of the log on one side: as they were useless for other purposes, these were converted into school-benches, the rounded part down. They had each four supports, consisting of straddling wooden legs, set into augurholes. Our own legs swayed in the air, for they were too short to touch the floor. Oh, what an awe fell over me, when we were all seated and silence reigned around!

"The children were called up, one by one, to Aunt Delight, who sat on a low chair, and required each, as a preliminary, to make his manners, consisting of a small sudden nod or jerk of the head. She then placed the spelling-book—which was Dilworth's—before the pupil, and with a buck-handled penknife pointed, one by one, to the letters of the alphabet, saying, 'What's that?' If the child knew his letters, the 'what's that?' very soon ran on thus:

"'What's that?'
"'A.'
"'Stha-a-t?'
"B.'
"'Sha-a-t?'
"'C.'
"'Sha-a-t?'
"'D.'
"'Sha-a-t?'
"'È.' &c.

"I looked upon these operations with intense curiosity and no small respect, until my own turn came. I went up to the school-mistress with some emotion, and when she said, rather spitefully, as I thought, 'Make your obeisance!' my little intellects all fled away, and I did nothing. Having waited a second, gazing at me with indignation, she laid her hand on the top of my head, and gave it a jerk which made my teeth clash. I believe I bit my tongue a little; at all events, my sense of dignity was offended, and when she pointed to A, and asked what it was, it swam before me dim and hazy

Vessels of war in the time of William the Conqueror.

(From *Peter Parley's Common School History.)*

and as big as a full moon. She repeated the question, but I was doggedly silent. Again, a third time, she said, 'What's that?' I replied: 'Why don't you tell me what it is? I didn't come here to learn you your letters!'

"... Up to the age of ten or twelve years, I had made little acquaintance with literature. Beyond my school-books, I had read almost nothing. My father had a considerable library, but it consisted mostly of theology, a great deal of it in Latin, and in large folios. Into such a forbidding mass, I never penetrated, save only that I sometimes dipped into a big volume, which happened to be in large print. This was in English, and was, I suspect, some discussion of Calvin's Five Points; still it attracted my attention, and sometimes, especially of a rainy day, when I could hear the big drops thump upon the shingles over my head—for the library was in the second loft, and led by an open stairway to the attic—I read whole pages of this book aloud, spelling out the large words as well as I could. I did not understand a sentence of it, but I was fascinated with the fair large type. This circumstance I have never forgotten, and it should not be overlooked by those who make books for children, for in this case, I was but a representative of others of my age.

"When I was about ten years old, my father brought from Hartford, *Gaffer Ginger, Goody Two Shoes,* and some of the rhymes and jingles, now collected under the name of Mother Goose,—with perhaps a few other toy books of that day. These were a revelation. Of course I read them, but I must add with no real relish.

"Somewhat later one of my companions lent me a volume containing the stories of *Little Red Riding Hood, Puss in Boots, Blue Beard, Jack the Giantkiller,* and some other of the tales of horror, commonly put into the hands of youth, as if for the express purpose of reconciling them to vice and crime. Some children, no doubt, have a ready appetite for these monstrosities, but to others they are revolting, until by repetition and familiarity, the taste is sufficiently degraded to relish them. At all events, they were shocking to me. Even *Little Red Riding Hood,* though it seized strongly upon my imagination, excited in me the most painful impressions. I believed it to be true; at least it was told with the air of truth, and I regarded it as a picture of life. I imagined that what happened to the innocent child of the cottage, might happen to me and to others. I recollect, while the impression was fresh in my mind, that on going to bed, I felt a creeping horror come over me, as the story recurred to my imagination. As I dwelt upon it, I soon seemed to see the hideous jaws of a wolf coming out of the bedclothes, and approaching as if to devour me. My disposition was not timid, but the reverse; yet at last I became so excited, that my mother was obliged to tell me that the story was mere fiction.

"... This general impression, however, remained on my mind, that children's books were either full of nonsense, like 'hie diddle diddle' in Mother Goose, or full of something very like lies, and those very shocking to the mind, like *Little Red Riding Hood.* From that time my interest in them was almost wholly lost. I had read *Puss in Boots,* but that seemed to me without meaning, unless it was to teach us that a Good Genius

West Lane School House, which Goodrich attended, 1799-1803. ■ (From *Samuel Griswold Goodrich, Creator of Peter Parley* by Daniel Roselle.)

may cheat, lie, and steal; in other words, that in order to show gratitude to a friend, we may resort to every kind of meanness and fraud. I never liked cats, and to make one of that race—sly, thieving, and bloodthirsty by instinct—the personification of virtue, inclined me, so far as the story produced any moral effect, to hate virtue itself." [Samuel Griswold Goodrich, *Recollections of a Lifetime,* Volume I, Gale Research, 1967.[1]]

1808. "It was in the autumn . . . that a sudden change took place in my prospects. My eldest sister had married a gentleman by the name of Cooke, in the adjacent town of Danbury. He was a merchant, and being in want of a clerk, offered me the place. It was considered a desirable situation by my parents, and overlooking my mechanical aptitudes, they accepted it at once, and at the age of fifteen I found myself installed in a country store.

"I was not long in discovering that my new vocation was very different from what I had expected, and very different from my accustomed way of life. My habits had been active, my employments chiefly abroad—in the open air. I was accustomed to be frequently on horseback, and to make excursions to the neighboring towns; I had also enjoyed large personal liberty, which I failed not to use in rambling over the fields and forests. All this was now changed. My duties lay exclusively in the store, and this seemed now my prison. From morning to night I remained here, and as our business was not large, I had many hours upon my hands with nothing to do, but to consider the weariness of my situation. My brother-in-law was always present, and being a man of severe aspect and large ubiquitous eyes, I felt a sort of restraint, which, for a time, was agonizing. I had consequently pretty sharp attacks of homesickness, a disease which—save that it is not dangerous—is one of the most distressing to which suffering humanity is exposed.

"I was, then, eighteen years of age, installed in a dry-goods store at Hartford, under a respectable and reasonable master. I had been sufficiently educated for my station. My parents had now removed from Ridgefield to Berlin, a distance of but eleven miles from my present residence, so that I had easy and frequent communication with them. My uncle, Chauncey Goodrich, then a Senator of the United States, lived in an almost contiguous street, and while in the city, always treated me with the kindness and consideration which my relation to him naturally dictated. In general, then, my situation was eligible enough; and yet I was unhappy.

"The truth is, I had now been able to sit in judgement upon myself—to review my acquirements, to analyze my capacities, to estimate my character—to compare myself with others, and see a little into the future. The decision was painful to the ambition which lurked within me. I had all along, unconsciously, cherished a vague idea of some sort of eminence, and this unhappily had nothing to do with selling goods or making money. I had lived in the midst of relations, friends, and alliances, all of which had cultivated in me trains of thought alien to my present employment. My connections were respectable: some of them eminent, but none of them rich; all had acquired their positions without wealth, and I think it was rather their habit to speak of it as a very secondary affair. Brought up under such influences, how could I give my heart to trade? It was clear, indeed, that I had missed my vocation.

"Full of this conviction, I besought my parents to allow me to quit the store, and attempt to make my way through college. Whether for good or ill, I know not, but they decided against the change, and certainly on substantial grounds. Their circumstances did not permit them to offer me any considerable aid, and without it they feared that I should meet with insuperable difficulties. I returned to the store, disheartened at first, but after a time my courage revived, and I resolved to re-educate myself. I borrowed some Latin books, and with the aid of George Sheldon, I passed through the Latin Grammar, and penetrated a little way into Virgil. This was done at night, for during the day I was fully occupied.

"At the same time, I began—with such light and strength as I possessed—to train my mind—to discipline my thoughts, then as untamed as the birds of the wilderness. *I sought to think*—to think steadily, to acquire the power of forcing my understanding up to a point, and make it stand there and do its work. I attempted to gain the habit of speaking methodically, logically, and with accumulating power, directed to a particular object. I did all this as well by study as practice.

". . . I relearned the elements of geography; I revised my history, my chronology, my natural history—in all of which I had caught casual glimpses of knowledge. Finding my memory bad for dates, I made a list of chronological eras, from the Creation down, and riveted them by repetition, in my memory. What I read, I read earnestly. I determined to pass no word without ascertaining its meaning, and I persevered in this, doggedly, for five and twenty years."[1]

1817. "I remember very well the tide of emigration through Connecticut, on its way to the West, during the summer. . . . Some persons went in covered wagons—frequently a family consisting of father, mother, and nine small children, with one at the breast—some on foot and some crowded together under the cover, with kettles, gridirons, feather-beds, crockery, and the family Bible, Watts' Psalms and Hymns, and Webster's Spelling-book—the lares and penates of the household. Others started in ox-carts, and trudged on at the rate of ten miles a day. In several instances I saw families on foot—the father and boys taking turns in dragging along an improvised hand-wagon, loaded with the wreck of the household goods—occasionally giving the mother and baby a ride. Many of these persons were in a state of poverty, and begged their way as they went. Some died before they reached the expected Canaan; many perished after their arrival, from fatigue and privation; and others, from the fever and ague, which was then certain to attack the new settlers.

"It was, I think, in 1818, that I published a small tract, entitled 'T'other side of Ohio'—that is, the other view, in contrast to the popular notion that it was the paradise of the world. It was written by Dr. Hand—a talented young physician of Berlin—who had made a visit to the West about these days. It consisted mainly of vivid but painful pictures of the accidents and incidents attending this wholesale migration. The roads over the Alleghanies, between Philadelphia and Pittsburg, were then rude, steep, and dangerous, and some of the more precipitous slopes were consequently strewn with the carcases of wagons, carts, horses, oxen, which had made shipwreck in their perilous descents. The scenes on the road—of families gathered at night in miserable sheds. . . .

". . . I turned my attention to books for education and books for children, being strongly impressed with the idea that there was here a large field for improvement. I wrote, myself, a small arithmetic, and half a dozen toy-books, and published them, though I have never before confessed their authorship. I also employed several persons to write school histories, and educational manuals of chemistry, natural philosophy, &c., upon plans which I prescribed—all of which I published; but none of these were very successful at that time. Some of them, passing into other hands, are now among the most popular and profitable school-books in the country. William C. Woodbridge, one of the teachers of the Deaf and Dumb Asylum, at this time projected a school geography, in which I assisted him—mostly in preparing the details of the work for the press, and in the mechanical department. When an edition of it was finally ready—after long and anxious labor, both on his part and mine—the state of my health compelled me to relinquish it. This work acquired great popularity, and became the starting-point of a new era in school geographies, both in this country and in England." [Samuel Griswold Goodrich, *Recollections of a Lifetime,* Volume II, Gale Research, 1967.[2]]

February 2, 1818. Married Adeline Gratia Bradley, the daughter of Senator Stephen Bradley of Vermont, a colleague and friend of Uncle Chauncey Goodrich.

1821-1822. Wife died. ". . . Clouds and darkness began to gather around my path. By a fall from a horse, I was put upon crutches for more than a year, and a cane for the rest of my life. Ere long death, entered my door, and my home was desolate. I was once more alone—save only that a child was left me, to grow to womanhood, and to die a youthful mother, loving and beloved—leaving an infant soon to follow her to the tomb. My affairs became embarrassed, my health failed, and my only hope of renovation was in a change of scene."[2]

1823. Visited Europe. "When I left America, I had it in mind to render my travels subservient to a desire I had long entertained of making a reform—or at least an improvement—in books for youth. I had made researches in London, France, and Germany, for works that might aid my design. It is true I had little success, for while scientific and classical education was sedulously encouraged on the continent as well as in England, it seemed to be thought, either that popular education was not a subject worthy of attention, or that Dilworth and Mother Goose had done all that could be done. In this interview with the most successful and most efficient teacher of the age, I had the subject still in mind; and discerning by what she had accomplished, the vast field that was open, and actually inviting cultivation, I began from this time to think of attempting to realize the project I had formed. It is true that, in some respects the example I had just contemplated was different from my own scheme. Hannah More had written chiefly for the grown-up masses; I had it in contemplation to begin further back—with the children. Her means, however, seemed adapted to my purpose: her success, to en-

Peter Parley instructing youngsters in *The First Reader*. ■(From *Samuel Griswold Goodrich, Creator of Peter Parley* by Daniel Roselle.)

courage my attempt. She had discovered that truth could be made attractive to simple minds. Fiction was, indeed, often her vehicle, but it was not her end. The great charm of these works which had captivated the million, was their verisimilitude. Was there not, then, a natural relish for truth in all minds, or at least was there not a way of presenting it, which made it even more interesting than romance? Did not children love truth? If so, was it necessary to feed them on fiction? Could not history, natural history, geography, biography, become the elements of juvenile works, in place of fairies and giants, and mere monsters of the imagination? These were the inquiries that from this time filled my mind."[2]

January 2, 1826. Married nineteen-year-old English girl, Mary Boott.

1827. "Though I was busily engaged in publishing various works, I found time to make my long meditated experiment in the writing of books for children. The first attempt was made . . . and bore the title of the *Tales of Peter Parley about America*. No persons but my wife and one of my sisters were admitted to the secret—for in the first place, I hesitated to believe that I was qualified to appear before the public as an author, and in the next place, nursery literature had not then acquired the respect in the eyes of the world it now enjoys. It is since that period, that persons of acknowledged genius—Scott, Dickens, Lamartine, Mary Howitt, in Europe, and Abbott, Todd, Gallaudet, Miss Sedgwick, Mrs. Child, and others, in America, have stooped to the composition of books for children and youth.

"I published my little book, and let it make its way. It came before the world untrumpeted, and for months seemed not to attract the slightest attention. Suddenly I began to see notices of it in the papers, all over the country, and in a year from the date of its publication, it had become a favorite. In 1828, I published the *Tales of Peter Parley about Europe;* in 1829, *Parley's Winter Evening Tales;* in 1830, *Parley's Juvenile Tales,* and *Parley's Asia, Africa, Sun, Moon, and Stars.* About this time the public guessed my secret—it being first discovered and divulged by a woman—Mrs. Sarah J. Hale, to whom, by the way, I am indebted for many kind offices in my literary career—yet I could have wished she had not done me this questionable favor. Though the authorship of the Parley books has been to me a source of some gratification, . . . it has also subjected me to endless vexations."[2]

1828-1832. ". . . I had now obtained a humble position in literature, and was successful in such unambitious works as I attempted. I gave myself up almost wholly for about four years . . . to authorship, generally writing fourteen hours a day. A part of the time I was entirely unable to read, and could write but little, on account of the weakness of my eyes. In my larger publications, I employed persons to block out work for me; this was read to me, and then I put it into style, generally writing by dictation, my wife being my amanuensis. Thus embarrassed, I still, by dint of incessant toil, produced five or six volumes a year, mostly small, but some of larger compass."[2]

Spring, 1832. "In the midst of these labors . . . I was suddenly attacked with symptoms, which seemed to indicate a disease of the heart, rapidly advancing to a fatal termination. In the course of a fortnight I was so reduced as not to be able to mount a pair of stairs without help, and a short walk produced palpitations of the heart, which in several instances almost deprived me of consciousness. There seemed no hope but in turning my back upon my business, and seeking a total change of scene and climate. In May I embarked for England, and after a few weeks reached Paris. I here applied to Baron Larroque, who, assisted by L'Herminier—both eminent specialists in diseases of the heart—subjected me to various experiments, but without the slightest advantage. At this period I was obliged to be carried up stairs, and never ventured to walk or ride alone, being constantly subject to nervous spasms, which often brought me to the verge of suffocation.

"[I] came to the conclusion that in feeding the mind of children with facts, with truth, and with objective truth, we follow the evident philosophy of nature and providence, inasmuch as these had created all children to be ardent lovers of things they could see and hear and feel and know. Thus I sought to teach them history and biography and geography, and all in the way in which nature would teach them—that is, by a large use of the senses, and especially by the eye—the master organ of the body as well as the soul. I selected as subjects for my books, things capable of sensible representation, such as familiar animals, birds, trees, and of these I gave pictures, as a starting point. The first line I wrote was, 'Here I am; my name is Peter Parley,' and before I went further, gave an engraving representing my hero, as I wished him to be conceived by my pupils. Before I began to talk of a lion, I gave a picture of a lion—my object being, as you will perceive, to have the child start with a distinct image of what I was about to give an account of. Thus I secured his interest in the subject, and thus I was able to lead his understanding forward in the path of knowledge.

"It is true that occasionally I wrote and published a book, aside from this, my true vocation; thus I edited the *Token,* and published two or three volumes of poetry. But out of all my works, about a hundred and twenty are professedly juvenile; and forty are for my early readers, advanced to maturity. It is true that I have written openly, avowedly, to attract and to please children; yet it has been my design at the same time to enlarge the circle of knowledge, to invigorate the understanding, to strengthen the moral nerve, to purify and exalt the imagination. Such have been my aims; how far I have succeeded, I must leave to the judgment of others. One thing I may perhaps claim, and that is, my example and my success have led others—of higher gifts than my own—to enter the ample and noble field of juvenile instruction by means of books; many of them have no doubt surpassed me, and others will still follow, surpassing them. I look upon the art of writing for children and youth, advanced as it has been of late years, still as but just begun."[2]

1851. Appointed *Consul of the United States of America at Paris.*

1854. Visited Italy with his family.

May 9, 1860. Died of a heart ailment in New York City.

FOR MORE INFORMATION SEE: Recollections of a Lifetime; or, Men and Things I Have Seen, Miller, Orton, 1856, reprinted, Gale, 1967; Alice M. Jordan, *From Rollo to Tom Sawyer, and Other Papers,* Horn Book, 1948; June B. Mussey, editor, *Yankee Life by Those Who Live It,* Knopf, 1947; D. Roselle, "What Ever Became of Peter Parley?," *Social Education,* January, 1957; Brian Doyle, editor, *Who's Who of Children's Literature,* Schocken Books, 1968; Daniel Roselle, *Samuel Griswold Goodrich, Creator of Peter Parley: A Study of His Life and Work,* State University of New York Press, 1968; Helen S. Canfield, "Peter Parley," *Horn Book,* April-August, 1970.

GRAMATKY, Hardie 1907-1979

OBITUARY NOTICE—See sketch in *SATA* Volume 1: Born April 12, 1907, in Dallas, Tex.; died April 29, 1979, in Westport, Conn. Author and illustrator best known for his series about a tugboat called "Little Toot." Gramatky began the series in 1939 with the now-famous *Little Toot.* Rated by the Library of Congress as one of the all-time greats in children's literature, it has inspired everything from parade floats to the naming of the Los Angeles Library bookmobile service. Translated into several languages, with sales in the millions, the book was adapted as a motion picture by the Walt Disney Studios in 1939. The final volume in the tugboat series, *Little Toot Through the Golden Gate,* was published in 1975. Gramatky worked as head animator for Walt Disney Productions during the early 1930's, but turned to free-lance work in 1944. An award-winning artist as well as an author, he produced watercolors which are now displayed in museums, including the Art Institute of Chicago and the Springfield Museum of Fine Art. Gramatky is one of twenty-nine honorary members of the American Watercolor Society. *For More Information See: Illustrators of Children's Books, 1744-1945,* Horn Book, 1945, reprinted, 1970; *Story and Verse for Children,* 3rd edition, Macmillan, 1965; *Contemporary Authors,* Volume 1-4, revised, Gale, 1967; *Books Are by People: Interviews With 104 Authors and Illustrators of Books for Young People,* Citation Press, 1969; *Anthology of Children's Literature,* Houghton, 1970; *Who's Who in the World,* 2nd edition, Marquis, 1973; *American Picturebooks from "Noah's Ark" to "The Beast Within,"* Macmillan, 1976; *Authors in the News,* Volume 1, Gale, 1976. *Obituaries: New York Times,* May 1, 1979; *Publishers Weekly,* May 14, 1979; *AB Bookman's Weekly,* May 21, 1979; *Horn Book,* August, 1979; *School Library Journal,* September, 1979; *Contemporary Authors,* Volume 85-88, Gale, 1980.

GREENE, Ellin 1927-

PERSONAL: Born September 18, 1927, in Elizabeth, N.J.; daughter of Charles M. and Dorothea (Hooton) Peterson; married K. Richard Greene, June 24, 1962 (marriage ended, 1976). *Education:* Douglass College, A. B., 1953; Rutgers University, M.L.S., 1957, Ed.D., 1979. *Home:* 113 Chatham Lane, Point Pleasant, N.J. 08742. *Office:* University of Chicago, Graduate Library School, 111 East 57th St., Chicago, Ill. 60637.

CAREER: Free Public Library, Elizabeth, N.J., children's librarian, 1953-57, specialist in group work with children,

"Open your mouth and make some of those fine courteous remarks that ye're so famous for making," they cried again. ■ (From *Midsummer Magic: A Garland of Stories, Charms, and Recipes* by Ellin Greene. Illustrated by Barbara Cooney.)

ELLIN GREENE

1957-59; New York Public Library, New York, N.Y., assistant storytelling and group work specialist, 1959-64, children's specialist in Bronx, 1964-65, storytelling specialist and assistant coordinator of children's services, 1965-67; Rutgers University, New Brunswick, N.J., adjunct faculty member in children's literature, storytelling, and library service to children, 1968-79; National College of Education, Evanston, Ill., children's literature specialist, 1976-77; Graduate Library School, University of Chicago, Ill., associate professor and dean of students, 1980—. Juror of children's films for Educational Film Library Association; lecturer and consultant.

MEMBER: Children's Literature Association, Rutgers Advisory Council on Children's Literature, National Association for the Preservation and Perpetuation of Storytelling (board member), American Association of University Women, American Library Association, National Council of Teachers of English, ALA Association for Library Service to Children, Authors Guild, Authors League of America, American Crafts Council, Arrow Book Club (advisory board). *Awards, honors:* Psi Chi; Tangley Oaks fellowship, 1977-78; Rutgers Graduate/Law fellowship, 1978-79.

WRITINGS: Recordings for Children: A Selected List, New York Public Library, 1964; *Stories: A List of Stories to Tell and Read Aloud,* 6th edition, New York Public Library, 1965; *Films for Children: A Selected List,* New York Library Association, 1966; (reteller) Mary E. Wilkins, *The Pumpkin Giant* (juvenile), Lothrop, 1970; (reteller) Mary E. Wilkins, *Princess Rosetta and the Popcorn Man* (juvenile), Lothrop, 1971; (with Madalynne Schoenfield) *A Multimedia Approach to Children's Literature: A Selective List of Films, Filmstrips, and Recordings Based on Children's Books,* American Library Association, 1972, 2nd edition, 1977; (compiler) *Clever Cooks: A Concoction of Stories, Charms, Recipes, and Riddles,* Lothrop, 1973, published as *Clever Cooks: A Ready-Mix of Stories, Recipes and Riddles,* Scholastic Book Services, 1977; (editor) Laurence Housman, *The Rat-Catcher's Daughter* (stories), Atheneum, 1974; (with Augusta Baker) *Storytelling: Art and Technique,* Bowker, 1977; (compiler) *Midsummer Magic: A Garland of Stories, Charms, and Recipes,* Lothrop, 1977. Contributor to *World Book Encyclopedia, Top of the News,* and *School Library Journal.*

WORK IN PROGRESS: An anthology of articles on storytelling, *Storytellers on Storytelling,* and an anthology of flower stories and cookery for juveniles.

SIDELIGHTS: "I have a deep interest in literature, especially imaginative literature, including folk and fairy tales, fantasy, and poetry for both adults and children.

"I believe imaginative literature keeps us in touch with what is most human in us. As a librarian/teacher I am interested in introducing this literature to children and adults, especially through the art of storytelling. I also attempt to do this through my books.

"As a doctoral student in creative arts education, my special area of research was the relationship between childhood fantasy play and later literary creativity. This research continues."

HOBBIES AND OTHER INTERESTS: Dance, theater, gardening, the seashore, yoga, meditation.

FOR MORE INFORMATION SEE: Horn Book, October, 1973, April, 1978, June, 1978.

GRIMSHAW, Nigel (Gilroy) 1925-

PERSONAL: Born November 5, 1925, in Manchester, England; son of Harold C. (a scientist) and Gladys Jeanne Grimshaw; married Margarete Apell, February 25, 1950; children: Rosemary, Mark, Peter, John. *Education:* Victoria University of Manchester, B.A. (with honors), 1950; University of Nottingham, M.A., 1976. *Home and Office:* 3 Plane Trees, Rosedale E., Pickering, North Yorkshire, England. *Agent:* Bolt & Watson Ltd., 8-12 Old Queen St., Storey's Gate, London SW1H 9HP, England.

NIGEL GRIMSHAW

CAREER: Teachers Training College, Bangkok, Thailand, lecturer in English, 1958-62; Frances Bacon Grammar School, St. Albans, England, teacher of English and department head, 1962-65; Kesteven College of Education, Grantham, England, senior lecturer in English, 1965-80. *Military service:* Royal Navy, 1943-47. *Member:* International P.E.N., Society of Authors.

WRITINGS—For children: *Tiger Gold,* Longmans, Green, 1964; *The Painted Jungle,* Longmans, Green, 1965; *The Sign of Indra,* Longmans, Green, 1967; *The Angry Valley,* Longmans, Green, 1970; (with Paul Groves) *Up Our Way,* Edward Arnold, 1972; (with Paul Groves) *Living Our Way,* Edward Arnold, 1973; *Join the Action,* Edward Arnold, 1973; *Bluntstone and the Wildkeepers,* Faber, 1974; *Action Replay,* Edward Arnold, 1975; *Going Our Way,* Edward Arnold, 1975; *The Wildkeepers' Guest,* Faber, 1978; *13 Ghosts,* Edward Arnold, 1976; *13 Weird Tales,* Edward Arnold, 1977; *13 Scifi Stories,* Edward Arnold, 1979; *Into Action,* Edward Arnold, 1980.

WORK IN PROGRESS: Another novel for children; textbooks.

SIDELIGHTS: "My first children's novel began as a story I told my own children during a rather wet holiday in Wales. Since that was intentionally comic, I wrote *The Wildkeepers' Guest* in a more serious mode as a companion piece."

GUNDREY, Elizabeth 1924-

PERSONAL: Born 1924, in London, England; married a psychiatrist; children: one son. *Education:* University of London, B.A. (honors in history), 1946. *Home:* 19 Fitzjohns Ave., London NW3 5JY, England.

CAREER: Author, editor. Formerly feature writer for *News Chronicle* and home editor of *House and Garden* and *Housewife; Shopper's Guide,* London, England, founder and editor, 1957-64. Was also editorial director for Spectator Publications. *Member:* Society of Authors.

WRITINGS—Juvenile: *Fun Foods,* Galts, 1971; *Then—1745, 1815, 1832, 1848, 1901, 1920,* Peter Way, 1972; *Making Decorations,* Pan, 1973; *Sewing Things,* Pan, 1973; *Fun with Flowers,* Galts, 1973; *Fun Dressing-Up,* Galts, 1973; *Growing Things,* Pan, 1973; *Make Your Own Monster,* Pan, 1973; (with Martin Mayhew and Cherille Mayhew) *Fun with Art,* Galts, 1973; *Collecting Things,* Pan, 1974; *The Summer Book,* Methuen, 1974; *You and Your Money,* Evans, 1976; *All Your Own,* Hamlyn, 1977; *Kings and Queens,* Pan, 1977; *Send Off for It,* Hamlyn, 1978; *Joining Things,* Severn House, 1978; *The Winter Book,* Methuen, 1978; *Fun in the Garden,* Pan, 1978; *Exploring England by Bus,* Hamlyn, 1981; *Sparing Time: Guide to Helping Others,* Allen & Unwin, 1981.

Adult: *Your Money's Worth,* Penguin, 1962; *At Your Service,* Penguin, 1954; *A Foot in Your Door,* Muller, 1965; *Value for Money,* Hodder & Stoughton, 1966; *Jobs for Mothers,* Hodder & Stoughton, 1967; (with Jean Carper) *Stay Alive! How to Prevent Accidents in the Home,* MacGibbon & Kee, 1967; (editor) *The Book of Egg Cookery,* Spectator Publications, 1969. Also author and editor of numerous books for adults on consumer economics, industrial hygiene, careers, cookery, interior decoration, etc. Contributor to the *Guardian, Sunday Times, Daily Mail, Daily Mirror,* and other news-

ELIZABETH GUNDREY

papers in England, to the British Broadcasting Corporation, and to various television programs.

SIDELIGHTS: "I came into children's writing after a quite dissimilar career—writing on consumer affairs—very factual, technical stuff for adult readers. I'd edited a magazine that published test reports, written various books on consumer protection or education, and had done quite a bit of press and television work in this field.

"Suddenly I got tired of so much critical and analytical writing. I wanted to do something more creative—more fun! In a way, I rolled the years back to my own childhood and the interests I'd enjoyed then—many of them stimulated by my mother. Painting, making things, enjoying the English countryside and all wildlife, Britain's marvellous history and architectural heritage, all this began to surface again.

"Soon it all got a fresh stimulus from a late marriage (to an Australian psychiatrist resident in England), for my husband shared many of these interests, and then by the adoption of a nine year-old son, who began to show an enthusiasm for the wildlife and history, though not for the crafts that I enjoy so much.

"I found I had a way of 'talking' to children through my books which seemed to stimulate a response. I love getting letters from children and replying to them. I now write on similar subjects for adults too—having discovered that a number of my children's books were finding their way into adult hands!"

HALL, Donald (Andrew, Jr.) 1928-

PERSONAL: Born September 29, 1928, in New Haven, Conn.; son of Donald Andrew (a businessman) and Lucy (Wells) Hall; married Kirby Thompson, September 13, 1952 (divorced, 1969); married Jane Kenyon (a poet), 1972; children: (first marriage) Andrew, Philippa. *Education:* Attended Philips Exeter Academy, 1944-47; Harvard University, B.A., 1951; Oxford University, B.Litt., 1953; attended Stanford University, 1953-54. *Home:* Eagle Pond Farm, Danbury,

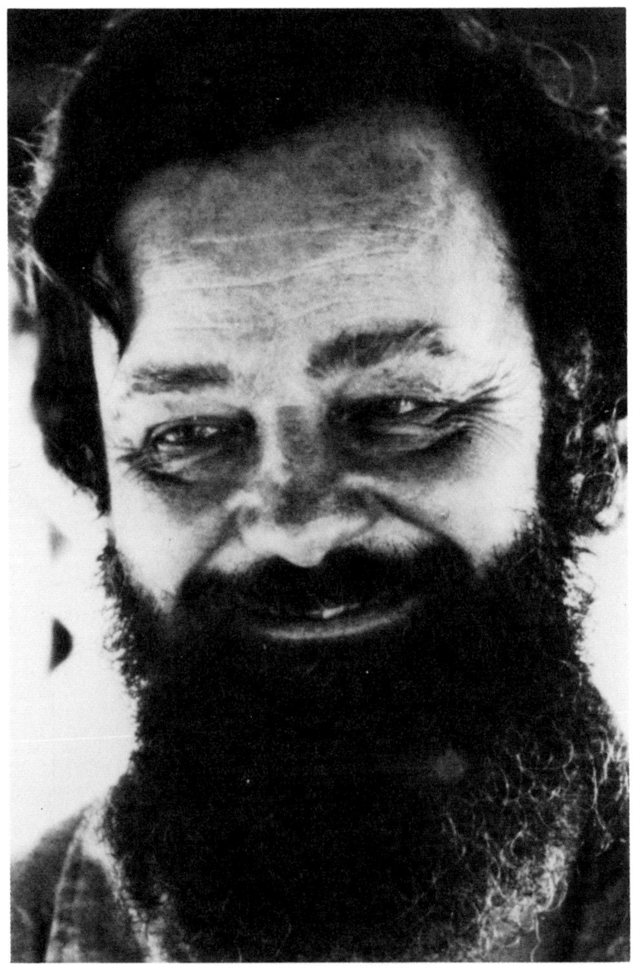

DONALD HALL

. . . And in March they tapped the sugar maple trees and boiled the sap down . . . . ■ (From *Ox-Cart Man* by Donald Hall. Illustrated by Barbara Cooney.)

N.H. 03230. *Agent:* Gerard McCauley, Box AE, Katonah, N.Y.

CAREER: Harvard University, Cambridge, Mass., junior fellow in the Society of Fellows, 1954-57; University of Michigan, Ann Arbor, assistant professor, 1957-61, associate professor, 1961-66, professor, 1966-75; editorial consultant for Harper & Row, 1964-80. *Member:* P.E.N., Modern Language Association, American Association of University Professors. *Awards, honors:* Lloyd McKim Garrison prize for poetry, Harvard, 1951; John Osborne Sergeant prize for Latin translation, Harvard, 1951; Newdigate Prize, Oxford University, 1952, for "Exile"; Academy of American Poets' Lamont Poetry Selection, 1955, for *Exiles and Marriages*; Edna St. Vincent Millay award of the Poetry Society of America, 1956; recipient of two Guggenheim fellowships; honorary Doctorate of Humane Letters degree, 1980, from Plymouth State College.

WRITINGS: (Editor) *The Harvard Advocate Anthology,* Twayne, 1950; *To the Loud Wind, and Other Poems,* Regasus Publications, Harvard Advocate, 1955; *Exiles and Marriages* (poems), Viking, 1955; (editor with Robert Pack and Louis Simpson) *New Poets of England and America* (introduction by Robert Frost), Meridian, 1957; *The Dark Houses* (poems), Viking, 1958; *Andrew the Lion Farmer* (juvenile; illustrated by Jane Miller), F. Watts, 1959, second edition (illustrated by Ann Reason), Methuen, 1961.

String Too Short to Be Saved (autobiography; illustrated by Mimi Korach), Viking, 1961, revised edition, Godine, 1979; (editor) *Whittier,* Dell, 1961; (editor) *Contemporary American Poetry,* Penguin, 1962; (editor) *A Poetry Sampler,* F. Watts, 1962; (editor with Robert Pack) *New Poets of England and America: Second Selection,* Meridian, 1962; (with Warren Taylor) *Poetry in English,* Macmillan, 1963; (editor with Stephen Spender) *The Concise Encyclopedia of English and American Poets and Poetry,* Hawthorn, 1963; *A Roof of Tiger Lilies* (poems), Viking, 1964; *Henry Moore: The Life and Work of a Great Sculptor,* Harper, 1966; (contributor) Walter Lowenfels, *Where Is Vietnam?: American Poets Respond,* Doubleday-Anchor, 1967; (editor) *The Modern Stylists: Writers on the Art of Writing* (young adult), Free Press, 1968; (editor) *A Choice of Whitman's Verse,* Faber, 1968; (editor) *Man & Boy,* F. Watts, 1968; *The Alligator Bride: Poems New & Selected,* Harper, 1969.

Writing Well (textbook), Little, Brown, 1973, 3rd edition, 1979; *A Writer's Reader* (textbook), Little, Brown, 1976, 2nd edition, 1979; *Riddle Rat* (juvenile), Warne, 1977; *Kicking the Leaves* (poems), Harper, 1978; *Remembering Poets,* Harper, 1978; *Ox-Cart Man* (juvenile; Junior Literary Guild selection), Viking, 1979; *To Keep Moving* (essays), Seneca Press, 1980; *To Read Literature* (textbook), Holt, 1980; *Oxford Book of American Literary Anecdotes,* Oxford University Press, 1981. Poetry editor of the *Paris Review.*

Plays: "An Evening's Frost," first produced at Theatre de Lys, New York, N.Y., October 11, 1965.

WORK IN PROGRESS: "Working on poems every day. . . ."

SIDELIGHTS: Hall started to write poetry at the age of fourteen. "I worked very hard at it. I'd go up to my room after school and write poetry. I began to write poems in order to be loved by women. This is the general truth, I think."

Between the ages of thirteen and fourteen or so, he "hesitated between becoming a great actor or a great poet." He does act occasionally, but believes that the lecture circuit, an indulgence he is naturally quite fond of, allows him to play both roles at once. He also feels that the lecture circuit "is revolutionizing the life of the American poet, and probably his poetry as well. . . . I want to write poems in which the sound itself keeps the listeners intent. . . . The listener doesn't have to understand this poem intellectually, but to enjoy it as a sensual object, to take it into the ears and be moved by it. . . ."

On the writing of prose, Hall had this advice: "A writer of bad prose, in order to become a writer of good prose, must alter his character. He does not have to become good in terms of conventional morality, but he must become honest in the expression of himself, which means that he must know himself. . . . For some people, some of the time, this simply means *not* telling deliberate lies. For most people, it means learning when they are lying and when they are not. It means learning the real names of their feelings."

Hall lives in New Hampshire at Eagle Pond Farm to which his great-grandfather had moved in 1865. "It was really the place of solitude, the place of dreaming and writing; the beginning of my life as a writer is associated with this place. For many years, I never thought that it would be possible to live here, in this house that I loved so much. If my grandmother had died at a normal age—say, ninety—it would have gone to strangers. But she hung on until ninety-seven by which time it was possible for me to make the down payment to afford the mortgage, to give up teaching and to live here. I have never done anything so smart in my life.

"The house is a wonderful repository. As I sit at my desk, I can look up at an old photograph of my grandmother dressed to the teeth for the prize-speaking day when she was a junior at high school. And I can walk upstairs and look at the dress itself. Nothing was ever thrown away. There are three spinning wheels upstairs, twenty-five quilts, four high chairs, everything in the world. My great-grandfather was born in 1826, and we still have some of his underwear packed away in chests. You never know when it might come in handy. . . .

"It is this kind of spirit which pervades *Ox-Cart Man*. I heard the story from my cousin Paul Fenton, my grandfather's nephew. Paul told me he had heard it when he was a boy from an old man who told him that *he* had heard it when he was a boy, from an old man. It is always told as a true story, and I believe it. I was thrilled with it, thinking of man's past life described in cyclical fashion, dying in order to be born again, as if human beings could be perennial plants." Hall wrote *Ox-Cart Man* first as a poem for the *New Yorker*.

FOR MORE INFORMATION SEE: Time, December 5, 1955; *Christian Science Monitor,* October 2, 1958; *New York Times Book Review,* November 30, 1958, December 11, 1966, May, 1967; *New Statesman,* November 27, 1964; *Encounter,* March, 1965; *Virginia Quarterly Review*, Spring, 1965; *Publishers Weekly,* February 28, 1977.

HAMILTON, Elizabeth 1906-

PERSONAL: Born April 3, 1906, in County Wicklow, Ireland; daughter of John Douglas and Mary (Garnett) Hamilton. *Education:* University of London, B.A. (first class honors in classics), 1928, M.A. (with distinction), 1932. *Religion:* Roman Catholic. *Home:* 84 Vicarage Ct., Vicarage Gate, London W8 4HG, England. *Agent:* Curtis Brown Ltd., 1 Craven Hill, London W.1, England.

CAREER: Royal School for Daughter of Officers, Bath, England, Latin and Greek teacher, 1940-52; also taught Latin and Greek at Sacred Heart Convent in London; author, 1942—. *Member:* P.E.N.

WRITINGS: The Year Returns, M. Joseph, 1952; *A River Full of Stars,* Deutsch, 1954, Norton, 1955; *First Book of Caves,* F.Watts, 1956; *Simon,* Deutsch, 1956; *Put Off Thy Shoes,* Scribner, 1957; *Saint Teresa,* Scribner, 1959 (published in England as *The Great Teresa,* Chatto & Windus, 1960); *An Irish Childhood,* Chatto & Windus, 1963; *Heloise,* Doubleday, 1967; *The Desert My Dwelling Place* (biography of Charles de Foucauld), Hodder & Stoughton, 1968; *I Stay in the Church,* Vision Press, 1975; *Cardinal Suenens: A Portrait,* Doubleday, 1975; *Servants of Love: Spirituality of Teresa of Avila,* Our Sunday Visitor, 1975; *The Voice of the Spirit: Spirituality of St. John of the Cross,* Our Sunday Visitor, 1976; *The Ways of the Spirit: Spirituality of Cardinal Suenens,* Our Sunday Visitor, 1976; (editor) *Your God?,* Our Sunday Visitor, 1978; *In Celebration of Cats,* Scribner, 1979; *Nicholas Postgate* (foreword by Cardinal Hume, OSB) Darton Longman & Todd, 1980. Contributor to *The Month, New York Times, John O'London,* and *Catholic World.*

ELIZABETH HAMILTON

. . . She suddenly noticed something—something high above her on the cave's ceiling. It was an enormous red picture of an animal that looked like a bull. ■ (From *The First Book of Caves* by Elizabeth Hamilton. Illustrated by Bette J. Davis.)

WORK IN PROGRESS: A book on animals.

SIDELIGHTS: "My childhood was wonderful! I spent my first eight years in Ireland with a menagerie of donkeys, horses, cats, dogs, and a garden.

"At the age of eight my parents and I went to Florida where my parents hoped to fruit farm—a failure. We returned to England where I went to school. I largely owe my capacity to write to my Greek professor who, if he didn't like a translation, would throw it back at me saying, 'For goodness sake, put it into English!' Later, I taught Latin and Greek in several schools. I liked my pupils tremendously (I *love young* people), but did not care for the atmosphere of the schools.

"Traveling gives me great pleasure and I have traveled widely (France, Belgium, Spain, Norway, Portugal, Germany, Israel, Jordon, the Sahara, and the United States). I have enjoyed all my journeys, especially the months I spent in Israel and Jordan where I wrote *Put Off Thy Shoes,* and the time spent in the Sahara writing about Charles de Foucauld. My most enjoyable undertaking, however, was the life of Cardinal Suenens whom I visited at regular intervals. It was also a wonderful experience to help Cardinal Hume, the Archbishop of Westminster, with his books. My latest book, *In Celebration of Cats,* is very popular with teenagers and younger children."

HOBBIES AND OTHER INTERESTS: "I love poetry, music, the country, animals, nature, and cats."

FOR MORE INFORMATION SEE: Horn Book, January-December, 1947, January-December, 1948.

HANEY, Lynn 1941-

PERSONAL: Born February 12, 1941 in Pittsburgh, Pa.; daughter of John J. (a civil servant) and Kay (a teacher) Haney. *Education:* University of Pittsburgh, B.A., 1963; Sorbonne, University of Paris, graduate study, 1963-64. *Politics:* Democrat. *Home and office:* Box 145, Stonington, Conn. 06378.

CAREER: Christian Dior (fashion design firm), Paris, France, interpreter, 1965-66; National Endowment for the Arts, Washington, D.C., assistant to the director of public relations, 1966-68; *New York Times,* New York, N.Y., clerk, 1969-73; writer, 1973—. *Member:* Authors Guild, Dramatists Guild, American Civil Liberties Union. *Awards, honors:* Publishers merit award from *New York Times* for article on plastic surgery; Western Writers award for best nonfiction juvenile, 1975, for *Ride 'Em, Cowgirl!.*

WRITINGS: The Lady Is a Jock, Dodd, 1973; *The Memoirs of Mason Reese: In Cahoots with Lynn Haney,* Dodd, 1974; *Ride 'Em, Cowgirl!* (juvenile), Putnam, 1975; *Chris Evert: The Young Champion* (juvenile), Putnam, 1976; *Perfect Balance: The Training of an Elite Gymnast* (juvenile), Putnam, 1979; *Naked at the Feast: A Biography of Josephine Baker,* Dodd, 1980; *I Am a Dancer,* Putnam, 1980.

HOBBIES AND OTHER INTERESTS: Skiing, sailing, scuba diving.

FOR MORE INFORMATION SEE: Publishers Weekly, February 14, 1977; *The Compass,* May 11, 1979.

(From *Perfect Balance: The Training of an Elite Gymnast* by Lynn Haney. Photograph by Bruce Curtis.)

LYNN HANEY

HARRIS, Janet 1932-1979

OBITUARY NOTICE—See sketch in *SATA* Volume 4: Born April 17, 1932, in Newark, N.J.; died December 6, 1979, in Freeport, N.Y. Political activist, historian, educator, and writer. A firm opponent of racism, sexism, and war, Harris wrote a number of books on social revolution. Among her publications, which include both adult and juvenile titles, are *The Long Freedom Road: The Civil Rights Story, Students in Revolt, Crisis in Corrections,* and *The Prime of Ms. America. For More Information See: Contemporary Authors,* Volume 33-36, revised, Gale, 1978. *Obituaries: Contemporary Authors,* Volume 93-96, Gale, 1980; *Publishers Weekly,* January 18, 1980.

My castle has a lot of doors;
Each one is numbered too.
No matter which you open first,
Two pages wait on you.

—L.J. Bridgman

HARTLEY, Ellen (Raphael) 1915-

PERSONAL: Born January 1, 1915, in Dortmund, Germany; naturalized American citizen; daughter of Gustave and Elizabeth (Steinweg) Raphael; married William B. Hartley (a writer), October, 1957. *Education:* Attended German schools; completed equivalent of junior college; New York University, special courses; Florida International University, B.S. in social work, 1976. *Home and office:* 5747 Southwest 82nd St., South Miami, Fla. 33143.

CAREER: Sales Management magazine, New York, N.Y., assistant advertising production manager, 1952-55, head of records and research department, 1955; University of Miami School of Medicine, Department of Family Medicine, Miami, Fla., social work aide, 1975-76; Fellowship House, Psycho-Social Rehabilitation Center of Dade County, Inc., Miami, Fla., social worker, 1977—. *Military service:* Women's Auxiliary Air Force, England, 1941-46; became flight sergeant, Intelligence Staff, Royal Air Force Bomber Command. *Member:* Society of Magazine Writers.

WRITINGS: The Ellen Knauff Story, Norton, 1952; (with husband, William B. Hartley) *Your Important Years,* Popular Library, 1962; (with William B. Hartley) *A Woman Set Apart,* Dodd, 1963; *Young Living,* Popular Library, 1963: (with William B. Hartley) *Osceola—The Unconquered Indian,* Hawthorn, 1973; (with William B. Hartley) *The Alligator: King of the Wilderness* (juvenile), Nelson, 1977. Contributor of almost two hundred articles, alone or in collaboration with husband, to *Cosmopolitan, Ingenue, Redbook, Golf Digest, Good Housekeeping, Reader's Digest, Coronet, Pageant, Argosy, Saga, Popular Mechanics,* and other magazines.

WORK IN PROGRESS: Several books independently or in collaboration with William B. Hartley.

SIDELIGHTS: "I was born in Germany and lived in several European countries including England during World War II before settling down in Miami, Florida. My first book, *The Ellen Knauff Story* was written on the suggestion of friends who considered me a 'writer.' When the book was published I slowly started to agree with my friends.

ELLEN HARTLEY

"Until that time, I had been a voracious reader of any books I could lay my hands on—from Jack London and Shakespeare to medical textbooks written in German and borrowed from a cousin studying medicine. By concentrating when children's books were read to me, I had taught myself to read by age four, and started to devour the books found in my parents' library. I still devour books.

"I don't believe you can 'teach' writing. Books were my teachers. You can teach language, grammar, spelling, phonetics, and so on. You can even pass on a number of professional guidelines, such as article construction and how to write a query that will convince an editor to make an assignment, but you can't teach writing; you can only develop talent. It takes as much time to become a professional writer as it takes to become a doctor or a lawyer. Many books must be read before you learn how to write one. An eclectic taste in reading is another prerequisite for any aspiring writer, and it includes poetry. The person who specializes in reading fiction alone will not learn to work in non-fiction, and vice versa. The reading of poetry is essential to master the expression of feelings—so is listening to people talk. No person unable to listen can write realistic dialogue.

"Some years ago, while covering a magazine article at Duke University, Durham, N.C., I interviewed Carl Eisdoerfer, Ph.D., M.D., then professor of psychiatry and medical psychology at Duke. Dr. Eisdoerfer insisted that in order to remain active and keep up-to-date with an ever-changing society and an increasing pool of knowledge, all degrees issued should self-destruct after five years.

"Dr. Eisdoerfer must have convinced me of the need to keep my own education up to date. I enrolled at Florida International University, majoring in social work, did four years of academic work in less than half the time, and graduated 'with honors' in 1976. The four years of academic work before I reached my Bachelor of Science in social work degree were required because of lost and irreplaceable documents. I could not prove that I ever went to school!

"I have since worked with former mental patients (schizophrenics and depressives) as a social worker in a halfway house, helping them to avoid the vicious cycle of rehospitalization. Fellowship House in Miami, Florida, has been able to help better than eighty per cent of its members (as we call the people with whom we work) to find their way back into the mainstream of life—including regular jobs. Yes, I am working on a book on the subject.

"My orchid growing hobby has been abandoned out of necessity. My writing partner, William B. Hartley, and I received a *Redbook* assignment to cover the entire Gulf of Mexico coast from Florida deep into Mexico. There were to be stops in New Orleans and other important tourist locations in Alabama, Mississippi, Louisiana and Texas. While one of *Redbook's* famous travel sections grew healthily, the orchids grew sick and/or out of their pots. I could never again find the time to remedy the neglect. The survivors were happily accepted by my neighbor as a donation to her church fair.

"I am also far too busy living to have much time to worry about the fact that, since 1974, I have been diagnosed as having incurable cancer. It has not prevented me from working full time as a writer, social worker, and a contributing editor and reviewer for *Fine Dancing,* a Florida gourmet magazine that has recently extended its coverage to New York City. Thanks to the most modern medical care, I have yet to miss one day's work because of illness. I have no plans for retirement and expect to continue working as a social worker and writer for the rest of my life."

HOBBIES AND OTHER INTERESTS: Music (classics through jazz), gardening, animals, theater, travel.

FOR MORE INFORMATION SEE: Miami News, February 7, 1962; *Miami Herald,* February 26, 1963; *Publishers Weekly,* February 28, 1977.

HARTLEY, William B(rown) 1913-

PERSONAL: Born July 21, 1913, in South Norwalk, Conn.; son of Ralph George (a clergyman) and Genevra Vivien (Brown) Hartley; married Ellen Raphael (a writer), October, 1957. *Education:* Horace Mann Preparatory School, graduate, 1932; Colgate University, A.B., 1936. *Home and office:* 5747 Southwest 82nd St., South Miami, Fla. 33143.

CAREER: Fawcett Publications Men's Group, New York, N.Y., production editor, 1936-40; *True,* New York, N.Y., production and assistant editor, 1940-41; *Click,* New York, N.Y., managing editor, 1941-43; *Modern Screen,* New York, N.Y., managing editor, then editor, 1947-51; *Redbook,* New York, N.Y., executive editor, 1951-55; consultant to publishers, 1955-56. *Military service:* U.S. Army, 1943-47; served with 10th Mountain Division (ski troops), and with Academic Division, Army Information School. *Member:* American Society of Journalists and Authors.

WRITINGS: The Cruel Tower, Appleton, 1955; (with wife, Ellen R. Hartley) *Your Important Years,* Popular Library,

William Hartley with wife, Ellen.

Miami children with two-and-a-half-foot gator caught in backyard. ■ (From *The Alligator: King of the Wilderness* by William and Ellen Hartley. Photograph courtesy of *Miami Herald.)*

1962; (with Ellen R. Hartley) *A Woman Set Apart,* Dodd, 1963; (with Ellen R. Hartley) *Osceola—The Unconquered Indian,* Hawthorn, 1973; (with Ellen R. Hartley) *The Alligator: King of the Wilderness* (juvenile), Nelson, 1977. More than nine hundred articles published independently, or in collaboration with wife, for *Redbook, Good Housekeeping, Reader's Digest, Saturday Evening Post, True, Saga, Popular Mechanics, Cavalier, Science Digest, Kiwanis, Friends,* and other magazines. Author of fifteen radio scripts, 1943-44.

WORK IN PROGRESS: Several books independently or in collaboration with Ellen Hartley.

SIDELIGHTS: "All of my books, including those written in collaboration with Ellen R. Hartley, have had some basis either in personal experience or as a result of one of our magazine articles. For example, I spent college vacations working as a steeplejack—a risk worker who repairs church steeples, high water towers, flag poles, smoke stacks, etc. The top rigger (head steeplejack) in my gang used to say, 'We do any job other workers are scared to do.' I first capitalized on this experience by writing a steeplejack story for *Esquire* while still in college. And many years later I based the novel *The Cruel Tower* on episodes in the lives of steeplejacks. This book later became a paperback and a motion picture.

"Ellen Hartley and I wrote an article for the old *Coronet* magazine on an Episcopal deaconess who served the Mikasuki Seminole Indians of Florida as a missionary. While preparing the article, we found that Dss. Harriet M. Bedell had also been an adventurous missionary in early Oklahoma, and in Alaska above the Arctic Circle.

"An editor at Dodd, Mead read our *Coronet* article and phoned to ask if we thought an interesting biography could be written about the aged woman. We certainly did. The result was *A Woman Set Apart.* This book was later published in German under the title: *Eine Tapfere Frau.*

"The book on alligators, *King of the Wilderness,* started with a magazine article in one of the science magazines. At the time, alligator poaching was widespread in the Florida Everglades and I volunteered to accompany a game warden on a night patrol to catch poachers. It was a bitterly cold night. (Florida can be surprisingly cold in winter.) To add to the discomfort, we covered about 125 miles of wilderness in an airboat with lights turned off. An airboat is propelled by an airplane propeller and can even skim over a few inches of water at high speeds. I imagine our average speed was about 55 mph. We arrested no poachers, but I collected good article material and the idea of a book on alligators.

"Ellen Hartley and I have written all kinds of articles on many subjects. Some have involved an element of danger, others (such as our science articles) have required extensive and demanding research. But I can think of no book, story or article that we've disliked writing.

"Although our book *The Alligator: King of the Wilderness* was planned by the publisher for young readers, we designed it for appeal to adult readers as well. I strongly believe that in almost every instance a general book should appeal to readers of all ages. I'm sure that Stevenson didn't write *Treasure Island* while telling himself, 'This is for readers between the ages of twelve and fourteen.' He wrote an excellent story a ninety-year-old may also enjoy.

"Magazine articles, however, must be tailored to the interests of the magazine's specific audience. An article idea for *Good Housekeeping* would probably be unacceptable in *Playboy*, and vice versa.

"Writing is a profession, just as medicine and law are professions. I have no use for the silly people who think they can write because Aunt Mary says their letters are wonderful. The writer must go through a lengthy learning process before he becomes a competent professional. He must do most of the learning by himself, and there are no shortcuts. A successful beginner may be fortunate enough to sell a book or a magazine piece, but it's usually his last unless he begins to learn the skills of writing.

"One curious point that laymen rarely understand: a writer is working all of his waking hours. I may take time off to garden, play the piano, jog or read, but I'm considering writing problems most of the time. All of the time, in fact, although I may not even be aware of it. You learn to do this automatically both with the conscious and the subconscious areas of the mind.

"Is there fun to it? Yes, a great deal. When you deal with a wide variety of subjects, you rarely get bored. I would hate to be pigeonholed as a specialist in anything but living."

HOBBIES AND OTHER INTERESTS: Piano, gardening, swimming, mountain-climbing, woodcraft and travel.

FOR MORE INFORMATION SEE: Miami News, February 7, 1962; *Miami Herald,* February 26, 1963; *Publishers Weekly,* February 28, 1977.

HATLO, Jimmy 1898-1963

OBITUARY NOTICE: Born September 1, 1898, in Providence, R.I.; died November 30, 1963. Cartoonist. Creator of the "They'll Do It Every Time" and "Little Iodine" series, Hatlo began his career as a sports and editorial cartoonist for the *Los Angeles Times.* He subsequently spent fifteen years with the Hearst newspaper chain as an editorial cartoonist. Hatlo's works were syndicated in the United States and abroad. In 1949 "Little Iodine" became a motion picture under the direction of Mary Pickford and Buddy Rogers. *For More Information See: Who Was Who in America,* Volume IV, Marquis, 1968; *The World Encyclopedia of Comics,* Volume I, Chelsea House, 1976. *Obituaries: New York Times,* December 2, 1963; *Time,* December 13, 1963; *Newsweek,* December 16, 1963; *Contemporary Authors,* Volume 93-96, Gale, 1980.

WALTER WILLIAM HERBERT

(From *Eskimos* by Wally Herbert. Painting by the author.)

HERBERT, Walter William 1934-
(Wally Herbert)

PERSONAL: Born October 24, 1934, in York, England; son of Walter William (in armed services) and Helen (Manton) Herbert; married Marie Rita McGaughey (a writer), December 24, 1969; children: Kari Elizabeth, Pascale. *Education:* Educated in Lichfield, Staffordshire, England. *Address:* c/o Royal Geographical Society, 1 Kensington Gore, London SW7, England. *Agent:* Julian Bach Literary Agency Inc., 3 East 48th St., New York, N.Y. 10017; and George Greenfield, John Farquharson Ltd., Bell House, Bell Yard, London WC2A 2JR, England.

CAREER: Polar explorer and writer. Falkland Islands Dependencies Survey, Hope Bay Antarctica, surveyor, 1955-58; member of expedition to Lapland and Spitzbergen, 1960; surveyor with New Zealand Antarctic Expedition, mapped 41,000 sq. miles of previously unexplored territory and retraced the route of Roald Amundsen on the 50th anniversary of his attainment of the South Pole, 1960-62; planned and prepared for trans-Arctic expedition, 1964-66; led expedition to northwest Greenland, testing equipment and techniques for the trans-Arctic expedition, 1966-67; led British trans-Arctic expedition which made the 3,800 mile first surface crossing of the Arctic Ocean from Alaska, via the North Pole, to Spitzbergen, 1968-69; led expedition to northwest Greenland to make film about Polar Eskimos, 1971-73; led expedition to Lapland, 1975; planned and prepared for expedition to Greenland, 1976; led expedition making first attempt at circumnavigation of Greenland by dog sledge and skin boat, 1977-81. *Military service:* British Army, Royal Engineers, 1952-55. *Member:* World Expeditionary Association (honorary joint president), Royal Geographical Society (fellow), British Schools Exploring Society (honorary member), Lansdowne Club, Explorers Club of New York (fellow). *Awards, honors:* Polar Medal from Queen Elizabeth, 1962, for explorations in Antarctica; Livingstone Gold Medal of Royal Scottish Geographical Society, 1969, for polar explorations; bar to Polar Medal, 1969, for first surface crossing of Arctic Ocean; Founder's Gold Medal of Royal Geographical Society, 1970, for outstanding contributions to Arctic and Antarctic exploration and survey; German State Literary prize, 1977, for *Eskimos.* A range of mountains and a plateau in the Antarctic and a mountain in the Arctic are named for Herbert.

WRITINGS: A World of Man, Eyre & Spottiswoode, 1968, Putnam, 1969; *Across the Top of the World,* Longmans,

Green, 1969; (contributor) W. Noyce and I. McMorren, editors, *World Atlas of Mountaineering*, Nelson, 1969; *The Last Great Journey on Earth*, Putnam, 1971; *Polar Deserts*, F. Watts, 1971; *Eskimos*, F. Watts, 1976; (contributor) A. Ballantine and J. Blashford-Snell, editors, *Expeditions the Experts Way*, Faber, 1977; *North Pole*, Sackett & Marshall, 1978; (contributor) *The Bell House Book*, Hodder & Stoughton, 1978; *The First Circumnavigation of Greenland*, Doubleday, 1981; *The Cry of the Hunter*, Weidenfeld, 1981; *The Polar Eskimo*, Time-Life Books, 1981; *King Dog* (novel), Collins, 1982.

Contributor of articles to *Geographical Magazine* and *Geographical Journal*.

SIDELIGHTS: Herbert felt he was born sixty or seventy years too late to make his fortune as a polar writer. In *A World of Men* Herbert said that he wrote, not with the purpose of answering questions, but "because the feeling needs expression and adventure needs its advocate."

British Prime Minister Harold Wilson called Herbert's North Pole journey "a feat of endurance and courage which ranks with any in polar history." Herbert's patron, Prince Philip, described the journey as ranking "among the greatest triumphs of human skill and endurance." And yet, Herbert noted that while the National Geographic Society has recognized his Arctic crossing as a truly "epic" trek, none of his polar journeys have been featured or even referred to in the text of their magazine on the grounds that his journeys are "too long." In his words: "Since each of my journeys is longer than the last it would seem that I have made my choice between instant fame and a place in history as a pioneer, and have settled for the latter."

FOR MORE INFORMATION SEE: Times Literary Supplement, January 8, 1970.

GRETE JANUS HERTZ

HERTZ, Grete Janus 1915-
(Grete Janus)

PERSONAL: Born November 21, 1915, in Copenmagen, Denmark; daughter of Janus Nielsen (a schoolmaster) and Karla (Pedersen) Nielsen; married Mogens Hertz (an artist), August 8, 1944; children: Ole, Birgitte. *Education:* Rysensteen Gymnasium, 1934, Zahles Seminarium, teacher's certificate, 1937; University of Copenhagen, M.A. in psychology, 1945. *Home:* 3760 Gudhjem, Denmark, and Strandboulevarden 94, Copenhagen, Denmark.

CAREER: Teacher at various schools in Copenhagen, 1937-46; school psychologist in Copenhagen, 1939-46; translator, 1955—; free-lance writer, 1968—. *Awards, honors:* Critici in Erba Prize from Bologna Children's Book Fair, 1975, for *Das Gelbe Haus*.

WRITINGS—For children: *Bamse* (illustrated by husband, Mogens Hertz), H. Hirschsprung, 1946, second edition, Carlsen Verlag, 1968, published as *Teddy*, Lothrop, 1964; *Tit-tit lille far*, Gads Forlag, 1962, translation by Margaret Young Gracza published as *Hi, Daddy, Here I Am*, Lerner, 1964; *Fartars Halmhatt*, 1962, translation by Marianne Helweg published as *Grandfather's Straw Hat* (edited by Kay Ware and Lucille Sutherland), McGraw, 1964; *Da Lena og Lisa havde rode hunde*, 1964, translation by Kay Ware and Lucille Sutherland published as *When Lena and Lisa had Measles*, McGraw, 1964; *Das Gelbe Haus* (title means "The Yellow House"), Carlsen Verlag, 1975.

Not in English: (Under name Grete Janus; illustrated by husband, Mogens Hertz) *Da Ole gik til begeren* (title means "When Ole Went to the Bakers"), Gyldendal, 1966; (editor) *Dig og mig og vi to (Boernerim og sange)* (title means "Mother Goose Rhymes from Denmark [Nursery Rhymes]"), Illustrationsforlaget, 1971; *Ide bog for rare voksne* (title means "Handbook for Adults Who Wish to Entertain Small Children"), Wöldike, 1980; *Strik dyr og ting at bar ret* (title means "A Knitting Book for Beginners"), Borgen, 1980; *Kasper og hans venner* (title means "Kasper's Friends: Five Titles about Kindergarten Children"), Delta, 1980. Contributor of several hundred psychology articles in weekly magazines and newspapers.

SIDELIGHTS: "I like to write and have been doing so since I was sixteen years old. My husband and I live on Bornholm, a small island in the Baltic Sea near Sweden, but we also have a flat in Copenhagen. From my daughter, who is a kindergarten teacher, and my son's two children, I still get a lot of inspiration for books and articles."

Hertz has been a free-lance journalist since she was sixteen. Her books have been translated into German, Swedish, Japanese, French, Finnish, Norwegian, and English.

And he who gives a child a treat
Makes joy-bells ring in Heaven's street,
And he who gives a child a home,
Builds palaces in Kingdom come.

—John Masefield

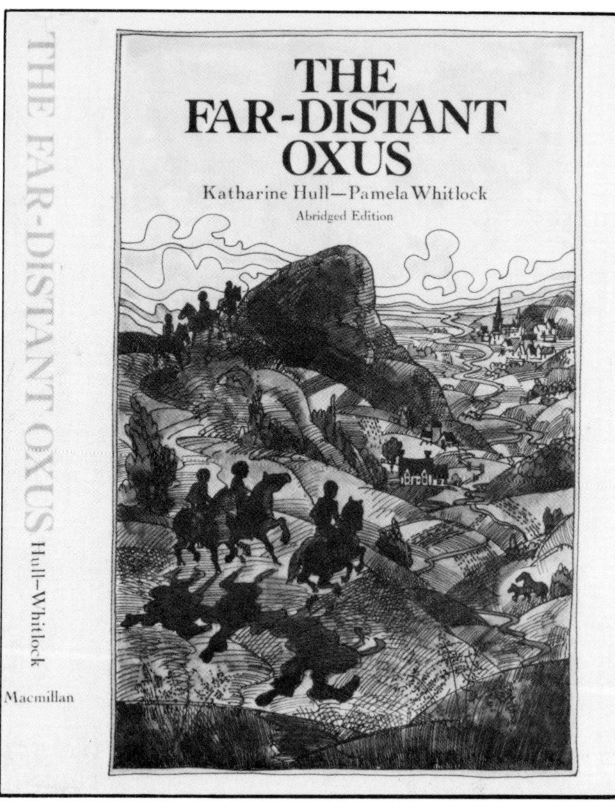

(From *The Far-Distant Oxus* by Katharine Hull and Pamela Whitlock. Jacket illustrated by Carl W. Stuecklen.)

HULL, Katharine 1921-1977

PERSONAL: Born July 18, 1921; died November 13, 1977, in London, England; daughter of Sir Hubert Hull; married Paul Buxton (a British diplomat); children: Charles, Mary, Tracy. *Education:* Educated at St. Mary's Convent, Ascot, England, and Lady Margaret Hall, Oxford University, England.

CAREER: Served in the Royal Air Force during World War II, became a flight lieutenant.

WRITINGS: (With Pamela Whitlock) *The Far-Distant Oxus* (juvenile; illustrated by Pamela Whitlock), J. Cape, 1937, Macmillan, 1938, abridged edition with foreword by Arthur Ransome, Macmillan, 1969; *Escape to Persia* (illustrated by Pamela Whitlock), J. Cape, 1938, Macmillan, 1939; *Oxus in Summer* (illustrated by Pamela Whitlock), J. Cape, 1939, published in America with illustrations by Charles E. Pont, Macmillan, 1940; *Crowns* (illustrated by Pamela Whitlock), J. Cape, 1947.

How beautiful is youth! how bright it gleams
With its illusions, aspirations, dreams!
Book of Beginnings, Story without End,
Each maid a heroine, and each man a friend!

—Henry Wadsworth Longfellow

HYNDMAN, Jane Andrews 1912-1978 (Lee Wyndham)

OBITUARY NOTICE—See sketch in *SATA* Volume 1: Born December 16, 1912, in Russia; died March 18, 1978, in Morristown, N.J. Journalist, lecturer, and author of about thirty books, best known for her juvenile book, *Candy Stripers.* Hyndman, probably better known by her pseudonym Lee Wyndham, was the author of a syndicated children's book column "The Junior Book Shelf." She was also children's book editor for the *Morristown Daily Record* and the *Philadelphia Inquirer.* For thirteen years, Hyndman lectured on writing for children and teenagers at New York University's Washington Square Writing Center. A widely-used textbook resulted from her teaching, *Writing for Children and Teenagers.* She once stated, "Writing for young people is a great responsibility. An author can help mold character and even influence a young person's choice of and training for a career." An illustration of this is her book *Candy Stripers,* which has sold close to one million copies and which has inspired numerous teenage girls to become hospital volunteers. A love of ballet spurred Hyndman to write a number of books with dance as their setting. The most popular of these are the "Susie" series of books. Hyndman worked closely with the Institute of Children's Literature, and was on the board of directors of the Society of Children's Book Writers. *For More Information See: Contemporary Authors,* Volume 7-8, revised, Gale, 1969; *Authors of Books for Young People,* 2nd edition, Scarecrow, 1971; *Who's Who in the East,* 14th edition, Marquis, 1973; *The Writers Directory, 1976-78,* St. Martin's, 1976. *Obituaries: Publishers Weekly,* April 10, 1978; *Contemporary Authors,* Volume 89-92, Gale, 1980.

JOHNSON, D(ana) William 1945-

PERSONAL: Born May 30, 1945, in Helena, Mont.; son of Elwood Carl and H. Lucille (Thorsen) Johnson. *Education:* Montana State University, B.A., 1971. *Politics:* "TRUTH—practically the answer to everything." *Religion:* "TRUTH—practically the answer to everything." *Home:* 374 Fore St., Portland, Maine 04112.

D. WILLIAM JOHNSON

As Lewis watched the sun rise through blustery clouds, the day seemed a bleak one. The trees stood bent in the wind, and the snow was so deep that his house was hidden, as lost as his muffler. ■ (From *The Willow Flute: A North Country Tale* by D. William Johnson. Illustrated by the author.)

CAREER: Commercial illustrator, animation and graphic designer, and painter, 1971—. Design consultant. *Awards, honors:* Nomination for Caldecott Medal, from American Library Association, 1975, for *The Willow Flute.*

WRITINGS—Self-illustrated children's books: *The Willow Flute: A North Country Tale,* Little, Brown, 1975; (adapter) *Jack and the Beanstalk,* Little, Brown, 1976; *The Tiger and the Rabbit,* Houghton, 1977. Creator of commercial brochures, television advertisements, and animations.

WORK IN PROGRESS: "I am immersed in creating stained glass pieces and windows—designing for the Phoenix Studio in Portland, as well as design and construction of private commission work. It is the *most* absorbing media I've worked within and wonderfully exciting work."

SIDELIGHTS: "I have lived a year each in Italy and England. I also spent eight summers on a remote fire station tower in Montana—four months of isolation at a stretch gets you in touch with yourself. Now I am in Portland, Maine—at last, somewhere perfect. I am no longer a lone traveler at this point, thank God, but my family dates back to the year 104 A.D.—to Bronze Age chieftain King O'Lorcaine of Ireland. Nice genes.

"I am not a good member of clubby things. I try to be a good member of the human race . . . not always easy. If I ever get there, I'll join a club, maybe the Intergalactic Federation. But I am active in environmental concerns—anti-nuclear power and pro-everything else—a dyed-in-the-wool Gemini."

KALB, Jonah 1926-

PERSONAL: Born September 17, 1926, in New York, N.Y.; son of Herman and Helen (Busch) Kalb; married Mary Jeannie Astier, July 23, 1950; children: Laura Margaret, Eugene Herman. *Education:* Oberlin College, B.A., 1949. *Home:* 17 North St., Lexington, Mass. 02173. *Office:* Witan Corp., 27 Montvale Ave., Woburn, Mass. 01801.

CAREER: Kalb & Schneider, Inc. (advertising agency), Boston, Mass., president, 1963-70; Sensitivity Games, Inc., Boston, Mass., chairman, 1970-73; Witan Corp. (consulting firm), Woburn, Mass., president, 1973-77; Digital Equipment Corporation, Maynard, Mass., corporate director of advertising, 1977—. Vice-president of Longwood Management, 1973-74; member of board of directors of Lythorn Corp., 1965-70, and Visual Learning Corp., 1968-70. *Military service:* U.S. Army, 1952-54.

WRITINGS—For young people: (With David S. Viscott, M.D.) *Language of Sensitivity,* six volumes, Peter H. Wyden, 1973; (with David Viscott, M.D.) *What Every Kid Should Know,* twelve volumes, American Greetings, 1974, revised edition (includes six of the earlier volumes), Houghton, 1976; *How to Play Baseball Better Than You Did Last Year,* Macmillan, 1974; *The Kids' Candidate* (fiction), Houghton, 1975; *The Easy Baseball Book,* Houghton, 1976; *The Goof That Won the Pennant* (fiction), Houghton, 1976; *The Easy Hockey Book,* Houghton, 1977.

Roger's uniform was too big. Betcha's was too tight. Phantom's was so big that the pants reached almost to his ankles. ■ (From *The Goof That Won the Pennant* by Jonah Kalb. Illustrated by Sandy Kossin.)

SIDELIGHTS: "Boys. The subject is boys. Not that I dislike girls. I don't. I married one. Have another as a daughter. But most authors of children's books are women. Most editors are women. Most librarians who buy most children's books are women. Most teachers who teach them are women. I'm not blaming anyone. It's just the way things are. But the effect is—boys don't read.

"I try to write mostly for boys. And among the eight to thirteen-year-olds, sports books, I believe, are most likely to attract them. So I write mostly sports books. Mostly baseball, in fact.

"I grew up in the big city—New York. I was a pretty smart kid, but I had this little, minor problem. I couldn't speak. That is, I stuttered. And a lot of people laughed. and I was terribly embarrassed. And words became very, very important to me. And mostly, I wouldn't speak, in anticipation of that embarrassment, and pain, and laughter.

"I found, in sports, my refuge. Nobody ever laughed when I hit. And, in fact, I rarely stuttered when playing ball, a phenomenon yet to be satisfactorily explained. I never stuttered when I sang, either, but I couldn't handle the pitch.

"So I kept my mouth shut and swung, and found, in baseball, the anchor of my early days. And by the time real pitchers knew how to throw curves, which I could not hit, I was okay in the speech department. I never did learn how to sing, though.

"As an adult, I wandered into baseball coaching, looking for stutterers who needed anchors. I didn't find too many—one or two—but I found a lot of non-readers. Five kids on my first little league team were 'reluctant' readers, to put it most politely. I searched. I asked. I found, not without some justification, that they said they couldn't find any books which told them anything they wanted to know. So I wrote my first real book. How to play baseball better. They wanted to know that.

"And then some lady reviewer in the *New York Times* said the book was no good because it was a how-to book, and how-to books and kids don't mix. Bet you anything she was a lady author herself, writing books about pretty stones or poetry or novels about deeply sensitive girls whose grandmothers had just died. *She* knew what kids wanted. But my book sold 40,000 copies!

"Absolute best training for children's authors writing for middle-aged juveniles (nine to thirteen) is the advertising profession. It pays well, and teaches the writer to get into the mind of a twelve-year-old. I love advertising. It's really hard to keep things simple. I love baseball. Probably for the same reason. It's a very complicated game that boils down to hitting a small white pellet with a medium size piece of wood. Hate writing. Love having written (stolen from Dorothy Parker). And yes, I love girls, too."

Fairy land,
Where all the children dine at five,
And all the playthings come alive.
—Robert Louis Stevenson

(From *The Dangers of Noise* by Lucy Kavaler. Illustrated by Richard Cuffari.)

KAVALER, Lucy 1930-

PERSONAL: Born August 29, 1930, in New York, N.Y.; daughter of L. I. (a banker) and Helen (Vishniac) Estrin; married Arthur R. Kavaler (a publisher), November 9, 1949; children: Roger, Andrea. *Education:* Oberlin College, B.A. (magna cum laude), 1949. *Residence:* New York, N.Y. *Agent:* Harold Ober Associates, 40 East 49th St., New York, N.Y. 10017.

CAREER: P. W. Communications, New York, N.Y., executive editor of medical publication, 1975—; author. *Member:* P.E.N., American Center (member of executive board, 1972-77), Society of Magazine Writers (member of executive council, 1971-72), National Association of Science Writers, Authors Guild. *Awards, honors:* Advanced science writing fellowship from Columbia University Graduate School of Journalism, 1969-70.

WRITINGS: The Private World of High Society, McKay, 1960; *Mushrooms, Molds, and Miracles,* John Day, 1965; *Freezing Point* (ALA Notable Book), John Day, 1970; *Noise: The New Menace,* John Day, 1975.

Juveniles: *The Wonders of Algae* (ALA Notable Book), John Day, 1961; *The Artificial World Around Us,* John Day, 1963; *The Wonders of Fungi,* John Day, 1964; *The Astors, an American Legend,* Dodd, 1966; *Dangerous Air,* John Day, 1967; *Cold Against Disease,* John Day, 1971; *Life Battles Cold,* John Day, 1973; *The Dangers of Noise,* Crowell, 1978. Contributor of articles to magazines including *Redbook, Natural History, Woman's Day, Smithsonian, McCall's,* and *Family Circle.*

SIDELIGHTS: "My career as a published author began when I was six years old, and my mother sent a poem of mine on snowflakes to a children's magazine. I was paid one dollar, which I spent that very day in Woolworth's. There was never any doubt in my mind thereafter that I was going to be a writer.

"My first professional writing was romantic fiction for popular magazines, and I also began writing features for the Sunday magazine section of a large New York City newspaper. I did a series of articles on dancing schools, debutantes, and society. A book publisher called and asked if I could turn this into a book. As book writing had always been my goal, I quickly agreed.

"I kept writing newspaper features and was given an assignment to write an article on how perfume is made. I made an appointment with a perfume manufacturer, but when I got there, he kept me waiting for nearly an hour. But during that hour something happened that changed the course of my career. I picked up a newsletter lying on the table in the waiting room and it had an article about algae, the one-celled plant. I was fascinated by the possibilities of this little-known topic, and kept thinking about it all the time I was asking questions about perfume.

"When I went home, I realized that I had my subject for my first book for young readers. It was the start—leading me

LUCY KAVALER

into both juvenile and adult books on subjects in the natural sciences."

Kavaler's works are included in the Kerlan Collection at the University of Minnesota.

FOR MORE INFORMATION SEE: Horn Book, June, 1964, August, 1976.

KEATING, Lawrence A. 1903-1966 (John Keith Bassett, H. C. Thomas)

PERSONAL: Born January 21, 1903, in Chicago, Ill.; died June 16, 1966; son of Thomas F. and Eliza F. Keating; married Ethel Milzer, 1934. *Education:* Marquette University, Ph.B. in journalism, 1926. *Home:* 2508 North Stowell Ave., Milwaukee, Wis.

CAREER: Free-lance writer, 1932-66. Assistant director of public information, American Red Cross, 1942-45; instructor in writing courses at Northwestern University, 1941-60, and later at Marquette University and University of Wisconsin. *Member:* Authors League, Sigma Delta Chi, Milwaukee Fictioneers (former president), City Club of Milwaukee (former vice-president and director).

WRITINGS: Riding the Range, Clode, 1932; *Riders of the Valley Range,* Clode, 1932; *Peace River Justice,* Clode, 1932; *Sunset Range,* Clode, 1933; *The Deputy of San Riano,* Clode, 1933; *Silver River Ranch,* Clode, 1934; *Fleming's Folly,* Clode, 1934; *Comrades of Kiowa Valley,* Clode, 1936; *The Bar K,* Phoenix, 1939; *Men in Aprons,* Mills, 1944; *The Highview Mystery,* Messner, 1944; *Jerry Dowd,* 1955; *False Start,* Westminster, 1955; *Kid Brother,* Westminster, 1956; *Freshman Backstop,* Westminster, 1957; *Junior Miler* (Junior Literary Guild selection), Westminster, 1958; *Senior Challenge,* Westminster, 1959; *Runner-Up* (Junior Literary Guild selection), Westminster, 1961; (with Jerry J. Joswick) *Combat Cameraman,* Chilton, 1961; *Wrong-Way Neelen* (Junior Literary Guild selection), Westminster, 1963; *Ace Rebounder,* Westminster, 1964; *Fleet Admiral: The Story of William F. Halsey,* Westminster, 1965; *The Comeback Year,* Westminster, 1966.

Under pseudonym John Keith Bassett: *Trailers of the Sage,* Greenberg, 1935.

Under pseudonym H. C. Thomas: *Comrades of the Colt,* Greenberg, 1936; *The Last Kenton,* Phoenix, 1939; *A Boy Sailor with John Paul Jones,* Whitman Publishing, 1946; *A Boy Fighter with Andrew Jackson,* Whitman Publishing, 1947.

HOBBIES AND OTHER INTERESTS: Music and horseback riding.

Child! do not throw this book about;
Refrain from the unholy pleasure
Of cutting all the pictures out!
Preserve it as your chiefest treasure.

—Hilaire Belloc

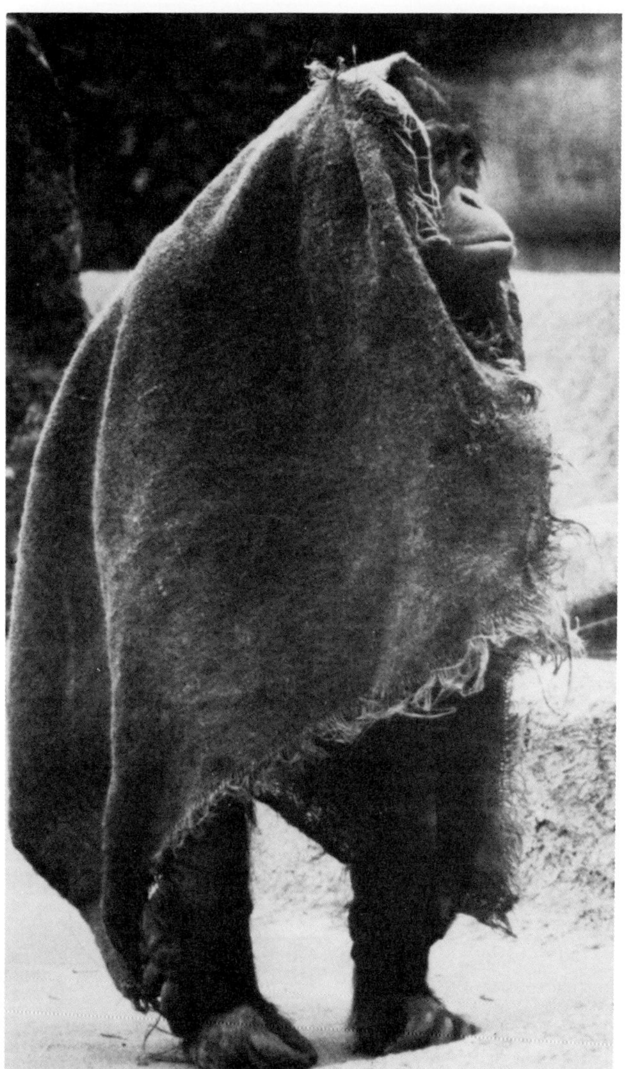

An orangutan will use any available material, here a piece of burlap, to cover its head. ■ (From *Watching the Wild Apes* by Bettyann Kevles. Photograph by Miriam Austerman.)

KEVLES, Bettyann 1938-

PERSONAL: Born August 20, 1938, in New York, N.Y.; daughter of David Marshal (a lawyer) and Sondra (a theatrical producer; maiden name, Alosoroff) Holtzmann; married Daniel Jerome Kevles (a historian), May 18, 1961; children: Beth, Jonathan. *Education:* Vassar College, B.A., 1959; Columbia University, M.A., 1961. *Home:* 575 La Loma Rd., Pasadena, Calif. 91105. *Agent:* Larry Sternig Literary Agency, 742 Robertson St., Milwaukee, Wis. 53213.

CAREER: Sunbeam, Northridge, Calif., editor and writer, 1967-69; Westridge School, Pasadena, Calif., instructor in history, 1970-76. *Awards, honors:* Best older juvenile award from New York Academy of Science, 1977, and best nonfiction *Boston Globe-Horn Book* award, 1978, for *Watching the Wild Apes.*

BETTYANN KEVLES

WRITINGS: Watching the Wild Apes: The Primate Studies of Goodall, Fossey, and Galdikas, Dutton, 1976; *Listening In,* Scholastic Magazine Press, 1979; *Thinking Gorillas,* Dutton, 1980. Science fiction and spy stories represented in anthologies.

WORK IN PROGRESS: The Abduction of Esther Lyons, an historical reconstruction.

SIDELIGHTS: "Until completing the *Wild Apes,* most of my writing has been fictional, and a lot of it was science fiction, mostly short stories. My research has proven to me that finding out what is really happening is as exciting as fantasy, and has fed my imagination so that I have more fiction planned.

"My other projects at the moment include the reconstruction of a fascinating abduction and trial in Cardiff, Wales, that happened a hundred and ten years ago. The chase is almost as thrilling as the writing, and makes life varied as well as fulfilling. Other projects include several science-fiction novels for young adults."

FOR MORE INFORMATION SEE: Horn Book, June, 1977, October, 1977.

There was an Old Man with a beard,
Who said, 'It is just as I feared!—
Two Owls and a Hen,
Four Larks and a Wren,
Have all built their nests in my beard!'

—Edward Lear

KEY, Alexander (Hill) 1904-1979

OBITUARY NOTICE—See sketch in *SATA* Volume 8: Born September 21, 1904, in La Plata, Md.; died July 25, 1979, in Eufaula, Ala. Illustrator, free-lance writer, and author. Key illustrated his first book at the age of nineteen while still a student, and later taught art at the Studio School of Art in Chicago. He was most noted for his children's books, and indeed came to feel that "the young are the only ones worth writing for." One of his better-known books, *Escape to Witch Mountain,* became a Walt Disney movie in 1975. Several of Key's books were chosen as Junior Literary Guild selections, including *The Golden Enemy. The Forgotten Door* was honored with various awards, among them the Lewis Carroll Shelf Award for 1972. His last book, *The Case of the Vanishing Boy,* was published posthumously. *For More Information See: Contemporary Authors,* Volume 5-6, revised, Gale, 1969; *Authors of Books for Young People,* 2nd edition, Scarecrow, 1971; *The Writers Directory, 1980-82,* St. Martin's, 1979. *Obituaries: Publishers Weekly,* August 20, 1979; *School Library Journal,* November, 1979; *Contemporary Authors,* Volume 89-92, Gale, 1980.

KING, Marian

PERSONAL: Born in Washington, D.C.; daughter of Joseph and Jeannette (Michel) King. *Education:* Attended Miss Madeira's School; studied abroad. *Home:* 4501 Connecticut Ave., Washington, D.C. 20008.

CAREER: Author, 1928—. Served with British Supply Missions, Washington, D.C., 1940-45. Was children's book editor for the *National Observer.* Lecturer throughout country. *Member:* Authors Guild, Children's Book Guild (Washington, D.C.), American Women's Newspaper Club, Marquis Biographical Library Society (advisory member), and many religious, literary, and art circles.

WRITINGS: A.B.C. Game Book, Morrow, 1928; *The Mirror of Youth,* Longmans, Green, 1929; *Kees* (Junior Literary Guild selection), Harper, 1930; *The Story of Athletics,* Harper, 1931; *The Dutch Mother Goose,* Donahue, 1931; *Amon, A Lad of Palestine,* Houghton, 1932; *Skeeta,* Whitman, 1933; *The Golden Cathead,* Whitman, 1933; *Kees and Kleintje* (Junior Literary Guild selection), Whitman, 1934; *A Boy of Poland,* Whitman, 1935; *Sean and Sheela,* Whitman, 1937; *It Happened in England,* Whitman, 1939; *Piccolino,* Whitman, 1939.

Elizabeth: The Tudor Princess, Lippincott, 1940; *Young King David,* Lippincott, 1948; *The Coat of Many Colors,* Lippincott, 1950; *Life of Christ,* National Gallery of Art, 1953; *Young Mary Stuart, Queen of Scots,* Lippincott, 1954; *Portraits of Children in the National Gallery of Art,* National Gallery of Art, 1954-55; *A Gallery of Children,* Lippincott, 1955, Acropolis, 1967; *Portrait of Jesus,* Lippincott, 1957; *A Gallery of Mothers and Their Children,* Lippincott, 1958.

What Would You Do?, Robert B. Luce, 1962; *Mary Baker Eddy: Child of Promise,* Prentice-Hall, 1968; *Star of Bethlehem,* Harvey, 1968; *The Ageless Story of Jesus,* Acropolis, 1970; *Micco & Piccolino,* Harvey House, 1972; (with others) *Gallery of Famous Artists,* Highlights, 1974; *Adventures in Art,* Harry N. Abrams, 1978. Contributor of articles, stories, and book reviews to *Christian Science Monitor, Playmate, Washington Post and Times Herald, Saturday Review, High-*

lights, Boys' Life, Junior Red Cross Magazine, and to church periodicals.

ADAPTATIONS: "A Gallery of Children," narrated by Joan Kennedy, was produced for WETA public television and won two Emmies; "Adventures in Art," narrated by Julie Harris, was produced for WETA public television, 1980.

SIDELIGHTS: "I am a native of Washington, D.C. I attended Miss Madeira's School and later studied abroad. Much of my career as a writer and lecturer has been devoted to bringing out the art, beauty, and power of spiritual worth as portrayed by the great Biblical characters and by great painters. The goal of many of my books has been to illumine the religious heritage of our nation. I have written historical and religious biographies, short novels created from real life situations, short stories, poetry, art books and art pieces for magazines. All of these, although written for young people and children, have been read and enjoyed by adults as well.

"As far back as I can remember, I was surrounded by books. Under my parents' guidance, they were excellently chosen. Even at that time historical biography, the Bible, and the classic poets were my favorites. When I was about ten years old I learned that the information in a series of volumes I was reading on foreign countries was not factually accurate. I resolved at that time that if I ever wrote a story or book every bit of the background, including customs and history, would be factually authentic.

"When I began to write seriously and to gather material for my early story books, I went to Europe and travelled through the countries I had chosen to write about. I lived with the people, absorbing their customs, characteristics and culture. For my historical and religious biographies, I spent many months searching every available source for authentic background, researching material, talking with authors, historians, and scholars. This pattern has been followed in all my historical and religious books. Even in the dialogue no fictitious conversations have been used. I used only original conversations found in documents, state papers, correspondence, and the spoken word in the Bible. When each manuscript was completed I sent it to the best known authority on the subject to have his verification and imprint of authenticity. Even in my fictionalized stories I used authentic backgrounds based on the manners, customs, music, arts and history of the countries in which I set my stories. In any folklore used pertaining to the specific country involved, it was authentically translated and approved and verified by scholars in the field. A most gratifying part of my research was the wonderful assistance, interest, willing and complete cooperation I received from my colleagues and all other persons with whom I worked.

"Although I find writing an exacting task, it is also a gratifying one. I have endeavored in my writings to convey the spiritual, cultural and artistic good and beautiful ideals to my readers.

"In all I have written twenty-nine books. Two of these appeared in portfolio form for the National Gallery of Art at their request. Each experience opens up many new avenues in the field of the arts and humanitarian services, and the contacts I make often bring lasting friendships.

"In addition to writing books, I have contributed to numerous publications. I have lectured throughout the country. I still accept speaking engagements from various faiths and denominations as well as from other interested organizations.

MARIAN KING

My only desire is to bring to my audience the knowledge, the humanitarian, religious and cultural backgrounds I have been privileged to share. I never write my speeches. I may have a note or two and I often read from my books to cite various points I am making. The material flows from a feeling of response I get from the audience. I generally open my talks with the reading from Proverbs, Chapter 16, Verses 1 and 3—'The preparations of the heart in man, and the answer of the tongue, is from the LORD.'—'Commit thy works unto the LORD and thy thoughts shall be established.' It is also my practice to have a question-and-answer period after the lectures.

"I have served as volunteer with the Hospitality Information Service at Meridian House in Washington, D.C., which serves only diplomats and their families and which is sponsored by the wives of members of the President's Cabinet. I have had many citations from various charitable and religious organizations as a result of the contributions of my books and other material to such organizations which have assisted them in their endeavors to help those in need. However, my best reward is that my books, lectures, and personal contacts help others. Any sense of spiritual good that I can convey to them to enrich their well-being is the pinnacle of my satisfaction and gratification.

"From early childhood I was always inspired by the spiritual qualities expressed by my parents. I have sought to share these qualities with others through my writings and lectures.

All that I may have accomplished I most humbly and gratefully owe to God to whom I have always turned for guidance.

"I still make my home in the nation's capital, where my leisure time activities are many and varied, including visits to art galleries and museums, the theatre, opera, concerts and ballets. I enjoy swimming and walking and, although I no longer participate, I enjoy tennis tournaments and horse shows."

FOR MORE INFORMATION SEE: Horn Book, January-December, 1948; *Washington Post Magazine,* March 4, 1979.

KOOB, Theodora (Johanna Foth) 1918-

PERSONAL: Born September 16, 1918, in Jersey City, N.J.; daughter of George F. and Theodora K. (Schmidt) Foth; married Robert A. Koob (U.S. Army officer), June 24, 1942 (divorced, 1973); children: George, Joseph, Stephen, Katherine. *Education:* New York University, B.S., 1941, M.A., 1945, Ph.D., 1946; New York College of Music, teacher's certificates in voice and piano. *Politics:* No affiliation. *Religion:* Roman Catholic. *Address:* Box 307, Scotland, Pa. 17254.

CAREER: School teacher at various times, all classes from kindergarten through college-level English, in New Jersey, New York, Okinawa, and France; Shippensburg State College, Shippensburg, Pa., professor of English, 1964-80. On Okinawa, established the American Dependent School System, grades 1-12. Also teacher of voice and piano, intermittently, at places where her Army husband was stationed. Active in Boy Scouts and Girl Scouts. Full-time writer, 1980—.

WRITINGS: Johann of the Trembling Hand, Bruce, 1960; *Surgeon's Apprentice,* Lippincott, 1963; *Benjy Brant: Dragooning with the Swamp Fox,* Lippincott, 1965; *The Tacky Little Icicle Shack,* Lippincott, 1966; *The Green Goose,* Lippincott, 1967; *This Side of Victory,* Lippincott, 1967; *Hear a Different Drummer,* Lippincott, 1968; *The Deep Search,* Lippincott, 1971. Contributor to periodicals.

WORK IN PROGRESS: Three children's and young adult books, two revolutionary American novels and an American historical biography.

SIDELIGHTS: Koob speaks French and German; can read Italian, Spanish and Portuguese. "I am translating Heinrich Heine's lyric poetry and am working on biographies and

(From *Benjy Brant: Dragooning with the Swamp Fox* by Theodora Koob. Illustrated by Leonard Vosburgh.)

THEODORA KOOB

resuming work with children's and young adult books. I retired in 1980 and may someday enter the ministry."

HOBBIES AND OTHER INTERESTS: Bridge, cooking, and chess.

FOR MORE INFORMATION SEE: Horn Book, June, 1963, February, 1966.

KRUMGOLD, Joseph (Quincy) 1908-1980

OBITUARY NOTICE—See sketch in *SATA* Volume 1: Born April 9, 1908, in Jersey City, N.J.; died of a stroke, July 10, 1980, in Hope, N.J. Producer, screenwriter, and author. Krumgold wrote scripts and produced motion pictures for several film companies, including Metro-Goldwyn-Mayer (MGM), Paramount, RKO, Columbia, and Republic. He is best known, however, for his highly acclaimed children's books. Krumgold won Newbery Awards from the American Library Association for his books *And Now Miguel* and *Onion John,* becoming the first author ever to receive the award twice. His other works include *Thanks to Murder* and *Sweeney's Adventure. For More Information See: More Junior Authors,* Wilson, 1963; *Famous Modern Storytellers for Young People,* Dodd, 1968; *Contemporary Authors,* Volume 9-12, revised, Gale, 1974; *Encyclopedia of Mystery and Detection,* McGraw, 1976. *Obituaries: New York Times,* July 16, 1980; *Publishers Weekly,* August 1, 1980; *AB Bookman's Weekly,* September 1, 1980; *Contemporary Authors,* Volume 101-104, Gale, 1981.

LAMBERT, Saul 1928-

PERSONAL: Born March 12, 1928, in New York, N.Y.; son of Abraham (a vendor) and Esther (a garment worker; maiden name, Nistel) Lambert; married Emily Whitty, May 27, 1955 (divorced); children: Jonathan Whitty, Katherine Aviva. *Education:* Brooklyn College, B.A., 1949. *Home:* 153 Carter Rd., Princeton, N.J. 08540. *Agent:* Leslie Korda, 34 West 65th St., New York, N.Y.

CAREER: Free-lance illustrator. Worked as an advertising assistant in New York City, 1955-57. *Exhibitions:* Art Directors Club, New York and Chicago; Communication Arts Exhibition; Artists Guild of Chicago; Bolles Gallery, New York; City Center Gallery, New York; annual exhibitions at Society of Illustrators, New York. *Military service:* U.S. Army, corporal, 1951-53. *Awards, honors:* Award of Distinctive Merit, Art Directors Club, New York, 1960, 1961, Chicago, 1963; Award for Excellence, Society of Illustrators, New York, 1961, 1964; Best of Category, Artists Guild, Chicago, 1967; Award of Excellence, American Institute of Graphic Artists, 1967; Award for Excellence, Communication Arts, 1968; twenty-five Certificates of Merit, Society of Illustrators, New York.

WRITINGS—Self-illustrated: *Mrs. Poggi's Holiday,* Random House, 1969.

Illustrator: Charles Perrault, *Fairy Tales,* Macmillan, 1963; James P. Wood, *The Lantern Bearer: A Life of Robert Louis Stevenson,* Pantheon, 1965; Robert Arthur, *Mystery and More Mystery,* Random House, 1966; Robert Arthur, editor, *Spies and More Spies,* Random House, 1967; Emily Lambert, *The Man Who Drew Cats,* Harper, 1967; Robert Arthur, *Thrillers and More Thrillers,* Random House, 1968; *The Usurping Ghost,* Pantheon, 1969; Leon Garfield, *The Restless Ghost: Three Stories,* Pantheon, 1969; *Haiku,* Houghton, 1971; *Diary of a Madman,* Houghton, 1971; Joyce Harrington, *Five Profiles,* Houghton, 1971; Anne Frank, *The Diary of Anne Frank,* Houghton, 1972; *Miss Mandlebaum Came Back,* Houghton, 1972; Paula Fox, *Portrait of Ivan* (ALA Notable Book), Bradbury, 1969; Suzanne Ryer, *Transcripts H4,* Houghton, 1973; Linda Mancini, *Songs IV,* Houghton, 1973; Florence Fisher, *Search for Anna Fisher,* Reader's Digest, 1973; *Lady in Black of Boston Harbor,* Houghton, 1974; Thomas Rockwell, *Tin Cans,* Bradbury, 1975. Also illustrated for *Macmillan Reading Program,* "The Magic Word" series, called *Fourth Reader* by Marian Gartler, et. al., and *Gartler Readers* by Albert J. Harris and Marian Gartler.

WORK IN PROGRESS: A series of posters concerning spiritual values; "my own paintings."

SIDELIGHTS: "My basic concern in illustration is communicating. I use the medium which, I feel, best suits the point of view I have taken for that illustration. Therefore, I will use watercolors, pencil, oils or whatever."

FOR MORE INFORMATION SEE: Idea Magazine, Number 82, Japan, 1967; Martha E. Ward and Dorothy A Marquardt, *Illustrators of Books for Young People,* Scarecrow, 1975.

(From *Mystery and More Mystery* by Robert Arthur. Illustrated by Saul Lambert.)

LAMORISSE, Albert (Emmanuel) 1922-1970

PERSONAL: Born January 13, 1922, in Paris, France; died June 2, 1970, near Teheran, Iran; killed in a helicopter crash while filming a documentary; buried at Chateau de Meaulvuar, France; son of Albert Gusman (a businessman) and Elise (Decaux) Lamorisse; married Claude Jeanne Marie Duparc (a dancer), on November 24, 1947; children: Pascal, Sabine, and Fanny. *Education:* Attended Institut des Hautes Etudes Cinématographiques. *Religion:* Roman Catholic. *Home:* Paris, France.

CAREER: Motion picture writer, producer, and director, Began career as technical assistant for feature film, "Kairouan," Tunisia, 1946; cameraman for documentary, "Guatemala," 1955; creator of his own award-winning films. Inventor of Helevision, a system of aerial photography, and of board game, "Risk." *Awards, honors:* Chevalier of the Order of Arts and Letters (France); recipient of numerous awards, including, for "Crin Blanc," Grand Prix for short films, Cannes Film Festival, 1953; Prix Jean Vigo; International Prize for Youth; Epi d'Or of Rome; for "Le Ballon Rouge," Academy Award for best original screenplay, 1956; Grand Prix for short films, Cannes Film Festival, 1956; Grand Prix of the French Cinema; West German film critics prize for best foreign film, and similar awards in Japan, England, Mexico, the United States, and Switzerland; for "Le Voyage en Ballon," Blue Ribbon of the French Movie and Television Critics Association, 1960; Concours Technique International du Film, Prague; Prix de l'Office Catholique, Venice; Festival International de l'Enfance, La Plata; San Gregorio Prize, International Festival of Religious Films. *The Red Balloon* was a *New York Times* Choice of Best Illustrated Children's Books of the Year, 1957.

WRITINGS—Published screenplays: (With Jacques Prevert) *Bim, le petit ane* (self-illustrated with photographs from the film), Le Guilde du livre, 1951, translation by Roger Lubbock published as *Bim, the Little Donkey,* Putnam (London), 1957, Doubleday (translation by Bette Swados and Harvey Swados), 1973; (with Denys Colomb de Daunant) *Crin-Blanc,* Hachette, 1953, translation published as *White Mane,* Dutton, 1954, also published as *The Wild White Stallion,* Putnam

From there he called his balloon, which came to him at once . . . . ■(From *The Red Balloon* by Albert Lamorisse. Photograph taken during the filming of the movie "The Red Balloon.")

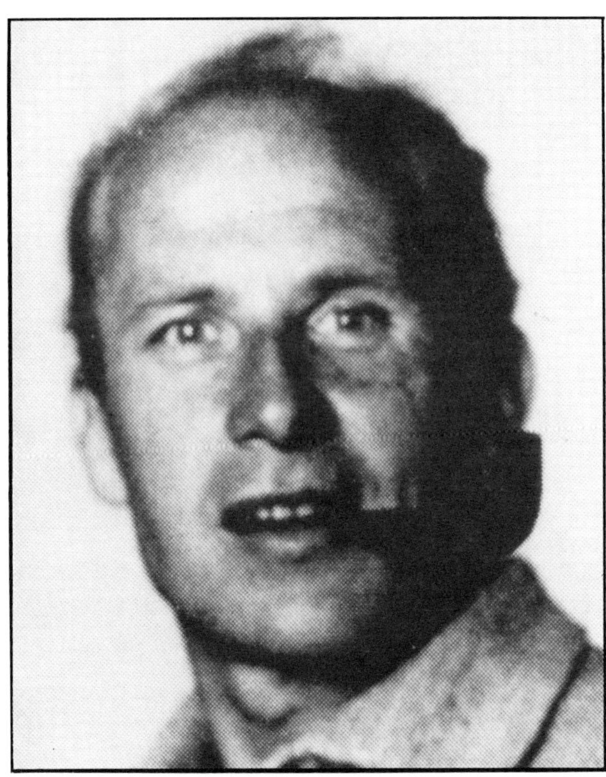

ALBERT LAMORISSE

(London), 1955; *Le ballon rouge* (illustrated with photographs from the film), Hachette, 1956, translation published as *The Red Balloon,* Doubleday, 1957; *Le voyage en ballon* (illustrated with photographs from the film), Hachette, 1960, translation by Malcolm Barnes published as *Trip in a Balloon,* Doubleday, 1960; *Fifi la Plume,* Hachette, 1965.

Screenplays; all original French productions; released in the U.S. as indicated: "Djerba," 1947; "Bim, le petit ane," 1949; "Crin Blanc," 1952 (released in U.S. as "White Mane," United Artists, 1953); "Le Ballon Rouge," 1956 (released in U.S. as "The Red Balloon," Lopert, 1957); "Le Voyage en Ballon," Filmsonor-Films Montsouris, 1960 (released in U.S. as "Stowaway in the Sky," Lopert, 1962); "Fifi la Plume," 1965; "Versailles," 1967; "Paris jamais vu," (title means "Paris Rediscovered"), 1968; "Le Vent des amoureux" (title means "The Lovers' Wind"), 1978.

SIDELIGHTS: Lamorisse was born and raised in Paris, Although he did rather poorly in school, after completing secondary school he audited classes at the Institut des Hautes Etudes Cinématographiques. Supposedly, he did not take a serious interest in work until he began his film career as a scriptwriter and photographer in 1945.

Though the filmic output of Lamorisse is relatively slight, his films are award-winning and of such a nature as to have become classics. His most noted works are his shorter films, projects full of dream-like fantasy and wonderment, all done with an eye toward the poetic.

The first of these is "White Mane," which details the friendship of a boy and a wild horse. In the film, which was shot in the wet flatlands of the South of France where wild horses roam and the landscape is desolate, a young boy eagerly attempts to possess a beautiful stallion. He gradually gains the animal's confidence, and triumphantly rides off astride the horse into the sea. With this film Lamorisse came to the fore of French filmmaking; and indeed gained world-wide attention. It has been shown before the Queen of England and the King of Greece, and in scores of countries outside France.

In his next films, Lamorisse's range of vision was freed from the ground. He explained to Howard Thompson of the *New York Times,* "From the air, the world becomes a table top. Man's efforts to transform nature seem so illogical when seen from high up, when he is seen in true perspective as part of earth and nature."

"The Red Balloon" was seven years in the making—due to deliberate and painstaking work. Lamorisse went through forty-two scenarios before he arrived at one with which he was pleased. And also, as he told Thompson, "I wait simply because I must be inspired." And the Oscar-winning "The Red Balloon" is just that. With the streets of Paris as a backdrop, a little boy adopts a stray red balloon, which faithfully follows behind him on his ramblings through the city. He must defend it from tormentors intent on destroying it. Lamorisse's own son, Pascal, played the main role, and his daughter, Sabine, also played a small part. The unique atmosphere of Paris permeates the film, and the filmmaking has been called triumphant.

While making "Stowaway in the Sky"—a full-length film in which a boy (again played by Pascal) and his grandfather go aloft in a hot air balloon—Lamorisse developed Helevision. Presented with the problems of vibrations inordinately shaking a camera which is mounted in a helicopter, Helevision allows for mounting so that vibrations are cushioned and minimized. The result is as if the camera were mounted on a solid track, all the while seeming to float in the sky. So in "Stowaway in the Sky," the audience follows a seventy-foot orange balloon as it skims the countryside above such spectacles as Notre Dame, the Eiffel Tower, a bullfight, a forest fire, a stag hunt, and a sailboat race, without the interference of vibrations common in the use of a helicopter.

Logistically, the filming was arduous. Each time the balloon went up or came down, Lamorisse had to get government permits. And once, an unscheduled landing occurred when the balloon exploded. The occupants, including his son, narrowly escaped injury as the basket tumbled to the ground. Being the true inventive artist, Lamorisse incorporated the accident into the plot. As he told *Times* magazine, "Poetry is always an accident in cinema."

Lamorisse's feature-length films met with less acclaim and success than had his early short and medium-length films, so at the time of his death he was concentrating on documentary shorts. He was killed in a helicopter crash while filming near Teheran. That film, "The Lover's Wind," was later edited from his notes, garnering a nomination for an Oscar as best feature documentary for the Academy Awards of 1978.

Lamorisse courted adventure, which was not always beneficent in return. In 1952, he was in the Gap region of France working on a film about two bears and a boy when he was caught in an avalance. The accident sent him to the hospital for five months and cost him a year of mobility. And too, Lamorisse cultivated inventiveness, a sense which extended even beyond the world of film. He was the inventor of the

. . . One day, on his way to school, he caught sight of a fine red balloon, tied to a street lamp. ■ (From *The Red Balloon* by Albert Lamorisse. Photograph taken during the filming of the movie "The Red Balloon.")

game "Risk," a widely-selling board game of strategy and international finesse. He was a licensed helicopter pilot as well as a balloonist. And the Lamorisse family at times created their own dishware and printed their own fabrics.

But film is the medium in which he created his classics. Lamorisse summed up this view of his art for Thompson, "To me cinema is a living art, the only one that has so many varied forms of expression. My own is a kind of visual movement. . . ."

HOBBIES AND OTHER INTERESTS: Making wine, skiing, fencing, riding, and swimming.

FOR MORE INFORMATION SEE: Time, October 24, 1960; *New York Times,* June 17, 1962. Obituaries: *New York Times,* June 4, 1970; *Time,* June 15, 1970; *Current Biography Yearbook, 1970.*

LAMPMAN, Evelyn Sibley 1907-1980 (Lynn Bronson)

OBITUARY NOTICE—See sketch in *SATA* Volume 4: Born April 18, 1907, in Dallas, Ore.; died of cancer, June 13, 1980, in Portland, Ore. Author. Lampman wrote many children's books for which she won several honors, including the Dorothy Canfield Fisher Memorial Children's Book Award for *City Under the Back Steps,* 1962, and Western Writers of America Spur Award for *Cayuse Courage,* 1970. As educational director of a Portland radio station she wrote scripts which were aired in the public schools. Tapes of the programs were made for educational use. She won two Jean Hersholt awards for radio script writing. Her numerous books include *Bargain Bride, Crazy Creek,* and *Coyote Kid. For More Information See: Contemporary Authors,* Volume 15-16, revised, Gale, 1975; *More Junior Authors,* Wilson, 1963; *Who's Who of American Women,* 8th edition, Marquis, 1973; *Who's Who Among Pacific Northwest Authors,* 2nd edition, Pacific Northwest Library Association, 1969. *Obituaries: New York Times,* June 14, 1980; *Washington Post,* June 16, 1980; *Contemporary Authors,* Volume 101-104, Gale, 1981.

LEAVITT, Jerome E(dward) 1916-

PERSONAL: Born August 1, 1916, in Verona, N.J.; son of Thomas Edward (a painter) and Clara (Sonn) Leavitt. *Education:* New Jersey State Teachers College, B.S., 1938; New York University, M.A., 1942; University of Colorado, graduate student, 1950; Northwestern University, Ed.D., 1952; University of Arizona, visiting scholar, 1959. *Home:* 1338 East Almendria Dr., Fresno, Calif. 93710. *Office:* School of Education, California State University, Fresno, Calif. 93740.

CAREER: Heights Elementary School, Roslyn Heights, N.Y., teacher, 1938-42; Sperry Gyroscope Co., Inc., Brooklyn, N.Y., instructor, 1942-45; Canyon Elementary School, Los Alamos, N.M., principal, 1945-49; Northwestern University, Evanston, Ill., instructor, 1950-52; Portland State College, Portland, Ore., professor, 1952-66; University of Arizona, Tucson, professor, 1966-69; California State University, Fresno, professor, 1969—. Evaluation of Arkansas experiment in teacher education, research associate; U.S.

JEROME LEAVITT

State Department, American specialist in education, in Cyprus. *Member:* Association for Childhood Education, National Education Association, National Society for College Teachers of Education, Writers Guild, Association for Supervision and Curriculum Development, American Humane Association.

WRITINGS: Tools for Building, Childrens, 1955; (editor) *Nursery-Kindergarten Education,* McGraw, 1958; *Carpentry for Children,* Sterling, 1959; (with Huntsberger) *Terrariums and Aquariums,* Childrens, 1961; *America and Its Indians,* Childrens, 1961; (editor) *Readings in Elementary Education,* W. C. Brown, 1961; (with Salot) *The Beginning Kindergarten Teacher,* Burgess, 1965; *By Land, By Sea, By Air,* Putnam, 1969; (editor) *The Battered Child,* General Learning, 1974. Compiler, *Bibliography, Programmed Learning,* annually, 1961-66. Contributor to magazines and professional journals. Editor of special issues of *Education* magazine on nursery-kindergarten education, education around the world, and fine and industrial arts.

WORK IN PROGRESS: Child Abuse and Neglect.

SIDELIGHTS: "Most of my writing is a result of a felt need on my part. In some cases this is to provide informational material that is lacking, which was true in the case of *Nursery-Kindergarten Education.* With *America and Its Indians* the objective was to provide accurate up-to-date material for children on our native Americans."

HOBBIES AND OTHER INTERESTS: Gardening, remodeling houses.

FOR MORE INFORMATION SEE: National Elementary Principal, June, 1949.

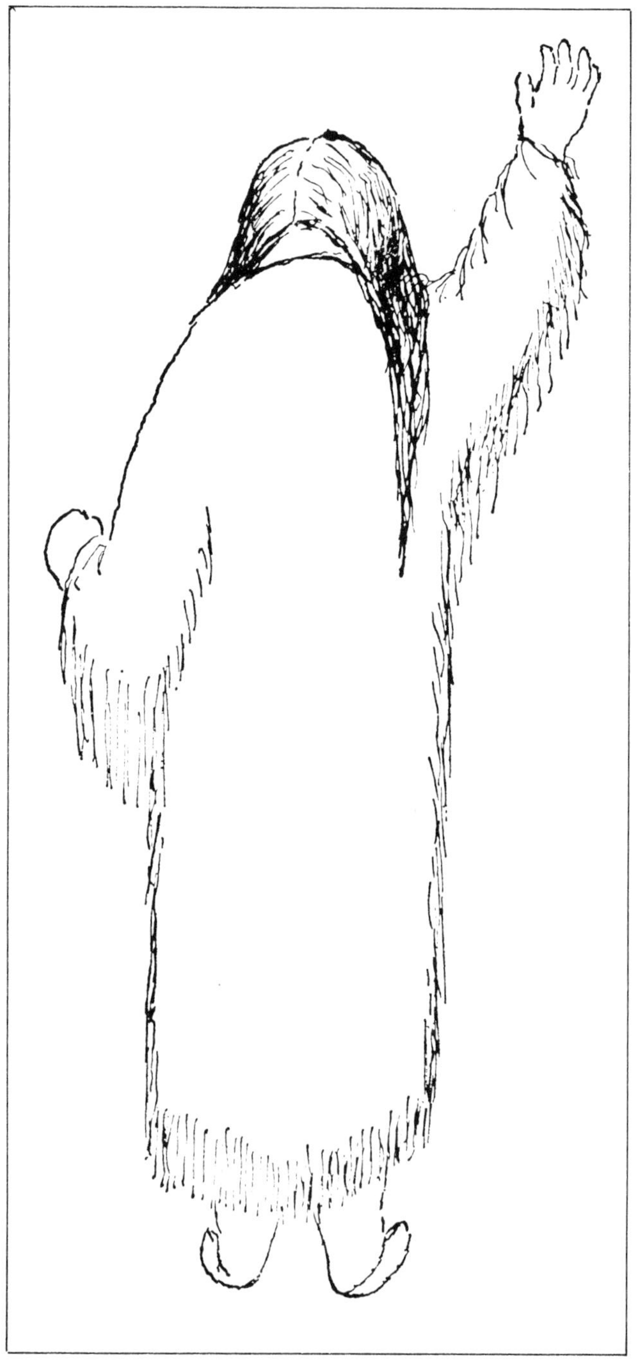

(From *The World of Manabozho: Tales of the Chippewa Indians* by Thomas B. Leekley. Illustrated by Yeffe Kimball.)

LEEKLEY, Thomas B(riggs) 1910-

PERSONAL: Born March 9, 1910, in Parker, S.D.; son of Thomas B. (a retail lumber merchant) and Beulah (Briggs) Leekley; married Dorothy O'Hora, August 25, 1937; children: John Robert, Dorothy Anne. *Education:* Dakota Wesleyan University, A.B.; University of South Dakota, M.A.; further studies at University of Colorado, 1936, University of Pennsylvania, 1938-42. *Politics:* Democrat. *Religion:* Roman Catholic. *Home address:* Box 80-3, RFD 2, Killingworth, Conn. 06417. *Agent:* McIntosh and Otis, 18 East 41st St., New York, N.Y. 10017. *Office:* One Fifth Ave., New York, N.Y. 10003.

CAREER: South Dakota high schools, instructor in English and history, 1935-37; University of Pennsylvania, Philadelphia, instructor in English, 1937-44; *Time,* Old Saybrook, Conn., manager, manufacturing operations, 1944-64; *Newsweek,* Dayton, Ohio, New York, N.Y., vice-president of manufacturing, 1965-76 (retired); graphic arts consultant, 1976—. Active in Democratic political affairs, Upper Darby, Pa. and in Conn.

WRITINGS—For young people: *King Herla's Quest, & Other Medieval Stories from Walter Map,* Vanguard, 1956, reissued as *The King the Merman,* Blackie, 1972; *The Riddle of the Black Knight & Other Stories from the Middle Ages Based on the Gesta Romanorum,* Vanguard, 1957; *Rescue for Brownie,* Vanguard, 1959; *The World of Manabozho; Tales of the Chippewa Indians,* Vanguard, 1965.

WORK IN PROGRESS: The Lynx in the Lake, a book about the Canadian wilderness.

SIDELIGHTS: "Why do people write books? Is that the question? In my case I believe it is because, at a few times in my life, something inside me insistently wanted out, so that I and others could see it. Children certainly know about something inside wanting out. Perhaps even yet there remains a bit of child in me.

"At any rate when I wrote, first *King Herla,* and then *Riddle of the Black Knight,* it was because I knew two sets of medieval stories which I thought wanted telling, and which some boys and girls, but not all, would like to read. When I did *Brownie* it was because I remembered an event from my boyhood. It kept coming back to ask that I tell others what had happened. Under editorial revision *Brownie* became a different book than I had planned, but that is a different story. I wrote *Manabozho* when some memories of Indians I had seen in Minnesota and western South Dakota led me to a collection of folklore which I thought should be told so that children could enjoy them. Always two elements seem to go together: Something inside wants out, but it wants out in order to be seen or read.

"In this respect few boys or girls, few men or women are unique. Most begin with mud pies or building blocks, progress through doll houses and graffiti, and end by growing roses, making pots, painting pictures, or carving canes from diamond willows. At first whatever wants out is satisfied with being seen. A little later it wants to be seen by people who can tell good things from bad. Perhaps he who once simply scrawled graffiti may learn to write verses or to paint pictures.

"Of course nothing is quite so simple as that. Many stories never come right and end in the wastebasket just as many

THOMAS B. LEEKLEY

pots break and many roses canker. It was my father who carved canes from diamond willow. One he had planned to give Theodore Roosevelt developed a long twisted crack while he was letting it dry and season. He kept the unfinished cane a long time while he studied that crack and tried to make something of it; he even thought of calling the crack the 'River of Doubt' after a stream Roosevelt had discovered on an exploring trip in South America. But in the end he gave up and left the half-finished stick in the attic.

"I have another problem, not just peculiar to me but to a lot of other people who try to write. Nothing I write comes out the way I want it the first time, or even the second or the third time. Whenever I try to create quickly I spoil what I am making. Sometimes I spoil it however long I work upon it. Yet if the idea for the story still wants out I try to help it.

"Here is an example of what I mean: Ten years ago, crossing a stormy wilderness lake in Northern Ontario, I saw a swimming lynx parting the whitecaps just beside my boat. For ten years I have tried to capture that lynx on paper. So far whatever there was of vision in that sight resists my efforts. But so far, unlike my father's diamond willow cane, the story hasn't cracked. It still insists that it wants out so that it can be read and even understood by others. So, after I have again given it time to season, I shall have another try. That's not the way all writers have to work, but many do and I am one of them."

LEUTSCHER, Alfred (George) 1913-

PERSONAL: Surname is pronounced *Loo*-cher; born of Dutch parents, October 30, 1913, in London, England; son of Izaak and Lammegien (Huizinga) Leutscher; married Phyllis Muriel Carter, July 13, 1940 (deceased); married Barbara Joan Farr, December 13, 1971; children: (stepchildren) Kevin Maurice Farr, Victoria Jayne Farr, Anthony John Farr. *Education:* Birkbeck College, London, B.Sc. (honors), 1940. *Office:* Pixies Halt, Kedington, Haverhill, Suffolk CB9 7QU, England.

ALFRED LEUTSCHER

CAREER: British Museum (Natural History), South Kensington, England, guide lecturer, 1946-50, senior guide lecturer, 1950-73; writer, 1973—. Guest on radio and television programs. *Military service:* British Army, Royal Service Corps and Education Corps, 1941-46. *Member:* British Naturalists Association (president), Wildlife Fund (committee member of Wildlife Youth Service), London Natural History Society, Zoological Society of London (fellow).

WRITINGS: Vivarium Life, Cleaver-Hume, 1952, 2nd edition, 1961; *Quiz Book on Animals,* Daily Mail Publications, 1956; *Quiz Book on Birds,* Daily Mail Publications, 1957.

The Wonderful World of Reptiles, Bruce & Gawthorn, 1960; *Pictorial Animal Book,* Daily Mail Publications, 1961; *Tracks and Signs of British Animals,* Cleaver-Hume, 1961; *A Study of Reptiles and Amphibians,* Blandford, 1963; *The Curious World of Snakes,* Bodley Head, 1963; *Life in Freshwaters,* Bodley Head, 1964; (translator) A. vanden Nieuwenhuizen, *Tropical Aquarium Fishes,* Constable, 1965; (translator) P. Brohmer and G. Stehli, *The Young Specialist Looks at Animals,* Burke Publishing, 1965; (translator) R. Mertens, *The Young Specialist Looks at Reptiles,* Burke Publishing, 1966; (translator) Hans Haas, *The Young Specialist Looks at Fungi,* Burke Publishing, 1969; *Field Natural History: An Introduction to Ecology,* G. Bell & Son, 1969.

(With Francis Rose, M. Chinery, C. M. Yonge, T. Bagenal, K. Williamson, and R. Fitter) *Shell Natural History of Britain,* Rainbird, 1970; *Ecology of Waterlife,* F. Watts, 1971; *Dinosaurs and Other Prehistoric Animals,* Paul Hamlyn, 1971, published in America as *Dinosaurs & Other Ancient Reptiles & Mammals,* Grosset, 1975; *Woodland Life: Badgers,* F. Watts, 1973; *Woodland Life: Deer,* F. Watts, 1973; *Woodland Life: Squirrels,* F. Watts, 1973; *Woodland Life: Woodpeckers,* F. Watts, 1973; (with other) *Book of the British Countryside,* Reader's Digest Press, 1973; *Epping Forest: Its History and Wildlife,* David & Charles, 1974; *The Ecology of Towns,* F. Watts, 1975; *Keeping Reptiles and Amphibians,* David & Charles, 1976; *The Ecology of Woodlands,* F. Watts, 1977; *Nature Trail Book of Ponds and Streams,* Reader's Digest Press, 1977; *Ecology of Mountains,* F. Watts, 1978; (consultant editor) *Joy of Nature,* Reader's Digest Press, 1978; (consultant editor) *Nature Trail of Wild Animals,* Osborne Publishing, 1978; *Spotters Guide to Animals, Tracks and Signs,* Osborne Publishing, 1979; *Prehistoric Man (History in Pictures),* Volume I, Macmillan, 1979. Also author of *Animals and Their Young,* 1962. Contributor to magazines.

SIDELIGHTS: "My most rewarding experience has been in talking to and writing for the young generation (my sternest critics!). As an outlet for the enduring young mind, natural history knows no bounds, and it has been my humble privilege to encourage youngsters to follow in my footsteps.

"My love of nature stems from early childhood. Mother used to tell me that I often escaped from the playpen in the garden, to explore the exciting world of nature in the herbaceous border, collecting caterpillars, worms, spiders and other treasures which were lovingly gathered as my first 'pets.' I then went through the usual juvenile phase of keeping tadpoles, fancy mice, goldfish and similar conventional pets, but was always keen to meet the real wildlife of the countryside.

"I have always stressed the importance of taking an active part in nature pursuits, pointing out that books, lectures, radio, museum visits and other media are only guidelines to personal and practical studies, especially in the field. Even a town garden in a city environment has something to offer. My garden in London is akin to a small nature reserve, designed to attract wildlife. Indoors it is nothing unusual to find an animal or two sharing our home—a python in the bedroom, a crocodile in the bath, or a bush-baby in the morning room.

"At the moment I am 'resting' and adjusting to retirement, but no doubt the urge will come to put pen to paper once more."

LLOYD, Norman 1909-1980

OBITUARY NOTICE: Born November 8, 1909, in Pottsville, Pa.; died of leukemia, July 31, 1980, in Greenwich, Conn. Musician, educator, and author. Lloyd began his career in music as a pianist for silent films and then taught at the Juilliard School of Music and Oberlin College Conservatory of Music. While at Juilliard he devised a new method for teaching music theory to students. Instead of using textbooks, Lloyd relied primarily on discussions with composers and other people active in the field of music. His works include *Fireside Book of Folksongs, Fundamentals of Sight Singing,* and *Keyboard Improvisation. For More Information See: ASCAP Biographical Dictionary of Composers, Authors, and Publishers,* American Society of Composers, Authors, and Publishers, 1966; *Who's Who in America,* 38th edition, Marquis, 1974; *Contemporary Authors,* Volume 37-40, revised, Gale, 1979. *Obituaries: New York Times,* August 1, 1980; *Contemporary Authors,* Volume 101-104, Gale, 1981.

Witch Dole had a long cold nose and a wrinkled skin; poisonous snakes oozed around her hat; skulls dangled from her ears; and, high up on her crooked back, sat Scratch, her cat. ■ (From *Ratsmagic* by Christopher Logue. Illustrated by Wayne Anderson.)

LOGUE, Christopher 1926-
(Count Palmiro Vicarion)

PERSONAL: Born November 23, 1926, in Portsmouth, Hampshire, England. *Home:* 18 Denbigh Close, London W11 2QH, England. *Agent:* Tesse Sayle, 11 Jubilee Place, London SW3 3TE, England.

CAREER: Poet. *Military service:* British Army, 1944-48.

WRITINGS—All poetry, except as indicated: *Wand and Quadrant,* [Paris], 1953; *Seven Sonnets,* [Paris], 1954; *Devil, Maggot and Son,* [Amsterdam], 1954, limited edition, P. Russell, 1956; *The Weekdream Sonnets,* Jack Straw (Paris), 1955; *The Song of the Dead Soldier,* Villiers Publications, c.1956; *The Man Who Told His Love: Twenty Poems Based on P. Neruda's "Los Cantos d'amores,"* Scorpion Press, 1958, 2nd edition, 1959; *A Song for Kathleen,* Villiers Publications, 1958; *Memoranda for Marchers,* [London], 1959;

Songs, Hutchinson, 1959, McDowell, Obolensky, 1960; (compiler) *Count Palmiro Vicarion's Book of Limericks,* Olympia Press (Paris), 1959.

Songs from "The Lily-White Boys," Scorpion Press, 1960; (translator and adapter) Homer, *Patrocleia: Book 16 of Homer's Illiad Freely Adapted into English,* Scorpion Press, 1962, published in America as *Patrocleia of Homer: A New Version by Christopher Logue,* University of Michigan Press, 1963; *The Arrival of the Poet in the City: A Treatment for a Film,* Mandarin Books, 1964; *I Shall Vote Labour,* Turret Books, 1966; *Christopher Logue's ABC,* Scorpion Press, 1966; *True Stories,* Four Square Books, 1964, 1973; *The Establishment Songs,* Poet & Printer, 1966; (translator and adapter) Homer, *Pax, from Book XIX of the Illiad,* Turret Books, 1967, also published as *Pax,* Rapp & Carroll, 1967; (with Wallace Southam and Patrick Gower) *Gone Ladies* (contemporary poetry set to music; words by Logue, music by Southam, and arrangement by Gower), Turret Books, 1968; (under pseudonym Count Palmiro Vicarion) *Lust,* Ophelia Press, 1969; *The Girls,* Turret Books, 1969; *New Numbers,* J. Cape, 1969, Knopf, 1970.

Twelve Cards, [London], 1972; *The Crocodile,* [London], 1976; *ABECEDARY,* [London], 1977; *Ratsmagic* (juvenile; prose), J. Cape, 1977, Pantheon Books, 1979; (reteller) *Puss in Boots* (juvenile; prose), Greenwillow, 1977; *The Magic Circus* (prose), J. Cape, 1979; *An Anthology of Comic Verse for Children,* [London], 1979; *War Music,* [London], 1981; *Ode to the Dodo* (collected verse), [London], 1981. Also author of twenty-six illustrated verse posters.

Plays: "The Lilywhite Boys," presented at the Royal Court Theatre, 1959; "The Trial of Cob and Leach," presented at the Royal Court Theatre, 1959; "Antigone," presented at the Royal Court Theatre, 1961; "Friday," produced at the Royal Court Theatre, 1971; "War Music," produced by the Prospect Theatre Company at the Old Vic Theatre, 1978.

Author of screenplays for films: "Savage Messiah," Metro-Goldwyn-Mayer, 1972; "The End of Arthur's Marriage," produced by the BBC.

ADAPTATIONS—Recordings: Logue's poems have been issued in London, under the titles "Red Bird," 1961, "Poets Reading," 1961, "The Death of Patrocleia," 1962, and "Loguerhythms," 1967.

SIDELIGHTS: Beginning in 1958 with "To My Fellow Artists," Logue has made many of his poems into posters. When asked by Davina Lloyd if his "prime motive in making posters [is] to get poems out," Logue answered: "One doesn't always know one's own motives. A poster seems two things: both a means to an end and an end in itself. The Iliad would go marvellously on a poster except that it would be a [very] large poster. . . .As for poetry, this fostered, pampered child of the arts, you suddenly realize it's a wide open thing, not a literary thing. . . .I simply feel that I'd like to publish all my poems as posters. For one thing it is easier for people who don't associate themselves with book poems, which is the majority of us. Turner liberated colour from form. At the other end of the scale, the poster can liberate the poem from a book. . . .Now, particularly in America, there is a fantastic upsurge of people doing posters just as creative objects which just are by their very nature multiples. Within this given situation the idea of putting poems with designs or images on them could hardly be more natural. It is an obvious extension of graphic activity."

FOR MORE INFORMATION SEE: Books and Bookmen, May, 1967; *London Magazine,* August, 1968, October, 1969.

LOVELACE, Maud Hart 1892-1980

OBITUARY NOTICE—See sketch in *SATA* Volume 2: Born April 25, 1892, in Mankato, Minn.; died March 11, 1980, in California. Author. Lovelace began writing at the age of nineteen while attending the University of Minnesota. She produced various adult historical novels, several of them written with her husband, Delos. She is best known in the realm of children's literature for her "Betsy-Tacy" series of books, which were inspired by her girlhood in Mankato, Minnesota. The journals Lovelace kept as a young student formed the basis for books about Betsy in high school, and indeed the majority of her characters were patterned after friends and relatives. They became so well-known that in 1961 a Betsy-Tacy Day was sponsored in Mankato, with Lovelace and her "characters" returning for the occasion. *For More Information See: The Junior Book of Authors,* 2nd edition, revised, Wilson, 1951; *Contemporary Authors,* Volume 5-8, revised, Gale, 1969; *Author's and Writer's Who's Who,* 6th edition, Burke's Peerage, 1971; *Who's Who of American Women,* 8th edition, Marquis, 1973. *Obituaries: Horn Book,* June, 1980.

LOWRY, Lois 1937-

PERSONAL: Born March 20, 1937, in Honolulu, Hawaii; daughter of Robert E. (a dentist) and Katharine (Landis) Hammbersberg; married Donald Grey Lowry (an attorney),

LOIS LOWRY

February is the worst month in New England. I think so, anyway. ■ (From *A Summer to Die* by Lois Lowry. Illustrated by Jenni Oliver.)

June 11, 1956 (divorced, 1977); children: Alix, Grey, Kristin, Benjamin. *Education:* Attended Brown University, 1954-56; University of Maine, B.A., 1972, also graduate study. *Religion:* Episcopalian. *Home:* 34 Mt. Vernon St., Boston, Mass. 02108.

CAREER: Free-lance writer and photographer, 1972—. *Awards, honors:* International Reading Association award for children's literature, 1978, for *A Summer to Die*.

WRITINGS—All juveniles, except as noted: *Black American Literature* (textbook), J. Weston Walsh, 1973; *Literature of the American Revolution* (textbook), J. Weston Walsh, 1974; *A Summer to Die* (*Horn Book* honor list), Houghton, 1977; *Find a Stranger, Say Goodbye,* Houghton, 1978; *Here in Kennebunkport* (book of photographs), Durrell, 1978; *Anastasia Krupnik,* Houghton, 1979; *Autumn Street,* Houghton, 1980. Contributor of stories, articles, and photographs to magazines, including *Redbook, Yankee,* and *Down East,* and to newspapers.

SIDELIGHTS: "I remember the feeling of excitement that I had, the first time that I realized each letter had a sound, and the sounds went together to make words; and the words became sentences, and the sentences became stories. I was very young—not yet four years old. It was then that I decided that one day I would write books.

"That was an aspiration that I never set aside. Under my photograph—me, seventeen, blonde, laughing—in a 1954 high school yearbook—are the words 'future novelist.'

"But it was to be a long time before the ambition was fulfilled. There were children to raise, education to complete, experience to learn from, and losses to mourn.

"Now, when I write, I draw a great deal from my own past. There is a satisfying sense of continuity, for me, in the realization that my own experiences, fictionalized, touch young readers in subtle and very personal ways.

"Once, when I was speaking to a group of teachers and librarians, a member of the audience asked me what my purpose was, what my intention was, in writing books for adolescents. I answered that it was to make a reader feel less alone. I remember feeling irritated at the person who asked, for asking what seemed an unanswerable question; and at myself, for having answered it hastily and, I thought, inadequately. But on reflection, I think my answer was not, after all, a bad one. Adolescence is very often a painfully lonely time; and it is a time when communication is difficult. A book can be a vehicle for communication; and a book can alleviate the sense of isolation that sometimes makes growing up lonely. Walking through a scary place is easier if you know that someone else has walked there once, and survived.

"I live now on Beacon Hill, in Boston, on a street that has brick sidewalks and gaslights and a wonderful quiet feeling of the past. I am told that Herman Melville once lived in the house where I now live, and with a writer's sense of the romantic and the impossible, I like to think that his ghost still hovers here benevolently.

"I like all sorts of people, the ocean sailboats, music, and movies. Most of all I like the excitement I still feel, as I did when I was not quite four, when words go together to make sentences, and the sentences become stories."

FOR MORE INFORMATION SEE: Publishers Weekly, February 28, 1977; *Horn Book,* August, 1977, June, 1978.

LUGER, Harriett M(andelay) 1914-

PERSONAL: Born July 21, 1914, in Vancouver, British Columbia, Canada; daughter of Leo Leon and Mollie (Benjamin) Mandelay; married Charles Luger (an instructor in botany), December 5, 1942; children: Carolyn (Mrs. Paul Slayback), Allen, Eleanor. *Education:* University of California at Los Angeles, B.A., 1936. *Home:* 3427 West 225th St., Torrance, Calif. 90505.

CAREER: Free-lance writer. *Member:* Authors Guild, California Writers Guild.

WRITINGS—All for young people: *Bird of the Farallons,* Young Scott, 1971; *The Last Stronghold,* Young Scott, 1972; *Chasing Trouble,* Viking, 1976; *The Elephant Tree,* Viking, 1978; *Lauren,* Viking, 1979.

WORK IN PROGRESS: An unnamed young adult novel.

SIDELIGHTS: "Until a few years ago when I officially signified my wish to be a citizen of the United States, I had dual citizenship in this country and Canada, having been born in Vancouver, B.C. of parents who were U.S. citizens. Before I was a year old my parents left Canada for New Orleans where we lived briefly. Then we went to El Paso, Texas, and it was there that I spent my early childhood. We came to California when I was ten, and I grew up in Hollywood during its glory years, proud to live in the glitter, convinced that its glamor would in some way rub off on me, and I would shine like a star. In fact, it never touched me. I trudged to school in decent, clean clothes, learned my lessons, played after school just as I had done in El Paso. When, in Le Conte Junior High I was chosen to edit the *Le Contean,* the school annual, the event went monumentally unnoticed.

"I went on to Hollywood High, quietly progressing through the three-year curriculum (junior high included the ninth grade)—almost flunking physics but redeeming myself by being managing editor of the *Hollywood High School News.* More important than the prestige of the position was the contact with Mr. William Thorpe, the journalism teacher, who made me aware of sloppy writing. In 1932 I entered UCLA and graduated four years later with a B.A. degree. Few took note and fewer have remembered that mine was the second highest grade in the English comprehensive, a formidable test required of all English majors. I have forgotten the questions that I answered with such distinction, I do remember an excellent creative writing course on the short story given by a man named Hubbell.

"The pre-World War II recovery from the Depression was still several years in the future, and jobs continued to be hard to get. I had worked for Perfection Bakeries during my college years, selling baked goods over immaculate glass counters in stores scattered through the Los Angeles metropolitan area. After graduation, for a little while I worked as a salesperson and then office clerk in several department stores in downtown Los Angeles. I returned to UCLA as a stenographer in the College of Agriculture where I met my husband. We married during World War II while he was serving as an aerial navigator. When the war ended, chance dictated that we settle in the southwestern portion of Los Angeles County. We have lived in such places as Gardena, Haw-

HARRIET LUGER

I saw two bright, black, shiny beads, two little round ears barely sticking above the short, dark fur of the head, stubby whiskers, and long, ugly front teeth. I don't know what *he* saw, but whatever it was made him mad. ■(From *Chasing Trouble* by Harriet Luger. Illustrated by Diane de Groat.)

thorne, Redondo Beach, and finally Torrance, where we raised our family. When we were not creating and rearing children, my husband, Charlie, has been a botanist at El Camino College, and I have been a spy, keeping under surveillance everyone who passes before me, as well as the terrain, as far as I can see, for significant information. What I pick up, I put in my books, which I started writing ten years ago when my son, Allen, found an oil-soaked bird on Torrance Beach and brought it home.

"Practically right from the beginning I have loved stories and wanted to make my own. As I read I wrote, first for entertainment, then to live other lives than mine. Gradually, I came to realize the possibilities in fiction. It is possible to entertain, to instruct, propagandize, illuminate the internal landscape, stimulate the intellect, or inspire—within the framework of a story. One can do one or several of these things, the only requirement being that the story must have a life of its own that draws the reader to participate in it from its beginning until it is finished. This means that it must be shaped and modelled and polished. It must have a logical progression from beginning to middle to end with characters who live and a problem that the reader cares about enough to want it solved.

"Four of the five juvenile books I have written have required research. For the *Bird of the Farallons,* I learned how the common murre pursues its life so that I could write a story about the oil-soaked bird who was found on a Southern California beach. I read the greater part of what is written about the Modoc War and as much as I could find about the Modoc people for *The Last Stronghold,* which deals with the only Indian war fought in the state of California. I discovered how a pocket gopher spends his time for *Chasing Trouble,* as well as learning specifically how an eco-system works. *Lauren* required that I visit a free clinic, County Health Centers, a welfare office, and speak to as many young adults as possible for my story dealing with the choices a seventeen-year-old high school senior has to consider when she finds herself pregnant. Only *The Elephant Tree,* my fourth book, required little research. As important and informative as this research may be, in no case was it the reason for the book. Each of the stories is about a personal problem which had to be solved and about the growth of the individual who works out its solution.

"The action in all my books takes place in California. It is possible that sometime in the future I shall lay the scene elsewhere, but I doubt it. California is where I have lived my life, where I have met the world. It contains almost the whole world in its boundaries, actually. With the exception of the tropics, all the climates occur here, from glacial arctic cold to searing desert heat. It has old mountains and new, great plains, a long seashore, many hills. The social environment varies as much as the natural. Great cities, villages, wildernesses—each exerts its own pressures which pull and buffet the individual. The names, Los Angeles and San Francisco, have come to possess special auras which apply only to themselves—but they are also any metropolis where people crowd each other. Every spot on earth is unique, but in my opinion the vigor and squalor of California cities and the various conditions of its varied landscape can be understood by people living almost anywhere on this planet. To me, at least, it is the world."

FOR MORE INFORMATION SEE: Publishers Weekly, February 23, 1976.

LYTTLE, Richard B(ard) 1927-

PERSONAL: Surname is pronounced "*lit*-il"; born June 9, 1927, in Los Angeles, Calif.; son of Herbert George (a businessman) and Florence (Burleson) Lyttle; married Jean Haldeman (a teacher), December 17, 1949; children: Herbert G. (deceased), Matthew H., Jenny G. *Education:* Attended Thacher School; University of California, Berkeley, B.A., 1950. *Home and office:* Box 403, Point Reyes Station, Calif. 94961.

CAREER: Rancho Dos Rios, Ojai, Calif., cowboy and ranch hand, 1950-54; *Oxnard Press-Courier,* Oxnard, Calif., reporter and editor, 1954-62; *Independent-Journal,* San Rafael, Calif., reporter and editor, 1962-67. Free-lance writer. *Military service:* U.S. Navy, 1945-46. *Member:* Inverness Yacht Club (commodore, 1969). *Awards, honors:* Matrix award, Los Angeles alumnae chapter of Theta Sigma Phi, for best news story in a community daily, 1957.

WRITINGS—All juveniles; all published by Doubleday, except as indicated: *Challenged by Handicap,* Reilly & Lee,

RICHARD B. LYTTLE

1971; *Polar Frontiers: About The Arctic, The Antarctic and Mankind,* Parents' Magazine Press, 1972; *The Complete Beginners' Guide to Bicycling,* 1974; *Paints, Inks and Dyes: The Story of Colors at Work,* Holiday House, 1974; *A Year in the Minors* (Junior Literary Guild selection), 1975; *The Complete Beginners' Guide to Backpacking,* 1975; *Basic Hockey Strategy,* 1976; *How to Beat the High Cost of Sailing* (adult), Regnery, 1976; *Soccer Fever: A Year With the San Jose Earthquakes,* 1977; (with Edward F. Dolan, Jr.) *Bobby Clark,* 1977; (with Edward F. Dolan, Jr.) *Archie Griffin,* 1977; (with Edward F. Dolan, Jr.) *Martina Navratilova,* 1977; *The Complete Beginners' Guide to Physical Fitness,* 1978; *Basic Volleyball Strategy,* 1978; (with Edward F. Dolan, Jr.) *Fred Lynn,* 1978; (with Edward F. Dolan) *Janet Guthrie,* 1978; (with Edward F. Dolan, Jr.) *Scott May,* 1978; *The Complete Beginners' Guide to Skiing,* 1978; *Getting Into Pro Basketball,* F. Watts, 1979; *Jogging and Running,* F. Watts, 1979; (with Edward F. Dolan, Jr.) *Kyle Rote, Jr.,* 1979; (with Edward F. Dolan, Jr.) *Jimmy Young,* 1979; (with Edward F. Dolan, Jr.) *Dorothy Hamill,* 1979; *The Complete Beginners' Guide to Hi Fi,* 1980; *People of the Dawn,* Atheneum, 1980.

SIDELIGHTS: "My efforts to become a writer ran side by side with my search for space. At first, there was not much space, and without a nook I could call my own, a quiet spot with a chair and some kind of horizontal surface that would support a typewriter, I could do very little writing. Ours was the common problem of a growing family in a small house, or rather houses. We moved often.

"Early one morning, however, I made an important discovery. Between the hours of 2 and 6 a.m. our kitchen was abandoned, absolutely empty, and this situation apparently came to pass every day. It seemed a shame to let such quiet time and such a good space go to waste. So, with some coffee steaming on the stove and a typewriter on the kitchen table, I began to write regularly.

"My stories did not sell at first, and the early sales, when they did finally begin, could best be described as rare. But I found consolation in my discovery. Space seemed to be the key to writing.

"There were some difficulties and frustrations. In one house, the kitchen was so close to the bedroom that my typing kept the children awake. I moved into the garage. The family car was noble company, but for me the garage always held a dark mood of exile. Later, after another move, I decided to make space by building a small shack at the back of the lot. The project taught me something of the dark mysteries of rough carpentry, but the shack was hardly finished before we moved once again.

"To my joy, however, the next house had a garret. Yes, a real room under the eaves with a small window, a room no one else wanted. It was hot in the summer and mighty cool in the winter, and there were a few spiders who refused to abandon their shadowy realm. But how minor these defects were to me. Here at last was real space of my own, my first office!

"That little room at the top of the stairs, cramped as it was, opened the way to modest success. Before long I was able to change from a full to a part-time job, a switch that let me spend more time writing and at last, drop the pre-dawn stint from my schedule. Being able to work normal hours in my own office was a great satisfaction, perhaps the greatest satisfaction I have had as a writer.

"Many other satisfying things have since occurred. For one thing, we were lucky enough to buy a house of our own. Naturally, I made sure that it had a spare bedroom I could convert into a handsome office. Jean and I do not plan to move again, not for a few years, anyway. By more good luck, I was able to give up the part-time job and make writing my full-time business.

"It's good to be a writer, to be your own boss, to have a family and friends who are helpful and interested in your work. And it's particularly good to have a space you can call your own."

Childhood shows the man as morning does the day.
—John Milton

Between the dark and the daylight,
When the night is beginning to lower,
Comes a pause in the day's occupations,
This is known as the Children's Hour.
—Henry Wadsworth Longfellow

LYTTON, Edward G(eorge) E(arle) L(ytton) Bulwer-Lytton, *Baron* 1803-1873 (Pisistratus Caxton)

PERSONAL: Born May 25, 1803, in London, England; died January 18, 1873, in Torquay, England; son of William Earle (a general) and Elizabeth Barbara (Lytton) Bulwer; married Rosina Doyle Wheeler, 1827 (separated, 1836); children: Emily, Edward Robert. *Education:* B.A. and M.A., Trinity College, Cambridge. *Home:* Knebworth, Herfordshire, England.

CAREER: Novelist, playwright, and statesman. Began writing poetry for diversion as a college student; forced to rely on his writings for income, beginning 1827; became a member of Parliament on a reform ticket, 1831-41; editor of the *New Monthly* magazine, 1831-32; returned to Parliament as a conservative candidate, 1852, appointed Colonial Secretary, 1858-59; elected Lord Rector of Glasgow University, 1856 and 1858; retired from active politics, 1866. *Awards, honors:* Cambridge University Chancellor's Medal, 1825, for poem, "Sculpture"; made baronet, 1838; raised to the House of Peers as Baron Lytton of Knebworth, 1866; honorary degrees from Oxford and Cambridge Universities.

EDWARD G.E.L. BULWER-LYTTON, BARON LYTTON

WRITINGS—Novels: *Falkland,* H. Colburn, 1827, new edition, edited by Herbert Van Thal, Cassell, 1967; *Pelham; or, The Adventures of a Gentleman,* three volumes, H. Colburn, 1828, new edition, edited by Jerome J. McGann, University of Nebraska Press, 1972; *The Disowned,* H. Colburn, 1829; *Devereux: A Tale,* three volumes, H. Colburn, 1829; *Paul Clifford,* three volumes, H. Colburn & R. Bentley, 1830; *Eugene Aram: A Tale,* Harper, 1832; *Asmodeus at Large,* Carey, 1833; *Godolphin,* three volumes, R. Bentley, 1833; *The Pilgrims of the Rhine,* Harper, 1834 [another edition illustrated by Daniel Maclise and others, Routledge, 1891].

The Last Days of Pompeii, Harper, 1834, reissued, Heron Books, 1968 [other editions illustrated by Lancelot Speed, Service & Paton, 1897; Paul Hardy, Bell's Reading Books, 1914; Frederick Coffay Yohn, Scribner's, 1926; Val Biro, Vision Press, 1948; adaptations for children include editions edited by Josephine Field, J. Crowther, 1944; Lou P. Bunce, Globe Book, 1960; E. F. Dodd, Macmillan, 1961; E. Tydeman, Oxford University Press, 1961]; *Rienzi: The Last of the Roman Tribunes,* three volumes, Saunders & Otley, 1835, reissued, Lippincott, Scholarly Press, 1971; *Ernest Maltravers,* three volumes, Saunders & Otley, 1837; *Leila; or, The Siege of Granada,* Longmans, 1838; *Calderon the Courier: A Tale,* Carey, Lea, 1838; *Alice; or, The Mysteries* (a sequel to *Ernest Maltravers*), Saunders & Otley, 1838.

Night and Morning, three volumes, Saunders & Otley, 1841; *Zanoni* (an adaptation of his *Zicci* which appeared in the *Monthly Chronicle,* 1841), Saunders & Otley, 1842, reissued as *Zanoni: A Rosicrucian Tale,* Rudolf Steiner, 1971; *The Last of the Barons,* J. Winchester, 1843 [another edition illustrated by Fred Pegram, Service & Paton, 1897; adaptations for children include an edition edited by C. E. Smith, T. C. & E. C. Jack, 1910]; *Lucretia; or, The Children of the Night,* three volumes, Saunders & Otley, 1846; *Harold: The Last of the Saxon Kings,* three volumes, R. Bentley, 1848, reissued, Dutton, 1970; *The Caxtons: A Family Picture,* three volumes (first published in *Blackwood's* magazine, 1845-49), W. Blackwood, 1849, a later edition (illustrated by Chris Hammond), Putnam, 1889, reprinted, Scholarly Press, 1971.

(Under pseudonym Pisistratus Caxton) *"My Novel"; or, Varieties in English Life,* four volumes (first published in *Blackwood's* magazine, 1850-53), W. Blackwood, 1853; (under pseudonym Pisistratus Caxton) *What Will He Do with It?,* four volumes (first published in *Blackwood's* magazine), W. Blackwood, 1859; *A Strange Story: A Novel* (first published in *All the Year Round,* 1861), Harper, 1862; *The Wooing of Master Fox* (adapted for children by O. D. Martin), Ashmead & Evans, 1866; *The Coming Race,* W. Blackwood, 1871, new edition, Philosophical Publishing, 1973 [another edition published as *Vril: The Power of the Coming Race,* Rudolf Steiner, 1972]; *The Parisians* (illustrated by Sydney Hall), four volumes (first published in *Blackwood's* magazine, October, 1872 to January, 1874), W. Blackwood, 1873; *Kenelm Chillingly: His Adventures and Opinions,* Harper, 1873; *Pausanius the Spartan: An Unfinished Historical Romance,* edited by his son, Edward Robert Bulwer-Lytton Lytton, Routledge, 1876; *The Haunted and the Haunters* (published with *A Strange Story),* Lippincott, 1879.

Plays: *The Duchess de La Vallière* (five-act; first produced January 4, 1837), Saunders & Otley, 1836; *The Lady of Lyons; or, Love and Pride* (five-act; first produced in Covent Garden, at the Theatre Royal), Harper, 1838; *The Sea-Captain; or, The Birthright!* (five-act), Saunders & Otley, 1839, Turner & Fisher, 1840 [rewritten and revived under the title *The Rightful Heir* (five-act; first produced at the Lyceum Theatre, October 3, 1868), Harper, 1868]; *Richelieu; or, The Conspiracy* (five-act), Saunders & Otley, 1839; *Money* (five-act comedy; produced at the Park Theatre), Saunders & Otley, 1840; *Not so Bad as We Seem; or, Many Sides to a Character* (five-act comedy; first produced at Devonshire House), Harper, 1851; *Walpole; or, Every Man Has His Price* (five-act comedy in rhyme), W. Blackwood, 1869.

Poems: *Ismael: An Oriental Tale, with Other Poems,* J. Hatchard, 1820; *Delmour; or, A Tale of Syphid and Other Poems,* Carpenter & Son, 1823; *Sculpture: A Poem,* [Cambridge], 1825; *Weeds and Wildflowers,* privately printed, 1826; *O'Neill; or, The Rebel,* H. Colburn, 1827; *The Siamese Twins: A Satirical Tale of the Times,* Harper, 1831; *Eva: A True Story of Light and Darkness,* Saunders & Otley, 1842; *The Crisis: A Satire of the Day,* J. Olliver, 1845; *The New Timon: A Romance of London,* H. Colburn, 1846; *King Arthur,* H. Colburn, 1848-49; *Saint Stephen's,* [Edinburgh], 1860; (under pseudonym Pisistratus Caxton) *The Boatman* (first published in *New Monthly*), W. Blackwood, 1864; *The Lost Tales of Miletus,* J. Murray, 1866 [another edition published as *The Secret Way: A Lost Tale of Miletus,* Lothrop, 1889].

Letters: *A Letter to a Late Cabinet Minister on the Present Crisis,* Saunders & Otley, 1834; *Confessions of a Water-Patient in a Letter to W. Harrison Ainsworth,* H. Colburn, 1845; *Letters to John Bull: Esquire,* Chapman & Hall, 1851; *Letters of the Late Edward Bulwer: Lord Lytton to His Wife,* Sonnenschein, 1884, reprinted, AMS Press, 1976; *Letters of Bulwer-Lytton to Macready,* privately printed (Carteret Book Club), 1911; *Bulwer and Macready: A Chronicle of the Early Victorian Theatre,* University of Illinois Press, 1958.

Other: *Conversations with an Ambitious Student in Ill-Health, with Other Pieces,* Harper, 1832 (published in England as *The Student: A Series of Papers,* Saunders & Otley, 1835); *England and the English,* Harper, 1833, new edition, edited by Standish Meacham, University of Chicago Press, 1972; *Athens: Its Rise and Fall,* Saunders & Otley, 1837; *Caxtoniana: A Series of Essays of Life, Literature, and Manners,* Harper, 1863; *Miscellaneous Prose Works,* R. Bentley, 1868.

Translator: Johann Christoph Friedrich von Schiller, *The Poems and Ballads of Schiller,* W. Blackwood, 1844; J. C. Friedrich von Schiller, *Lay of the Bell,* [London], 1864; (and editor) Quintus Horatius Flaccus, *The Odes and Epodes of Horace,* W. Blackwood, 1869.

Collections: *The Poetical Works of the right Honorable Lord Lytton,* Routledge, 1859; *The Dramatic Works of the Right Honorable Lord Lytton,* Routledge, circa 1873, reprinted, Books for Libraries, 1972; *Speeches of Edward: Lord Lytton,* W. Blackwood, 1874; C. L. Bonney, editor, *The Wit & Wisdom of E. Bulwer-Lytton,* Folcroft, 1883; *The Novels and Romances of Edward Bulwer Lytton,* G. D. Sprout, 1896; *The Works of Edward Bulwer Lytton,* 18 volumes, reprinted, Scholarly Press, 1976.

ADAPTATIONS—Movies: "The Last Days of Pompeii," Pasquali American, 1913, RKO Radio Pictures, starring Preston Foster and Basil Rathbone, 1935, United Artist, 1960; "Eugene Aram," Thomas A. Edison, 1915; "In the Name of Love," adaptation of *The Lady of Lyons,* starring Ricardo Cortez and Wallace Beery, Famous Players-Lasky, 1925; "Cardinal Richelieu," starring George Arliss and Maureen O'Sullivan, 20th Century Pictures, 1935; "Night Comes Too Soon," adaptation of *The Haunted and the Haunters,* Butcher's Film Productions, 1947.

Plays: Benjamin N. Webster, *Paul Clifford: The Highwayman of 1770* (three-act), [London], 1833; Edward Ball, *Paul Clifford* (three-act), [London], circa 1835; William T. Moncrieff, *Eugene Aram; or, Saint Robert's Cave,* [London], 1835; William B. Bernard, *Lucille; or, The Story of a Heart* (three-act; adaptation of *Pilgrims of the Rhine*), John Miller, 1836; Louisa H. Medina, *The Last Days of Pompeii,* Samuel French, 1858; L. H. Medina, *Ernest Maltravera* (three-act), [New York], 1860; Giovanni Peruzzini, *Jone; or, The Last Days of Pompeii* (four-act opera; music by Errico Petrella), Academy of Music (New York), 1863; John Broughman, *Night and Morning,* [London], 1883; Elizabeth C. J. Abbott, *The Last Days of Pompeii,* Oxford University Press, 1929.

SIDELIGHTS: **March 25, 1803.** Born in London into a family torn by marital discord. "I was born just at the time when my mother's married life was saddest. For in unions, however ill-assorted, so long as there are good qualities on either side, it takes some few years before one can part with hope. And at first, though my father's temper was of the roughest, yet he was very much in love; and love had a good-humour of its own. But gradually the temper rose superior to the love; and gout, to which from early youth my father had been occasionally subjected, now suddenly fixed upon him premature and almost habitual residence. He bore pain with the fierce impatience common to the strong when they suffer; and it exasperated all the passions which, even in health and happiness, that powerful and fiery organisation could but imperfectly control. . . ." [The Earl of Lytton, *The Life of Edward Bulwer-Lytton,* Volume I, Macmillan, 1913.[1]]

"Out of jealousy for my mother's love, my father had positively disliked me; for the same cause my grandmother took me into open aversion—an aversion unsoftened to her dying day; and my grandfather, who ought, if conscious of the future, to have welcomed and petted me, as the one of his grandsons destined to live the most amongst books, did not suffer me to be four-and-twenty hours in the house before he solemnly assured his daughter 'that I should break her heart, and (what was worse) that I should never know my A.B.C.' He maintained this ill opinion of my disposition and talents with the obstinacy which he carried into most of his articles of belief; and I cannot call to mind ever having received from him a caress or a kind word.

"Behold the great event of my infant life—my Siege of Troy, my Persian Invasion, my Gallic Revolution—the Arrival of my Grandfather's Books!

"The learned Deluge flowed into the calm still world of Home; it mounted the stairs, it rolled on, floor upon floor; the trim face of drawing-rooms vanished before it; no attic, the loftiest, escaped from the flood.

"But the grand reservoir, the Lake Moeris of the whole inundation, was the great dining-room; and there, when the flood settled, I rested mine infant ark.

"So the house, with all its new treasures, was given up to me. Having duly visited all the lesser, if loftier, settlements of the immigration, I finally, as I before said, settled myself habitually in the dining-room, which I regarded as the central camp of the invading hordes. Words cannot paint the sensations of awe, of curiosity, of wonder, of delight, with which I dwelt in that City of the Dead. . . ." [The Earl of Lytton, K.G., *Bulwer-Lytton,* Home & Van Thal Ltd., 1948.[2]]

". . .For, as I never remember a time when I could not read, so I never remember a time when I had not a calm and intimate persuasion that, one day or other, I was to be somebody, or do something. It was no feverish desire of fame that

(From the movie "Cardinal Richelieu," based on the play "Richelieu," starring George Arliss. Copyright 1935 by Twentieth Century Pictures, Inc.)

(From *The Last Days of Pompeii* by Edward Bulwer Lytton. Illustrated by F. C. Yohn.)

preyed upon me, such as disturbs, the childhood of the ambitious; it was a confidence in the days to come, which was attended with small curiosity, and never troubled by the modesty of a doubt."[1]

1812. Of his first school experience, Lytton wrote: ". . . The school hours were to me hours of relief, for I was quick and docile, and my master could find no fault with me. But when the school broke up, that hour of release, so dear to others, was regarded by me with unutterable terror. Then the lesser boys would come round me to taunt the griefs which they themselves, I suppose, must once have felt. They had nothing of which to accuse me, except that I was homesick. But in the eyes of schoolboys that is the worst offence. There I learnt betimes that, with the unfeeling, feeling is a crime, and there betimes I sought the refuge of dissimulation. To put a good face on the matter, to laugh with those who laughed, to pretend that a day or two had sufficed to cure all longing for my mother and my home—this was my only policy. And the attempt to practise it cost me more pain than all the tears with which, when I could steal away unobserved, I gave vent to my first sorrows. . . .

"I did not remain in that school above a fortnight. My misery was so great that it affected my health; and my mother, coming to see me, was so shocked at my appearance, and at my narrations, that she took me away. But the experience I had undergone, short though it was, had no trivial effect on my character. It long damped my spirits, and chilled that yearning for childish friendships which is an instinct with childhood. On the other hand, it left on my mind a hatred of cruelty and oppression which, I trust, has never faded away."[1]

1814. Studied under a tutor at Ealing.

1820. Suffered emotional distress over his first love. "She was married. She, whose heart, whose soul, whose every thought and feeling, all were mine to the last, she who never spared even a dream to another—lost, lost to me for ever!

"When that tragedy was over, I felt myself changed for life. Henceforth melancholy became an essential part of my being; henceforth I contracted the disposition to be alone and to brood. I attained to the power of concentrating the sources of joy and sorrow in myself. My constitution was materially altered. It was long before I knew again the high animal spirits which delight in wild sport and physical action. Till then I had been irascible, combative, rash, foolhardy. Afterwards, my temper grew more soft and gentle, and my courage was rather the result of pride and jealous honour than the fearless instinct that rejoiced in danger. My ambition, too, became greatly subdued, nor did it ever return to what it was in boyhood."[1]

1824-1826. Travelled throughout Europe. ". . . I wrote some poems, which I privately printed at Paris, under the name of *Weeds and Wildflowers.* They have never been published, and I do not think ten copies have been given away. I also recast and nearly completed the sombre tale of *Falkland.* Besides these achievements, I studied with critical attention the standard French authors. At last, finding that literary occupation of this nature only fed my melancholy, I made a determined resolve to wrestle with myself against it. I left Paris abruptly, took an apartment at Versailles, where I did not know a soul, and tried the effect of healthful physical exercise in restoring the mind to that cheerful view of life which is essential to its just equilibrium. I had with me my favourite Andalusian horse, and, rising early, I forced myself to ride out daily, in all weathers, for nine or ten hours, till it grew dark. I returned home sufficiently fatigued to ensure a good appetite and a sound sleep. All my life through, I have found the necessity of intervals of complete solitude for the cure of the morbid symptoms which half solitude engenders."[1]

August 30, 1827. Married Rosina Wheeler despite the strong protestations of his mother. ". . . I am going to be married!!! And that very soon, perhaps in less than a month. My intended is very beautiful, very clever, very good, and I believe likes me passing well. Moreover she is well born and well connected. . . . But, alas! the human heart is most inscrutable and I feel at this moment only one bright and cheering consolation, viz.:—that I have for once in my life acted well. . . . My plan is, after marriage, to hire a large old-fashioned house in the country, live very retired for three years, give myself wholly up to literature, in which I hope to earn somewhat of that breath of fools which the knaves wisely called reputation. . . .

"The poor author! how few persons understand and forbear with and pity him! He sells his health and youth to a rugged task master. And O blind and selfish world, you expect him to be as free of manner, and as pleasant of cheer, and as equal of mood, as if he were passing the most agreeable and healthful existence that pleasure could afford or medicine invent to regulate the nerves of the body."[1]

1831. Elected to Parliament.

1833. Second honeymoon to Italy resulted in the first serious marital strife. "I am now convinced of what I have long believed: I am only fit to live alone. God and Nature afflicted me with unsocial habits, weak nerves and violent passions. Everything in my life has tended to feed these infirmities until they have become a confirmed and incurable disease, which nothing but a gentle pity, a forbearing, soothing, watchful compassion—as of a nurse over a madman—can render bearable to me or to others. God forbid that any should so sacrifice herself for me! Willingly I retire from a struggle with the world, which I have borne so long and with such constitutional disadvantages."[1]

A final separation ensued three years later. He wrote to Rosina: "I shall submit no longer to continued disrespect and the gnaw and tooth of eternal reproach. My mind is made up finally and irrevocably. We must part. You shall no longer complain that I keep you in a 'County jail.' Take your own residence where you will. I grudge not your happiness or liberty. I demand only no more to sacrifice my own. You have no longer affection for me—*you have completely and eternally eradicated all mine for you,* but I have still the memories of the Past, and still wish most sincerely to make you as comfortable as I can."[2]

1837. Wrote his first play. ". . . 'The Duchess de La Vallière,' the most polished in point of diction, and the highest in point of character, went the first night thro' an ordeal which a play a thousand times better could not have braved unscathed. The practical dramatist knows that there is no fault more perilous to a play than that of being too long; but from some grievous error in stage management the length of mine had been overlooked, and the curtain did not fall till half past eleven! viz:—nearly two hours after the proper and orthodox close of a five-act play."[1]

(From the movie "The Last Days of Pompeii," starring Basil Rathbone and Louis Calhern. Copyright 1935 by RKO Radio Pictures, Inc.)

1841. Resigned seat in House of Commons.

1843. Mother's death plunged Lytton into unrelenting bereavement. "No one else knew my mother as I did, and I never till now knew half her great qualities and noble heart. In her I have lost a thousand ties in one. It was almost the great affection of my life. Her weary death-bed was sad beyond words, and yet it was no disease from which one can say 'Happy are those released.' She was so young of heart and mind, so full of energy and will. The soul seemed to live on when the body was a shadow. All about her was so high-hearted even in suffering and death. Hitherto I have had one shelter in this dreary world—it is now gone for ever. Nothing that reminds me I have ever been young is left. Every hour that poor face is before me. In vain I had preparation; to the last I clung to hope. After they said she was dead I felt her hand press mine. I have but one comfort, such as it is, that I am comfortless. I should loathe myself if I grieved less. I believe and I hope that that grief will last; it is the last earthly link between us. I would not break it for all the joys or triumphs I dreamed of at sixteen. . . ." [The Earl of Lytton, *The Life of Edward Bulwer-Lytton,* Volume II, Macmillan, 1913.[3]]

1844. Complete breakdown in health. "Sometimes, indeed, thoroughly overpowered and exhausted, I sought for escape. The physicians said 'Travel,' and I travelled. 'Go into the country,' and I went. But at such attempts at repose all my ailments gathered round me—made themselves far more palpable and felt. I had no resource but to fly from myself—to fly into the other world of books, or thought, or reverie—to live in some state of being less painful than my own. As long as I was always at work it seemed that I had no leisure to be ill. Quiet was my hell.

"At length the frame thus long neglected, patched up for a while by drugs and doctors, put off and trifled with as an intrusive dun, like a dun who is in his rights—brought in its arrears, crushing and terrible, accumulated through long years. Worn out and wasted, the constitution seemed wholly inadequate to meet the demand.

"The exhaustion of toil and study had been completed by great anxiety and grief. I had watched with alternate hope and fear the lingering and mournful death-bed of my nearest relation and dearest friend—of the person around whom was entwined the strongest affection my life had known—and when all was over, I seemed scarcely to live myself."[3]

1847-1851. Resumed occupation of country squire. "My time at present if occupied in repairing farms, opening schools, etc. There are two things in life which bring a man in connection with that grave happiness called Duty. One is a fortunate marriage, the other a landed property. As I missed the one, I am pleased to see that the other compels one, *nolens volens,* to rouse oneself from one's egoism, and to one's amaze act for other people. . . ."[3]

April, 1848. Daughter Emily died at age twenty. Ex-wife began a series of attacks designed to provoke public embarrassment.

1858. Had his ex-wife certified as insane, after she vilified him in many attacks which he considered slanderous. "That which I desire is affection, and this it is which captivates me. I cannot exist without the interchange of affection, and I can find affection nowhere so strong and so pure as in the heart of a woman. Therefore a woman's love has been necessary to my existence, and I have paid for it the usual penalty, in error and in scandal. This *besoin d'aimer* has involved me in the most serious errors of my life, embarrassed me in complicating all my duties, and often placed me unhappily at war with the world. I grant this; yet had I, when I could no longer love and esteem my wife, somewhere about the age of 26, shut my heart to the want it craved for, sure am I that though in the eyes of the world I should have been a more respectable man, I should have become a much more unamiable one. It has been the interchange of affection with some loving and loyal nature that has kept me from becoming a cold and ambitious egotist, and in reality reconciled me with the world with which, in seeming, it often placed me at war."[3]

1866. Concluded active political career. Raised to peerage as Baron Lytton.

January 18, 1873. Died in Torquay, England as a result of an ear disease which had plagued him for many years. "I am not sure that I could not give a more truthful picture of the Nile, which I have never beheld except in my dreams, than I could of the little lake at the bottom of my own park, on the banks of which I loitered out my schoolboy holidays, and (could I hallow their turf as Christian burial-ground) would desire to choose my grave."[3]

FOR MORE INFORMATION SEE: Thomas H. Escott, *Edward Bulwer: First Baron Lytton of Knebworth,* Routledge, 1910, reprinted, Kennikat, 1970: The Earl of Lytton, *The Life of Edward Bulwer-Lytton,* Volumes I and II, Macmillan, 1913; Victor A.G.R. Bulwer-Lytton, Earl of Lytton, *Bulwer-Lytton,* Swallow Press, 1948; (for children) John and H.S.N.K. Cournos, *Famous British Novelists,* Dodd, 1952; Edward G.E.L. Bulwer-Lytton, Baron Lytton, *Bulwer and Macready: A Chronicle of the Early Victorian Theatre,* University of Illinois Press, 1958; Ellen Moers, *Dandy,* Viking, 1960; Sybilla Jane Flower, *Bulwer-Lytton,* Newbury Books, 1973.

'Tis the good reader that makes the book.

—Ralph Waldo Emerson

ALISTAIR MacLEAN

MacLEAN, Alistair (Stuart) 1923-
(Ian Stuart)

PERSONAL: Born 1923, in Glasgow, Scotland. *Education:* Attended University of Glasgow. *Home:* Geneva, Switzerland. *Office:* c/o William Collins Sons & Co. Ltd., 14 St. James Place, London SW1, England.

CAREER: Former teacher of English and history in Glasgow; writer, 1955—. *Military service:* Royal Navy. *Member:* Writers' Guild.

WRITINGS—All novels: *H.M.S. Ulysses,* Collins, 1955, Doubleday, 1956, also published in omnibus volume with works by other authors, Books Abridged, 1956; *The Guns of Navarone,* Doubleday, 1957; *South by Java Head,* Doubleday, 1958; *The Secret Ways,* Doubleday, 1959, (published in England as *The Last Frontier,* Collins, 1959).

Night Without End, Doubleday, 1960, also published in an omnibus volume with works by other authors, Doubleday, 1960; *Fear is the Key,* Doubleday, 1961; *The Golden Rendezvous,* Doubleday, 1962, condensed version, Reader's Digest, 1963; *Lawrence of Arabia* (juvenile), Random House, 1962 (published in England as *All About Lawrence of Arabia,* W. H. Allen, 1962); *Ice Station Zebra,* Doubleday, 1963; *When Eight Bells Toll,* Doubleday, 1966; *Where Eagles Dare,* (Companion Book Club and Readers Book Club selections),

It was more than just a ceremonial tour, it was a completely triumphal one; everywhere they were met with the most overwhelming enthusiasm.

Damascus went mad with joy. ■ (From *Lawrence of Arabia* by Alistair MacLean. Illustrated by Gil Walker.)

Doubleday, 1967; *Force 10 from Navarone,* Doubleday, 1968; *Puppet on a Chain,* Doubleday, 1969.

Caravan to Vaccares, Doubleday, 1970; *Bear Island,* Doubleday, 1971; *Captain Cook,* Doubleday, 1972; *Alistair MacLean Introduces Scotland,* edited by Alastair M. Dunnett, McGraw-Hill, 1972; *The Way to Dusty Death,* Doubleday, 1973; *Breakheart Pass,* Doubleday, 1974; *Circus,* Doubleday, 1975; *The Golden Gale,* Doubleday, 1976; *Seawitch,* Doubleday, 1977; *Goodbye California,* Doubleday, 1977; *Athabasca,* Doubleday, 1980.

Under pseudonym Ian Stuart: *The Snow on the Ben,* Ward, Lock, 1961; *The Black Shrike,* Scribner, 1961; *The Dark Crusader,* Collins, 1961, published under name Alistair MacLean, Collins, 1963; *The Satan Bug,* Scribner, 1962.

Screenplays: "The Guns of Navarone," "Where Eagles Dare," "Breakheart Pass," "Caravan to Vaccares," "When Eight Bells Toll," "Puppet on a Chain," "Force 10 from Navarone," "Golden Rendezvous."

WORK IN PROGRESS: "River of Death" scheduled for publication in 1981.

SIDELIGHTS: Alistair MacLean, the son of a Scots minister, was brought up in the Scottish Highlands. In 1941 at the age of eighteen, he joined the Royal Navy and began five years of service as a torpedo-man in the East Coast Convoy Escorts. He fired only one torpedo during the war, though under fire several times and was wounded once, but the two and half years spent aboard a cruiser was later to give him the background for *H.M.S. Ulysses,* his first novel, the outstanding documentary novel on the war at sea.

After the war, MacLean graduated in arts with honours from Glasgow University and took up teaching. In his spare time he wrote short stories, one of which won him a £100 first prize in a Glasgow *Herald* competition. This short story was spotted by Ian Chapman of Collins who encouraged MacLean to write a full-length book, which he did in the evenings of three months. The result was *H.M.S. Ulysses,* which launched him as an international novelist. A Book Society Choice, it became the first novel ever to sell 250,000 hardcover copies in the first six months after publication in England.

Furthermore, he has found that he is a natural screen-writer. Elliott Kastner, the American film producer, noticed on a trip to London that MacLean's paperbacks dominated every station bookstall and he suggested that MacLean should try his hand at an original screenplay. MacLean was uncertain but when Kastner sent him some specimen screenplays, MacLean at once decided he could do better. He did. "Where Eagles Dare" the film which resulted, was a box office smash as was the book which he then derived from it. A number of his books have now been made into films including the famous "Guns of Navarone."

Alistair MacLean titles have been translated by many countries and these include: Czechoslovakia, Denmark, Finland, France, Germany, Greece, Greenland, Holland, Iceland, Japan, Norway, Persia, Poland, South Africa, Spain, Sweden, Yugoslavia.

In February of 1976, the year of a special campaign to celebrate the publication of his twenty-first bestseller, using the slogan—MACLEAN MEANS ACTION—Fontana paperbacks played a big part. Up to that time, it was Ian Fleming who held the record for one million sellers, having thirteen titles to his name. But MacLean has eighteen, all of which have topped the million, plus *The Guns of Navarone* that has gone over the 1½ million.

Besides the screenplays written by MacLean, some of his other novels have been brought to the screen, including *Fear is the Key, Ice Station Zebra, The Secret Ways, South by Java Head, The Satan Bug,* and *Bear Island.*

David Depledge wrote: "He (MacLean) has made his name by writing superb and highly filmable adventure novels. . . . Writing, to Alistair MacLean, is a business. His workroom is in the attic, cut off even from his family." Depledge continues: "The script for *Where Eagles Dare* was the first he had ever attempted, but having accepted the challenge of doing something new he quickly became fascinated by the technical demands. . . . He works quickly, completes a film script in one to two months and a novel in less. If he gets behind schedule . . . he just works longer hours."

HOBBIES AND OTHER INTERESTS: Science, astronomy, and travel.

FOR MORE INFORMATION SEE: Books and Bookmen, May, 1968; *Life,* November 26, 1971; *Contemporary Literary Criticism,* Volume 3, Gale, 1975.

GLADYS MALVERN

MALVERN, Gladys (?)-1962 (Sabra Lee Corbin, Vahrah von Klopp)

PERSONAL: Died November 16, 1962; sister of Corinne Malvern (an author and illustrator).

CAREER: Author of books for children. Malvern was a child actress, growing up to become a leading lady. She also worked as an advertising manager in Los Angeles for 12 years. *Awards, honors:* Julia Ellsworth Ford Prize for *Valiant Minstrel,* 1943.

WRITINGS: (Under pseudonym Vahrah von Klopp) *Kin,* Dodd, 1931; *If Love Comes* (illustrated by John A. Maxwell), C. Kendall, 1932; *Love Comes Late,* Greenberg, 1934; (under pseudonym Sabra Lee Corbin) *Let's Call It Love,* Hillman-Curl, 1938; (with sister, Corinne Malvern) *Brownie: The Little Bear Who Liked People,* McLoughlin, 1939; (with C. Malvern) *The Story Book of Brownie and Rusty,* McLoughlin, 1940; *Dancing Star: The Story of Anna Pavlova* (illustrated by Susanne Suba), J. Messner, 1942, reprinted, 1967; *Curtain Going Up! The Story of Katherine Cornell,* J. Messner, 1943, reprinted, 1962; *Valiant Minstrel* (illustrated by Corinne Malvern), J. Messner, 1943; *Jonica's Island* (illustrated by C. Malvern), J. Messner, 1945; *Good Troupers All: The Story of Joseph Jefferson,* M. Smith, 1945.

Gloria: Ballet Dancer, J. Messner, 1946; *Ann Lawrence of Old New York* (illustrated by C. Malvern), J. Messner, 1947; *According to Thomas,* R. M. McBride, 1947; *Your Kind Indulgence: A Romance of the Theatre in Old New York* (illustrated by C. Malvern), J. Messner, 1948; *Eric's Girls* (illustrated by C. Malvern), J. Messner, 1949; *Meg's Fortune* (illustrated by C. Malvern), J. Messner, 1950; *Prima Ballerina,* J. Messner, 1951; *Behold Your Queen!* (illustrated by C. Malvern), Longmans, Green, 1951, reprinted, McKay, 1964; *Tamar* (illustrated by C. Malvern), Longmans, Green, 1952; *Dear Wife* (illustrated by C. Malvern), Longmans, Green, 1953; *Hollywood Star,* J. Messner, 1954; *The Foreigner: The Story of a Girl Named Ruth* (Junior Literary Guild selection; illustrated by C. Malvern), Longmans, Green, 1954, reprinted, McKay, 1967; *Mamzelle: A Romance for Teen-Age Girls Set in the Days of Dolly Madison,* M. Smith, 1955.

Saul's Daughter (illustrated by Vera Bock), Longmans, Green, 1956; *Stephanie,* M. Smith, 1956; *My Lady, My Love: An Historical Junior Novel about Isabella of Valois,* M. Smith, 1957; *Curtain's at Eight: A Gladys Malvern Presentation,* M. Smith, 1957; *There's Always Forever* (illustrated by Allan Thomas), Longmans, Green, 1957; *Rhoda of Cyprus,* M. Smith, 1958; *The Great Garcias* (illustrated by Alan Moyler), Longmans, Green, 1958; *Rogues and Vagabonds: A Novel about the First Acting Troupe to Play in America,* M. Smith, 1959; *Blithe Genius: The Story of Rossini* (illustrated by Donald Bolognese), Longmans, Green, 1959; *Dancing Girl,* M. Smith, 1959; *On Golden Wings: The Story of Giuseppe Verdi,* M. Smith, 1960; *Patriot's Daughter: The Story of Anastasia Lafayette for Teen-Age Girls,* M. Smith, 1960; *The Secret Sign,* Abelard-Schuman, 1961; *Wilderness Island,* M. Smith, 1961; *So Great a Love,* M. Smith, 1962; *Heart's Conquest,* M. Smith, 1962; *The Queen's Lady,* M. Smith, 1963; *The World of Lady Jane Grey,* Vanguard Press, 1964; *The Six Wives of Henry VIII,* Vanguard Press, 1969, reissued, 1972.

SIDELIGHTS: "I grew up traveling with theatrical companies. And I can remember walking along the streets of strange

Marguerite leaned over her, speaking softly. "You-want something, Madame?"

Pavlova smiled, a faint, rather twisted smile. "Bring me-my-swan costume," she whispered. ▪ (From *Dancing Star: The Story of Anna Pavlova* by Gladys Malvern. Illustrated by Susanne Suba.)

towns at evening, and looking into lamp-lit rooms where there were many books. 'Will the time ever come,' I thought enviously, 'when I can have a place for my books—and just *write?*'

"I spent most of my allowance on books. But I was forever having to leave them behind because our baggage must be kept down.

"Even then I was writing—anywhere, everywhere. Sometimes in a dressing room, waiting for my cue, an idea for a poem would flash over me, but there was never any writing paper. But there was always a good-sized mirror on the shelf, which I would turn about to its paper side and scribble upon feverishly! It didn't matter that I must leave my masterpiece behind, or that nobody else would read it unless he was in the habit of turning large mirrors back-side-fore. My poem was *written*.

"I write almost every day, starting at one in the afternoon and keeping at it until dinner. I'm rarely interrupted, except by [my sister] Corinne's impertinent Siamese cat, who takes a particular delight in sitting right on my manuscript. He pokes his brown paw at the jumping typewriter keys, which doesn't help my typing at all. But I'm convinced he wants to help, and some day I'll put him in a book, too.

"It is especially much fun when Corinne is illustrating a book of mine, for then my characters appear as she sees them. Naturally these characters are very real to me, and I'm delighted when I can watch her pen bring Ann, Peter, Elnathan, and the rest right out into the open."

FOR MORE INFORMATION SEE: Young Wings, July, 1945, June, 1947, June, 1951; Stanley J. Kunitz and Howard Haycraft, editors, *Junior Book of Authors*, second revised edition, Wilson, 1951; H. Finch, "Meet Gladys Malvern," *Scholastic*, November 5, 1952; Martha E. Ward and D. A. Marquardt, editors, *Authors of Books for Young People*, Scarecrow Press, 1964. *Obituary: Publishers Weekly*, January 7, 1963.

MARKS, Margaret L. 1911(?)-1980

OBITUARY NOTICE: Born about 1911 in London, England; died of cancer, June 30, 1980, in Leesburg, Va. Painter, translator, and teacher. Marks exhibited her paintings in Virginia and in New York, N.Y., where she held a show at the Ward-Nasse Gallery in 1980. She also translated foreign folk song lyrics into English, many of which were published in children's song books by Time, Inc. *Obituaries: Washington Post*, July 1, 1980; *Contemporary Authors*, Volume 101-104, Gale, 1981.

McEWEN, Robert (Lindley) 1926-1980

OBITUARY NOTICE: Born June 23, 1926; died in 1980 in Berwickshire, Scotland. Lawyer, illustrator, and author. McEwen contributed to the *Listener*, wrote a column for the *Spectator*, and authored a number of legal textbooks, including *The Law of Monopolies* and *Gatley on Libel and Slander*. He illustrated Gavin Maxwell's *Ring of Bright Water* and *Raven, Seek Thy Brother*, as well as Iris Origo's *Giovanna and Jane*. *For More Information See: Who's Who*, 131st edition, St. Martin's, 1979. *Obituaries: AB Bookman's Weekly*, July 14-21, 1980; *Contemporary Authors*, Volume 101-104, Gale, 1981.

That place that does contain
My books, the best companion, is to me
A glorious court where hourly I converse
With the old sages and philosophers.

—John Fletcher and Francis Beaumont

A house full of books, and a garden of flowers.

—Andrew Lang

I keep a look out for car doors that are open. ■ (From *The Bear's Bicycle* by Emilie Warren McLeod. Illustrated by David McPhail.)

McLEOD, Emilie Warren 1926-

PERSONAL: Born December 2, 1926, in Boston, Mass.; daughter of Shields (a physician) and Alice (Springfield) Warren; children: Sara K., Susan W., Stuart C. *Education:* Mount Holyoke College, B.A., 1948. *Home:* 90 Commonwealth Ave., Boston, Mass. 02116. *Office:* Unicorn Books, 306 Dartmouth St., Boston, Mass. 02116.

CAREER: Houghton Mifflin Co., Boston, Mass., assistant editor of children's books, 1950-52; Atlantic Monthly Press, Boston, Mass., children's book editor, 1956-77, associate director, 1976-77; Unicorn Books, Boston, Mass., director-editor, 1977—. Shared Educational Services, director, 1969—. *Member:* American Library Association, Mount Holyoke Alumnae Association, New England Library Association, World Guild Children's Book Council, Children's Book Writers, IBBY.

WRITINGS—For children: *The Seven Remarkable Bears,* Houghton, 1954; *Clancy's Witch,* Atlantic Monthly Press, 1959; *One Snail and Me,* Atlantic Monthly Press, 1962; *The Bear's Bicycle,* Atlantic Monthly Press, 1975.

SIDELIGHTS: "My books have been few and far between, written—first from my own childhood, then from my children's—and only when they are complete in my own mind. I wish I had time to write for fun, to write books without knowing how they will end.

"When I am not working I'd rather sail than do anything else. Next best is reading. I like surprises—in what I read and what I write—and in real life.

"I wish I could draw."

EMILIE WARREN McLEOD

MARION MEADE

MEADE, Marion 1934-

PERSONAL: Born January 7, 1934, in Pittsburgh, Pa.; daughter of Surain (a physicist) and Mary (Homeny) Sidhu; children: Alison Linkhorn. *Education:* Northwestern University, B.S., 1955; Columbia University, M.S., 1956. *Residence:* New York, N.Y. *Agent:* Julia Coopersmith, 10 West 15th St., New York, N.Y. 10011.

CAREER: Author.

WRITINGS: *Bitching,* Prentice-Hall, 1973; *Free Woman: The Life and Times of Victoria Woodhull* (juvenile), Knopf, 1976; *Little Book of Big Riddles* (juvenile), Harvey House, 1976; *Little Book of Big Bad Jokes* (juvenile), Harvey House, 1977; *Eleanor of Aquitaine,* Hawthorn, 1977; *Stealing Heaven: The Love Story of Heloise and Abelard,* Morrow, 1979; *Madame Blavatsky: The Woman Behind the Myth,* Putnam, 1980. Contributor to *New York Times, Village Voice, McCall's, Woman's Day, Commonweal, Cosmopolitan,* and *Aphra.*

MEADOW, Charles T(roub) 1929-

PERSONAL: Born December 16, 1929, in Paterson, N.J.; son of Abraham (a textile worker and union leader) and Florence (Troub) Meadow; married Harriet Riess, September 9, 1956 (divorced); married Mary Louise Shinskey, June 24, 1972; children: (first marriage) Debra Lynne, Sandra Lee; (second marriage) Alison Maria, Benjamin Niland. *Education:* University of Rochester, A.B., 1951; Rutgers University, M.S., 1954. *Home:* 847 Ardleigh St., Philadelphia, Pa. 19118. *Office:* School of Library and Information Science, Drexel University, Philadelphia, Pa. 19104.

CAREER: U.S. Department of the Navy, Bureau of Ships, Washington, D.C., mathematician at David Taylor Model Basin, 1954-55; RAND Corp., Santa Monica, Calif., assistant mathematician in Systems Development Division, 1955-56; General Electric Co., Phoenix, Ariz., and Washington, D.C., unit manager, 1956-59, consulting analyst, 1959-60; International Business Machines Corp. (IBM), Federal Systems Division, Gaithersburg, Md., development mathematician,

1960-62, senior programmer, 1962-67, manager of information sciences, Center for Exploratory Studies, 1967-68; National Bureau of Standards, Center for Computer Sciences and Technology, Washington, D.C., chief of Systems Development Division, 1968-71; Atomic Energy Commission, Washington, D.C., assistant director of Division of Management Information and Telecommunications, 1971-74; Drexel University, Philadelphia, Pa., professor of information science, 1974—; *Journal of the American Society for Information Science,* New York, N.Y., editor, 1977—. Adjunct lecturer, University of Maryland, School of Library and Information Services, 1967-72. Executive secretary, Committee on Scientific and Technical Information, Federal Council for Science and Technology, 1970-71; member of advisory committee, Office of Library, Personnel Resources, American Library Association, 1970-77.

MILITARY SERVICE: U.S. Marine Corps, 1951-53; became first lieutenant. *Member:* Association for Computing Machinery, American Society for Information Science (vice-president, commission on long range planning, 1974-76), Institute of Information Scientists, Sigma Xi. *Awards, honors:* Honorable mention, Children's Science Book Award, 1976, from New York Academy of Science for *Sound and Signals: How We Communicate.*

WRITINGS: The Analysis of Information Systems, Wiley, 1967, 2nd edition, 1973; *The Story of Computers* (juvenile), Harvey House, 1970; *Man-Machine Communication,* Wiley, 1970; *Sounds and Signals: How We Communicate* (juvenile), Westminster, 1975; *Applied Data Management,* Wiley, 1976; (with P. Atherton) *Basics of Online Searching,* Wiley, 1980. Contributor to *Annual Review of Information Science and Technology,* Encyclopaedia Britannica, 1970, to *Encyclopedia of Computer Science and Technology,* 1978, and to other publications.

CHARLES T. MEADOW

SIDELIGHTS: "I think of myself as an information scientist, rather than a writer. I have written several adult text books and I consider that sort of writing as part of my life as a scientist and teacher. My children's books are done mostly for fun. As a student, listening to teachers and reading the assigned text books, I was always struck with the fact that some people did and some did not have the knack of explaining a subject to the relatively uninitiated reader or listener. I am a believer in the dictum that any scientist should be able to explain his or her work in a few words to a layman.

"I became interested in writing about computers and communications for children when my own children began to reach the age where I thought they could understand these things if they wanted to. And so I began work on a book on computers for young people who had no mathematics or previous computer instruction. When it was published, or anyway when it was begun, there was no work I know of that explained how a real computer worked, at the juvenile level. Before I had finished, I felt that my next effort would be to try to explain the basic elements of communications to the same audience.

"In spite of the fun of doing children's books, they are in some ways harder to write than adult books. A reputation as a worker in the field doesn't necessarily sell the book, or even sell the publisher on oneself as an author. One has to start all over again. I am particularly indebted to one of the most delightful people I have known, Zola Harvey, for his faith in me and willingness to publish my first children's book, *The Story of Computers.* Working with him and his staff at Harvey House was a wonderful experience, much different from any other publishing experience I have had.

"We are going to see computers and other information machines make enormous changes in our lives, and I hope to be writing about them for readers at all levels."

HOBBIES AND OTHER INTERESTS: Photography, travel.

MILTON, Hilary (Herbert) 1920-

PERSONAL: Born April 2, 1920, in Jasper, Ala.; son of Hilary Herbert and Erline (Moore) Milton; married Patty Sanders (a writer), September 26, 1952; children: Michelle Sanders, David Rodgers. *Education:* Attended Alabama Polytechnic Institute (now Auburn University), 1938, and Birmingham-Southern College, 1939-40; University of Alabama, A.B., 1948, M.A., 1949. *Politics:* Independent. *Religion:* Protestant. *Home:* 3540 Oakdale Dr., Birmingham, Ala. 35223. *Office:* Department of English, Samford University, 800 Lakeshore Dr., Birmingham, Ala.

CAREER: University of Alabama, Tuscaloosa, instructor in business writing, 1948-51; civilian educational specialist in Montgomery, Ala., 1951-52, informational specialist in St.

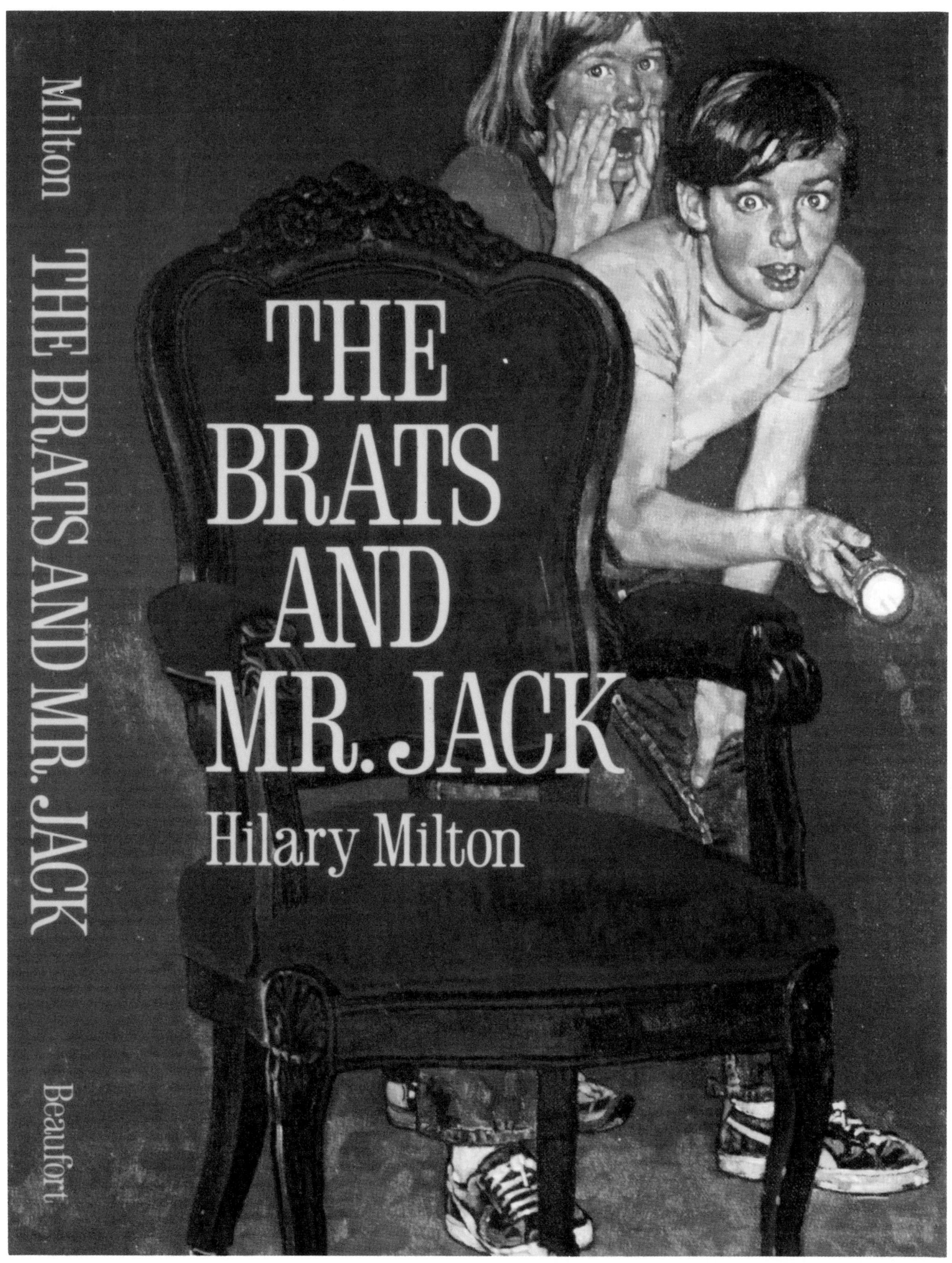

(From *The Brats and Mr. Jack* by Hilary Milton. Jacket illustrated by Robert Chronister.)

Louis, Mo., 1952-55; Department of the Air Force, Washington, D.C., editorial director, 1955-56, speech writer, 1956-62; National Aeronautics & Space Administration (NASA), Washington, D.C., report writer, 1962-70; full-time research and writing, 1970-71; Samford University, Birmingham, Ala., writer-in-residence, 1971—. Special lecturer at George Washington University, 1960. *Military service:* U.S. Army Air Forces, 1942-45. *Awards, honors: November's Wheel* was chosen a most notable book, 1976, by the National Council of Social Studies.

WRITINGS: Steps to Better Writing, Spartan, 1962; *The Gitaway Box* (novel), Luce, 1968; *The House of God and Minnie May* (novel), Luce, 1969; *The Tipple Bell* (novel), Luce, 1970; *November's Wheel,* Abelard, 1976; *Emergency: 10-33 on Channel 11!* (novel), F. Watts, 1977; *Nowhere to Run,* F. Watts, 1978; *Mayday! Mayday!* (novel), F. Watts, 1979; *The Longest Highway* (novel), David C. Cook, 1979; *Blind Flight* (novel), F. Watts, 1980; *The Brats and Mr. Jack,* Beaufort Books, 1980. Author of writing instruction manuals. Contributor of articles on U.S. space activities to encyclopedias; contributor of articles to educational and government publications.

WORK IN PROGRESS: Three novels: *Two From the Dead, Siege!,* and *Last One Up Springs for Pizza.*

SIDELIGHTS: "Though I was born in Jasper, I grew up and attended public school in Bessemer, Alabama, a mining and steel–mill town ten or so miles from Birmingham. As the son of an elementary school teacher and a home builder, I learned early to use both my mind and my hands. My father's tools were very useful for me during the Great Depression, for I was able to make-do—build my own wagons, scooters, rubber guns, and other toys. And my mother's love for books, especially collections of poems, was a source of encouragement when I first tried to write.

"As a youngster during the Depression, I learned much about people, especially the willingness of strong-minded people to struggle through the rough period, maintaining their dignity and pride, despite the severest of disadvantages. I still remember how we got along without—and many of the characters in my stories reflect my admiration for the people I knew then. My book, *November's Wheel* captures the early thirties, as seen through the eyes of a young boy.

"Although I spent sixteen years in and around Washington, D.C., I still prefer to set my stories in the South. That, of course, is largely because I know the South and its people. I do not believe, however, that the stereotyped southerner has to be used in 'southern' stories. Adventure stories of airplane crashes and rescue attempts, sophisticated novels of intrigue and interlocking conflicts, and certainly animal stories of all kinds can be set in the South as easily as anywhere else.

"Many of the stories I write are about people caught in dilemmas not of their own making, characters who have the courage and self-reliance necessary to work out their own solutions. As a kind of philosophy, I believe in people, not movements, and have the utmost faith in the ability of a free people to survive. This faith stems from the jobs I had as a teen—I worked as a life guard, a nightwatchman, a truck driver, and an iron ore miner.

"My wife has been most helpful in all my writings. She often has to listen to my plans before I begin a new book; and always she reads the manuscript before it's submitted to a publisher. I don't believe my first published novel would have gotten off the ground without her encouragement."

HILARY MILTON

HOBBIES AND OTHER INTERESTS: "My family, photography, target shooting (but *no* hunting), and the two-way radio."

FOR MORE INFORMATION SEE: Publishers Weekly, February 28, 1977.

MONCURE, Jane Belk (Bruce Wannamaker)

PERSONAL: Born in Orlando, Fla.; daughter of J. Blanton (a Presbyterian minister) and Jennie (Wannamaker) Belk; married Dr. James Ashby Moncure (vice president of Elon College), June 14, 1952; children: James Ashby, Jr. *Education:* Virginia Commonwealth University, B.S. in Ed.; Columbia University, M.A. in early childhood education, 1954. *Religion:* Christian. *Home:* 1046 Briarcliff Rd., Burlington, N.C. 27215.

CAREER: Teacher, author, and consultant. Woodward School, New York, N.Y., teacher, 1952-53; Adelphi College, Garden City, N.Y., summer guest instructor, 1953; First Presbyterian Church Nursery School, New York, N.Y., teacher-director, 1953-54; Southside Day Nursery, Richmond, Va., director-teacher, 1954-56; Town and Garden

JANE BELK MONCURE

School, Richmond, Va., director-teacher, 1957-64; Richmond (Va.) public schools, junior primary teacher, 1964-66; Virginia Commonwealth University, Richmond, instructor in early childhood education, 1966-71; Stanford University Research Grant, Richmond, Va., Project Follow Through program tester, 1971; Virginia Union University, Richmond, Va., professional staff member, language arts project, 1972-73; University of Richmond, Richmond, Va., instructor in early childhood education, 1973-74; Burlington Day School, Burlington, N.C., kindergarten teacher, 1974-78; author and teacher consultant in early childhood education, 1978—. Part-time consultant on day care for children under six, Department of Welfare and Institutions, Richmond, Va. Conductor with husband of University of Richmond Summer School Abroad Program, 1963-70.

MEMBER: Virginia Association for Early Childhood Education (first president, 1956), University of Richmond Faculty Wives Club (president, 1964), Southern Association on Children Under Six, National Association for the Education of Young Children, Delta Kappa Gamma, International Council of Richmond. *Awards, honors:* Early Childhood Education award for outstanding service to young children, 1979, from the Virginia Association for Early Childhood Education.

WRITINGS—All juveniles: *Pinny's Day at Play School,* Lothrop, 1955; *Bunny Finds a Home,* Orion, 1962; *Flip: The True Story of a Dairy Farm Goat,* Farrar, 1964.

Creative dramatics, creative expression and nonsense rhyme books; all published by Child's World: *How Do You Feel?,* 1973; *Rhyme Me a Rhyme,* 1976; *A Rabbit Has a Habit,* 1976; *All About Me,* 1976; *Riddle Me a Riddle,* 1977; *A Beach in My Bedroom,* 1978; *Tick-Tock, The Popcorn Clock,* 1978; *Birds, Baboons and Barefoot Bears,* 1978; *Skip Aboard a Space Ship,* 1978; *If a Dinosaur Came to Dinner,* 1978; *Magic Monsters Count to Ten,* 1979; *Magic Monsters Look for Colors,* 1979; *Magic Monsters Look for Shapes,* 1979.

Language arts books; all published by Child's World: *"Wait,"... Says His Father,* 1975; *What Does a Koala Bear Need?,* 1976; *Where Things Belong,* 1976; *All By Myself,* 1976; *A New Boy in Kindergarten,* 1976; *My Baby Brother Needs a Friend,* 1979; *I Never Say I'm Thankful, But I Am,* 1979.

"Sound Box" series; all published by Child's World: *My "B" Sound Box,* 1977; *My "F" ...,* 1977; *My "H" ...,* 1977; *My "S" ...,* 1977; *My "T" ...,* 1977; *My "D" ...,* 1978; *My "L" ...,* 1978; *My "P" ...,* 1978; *My "R" ...,* 1978; *My "W" ...,* 1978; *My "C" ...,* 1978; *My "K" ...,* 1978; *My "J" ...,* 1979; *My "M" ...,* 1979; *My "N" ...,* 1979; *My "Q" ...,* 1979; *My "V" ...,* 1979; *My "XYZ" ...,* 1979.

Science and Social Science series; all published by Child's World: *Try on a Shoe,* 1973; (under pseudonym Bruce Wannamaker) *A Trip to the Farm,* 1974; (under pseudonym Bruce Wannamaker) *A Trip to the Zoo,* 1974; *Plants Give Us Many Kinds of Food,* 1975; *Spring Is Here!,* 1975; *The Bunny Who Knew all About Plants,* 1975; *Summer Is Here!,* 1975; *Winter Is Here!,* 1975; *Fall Is Here!,* 1975; *People Who Help People,* 1975; *Animal, Animal Where Do You Live?,* 1975; *One Little World,* 1975; *Thank You, Animal Friends,* 1975; *People Who Come to My House,* 1975; *See My Garden Grow,* 1976; *What Do the Animals Do in the Zoo?,* 1976; *Pets are Smart,* 1976; *What Will It Be?,* 1976; *Just the Right Place!,* 1976; *Jobs People Do,* 1976; *What Will It Rain?,* 1977; *Barbara's Pony, Buttercup,* 1977; *What Causes It?,* 1977.

"Special Day" series, arts and crafts holiday books; all published by Child's World: *Our Thanksgiving Book,* 1976; *Our Valentine...,* 1976; *Our Easter...,* 1976; *Our Birthday...,* 1977; *Our Christmas...,* 1977; *Our Halloween...,* 1977; *Our Mother's Day...,* 1977.

Religious education series; all published by Standard Publishing: *My Baby Brother Needs Me,* 1979; *But I'm Thankful, I Really Am,* 1979; *The Gift of Christmas,* 1979; *The Boy Samuel,* 1979.

Also author of *Alphabet Books* (set of five books, including: "Play with 'A & T'"; "Play with 'E & D'"; "Play with 'I & G'"; "Play with 'O & G'"; "Play with 'U & G'"), Child's World, 1973.

Author of materials for early childhood education; all published by Child's World: *Fold Out Picture Charts* ("Plants Provide Food," "Animal Homes," "Pets," "Kinds of Animals," "Health and Body Care," "People in the Neighborhood," "Take a Walk in Spring: Summer: Fall: Winter"), 1969; *Teaching Picture Sets* ("Nonsense Rhymes," "Animals of the Wild"), 1970-71; *Table Games* ("Guess Whose Feet? Ears? Tail?," "What's Going Through the Tunnel?," "Which Piece Fits?," "What Belongs Where?"), 1972; *Time-Line Sequence Stories:* ("Going Places by Land," "Going Places by Sea," Going Places by Air," "Communication

As Buttercup galloped past, one of the boys threw a lighted firecracker into the air. ■ (From *Barbara's Pony, Buttercup* by Jane Belk Moncure. Illustrated by Franz Altschuler.)

From the Beginning," "Reptiles: From Dinosaurs to Alligators"), 1977.

SIDELIGHTS: "I had a happy childhood with summers on my grandparents' farm in South Carolina where my first delights were ducks and chicks, tadpoles and turtles, piglets and puppies.

"On the farm I fell in love with living things, planted my own little garden and milked my own cow. Most of all I enjoyed the summer evenings when 'Papoo,' my grandfather, told us wonderful stories of his adventures as a boy. He always stopped at the most exciting part of a story and we had to wait til the next night to hear the rest of the story. Sometimes his stories continued from one summer to the next. During the winter months 'Papoo' wrote us letter-stories about pirates and trips to the bottom of the sea. This stimulated my imagination and I began writing letter-stories to my grandfather.

"My parents also encouraged me to write poems and stories when I was very young. My father took us camping in the mountains of North Carolina where he had lived as a boy. I came to love the woodlands and developed a deep respect for nature and living things.

"My first teacher helped me write stories and make my very own books. As a teacher I always encourage young children to create their very own books because I remember how good it felt to be an author when I was six!

"I believe every person has the gift for creative writing. It is buried deep inside like a treasure waiting to be uncovered. I have lived half of my life with children. I am ever learning from them. I always keep a pencil and paper near me, and my books have come directly from my experiences with young people. A word, an action, sparks an idea and I begin writing it down.

"Our son's pet bunny and pet goats were both featured in several of my stories. When Jim was five years old, we took him to Europe, as my husband was teaching a European history course for college students. Jim fell asleep in New York and woke up in Paris. He said, 'Across the sea is just next door, isn't it?' That sentence sparked the idea for my book, *One Little World.* When we were in Holland I watched a little boy take off his wooden shoe and count his toes. That sparked the idea for my book, *Try On a Shoe.* The story, *Barbara's Pony Buttercup,* is a true story. Buttercup was my pony and Barbara is my sister.

"If you read my 'Special Day Books' the children's names belong to real children in my class. They really said and did the things I wrote about.

"'The Sound Box Books' were first drawn on a blackboard in my classroom before they became books.

"Lori really did say, 'I have a beach in my bedroom.' David really had an imaginary friend, a dinosaur which is my *If a Dinosaur Came to Dinner.* One morning Jeff came to school sporting a cotton beard in imitation of his father. One of his friends said, 'Jeff, you'll have to wait till you grow up to have a real beard.' That sentence sparked the book, *'Wait,' Says His Father* and so it goes with every book I write. I am never bored because there is always something new to discover, wish for, dream about or imagine.

"Writing takes patience and discipline, but I love it. My real reward comes when someone writes to me and says, 'I liked your book.' I hope someday that may happen to you, too."

Presently an author of books and educational materials for children, Moncure's writing career covers some twenty-five years. With her husband she has done extensive study and travel in foreign countries and has visited schools for young children in Germany, Holland, France, Switzerland, England, Spain, Italy and Greece. Moncure lives with her husband in Burlington, N.C. Her son, James A. Moncure II, is a student at the University of North Carolina.

FOR MORE INFORMATION SEE: Early Years, September, 1978-79; *Instructor* Magazine, September, 1978; *Burlington Daily Times,* March 29, 1979.

He was swarthy and wore a red bandanna over long, curly hair. His belt and bandolier were hung about with tools and oddments which clinked and jangled. ■ (From *Secret Island* by S.E. Moore. Illustrated by Judith Gwyn Brown.)

MOORE, Ruth

PERSONAL: Daughter of William D. (a lawyer) and Ethel (Sledd) Moore; married Raymond W. Garbe, 1967. *Education:* Washington University, St. Louis, Mo., A.B., M.A. *Home:* 860 Lake Shore Dr., Chicago, Ill. 60611.

CAREER: Chicago Sun-Times, Chicago, Ill., reporter, 1943-71, Washington correspondent, 1943-50. Commission on Chicago Historical and Architectural Landmarks, Chicago, commissioner, 1973—; University of Chicago, Chicago, president of woman's board, 1974-78. *Member:* Women's National Press Club (Washington, D.C.), Press Club (Chicago), Prairie Avenue Historic District (chairman, 1973—), Chicago Architecture Foundation (president, 1978-79), Phi Beta Kappa. *Awards, honors:* D.Litt. from McMurray College, 1955; Friends of Literature annual award, 1955; national awards from National Municipal League and American Association of Planning Officials; Washington University, alumni citation, 1963.

WRITINGS: Man, Time, Fossils, Knopf, 1953; *Charles Darwin: A Great Life in Brief,* Knopf, 1955; *The Earth We Live On,* Knopf, 1956; *The Coil of Life,* Knopf, 1960; *Evolution,* Time, Inc., 1962, revised edition, 1969; *Niels Bohr: The Man, His Science and the World They Changed,* Knopf, 1966; *Ape Into Man,* Little, Brown, 1974, revised edition, published as *Ape Into Human,* Little, Brown, 1980; *Man in the Environment,* Knopf, 1975.

MOORE, S. E.

PERSONAL: Born in Berkeley, Calif.; daughter of John W. (in U.S. Navy) and Constance (Eustis) Moore. *Education:* Wellesley College, B.A.; University of Lausanne, further study. *Agent:* Paul R. Reynolds, Inc., 12 East 41st St., New York, N.Y. 10017.

CAREER: Has lived and worked in Switzerland, American Samoa and India, and on both coasts of the United States as a member of an international organization. Has also done journalistic and editorial work. Full-time writer, 1979—. *Military service:* U.S. Navy Women's Reserve (WAVES), communications officer and aviation safety officer during World War II; became lieutenant junior grade; her communication group received the Presidential Unit Citation. *Member:* Author's Guild.

WRITINGS: Diego (juvenile), Harcourt, 1972; *Secret Island,* Four Winds, 1977.

WORK IN PROGRESS: A book on the adventures of teaspoon-size dolls; another adventure novel; a memoir and other nonfiction works.

SIDELIGHTS: "I come from a family of writers, musicians, ministers, teachers and lawyers, all of whom loved language and used it vividly, who lived with relish and daring, who faced difficulties with determination and hurt with compassion, and most of whom believed that faith makes you 'absolutely fearless, ridiculously happy—and always in trouble.' Add to that heritage, travel to far countries, friendships with people of many languages and backgrounds, and you may turn into a writer, as I did.

"From that background, I write the kind of stories I myself like to read: about persons (or animals) faced with danger or difficulty or in conflict with outside or inside forces. I like to give a hero or heroine a chance to work out his difficulties and to see him change as he does it. I like adventures to be as real as possible and full of action: sailing small boats, or flying small planes, or acting on the stage, things that I have done myself, and in places where I have lived, especially in wild country near rivers or lakes or the sea."

HOBBIES AND OTHER INTERESTS: The sea, the theater and other arts, history, foreign languages.

FOR MORE INFORMATION SEE: Horn Book, April, 1978.

MORRESSY, John 1930-

PERSONAL: Born December 8, 1930, in Brooklyn, N.Y.; son of John Emmett and Jeanette (Geraghty) Morressy; married Barbara Turner, August 11, 1956. *Education:* St. John's University, Jamaica, N.Y., B.A., 1953; New York University, M.A., 1961. *Residence:* East Sullivan, N.H. 03445. *Agent:* James Oliver Brown, James Brown Associates, 25 West 43rd St., New York, N.Y. 10036. *Office:* Department of English, Franklin Pierce College, Rindge, N.H. 03461.

CAREER: Teacher, intermittently 1956-63; St. John's University, Jamaica, N.Y., instructor in English, 1963-66; Monmouth College, West Long Branch, N.J., assistant professor of English, 1966-67; Franklin Pierce College, Rindge, N.H., 1968—, began as associate professor, currently professor of English and writer in residence. *Military service:* U.S. Army, 1953-55. *Member:* Authors Guild of America, Science Fiction Writers of America.

WRITINGS: The Blackboard Cavalier (novel), Doubleday, 1966; *The Addison Tradition* (novel), Doubleday, 1968; *Starbrat* (novel), Walker, 1972; *Nail Down the Stars* (novel), Walker, 1973; *The Humans of Ziax II* (juvenile), Walker, 1974; *A Long Communion* (novel), Walker, 1974; *Under a Calculating Star* (novel), Doubleday, 1975; *The Windows of Forever* (juvenile), Walker, 1975; *A Law for the Stars,* Laser Books, 1976; *The Extraterritorial* (novel), Laser Books, 1977; *Frostworld and Dreamfire* (novel), Doubleday, 1977; *The Drought on Ziax II* (juvenile), Walker, 1978; *Ironbrand* (novel), Playboy, 1980. Contributor of short stories, light verse, essays, and poetry to magazines ranging from *Esquire* to *Fantasy and Science Fiction* and *Omni.*

WORK IN PROGRESS: Fantasy trilogy and a novel about religion in the worlds of the future.

SIDELIGHTS: "I've been writing fiction for more than half my life, and I enjoy doing it even more now than when I began. Experience has not made writing any easier for me. Quite the reverse: the longer I work at it, the more I realize

JOHN MORRESSY

how very difficult it is to write well. If I've learned anything, it's that good writing is not easy, and easy writing is usually not good.

"The difficulty is probably the best thing about writing. There is always something new to learn, and all the old things still to be remembered. A writer's life need never be boring.

"Somehow, I seem to have arranged to have just the proper childhood for a writer. I was an only child. I had a serious illness that kept me confined to bed for a long time. I read everything I could lay my hands on (I still do that), and took to making up long, complicated stories of my own. A lot of other writers, Orwell, Trollope, and Kipling among them, have admitted to doing exactly the same thing, so it appears to be part of the basic training.

"Reflecting on this, I'm glad and grateful that I was born in 1930. If I were a child today, confined to my bed, I'd probably watch television. By the time I was twelve, I'd have no more imagination than a bread pudding.

"I write slowly. A thousand words is a good day's work. I do first drafts in longhand, revise until the manuscript is all but indecipherable, set it all aside for a while, then type the final copy myself. This is a time-consuming way to work, but somehow, the books get written.

". . . But the Earthmen have intelligence, and yet they, too, kill," the Ru-Imbur said. ■ (From *The Drought on Ziax II* by John Morressy. Illustrated by Stanley Skardinski.)

"My wife has always been a great help. Unfortunately, she has not yet mastered the knack of praising every word I write, but she's very good in all other respects. She is cheerful pleasant company, even though a writer's wife leads a very lonely life much of the time. I'm grateful for her patience.

"That is enough autobiography. John Dryden, a writer I greatly admire and respect, once wrote, 'Anything, though never so little, which a man speaks of himself, in my opinion is still too much.' I find myself agreeing.

"Since I don't want to go on about myself, and since I have no magical advice to pass on, I'd like to answer questions. There are certain questions everyone seems to ask writers, and the answers are so simple that people think the writer is joking when he gives them. I'm going to answer five of those standard questions very honestly. I'm not joking here at all.

"*How does one become a writer?* 'He writes. He sits down and writes his story, or play, or novel, and keeps at it until the work is finished. He rewrites and revises and polishes until he can't bear the sight of his own words on paper. As soon as one work is finished, he starts on the next. People who talk about writing, or intend to write just as soon as they have time, or really wish they could settle down to their writing, are not writers. Writers are people who write. If you want to write, do it. It's that simple.

"*Where can I learn to be a writer?* 'I'm not certain that anyone can learn to be a writer, any more than one can learn to be tall, or blue-eyed, or left-handed. You have to start out with a certain talent, or all the learning in the world can't help you. But if you have the talent to start with, the best place to learn is the library. The best teachers are the people who have written good books. Read them. Study them. Reread them and study them some more, all your life. Even if you never become a writer, you'll be a more interesting person.

"*Where does one find inspiration?* 'Inspiration is baloney. Anyone who sits around waiting for inspiration to strike is going to do a lot of sitting and not much writing.

"*Is there a certain atmosphere, or climate, or time of day, that is best for writing?* 'If a writer is serious about his work, he can do it anytime, anyplace, under almost any conditions. Preference is something else. We all have our preferences, but what works for me might not work for others. Sometimes it doesn't work even for me. Advice about a "right" time or a "right" place or "ideal" conditions for writing can be interesting shop talk, but it's usually completely useless.

"*How do I know if I'm really a talented writer?* 'Asking people doesn't help, unless the people you ask are editors. The only way to find out is to write the best piece you can, and send it out to the places you think might want to publish it, starting with the one that would be most likely and working down the list, one by one, until someone accepts it."

FOR MORE INFORMATION SEE: Times Literary Supplement, February 2, 1967; *New York Times Book Review,* July 28, 1968; *Best Sellers,* August 15, 1968; *Christian Science Monitor,* August 29, 1968; *Choice,* November, 1968; *Virginia Quarterly Review,* winter, 1969.

MOSKIN, Marietta D(unston) 1928-

PERSONAL: Born April 30, 1928, in Vienna, Austria; came to the United States in 1946, naturalized citizen, 1952; daughter of Felix C. and Clara (Ettinger) Dunston; married Donald Moskin (in real estate), September 5, 1958; children: James, Linda. *Education:* Barnard College, B.A., 1952; University of Wisconsin, Madison, M.A., 1955. *Residence:* New York, N.Y.

CAREER: Tax Foundation, Inc., New York City, economic research assistant, 1952-53; Savings Banks Trust Co., New York City, economic research assistant, 1955-56; General Motors Co., New York City, economic research assistant, 1956-58; writer and reviewer of children's books, 1958—. *Awards, honors:* Shirley Kravitz Children's Book Award from Association of Jewish Libraries, 1976, for *Waiting for Mama.*

WRITINGS—For children, except as noted: *The Best Birthday Party,* John Day, 1964; *With an Open Hand,* John Day, 1967; *A Paper Dragon,* John Day, 1968; *Hop, Run, Jump,* translation from German by Rose Demeter, John Day, 1968;

Maybe this month Mama will come, Becky thought. Maybe a letter will come to tell us that she is on her way. ■(From *Waiting for Mama* by Marietta Moskin. Illustrated by Richard Lebenson.)

The Bamboo School in Bali, translation from Dutch by Jef Last and U. P. Tisna, John Day, 1969; *The Different Child Grows Up* (adult), translation from German by Maria Egg, John Day, 1969.

Toto, Coward, 1971; *I Am Rosemarie,* John Day, 1972; *Lysbet and the Fire Kittens,* Coward, 1973; *Waiting for Mama,* Coward, 1975; *Adam and the Wishing Charm,* Coward, 1977; *Day of the Blizzard,* Coward, 1978; *In Search of God: The Story of Religion,* Atheneum, 1979; *In the Name of God: Religion in Everyday Life,* Atheneum, 1980.

Work anthologized in *Round About the City,* Crowell, 1966.

WORK IN PROGRESS: A teenage novel, tentatively titled *Dream Lake,* to be published by Atheneum.

SIDELIGHTS: "I can't remember a time when I didn't want to write poems or stories. And I did, as soon as I could write—first in German, then in Dutch after my family moved from my native Austria to Holland, where I had most of my elementary schooling. During World War II we spent several years in a number of concentration camps where I continued to spin a fantasy world of poetry and stories for myself on hoarded scraps of paper.

"After our liberation I had access to a library of English language books provided by the British Red Cross. The books ranged from such classics as Dickens, Scott and Thackeray through modern English and American bestsellers, such as *A Tree Grows in Brooklyn* or *How Green Was My Valley.* I read my way through that library and in the process I acquired a serviceable working knowledge of the English language. My own literary efforts turned to English too. Soon I found that I could express myself better in English than in any other language.

"It is a long step, though, from learning a language to mastering its nuances well enough to write with ease and style. I wrote for myself all through my college years and when I graduated with degrees in economics I wrote well enough to produce the written reports and surveys my jobs required. On the side, I continued to write fiction and poetry for my growing 'literary' file.

"Marriage and the birth of my first child gave me more leisure to work on writing projects. At the same time I began to review children's books for the Child Study Association on a volunteer basis. Suddenly my writing efforts took a new direction. I found that I enjoyed writing for children—sharing with them my own discoveries of new ideas and facts and my own reactions to the wonders of this world. Children read with open minds, but they can neither be fooled nor manipulated. Facts brought to them must be true, situations presented to them must be reasonable and logical, the flow of the story must be fast-paced to keep their interest and yet flow smoothly enough to capture their feelings and emotions. For an author, it is a challenge to write for such a demanding readership.

"In my books I have tried to draw as often as possible on my own experiences and remembered feelings. I hope that I can help my readers to expand their horizons and to make them understand, through my words, different ways of living, different emotions, circumstances different from their own. This reaching out and sharing is to me one of the great joys of writing for young people."

HOBBIES AND OTHER INTERESTS: New York City history, comparative religion, archaeology.

FOR MORE INFORMATION SEE: Horn Book, February, 1972, 1973, 1977; *Publishers Weekly,* February 14, 1977, February 23, 1977.

MARIETTA D. MOSKIN

I am a man, but some people say that I have never grown up. They say that I'm a kid at heart. ■
(From *A Man's Work* by Donald Myrus. Illustrated by William Steinel.)

DONALD MYRUS

MYRUS, Donald (Richard) 1927-

PERSONAL: Born September 22, 1927, in Baldwin, N.Y.; son of Richard T. and Hazel (Sawtelle) Myrus; married Joyce Dietz, September 9, 1959; children: Richard Benjamin, Noah. *Education:* University of Chicago, student, 1948-49; Muhlenberg College, A.B., 1950. *Home:* 9 Hillside Pl., Seacliff, N.Y. 11579. *Office:* Penthouse/Omni, 909 Third Ave., New York, N.Y. 10022.

CAREER: New York Daily News, New York, N.Y., copy boy, 1951-52; *Schenectady Union-Star,* Schenectady, N.Y., reporter, 1952-54; Maco Magazine Corp. and Ridge Press, editor, 1955-59; *American Gun,* founder and managing editor, 1960; Macmillan Co., New York, N.Y., senior editor of adult books, 1961-63; Grosset & Dunlap, Inc., New York, N.Y., chief editor, 1964; Ford Foundation, New York, N.Y., writer, 1964-65; Playboy Press, Chicago, Ill., director, 1966-73; Penthouse Press and Omni Society, New York, N.Y., director, 1979—. *Military service:* U.S. Navy, 1945-46. *Awards, honors:* Boys' Clubs of America, Best Book Award, 1963, for *Keeping Up with the Astronauts;* Child Study Association citation and American Institute of Graphic Arts design citation for *Story in the Sand.*

WRITINGS: The Astronauts, Grosset, 1961, revised editions published as *Keeping Up with the Astronauts,* Grosset, 1962, 1963; *Collectors' Guns,* Arco, 1961; (with Albert Squillace) *Story in the Sand,* Macmillan, 1963; *I Like Jazz,* Macmillan, 1964; *A Man's Work,* Macmillan, 1965; *Ballads, Blues, and the Big Beat,* Macmillan, 1966; (editor) *Law & Disorder: The Chicago Connection & Its Aftermath,* privately printed, 1968; (co-editor) *The Photography Catalog,* Harper, 1976; *Dog Catalog,* Macmillan, 1978; (co-editor with Ben Bova) *The Best of Omni Science Fiction,* Doubleday Science Fiction Books Club, 1980.

NELSON, Mary Carroll 1929-

PERSONAL: Born April 24, 1929, in College Station, Tex.; daughter of James Vincent (an army officer) and Mary (Langton) Carroll; married Edwin Blakely (a retired Army officer; now research consultant), June 27, 1950; children: Patricia Ann, Edwin Blakely, Jr. *Education:* Barnard College, B.A., 1950; University of New Mexico, M.A., 1963, further graduate study, 1969-70. *Politics:* Republican. *Religion:* Catholic. *Home:* 1408 Georgia N.E., Albuquerque, N.M. 87110.

CAREER: Teacher most of the time since 1957, presently art teacher at Sunset Mesa School, Albuquerque, N.M. Professional artists. *Member:* National Writers Club, Rio Grande Writers Association, National League of American Pen Women (member of chapter board, 1970-74; member of state

MARY CARROLL NELSON

board, 1972-74), New Mexico Watercolor Society (member of board, 1970-73). *Awards, honors:* Various exhibition awards for paintings.

WRITINGS—American Indian biography series for young people; all published by Dillon: *Pablita Velarde: The Story of an American Indian,* 1971; *Maria Martinez,* 1972; *Annie Wauneka,* 1972; *Michael Naranjo,* 1975; *Robert L. Bennett,* 1976.

Other: (With Robert E. Wood) *Watercolor Workshop,* Watson-Guptill, 1974; (with Ramon Kelley) *Ramon Kelley Paints Portraits and Figures,* Watson-Guptill, 1977; *The Legendary Artists of Taos,* Watson-Guptill, 1980. Contributing editor of *American Artist.* Contributor to art periodicals.

WORK IN PROGRESS: Young Children Can Learn Anything, a book about teaching; *Stories for Children; Painting Western Subjects.*

SIDELIGHTS: "I'm an Army brat. My husband is now a retired Army officer and we have two grown Army brats of our own. Moving around in the Army as we did for so long gave me many opportunities to meet new people. I like talking with other people about their lives. Since I've moved often, I'm especially curious about those who have stayed put or had one career for years. We are now settled in Albuquerque, New Mexico.

"I paint and I teach art to children. For thirteen years I taught first grade. All of my interests combine in my writing.

"There is a vast difference between writing and being published. Although my articles about art had appeared in publications, I had not had a book of mine in print until Dillon Press published *Pablita Velarde: The Story of an American Indian* in 1971—and that happened by a fluke.

"Pablita is a famous Indian painter of Santa Clara Pueblo in New Mexico. She's a friend of mine. We belong to the same branch of the National League of American Pen Women. When my husband went to Viet Nam in 1969 I decided to work on a series of reading books for elementary children and I asked Pablita if I could write about her in my fourth-grade reader.

"She courteously agreed and later showed me a letter she'd had from Dillon Press which was just starting its 'American Indian Biography' series. Pablita suggested I answer the letter and explain that I could author the book on her life, rather than the short story I intended.

"As it turned out, I wrote five books for Dillon. Each of these are about heroes. Maria and her husband Julian shared their discovery of the way to create black pottery as their ancestors did with all of those who wanted to learn in their pueblo. Annie Wauneka is a leader of the Navajos. Through her effort tuberculosis has been defeated as the number one killer of her people. Michael Naranjo was blinded in Viet Nam, but he has become one of our finest sculptors. Robert Bennett rose through the ranks of the Bureau of Indian Affairs to become the first Indian director in 200 years. You can imagine how exciting it has been for me to come to know these people and tell their story for young and older readers to enjoy.

"To me all artists are heroes because they bravely create beautiful or meaningful things for the rest of us to share even though they have no financial security. Much of my writing is about artists. I write books and articles that tell how artists work and survive; all of these are illustrated with the lovely paintings, prints and sculptures done by the subjects of the stories.

"My other writing is not really secret, but is unpublished. I write fantasies for children about fairies, UFOs, gnomes and those things we think about inside that some say are unreal. I believe the most important side of life is that which is unseen—the hunches and intuitions that come unbidden into our minds and prove to be right, the ideas and inspirations that lead us to our finest creative efforts—all these prompt my stories. I often share them with my classes and, perhaps, some day I'll illustrate them for the market. Who knows? That's one of the thrills of being a writer; you never know what will happen next."

Nelson's works are included in the Kerlan Collection at the University of Minnesota.

FOR MORE INFORMATION SEE: Publishers Weekly, February 23, 1976.

(From *The March of the Lemmings* by James R. Newton. Illustrated by Charles Robinson.)

JAMES R. NEWTON

NEWTON, James R(obert) 1935-

PERSONAL: Born December 22, 1935, in Yakima, Wash.; son of James Thompson and Daisy (Coffee) Newton; married Kay M. Fredenburg (a teacher), December 28, 1954; children: Cindy Kay, Mark Andrew. *Education:* Pacific Lutheran University, B.A., 1965; also attended Seattle Pacific University, Western Washington State College, and Central Washington State College. *Religion:* Roman Catholic. *Home:* 14917 82nd Ave. N.W., Gig Harbor, Wash. 98335.

CAREER: Franklin Pierce School District, Tacoma, Wash., elementary school teacher, 1965—. *Member:* National Education Association, Washington Education Association, Franklin Pierce Education Association.

WRITINGS: The March of the Lemmings (juvenile nonfiction), Crowell, 1976; *Forest Log* (juvenile nonfiction), Crowell, 1980. Contributor to *Ranger Rick.*

WORK IN PROGRESS: Research on "nature's mysteries"; a third juvenile nonfiction tentatively entitled *Forest-Fire-Forest.*

SIDELIGHTS: "I spend as much time as I can in field and forest. It is there that I feel closest to my creator, and I never cease to be fascinated by the innumerable mysteries of His creation."

FOR MORE INFORMATION SEE: Horn Book, April, 1977.

CHARLES NORDHOFF

NORDHOFF, Charles (Bernard) 1887-1947

PERSONAL: Born February 1, 1887, in London, England; brought to the United States by his American parents at the age of three; died April 11, 1947, in Santa Barbara, Calif.; son of Walter and Sarah Cope (Whitall) Nordhoff; married Pepé Teara (a native of Tahiti), December 4, 1920 (divorced); married Laura Grainger Whiley, 1941; children: (first marriage) Sarah, Margaret, Jane, Charles, Mary, James. *Education:* Attended Stanford University for one year; Harvard University, B.A., 1909. *Home:* Hope Ranch, Santa Barbara, Calif.

CAREER: Author. Worked on his father's ranch in Mexico for two years following his graduation from Harvard, 1909-11; secretary and treasurer of a tile and firebrick manufacturing firm in California, 1911-16; met his future collaborator, James Norman Hall, while serving in the Lafayette Flying Corps during World War I; after the war, Nordhoff emigrated with Hall to Tahiti where they began the writing partnership that continued until Nordhoff's death in 1947. *Military service:* Enlisted as a driver in the French Ambulance Corps, 1916; served as a pilot in the Lafayette Flying Corps (a squadron of American volunteers in the French Army), and finally transferred to the U.S. Air Service, 1917-19; became a first lieutenant. *Awards, honors:* Croix de Guerre with star and citation, during World War I.

WRITINGS—Novels: *The Fledgling,* Houghton, 1919; *The Pearl Lagoon,* Atlantic, 1924; *Picaro,* Harper & Brothers, 1924; *The Derelict: Further Adventures of Charles Selden and His Native Friends in the South Seas,* Little, Brown, 1928; *The Island Wreck,* Methuen, 1929.

With James Norman Hall; all novels, except as indicated: *The Lafayette Flying Corps* (history), Houghton, 1920, reissued, Kennikat, 1964; *Faery Lands of the South Seas* (nonfiction; illustrated by George A. Picken), Harper & Brothers, 1921; *Falcons of France: A Tale of Youth and the Air* (illustrated by A. Vimnera), Little, Brown, 1929.

Mutiny on the Bounty, Little, Brown, 1932 [other editions include those illustrated by Fletcher Martin, Heritage Press, 1947; N. C. Wyeth, Franklin Library, 1978; school editions for children include those published by Globe Book, 1952, and Houghton, 1962], also published in England as *Mutiny!,* Chapman & Hall, 1933; *Men Against the Sea,* Little, Brown, 1934, reprinted, 1962; *Pitcairn's Island,* Little, Brown, 1934, reprinted, 1962; *The Bounty Trilogy* (includes *Mutiny on the Bounty, Men Against the Sea,* and *Pitcairn's Island;* illustrated by Henry C. Pitz), Little, Brown, 1936 [another edition illustrated by N. C. Wyeth, Little, Brown, 1940; a school edition for children published by Globe Book, 1953]; *The Hurricane,* Little, Brown, 1936 [another edition with illustrations from the Samuel Goldwyn film production, Chapman & Hall, 1938].

The Dark River, Little, Brown, 1938; *No More Gas,* Little, Brown, 1940; *Botany Bay,* Little, Brown, 1941, reissued, C. Chivers, 1973; *Men Without Country,* Little, Brown, 1942; *The High Barbaree,* Little, Brown, 1945.

These lagoons swarm with strange forms of life unknown in northern waters. ■(From *Faery Lands of the South Seas* by James Norman Hall and Charles Nordhoff. Illustrated by George A. Picken.)

ADAPTATIONS—Movies and filmstrips: "Mutiny on the Bounty" (motion pictures), Metro-Goldwyn-Mayer, starring Charles Laughton and Clark Gable, 1935, excerpts for school use, Teaching Film Custodians, 1944, Metro-Goldwyn-Mayer, starring Marlon Brando, Trevor Howard, and Richard Harris, 1962; "Mutiny on the Bounty" (filmstrip; excerpts from the 1962 motion picture), Films Inc., 1975; "The Hurricane" (motion pictures), United Artists, starring Dorothy Lamour and Mary Astor, 1938, Paramount Pictures Corp., starring Jason Robards, Mia Farrow, Max Von Sydow, Trevor Howard, and Timothy Bottoms, 1979; "The Tuttles of Tahiti" (motion picture), adaptation of *No More Gas,* starring Charles Laughton, RKO Radio Pictures, 1942; "Passage to Marseille" (motion picture), adaptation of *Men Without Country,* starring Humphrey Bogart, Sydney Greenstreet, Claude Rains, and Peter Lorre, Warner Brother Pictures, 1944; "High Barbaree" (motion picture), starring Van Johnson and June Allyson, Loew's Inc., 1947; "Botany Bay" (motion picture), starring Alan Ladd and James Mason, Paramount Pictures Corp., 1953.

SIDELIGHTS: **1887.** Born in London where his father was a correspondent for the *New York Herald.* Two years later the family returned to the United States to live in a converted incubator building on the Hudson called "The Roost."

1890. Moved to a ranch in Baja, California, where he soon learned to hunt, sail and fish. Close to both the soil and the sea, Nordhoff gained self-reliance.

1894. Sent to a classical school for boys in Pasadena.

1906-1909. Transferred from Stanford University to Harvard University from which he graduated. Worked at several odd jobs over the next seven years: supervised a sugar cane plantation in Mexico, established the California China Company (a tile business) with his father, became an ambulance driver in France.

June, 1917. Joined the French foreign legion and attended flight school, where he became a flying enthusiast. "I began to float about in a world of utter celestial loneliness, dazzlingly pure sun, air like the water of a coral atoll, and beneath me a billowy sea of clouds, stretching far away to infinity. Here and there, from the cloudy prairies, great fantastic mountain ranges reared themselves; foothills and long divides, vast snow peaks, impalpable sisters of Orizaba and Chimborazo, and deep gorges, ever narrowing, widening, or deepening, across whose shadowy depths drove ribbons of thin gray mist." [Paul Briand, Jr., *In Search of Paradise,* Duell, Sloan and Pearce, 1966.[1]]

1918. Mother submitted his letters dealing with his war experience to *Atlantic Monthly.* "For myself, there is nowhere and nobody I would rather be at present than here and a pilot. No man in his senses could say he enjoyed the war; but as it must be fought out, I would rather be in aviation than any other branch. A pleasant life, good food, good sleep, and two to four hours a day in the air. After four hours (in two spells) over the lines, constantly alert and craning to dodge scandalously accurate shells and suddenly appearing Boches, panting in the thin air at twenty thousand feet, the boys are, I think, justified in calling it a day. I have noticed that the coolest men are a good bit let down after a dogged machine-gun fight far up in the rarefied air. It may seem soft to an infantry-man—twenty hours of sleep, eating, and loafing; but in reality the airman should be given an easy time outside of flying."[1]

(From *Mutiny on the Bounty* by Charles Nordhoff and James Norman Hall. Illustrated by Fletcher Martin.)

1919. Assigned as a co-editor with James Norman Hall of a history on the Lafayette Flying Corps. Hall recalled his first impression of Nordhoff: "We made little progress toward friendship in our first conversations. The fact that I was from Iowa was anything but in my favor with Nordhoff, although his only comment when he learned this was that his state, California, was 'lousy with Iowans.'. . .

"Once I got to know him [however] my liking for him increased daily. I had never before met a man who had a wider store of information upon so many unrelated subjects. I discovered, later, that some of it was misinformation, but he spoke upon whatever subject with such an air of authority that one was ready to believe whatever he said. He loved to exaggerate, to astonish people by making extravagant statements with the gravest air, but it was all a kind of game with him. He was often surprised—shocked, rather—that he got away with so many of them. But in the field of natural history he was deeply learned, particularly about game birds, their habits, haunts, migrations, and the like. He loved wild birds far better than people. He told me that his father had

"Stand back, you others!" said Bligh. "Up with your weapon, you mutinous villain! I'll soon prove whether you are a man or not! ■ (From "Men Against the Sea," in *The Bounty Trilogy* by Charles Nordhoff and James Norman Hall. Illustrated by N. C. Wyeth.)

(From the movie "Botany Bay," starring Alan Ladd, Patricia Medina, and James Mason. Copyright 1953 by Paramount Pictures Corp.)

(From *Falcons of France* by Charles Nordhoff and James Norman Hall. Illustrated by A. Vimnèra.)

(From the movie "High Barbaree," starring Van Johnson, June Allyson, and Cameron Mitchell. Copyright 1947 by Loew's, Inc.)

given him the best possible education as a youngster—that is, no education at all except what he had been able to pick up for himself on the lonely ranch in Lower California. He had not learned to read and write until he was twelve. At least, so he insisted, but this may have been one of his exaggerations that he held fast to until he believed it himself.

"One thing that brought us together quickly was the dream we held in common: to visit the South Seas; many an evening we spent discussing this possibility.

"'Why shouldn't we go as soon as we are demobilized?' Nordhoff said. 'We'll both be at loose ends. We are not married and have no jobs to return to.'

"And so that was agreed upon. Neither of us would make any new commitments. As soon as we had finished the Lafayette Corps History that dream was to become a reality." [James Hall, *My Island Home,* Little, Brown, 1952. [2]]

January, 1920. Embarked on a South Seas adventure with Hall. "After being in France for these past few years and seeing what civilization had done to mankind, I want to get as far away from it as possible; so, if the South Seas are as I hope they are, that is where I want to spend the rest of my life."[1]

December 4, 1920. Married Pepé Teara, a Tahitian girl.

1921. Collaborated with Hall on *Faery Lands of the South Seas.* Also wrote his own juveniles, although literary work was most successful when Nordhoff collaborated with Hall. An editor commented that friendship was the mainspring of this collaboration. "What a contrast, those two young men! Nordhoff slightly scornful, very ambitious, Hall modest to a fault; Nordhoff skeptical and distrusting, Hall with no formulated belief but trusting absolutely in good. Both had a compelling sense of beauty; but for Nordhoff it was the beauty of strength and the outward world, for Hall the fairness of the inner, poetry and dream. Nordhoff was strikingly handsome in those days, a young David straight as a javelin, with aristocratic features and a manner that showed friendliness was not to be imposed upon. Hall wore a homely pleasantness about him reminding one, in spite of his soldiering abroad, of the good earth of his father's farm. Nordhoff had his inhibitions, too, but he was full of confidence and too eager to let doubts raise their interrogating heads. . . ."[2]

1929. Another Hall-Nordhoff book, *Falcons of France,* was published. Hall recalled their next and most successful collaboration: " . . . After we had written *Falcons of France,* Nordhoff said: 'Why don't we go on writing together? Two heads are better than one, and neither of us seems to be making much progress writing alone.' I was more than willing, so we began searching around for a story that both of us would be interested in. Nordhoff suggested that we might continue his boy, Charles Selden: bring him back to the South Seas, after the war, and put him through another series of adventures, concerning a hurricane, perhaps. But I was not greatly interested in boys' books, although publishers had told us that a good boy's book was like an investment in government bonds, bringing in small but steady returns, sometimes over a period of many years.

"One day I said to Nordhoff: 'Have you ever heard of the *Bounty* mutiny?'

"'Of course,' he replied. 'Who hasn't, who knows anything about the South Seas?'

"'Well, what about that for a story?'

"Nordhoff shook his head. 'Someone must have written it long since.'

"'I doubt it,' I replied. 'The only book I have seen is Sir John Barrow's factual account of the mutiny. Barrow was Secretary of the British Admiralty at that time. His book was published in 1831.'

"I saw in my friend's eyes a Nordhoffian glow and sparkle which meant that his interest was being aroused. 'By the Lord, Hall!' he said. 'Maybe we've got something there! I wish we could get hold of a copy of Barrow's book.'

"'I have it,' I replied. 'I bought it in Paris during the war.'

"The result was that Nordhoff took the book home to read and the next day he was back, and he was in what I can only call a 'dither' of excitement. 'Hall, what a story! What a story!' he said, as he walked up and down my veranda.

"'It's three stories,' I replied. 'First, the tale of the mutiny; then Bligh's open-boat voyage, and the third, the adventures of Fletcher Christian and the mutineers who went with him to Pitcairn Island, together with the Tahitian men and women who accompanied them. It's a natural for historical fiction. Who could, possibly, invent a better story? And it has the merit of being true.'

"'You're right, it *is* a natural,' said Nordhoff, 'but . . . ' he shook his head, glumly. 'It must have been written long since. It's incredible that such a tale should have been waiting a century and a half for someone to see its possibilities.'

"Nevertheless, after having made the widest inquiries and the most painstaking researches, the only book we discovered concerned with the *Bounty* mutiny—outside of Bligh's own narrative, Sir John Barrow's account, and others written by British seamen such as Captain Staines and Pipon who had written of Pitcairn after the discovery of Christian's refuge by Captain Folger, in 1808—was a tale called *Aleck, the Last of the Mutineers, or, The History of Pitcairn Island,* published anonymously by J. S. & C. Adams, at Amherst, Massachusetts, in 1845. This book was designed for young readers, and was made up of a compilation, culled from other books, of the facts then known about the *Bounty* mutiny."[2]

1930. Continued to spend his middle years in repose in Tahiti. "A man will, usually, find a few congenial souls wherever he goes. I live here because I like a tropical climate, fishing in tropical waters, and going to seed slowly and pleasantly.

"I have . . . said that I enjoy going to seed. I am clear-sighted enough to realize what is happening, but I don't care. I don't in the least object. I am now in my forty-third year. Thus far I have had as wide an experience of life as a man could wish. I have learned many things and unlearned many. I have arrived, by hard thinking, at various conclusions with respect to the meaning of life and of man's place in the universe; more particularly, my own place. By hard thinking I have discarded, in turn, these conclusions. I shall form no new ones. I no longer care whether or not there is meaning in life, or whether or not I am entitled to a place in the cosmical scheme. I have now had the place for a considerable number

(From the movie "Mutiny on the Bounty," starring Marlon Brando and Trevor Howard. Produced by Metro-Goldwyn-Mayer, 1962.)

(From the movie "Hurricane," starring Thomas Mitchell, Jon Hall, and Mary Astor. Copyright 1937 by Samuel Goldwyn, Inc.)

Bligh paced the quarter-deck angrily as the boat approached. By nature a man who brooded over grudges till they were magnified out of all proportion to reality, the captain was ready to explode.... ■(From the movie "Mutiny on the Bounty," starring Charles Laughton. Copyright 1935 by Metro-Goldwyn-Mayer Corp.)

(From the movie "Hurricane," starring Jason Robards and Mia Farrow. Copyright © 1979 by Dino De Laurentiis Corp.)

(From the movie "Passage to Marseille," starring Humphrey Bogart and Peter Lorre, adapted from the novel, *Men Without Country*. Copyright 1944 by Warner Brothers Pictures.)

(From the movie "Tuttles of Tahiti," starring Charles Laughton and Jon Hall, adapted from the novel, *No More Gas*. Copyright 1942 by RKO Radio Pictures, Inc.)

of years, and in view of that fact I can afford to be content. Fly from Tahiti? For what reason? And where to?"[2]

1931. Blamed his wife for the death of his son. Marriage disintegrated in the wake of excessive drinking, infidelity and violence. "I came to Tahiti taproots and all, and they are now comfortably embedded here. Nevertheless, I realize that I am an exotic plant and must suffer the consequences of the change of habitat. My growth here has been sickly, but my decay will, I believe, be luxuriant and low."[2]

1937. Resisted Hall's suggestions to return to the United States. "What chance would I have to go to seed [in America]? I would not be permitted to. I would be bribed, or forced out of my quite natural inclination to go downhill. I would be driven uphill to the very end, and so cheated out of my birthright to an agreeable old age. And think of the freedom of a special kind that one has here: freedom from the influence of the mass mind, with its intolerance, its disregard of minority rights and opinions, its profound belief in material progress, and that science will, ultimately, solve all the riddles of the universe. It is impossible for the individual, living within the scope of this mighty influence, not to be affected by it.

". . . I mean to depart from the practice of most men of our years. They cling to the fiction that they are still vigorous youngsters until, at the age of forty-five or thereabout, the fact that they have long been middle-aged is forced upon them. Then they persist in being middle-aged until they are ready to topple into their graves, crowding their old age into a scant year or two.

"But consider my happy prospect. I may have thirty, even forty years to spend in this pleasant old-man's garden. I shall have time to enjoy to the full an old man's pleasures. I shall read old books and care nothing about the new ones. I needn't try to keep abreast of the world's doings, and who would care to, in these times? My fishing will keep me healthy in body, and the humdrum existence we live here will keep me tranquil in mind. . . ."[2]

1941. Returned to the United States where he married Laura Grainger Whiley.

April 11, 1947. Died in California. Nordhoff never returned to his tropical paradise. "How many men want to discover themselves? We already know too much to wish to make further explorations."[2]

HOBBIES AND OTHER INTERESTS: Anthropology and fishing.

FOR MORE INFORMATION SEE: Harry R. Warfel, *American Novelists of Today,* American Book Co., 1951; James Hall, *My Island Home,* Little, Brown, 1952; Frank Northen Magill, *Cyclopedia of World Authors,* Harper, 1958; Paul L. Briand, *In Search of Paradise: The Nordhoff-Hall Story,* Duell, 1966.

Obituaries: *New York Times,* April 12, 1947; *Newsweek,* April 21, 1947; *Time,* April 21, 1947; *Publishers Weekly,* May 3, 1947; *Wilson Library Bulletin,* June, 1947.

Come, my best friends, my books, and lead me on.
—Abraham Cowley

(From *Frogs, Toads & Newts* by F. D. Ommanney. Illustrated by Deborah Fulford.)

OMMANNEY, F(rancis) D(ownes) 1903-1980

PERSONAL: Born April 22, 1903, in England; died in 1980 in Cobham, England; son of Francis Frederick (a lawyer) and Olive Caroline (Owen) Ommanney. *Education:* Attended Aldenham School, Elstree, Hertfordshire, England, 1915-18; Royal College of Science, London, England, A.R.C.Sc. and B.Sc. (honors), 1926; Ph.D. (London), 1934. *Residence:* Somerset, England. *Agent:* Curtis Brown Ltd., 1 Craven Hill, London W2 3EP, England.

CAREER: East London College, University of London, England, assistant lecturer in zoology, 1926-29; Colonial Office, London, England, scientific officer on "Discovery" Committee, 1929-39; British Council, London, England, science editor, 1946-47; Colonial Office, scientific officer on Mauritius-Seychelles Fisheries Survey in Indian Ocean, 1947-50; Marine Fisheries Research Organization, Zanzibar, chief scientific officer, 1951-52; Singapore Regional Fisheries Research Station, Singapore, director, 1952-57; University of Hong Kong, Hong Kong, reader in marine biology, 1957-60. UNESCO, adviser in oceanography, Pusan, South Korea, 1964. *Military service:* Royal Naval Volunteer Reserve, 1940-46; became lieutenant commander.

MEMBER: Marine Biological Association, Institute of Biology (fellow), Royal Society of Literature (fellow), Linnean Society (fellow), Challenger Society, Travellers' Club, Royal Society of Arts and Science (fellow). *Awards, honors: Sunday Times* gold medal for the best travel book of the year, 1938, for *South Latitude;* bronze Polar Medal, 1942, for work in the Antarctic, 1929-39.

WRITINGS: Below the Roaring Forties, Longmans, Green (New York), 1938; *North Cape,* Longmans, Green (London), 1939; *The House in the Park* (autobiographical), Longmans, Green (London), 1944; *The Ocean,* Oxford University Press, 1949; *The Shoals of Capricorn,* Harcourt, 1952; *Isle of Cloves,* Longmans, Green (London), 1954; *Eastern Windows,* Longmans, Green (London), 1957; *Fragrant Harbour,* Doubleday, 1957; (with editors of *Life*) *The Fishes,* Time-

Life, 1963; *A Draught of Fishes,* Longmans, Green (London), 1965; *Lost Leviathan: Whales and Whaling,* Anchor Press, 1971; *Frogs, Toads & Newts,* McGraw, 1975.

SIDELIGHTS: Ommanney took part in three Antarctic expeditions with the research ship, "Discovery II," from 1929-36; on the third expedition he went to the assistance of explorer Lincoln Ellsworth at Little America after Ellsworth's Antarctic transcontinental flight that took him to Australia. During 1947-50 he participated in a fishing survey covering more than 25,000 miles of the western Indian Ocean. All but two of his books are based on travels and experiences on expeditions and surveys.

FOR MORE INFORMATION SEE—Obituaries: *AB Bookman's Weekly,* October 6, 1980; *Contemporary Authors,* Volume 101-104, Galc, 1981.

PALLAS, Norvin 1918-

PERSONAL: Born April 4, 1918, in Cleveland, Ohio; son of Rudolph and Elsa (Laurence) Pallas. *Education:* Attended public schools in Cleveland, Ohio. *Home:* 3823 Behrwald Ave., Cleveland, Ohio 44109.

CAREER: Free-lance writer and part-time accountant.

WRITINGS—All published by Washburn, except as noted: *The Secret of Thunder Mountain,* 1951; *The Locked Safe Mystery,* 1954; *The Star Reporter Mystery,* 1955; *The Singing Trees Mystery,* 1956; *The Empty House Mystery,* 1957; *The Counterfeit Mystery,* 1958; *The Stolen Plans Mystery,* 1959; *The Scarecrow Mystery,* 1960; *The Big Cat Mystery,* 1961; *The Missing Witness Mystery,* 1962; *The Baseball Mystery,* 1963; *The Mystery of Rainbow Gulch,* 1964; *The Abandoned Mine Mystery,* 1965; *The S. S. Shamrock Mystery,* 1966; *The Greenhouse Mystery,* 1967; *Code Games,* Sterling, 1971, Piccolo, 1973; (with Norris and Ross McWhirter) *Guinness Game Book,* Bantam, 1974; (with Norris and Ross McWhirter) *Guinness Book of Games & Puzzles,* Corgi/Carousel, 1974; *1975 Guinness Game Book,* Bantam, 1975; *Calculator Puzzles, Tricks & Games,* Sterling, 1976; (with Norris McWhirter) *Guinness New Game Book,* Sterling, 1978; *Short Short Stories,* Newbery House, 1981. Contributor to newspapers, to poetry anthologies, and to puzzle magazines.

WORK IN PROGRESS: "My present efforts are directed toward the mathematical and adult mystery fields."

SIDELIGHTS: "When I was a child we read and read, often the same books over and over. I believe I may have read *Huckleberry Finn* as many as fifty times. Does any present-day child do that? One reason of course was that our selections were limited to our own small collections or the meager offerings in the public library, where the most popular books were usually out anyway.

"On our trips downtown we always ended in the book department, where we were allowed to purchase a book of our own choice. What a delicious smell of shelves and shelves of new books! How eager we were to get home where we might race through the book, and then start right over again to read it more leisurely.

"This was before television, but we had our radio and movies (no ratings required) and other distractions, so we were not merely filling our idle hours with books. What difference has television made? It is not merely the time devoted to it, but seemingly a change of attitudes. The pictures flash effortless before the eyes. There is swift movement, often unmotivated or irrational, which is all right because there is no time to think. The television set is a pacemaker, with which you must keep up. You cannot approach it only when you are ready, skim lightly or plod slowly and digest.

"The problem is that the youngster may so adjust to television that he expects the same thing from books, and when he doesn't get it he is lost and frequently abandons the quest. Television and movies have strong visual appeal, without much depth. Books are more contemplative, deeper; you become acquainted with the characters and way of life presented. When you see a good television program, you may have difficulty recalling it a month later. When you read a good book, you may someday tell your grandchildren about it.

"There are still omnivorous readers among children today, but perhaps most children approach books tentatively, reluctantly. Are they aware of what they are missing, of what may be lost to them forever if they do not seize the opportunity now? Most knowlege, most understanding, most appreciation of the good things life has to offer come by way of the printed word. Without it, a person is limited to his own personal experiences. His immediate environment contains him like a strait-jacket. Books are a road to an expanded life, to freedom!

"As a boy I produced a family newspaper for several years, and later served on the high school newspaper staff. This gave me the background I later used in my juvenile mysteries. Why did I write juveniles? Well, I wrote adult material, too, but my juveniles were more successful. People said I had a greater feeling for children than I did for adults. Why did I write mysteries? I have always had a strong mathematical bend, which I think led me into the construction of strong

NORVIN PALLAS

1,234 - 463 and find out what you'll be after eating four gallons of ice cream. ■(From *Calculator Puzzles, Tricks & Games* by Norvin Pallas. Drawing by Joyce Behr.)

plots. At the time I began my juvenile mystery series, I believe I brought something new to the field. These were complicated, logical, adult-style plots (even adult readers were not very successful in guessing the outcomes), but without violence, with idealistic protagonists trying to accomplish decent things, the characters acting the way I thought real people should act. My juveniles did not do impossible things, solving mysteries that baffled the police, with heroic feats beyond their capacity, or narrow escape after narrow escape without the law of averages ever overtaking them, immune from disaster. Occasionally they experienced heart-breaking failures.

"I did not care to write about alcoholic parents, which is a problem a child can learn to adjust to somehow but cannot solve. I did not write about dope, feeling that any children fooling around with that stuff after all the warnings given to them would be too stupid to be attracted to my books anyway. I did not burden them with rape or abortions, which is essentially an adult problem, touching children only when they are propelled too quickly into the adult world. I figured that my readers were children, but I respected them for it, and did not talk down to them. Should we try to protect children from the realities of the world? No. Should we offer them a view of the more sublime values of life? Yes.

"I would have liked to write something other than mysteries, but I was told that the juvenile market was not that auspicious, and that only books with an assured market could be published. In my view the test of a worthy book is whether the author is sincerely trying his best, or is writing down to popular ideas, pandering the low tastes, seeking out the worst in people instead of the best, looking for a quick buck, or maybe desperately trying anything. Such books are not worthy of your time or money, and when you or the library purchase them, demand them, grub in them, you are helping to prevent more worthy books from ever seeing the light of day."

HOBBIES AND OTHER INTERESTS: Cryptography, math, puzzles, and games.

PAUL, James 1936-
(J. C. Kocsis)

PERSONAL: Born April 27, 1936, in Buffalo, New York. *Education:* Studied at Fleisher Art Memorial School; attended Philadelphia College of Art where he studied under Jacob Landau. *Home:* Philadelphia, Pennsylvania.

Sometimes he wasn't lucky enough to wake up in time, and then the lid came off and he dreamed.

Now Calvin tried to slam the lid down on the Indian again. The Indian wasn't a dream, although Calvin kept thinking of him that way to keep the lid on his memory. ■(From *Edge of Two Worlds* by Weyman Jones. Illustrated by J. C. Kocsis.)

CAREER: Artist and illustrator. Held his first one-man show at the age of fourteen; began illustrating magazines and books following his service in the Army; has been a member of the faculty of the Philadelphia College of Art since 1965. James Paul has worked with the American Camping Association and the YMCA specializing in American Indian Folklore, since 1949. *Military service:* Inducted into the Army during the late 1950's; served in Germany.

ILLUSTRATOR—Under pseudonym J. C. Kocsis: Henri Bosco, *Boy and the River,* Pantheon, 1957; Judith Unger Scott, *The Art of Being a Girl,* Macrae, 1963; Alberta Armer, *Steve and the Guide Dogs,* World Publishing, 1965; James Reeves, *Strange Light,* Rand McNally, 1966; Elizabeth Ladd, *Trouble on Heron's Neck,* Morrow, 1966; A. Armer, *Troublemaker,* World Publishing, 1966; Anne Huston and J. H. Yolen, *Trust a City Kid,* Lothrop, 1966; Lyn Harmon, *Flight to Jewell Island,* Lippincott, 1967; Aline Glasgow, *Journey of Akbar,* Dial, 1967; Myrtle Shay, *Two on the Trail,* Bobbs-Merrill, 1967; Weyman Jones, *Edge of Two Worlds,* Dial, 1968, reissued, Dell, 1970; Giuliana Boldrini, *Etruscan Leopards* (translated by Isabel Quigley), Pantheon, 1968.

SIDELIGHTS: Paul painted his first two pictures at the age of twelve using a small set of oil paints he had received as a Christmas gift. His parents were so impressed with his efforts that they engaged two professional artists to train him. Two years later, after numerous commissions, he was holding his first one-man show. From that time on, Paul has devoted himself to art and illustration.

FOR MORE INFORMATION SEE: Lee Kingman, and others, compilers, *Illustrators of Children's Books, 1957-1966,* Horn Book, 1968.

(From *Alice's Adventures in Wonderland* [*and*] *Through the Looking-Glass* by Lewis Carroll. Illustrated by Mervyn Peake.)

PEAKE, Mervyn 1911-1968

PERSONAL: Born July 9, 1911, in Kuling, Central China; died November 18, 1968 at Burcot, Oxfordshire, England; son of Ernest Cromwell (a doctor) and Elizabeth (Powell) Peake; married Maeve Gilmore (a painter), 1937; children: Sebastian, Fabian, Clare. *Education:* Attended grammar school in Tientsin, China, Eltham College and Royal Academy Schools in England. *Home:* 1 Drayton Gardens, London, S.W. 10, England. *Agent:* David Higham Associates, 76 Dean St., Soho, London, W.1, England.

MERVYN PEAKE

CAREER: Author, poet, painter (was Britain's official artist sent to the liberated German concentration camp at Belsen), and illustrator of his own and other books. From 1964 until his death, Peake had been hospitalized for treatment of encephalitis, which he contracted in 1956. He was far too ill to work or to understand that new editions of his books were being published. *Military service:* British Army; served as an engineer then as an official military artist during World War II. *Member:* Royal Society of Literature (fellow).

EXHIBITIONS: Royal Academy, London, 1931; Soho Group, Regal Restaurant, Soho, London, 1931; The "20s Group," Wethern Gallery, London, 1932; The Gallery, Sark, England, 1933; Cooling Galleries, London, 1934; R.B.A., London, 1935; Leger Galleries, London, 1936; Calmann Gallery, London, 1938; Leicester Galleries, London, 1939; "Satirical Drawings of our Time," Delius Giese Gallery, London, 1939; National Gallery, Washington, D.C., 1943; Adams Gallery,

London, 1946; Arcade Gallery, London, 1946; Waddington Galleries, Dublin, Ireland, c.1956; Collectors Gallery, London, c.1957, c.1958; Waddington Gallery, London, c.1957; Upper Grosvenor Galleries, London, c.1967; Eltham College, London, 1969; Swansea University, Swansea, England, 1970; National Book League Exhibition, London, 1972. *Awards, honors:* Heinemann Award for Literature, for *Gormenghast* and *The Glassblowers,* 1951.

WRITINGS: Shapes and Sounds (poems), Chatto & Windus, 1940; (self-illustrated) *Captain Slaughterboard Drops Anchor,* Eyre & Spottiswoode, 1942, Macmillan, 1967, Academy Edition, 1973; (self-illustrated poems) *Rhymes Without Reason* (poems), Eyre & Spottiswoode, 1944; *The Glassblowers* (poems), Eyre & Spottiswoode, 1945; *The Drawings of Mervyn Peake,* Grey Walls Press, 1945; *Titus Groan,* Eyre & Spottiswoode, 1945, published in America, with *Gormenghast* and *Titus Alone,* as *The Gormenghast Trilogy,* Weybright & Talley, 1967; (self-illustrated) *Craft of the Lead Pencil,* Wingate, 1946; (self-illustrated) *Letters from a Lost Uncle,* Eyre & Spottiswoode, 1947; *Gormenghast,* Eyre & Spottiswoode, 1950; *Mr. Pye,* Heinemann, 1954, Penguin, 1972; *Figures of Speech,* Gollancz, 1954; *Boy in Darkness,* Eyre & Spottiswoode, 1956, Ballantine, 1957; *Titus Alone,* Eyre & Spottiswoode, 1959, revised edition, 1970, (self-illustrated) *Rhyme of the Flying Bomb* (poems), Dent, 1962; *Poems and Drawings,* Keepsake Press, 1965; *A Reverie of Bone, and Other Poems,* Bertram Rota, 1967; *Mervyn Peake: A Book of Nonsense,* Peter Owen, 1972. Author of play, "The Wit to Woo," performed at Arts Theatre, London, 1958.

(From "The Three Spinners" in *Household Tales* by the Brothers Grimm. Illustrated by Mervyn Peake.)

(From *Treasure Island* by Robert Louis Stevenson. Illustrated by Mervyn Peake.)

Illustrator: *Ride a Cock-Horse and Other Nursery Rhymes,* Chatto & Windus, 1940, 1972; Lewis Carroll (pseudonym of Charles L. Dodgson), *The Hunting of the Snark,* Chatto & Windus, 1941, 8th edition, 1973; Samuel Taylor Coleridge, *The Rime of the Ancient Mariner,* Chatto & Windus, 1943, 3rd edition, 1971; E. M. Joad, *Adventures of the Young Soldier,* Faber & Faber, 1943; Q. Crisp, *All This and Bevin Too,* Nicholas & Watson, 1943; A. M. Laing, *Prayers and Graces,* Gollancz, 1944; C. Hole, *Witchcraft in England,* Batsford, 1945; Brothers Grimm, *Household Tales,* Eyre & Spottiswoode, 1946; M. C. Collis, *Quest for Sita,* Faber & Faber, 1946, John Day, 1947; Robert Lewis Stevenson, *Dr. Jekyll and Mr. Hyde,* Cassell, 1948; Robert Lewis Stevenson, *Treasure Island,* Eyre & Spottiswoode, 1949; D. K. Haynes, *Thou Shalt Not Suffer a Witch,* Methuen, 1949.

J. D. Wyss, *The Swiss Family Robinson,* Heirloom Library, 1950; H. B. Drake, *The Book of Lyonne,* Falcon, 1952; E. C. Palmer, *The Young Blackbird,* Wingate, 1953; Lewis Carroll (pseudonym of Charles L. Dodgson), *Alice's Adventures in Wonderland,* Wingate, 1954; Lewis Carroll (pseudonym of C. L. Dodgson), *Through the Looking Glass,* Wingate, 1954; P. B. Austin, *The Wonderful Life and Adventures of Tom Thumb* (two volumes), Radio Sweden, 1954-55; A. Sander, *Men: A Dialogue Between Women,* Cresset, 1955; H. B. Drake, *Oxford English Course for Secondary Schools*

(Book I), Oxford University Press, 1957; A. M. Laing, *More Prayers and Graces,* Gollancz, 1957; A. Judah, *The Pot of Gold and Two Other Tales,* Faber & Faber, 1959; H. de Balzac, *Droll Stories,* Cassell, 1961.

Collections: *Selected Poems of Mervyn Peake,* Faber & Faber, 1972; *The Drawings of Mervyn Peake* (introduction by Hilary Spurling), Davis-Poynter, 1974; *Mervyn Peake: Writings and Drawings* (compiled by Maeve Gilmore and Shelagh Johnson), St. Martin's, 1974.

SIDELIGHTS: **July 9, 1911.** Born in Kuling, Central China, the son of an Anglo-Swiss father and a Welsh mother. When only five months old moved to Tientsin (Northern China) where the scenes of poverty and deprivation served as material on which his later works were based.

1921. At the age of ten, wrote and illustrated *Ways of Travelling* combining elements of reality of life in China with adventures and fantasy. "The first travelling I ever did was in a mountain-chair, from Kuling, when I was only five months old. I was carried shoulder high by four very surefooted Chinese, while one false step on uneven ground would carry all five of us hundreds of feet below. From the chair I went on to a Yangtzse river steamer. The steamer was very nice and comfortable. I know, because I have been on some since. They are much smaller than any ordinary sea steamer.

"I used to go to school on a donkey, and it was great fun, because he used to gallop like anything. . . .

"I once rode in a Peking cart in Tsang-Chow. There is a mule between two shafts pulling a covered over cart. The cart has no springs, so that it bumps terribly, so that it makes your bones very sore.

"The driver sits on the shafts very near the mule's tail. The people inside are usually very cramped.

"I have been on many train journeys, but my longest was from China across Siberia to England. It took us just twelve days from Tientsin to London. We passed through Russia and we had Russian tea. Many of the Russian women sold us eatables like bread, milk and eggs.

"My longest sea trip was from England to China in a Japanese steamer around the Cape. The whole journey took two months, and it was pretty risky because at that time the war was on and the German submarines were out." [Maeve Gilmore and Shelagh Johnson, *Mervyn Peake,* St. Martin's Press, 1974. [1]]

(From *The Hunting of the Snark* by Lewis Carroll. Illustrated by Mervyn Peake.)

Mervyn Peake and his wife, Maeve.

1922. Peake returned with his family to England where he entered Eltham College.

1927-1929. After attending Croydon School of Art for one year, Peake was accepted as a student at the Royal Academy Schools. During this period he wrote and painted with equal vigor.

1937. Married art student, Maeve Gilmore. They had three children, two boys and a girl.

1939. *Captain Slaughterboard Drops Anchor* brought him initial public recognition.

1940. Began army training but was invalided out three years later after suffering a nervous breakdown precipitated by the rigors of army life.

1945. Officially assigned to visit Belsen concentration camp to draw the scenes there. Gained a reputation as an artist, illustrator, novelist, and poet. "To make a drawing is to record an idea: an idea of a particular breed that can only be expressed through making marks on a piece of paper. This process alone can arrest, transmute, and give it permanence. For drawing should be an attempt to hold back from the brink of oblivion some fleeting line or rhythm, some mood, some shape or structure suddenly perceived, imaginary or visual. Something *about* a head that calls out to be recorded: something *about* the folds of a long cloth: the crawling wave; the child; the tear; the brood of shadows. That movement of the arm that hinted fear: that gesture that spelt amazement: the dream; the alleyway; clown; broker; stone or lizard. The quicksands closing on a centaur's head tokens no more of magic than the penny loaf. They both exist. Neither be afraid of the unorthodox subject nor in finding delight in the contemplation of commonplace things. Anything, seen without prejudice, is enormous."[1]

1946. *Titus Groan,* the first book in his *Gormenghast Trilogy,* was a financial and critical success and allowed Peake to rent a house on Sark, an island in the English Channel where his family lived for three years.

The trilogy was met with mixed reviews in America. Stephen J. Laut wrote: "The entire pseudo-medieval setting has all the surrealism of a nightmare; the characters are as wild a collection of grotesques as one could find. The strange anachronisms which dot the tale contribute to a strange timelessness which makes it quite impossible to pin down just when these weird events occur. Bizarre landscape, odd customs and climate make the locale of the work equally as mysterious." But, Laut added, "here reality escapes and no motives for the overwhelming fantasy are visible. . . . Mervyn Peake, unfortunately, is no Tolkien, nor a T. H. White, nor even a Malory."

Ostermann, however, was convinced that the trilogy was "an eccentric, poetic masterpiece." He wrote: "The *Gormenghast* is about Titus Groan and his accent toward manhood. And yet to speak of these novels as being 'about' something is as inadequate as saying the Odyssey is about a man trying to get home to his wife. Such fiction as this is first and foremost about itself. Their life is their own—a bizarre, often awful life. And it imposes itself with obsessive force on the reader." Ostermann described Peake's language, "which now surges and booms like tidal surf, now curls out to trap heaven and hell in silken loops," as one of the primary sources of life in the novels. "Language and scenes combine the lyrical and the monstrous, and it would be hard to find their equivalent in contemporary fiction. . . . They are, in short, a triumph. The author's inventiveness does not falter; he retains mastery of theme and story despite the more than 13 years of writing involved."

Long before the advent of the hippies, Peake, with his long hair, flamboyant clothes, and jewelry, was a familiar sight in Chelsea.

1949. Returned to London where he taught two days a week at the Central School of Art. "What a city for the 'head-hunter!' From Half-Moon Street, where some cog in Schiaparelli's dazzling wheel picks its feline, yet metallic way, like a clockwork leopard through a crowd of beasts less elegant, to where, in the Limehouse undergrowths, an old woman stops to pull from her ragged pocket her grandchild's yellow sock and wipes the sweat from her wrinkled neck.

"The endless, generous profligacy of every sliding second—and nothing moves but has its repercussions. A hundred tales, and labelled ways of life, each with its rhythm and jargons. But how few they are, these trades, compared with the subtle, secret, nameless paths that, once upon a time, shone like a sun-glance in the early mind. The paths, the phantom-trades, or trails have been lost for ever. The talents that never bore fruit or even flowered: the forgotten talents; the murdered talents; the shamefaced talents; the talents of such forlorn uniqueness that they have no bearing upon the theme of keeping alive or of embodiment; the talents that were so original that they were broken beneath the stamping feet of boyhood as something too delicate to be allowed."[1]

1951. After the death of his father, Peake moved his family into his father's home in Wallington, Surrey. Concern for his own creative work began to supersede his interest in book illustrations. Besides writing books and poetry he also wrote several plays, which were mostly unsuccessful. "This is the problem of the artist—to discover his language. It is a lifelong search for when the idiom is found it has then to be developed and sharpened. But worse than no style is a mannerism—a formula for producing effects, the fruit of suicide.

"If I am asked whether all this is not just a little 'intense'—in other words, if it is suggested that it doesn't really matter, I say that it matters fundamentally. For one may as well be asked, 'Does life matter?'—'Does man matter?' If man matters, then the highest flights of his mind and his imagination matter. His vision matters, his sense of wonder, his vitality matters. It gives the lie to the nihilists and those who cry 'Woe!' in the streets. For art is the voice of man, naked, militant, and unashamed."[1]

1957. Admitted to a hospital with a nervous breakdown. Upon his discharge Peake showed early symptoms of Parkinson's Disease which severely affected his work.

1961. Parkinson's Disease forced him to give up his teaching job and confined him to a nursing home. With his wife's help two anthologies were edited and published in 1965 and 1967.

1968. Died at Burcot, Oxfordshire, England.

"If I could see not surfaces
But could express
What lies beneath the skin
Where the blood moves
In fruit or head or stone,
Then would I know the one
Essential
And my eyes
When dead
Would give the worm
No hollow food."[1]

Titus Groan, Mr. Pye, and *Rhyme of the Flying Bomb* were adapted for radio plays.

FOR MORE INFORMATIONS SEE: E. Merzl, "Ghosts and Things by Mervyn Peake," *American Artist,* February, 1955; B. M. Miller and others, compilers, *Illustrators of Children's Books, 1946-1956,* Horn Book, 1958; M. Moorcock, "Architect of the Extraordinary. The Work of Mervyn Peake," *Vector,* June, 1960; E. Morgan, "The Walls of Gormenghast," *Chicago Review,* Autumn/Winter, 1960; M. Moorcock, "Mervyn Peak: An Appreciation," *Science Fantasy,* 1963; H. Tube, "Mervyn Peake," *Spectator,* July, 1966; *Best Sellers,* November 1, 1967; *National Observer,* November 6, 1967, December 11, 1967; Brian Doyle, *The Who's Who of Children's Literature,* Schocken Books, 1968; *Book World,* January 7, 1968; R. Wittington-Egan, "Dumb Stones and Singing Bones," *Contemporary Review,* April, 1968; *New York Times,* November 19, 1968; M. Moorcock, "Mervyn Peake," *New Worlds,* February, 1969; Maeve Gilmore, *A World Away,* Gollancz, 1970; H. Brogan, "The Gutters of Gormenghast," *Cambridge Review,* November 23, 1973; Maeve Gilmore and Shelagh Johnson, *Mervyn Peake: Writings & Drawings,* St. Martin's Press, 1974.

Obituaries: *London Times,* November 19, 1968; *New York Times,* November 19, 1968; *Antiquarian Bookman,* December 9, 1968, December 23-30, 1968; *Books Abroad,* Spring, 1969.

PIAGET, Jean 1896-1980

OBITUARY NOTICE: Born August 9, 1896, in Neuchatel, Switzerland; died September, 1980, in Geneva, Switzerland. Psychologist, educator, and author. Piaget was one of the first psychologists to explore the development of intelligence in children. Searching for an "embryology of intelligence," he worked with and observed hundreds of children in his more than forty years at the University of Geneva. Piaget's revolutionary theory on the intelligence of children proposes that a child's mind is neither a blank page to be filled with information nor a smaller version of the adult mind; rather it is active from birth and progresses through a number of developmental stages until the approximate age of fifteen, when logical thinking is finally mastered. Piaget wrote numerous books advancing this and his other theories, including *The Language and Thought of the Child, The Origins of Intelligence in Children,* and *The Psychology of the Child. For More Information See: Who's Who,* 126th edition, St. Martin's, 1944; *Current Biography,* Wilson, 1958; *Who's Who in the World,* 2nd edition, Marquis, 1973; *Contemporary Authors,* Volume 21-24, revised, Gale, 1977. *Obituaries: Time,* September 29, 1980; *Newsweek,* September 29, 1980; *Contemporary Authors,* Volume 101-104, Gale, 1981.

POE, Edgar Allan 1809-1849

PERSONAL: Born January 19, 1809, in Boston, Massachusetts; died October 7, 1849, in Baltimore, Maryland; buried in the Westminster Presbyterian Churchyard, Baltimore, Maryland; son of David, Jr. (a lawyer-turned actor; died, 1810) and Elizabeth (an English actress; maiden name, Arnold; died, 1811) Poe; unofficially adopted, 1811, by John (a Richmond, Virginia tobacco merchant) and Frances Allan; married Virginia Clemm (his cousin), May 16, 1836 (died, 1847). *Education:* Attended the Manor House School, Stoke Newington, England, 1815-1820; University of Virginia, student, 1826; United States Military Academy at West Point, cadet, 1830-1831 (dismissed).

CAREER: Poet, short-story writer, critic. Member of the staff of the *Southern Literary Messenger,* Richmond, Virginia, 1835-1837, assistant editor, 1836-1837; co-editor, *Burton's Gentleman's Magazine,* Philadelphia, 1839-1840; literary editor, *Graham's Lady's and Gentleman's Magazine,* 1841-1842; on the staff of the *Evening Mirror,* New York City, 1845; editor of the *Broadway Journal,* 1845, owner, 1845-1846. Many of Poe's writings first appeared in such periodicals as *Burton's Gentleman's Magazine, Graham's Lady's and Gentleman's Magazine,* the Philadelphia *Saturday Courier,* the *Southern Literary Messenger,* and the *Evening Mirror. Military service:* Enlisted in the United States Army under the name "Edgar A. Perry," 1827; became regimental sergeant-major, January, 1929; discharged, April, 1829.

Edgar Allan Poe, daguerreotype by Mathew Brady.

(From "Lenore" in the *Poems of Edgar Allan Poe.* Illustrated by W. Heath Robinson.)

WRITINGS—Separately published works: (By "a Bostonian") *Tamerlane and Other Poems,* Calvin F. S. Thomas, 1827, facsimile edition reproduced on microfiche, University Microfilms, 1968; *Al Araaf, Tamerlane, and Minor Poems,* Hatch and Dunning, 1829, facsimile edition, Norwood, 1976; *Poems,* Elam Bliss, 1831, facsimile edition, Columbia University Press, 1936; *The Narrative of Arthur Gordon Pym,* Harper and Brothers, 1838, reissued, David R. Godine, 1973 [other editions illustrated by A. D. McCormick and Rene Clark; another edition published as *The Mystery of Arthur Gordon Pym,* with a sequel by Jules Verne, edited by Basil Ashmore, Associated Booksellers, 1961]; *The Conchologist's First Book,* Haswell, Barrington, & Haswell, 1839, second edition, 1840; *Tales of the Grotesque and Arabesque,* two volumes, Lea & Blanchard, 1840, reprinted, Peter Smith, 1965; *Prose Romances: The Murders in the Rue Morgue and The Man That Was Used Up,* W. H. Graham, 1843, facsimile edition, St. John's University Press, 1968; *The Raven, and Other Poems,* Wiley & Putnam, 1845, facsimile edition, Columbia University Press, 1942; *Tales,* Wiley & Putnam, 1845, facsimile edition reproduced on microfiche, University Microfilms, 1968; *Eureka: A Prose Poem,* Putnam, 1848, new edition, Transcendental, 1973; *The Literati,* J. S. Redfield, 1850; *Politan: An Unfinished Tragedy,* George Banta, 1923, facsimile edition reproduced on microfiche, University Microfilms, 1968.

Collections: *The Works of the Late Edgar Allan Poe, With Notices of His Life and Genius,* two volumes, edited by N. P. Willis, J. R. Lowell and R. W. Griswold, J. S. Redfield, 1850, reproduced on microfiche, University Microfilms, 1974; *The Poetical Works of Edgar Allan Poe* (illustrated by Waller H. Paton, John M. Whirter and others), W. J. Widdleton, 1870; *The Life and Poems of Edgar Allan Poe,* W. J. Widdleton, 1877, reprinted, with an introductory letter by Sarah H. Whitman, Haskell House, 1974; *The Works of Edgar Allan Poe,* ten volumes (illustrated by Albert E. Sterner; edited by Edmund C. Stedman and George E. Woodberry), Stone & Kimball, 1894-1895, reprinted, Books for Libraries, 1971.

The Complete Works of Edgar Allan Poe, seventeen volumes, edited by James A. Harrison, Crowell, 1902, reissued, AMS Press, 1965; *The Poems of Edgar Allan Poe,* edited by Killis Campbell, Ginn, 1917, reissued as *Poems,* Russell, 1962; *The Complete Tales and Poems of Edgar Allan Poe,* Modern Library, 1938, reissued, 1965; *Complete Poems of Edgar Allan Poe* (illustrated by Hugo Steiner-Prag; edited by Louis Untermeyer), Heritage Press, 1943; *The Complete Poems and Stories of Edgar Allan Poe,* two volumes (illustrated by E. McKnight Kauffer), Knopf, 1946, reissued, 1964; *The Letters of Edgar Allan Poe,* two volumes, edited by John W. Ostrom, Harvard University Press, 1948, reissued as *Letters,* with supplementary chapter, Gordian, 1966; *Poe: Complete Poems,* edited by Richard Wilbur, Dell, 1959; *Literary Criticism of Edgar Allan Poe,* edited by Robert I. Hough, University of Nebraska Press, 1965; *Complete Stories and Poems,* Doubleday, 1966; *Complete Poetry and Selected Criticism,* edited by Allen Tate, New American Library, 1968; *The Complete Tales and Poems of Edgar Allan Poe,* Random House, 1975.

Selections: *The Assignation, and Other Tales,* J. W. Lovell, 1884; *Monsieur Dupin, the Detective Tales of Edgar Allan Poe* (illustrated by Charles R. Macauley), McClure, Phillips, 1904; *Tales of Mystery and Imagination,* Dutton, 1908, reissued, 1968 [other editions published by Oxford University Press, 1928, reissued, 1972, and one, illustrated by Harry Clarke, by Tubor, 1933, reissued, Minerva, 1977]; *The Last Letters of Edgar Allan Poe to Sarah Helen Whitman,* edited by James A. Harrison, Putnam, 1909, reissued, Norwood, 1977; *The Letters from George W. Eveleth to Edgar Allan Poe,* edited by Thomas O. Mabbott, New York Public Library, 1922, reissued, Norwood, 1978; *Edgar Allan Poe Letters Till Now Unpublished, in the Valentine Museum,* Lippincott, 1925, reprinted, Haskell House, 1973; *Doings of Gotham,* J. E. Spannuth, 1929, reprinted, Folcroft, 1974.

The Masque of the Red Death, and Other Tales (engravings by J. Buckland Wright), Halcyon, 1932; *Representative Selections,* edited by Margaret Alterton and Hardin Craig, American Book, 1935, revised edition, Hill and Wang, 1962; *Edgar Allan Poe,* edited by Philip Van Doren Stern, Viking, 1945, reissued, Penguin, 1977; *Selected Prose and Poetry,* edited, with an introduction by W. H. Auden, Holt, 1950, reissued as *Selected Prose, Poetry, and Eureka,* 1968; *Selected Poetry and Prose,* edited by Thomas A. Mabbott, Modern Library, 1951, reissued, 1958; *Tales,* Dodd, 1952; *Selected Writings,* edited by Edward Davidson, Houghton, 1956; *Poems and Essays,* Dutton, 1958.

The Fall of the House of Usher, and Other Tales, New American Library, 1960; *Eight Tales of Terror* (illustrated by Irv Docktor, edited by John P. Roberts), Scholastic Book Services, 1961; *Stories,* Platt, 1961; *Tales and Poems* (illustrated by Russell Hoban), Macmillan, 1963; *Great Tales of Horror,* edited by David Sohn, Bantam, 1964; *Eighteen Best Stories by Edgar Allan Poe,* edited by Vincent Price and Chandler Brossard, Dell, 1965; *Poems* (drawings by Ellen Raskin), Crowell, 1965; *Poems,* edited by Floyd Stovall, University Press of Virginia, 1965; *Introduction to Poe, a Thematic Reader,* edited by Eric W. Carlson, Scott, Foresman, 1967; *The Pit and the Pendulum, and Five Other Tales* (illustrated by Rick Schreiter), F. Watts, 1967; *Selected Writings, Poems, Tales, Essays, and Reviews,* edited by David Galloway, Penguin, 1967; *Collected Works of Edgar Allan Poe,* Volume 1, edited by Mabbott, Belknap, 1969, Volumes 2 and 3, 1978; *The Gold Bug, and Other Tales of Mystery* (illustrated by Al Davidson), Childrens Press, 1969.

Great Short Works of Edgar Allan Poe, edited by G. R. Thompson, Harper, 1970; *Seven Tales,* with a French translation and essay by Charles Baudelaire, edited by W. T. Bandy, Schocken, 1971; *The Illustrated Edgar Allan Poe,* Drake, 1975; *The Science Fiction of Edgar Allan Poe,* edited by Harold Beaver, Penguin, 1976; *The Short Fiction of Edgar Allan Poe,* annotated by Stuart and Susan Levine, Bobbs-Merrill, 1976.

ADAPTATIONS—Movies and filmstrips: "The Raven" (motion pictures), American Eclair Company, 1912, Essanay Film Manufacturing Company, 1915, Universal Pictures, starring Bela Lugosi and Boris Karloff, American Art and History Films, 1953, American International Pictures, starring Vincent Price, Peter Lorre and Boris Karloff (this version adapted into book form by Eunice Sudak, Lancer Books, 1963); "The Raven" (filmstrip), Brunswick Productions, 1969; "The Raven" (motion picture), Texture Films, 1973; "The Raven" (filmstrip), Texture Films, 1976.

"The Bells" (motion picture), Thomas A. Edison, Inc. 1913; "The Murders in the Rue Morgue" (motion pictures), Sol. A. Rosenberg, 1914, Universal Pictures, 1932; "Phantom of the Rue Morgue" (motion picture), Warner Brothers Pictures, 1954.

"The Black Cat" (motion pictures), Universal Pictures, starring Boris Karloff and Bela Lugosi, 1934, Universal Pictures, starring Basil Rathbone, Broderick Crawford and Alan Ladd, 1941, University of Southern California, 1956; "The Black Cat" (filmstrip), Brunswick Productions, 1966; "The Black Cat" (filmstrip), Prentice-Hall, 1977; "The Crime of Doctor Crespi" (motion picture), adaptation of "The Premature Burial," Republic Pictures, 1935; "The Premature Burial" (motion picture), American International Pictures, starring Ray Milland, 1962; "The Tell-Tale Heart" (motion picture), Metro-Goldwyn-Mayer, 1941; "Heartbeat" (motion picture), adaptation of "The Tell-Tale Heart," General Television Enterprises, 1950; "The Tell-Tale Heart" (motion pictures), Learning Corporation of America, 1953, Columbia Pictures, narrated by James Mason, 1953, Rothschild Film Corp., starring Michael Kane, 1959, CBS Films, starring Michael Kane, 1959; "Tell-Tale Heart" (filmstrip), Brunswick Productions, 1966; "Tell-Tale Heart" (motion picture), American Film Institute, 1971; "The Tell-Tale Heart" (filmstrip), Listening Library.

"Masque of the Red Death" (motion pictures), American International Pictures, starring Vincent Price, 1954, American International Pictures, 1964; "The Masque of the Red Death" (filmstrip), Brunswick Productions, 1966; "Masque of the Red Death" (motion picture), Contemporary Films/

(From the movie "The Mystery of Marie Roget," starring Maria Ouspenskaya. Copyright 1942 by Universal Pictures Co.)

(From the movie "The Black Cat," starring Broderick Crawford. Copyright 1941 by Universal Pictures.)

(A lithograph of *The Raven* by French Impressionist painter Edouard Manet.)

McGraw-Hill, 1970; "Masque of the Red Death" (filmstrip), Listening Library, 1976; "The Gold Bug" (filmstrip), Encyclopaedia Britannica Films, 1956; "Manfish" (motion picture), adaptation of "The Gold Bug" and "The Tell-Tale Heart," United Artists, starring Lon Chaney, Jr., 1956; "The Fall of the House of Usher" (motion pictures), Brandon Films, 1959, American International Pictures, starring Vincent Price, 1960, Encyclopaedia Britannica Educational Corp., 1976; "A Discussion of Edgar Allan Poe's 'The Fall of the House of Usher'" (motion picture), Encyclopaedia Britannica Educational Corp., with Ray Bradbury discussing the short story and the preceeding film, 1976; "The Fall of the House of Usher" (filmstrip), Brunswick Productions, 197(?).

"Pit and the Pendulum" (motion picture), American International Pictures, starring Vincent Price, 1961; "The Pit" (motion picture), British Film Institute, 1961, released in the United States by Films Incorporated, 1971; "The Pit and the Pendulum" (motion picture), Murray Cowell, 1966; "The Pit and the Pendulum" (filmstrip), Brunswick Productions, 1966; "The Pit and the Pendulum" (animated motion picture), Conestoga College of Applied Arts and Technology, 1975; "Tales of Terror" (motion picture), adaptations of "Morella," "The Black Cat" and "The Case of M. Valdemar," American International Pictures, starring Vincent Price, Peter Lorre and Basil Rathbone, 1962; "The Haunted Palace" (motion picture), American International Pictures, starring Vincent Price, Debra Paget and Lon Chaney, 1963; "The Tomb of Ligeia" (motion picture), American International Pictures, starring Vincent Price, 1965; "War-Gods of the Deep" (motion picture), adaptation of "City in the Sea," American International Pictures, starring Vincent Price and Tab Hunter, 1965; "Annabel Lee" (filmstrip), Brunswick Productions, 1966; "Annabel Lee" (motion picture), Productions Unlimited, narrated by Vincent Price, 1973; "The Oblong Box" (motion picture), American International Pictures, 1969; "Poe's Short Stories" (filmstrip; with teacher's guide), Popular Science Audio-Visuals, 1969; "Spirits of the Dead" (motion picture), American International Pictures, narrated by Vincent Price, starring Peter Fonda, Jane Fonda, Brigitte Bardot, and Terence Stamp, 1969.

"The Facts in the Case of M. Valdemar" (filmstrip; with captions), Brunswick Productions, 1970; "To Helen" (filmstrip; with captions), Brunswick Productions, 1970; "Ulalume" (filmstrip; with captions), Brunswick Productions, 1970; "The Cask of Amontillado" (filmstrip; with captions), Brunswick Productions, 197(?); "The Cask of Amontillado" (filmstrip), Listening Library, 1976; "Master Storytellers, Set 2" (filmstrips), Random House, 1977.

Plays: Robert Brome, *Edgar Allan Poe's "Masque of the Red Death,"* (one-act), Eldridge Publishing, 1963; Brome,

. . . The gigantic animal had seized Madame L'Espanaye by the hair (which was loose, as she had been combing it), and was flourishing the razor about her face . . . . ■ (From *Tales of Edgar Allan Poe* by Edgar Allan Poe. Illustrated by Fritz Eichenberg.)

As the sailor looked in, the gigantic animal had seized Madame L'Espanaye by the hair (which was loose, as she had been combing it), and was flourishing the razor about her face, in imitation of the motions of a barber. ■ (From *The Murders in the Rue Morgue* by Edgar Allan Poe. Illustrated by Rick Schreiter.)

Edgar Allan Poe's "The Tell-Tale Heart," (one-act), Eldridge Publishing, 1966; Brome, *Edgar Allan Poe's "The Cask of Amontillado,"* Eldridge Publishing, 1968; Steven Berkoff, *The Fall of the House of Usher,* J. Calder, 1977 (also includes *East* and *Agamemnon*).

Recordings: "The Gold Bug," read by Vincent Price, Caedmon Records, 1974; "The Imp of the Perverse, and Other Tales," read by Vincent Price, Caedmon Records, 1974; "Edgar Allan Poe," read by Basil Rathbone, Caedmon Records; "The Invisible Man" by H. G. Wells and "Selected Stories of Edgar Allen Poe" (8 cassettes), Books on Tape.

Recorded exclusively for American Forces Radio and Television Service: "The Black Cat," starring Peter Lorre, 1972; "The Cask of Amontillado and The Scapegoat," 1972; "The Cask of Amontillado," 1974; "Hall of Fantasy: The Tell-Tale Heart," 1974; "Never Bet the Devil Your Head," starring John Dehner, 1974.

SIDELIGHTS: **January 19, 1809.** Born in Boston, Mass., son of actress Elizabeth (Arnold) and actor David Poe. Elizabeth was: "The childish figure, the great, wide-open mysterious eyes, the abundant curling hair confined in the quaint bonnet of a hundred years ago and shadowing the brow in raven masses, the high waist and attenuated arms clasped in an Empire robe of faint, flowered design, the tiny but rounded neck and shoulders, the head proudly erect. It is the face of an elf, a sprite, an Undine. . . ." [Wolf Mankowitz, *The Extraordinary Mr. Poe,* Simon & Schuster, 1978.[1]] Soon after his marriage, David Poe developed a "dependency on drink."

October 19, 1810. A Norfolk, Va. newspaper clipping of unknown origin recorded David Poe's death from consumption. In ill health from tuberculosis accelerated by her pregnancies—a third child, Rosalie, born—Poe's mother was forced to leave her oldest son, William Henry Leonard, in the care of his paternal grandparents, and returned with young Poe and Rosalie to Richmond, Virginia.

1811. Benefit performances were arranged for the ailing Mrs. Poe who was "the sole support of herself and her children." An advertisement of such a benefit appeared in a Richmond newspaper:

"TO THE HUMANE HEART

"On this night, Mrs Poe, lingering on the bed of disease and surrounded by her children, asks your assistance; and asks it perhaps for the last time. The generosity of a Richmond audience can need no other appeal. For particulars, see the Bills of the day."[1]

December 8, 1811. Elizabeth Poe, aged twenty-four, died of pneumonia.

December 9, 1811. With his inheritance—a miniature of his mother, a little painting she had made of the port in Boston where he was born, and a pocketbook containing locks of

(From *Tales of Mystery and Imagination* by Edgar Allan Poe. Illustrated by Harry Clarke.)

(From *Tales of Mystery and Imagination* by Edgar Allan Poe. Illustrated by Harry Clarke.)

both his mother's and father's hair—Poe was removed to the home of Scottish merchant John Allan who yielded under the pressure of demands made by his childless wife, Frances.

Poe's new family relationships were fragile from the start and were to grow into a mutual hatred between John Allan and himself.

Frances Allan's determination to keep the young Poe with them was aptly demonstrated by a letter of Poe's aunt, Eliza Poe. "Tis the Aunt of Edgar that addresses Mrs Allen [sic] for the second time, impressed with the idea that a letter if received could not remain unacknowledged so long as from the month of July, she is induced to write again in order to inquire in her family's as well as in her own name after the health of the child of her Brother, as well as that of his adopted Parents. I cannot suppose my dear Mrs Allen that a heart possessed of such original humanity as yours must without doubt be, could so long keep in suspense, the anxious inquiries made through the medium of my letter by letter by the Grand Parents of the Orphan of an unfortunate son, surely ere this allowing that you did not wish to commence a correspondence with one who is utterly unknown to you had you received it Mr Allen would have written to my Father or Brother if it had been only to let them know how he was, but I am confident that you never received it. . . ."[1]

1815-1820. Attended the Manor House School, Stoke Newington, England. "My earliest recollections of a school life are connected with a large, rambling, Elizabethan house, in a misty-looking village of England, where were a vast number of gigantic and gnarled trees, and where all the houses were excessively ancient. In truth, it was a dream-like and spirit-soothing place, that venerable old town.

"Encompassed by the massy walls of this venerable academy, I passed yet not in tedium or disgust, the years of the third lustrum of my life. The teeming brain of childhood requires no external world of incident to occupy or amuse it; and the apparently dismal monotony of a school was replete with more intense excitement than my riper youth has derived from luxury, or my full manhood from crime. Yet I must believe that my first mental development had in it much of the uncommon—even much of the *outre*." [John W. Robert-son, M.D., *Edgar A. Poe: A Psychopathic Study*, Putnam, 1923.[2]]

During these years Poe penned his first poetic lines.

"Last night with many cares and toils oppress'd
Weary . . . I laid me on a couch to rest—"[1]

Another early poem expressed pained love:

"Oh feast my soul, revenge is sweet
Louisa, take my scorn;—
Curs'd was the hour that saw us meet
The hour when we were born."[1]

March, 1825. Privately tutored for entrance to the University of Virginia.

February, 1826. Entered University of Virginia with but a portion of financial backing from his wealthy foster-father. One year later saw the young Poe in irretrievable debt, disappointed in love, and drinking seriously for the first time. A contemporary, Thomas Tucker, described Poe's drinking style: "He would always seize the tempting glass, generally unmixed with sugar or water—in fact, perfectly straight—and without the least apparent pleasure, swallow the contents, never pausing until the last drop had passed his lips. One glass at a time was all that he could take; but this was sufficient to rouse his whole nervous nature into a state of strongest excitement, which found vent in a continuous flow of wild, fascinating talk that irresistibly enchanted every listener with siren-like power."[1]

December, 1826. Returned to Richmond.

March, 1827. Left Allan's house for Boston.

1827. Desperate for a roof over his head and meals, enlisted in the U.S. Army giving his age as twenty-two and his name as Edgar A. Perry. Posted at Sullivan's Island, South Carolina. "This island is a very singular one. It consists of little else than the sea sand, and is about three miles long. Its breadth at no point exceeds a quarter of a mile. It is separated from the main land by a scarcely perceptible creek, oozing its way through a wilderness of reeds and slime, a favourite resort of the marsh-hen. The vegetation, as might be supposed, is scant, or at least dwarfish. No trees of any magnitude are to be seen. Near the western extremity, where Fort Moultrie stands, and where are some miserable frame buildings, tenanted, during summer, by the fugitives from Charleston dust and fever, may be found, indeed, the bristly palmetto; but the whole island, with the exception of this western point, and a line of hard, white beach on the seacoast, is covered with dense undergrowth of the sweet myrtle, so much prized by the horticulturalists of England. The shrub here often attains the height of fifteen or twenty feet, and forms an almost impenetrable coppice, burdening the air with its fragrance."[1]

January 1, 1829. Promoted to sergeant-major.

February, 1829. Frances Allan died.

1829. "I am young—not yet twenty—*am* a poet—if deep worship of all beauty can make me one—and wish to be so in the more common meaning of the word. I would give the world to embody one half the ideas afloat in my imagination . . . I am and have been from my childhood, an idler. It cannot therefore be said that

'I left a calling for this idle trade
A duty broke—a father destroyed—'
for I have no father—or mother."[2]

April, 1829. Released from the Army with testimonials from all of his officers recommending his sobriety, conduct, and high intelligence. John Allan later added the following introduction: "The youth who presents this is the same alluded to by Lt. Howard, Capt. Griswold, Col. Worth, our representative and the speaker, the Hon'ble Andrew Stevenson, and my friend Major Jno Campbell.

"He left me in consequence of some gambling at the University of Charlottesville, because (I presume) I refused to sanction a rule that the shop-keepers and others had adopted there, making Debts of Honour of all indiscretions. I have much pleasure in asserting that he stood his examination at the close of the year with great credit to himself. His history is short. He is the grandson of Quartermaster-Gen'l Poe of Maryland, whose widow, as I understand, still receives a pension for the services or disability of her husband. Frankly, Sir, do I declare that he is no relation to me whatever; that

This morning, about three o'clock, the inhabitants of the Quartier Saint-Roch were aroused from sleep by a succession of terrific shrieks, issuing, apparently, from the fourth story of a house in the Rue Morgue.... ■ (From *Tales of Mystery and Imagination* by Edgar Allan Poe. Illustrated by Arthur Rackham.)

(From the movie "The Tell-Tale Heart," produced by Learning Corporation of America.)

I have many whom I have taken an active interest to promote theirs; with no other feeling than that every man is my care, if he be in distress; for myself I ask nothing but I do request your kindness to aid this youth in the promotion of his future prospects. And it will afford me great pleasure to reciprocate any kindness you can show him. Pardon my frankness; but I address a soldier."[1]

Went to live with Aunt, Marie Poe Clemm, eleven year-old cousin, Henry, and seven year-old cousin Virginia Eliza ("Sis"). Mrs. Clemm became Poe's "Muddy," a childish word for "mother."

"TO MY MOTHER

"Because I feel that, in the Heavens above,
The angels, whispering to one another,
Can find, among their burning terms of love,
None so devotional as that of 'Mother,'
Therefore by that dear name I long have called you—
You who are more than mother unto me,
And fill my heart of hearts, where Death installed
—you,
In setting my Virginia's spirit free.
My mother—my own mother, who died early,
Was but the mother of myself; but you
Are mother to the one I loved so dearly,
And thus are dearer than the mother I knew
By that infinity with which my wife
Was dearer to my soul than its soul-life."[1]

1830. Entered West Point. In a letter addressed to his wealthy foster-father, Poe reviewed his life's circumstances and made an appeal for written permission to resign West Point. "Did I, when an infant, sollicit your charity and protection, or was it of your own free will, that you volunteered your services in my behalf? It is well known to respectable individuals in Baltimore, and elsewhere, that my Grandfather (my natural protector at the time you interposed) was wealthy, and that I was his favorite grandchild—But the promises of adoption, and liberal education which you held forth to him in a letter which is now in possession of my family, induced him to resign all care of me into your hands. Under such circumstances, can it be said that I have no *right* to expect any thing at your hands? You may probably urge that you have given me a liberal education. I will leave the decision of that question to those who know how far liberal educations can be obtained in 8 months at the University of Va. Here you will say that it was my own fault that I did not return—You would not let me return because bills were presented you for payment which I never wished nor desired you to pay. Had you let me return, ny [sic] reformation had been sure—as my conduct the last 3 months gave every reason to believe—and you would never have heard more of my extravagances. But I am not about to proclaim myself guilty of all that has been alledged against me, and which I have hitherto endured, simply because I was too proud to reply.

"I will boldly say that it was wholly and entirely your own mistaken parsimony that caused all the difficulties in which I was involved while at Charlotte[s]ville. The expences of the institution at the lowest estimates were $350 per annum. You sent me there with $110. Of this $50 were to be paid immediately for board—$60 for attendance upon 2 professors—and you even did not miss the opportunity of abusing me because I did not attend 3. Then $15 more were to be paid for room-rent—remember that all this was to be paid *in advance,* with $110.—$12 more for a bed—and $12 more for room furniture. I had, of course, the mortification of running in debt for public property—against the known rules of the institution, and was immediately regarded in the light of a beggar. You will remember that in a week after my arrival, I wrote to you for some more money, and for books—You replied in terms of the utmost abuse—if I had been the vilest wretch on earth you could not have been more abusive than you were because I could not contrive to pay $150 with $110. I had enclosed to you in my letter (according to your express commands) an account of the expences incurred amounting to $149—the balance to be paid was $3[9]—You enclosed me $40, leaving me one dollar in pocket. In a short time afterwards I received a packet of books consisting of, Gil Blas, and the Cambridge Mathematics in 2 vols: books for which I had no earthly use since I had no means of attending the mathematical lectures. But books must be had, if I intended to remain at the institution—and they were bought accordingly *upon credit.*

"In this manner debts were accumulated, and money borrowed of Jews in Charlottesville at extravagant interest—for I was obliged to hire a servant, to pay for wood, for washing, and a thousand other necessaries. It was then that I became dissolute, for how could it be otherwise? I could associate with no students, except those who were in a similar situation with myself—altho' from different causes—They from drunkenness, and extravagance—I, because it was my crime to have no one on Earth who care for me, or loved me. I call God to witness that I have never loved dissipation—Those who know me know that my pursuits and habits are very far from any thing of the kind. But I was drawn into it by my companions[.] Even their professions of friendship—hollow as they were—were a relief. Towards the close of the session you sent me $100—but it was too late—to be of any service in extricating me from my difficulties—I kept it for some time—thinking that if I could obtain more I could yet retrieve my character—I applied to James Galt—but he, I believe, from the best of motives refused to lend me any—I then became desperate, and gambled—until I finally i[n]volved myself irretrievably.

"If I have been to blame in all this—place yourself in my situation, and tell me if you would not have been equally so. But these circumstances were all unknown to my friends when I returned home—They knew that I had been extravagant—but that was all—I had no hope of returning to Charlottesville, and I waited in vain in expectation that you would, at least, obtain me some employment. I saw no prospect of this—and I could endure it no longer.—Every day threatened with a warrant &c. I left home—and after nearly 2 years conduct with which no fault could be found—in the army, as a common soldier—I *earned,* myself, by the most humiliating privations—a Cadets' warrant which you could have obtained at any time for asking. It was then that I thought I might venture to sollicit your assistance in giving me an outfit—I came home, you will remember, the night after the burial [of step-mother, Frances]—if she had not have died while I was away there would have been nothing for me to regret—*Your* love I never valued—but she I believed loved me as her own child. You promised me to forgive all—but you soon forgot your promise. You sent me to W. Point l[ike a beggar.] The same difficulties are threateni[n]g me as before at [Charlottesville]—and I must resign.

"As to your injunction not to trouble you with farther communication rest assured, Sir, that I will most religiously observe it. When I parted from you—at the steam-boat, I knew that I should nev[er] see you again.

(From the movie "The Raven," starring Bela Lugosi. Copyright 1949 by Film Classics, Inc.)

(From the movie "The Murders in the Rue Morgue," starring Bela Lugosi. Released by Universal Pictures, 1932.)

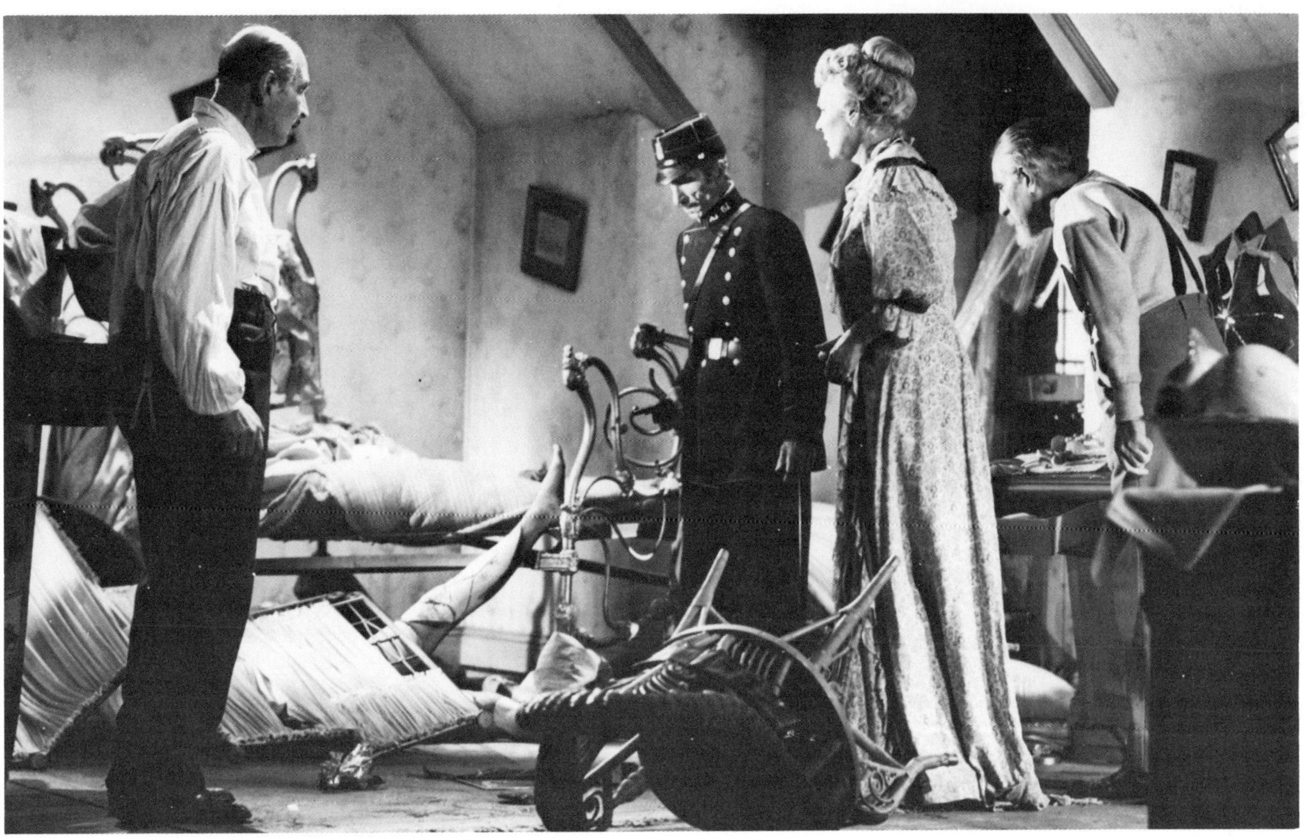

(From the movie "Phantom of the Rue Morgue," based on *The Murders in the Rue Morgue.* Copyright 1953 by Warner Bros. Pictures Corp.)

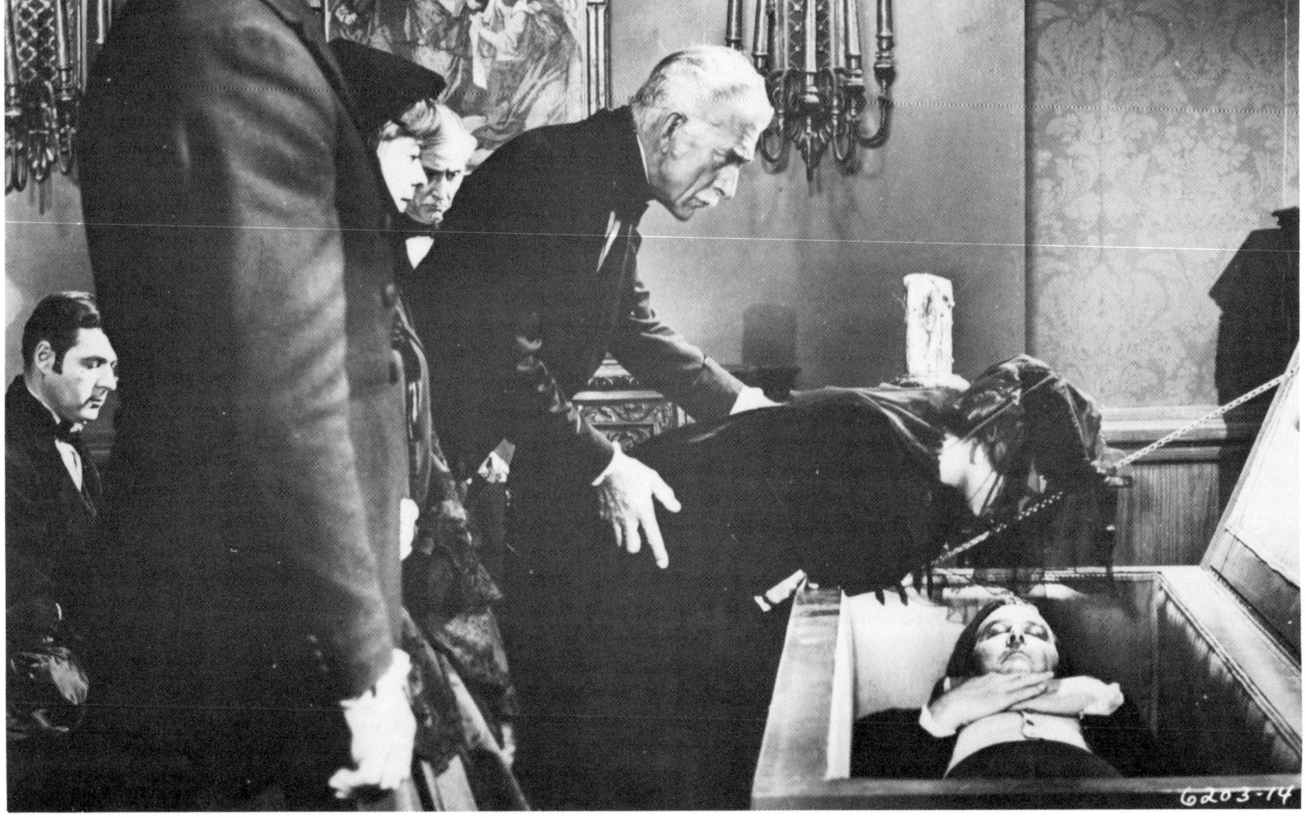

(From the movie "The Premature Burial." Released by American International Pictures, 1962.)

"I have no more to say—except that my future life (which thank God will not endure long) must be passed in indigence and sickness. I have no energy left, nor health, If it was possible, to put up with the fatigues of this place, and the inconveniences which my absolute want of necessaries subject me to, and as I mentioned before it is my intention to resign. For this end it will be necessary that you (as my nominal guardian) enclose me your written permission. It will be useless to refuse me this last request—for I can leave the place without any permission—your refusal would only deprive me of the little pay which is now due as mileage.

"From the time of writing this I shall neglect my studies and duties at the institution—if I do not receive your answer in 10 days—I will leave the point without—for otherwise I should subject myself to dismission." [John Ward Ostrom, editor, *The Letters of Edgar Allan Poe,* Volume I, Harvard University Press, 1948.[3]]

January 28, 1831. A court martial tried Cadet E. A. Poe:

"CHARGE 1st—Gross Neglect of Duty

"Specification 1st—In this, that he, the said Cadet Poe, did absent himself from the following parades and roll calls between the 7th January and 27th January 1831. . . .

"Specification 2nd—In this, that he, the said Cadet E. A. Poe, did absent himself from all Academical duties between the 15th and 27th January 1831. . . .

"CHARGE 2nd—Disobedience of Orders

"Specification 1st—In this, that he, the said Cadet Poe, after having been directed by the officer of the day to attend church on the 23rd of January 1831 did fail to obey such order. . . .

"Specification 2nd—In this, that he, the said Cadet Poe, did fail to attend the Academy on the 25th January 1831, after having been directed to do so by the officer of the day."[1]

Poe pleaded guilty to all but the first part of the first charge, putting himself beyond any recommendation for mercy.

February 19, 1831. Left West Point.

December, 1831. Another appeal to Allan for funds. "I am sure you could not refuse to assist me if you were well aware of the distress I am in. How often have you relieved the distress of a perfect stranger in circumstances less urgent than mine, and yet when I beg and entreat you in the name of God to send me succour you will still refuse to aid me. I know that I have no longer any hopes of being again received into your favour, but for the sake of Christ, do not let me perish for a sum of money which you would never miss, and which would relieve me from the greatest earthly misery. . . . If you wish me to humble myself before you I am humble—Sickness and misfortune have left me not a shadow of pride. . . ."[1]

During his periods of intensive application to writing, Poe became familiar with opium in the form of tincture of laudanum, a commonly used medicine. In his *Confessions of an Opium Eater* he detailed how the drug first increased his stamina and heightened his imaginative flights. ". . . At night when I lay awake in bed, vast processions moved along continually in mournful pomp; friezes of never-ending stories drawn from time before Oedipus or Priam, before Tyre, before Memphis. And, concurrently with this, a corresponding change took place in my dreams; a theatre seemed suddenly opened and lighted up within my brain, which presented nightly spectacles of more than earthly splendour."[1]

1832. Romantic interlude with Mary Devereaux. Devereaux explained their meeting and subsequent affair during the summer in Baltimore. ". . . My intimacy with Mr Poe isolated me a good deal. In fact my girlfriends were many of them afraid of him and forsook me on his account. I knew more of his male friends. He despised ignorant people, and didn't like trifling and small talk. He didn't like dark-skinned people. When he loved, he loved desperately. Though tender and very affectionate, he had a quick, passionate temper, and was very jealous. His feelings were intense and he had but little control of them. He was not well balanced; he had too much brain. He scoffed at everything sacred and never went to church. If he had had religion to guide him he would have been a better man. He said often that there was a mystery hanging over him he never could fathom. He believed he was born to suffer, and this embittered his whole life. Mrs Clemm also spoke vaguely of some family mystery, of some disgrace. . . . Mr Poe once gave me a letter to read from Mr Allan, in which the letter said, referring to me, that if he married any such person he would cut him off without a shilling.

"Eddie and I never talked of his poetry then or in later years. He would not have done that; he would have considered it conceited. We were young, and only thought of our love. Virginia [Poe's cousin] always carried his notes to me. . . . Eddie's favourite name was 'Mary,' he said. He used often to quote Burns, for whom he had a great admiration. We used to go walking together in the evenings. We often walked out of the city and sat down on the hills.[1]

1834. John Allan died making no mention of Poe in his will.

August, 1835. Returned to Richmond to work on the *Southern Literary Messenger.* In that year alone, Poe published in that paper nine stories, four poems, extracts from his drama *Politan,* critical notes, editorials, and thirty-seven reviews.

September 22, 1835. Poe secretly married his thirteen-year-old cousin, Virginia, in St. Paul's Episcopal Church, Baltimore.

May 16, 1836. Married openly in Richmond, Virginia where it was witnessed on oath that "Virginia E. Clemm is of the full age of twenty-one years."

"She whom I loved in youth, and of whom I now pen calmly and distinctly these remembrances, was the sole daughter of the only sister of my mother long departed. [Virginia] was the name of my cousin. We had always dwelled together, beneath a tropical sun, in the Valley of the Many-Colored Grass. No unguided footstep ever came upon the vale; for it lay far away among a range of giant hills. . . . Thus it was that we lived all alone, knowing nothing of the world without the valley,—I, and my cousin, and her mother."[1]

1837. Moved to New York.

1839-1840. Co-editor with W. E. Burton of *Burton's Gentleman's Magazine* in Philadelphia to which he contributed such stories as *The Man that was Used Up; William Wilson; Morella; The Conservation of Eiros and Charmion; and The Fall of the House of Usher.* The latter story, largely autobio-

(From "The Black Cat" in *The Works of Edgar Allan Poe.* Illustrated by Aubrey Beardsley.)

(From the movie "The Haunted Palace," based on the novel *The Fall of the House of Usher,* starring Lon Chaney, Vincent Price and Debra Paget. Copyright © 1963 by American International Pictures.)

(From the movie "Tales of Terror," based on the short stories of Poe, starring Vincent Price. Copyright © 1962 by American International Pictures.)

(From the movie "The Masque of the Red Death," starring Vincent Price. Released by American International Pictures, 1961.)

(From the movie "The Tomb of Ligeia," starring Vincent Price. Released by American International Pictures, 1965.)

(A promotional photo of Vincent Price reading from the works of Poe.)

graphical, offered a self-portrait of Poe at age thirty. "The character of his face had been at all times remarkable. A cadaverousness of complexion, an eye large, liquid, and luminous beyond comparison; lips somewhat thin and very pallid, but of a surprisingly beautiful curve, a nose of a delicate Hebrew model, but with a breadth of nostril unusual in similar formations; a finely moulded chin, speaking, in its want of prominence, of a want of moral energy; hair of a more than web-like softness and tenuity;—these features, with an inordinate expansion above the regions of the temple, made up altogether a countenance not easily to be forgotten."[1]

After a "falling out" with Burton, Poe left the magazine. To Burton, he wrote: "Upon the whole I am not willing to admit that you have greatly overpaid me. That I did not do four times as much as I did for the Magazine was your own fault. At first I wrote long articles, which you deemed unadmissible, and never did I suggest any to which you had not some immediate and decided objection. Of course, I grew discouraged, and could feel no interest in the journal.

"I am at a loss to know why you call me selfish. If you mean that I borrowed money of you—you know that you offered it, and you know that I am poor. . . . Place yourself in my situation and see whether you would not have acted as I have done. You first 'enforced,' as you say, a deduction of salary; giving me to understand thereby that you thought of parting company. You next spoke disrespectfully of me behind my back—this is an habitual thing; to those whom you supposed your friends, and who punctually reported to me, as a matter of course, every ill-natured word you uttered. Lastly, you advertised your magazine for sale without saying a word to me about it. I felt no anger at what you did—none in the world. Had I not firmly believed in your design to give up your journal, with a view of attending to the Theatre, I should never have dreamed of attempting one of my own. The opportunity of doing something for myself seemed a good one—(and I was about to be thrown out of business)—and I embraced it. Now I ask you, as a man of honor and as a man of sense,—what is there wrong in all this? What have I done at which you have any right to take offence?. . . . The charge of $100 I shall not admit for an instant. If you persist in it our intercourse is at an end, and we can each adopt our own measures."[1]

Burton responded with Poe's reinstatement. "I am sorry you have thought it necessary to send me such a letter. Your troubles have given a morbid tone to your feelings which it is your duty to discourage. I myself have been as severely handled by the world as you can possibly have been, but my sufferings have not tinged my mind with melancholy, nor jaundiced my views of society. You must rouse your energies, and if care assail you, conquer it. I will gladly overlook the past. I hope you will as easily fulfill your pledges for the future. We shall agree very well, although I cannot permit the magazine to be made a vehicle for that sort of severity which you think 'so successful with the mob!' . . . I accept your proposition to recommence your interrupted avocations with the Maga. Let us meet as if we had not exchanged letters. Use more exercise, write when feelings prompt, and be assured of my friendship. You will soon regain a healthy activity of mind and laugh at your past vagaries."[1] Poe responded with a contribution of his serial story, *The Journal of Julius Rodman*.

August, 1840. Planned the establishment of his own magazine, *Penn Magazine*. ". . . I am actuated by an ambition which I believe to be an honourable one—the ambition of serving the great cause of truth, while endeavouring to forward the literature of the country. . . . Hitherto my circumstances, as regards pecuniary matters, have been bad. In fact, my path in life has been beset with difficulties from which I hope to emerge by this effort. So far, my exertions have served only to enhance my literary reputation in some degree and to benefit *others* so far as money was concerned. If I succeed in the present attempt, however, fortune & fame must go hand in hand. My chances of establishing the Magazine depend upon my getting a certain number of subscribers previously to the first of December. This is rendered necessary by my having no other capital to begin with than whatever reputation I may have acquired as a literary man. Had I money, I might issue the first numbers without this list; but as it is, at least 500 names will be required to enable me to commence. I have no doubt in the world that this number can be obtained among those friends who aided me in the *Messenger;* but still it behooves me to use every exertion to ensure success."[3] Unable to solicit the proper backing for his magazine, Poe postponed the project and sought employment with George R. Graham of *Graham's Magazine*.

1842. ". . . My connection with *Graham's Magazine* ceased with the May number, which was completed by the first of April—since which period the conduct of the journal has rested with Mr. Griswold [who became Poe's self-appointed literary executor]. . . . I have no quarrel with either Mr Graham or Mr Griswold—although I hold neither in especial respect. . . . I am making earnest although secret exertions to resume my project of the *Penn Magazine,* and I have every confidence that I shall succeed in issuing the first number on the first of January [1843]."[1]

January, 1842. Wife diagnosed as tubercular.

Summer, 1842. Virginia suffered relapse of tuberculosis. Poe removed to a Saratoga spa to recover from abuse of drink and opium.

April 7, 1844. Established with his sick wife in a New York boarding house. Poe related their situation in a correspondence with "Muddy." ". . . We have just this minute done breakfast, and I now sit down to write you about everything. I can't pay for the letter, because the P.O. won't be open to-day. In the first place we arrived safe at Walnut St wharf. The driver wanted to make me pay a dollar, but I wouldn't. Then I had to pay a boy a levy to put the trunks in the baggage car. In the meantime I took Sis in the Depot Hotel. It was only a quarter past six, and we had to wait till seven. We saw the Ledger and Times—nothing in either—a few words of no account in the *Chronicle*. We started in good spirits, but did not get here until nearly three o'clock. We went in the cars to Amboy, about forty miles from N. York. When we got to the wharf it was raining hard. I left her on board the boat, after putting the trunks in the Ladies' cabin, and set off to buy an umbrella and look for a boarding-house. I met a man selling umbrellas, and bought one for twenty-five cents. Then I went up Greenwich St and soon found a boarding-house. It is just before you get to Cedar St, on the west side going up—the left-hand side. It has brown stone steps, with a porch with brown pillars. 'Morrison' is the name on the door.

"I made a bargain in a few minutes and then got a hack and went for Sis. I was not gone more than half an hour, and she was quite astonished to see me back so soon. She didn't expect me for an hour. There were two other ladies waiting on board—so she wasn't very lonely. When we got to the house we had to wait about half an hour before the room was ready. The house is old and looks buggy . . . the cheapest board I ever knew, taking into consideration the central situation and the living. I wish Kate could see it—she would faint. Last night, for supper, we had the nicest tea you ever drank, strong and hot,—wheat bread and rye bread—cheese—tea—cakes (elegant), a great dish (two dishes) of elegant ham, and two of cold veal, piled up like a mountain and large slices—three dishes of the cakes and everything in the greatest profusion. No fear of starving here. The landlady seemed as if she couldn't press us enough, and we were at home directly. Her husband is living with her—a fat, good-natured old soul. There are eight or ten boarders—two or three of them ladies—two servants. For breakfast we had excellent-flavoured coffee, hot and strong—not very clear and no great deal of cream—veal cutlets, elegant ham and eggs and nice bread and butter. I never sat down to a more plentiful or a nicer breakfast. I wish you could have seen the eggs—and the great dishes of meat. I ate the first hearty breakfast I have eaten since I left our little home.

"Sis is delighted, and we are both in excellent spirits. She has coughed hardly any and had no night sweat. She is now busy mending my pants which I tore against a nail. I went out last night and bought a skein of silk, a skein of thread, two buttons, a pair of slippers, and a pan for the stove. The fire kept in all night. We have now got four dollars and a half left. Tomorrow I am going to try and borrow three dollars, so that I may have a fortnight to go upon. I feel in excellent spirits, and haven't drank a drop—so that I hope soon to get out of trouble. The very instant I scrape together enough money I will send it on. You can't imagine how much we both do miss you. Sissy had a hearty cry last night because you . . . weren't there. We are resolved to get two rooms the first moment we can. In the meantime it is impossible we could be more comfortable or more at home than we are. It looks as if it were going to clear up now. Be sure and go to the P.O. and have my letters forwarded. As soon as I write Lowell's article, I will send it to you, and get you to get the money from Graham. . . .

"(P.S.) Be sure and take home the *Messenger* to Hirst. We hope to send for you." [George E. Woodberry, *The Life of Edgar Allan Poe, Personal and Literary,* Houghton, 1909.[4]]

March, 1845. Joined staff of *The Broadway Journal* and became its sole editor and proprietor.

January, 1846. *The Broadway Journal* realized its final publication. "Unexpected engagements demanding my whole attention, and the objects being fulfilled so far as regards myself personally, for which the *Broadway Journal* was established, I now, as its editor, bid farewell—as cordially to foes as to friends."[1]

1846. Moved to Fordham with his wife. Their new quarters and situation was reported by one of Poe's supporters, Mrs. Grove Nichols: "The cottage had an air of gentility that must have been lent to it by the presence of its inmates. So neat, so poor, so unfurnished, and yet so charming a dwelling I never saw. The floor of the kitchen was white as wheaten flour. A table, a chair, and a little stove it contained seemed to furnish it completely. The sitting room was laid with check matting; four chairs, a light stand, and a hanging bookshelf completed its furniture. There were pretty presentation copies of books on the little shelves, and the Brownings had posts of honor on the stand. With quiet exultation Poe drew from his inside pocket a letter he had recently received from Elizabeth Barrett Browning. He read it to us. It was very flattering. . . . On the bookshelf there lay a volume of Poe's poems. He took it down, wrote my name in it and gave it to me. I think he did this from a feeling of sympathy, for I could not be of advantage to him, as my two companions could. . . . He was at this time greatly depressed. Their extreme poverty; the sickness of his wife, and his own inability to write sufficiently accounted for this."[1]

In a December visit, Nichols noted: "I saw [Virginia] in her bed-chamber. Everything here was so neat, so purely clean, so scant and poverty stricken, that I saw the poor sufferer with such a heartache as the poor feel for the poor.

"There was no clothing on the bed, which was only straw, but a snow-white counterpane and sheets. The weather was cold, and the sick lady had the dreadful chills that accompany the hectic fever of consumption. She lay in the straw bed, wrapped in her husband's great coat, with a large tortoise-shell cat in her bosom. The wonderful cat seemed conscious of her great usefulness. The coat and the cat were the sufferer's only means of warmth, except as her husband held her hands, and her mother her feet. Mrs Clemm was passionately fond of her daughter, and her distress on account of her illness and poverty was dreadful to see.

"As soon as I was made aware of these painful facts, I came to New York and enlisted the sympathies and services of a lady, whose heart and hand were ever open to the poor and miserable. . . ."[1]

January 30, 1847. Virginia died. ". . . Six years ago, a wife, whom I loved as no man ever loved before, ruptured a blood-vessel in singing. Her life was despaired of. I took leave of her forever and underwent all of the agonies of her death. She recovered partially, and I again hoped. At the end of a year, the vessel broke again. I went through precisely the same scene. . . . Then again—again—again—and even once again, at varying intervals. Each time I felt all the agonies of her death—and at each accession of the disorder I loved her more dearly and clung to her life with more desperate pertinacity. But I am constitutionally sensitive—nervous in a very unusual degree, I became insane, with long intervals of horrible sanity. During these fits of absolute unconsciousness, I drank—God only knows how often or how much. As a matter of course, my enemies referred the insanity to the drink, rather than the drink to the insanity. I had, indeed, nearly abandoned all hope of a permanent cure, when I found one in the death of my wife. This I can endure as becomes a man. It was the horrible never-ending oscillation between hope and despair which I could not longer have endured, without total loss of reason. In the death of what was my life, then, I receive a new but—Oh, God!—how melancholy an existence."[1]

1848. The first of Poe's amorous letters to widow, Sarah Helen Whitman.

July, 1848. Met and fell in love with Mrs. Annie Richmond. ". . . A young woman about twenty-eight years of age—slender, or rather slight, and somewhat above the medium height. As she approached, with a certain *modest decision* of step altogether indescribable, I said to myself, 'Surely here I have found the perfection of natural, in contradistinction from artificial *grace*.' The second impression which she made on me, but by far the more vivid of the two, was that of *enthusiasm*. So intense an expression of *romance,* perhaps I should

(From *The Bells, and Other Poems* by Edgar Allan Poe. Illustrated by Edmund Dulac.)

(From *The Raven* by Edgar Allan Poe. Illustrated by Gustave Doré.)

call it, or of unworldliness, as that which gleamed from her deep-set eyes, had never so sunk into my heart of hearts before. I know not how it is, but this peculiar expression of the eye, wreathing itself occasionally into the lips, is the most powerful, if not absolutely the *sole* spell, which rivets my interest in woman. *'Romance,'* provided my readers fully comprehend what I would here imply by the word—'romance' and 'womanliness' seem to me convertible terms: and, after all, what man truly *loves* in woman, is simply, her *womanhood.* The eyes of Annie (I heard some one from the interior call her 'Annie, darling!') were 'spiritual gray'; her hair, a light chestnut: this is all I had time to observe of her." [*Complete Stories and Poems of Edgar Allan Poe,* Doubleday, 1966.[5]]

Divided in his passion between S. Whitman and A. Richmond, he drowned his confusions with drink spanning a period of several weeks.

October 1, 1848. Continued writing a series of famous love letters to Mrs. Whitman. "During a walk in the cemetery I said to you while the bitter, bitter, tears sprang to my eyes—'Helen [Mrs. Whitman] I love now—now for the first and only time'."[1]

Confessed his attempt to resolve the impossible choice between the women in his life by committing suicide: "I remember nothing distinctly from that moment [the parting with 'Annie'] until I found myself in Providence. I went to bed and wept through a long, long hideous night of Despair—When the day broke, I arose and endeavored to quiet my mind by a rapid walk in the cold, keen air—but all would not do—the Demon tormented me still. Finally I procured two ounces of laudanum, and without returning to my hotel, took the cars back to Boston. . . . When I arrived [in Boston] I wrote you [Annie] a letter in which I opened my whole heart to you—to you. . . . I told you how my struggles were more than I could bear. I then reminded you of that holy promise which was the last I exacted from you in parting—that promise that under all circumstances, you would come to me on my bed of death. I implored you to come then, mentioning the place where I should be found in Boston. Having written this letter, I swallowed about half the laudanum, and hurried to the Post Office, intending not to take the rest until I saw you—for I did not doubt for one moment, that Annie would keep her sacred promise. But I had not calculated on the strength of the laudanum, for before I reached the Post Office my reason was entirely gone, and the letter was never put in. Let me pass over—my darling sister—the awful hours that succeeded. A friend was at hand, who aided me. . . . It appears that, after the laudanum was rejected from my stomach, I became calm, and to a casual observer, sane—so that I was suffered to go back to Providence."[1]

A brief engagement with Mrs. Whitman was broken. Poe returned to Fordham. "Of one thing rest assured, from this day forth, I shun the pestilential society of literary women. They are a heartless, unnatural, venomous, dishonorable set, with no guiding principle but inordinate self-esteem."[1]

1849. ". . . I am so busy, now, and feel so full of energy. Engagements to write are pouring in upon me every day. I had two proposals within the last week from Boston. I sent yesterday an article to the *Am. Review,* about Critics and Criticism. Not long ago I sent one to the *Metropolitan* called Landor's Cottage it has something about 'Annie' in it, and will appear, I suppose in the March number. To the *S. L. Messenger* I have sent fifty pages of Marginalia, five pages to appear each month of the current year. I have also made permanent engagements with another magazine, called *The Gentlemen's.* So you see that I have only to keep up my spirits to get out of all my pecuniary troubles. The least price I get is $5 per 'Graham page,' and I can easily average 1½ per day—that is $7½. As soon as 'returns' come in I shall be out of difficulty."[1]

Due to his chronic bad luck, all of Poe's new plans fell through, tapping him of all of his new energies and rendering him exhausted and depressed. Laudanum, of which his tolerance was now enormous, catapulted him back into his dream-world.

April, 1849. Received an offer from Edward Patterson (son of a newspaperman) to back Poe's magazine now to be known as *The Stylus.* "Experience, not less than the most mature reflection on this topic, assured me that no cheap magazine can ever again prosper in America. We must aim high—address the intellect—the higher classes—of the country (with reference, also to a certain amount of foreign circulation) and put the work at $5:—going about 112 pp (or perhaps 128) with occasional wood-engravings in the first style of the art, but only in obvious illustrations of the text. Such a Mag. would begin to pay after 1000 subscribers; and with 5000 would be a fortune worth talking about;—but there is no earthly reason why, under proper management, and with energy and talent, the work might not be made to circulate, at the end of a few years—(say 5) 20,000 copies in which case it would give a clear income of 70 or 80,000 dollars—even if conducted in the most expensive manner. . . . I need not add that such a Mag. would exercise a literary and other influence never yet exercised in America. . . . During the second year of its existence, the *S. L. Messenger* rose from less than 1000 to 5000 subs., and that *Graham's,* in 8 months after my joining it, went up from 5000 to 52,000. I do not imagine that a $5 Mag. could even be forced into so great a circulation as this latter; but under certain circumstances, I would answer for 20,000. The whole income from *Graham's* 52,000 never went beyond $15,000:—the proportioned expenses of the $3 Mags. being so much greater than those of $5 ones.

"My plan, in getting up such work as I propose, would be to take a tour through the principal States—especially west and south—visiting the small towns more particularly than the large ones—lecturing as I went, to pay expenses—and staying sufficiently long in each place to interest my personal friends (old college and West Point acquaintances scattered all over the land) in the success of the enterprise. By these means, I could guarantee in 3 months (or 4) to get 1000 subs. in advance, with their signatures—nearly all pledged to pay at the issue of the first number. Under such circumstances, success would be certain. I have now about 200 names pledged to support me whenever I venture on the undertaking—which perhaps you are aware I have long had in contemplation—only awaiting a secure opportunity. . . ."[1]

Patterson was too inexperienced in negotiating such projects to conceal his enthusiasm. He outlined an offer in detail: "I will furnish an office and take upon myself the sole charge and expense of Publishing a Magazine (name to be suggested by you) to be issued in monthly numbers at Oquawka, Illinois, containing in every number, 96 pages . . . at the rate of $5 per annum. Of this magazine you are to have the entire editorial control, furnishing at your expense, matter for its pages, which can be transmitted to me by mail or as we may hereafter agree upon. . . . You can make your own bargains with authors and I am to publish upon the best terms I can

. . . and we are to share the receipts equally. . . . If my plan accords with your views, you will immediately select a title, write me to that effect, and we will both commence operations. We ought to put out the first number January next. Let me hear from you immediately."[1]

June, 1849. Left New York for Richmond to implement his plans for the magazine.

Interrupted his journey in Philadelphia. He wrote Mrs. Clemm: "My *dear, dear* Mother,—

"I have been *so* ill—have had the cholera, or spasms quite as bad, and can now hardly hold the pen[. . .]

"The very instant you get this, *come* to me. The joy of seeing you will almost compensate for our sorrows. We can but die together. It is no use to reason with me *now;* I must die. I have no desire to live since I have done 'Eureka.' I could accomplish nothing more. For your sake it would be sweet to live, but we must die together. You have been all in all to me, darling, ever beloved mother, and dearest, truest friend.

"I was never *really* insane, except on occasions where my heart was touched[. . .]

"I have been taken to prison once since I came here for getting drunk; but *then* I was not. It was about Virginia." [John Ward Ostrom, editor, *The Letters of Edgar Allan Poe,* Volume II, Harvard University Press, 1948.[6]]

Resumed his journey to Richmond. ". . . I got here with two dollars over—of which I enclose you one. Oh, God, my mother, shall we ever meet again? If possible, oh COME! My clothes are so horrible and I am so ill. Oh, if you could come to me, my mother. Write instantly—Oh do not fail. God forever bless you."[1]

July 19, 1849. In another letter to Mrs. Clemm: "You will see at once, by the handwriting of this letter, that I am better—much better in health and spirits. Oh, if you only knew how your dear letter comforted me! It acted like magic. Most of my suffering arose from that terrible idea which I could not get rid of—the idea that you were dead. For more than ten days I was totally deranged, although I was not drinking one drop; and during this interval I imagined the most horrible calamities. . . .

"All was hallucination, arising from an attack which I had never before experienced—an attack of *mania-à-potu.* May Heaven grant that it prove a warning to me for the rest of my days. If so, I shall not regret even the horrible unspeakable torments I have endured.

". . . I have not drank anything since Friday morning, and then only a little Port wine. *If possible,* dearest Mother, I *will* extricate myself from this difficulty for your *dear, dear sake.* So keep up heart.

"All is not lost yet, and 'the darkest hour is just before daylight.' Keep up heart, my own beloved mother—all may yet go well. I will put forth all my energies. When I get my mind a little more composed, I will try to write something."[6]

Poe's primary goal for journeying to Richmond to complete arrangements for the publication of *The Stylus* dissipated. His preoccupation became that of courting Mrs. Barrett Shelton.

September, 1849. Set out for Baltimore sick from abusive drinking. His doctor described him: "His face was haggard, not to say bloated, and unwashed, his hair unkempt and his whole physique repulsive. His expansive forehead . . . and those full-orbed and mellow, yet soulful eyes for which he was so noticeable when himself, now lusterless as shortly I could see, were shaded from view by a rusty, almost brimless, tattered and ribbonless palm leaf hat. His clothing consisted of a sack-coat of thin and sleezy black alpaca, ripped more or less at intervals of its seams, and faded and soiled, and pants of a steel-mixed pattern of casinett, half worn and badly fitting, if they could be said to fit at all. He wore neither vest nor neck cloth, while the bosom of his shirt was both crumpled and badly soiled. . . ."[1]

October 3, 1849. Removed to a hospital in an almost unconscious state.

October 7, 1849. Died in Baltimore. "And now we rushed into the embraces of the cataract, where a chasm threw itself open to receive us. But there arose in our pathway a shrouded human figure, very far larger in its proportions than any dweller among men. And the hue of the skin of the figure was of the perfect whiteness of the snow."[1]

FOR MORE INFORMATION SEE: Thomas O. Mabbott, editor, *Edgar Allan Poe* (bound with a reprint of Lambert A. Wilmer, *Recollections of Edgar A. Poe,* 1827), Folcroft, 1941; Sarah H. Whitman, *Edgar Allan Poe,* 1860, reprinted, Haskell House, 1973; Whitman, *Edgar Poe and His Critics,* 1860, reissued, Americanist Press, 1967; John H. Ingram, *Edgar Allan Poe: His Life, Letters, and Opinions,* two volumes, 1880, reissued, Folcroft, 1973; Edmund C. Stedman, *Edgar Allan Poe,* Houghton, 1881, privately printed, 1909, reprinted, Norwood, 1976; George E. Woodberry, *Edgar Allan Poe,* Houghton, 1885, reprinted, AMS Press, 1968; Joel Benton, *In the Poe Circle,* 1899, reprinted, Arden Library, 1978; John P. Fruit, *The Mind and Art of Poe's Poetry,* A. S. Barnes, 1899, reissued, Norwood, 1975.

James A. Harrison, *The Life of Edgar Allan Poe,* Crowell, 1902-1903, reprinted, Haskell House, 1970; Charles W. Kent and John S. Patton, editors, *The Book of the Poe Centenary,* 1909, reprinted, Norwood, 1975; Woodberry, *The Life of Edgar Allan Poe, Personal and Literary,* Houghton, 1909, reissued, Biblo & Tannen, 1965; Heinrich E. Bucholz, editor, *Edgar Allan Poe: A Centenary Tribute,* 1910, reprinted, Folcroft, 1972; John W. Robertson, M.D., *Edgar A. Poe: A Psychopathic Study,* Putnam, 1923; Sherwin Cody, *Poe: Man, Poet, and Creative Thinker,* Boni & Liveright, 1924, reissued, Kennikat, 1973; Hervey Allen, *Israfel, the Life and Times of Edgar Allan Poe,* two volumes, George H. Doran, 1926, reissued, single volume, Holt, 1960; Joseph W. Krutch, *Edgar Allan Poe: A Study in Genius,* 1926, reprinted, Russell, 1965; Celestine Cambiares, *The Influence of Edgar Allan Poe in France,* 1927, reprinted, Scholarly Press, 1971.

Elizabeth Poe and Vylla Wilson, *Edgar Allan Poe, a High Priest of the Beautiful,* Stylus, 1930, reissued, R. West, 1978; Killis Campbell, *The Mind of Poe, and Other Studies,* 1933, reprinted, Russell, 1962; Una Pope-Hennessy, *Edgar Allan Poe: 1809-1849,* 1934, reprinted, Scholarly Press, 1971; Edward Shanks, *Edgar Allan Poe,* 1937, reprinted, Folcroft, 1974, Norwood, 1974.

Arthur H. Quinn, *Edgar Allan Poe: A Critical Biography,* 1941, reprinted, Cooper Square, 1970; George D. Snell, *Shapers of American Fiction, 1798-1947,* Dutton, 1947; Dora M. Barnes, *Edgar Allan Poe,* 1949, reprinted, R. West, 1978; Marie Bonaparte, *The Life and Works of Edgar Allan Poe, a Psycho-Analytic Interpretation,* foreward by Sigmund Freud, Imago, 1949; N. Bryllion Fagin, *The Histrionic Mr. Poe,* Johns Hopkins Press, 1949; John H. Hewitt, *Recollections of Poe,* Emory University Library, 1949; H. L. Mencken, *Mencken Chrestomathy,* Knopf, 1949.

"Griswold on Poe," *Treasury of Intimate Biographies,* edited by Louis L. Snyder, Greenberg, 1951; Charles D. Baudelaire, *Baudelaire on Poe: Critical Papers,* translated by Lois and Francis Hyslop, Bald Eagle Press, 1952; Jay B. Hubbell, *The South in American Literature, 1607-1900,* Duke University Press, 1954; Edward H. Davidson, *Poe: A Critical Study,* Harvard University Press, 1957; H. L. Mencken, *Bathtub Hoax and Other Blasts and Bravos from the Chicago Tribune,* Knopf, 1958; Louis Untermeyer, *Lives of the Poets,* Simon & Schuster, 1959.

David M. Rein, *Edgar Allan Poe, the Inner Patterns,* Philosophical Library, 1960; R. W. Stallman and Arthur Waldhorn, editors, *American Literature: Readings and Critiques,* Putnam, 1961; Vincent Buranelli, *Edgar Allan Poe,* Twayne, 1961, second edition, 1977; William Bittner, *Poe: A Biography,* Little, Brown, 1962; Sidney P. Moss, *Poe's Literary Battles,* Duke University Press, 1963; Eric W. Carlson, editor, *Recognition of Edgar Allan Poe: Selected Criticism Since 1829,* University of Michigan Press, 1966, reissued, 1970; John Walsh, *Poe the Detective,* Rutgers University Press, 1968; Robert D. Jacobs, *Poe: Journalist and Critic,* Louisiana State University Press, 1969; Floyd Stovall, *Edgar Poe the Poet,* University Press of Virginia, 1969.

Patrick R. Quinn, *The French Face of Edgar Poe,* Southern Illinois University Press, 1971; John C. French, *Poe in Foreign Lands and Tongues,* Folcroft, 1973, reissued, Norwood, 1978; Philip Stern, *Edgar Allan Poe: Visitor from the Night of Time,* Crowell, 1973; Peter Haining, editor, *The Edgar Allan Poe Scrapbook,* Schocken, 1978; W. Mankowitz, *The Extraordinary Mr. Poe,* Simon & Schuster, 1978; David Sinclair, *Edgar Allan Poe,* Rowman & Littlefield, 1978.

For children: Elizabeth R. Mongomery, *The Story Behind Great Stories,* McBride, 1947; Laura Benet, *Famous American Poets,* Dodd, 1950; Gertrude and J. V. Southworth, *Heroes of Our America,* Iroquois, 1952; Frederick H. Law, *Great Americans,* Globe Book, 1953; Sarah K. Bolton, *Famous American Authors,* Crowell, 1954; Robert Cantwell, *Famous American Men of Letters,* Dodd, 1956; David E. Scherman and Rosemarie Redlich, *America: The Land and Its Writers,* Dodd, 1956; Benet, "Growing Pains," *Roads to Greatness,* edited by Louise Galloway, Crowell-Collier, 1962; Frances Helmstadter, *Picture Book of American Authors,* Sterling, 1962; Lettice U. Cooper, *Young Edgar Allan Poe* (illustrated by William Randell), Roy, 1964; Nora Stirling, *Who Wrote the Classics?,* Day, 1965; Benet, *Famous English and American Essayists,* Dodd, 1966; Harriet I. Davis, *Elmira: The Girl Who Loved Edgar Allan Poe* (illustrated by Eugene Karlin), Houghton, 1966; John T. Winterich, *Writers in America,* Davey, Daniel, 1968; Alan S. Paley, *Edgar Allan Poe, American Poet and Mystery Writer,* SamHar, 1975; Carla Hancock, *Seven Founders of American Literature,* Blair, 1976.

EDGAR ALLAN POE

Movies and filmstrips: "Edgar Allan Poe" (motion picture), Mutoscope and Biograph, directed by D. W. Griffith, 1909; "The Loves of Edgar Allan Poe" (motion picture), Twentieth Century-Fox, 1942; "Edgar Allan Poe" (filmstrip; with teacher's manual), Eye Gate House, 1952; "Edgar Allan Poe" (filmstrip; with captions), Encyclopaedia Britannica Films, 1954; "Edgar Allan Poe" (filmstrip; captioned, with teacher's guide), Young America Films, 1955; "Edgar Allan Poe: Background for His Works" (motion picture; with teacher's guide), Coronet Instructional Films, 1958; "Three Great Writers" (filmstrip; with teacher's manual), Eye Gate House, 1961; "Edgar Allan Poe" (motion picture), University of Southern California, Division of Cinema, 1962; "Symbolism in Literature" (motion picture; with study guide), Sigma Educational Films, 1966.

"Edgar Allan Poe" (motion pictures; with scripts and study guides), Filmstrip House, 1968: Part 1: His Life, Part 2: His Times, Part 3: His Works, Part 4: His Styles; "Edgar Allan Poe" (2 filmstrips; with discussion guide), Guidance Associates of Pleasantville, 1970; "That Strange Mr. Poe" (filmstrip; with script), Thomas S. Klise, 1970; "Edgar Allan Poe: The Man and His Work" (4 filmstrips; with teacher's manual), Eye Gate House, 1971; "Reading Poetry: Annabel Lee" (motion picture; with study guide), Oxford Films, narrated by Lorne Greene, 1971; "Edgar Allan Poe" (motion picture; with teacher's guide), Oxford Films, with Lorne Green, 1972(?); "The Spectre of Edgar Allan Poe" (motion picture), Cinerama, starring Cesar Romero, 1974.

PORTER, Katherine Anne 1890-1980

OBITUARY NOTICE: Born May 15, 1890, in Indian Creek, Tex.; died September, 1980, in Silver Spring, Md. Author best known for her only full-length novel, *Ship of Fools,* Porter primarily wrote short stories and novellas that were critically acclaimed but not financially successful. She did not become popular until after her novel was published. Porter received several awards for her writing, including the 1966 Pulitzer Prize and the National Book Award. Her other works include *Flowering Judas, Pale Horse, Pale Rider,* and *A Defense of Circe. For More Information See: Current Biography,* Wilson, 1963; *The Oxford Companion to American Literature,* 4th edition, Oxford University Press, 1965; *Contemporary Authors,* Volume 1-4, revised, Gale, 1967; *American Writers: A Collection of Literary Biographies,* Scribner, 1974. *Obituaries: Newsweek,* September 29, 1980; *Time,* September 29, 1980; *Publishers Weekly,* October 3, 1980; *Contemporary Authors,* Volume 101-104, Gale, 1981.

PRICE, Christine (Hilda) 1928-1980

OBITUARY NOTICE—See sketch in *SATA* Volume 3: Born April 15, 1928, in London, England; died January 13, 1980, in Albuquerque, N.M. Illustrator and writer of children's books on art history, dance, and folklore. Extensive travel provided Price with material for many of her books which include *The Story of Moslem Art, Three Golden Nobles, Sixty at a Blow, The Mystery of Masks,* and *Dance on the Dusty Earth. For More Information See: Contemporary Authors,* Volume 5-6, revised, Gale, 1963; *Author's and Writer's Who's Who,* 6th edition, Burke's Peerage, 1971; *Authors of Books for Young People,* 2nd edition, Scarecrow, 1971; *Who's Who of American Women,* 10th edition, Marquis, 1977; *The Writers Directory, 1980-82,* St. Martin's, 1979. *Obituaries: Contemporary Authors,* Volume, 93-96, Gale, 1980; *Publishers Weekly,* February 22, 1980; *School Library Journal,* April, 1980.

RAPHAEL, Elaine (Chionchio) 1933-

PERSONAL: Born March 14, 1933, in New York City; married Donald Alan Bolognese (an illustrator), 1954; children: two daughters. *Education:* Attended Cooper Union Art School. *Home:* New York and Vermont.

CAREER: Author and illustrator of children's books; has served as an instructor at Pratt Institute, Brooklyn, New York, Cooper Union Art School, New York University, and the Metropolitan Museum of Art's medieval museum, The Cloisters.

(From *Letters to Horseface* by F. N. Monjo. Illustrated and designed by Don Bolognese and Elaine Raphael.)

WRITINGS—All written and illustrated with husband, Don Bolognese: *The Sleepy Watchdog,* Lothrop, 1964; *Sam Baker, Gone West,* Viking, 1977; *Donkey and Carlo,* Harper, 1978.

Illustrator: Ian Serraillier, *Havelok the Dane,* Walck, 1967; Roger L. Green, *Tales of Ancient Egypt,* Walck, 1968; Margaret Hillert, *Circus Fun,* Follett, 1969; (with D. Bolognese) William Jay Smith, *Poems from Italy,* Crowell, 1972; Hila Colman, *Benny, the Misfit,* Crowell, 1973; (with D. Bolognese) F. N. Monjo, *Letters to Horseface,* Viking, 1975; (with D. Bolognese) Margaret Hodges, *Knight Prisoner: The Tale of Sir Thomas Malory and His King Arthur,* Farrar, Straus, 1976.

FOR MORE INFORMATION SEE: Doris de Montreville and Elizabeth D. Crawford, editors, *Fourth Book of Junior Authors & Illustrators,* H. W. Wilson, 1978.

Twinkle, twinkle, little bat!
How I wonder what you're at!
Up above the world you fly!
Like a teatray in the sky.

—Lewis Carroll
(pseudonym of Charles Lutwidge Dodgson)

(From *Shapes* by John J. Reiss. Illustrated by the author.)

REISS, John J.

PERSONAL: Born in Milwaukee, Wis. *Education:* Graduated from a teacher's college in Milwaukee, Wis.; graduate study done at Black Mountain College, N.C.

CAREER: Artist, designer, illustrator. Reiss is widely recognized for his advertising art; examples of his graphic art and designs have been exhibited through *Graphis* magazine in Europe, Africa, and Asia. *Awards, honors:* Co-recipient of the Milwaukee Art Directors Club gold medal, 1967.

WRITINGS—All self-illustrated: *Colors,* Bradbury, 1969; *Numbers,* Bradbury, 1971; *Shapes* (ALA Notable Book), Bradbury, 1974.

Illustrator: Jane Jonas Srivastava, *Statistics,* Crowell, 1973.

SIDELIGHTS: A native of Milwaukee, Wisconsin, Reiss graduated from State Teachers College in Milwaukee prior to doing graduate study in North Carolina. A well known graphic artist and designer, his work has been exhibited in Europe, Africa, and Asia.

The consensus among the critics seems to be that Reiss is a master of the instructional concept book for children. Each of his books has been highly praised by the reviewers. His first book, *Colors,* elicited this comment from *Library Journal,* "Color perception is a sensation—a fact empirically and beautifully demonstrated here. . . . But what the book primarily supplies is visual enjoyment; the color theory included does not obtrude, and is there to be discovered when viewers are ready. . . . A thoroughly successful introduction to color that outshines all previous attempts." *Publishers Weekly* offers similar praise for *Numbers.* "Using the same vibrant colors and simplicity of design that made his *Colors* such a successful color identification book, John Reiss has now created an equally dazzling counting and number recognition book." *Shapes,* the most recent of Reiss's works, has been as highly recommended as were the earlier books. As stated in the *Center for Children's Books Bulletin,* "Absolutely luscious in its spectrum of vivid colors, this is one of the most attractive of the several books that present to young children examples of such shapes as oval, circle, triangle, rectangle, and square. Reiss carries it a bit farther, showing how squares form a cube, or circles a sphere, and he tosses in a few more complex shapes at the close of the book to intrigue the audience: a hexagon, an octagon, a pentagon."

FOR MORE INFORMATION SEE: Library Journal, December 15, 1969; *Publishers Weekly,* December 6, 1971; *Center for Children's Books Bulletin,* December, 1974; Lee Kingman, and others, compilers, *Illustrators of Children's Books: 1967-1976,* Horn Book, 1978; Martha E. Ward and Dorothy A. Marquardt, editors, *Authors of Books for Young People,* 2nd edition, supplement, Scarecrow, 1979.

RESNICK, Seymour 1920-

PERSONAL: Born January 15, 1920, in New York, N.Y. *Education:* City College (now of the City University of New York), B.A., 1940; New York University, M.A., 1943, Ph.D., 1951. *Home:* 57 Tobin Ave., Great Neck, N.Y. 11021.

CAREER: Examiner-translator, Office of Censorship, 1942-44; New York University, New York City, instructor in Spanish, 1944-50; City College (now of the City University of New York), New York City, lecturer in Romance languages, 1951-52; Rutgers University, New Brunswick, N.J., instructor in Romance languages, 1953-57; high school teacher in Great Neck, New York, 1957-64; Queens College of the City University of New York, Flushing, N.Y., lecturer, 1959-64, associate professor, 1964-66, professor of Romance languages, 1967-79, department of Romance languages, chairman, 1979—. *Member:* Modern Language Association of America, American Association of Teachers Spanish and Portuguese.

WRITINGS: Welcome to Spanish: A Grammar and Reader for Beginners, Ungar, 1952; (with Doriane Kurz) *Embarrassing Moments in French, and How to Avoid Them,* Ungar, 1953; *Rapid Spanish,* Ungar, 1960; *Essential French Grammar,* Dover, 1962; *Essential Spanish Grammar,* Dover, 1963.

Editor: Eduardo Barrios, *Cuatro Cuentos,* Harper, 1951, reissued as *El Niño que Enloqueció de Amor, y Otros Cuentos,* Las Américas Publishing, 1966; (with Jeanne Pasmantier)
An Anthology of Spanish Literature in English Translatio
Ungar, 1958; *Selections from Spanish Poetry* (illu
Anne Marie Jauss), Harvey House, 1962
tier), *Highlights of Spanish Literature,* Un
American Poetry: A Bilingual Selection (ill
Jauss), Harvey House, 1964; (with J. Pasm
of Spanish Literature in Translation, Unga

I did not gaze too long
at her great beauty
lest I lose
my freedom.
■ (From *Selections from Spanish Poetry* edited by Seymour Resnick. Illustrated by Anne Marie Jauss.)

SIDELIGHTS: As an authority on the Spanish language, Resnick translated and edited a number of works. The author-editor collected a wide range of poetry in his book, *Spanish-American Poetry. Library Journal* observed, "This companion to the author's *Selections from Spanish Poetry* includes 'a range of poems from the times of the conquistadors through the 19th and 20th centuries. . . .'" Pura Belpre, writing in the same magazine, found Resnick's book "a good representative selection from the major Latin American poets."

RIESENBERG, Felix, Jr. 1913-1962

PERSONAL: First syllable of surname is pronounced "ree"; born August 5, 1913, in New York City; died March 22, 1962, in Florida; son of Felix (a writer, engineer, and sea captain) and Maud (Conroy) Riesenberg; married Priscilla Frances Alden, June 6, 1936; children: Joan Riesenberg Barrett Hoyt, Felix III. *Education:* Attended Columbia University, 1932-34. *Politics:* Republican. *Religion:* Catholic.

CAREER: Editor and author. San Francisco *News,* reporter, shipping editor, daily columnist, 1936-39. Was Pacific Coast correspondent for *Nautical Gazette,* technical advisor for Warner Brothers Pictures and Republic Studios, radio news editor for the Office of War Information. *Military service:* Served in the U.S. Maritime Service (Merchant Marine) during World War II; became lieutenant.

WRITINGS—All for young readers, except as indicated: *Yankee Skippers to the Rescue: A Record of Gallant Rescues on the North Atlantic by American Seamen,* Dodd, 1940, reissued, Books for Libraries, 1969; (for adults) *Golden Gate: The Story of San Francisco Harbor,* Knopf, 1940; *Full Ahead! A Career Story of The American Merchant Marine,* Dodd, 1941; *Salvage: A Modern Sea Story,* Dodd, 1942; *The Phantom Freighter,* Dodd, 1944; *The Man on the Raft,* Dodd, 1945; *Galapagos Bound! Smuggling in the Tuna Fleet,* Dodd, 1947; *The Crimson Anchor: A Sea Mystery,* Dodd, 1948; *The Mysterious Sailor: A Sea Adventure,* Dodd, 1949.

"or adults) *Waterfront Reporter* (illustrated by Chauncey 'tman), Rand McNally, 1950; *Great Men of the Sea* (illustrated by Rus Anderson), Putnam, 1955; *Balboa, Swordsman and Conquistador* (illustrated by Feodor Rojankovsky), Random House, 1956; (for adults) *Sea War: The Story of the U.S. Merchant Marine in World War II,* Rinehart, 1956, reissued, Greenwood Press, 1974; *The Story of the Naval Academy* (illustrated by William M. Hutchinson), Random House, 1958; *The Vanishing Steamer,* Westminster Press, 1958; (for adults) *The Golden Road: The Story of California's Spanish Mission Trail,* McGraw, 1962; *The Undercover Sloop,* Westminster Press, 1962.

SIDELIGHTS: Riesenberg first developed his sea legs as a deck boy when he was ten. Like his father and grandfather who were both sea captains, he would eventually sail the world. Riesenberg spent many summer vacations from school on board a ship, travelling to Europe, Africa, South America, and the West Indies. He later sailed the Atlantic and Pacific coasts of the United States.

Riesenberg followed his father's footsteps in yet another direction. Son, like father, published a number of books, drawing on experiences at sea for subject matter. The majority of Riesenberg's books were tales of high adventure at sea for boys. He has also written a history of San Francisco, a history of California's Spanish mission trail which has since become the heavily-travelled U.S. Highway 101, and a history of the U.S. Merchant Marine.

HOBBIES AND OTHER INTERESTS: A love of the sea even filtered into Riesenberg's leisure time. Model ship building was his hobby, and he also enjoyed boxing and swimming.

FOR MORE INFORMATION SEE: Springfield Republican, December 8, 1940; *Christian Science Monitor,* December 12, 1940; *New York Times Book Review,* December 22, 1940; *New York Herald Tribune Books,* November 15, 1942; *New York Herald Tribune Weekly Book Review,* November 11, 1945, April 27, 1947, May 9, 1948; *Christian Science Monitor,* July 8, 1948; *Saturday Review,* June 2, 1956; *San Francisco Chronicle,* June 5, 1956; *Christian Science Monitor,* June 14, 1956; *Chicago Sunday Tribune,* August 12, 1956; *New York Times Book Review,* October 7, 1962; *New York Herald Tribune Books,* October 14, 1962; Martha E. Ward and Dorothy A. Marquardt, *Authors of Books for Young People,* Scarecrow Press, 1964.

ROBINSON, Ray(mond Kenneth) 1920-

PERSONAL: Born December 4, 1920, in New York, N.Y.; son of Louis H. (a lawyer) and Lillian (Hoffman) Robinson; married Phyllis Cumins (a writer), September 18, 1949; children: Nancy, Stephen, Tad. *Education:* Columbia University, B.A., 1941, further study, Columbia Law School, 1941-42. *Home:* 530 East 90th St., New York, N.Y. 10028. *Agent:* Sterling Lord Agency, Inc., 660 Madison Ave., New York, N.Y. 10028. *Office: Seventeen* magazine, 850 Third Ave., New York, N.Y. 10022.

CAREER: Real, New York City, editor, 1955-57; *Pageant,* New York City, managing editor, 1957-59; *Coronet,* New York City, senior editor, 1959-61; *Good Housekeeping,* New York City, articles editor, 1961-69; *Seventeen* magazine, New York City, executive editor, 1969—. Instructor at New York University, 1977. *Military service:* U.S. Army, 1942-46. *Member:* American Society of Magazine Editors (executive committee).

WRITINGS: (With Constantine Callinicos) *The Mario Lanza Story,* Coward, 1960; (editor) *Baseball Stars, 1961,* Pyramid Books, 1961; *Ted Williams,* Putnam, 1962; *Stan Musial: Baseball's Durable Man,* Putnam, 1963; *Speed Kings of the Basepaths,* Putnam, 1964; *Greatest World Series Thrillers,* Random House, 1965; *Baseball's Most Colorful Managers,* Putnam, 1969; *The Greatest Yankees of Them All,* Putnam, 1969. Work represented in anthologies, including *Fireside Book of Baseball,* Simon & Schuster, 1956, *Second Fireside Book of Baseball,* Simon & Schuster, 1958, *Best Sports Stories of 1958,* Dutton, 1958, and *Best Short Stories of 1959,* Dutton, 1959.

ROCKWELL, Norman (Percevel) 1894-1978

PERSONAL: Born February 3, 1894, in New York, N.Y.; died November 8, 1978, in Stockbridge, Mass.; son of J. Waring (a businessman) and Ann Mary (Hill) Rockwell; married Irene O'Connor (a teacher), 1916 (divorced, 1929); married Mary Rhodes Barstow (a teacher), April 17, 1930 (died, 1959); married Mary L. Punderson (a teacher), October 25, 1961; children: Jarvis Waring, Thomas Rhodes, Peter (second marriage). *Education:* Attended National Academy of Design, Chase Art School, and Art Students' League. *Residence:* Stockbridge, Mass. 01262.

CAREER: Free-lance book and magazine illustrator, 1911-78. Rockwell painted magazine covers and illustrated magazines, including *Saturday Evening Post, Ladies' Home Journal, Boy's Life, American* magazine, *Woman's Home Companion,* and *McCall's.* He was art director for *Boy's Life* in the 1910's. His works are represented at the Metropolitan Museum of Art. *Military service:* Served in U.S. Navy during World War I. *Member:* Society of American Illustrators, Free Lance Artists American. *Awards, honors:* A.F.D. from University of Vermont, 1949, and University of Massachusetts, 1961; H.H.D. from Middlebury College, 1954; received Presidential Freedom Medal, 1977.

WRITINGS: My Adventures as an Illustrator as Told to Thomas Rockwell (memoirs), Doubleday, 1960; (with wife Molly Rockwell, and illustrator) *Willie Was Different: The Tale of an Ugly Thrushling* (for children), Funk, 1969; (author of introduction) J. C. Leyendecker, *The J. C. Leyendecker Poster Book,* Watson-Guptill, 1975.

Illustrator: Mark Twain, *Tom Sawyer,* Heritage Club, 1936; Twain, *The Adventures of Huckleberry Finn,* Heritage Club, 1936; *The Norman Rockwell Album,* Doubleday, 1961; Benjamin Franklin, *Poor Richard: The Almanacks for the Years 1733-1758,* Limited Editions Club, 1964, Heritage Press, 1965; Robert Coles, *Dead End School,* Little, Brown, 1968; Jan Wahl, *The Norman Rockwell Storybook,* Windmill Books, 1969; Thomas Rockwell, *Norman Rockwell's Hometown,* Windmill Books, 1970; Thomas S. Buechner, *Norman Rockwell: A Sixty Year Retrospective* (catalog), Abrams, 1972; (with George Mendoza) *Norman Rockwell's Americana ABC,* Dell, 1975; Michael Schau, editor, *The Norman Rockwell Poster Book,* Watson-Guptill, 1976; *The Second Norman Rockwell Poster Book,* (introduction by Donald Holden), Watson-Guptill, 1977; Glorina Taborin, *Norman Rockwell's Counting Book.* Harmony Books, c. 1977; *Norman Rockwell's Christmas Book,* Abrams, c. 1977; William Hillcourt, *Norman Rockwell's World of Scouting,* Abrams, c. 1977.

NORMAN ROCKWELL

SIDELIGHTS: **February 3, 1894.** Born in New York City, the second son of J. Waring and Ann Mary (Hill) Rockwell. "I was born . . . in the back bedroom of a shabby brownstone front on 103rd Street and Amsterdam Avenue in New York City. My only recollection of this apartment, from which we moved when I was two years old, is of a blank sunlit wall suddenly obscured by slowly moving sheets, shirts, socks, and brightly colored print dresses.

"The Rockwells are distinguished by their lack of distinction: no millionaires in the family, but no poor starving wretches; no philanthropists or saints, but no horse thieves or swindlers.

"There are, to begin with, scattered memories of my childhood. Auntie Paddock and her pince-nez, the horse-drawn fire engines clattering over the cobblestones, the vacant lots, playing on the stoops of brownstone fronts, sitting at the dining-room table in my family's apartment on a winter's evening, my head scrunched down on one elbow, a pencil clutched in my fist, drawing a picture of Mr. Micawber while my father reads *David Copperfield.* My mother sewing, her chair drawn up to the table to catch the light from the gas lamp with the large green glass shade fringed with red silk

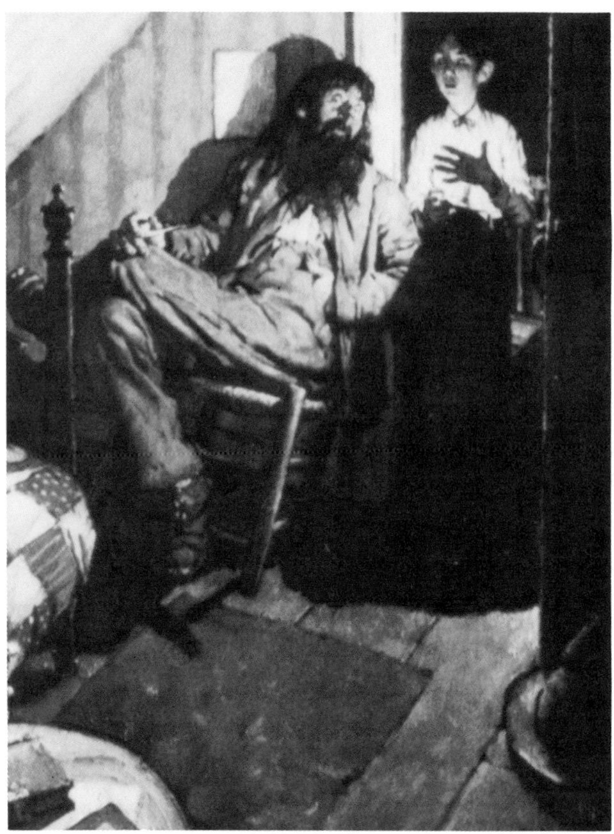

(From *The Adventures of Huckleberry Finn* by Mark Twain. Illustrated by Norman Rockwell.)

the pictures of African native ladies in the *National Geographic* magazines—not from a geographical point of view, I'm afraid, but from an anatomical one.

"We read the Rover Boys, Horatio Alger—*From Canal Boy to President, Phil, the Fiddler*—and G. A. Henty, who was considered a peg above the rest because it always said 'Based on Historical Fact' on the title pages of his books. We went over to Amsterdam Avenue to look under the swinging doors of saloons (it gave us a terrible thrill to see the feet of the men standing at the bar). We cheered the fire engines as they dashed past. I remember how when we heard the clang of the bell we'd gather on the sidewalk, jostling and shoving for a better place. The engine, drawn by three horses abreast, would career around the corner and we'd huzzah and wave our hats, then run for fear of being kindled by the cloud of sparks which rolled from the boiler. . . .

"Hungering to adventure to far exotic places, we dug holes to China in vacant lots under the square of sky encased in high smutty walls, and kneeling down, one ear pressed to the shallow bottom of the hole, listened intently. 'D'ya hear anything?' 'Yeah, yeah, I hear something. Quiet!' (Breathless silence.) 'Whatta ya hear?' 'Voices.' 'Whatta they saying?' 'They're talking Chinese; I can't understand them.'

"We boasted about our families. I was thought to be tops in culture because my family had two Caruso records. We climbed telegraph poles, played prisoner's base, sat on the stoops of our houses in the evenings watching the lamplighter climb his ladder and light the gas lamps. I guess we led the average life of the city kid around the turn of the century.

ribbons which hung above the center of the table; my brother Jarvis doing his homework beside me. And the dark room outside the wavering circle of gaslight; the ticking of the clock on the ornate plaster mantelpiece; the low rumble of a cart and the gruff snort of a horse in the street below. I'd draw Mr. Micawber's head, smudge it, erase it and start over, my tongue licking over my upper lip as I concentrated. Then I'd ask my father to read the description of Mr. Micawber again. Where it told about his head. And my father would read: '. . . a stoutish, middle-aged person, in a brown surtout and black tights and shoes, with no more hair on his head (which was a large one, and very shining) than there is upon an egg, and with a very extensive face . . .' So I'd draw Mr. Micawber again, struggling with his large, shiny head, as my father read on. . . .

"When I was six or seven my father's mother died and we moved in with my grandfather, who lived in a railroad apartment at 152nd Street and St. Nicholas Avenue. No trolley ran on St. Nicholas Avenue; there were two small elm trees in the point where two streets merged in front of our house and a mock fireplace with a plaster mantelpiece in the apartment. So we considered it a step up from 147th Street." [Norman Rockwell, *My Adventures as an Illustrator,* Doubleday, 1960.[1]]

Rockwell became a member of a boys' secret society, the Jamel Athletic Club (JAC). "The JAC . . . was devoted to knowledge. We made expeditions along the Hudson River or into an empty room in Jack Outwater's house to look at

(From *The Adventures of Tom Sawyer* by Mark Twain. Illustrated by Norman Rockwell.)

Triple self-portrait of Rockwell. ■ (From *Norman Rockwell's America* by Christopher Finch.)

"I really remember very little about my parents. They were very religious. Jarvis and I weren't allowed to play with our toys or read the funny papers on Sunday. I was a choir boy first at St. Luke's and then at the Cathedral of St. John the Divine. I didn't enjoy it much. At the cathedral we sang four services every Sunday, then there were rehearsals three afternoons a week after school and a dress rehearsal of the full choir on Friday evenings. So it was pretty hard work.

"We did do things together, though we certainly weren't a closely knit family. On Sundays, if my mother was too ill to go to church we would sing hymns in the parlor.

"My family spent every summer until I was nine or ten years old in the country at various farms which took in boarders. Those country boardinghouses weren't like the resorts of today. The advertisement in the New York papers would state: Tennis Court. But when you arrived, there wouldn't even be an old tennis ball kicking around on the floor, so you'd ask: 'Say, where's the tennis court?' And the farmer would reply: 'Oh, if you look under the hall stairs, you'll find the net. You string it anywhere in the meadow you want.'

"Those boardinghouses were just farms. The grownups played croquet or sat in the high slat-backed rockers which lined the long front porch. We kids were left to do just about anything we wanted. We helped with the milking, fished, swam in the river or the muddy farm pond, trapped birds, cats, turtles, snakes and one glorious morning a muskrat, smoked corn silk behind the barn, fell off wagons, horses, out of lofts—did everything, in fact, that country boys do except complain about the drudgery and boredom of the farm.

"It's queer: if I have no bad memories of my summers in the country, I also have few specific memories, memories of incidents of, say, just what I did during the summer I was eight years old or of my stay at the boardinghouse in Florida (New York). Of my winters in the city I have both a general impression—the sordidness, the filth, the drunks—and many memories of specific events and particular people. . . .But those summers, as I look back on them . . . have become a collection of random impressions—sights, sounds, smells—outside of time, not connected with a specific place or event and all together forming an image of sheer blissfulness, one long radiant summer. God knows, a country cur has just as many fleas as any city mongrel. But I didn't see them or, if I did, they were crowded out by the first sleepy cries of the whippoorwills at dawn—poor will, poor will, *whip* poor will—and long lazy afternoons spent fishing for bullheads, the emerald dragonflies darting around our heads (we called them darning needles and endowed them with a deadly sting). Oh, it sounds corny enough when I tell it, rather like those potboilers my grandfather used to paint. But that's the way I thought of the country then and still do in spite of myself.

"Later on I came to realize (reluctantly) that ugly things happen in the country as well as in the city. Still, that didn't change my ideas. I like the country better. . . .

"I would not have dwelt so long upon these summers I spent in the country as a child, except that I think they had a lot to do with what I painted later on.

"I sometimes think we paint to fulfill ourselves and our lives, to supply the things we want and don't have. . . .

"Maybe as I grew up and found that the world wasn't the perfectly pleasant place I had thought it to be I unconsciously decided that, even if it wasn't an ideal world, it should be and so painted only the ideal aspects of it—pictures in which there were no drunken slatterns or self-centered mothers, in which, on the contrary, there were only Foxy Grandpas who played baseball with the kids and boys fished from logs and got up circuses in the back yard. If there was sadness in this created world of mine, it was a pleasant sadness. If there were problems, they were humorous problems. The people in my pictures aren't mentally ill or deformed. The situations they get into are commonplace, everyday situations, not the agonizing crises and tangles of life.

"Of course, country people do fit into my kind of picture better than city people. Their faces are more open, expressive, lacking the cold veneer behind which city people seem to hide. I guess I have a bad case of the American nostalgia for the clean simple country life as opposed to the complicated world of a city.

"I think I've always wanted to be an artist. I certainly can't remember ever wanting to be anything else. Not that I awoke one morning with the full-blown idea swimming about in my head. It was gradual. I drew, then I found I liked to draw, and finally, after I had got to know something about myself and the people and things around me, I found that I didn't want to do anything else but draw.

"At first, though, my ability was just something I had, like a bag of lemon drops. Jarvis could jump over three orange crates; Jack Outwater had an uncle who had seen a pirate; George Dugan could wiggle his ears; I could draw. I never thought much about it. A bunch of us kids would be sitting around on the stoop and somebody would say, 'Let's go up to Amsterdam Avenue and look in the saloons.' 'Naw, we did that yesterday.' Silence. 'Say, Norm, draw something.' So I'd draw a lion or a fire engine on the sidewalk with a piece of chalk. But it was just as likely that someone would ask George Dugan to wiggle his ears.

"I was a skinny kid, not unhealthy but not robustly healthy either. My mother used to call me Snow-in-the-Face, because I was so pale. The other kids called me Mooney, because I wore glasses (round glasses were new then, the more usual type being long and narrow; our oculist was progressive so I had the rimless kind). How I hated that name Mooney.

"When I was ten years old I began a program of exercises to strengthen myself. Every morning I would do push-ups, deep knee bends, jumping jacks, et cetera, before the mirror in my room. But every morning when I picked myself up, panting, and looked in the mirror to see the improvement, I was confronted by the same long neck with that protruding Adam's apple which was such an embarrassment to me, the same narrow shoulders, jelly arms, and thin measly-looking legs. After a month or so I gave up the exercises.

"My parents bought me all sorts of orthopedic shoes to correct my pigeon toes, until I began to think I was some sort of a cripple. I used to practice walking with my toes turned out. If I heard someone coming up behind me on my way to school, I'd wrench my feet into a V and walk on the sides of my shoes. After a while I gave that up as a lost cause too.

"But my brother Jarvis, who was a year and a half older than I . . . was the best athlete in the school. He was a real boys' boy—adventurous, fearless, always ready to take a dare, strong, athletic. I remember there was a candy store about four blocks from our house in Mamaroneck (where, again

. . . I guess I'd rather break a leg than play with a girl, but Tige likes to swing. ■ (From *Norman Rockwell's Hometown* by Thomas Rockwell. Illustrated by Norman Rockwell.)

(Norman Rockwell art from the archives of the publishers Brown & Bigelow.)

by the way, we had moved when I was nine or ten) and some kid or other was always yelling: 'C'mon, last one to the store's a rotten egg.' Jarvis always came in first; I always came in last, puffing and blowing. There's always competition between brothers. I just couldn't compete with mine. Bob Titus, a big handsome athlete who had been my closest friend, drifted away from me and began to hang around with Jarvis.

"So when I got to be ten or eleven and began to be aware of myself and how I stood with the world, I didn't think too much of myself. I could see I wasn't God's gift to man in general or the baseball coach in particular. A lump, a long skinny nothing, a bean pole without the beans—that's what I was. I used to pull my sleeve over my hand when I walked along the street so that people would think I had only one hand and feel sorry for me. Or I'd develop a crooked limp.

"At that age boys who are athletes are expressing themselves fully. They have an identity, a recognized place among the other boys. I didn't have that. All I had was the ability to draw, which as far as I could see didn't count for much. But because it was all I had I began to make it my whole life. I drew all the time. Gradually my narrow shoulders, long neck, and pigeon toes became less important to me. My feelings no longer paralyzed me. I drew and drew and drew.

"My favorite memory of those days is of Miss Julia M. Smith, my eighth-grade teacher. She taught me what little I know about geography, arithmetic, grammar, et cetera. But I remember her mostly because she encouraged me in my drawing: every year she asked me to draw a Christmas picture on the blackboard in colored chalks; in history class I drew Revolutionary soldiers and covered wagons; in science, birds, lions, fish, elephants. That meant a lot to me; it was sort of a public recognition of my ability. . . . I *know* she saw where I was headed and, because she was a fine teacher, helped me along. God bless her."[1]

It was at this time that Rockwell decided that he definitely wanted to go to art school. "My brother and I never got an allowance. Our family never had enough money for that. We'd go out and earn our spending money at odd jobs. I had to scrape up the tuition for art schools, or I couldn't have gone." [Donald Walton, *A Rockwell Portrait,* Sheed Andrews and McMeel, 1978.[2]]

1908-1909. "During my first year in high school I went every Saturday to study art at the Chase School [of Fine and Applied Art] in New York City. After Thanksgiving the high school principal let me off every Wednesday so that I could attend the Chase School twice a week—Wednesdays and Saturdays. . . ."[1]

1910. Enrolled at the National Academy of Design. "In the middle of my sophomore year in high school, when I was sixteen years old, I quit and began to go to art school full time.

"I put everything into my work. A lot of artists do that: their work is the only thing they've got that gives them an identity. I feel that I don't have anything else, that I must keep working or I'll go back to being pigeon-toed, narrow-shouldered—a lump. When I was younger I used to work night and day, possessed by a sort of panic that I'd lose everything if I didn't drive myself. . . .

"I didn't study long at the National Academy. It was free, but stiff and scholarly—two-week poses, examinations, a lot of still life being done, no illustration, only fine arts. There was no camaraderie between teachers and students, and most of the students were a good deal older than I; many of them just stayed in the school on the off chance that they would be awarded the Prix de Rome. It was a generally stilted atmosphere, no sense of excitement among the students, just a sort of plodding doggedness.

"I switched to the Art Students League. Other students had told me something about the League and it sounded like the kind of school I wanted to go to."[1]

There Rockwell studied under George Bridgeman and Thomas Fogarty. "Mr. Bridgeman taught me not all I know about art but perhaps the most important part of what I know. . . . I worshiped George Bridgeman, absorbing his every word, not to the suffocation of my own ideas and abilities, but to the development of them. I entered Mr. Bridgeman's class raw; I came out browned to a turn.

"Oh, there were other influences. In illustration class . . . we studied the works of the great illustrators. Thomas Fogarty, who taught the class, would sketch the outlines of a story and discuss how to illustrate it with us—what scene in the story we should select, the characters, how they dressed, etc. He'd show us reproductions of illustrations which Pyle or Abbey or Remington had made for the story, pointing out how they'd managed to catch the tone of the story, why they'd used a dark instead of a light background, why they'd done a line drawing instead of a wash drawing.

"It's hard to say what one artist gets from studying the works of other artists. You learn how they use color, light, line—technique, technical triumphs or failures: a red chair on a fuchsia rug, a head painted so that it is the focal point of the portrait and yet doesn't stick out like a naked light bulb. But you don't, you can't, copy these things, putting a red chair and a fuchsia rug into your painting only because someone else did it successfully.

"I guess an artist just stores up in his mind what he learns from looking at the work of other artists. And after a while all the different things he has learned become mixed with each other and with his own ideas and abilities to form his technique, his way of painting. You start by following other artists—a spaniel. Then, if you've got it, you become yourself—a lion.

"I can't say who has influenced me really. Or at least I can't say *how* the artists I have admired have influenced me. Some of those I admire—Picasso, for example—have had no discernible effect (to say the least) on my work. Ever since I can remember, Rembrandt has been my favorite artist. Vermeer, Breughel, Velásquez, Canaletto; Dürer, Holbein, Ingres as draftsmen; Matisse, Klee—these are a few of the others I admire now. During my student days I studied closely the works of Edwin Austin Abbey, J. C. and Frank Leyendecker, Howard Pyle, Sargent, Whistler.

"Thomas Fogarty—a little birdlike man, slim, dapper, and very polite—was practical about teaching illustration. In giving an assignment most instructors asked their students to make an illustration of a broad subject such as 'Storm.' It is extremely easy to do a picture with such a general title. If you draw houses well, you do a picture of a house with some black clouds behind it. If scarecrows are your specialty, you draw a scarecrow with his coattails flying in the wind. Simple.

"But Mr. Fogarty would say to us, 'Gentlemen and ladies,' (the illustration class, unlike the life class, admitted ladies), 'the assignment for next week is the third story in this month's issue of *Adventure* magazine.' Then we'd have to read the story, select a scene to illustrate, get authentic costumes and props, etc. It was very much like an actual assignment from a magazine.

"Mr. Fogarty condemned all flights of fancy, insisting that our illustrations be faithful to the story in every detail. 'An illustration,' he used to say, 'is an illustration. Quite simply that. Nothing less, nothing more. An author's words in paint, gentlemen and ladies, an author's words in paint.' And pointing sharply to a student, he'd snap, 'Mr. Young, I see your mind. It is misguided. Not an excursion of your imagination, starting point the story. No. Emphatically not. But a meeting, Mr. Young, a meeting of artist and author.'

"For the same reasons Mr. Fogarty insisted on authenticity. If the author sat a character in a Windsor chair, the chair in the illustration had to be just that, even if it meant we all had to go up to the Metropolitan Museum to find out what a Windsor chair looked like."[1]

1911. "I was awarded a scholarship at the end of my first year in Mr. Fogarty's class. My charcoal drawing of a little boy in bed with the mumps, looking out of the window at the Fourth of July fireworks cascading down the night sky, was judged the best illustration made in class during the year. The scholarship covered my tuition for Mr. Fogarty's class during the next year. But by then it didn't mean much, for I was beginning to get jobs from children's magazines and didn't have time to attend his class regularly. (I continued to go to Mr. Bridgeman's class, however.)

"Then Mr. Fogarty sent me down to McBride, Nast & Company, which published books and a little magazine called *Travel,* and they gave me a children's book to illustrate. It was called *Tell Me Why Stories.* The child would ask his father or mother 'Why does the sun set?' or 'Why do rainbows appear in the sky?' Then the parent would explain by telling a little story. I did ten or twelve illustrations for the book and was paid a hundred and fifty dollars.

"On the strength of that, my first really professional job in illustration, I rented my first studio. E. F. Ward, another art student, and I went halves on the attic of a brownstone front on the upper West Side.

"Awhile after I finished the *Tell Me Why* job, Edward Cave, the editor of *Boys' Life,* asked me to illustrate a handbook on camping which he had written. He liked the way I handled the assignment and began to give me other stories to illustrate for *Boys' Life.* Then he made me art director of the magazine, paying me fifty dollars a month. I had to do the cover and one set of illustrations for each issue. I went into the office once a week to interview artists, assign stories, and approve the finished jobs. The extraordinary part of it was that I had to okay my own work. That part of being an art director wasn't difficult.

"With my illustrations for *Boys' Life* and *Tell Me Why* I felt I had a presentable portfolio of samples and began to make the rounds of the other children's magazines—*St. Nicholas, Youth's Companion*—and the book publishers. . . . I tramped around from art director to art director. . . . I would do anything—well, almost anything—to get an assignment."[1]

1916. ". . . I had a secret ambition: a cover on the *Saturday Evening Post.* In those days the cover of the *Post* was . . . the greatest show window in America for an illustrator. If you did a cover for the *Post* you had arrived.

"But I was scared. I used to sit in the studio with a copy of the *Post* laid across my knees. 'Must be two million people look at that cover,' I'd say to myself. 'At least. Probably more. Two million subscribers and then their wives, sons, daughters, aunts, uncles, friends. Wow! All looking at my cover.' And then I'd conjure up a picture of myself as a famous illustrator and gloat over it, putting myself in various happy situations: surrounded by admiring females, deferred to by office flunkies at the magazines, wined and dined by the editor of the *Post,* Mr. George Horace Lorimer.

"But the minute I thought of that name the spunk and dreams got soft and rotten. Mr. George Horace Lorimer had built the *Post* from a two-bit family journal with a circulation in the hundreds to an influential mass magazine with a circulation in the millions. He was THE GREAT MR. GEORGE HORACE LORIMER, the baron of publishing. What if he didn't like my work? I'd think. Supposing he denounced me as an instance of incompetence, banished me. He's got a lot of influence. I'd go down, down, down. The kids' magazines would drop me, then the dime novels and pulps would refuse to use me; I'd end up doing the wrappers for penny candies. And visions of a pale starving wretch with a huge Adam's apple lying in a flophouse on the Bowery would rise in my boiling brain.

"Well, one day as I was mentally rolling on my lousy cot . . . Clyde [Forsythe, a celebrated cartoonist and good friend of Rockwell's] came into the studio and asked me what in God's name made me moan so. I hemmed and hawed but finally told him. 'Why don't you do a cover and show it to them?' he said. Oh, I was scared; maybe they'd reject it; THE GREAT MR. GEORGE HORACE LORIMER was tough. 'For Lord's sake,' shouted Clyde, 'stop chewing on your tongue and do a cover . . . you're as good as anybody. Lorimer's not the Dalai Lama.' Then he set himself to encouraging me, convincing me I was good, the *Post* and Mr. Lorimer would love my work. Finally he extracted a promise from me that I'd think up some ideas for *Post* covers and do at least one of them during the next two weeks while he was away.

"So one cold morning in March . . . I set out for Philadelphia and the *Post* (and Mr. Lorimer, though I tried not to think of that). . . .

"When I asked to see Mr. Lorimer (I hadn't called for an appointment; I was afraid he'd refuse to see me), the receptionist asked me why. I explained and she said she'd call Walter M. Dower, the art editor, and would I please sit down. . . .

"Mr. Dower showed my paintings and sketches to Mr. Lorimer and brought back word that Mr. Lorimer was pleased, would accept the two finished paintings, and had okayed the three sketches for future *Post* covers. He added that I was to receive seventy-five dollars for each cover. (WOW!)

"I returned to Edgewood Hall [a boarding house] and asked Irene O'Connor, a schoolteacher I'd met there, to marry me. At first she refused, saying she was already engaged to an agricultural student at Michigan State. Then she accepted.

Rockwell's unpublished painting of Thackeray's heroine "Becky Sharp." ▪ (From *Norman Rockwell's America* by Christopher Finch.)

. . . There warn't no harm in a million of them; but that never made no difference to Aunt Sally; she despised snakes . . . . ■ (From *The Adventures of Huckleberry Finn* by Mark Twain. Illustrated by Norman Rockwell.)

We set a date and I went to work on my third *Post* cover—an old man playing baseball with a bunch of kids.

"But when I took it down to the *Post* the lid blew off the pot. Mr. Dower brought word out that Mr. Lorimer thought the old man was too rough and tramplike. Would I do the painting over? Of course. I stretched a new canvas and began again. 'Better,' said Mr. Dower. 'Mr. Lorimer thought it was better. But the old man's too old, he thought.' I did the painting over again. The boy was too small. I did that painting over five times before Mr. Lorimer accepted it. By the time he finally okayed it I had decided that doing *Post* covers wasn't all soup and fish; it appeared that life was going to be a bit more complicated than I had expected. (Mr. Lorimer later told me that he'd been testing me. I wonder if he ever knew how near I came to flunking his test.)

"But my disappointment at finding that life wasn't a golden chute the chute was mitigated by my first fan mail. I got five or six letters on the *Post* cover which had already been published. The public liked me!

"When I had added the *Post* cover to my portfolio the art directors of the other magazines began to give me assignments. . . ."[1]

1917. Enlisted in the Navy, where he was assigned to draw cartoons and make layouts for the camp newspaper. He also kept busy drawing portraits of the officers and sailors and continued his illustration and cover work.

1918. Received a special discharge. Continued his illustration and cover work and also did some advertising. "Over the years I've done many series of ads. But never under exclusive contract. I've always kept up my other work—*Post* covers, illustrations. And I've tried to accept only those jobs which I believe I'll enjoy doing.

"Thinking up ideas was the hardest work I did in those days. I never saw an idea happen or received one, whoosh, from heaven while I was washing my brushes or shaving or backing the car out of the garage. I had to beat most of them out of my head or at least maul my brain until something *came* out of it. It always seemed to me that it was like getting blood from a stone except, of course, that eventually something always came.

"There was one kind of idea which I didn't have to struggle over—the timely idea. I'd just keep my ear to the wind and, when I heard of a craze or fad or anything which everyone was talking about, I'd do a cover of it: the ouija board, the first radios, crossword puzzles, the movies.

"In 1920 the whole country was talking about Model T Fords and Henry Ford . . . so I did a cover (July, 1920) of a family riding in a Model T.

"The day after Lindbergh flew the Atlantic I called up the art editor at the *Post*. 'How about a cover on the pioneers of the air?' I asked. 'Okay,' he said. 'When can you get it to us? It'll have to be fast or we'll miss the boom; it won't be news.' 'Tomorrow afternoon,' I said. I hired a model, dug up an aviator's cap, and set to work. Twenty-six hours later I finished the cover, sent it to Philadelphia, and staggered off to bed.

1929. "Nineteen twenty-nine was the year of the speed traps. Instead of asking their citizens to pay taxes, all the small towns hired cops who set up speed traps and fined their victims heavily. Two or three industrious, clever cops could rake in over a thousand dollars a day. The towns grew fat. Finally the newspapers and the automobile clubs began to make a fuss and I heard about it and did a *Post* cover of a policeman holding a stop watch and hiding behind a town-limits sign.

"I did a cover based on the jazz craze (1929), one on the stock market crash (a butcher's boy, a housewife, a grandmother, a millionaire, and a dog, all staring at the stock market reports), one on the hundredth anniversary of baseball in 1939, the 1940 census, the hitchhiking fad (1940), the blackout, women war workers (Rosy the Riveter), the USO, soldiers returning from the war, television. . . .

"People sometimes suggest ideas too. Unwittingly, I mean. Someone comes into the studio and stands about talking to me or I see someone walking along the street. Gee, I think, noticing the way his ears stick up like two daffodils from the sides of his head or his peculiar stance, maybe one foot wrapped around the other, rocking back and forth, or the way he circles around a question, then pounces on it like a cat with a snake. Gee, I think, I'd like to paint that person. So then I mull him over in my mind, trying him out in different situations, trying to build something on his ears or stance or personality, and after a while, if I'm lucky, I come up with a *Post* cover.

"In those days before I began to photograph my models it was a problem to get anybody who could and would take the time to pose. I used to figure that, working from the model, it took me three days to paint a single figure. Sometimes longer. I'd draw the model in charcoal on the canvas, then paint over that. So I was forced to use many of the models who did have the available time over and over again. As with Mr. Van Brunt [one of Rockwell's regular models], this often brought the problem of overexposure. Neither the public nor Mr. Lorimer (nor, for that matter, the advertisers) wanted to see the same character more than once or twice a year even if he did have a nose with a bump, dog eyes, and an enormous mustache (or jutting lower lip).

"Thinking of Mr. Van Brunt and Harry Seal [another regular model] makes me wonder about why I painted old men and kids so much during the twenties and early thirties. Part of it, I guess, was my experience on the children's magazines. But more than that: early in my career I discovered that funny ideas, pure gags, were good, yes, but funny ideas with pathos were better. Not only pathos, though; just something deeper. An idea which is only humorous doesn't stay with people, but if the situation depicted has some overtones or undertones, something beyond humor, it sticks with people and they like it that much more. Take my cover of Van Brunt carrying a violin under his arm and looking quizzically at a saxophone to which is affixed a sign reading, 'Jazz it up with a *sax*.' His face and his baggy trousers and the idea of the old man 'jazzing it up with a sax' are comic, yet there's something more to it (at least I hoped there was when I painted the picture). The old confronted by the new and wondering what it's all about and whether he should take up the new ways or hold to the old, 'jazz it up with a sax' or continue to saw at his fiddle. Well, I don't know if that's something more than humor, but at the time I thought it was.

"Old men show their lives in their faces—the ups and downs and turn-arounds, the knocks and pushes. Van Brunt's face was more than just comic; in a sense, Antietam, Fredericksburg, the Wilderness, and Annabella were all in it. I guess that's why I painted old men so much.

"With kids . . . people think about their own youth. Nostalgia sets in. And yet the kids' antics are humorous, so the people laugh too. It's like Dickens: tragedy and comedy, tears and laughs in the same picture give it a greater impact.

"I used to think putting the characters in costume had a similar effect, gave sort of an added dimension to the picture: nostalgia again. But that wasn't the real reason I did so many costume pictures. I just loved to paint the costumes: a swirling scarlet cape; a flowered, bouncy bustle; rugged riding boots; lace collars; pantaloons with frills and furbelows upon a pretty leg. Costumes are colorful and picturesque; modern clothes are drab and dull. A fedora and a golfing cap don't compare, unless tattered and rotten, with a high top hat or brass guardsman's helmet."[1]

1929. Divorced first wife.

1930. Married Mary Rhodes Barstow, a schoolteacher. "Three months after our marriage Mary and I gave up the apartment in the Hotel des Artistes [New York City] and moved into the house on 24 Lord Kitchener Road in New Rochelle."[1]

1930's. Gradually, Rockwell began painting from photographs rather than models. "In the old days . . . I would sit and paint for hours before a living model, constantly commanding, 'Hold out your chin,' 'Turn a bit more this way,' or 'Straighten up!' And always I was painting against time, rushing to finish before the model's rest period, or before the light failed. I was under an awful tension, particularly as I would act out every one of those moves for the sitter in order to demonstrate my point. When quitting time came I was a wreck.

"Then I began to hear how effectively this or that illustrator was using the camera. At first I couldn't believe it. Later I became convinced that it was true, but felt that the method was somehow a bit dishonest, like cheating at solitaire. Still later, I decided that there might be some merit to it after all. It struck me that the Old Masters, with their inventiveness, would surely have found practical ways of utilizing the camera had it been available. So I began to experiment and discovered that, although the camera is a very tricky thing, it could be of legitimate assistance if employed judiciously. Frankly, I don't know whether my work is better or worse for it. I do know that it has helped to keep me working all these years.

"Painting from photographs can be a wholly creative performance if the artist himself is creative. To 'copy' the form, tone and color of a photographic print certainly is not creative. But one can be creative by modifying drawing, values and other aspects of the photo to realize the creative needs of the subject. The camera is no substitute for those creative faculties of mind and hand which have always produced art—and always will. The artist who can't draw or paint will never get anywhere trying to work from photographs. An unskilled artist, using photographs, can easily develop absurdities, such as the sun shining from two or three directions at once, or one object incorrect in size in relation to the whole, or perspective convergencies at variance one with another.

"It has never been natural for me to deviate from the facts of anything before me, so I have always dressed the models and posed them precisely as I have wanted them in my picture; then I have painted the thing before me. If a model has worn a red sweater, I have painted it red—I couldn't possibly have made it green. I have tried again and again to take such liberties, but with little success. But when working with photographs I seem able to recompose in many ways: as to form, tone, and color." [Arthur L. Guptill, *Norman Rockwell, Illustrator,* Watson-Guptill, 1946.[3]]

1938. "I was restless. I had lived in New Rochelle for over twenty years, and the town seemed tinged with everything that had happened to me during that time. The studio was somehow musty; the events of thirteen years were piled up in the corners—all the paintings I'd done, the parties, things I liked to remember and some I didn't—gathering dust. I had the feeling that a part of my life had ended. Mr. Lorimer was no longer editor of the *Post.* Most of my old models—Van Brunt, Harry Seal, Wilson, Van Vechtan—had either died or disappeared. It was time for a change.

"Mary and I decided to go to England. That would do as a starter. So in the summer . . . we sailed with our three sons—Jerry, Tommy (born in 1933), and Peter (born in 1936). Having read in some travel book that a trip was more enjoyable if it had a definite purpose, I determined to visit all the English illustrators whom I admired so much. . . ."[1]

Rockwell visited Arthur Rackham, Edmund Dulac, and George Belcher. "Those hours in the open air, riding down country lanes with the cows raising their heads to watch us pass and the warm dry smell of the newly cut hay and the birds singing in the hedgerows, recalling as they did my summers in the country as a child, made me receptive to the idea of buying a farm when, back in New Rochelle, Mary and I saw a real estate booklet listing houses for sale in Vermont. At any rate I jumped at the idea. My restlessness had not been cured by England. I had the feeling on our return to New Rochelle that it was beginning to run dry for me there, I'd got out of it about all I was ever going to. When I've lived in one place for too long ideas begin to come harder. Things go dead for me because I'm too familiar with them. They become a pattern. I need a change—new people, new surroundings—to set my mind thrashing again, stimulate me. That's why I take so many trips—to Europe, California. . . ."[1]

1939. Bought sixty acre farm in Arlington, Vermont. "The people we met were rugged and self-contained. None of that sham 'I am *so* GLAD to know you!' accompanied by radiant smiles. They shook my hand, said, 'How do,' and waited to see how I'd turn out. Not hostile but reserved with a dignity and personal integrity which are rare in suburbia, where you're familiar with someone before you know him. In Vermont you earn the right to be called by your first name.

"I'd met one or two hundred people I wanted to paint. Walt Squires, Clarence Decker, Nip Noyes. A whole raft of them. And ideas were jumping in my brain like trout on the Batten Kill at sunset. I'd found what I'd wanted—new people, new surroundings."[1]

1943. Studio burned and Rockwell lost original paintings, drawings, and a superb collection of irreplaceable antiques, costumes, books, prints, and clippings. "Until the fire, we were regarded as outlanders by some in Arlington. But when we were in trouble, they took us to their hearts. They represent what I admire most in the American character. Not that they're the only ones. You find honest, warmhearted, hardworking people much like them in all parts of the country.

Well, after two hours of saying who was bad at what and worse at what else, flipping coins, matching fingers, and drawing straws, the teams finally were chosen. ■ (Norman Rockwell art from the archives of the publishers Brown & Bigelow.)

But nowhere better. Here in New England the character is strong and unshakable."[2]

1951. Painted his most popular *Post* cover—a grandmother and grandson saying grace in a railroad station restaurant.

1952. Painted President Eisenhower and continued to paint the presidential candidates in every election thereafter.

1953. ". . . I left Arlington and moved to Stockbridge, Massachusetts. Restlessness again. And then I was having trouble with my work and thought that maybe a change of scene would help me. It didn't. I sank deeper into the muck. I was dissatisfied, doubted my ability; decisions made in the morning evaporated by three o'clock. I started to lean on advice, not sort it out, using the good, rejecting the bad. Among those I listened to were several psychiatrists from the Austin Riggs Center, a psychiatric institution in Stockbridge. And that, finally, was how I recovered from the crisis.

"I don't think I'm what you'd call a temperamental artist. For over forty years I've done commercial work, which involves deadlines and various other restrictions. . . . But every so often I get into a hassle over my work. I get all tied up in a knot. Why, I don't know. Usually I work my way through the crisis by myself. And it's a slow business, rather like getting up in the middle of the night in a strange house and trying to find the light switch. You bump into tables, bruising your shins; bang your head on doors; stumble over rugs; groping, straining your eyes, and all the while feeling that maybe the next step will be into nothing and you'll tumble down a stairway you can't see and split your skull."[1]

1959. Second wife died. Rockwell was sixty-five. "The remarks about my reaching the age of Social Security and coming to the end of the road, they jolted me. And that was good. Because I sure as hell had no intention of just sitting around for the rest of my life. So I'd whip out the paints and really go to it."[2]

1961. Presented with the Interfaith Award of the National Conference of Christians and Jews for his *Post* cover illustrating the Golden Rule. Generally, he was unimpressed by the many honors conferred on him; but this was a citation he treasured, because it recognized "his dedication to the highest ideals of amity, understanding and cooperation among men; and his artistic leadership in depicting with such exacting technique and unfailing humor the universal fact that all men, great and unknown, are members of the One Family of Man under God."[2]

October 25, 1961. Married Mary L. "Molly" Punderson, a retired Stockbridge schoolteacher.

December 14, 1963. The last Rockwell cover, a painting of John F. Kennedy which Rockwell had done earlier appeared on the *Post*. In forty-seven years, Rockwell had painted three hundred and seventeen covers for the *Post*, averaging six or seven a year.

1968. The Old Corner House Museum in Stockbridge, Mass. became a permanent house for displaying Rockwell's work. Among the more than one hundred and fifty works at the museum are "The Four Freedoms" and the originals of many of Rockwell's *Post* covers.

1969. First one-man show in Manhattan. The show was a huge, popular success although art critics gave it a lukewarm reception, as they always did with Rockwell's work. "I could never be satisfied with just the approval of the critics, and, boy, I've certainly had to be satisfied without it."[2] This show led to a country-wide touring exhibition of his works.

1973. New Rochelle, N.Y. celebrated a Norman Rockwell Day and renamed one of its streets Norman Rockwell Boulevard. A documentary on Norman Rockwell won an Academy Award as the best documentary of the year.

1976. "I guess a lot of us painters do last longer than most folks. Why is it? Well, maybe the secret to so many artists living so long is that every painting is a new adventure. So, you see, they're always *looking ahead* to something new and exciting. *The secret is not to look back.*"[2]

May 23, 1976. The citizens of Stockbridge celebrated a Norman Rockwell Day. At the end of the day he was brief but sincere in his comment to reporters, "I'm tired but proud."[2]

November 8, 1978. Died in Stockbridge, Mass. at the age of eighty-four. "People somehow get out of your work just about what you put into it, and if you are interested in the characters that you draw, and understand them and love them, why, the person who sees your picture is bound to feel the same say." [Norman Rockwell, *A Sixty-Year Retrospective,* Harry N. Abrams, Inc., 1972.[4]]

FOR MORE INFORMATION SEE: Norman Rockwell, *My Adventures as an Illustrator as Told to Thomas Rockwell* (memoirs), Doubleday, 1960; Thomas S. Buechner, *Norman Rockwell: Artist and Illustrator,* Abrams, 1970; *New York Times Magazine,* February 28, 1971; *Look,* June 1, 1971; *Saturday Evening Post,* summer, 1971, September, 1973, March, 1974, May, 1976, July, 1976, July, 1977, January, 1978; *Forbes,* June 1, 1972; *Ladies' Home Journal,* November, 1972; *Good Housekeeping,* April, 1976; *American Artist,* July, 1976; *Norman Rockwell and the Saturday Evening Post,* Rittenhouse, c. 1976; Donald Walton, *A Rockwell Portrait: An Intimate Biography,* Sheed Andrews & McMeel, 1978; *New York Times,* November 10, 1978; *Washington Post,* November 10, 1978.

ROGERS, W(illiam) G(arland) 1896-1978

PERSONAL: Born February 29, 1896, in Chicopee Falls, Mass.; died March, 1978 in Altoona, Penn.; son of Burt Teale (a businessman) and Nancy (Bean) Rogers; married Mildred Weston (a writer), October 5, 1934. *Education:* Amherst College, B.A., 1920; University of Pittsburgh, graduate study, 1927-29. *Home and office:* Greenwood Farm, RFD Box 209, Gallitzin, Pa. 16641. *Agent:* Dorothy Markinko, McIntosh & Otis, Inc., 18 East 41st St., New York, N.Y. 10017.

CAREER: Teacher in Massachusetts and Pennsylvania schools, 1921-30; *Springfield Union,* Springfield, Mass., reporter and art editor, 1931-43; Associated Press, New York, N.Y., arts editor, 1943-61; writer and book reviewer. Member of National Book Awards fiction juries, two years, of National Book Awards advisory committee, three years. *Military service:* U.S. Army, ambulance driver attached to French Army, 1917-19; received Croix de Guerre. *Member:* P.E.N., Phi Beta Kappa, Alpha Delta Phi.

WRITINGS: Fluent French for Beginners, Benjamin H. Sanborn, 1927; *Life Goes On* (novel), Liveright, 1929; (editor) *Le Voyage de M. Perrichon,* Oxford Book Co., 1930; *When This You See Remember Me: Gertrude Stein in Person,* Rinehart, 1948; (with Mildred Weston) *Carnival Crossroads: The Story of Times Square,* Doubleday, 1960; *A Picture Is a Picture: A Look at Modern Painting,* Harcourt, 1964; *Wise Men Fish Here: The Story of Frances Steloff and the Gotham Book Mart,* Harcourt, 1965; *What's Up in Architecture: A Look at Modern Building,* Harcourt, 1965; *Ladies Bountiful,* Harcourt, 1968; *Mightier Than the Sword: Cartoons, Caricature, Social Comment,* Harcourt, 1968; *Carl Sandburg, Yes: Poet, Historian, Novelist, Songster,* Harcourt, 1970; *Gertrude Stein Is Gertrude Stein Is Gertrude Stein,* Crowell, 1973; (translator) Jacques Georges-Picot, *The Real Suez Crisis,* Harcourt, 1977. Reviewer for *New York Times Book Review,* Saturday Review Syndicate, and other publications.

SIDELIGHTS: "It's hard to remember back to a time when I didn't want to write. An aunt, a schoolteacher, had written a book but that didn't influence me. One of my most important teachers at Amherst College was Robert Frost, but it was not his classes that made me want to write; it was because I already wanted to write that I went to his classes.

"I am quite sure it all began because I loved to read. There was a very good library in Springfield, Mass., where I grew up. The stacks were open to browsers and I read Henty, Scott, Irving, Cooper and many others. The best presents

W. G. ROGERS

at Christmas and on my birthdays were books. Though I studied mathematics and sciences, my favorite courses were Latin, English, French and history.

"If other people could write books, so could I, I used to say to myself. The way to find out was to try. There was no television to watch when I was a youngster, and there weren't many movies. Baseball and football games didn't draw huge crowds. So a boy read and, before long, he wrote. My first things were short skits . . . pretty bad ones, too . . . that my friends and I put on to celebrate holidays when we were in the army in wartime France. Then came a French textbook and next a novel. I wrote about things that interested me, that mattered to me, such as painting, architecture, other writers like my dear friend Gertrude Stein. At last it got so I couldn't imagine spending my time in any way except in writing. It was hard work but it was an ingrained habit. A good habit is just like a bad habit in one respect: it's almost impossible to get over it.

"I live at the top of the Allegheny Mountains in the middle of one hundred acres where it's quiet except for the barking of our collie. And when I'm not here, away from things, I like to be in the middle of things—principally in the middle of Paris."

She was laughed at madly and wildly praised. She was cheered for revitalizing English and reviled for abusing it. ■ (From *Gertrude Stein Is Gertrude Stein Is Gertrude Stein: Her Life and Work* by W. G. Rogers. Jacket illustrated by Nicholas Gaetano.)

Rogers died at Mercy Hospital in Altoona, Pennsylvania on March 1, 1978.

FOR MORE INFORMATION SEE: Amherst College Biographical Record, 1963; *Young Readers' Review,* April, 1966; *Best Sellers,* April 1, 1968, January 1, 1970, February 15, 1971; *Spectator,* August 30, 1968; *Punch,* September 11, 1968; *Observer Review,* September 29, 1968; *Publishers Weekly,* May 14, 1973.

SAROYAN, William 1908-
(Sirak Goryan)

PERSONAL: Born August 31, 1908, in Fresno, Calif.; son of Armenak (a Presbyterian preacher and a writer) and Takoohi (Saroyan) Saroyan; married Carol Marcus, February, 1943 (divorced, November, 1949); remarried Carol Marcus, 1951 (again divorced, 1952); children: Aram (a writer), Lucy. *Education:* Left high school at fifteen. *Home:* 114 rue la Boetie, Paris 8e, France.

CAREER: Began selling newspapers at the age of eight for the *Fresno Evening Herald;* while still in school he worked at various jobs, including that of telegraph messenger boy; after leaving school he worked in his uncle's law office, then held numerous odd jobs, including that of grocery clerk, vineyard worker, postal employee, and office manager of San Francisco Postal Telegraph Co. Co-founder of Conference Press, 1936. Organized and directed The Saroyan Theatre, August, 1942 (closed after one week). Writer in residence, Purdue University, 1961. *Military service:* U.S. Army, 1942-45. *Awards, honors:* Drama Critics Circle Award, 1940, for "The Time of Your Life"; Pulitzer Prize, 1940, for "The Time of Your Life" (Saroyan rejected the prize, saying he was opposed to the patronizing of art by the wealthy; "The Time of Your Life" was the first play to ever win both awards); California Literature Gold Medal, 1952, for *Tracy's Tiger.*

WILLIAM SAROYAN

WRITINGS: The Daring Young Man on the Flying Trapeze, and Other Stories, Random, 1934, 3rd edition, Modern Library, 1941; *A Christmas Psalm,* Gelber, Lilienthal, 1935; *Inhale and Exhale* (stories), Random, 1936, reprinted, Books for Libraries, 1972; *Those Who Write Them and Those Who Collect Them,* Black Archer Press, 1936; *Three Times Three* (stories), Conference Press, 1936; *Little Children* (stories), Harcourt, 1937; *A Gay and Melancholy Flux* (compiled from *Inhale and Exhale* and *Three Times Three),* Faber, 1937; *Love, Here is My Hat, and Other Short Romances,* Modern Age Books, 1938; *The Trouble with Tigers* (stories), Harcourt, 1938; *A Native American,* George Fields, 1938; *Peace, It's Wonderful* (stories), Modern Age Books, 1939; *3 Fragments and a Story,* Little Man, 1939; *The Hungerers: A Short Play,* S. French, 1939, reprinted, 1967; *My Heart's in the Highlands* (play; produced at Guild Theatre, New York, April 13, 1939; first published in *One-Act Play Magazine,* December, 1937), Harcourt, 1939, reprinted, S. French, 197?; *The Time of Your Life* (play; produced at Booth Theatre, New York, October 25, 1939), Harcourt, 1939; *Christmas, 1939,* Quercus Press, 1939.

"A Theme in the Life of the Great American Goof" (ballet-play; produced at Center Theatre, New York, January, 1940), published in *Razzle-Dazzle,* below; *Subway Circus* (play), S. French, 1940; *The Ping-Pong Game* (play), S. French, 1940; *Three Plays,* Harcourt, 1940; *A Special Announcement,* House of Books, 1940; *My Name is Aram* (stories; Book-of-the-Month Club selection), Harcourt, 1940, 4th edition, Harbrace Modern Classics, 1950, revised edition (illustrated by Don Freeman), Dell, 1966; *The Beautiful People* (play; produced and directed by the author at Lyceum Theatre, New York, April 21, 1940), Harcourt, 1941; *Saroyan's Fables,* Harcourt, 1941; *Love's Old Sweet Song* (play; produced at Plymouth Theatre, New York, May 2, 1940), S. French, 1941; *Harlem as Seen by Hirschfield,* Hyperion Press, 1941; *Hilltop Russians in San Francisco,* James Ladd Delkin, 1941; *Jim Dandy: A Play,* [Cleveland], 1941, reprinted as *Jim Dandy: Fat Man in a Famine,* Harcourt, 1947; "Across the Board on Tomorrow Morning," first produced at Pasadena (Calif.) Playhouse, February, 1941, produced at Theatre Showcase, March, 1942, another production produced and directed by the author at Belasco Theatre, New York, on the same bill with "Talking to You," also produced and directed by the author, August, 1942; *Hello Out There* (play; first produced at Lobeto Theatre, Santa Barbara, September, 1941, produced at Belasco Theatre, September, 1942), S. French, 1949; *Razzle-Dazzle* (short plays), Harcourt, 1942; *48 Saroyan Stories,* Avon, 1942; *The Human Comedy* (novel adapted from his film scenario), Harcourt, 1943, 4th edition, World Publishing, 1945, revised edition (illustrated by Freeman), Harcourt, 1971; *Thirty-One Selected Stories,* Avon, 1943; *Fragment,* Albert M. Bender, 1943; *Get Away Old Man* (play; produced at Cort Theatre, New York, November, 1943),

Harcourt, 1944; *Some Day I'll Be A Millionaire Myself*, Avon, 1944; *Dear Baby* (stories), Harcourt, 1944, reprinted, Faber, 1966; *The Adventures of Wesley Jackson* (novel), Harcourt, 1946, reprinted, Four Square Books, 1961; *The Saroyan Special,* Harcourt, 1948, revised edition (illustrated by Freeman), Books for Libraries, 1970; *The Fiscal Hoboes,* Press of Valenti Angelo, 1949; *Don't Go Away Mad, and Two Other Plays,* Harcourt, 1949; *A Decent Birth, A Happy Funeral* (play), S. French, 1949; *Sam Ego's House* (play), S. French, 1949.

The Assyrian, and Other Stories, Harcourt, 1950; *The Twin Adventures* (contains *The Adventures of Wesley Jackson* and a diary Saroyan kept while writing the novel), Harcourt, 1950; *Rock Wagram* (novel), Doubleday, 1951; *Tracy's Tiger* (fantasy), Doubleday, 1951, revised edition (illustrated by Henry Koerner), Ballantine, 1967; *The Bicycle Rider in Beverly Hills* (autobiography), Scribner, 1952; *The Laughing Matter* (novel), Doubleday, 1953; *Mama I Love You* (novel), Atlantic-Little, Brown, 1956; *The Whole Voyald* (stories), Atlantic-Little, Brown, 1956; *The Bouncing Ball* (an erroneous citation; given in some sources as a book published in 1957, but actually an early title for material published as *Mama I Love You*); *Papa You're Crazy* (novel), Atlantic-Little, Brown, 1957; *Pebbles on the Beach* (sometimes cited as a 1957 book of essays; no such book was published, however); *The Cave Dwellers* (play; produced in New York, October 19, 1957), Putnam, 1958; *The William Saroyan Reader,* Braziller, 1958; *The Slaughter of the Innocents* (play), S. French, 1958; *Once Around the Block* (play), S. French, 1959.

"The Paris Comedy; or, The Secret of Lily" (play), produced in Vienna, 1960, published as *The Paris Comedy; or, The Dogs, Chris Sick, and 21 Other Plays,* also published as *The Dogs, or The Paris Comedy, and Two Other Plays: Chris Sick, or Happy New Year Anyway, Making Money, and Nineteen Other Very Short Plays,* Phaedra, 1969; *Sam, the Highest Jumper of Them All, or, The London Comedy* (play; produced in London under Saroyan's direction, 1960), Faber, 1961; (with Henry Cecil) "Settled Out of Court" (play), produced in London, 1960; "High Time Along the Wabash" (play), produced at Purdue University, 1961; *Here Comes, There Goes, You Know Who* (autobiography), Trident, 1962; *Boys and Girls Together* (novel), Harcourt, 1963; *Me* (juvenile), Crowell-Collier, 1963; *Not Dying* (autobiography), Harcourt, 1963; *One Day in the Afternoon of the World* (novel), Harcourt, 1964; *After Thirty Years: The Daring Young Man on the Flying Trapeze,* Harcourt, 1964; *Best Stories of William Saroyan,* Faber, 1964; *Short Drive, Sweet Chariot* (reminiscences), Phaedra, 1966; (author of introduction) *The Arabian Nights* (illustrated by W. K. Plummer), Platt, 1966; *Look at Us; Let's See; Here We Are; Look Hard, Speak Soft; I See, You See, We All See; Stop, Look, Listen; Beholder's Eye; Don't Look Now But Isn't That You? (us? U.S.?),* Cowles, 1967; *I Used to Believe I had Forever, Now I'm Not So Sure,* Cowles, 1968; (author of foreword) Barbara Holden and Mary Jane Woebcke, *A Child's Guide to San Francisco,* Diablo Press, 1968; *Horsey Gorsey and the Frog* (illustrated by Grace Davidian), E. M. Hale, 1968; *Letters from 74 Rue Taitbout, or Don't Go, But If You Must, Say Hello to Everybody,* World, 1968; *Man With the Heart in the Highlands, and Other Stories,* Dell, 1968.

Days of Life and Death and Escape to the Moon, Dial, 1970; (editor and author of introduction) *Hairenik, 1934-39,* Books for Libraries, 1971; *Places Where I've Done Time* (autobiography), Praeger, 1972; *The Tooth and My Father* (short stories; illustrated by Suzanne Verrier), Doubleday, 1974; "The Rebirth Celebration of the Human Race at Artie Zabala's Off-Broadway Theater," first produced in New York City, July 10, 1975; *An Act or Two of Foolish Kindness,* Penmaen Press, 1976; *Morris Hirschfield* (introduction by Sidney Janis; critical notes by Oto Bihalji-Merin), Rizzoli International Publications, 1976; *Sons Come and Go, Mothers Hang in Forever* (illustrated by Al Hirschfeld), Franklin Library, 1976; *Chance Meetings,* Norton, 1978; *Obituaries,* Creative Arts, 1979; *Two Short Paris Summertime Plays of Nineteen Seventy-Four,* California State University, 1979. Also the author of *Coming Through the Rye* (play).

(From *Tracy's Tiger* by William Saroyan. Illustrated by Henry Koerner.)

Contributor to *Overland Monthly, Hairenik* (Armenian-American Magazine), *Story, Saturday Evening Post, Atlantic, Look, McCall's, Seventeen, Saturday Review,* and other publications.

Wrote lyrics and music for several songs for his play, *Love's Old Sweet Song;* other musical compositions include "An Italian Opera in English," "Notes for a Musical Review," and "Bad Men in the West" (a ballet scenario), all published in *Razzle-Dazzle;* with Ross Bagdasarian, wrote popular song, "Come On-a My House," 1951. Wrote and directed a short film of his own, "The Good Job," produced by Loew, 1942, based on his story "A Number of the Poor"; wrote a scenario for "The Human Comedy" for M-G-M, filmed in 1943; *The Time of Your Life* was filmed by United Artists,

I don't suppose anybody is willing to believe a tooth could come out of a boy's mouth and become another boy and go on and live a life of its own, but what do we care about people who don't believe? ■ (From *The Tooth and My Father* by William Saroyan. Illustrated by Suzanne Verrier.)

1948. A television adaptation of *The Time of Your Life* was produced on "Playhouse 90," October, 1958; "Ah Sweet Mystery of Mrs. Murphy" was produced by NBC-TV, 1959; "The Unstoppable Gray Fox" was produced by CBS-TV, 1962.

SIDELIGHTS: **August 31, 1908.** "On the last day of August in the year 1908 in the city of Fresno [California] I came into the world, sick to death with astonishment, anger and gladness. My father Armenak Saroyan was thirty-four years of age, my mother Takoohi Saroyan twenty-six." [William Saroyan, *The Bicycle Rider in Beverly Hills,* Scribner, 1952.[1]]

"According to the story, I came about among weeds and broken glass, while the bell of a Southern Pacific freight locomotive tolled in the hot August night from just across H Street, in Fresno, California.

"My father was on a vineyard in Sanger, twelve miles east, trying to gather the pieces together of a preacher without a pulpit and a poet without a reader.

"My mother was hushed and angry in the unlighted ramshackle house, because now here was one more, making four, two daughters born in Bitlis, in 1899 and in 1902, a son born in Erzeroum in 1905, and now another son, in 1908, myself. [William Saroyan, *Here Comes, There Goes You Know Who,* Trident Press, 1961.[2]]

July, 1911. "Now, my father, Armenak of Bitlis, as I think of him, the failed poet, the failed Presbyterian preacher, the failed American, the failed theological student, up and died in a way that was clearly damned foolish and deeply discourteous, and yet in another way a great kindness to me, since it put me into very real exile before I was three, and permitted me not to find my father a monster with a monstrous purpose, to do to my girl, my mother, the things that I was put into this life and world to do to her, without my knowledge of course but settled in my bones and nerves and mind and memory and sleep and all of the known senses and all of the unknown equivalent of senses and all of the unknown elements of human reality that nobody had yet so much as suspected as being there at all, died of a ruptured appendix one day, in the heat of a grand July afternoon . . . just asked for lots of water with which to try at least, to *try,* to quench his terrible thirst, the last thirst of life, and his wife, the mother, the woman, the girl, the first sexual party of my experience, letting me out of herself by that much enlarged channel into which she had not so long ago let him in, old Armenak, melancholy, in despair, died at the age of thirty-six, alive in Bitlis in 1874, dead in San Jose in 1911, and there she was with two daughters and two sons, my own kith and kin all of them, and I don't remember my father at all. . . .

"And so I could love and admire my father and did love and admire him, and at the same time refused to believe in his death, and permitted myself to believe that he would come back, somehow come back to me—the hell with the others, the rest of the kith and kin, my father would come back to me, for I had never known him at all, and they had, and I loved and admired him most, for to me he was a perfect man. . . . " [William Saroyan, *Sons Come and Go, Mothers Hang in Forever,* McGraw-Hill, 1976.[3]]

1911-1916. Lived in an orphanage while his mother (who visited him on weekends) worked as a maid. "She went off, taking with her the smell of mother, and to a man not yet three that's quite a smell. It's made of skin and soap and a little perspiration and a little powder from Woolworth's, but mainly of her, unaccountable, of the pieces broken and not picked up. She knew I wouldn't make a scene. I saw her go, and I saw the door close behind her, . . . "[2]

"It was only after having finally left the place that I, for one, began to see the orphanage as not having been anywhere near as rotten as it might have been, and it was quite simply true that the Irish cook's meat pie was one of the finest table experiences of my young life.

" . . . They tried their best to be mothers to the sons of unknown mothers, mad mothers, criminal mothers, and all

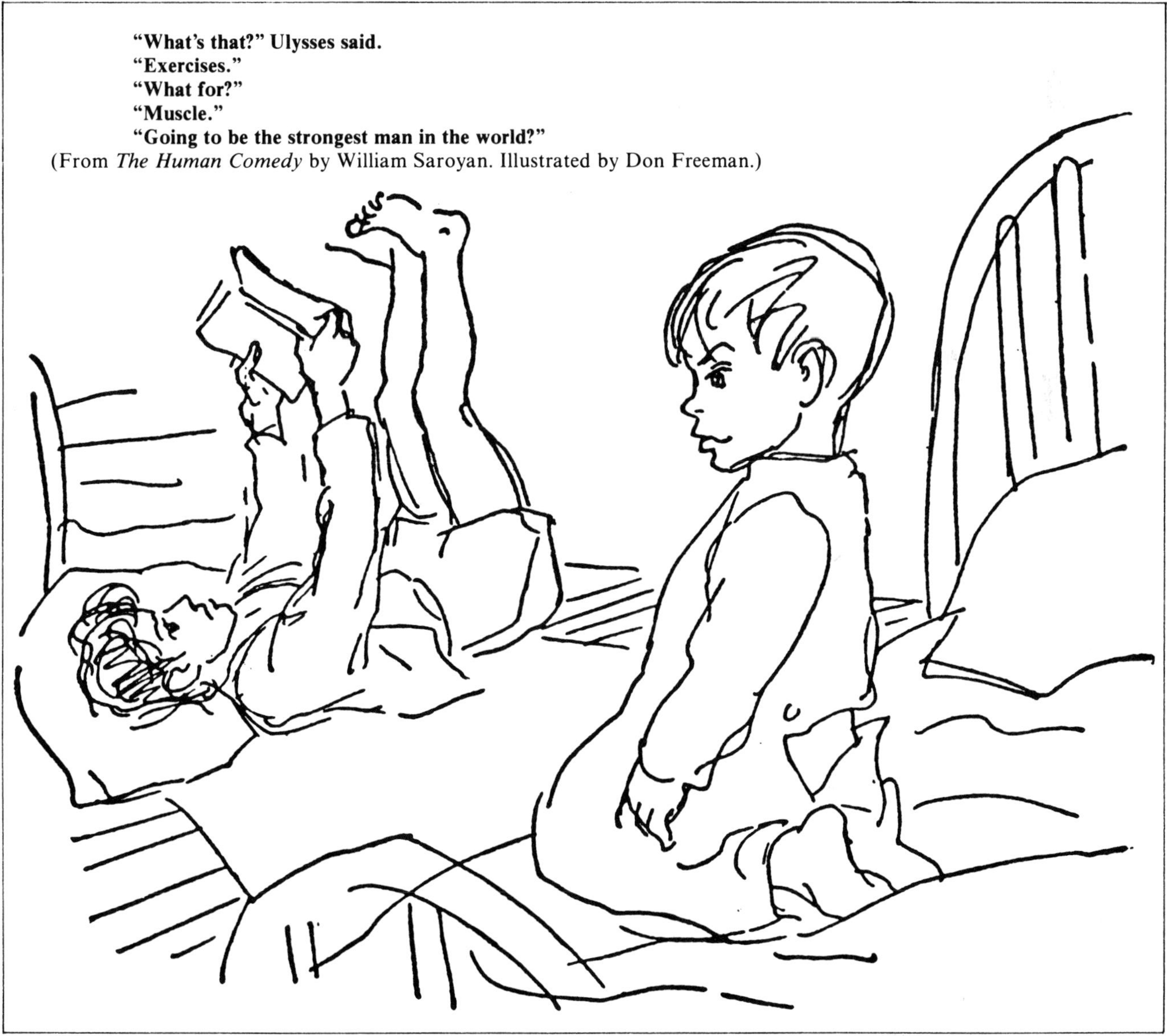

"What's that?" Ulysses said.
"Exercises."
"What for?"
"Muscle."
"Going to be the strongest man in the world?"
(From *The Human Comedy* by William Saroyan. Illustrated by Don Freeman.)

(From the stage production of "My Heart's in the Highlands," starring Sidney Lumet [the boy] and Harry Morgan. Presented by the Group Theatre, 1939.)

(From the stage production of "Hello Out There," starring Jennifer Jones and Harry Morgan. Presented by the Selznick Company at the Lobero Theater, Santa Barbara, California, 1942.)

Homer watched the old man to see if he was going to be all right, then went to the delivery desk and took up the telegram of death. ■ (From the movie "The Human Comedy," starring Mickey Rooney and Frank Morgan. Copyright 1943 by Loew's, Inc.)

(From the stage production of "The Time of Your Life," starring Julie Haydon and Gene Kelly. Produced at the Booth Theatre, 1939.)

One afternoon in 1918 an old Chinese who walked with a crooked stick came to my corner. . . . ■ (From *An Act or Two of Foolish Kindness* by William Saroyan. Wood engravings by Helen Siegl.)

kinds of other mothers. But the sons wouldn't have them, couldn't have them, had to have the original or no mother at all."[3]

1916. Reunited with family in Fresno. "I was a whistling boy, a singing boy, a laughing boy, a shouting, running, excited, delighted boy. I was also a brooding, miserable, angry, discontented, bitter, bored, lonely, unhappy one. I was both, and frequently simultaneously. I remember exulting in the fun of swimming at Thompson Ditch, at the headgate there, and then after swimming I remember sitting with my friends on the hot earth of the pasture bordering the ditch, in the wonderful light and heat of the August sun, and being miserable about my own impermanence, insignificance, meaninglessness, and feebleness."

"Boredom was the plague of my childhood. More—much more—than loneliness it filled my days and my soul. I was bored from the beginning, certainly from the moment I was cut off from my own home and my own family, from the moment my mother said deliberate goodbye to me in the waiting room of the orphanage. . . .

"This early boredom, this dissatisfaction with objects that I felt deeply and instinctively were substitutes, had something important to do with my reaching the decision to make writing my work. . . ."[1]

"My mother brought out the bundle of my father's writings when I asked if I might look at them. I was nine or ten and we were back in Fresno, in our own rented house on San Benito Avenue. This was an important event in my life, I may say. First, I was a little surprised that my mother had carefully kept something of my father's, for it had seemed a long time since he had come and gone, and what was the good of keeping worthless stuff like an unknown writer's writings, the writer himself long absent from a world that had moved along swiftly? Second, I was pleased that she believed I deserved to have a look at the stuff.

"I picked up the first notebook and just held it a moment. And then I read the stuff my father had written on the cover. It doesn't matter what the stuff actually was, I can't be sure of it, but I can be sure that after the name of it came his name, very clearly, in English, with that touch of foreignness which is in the handwriting of all men who are not English or American by birth."[2]

1921. " . . . I believed, for instance, at thirteen when I owned a typewriter that I could write a book in nine or ten days that would, in fact, change the order of the world and the nature of man, only to discover that what I wanted to say, what I knew I had to say, I *couldn't* say.

"The words wanted to come out so quickly and the entire book wanted itself written so quickly that no words at all would come out, or so few and such pathetic ones that I was plunged into profound anger and bitter despair.

"My family had always looked upon me as a little mad, and this fooling with a typewriter added to this reputation."[1]

1923. Left high school at the age of fifteen for an assortment of odd jobs: vineyard worker, office manager of the San Francisco Postal Telegraph Co., etc. " . . . My success as a telegraph messenger depended on my eyes. Consequently, *all* hope of effectiveness depended on them. My effectiveness as a messenger became inseparable from my hope to be effective as a writer.

"First, I needed the money the job brought me. That is, the Saroyan family needed it.

"Second, I needed the action of myself in the world. That is, the writer needed it.

"Third, I needed to go, to continue to go, to continue my study of rhythm, pace, speed, and effectiveness. I needed all this in order to understand who I was, who I could be, and how."[1]

1925. First story accepted for *The Overland Monthly*.

1928. Set out for New York to seek his fortune and recognition. "Why did I go to New York? "I went there because I was an immigrant, and all immigrants go to New York. My father went to New York, why shouldn't I go to New York? And I went there to see about improving my style. The bus ride gave me a pretty good idea about the size of the country, and New York gave me a pretty good idea about the size of a big city, and the way people live in a big city. They lived the same way people in Fresno lived, except that in November it began to snow.

"Now, when you're twenty, when you're three thousand three hundred and thirty-three miles from home, when you're a writer who hasn't made his fame and fortune, when it's snowing all the time and six million people are knocking themselves out trying to get through the slush on the sidewalk to a cup of coffee, you stop to think. You think, 'At this rate I'll never make my fame and fortune. I'm twenty years old. I've been in New York three and half months and I *still* haven't written a famous book. In less than two weeks it will be 1929, and what good will that do me, still unknown?' "[2] Considered his New York experience a failure and returned to California where Saroyan worked for the Cypress Lawn Cemetery Co. " . . . I was back in California after about five months in New York. I went back by chair car because it was all I could afford, and it was a good long, slow ride. I had failed again, for in my heart I had gone in the expectation of staying gone. Or at any rate until I might have gone back as a visitor, a man of fame and fortune. But I had gotten sick, and then I had gotten *homesick,* and I had gone back pretty much the same as I had been when I had left. Nothing and nobody. . ."[1]

1934. Gained first recognition with *The Daring Young Man on the Flying Trapeze.*

1935. First of many trips to Europe.

1939. Two plays, "My Heart's In the Highlands," and "The Time of Your Life," were produced to great acclaim. "From the beginning I got up early in the morning, and I wrote. I began with poems, and I moved along to stories and plays. I wrote all kinds of plays, and every one of them was without emotionality, because emotionality seemed phoney to me.

"Now, it happens that I write more plays more frequently than any other living playwright, and one play is different from the other, while each of them is directed to a human race, a horde if you like, which remains concealed behind the obsolete race which is dying of the bad habit of itself. . . ."[2]

1940. Rejected Pulitzer Prize for Drama, saying he was opposed to the patronizing of the arts by the wealthy.

1942-1945. Served in U.S. Army; stationed in London for part of his service. "Three times in my life I have been captured: by the orphanage, by school, and by the Army. I was four years in the orphanage, seven or eight in school, and three in the Army. Each seemed forever, though. But I'm mistaken. The fact is I was captured only once, when I was born, only that capture is also a setting free, which is what this is actually all about. The free prisoner."[2]

1943. Wrote *The Human Comedy,* a novel adapted from his scenario.

February, 1943. Married Carol Marcus.

September 25, 1943. Son, Aram, born in New York. "Soon enough, however, I began to meet him, when, even before he was a week old, he *wasn't* mad at me or anybody else. And I'm glad I *did* meet him, for such a meeting, a man meeting his son, even though even genetically it is now established that a son tends to inherit the character not of his father but rather of his father's mother's father's brother's son or something even more absurd and complicated than that—for such a meeting is a rather amazing event involving centuries of all manner of small and large accidents. [William Saroyan, *Chance Meetings,* W. W. Norton & Co., 1978.[4]]

January 17, 1946. Daughter, Lucy, born in San Francisco. "After meeting your father and mother, meeting your son and daughter is the rounding out of that part of the human experience."[4]

November, 1949. Divorced Carol Marcus.

1951. Remarried Carol Marcus.

1952. Re-divorced Carol Marcus. "Suicide was suicide, Divorce was divorce. I flipped a coin, and it came up divorce. The *second* divorce, that is, from the same little bride. I was bankrupt, in debt to the Tax Collector for about fifty thousand dollars, about half that much to others, most of them merchants who had sold her stuff. During the short second marriage I had bought her diamond rings, fancy dentistry, expensive furs, shoes and clothes. This hungry little girl with the pudgy, spongy flesh at which she worked better than half the day in order to be ready in the evening for her public at another party talked and laughed, and talked and laughed, and talked and laughed, and consulted her lawyer. She was a real Broadway musical comedy. Everybody loved her, men and women alike." [William Saroyan, *Places Where I've Done Time,* Praeger, 1972.[5]]

I began to inhale. Four minutes later I was still doing so. Naturally, the examining staff was a little amazed. ■ (From *My Name Is Aram* by William Saroyan. Illustrated by Don Freeman.)

1959. Plagued with income tax trouble, Saroyan went to Paris to live where he was often visited by his children. ". . .I was broke. I was in debt. My career as a writer was shot. I was fighting the world. I hated publishers, editors, agents, critics, book reviewers, newspapers, magazines, publicity agents, lawyers, dentists, and taxi drivers. I owed the Tax Collector so much money there just didn't seem to be any way I could possibly both pay him off and keep myself alive. . . ."[3]

"I had to have money, and I couldn't get any by any other means. My work was writing, so after the sensible breakfast of tea and bread and cheese every morning I went straight to work, and after I had done what I considered a fair day's work I took to the stairway again and went out to walk in the neighborhood.

"This is something all writers will understand.

"It is so good to have the day's work done that just to be out in the street, free, and to be walking, is a great joy."[4]

Reflecting on his career as a writer, Saroyan confesses: "The wisest thing any writer can do who is getting along in years and feeling it enough to know he can't do what he used to do is not to blow his brains out but to take it slow and easy, not feeling obliged to be a kind of hero of the world, and not being miserable about the fact that he has changed, as all things must, in time.

"That is the wise thing to do, but it isn't easy, and many a writer has had long years of terrible unhappiness about the fading of himself in himself, and of his name in the world. . . ." [William Saroyan, *Days of Life and Death and Escape to the Moon,* Dial, 1970.[6]]

FOR MORE INFORMATION SEE: Saturday Review of Literature, February 22, 1936; Edmund Wilson, *The Boys in the Back Room,* Colt Press, 1941; *New Republic,* March 9, 1953; *Saturday Evening Post,* August 16, 1958; *Theatre Arts,* December, 1958; *Newsweek,* March 2, 1959, September 10, 1962; *Time,* March 28, 1960, January 26, 1962; *New York Times,* January 7, 1962; *New York Times Book Review,* February 25, 1962; *Booklover's Answer,* September-October, 1963 (from which most of the above bibliography, by David Kherdian, and certain other information is taken by permission); David Kherdian, *A Bibliography of William Saroyan, 1934-1964,* J. Howell, 1965; Allan Lewis, *American Plays and Playwrights of the Contemporary Theatre,* Crown, 1965; Jean Gould, *Modern American Playwrights,* Dodd, 1966; Howard R. Floan, *William Saroyan,* Twayne, 1966.

SASEK, Miroslav 1916-1980

OBITUARY NOTICE—See sketch in *SATA* Volume 16: Born November 18, 1916, in Prague, Czechoslovakia; died May, 1980. Illustrator and author. Sasek, who was employed by Radio Free Europe for six years, wrote and illustrated the "This Is" series of children's books on travel in cities and countries around the world, including Paris, London, San Francisco, Israel, and Australia. *This Is London,* 1959, and *This Is New York,* 1960, were chosen among the best illustrated children's books of the year by the *New York Times. For More Information See: Books Are by People: Interviews with 104 Authors and Illustrators of Books for Young Children,* Citation Press, 1969; *Third Book of Junior Authors,* Wilson, 1972; *Contemporary Authors,* Volume 73-76, Gale, 1978. *Obituaries: Publishers Weekly,* June 27, 1980; *Contemporary Authors,* Volume 101-104, Gale, 1981.

SAVILLE, (Leonard) Malcolm 1901-

PERSONAL: Born February 21, 1901, in Hastings, Sussex, England; son of Ernest Vivian (a bookseller) and Fanny Ethel (Hayes) Saville; married Dorothy May McCoy, 1926; children: two sons, two daughters. *Education:* Richmond Hill School, Richmond, Surrey, England. *Home:* Chelsea Cottage, Winchelsea, East Sussex, TN36 4HU, England. *Agent:* A. P. Watt, Ltd., 26-28 Bedford Row, London, WC1R 4HL, England.

CAREER: Cassell & Co. (publishers), London, publicity work, 1920-22; Amalgamated Press, London, sales promotion manager, 1922-36; George Newnes Co. and C. Arthur Pearson Ltd. (publishers), London, copy writer and sales promotion manager, 1936-40, general books editor, 1957-66; *My Garden* magazine, London, associate editor and writer, 1947-52; Kemsley Newspapers, London, writer, 1952-55; full-time writer, 1966—. *Member:* Savage Club (London).

WRITINGS—Mostly juvenile: *Mystery at Witchend* (illustrated by G. E. Breary), George Newnes, 1943, reissued (illustrated by Bertram Prance), 1960, published in the United States as *Spy in the Hills,* Farrar & Rinehart, 1945; *Country Scrap Book for Boys and Girls,* National Magazine Co., 1944, 3rd edition, Gramol, 1946; *Seven White Gates* (illustrated by B. Prance), George Newnes, 1944; *The Gay Dolphin Adventure,* George Newnes, 1945; *Open-Air Scrap Book for Boys and Girls,* Gramol, 1945; *Trouble at Townsend,* Transatlantic Arts, 1945; *Jane's Country Year* (illustrated by Bernard Bowerman), George Newnes, 1946, 3rd edition, 1953; *The Riddle of the Painted Box* (illustrated by Lunt Roberts), Transatlantic Arts, 1947; *The Secret of Grey Walls,* George Newnes, 1947, revised edition, Armada, 1975; *Redshank's Warning* (illustrated by L. Roberts), Lutterworth, 1948; *Two Fair Plaits* (illustrated by L. Roberts), Lutterworth, 1948; *Lone Pine Five* (illustrated by B. Prance), George Newnes, 1949; *Strangers at Snowfell* (illustrated by Wynne), Lutterworth, 1949.

The Adventure of the Life-Boat Service, Macdonald & Co., 1950; *The Flying Fish Adventure* (illustrated by L. Roberts), J. Murray, 1950; *The Master of Maryknoll* (illustrated by Alice Bush), Evans Brothers, 1950, revised edition, Collins, 1971; *The Sign of the Alpine Rose* (illustrated by Wynne), Lutterworth, 1950; *All Summer Through* (illustrated by Joan Kiddell-Monroe), Hodder & Stoughton, 1951; *The Elusive Grasshopper* (illustrated by B. Prance), George Newnes, 1951; *The Buckinghams at Revenswyke* (illustrated by A. Bush), Evans Brothers, 1952, revised edition, Collins, 1971; *Coronation Gift Book,* Pitkin, 1952; *The Luck of Sallowby* (illustrated by Tilden Reeves), Lutterworth, 1952; *The Ambermere Treasure* (illustrated by Marcia Lane Foster), Lutterworth, 1953, published in the United States as *The Secret of the Ambermere Treasure,* Criterion, 1967; *Christmas at Nettleford* (illustrated by J. Kiddell-Monroe), Hodder & Stoughton, 1953; *The Neglected Mountain* (illustrated by B. Prance), George Newnes, 1953; *The Secret of the Hidden Pool* (illustrated by L. Roberts), J. Murray, 1953; *The Long Passage* (illustrated by Alice Bush), Evans Brothers, 1954; *Spring Comes to Nettleford* (illustrated by J. Kiddell-Monroe), Hodder & Stoughton, 1954; *Saucers Over the Moor* (illustrated by B. Prance), George Newnes, 1955, revised edition, Collins, 1972; *The Secret of Buzzard Scar* (illustrated by J. Kiddell-Monroe), Hodder & Stoughton, 1955; *Where the Bus Stopped,* Basil Blackwell, 1955.

Young Johnnie Bimbo (illustrated by L. Roberts), J. Murray, 1956; *Wings over Witchend,* George Newnes, 1956; *The Fourth Key* (illustrated by L. Roberts), J. Murray, 1957; *Lone Pine London,* George Newnes, 1957; *Treasure at the Mill* (illustrated by Harry Pettit), George Newnes, 1957; *King of Kings,* Nelson, 1958, revised edition, Lion Publishing, 1975, Our Sunday Visitor, 1977; *The Secret of the Gorge,* George Newnes, 1958; *Four-and-Twenty Blackbirds* (illustrated by Lilian Buchanan), George Newnes, 1959, reissued as *The Secret of Galleybird Pit,* Armada, 1968; *Mystery Mine,* George Newnes, 1959; *Small Creatures* (illustrated by John T. Kenney), Edmund Ward, 1959; *Sea Witch Comes Home,* George Newnes, 1960; *Malcolm Saville's Country Book,* Cassell, 1961; *Malcolm Saville's Seaside Book,* Cassell, 1962; *Not Scarlet but Gold* (illustrated by A. R. Whitear), George Newnes, 1962; *A Palace for the Buckinghams* (illustrated by A. Bush), Evans Brothers, 1963; *Three Towers in Tuscany,* Heinemann, 1963; *The Purple Valley,* Heinemann, 1964; *Treasure at Amorys* (illustrated by Terence Freeman), George Newnes, 1964.

MALCOLM SAVILLE

Dark Danger, Heinemann, 1965; *The Man with Three Fingers,* George Newnes, 1966, revised edition, Collins, 1971; *The Thin Grey Man* (illustrated by Desmond Knight), Macmillan, 1966; *White Fire,* Heinemann, 1966; *Come to London: A Personal Introduction to the World's Greatest City,* Heinemann, 1967; *Strange Story,* Mowbray, 1967; *Power of Three,* Heinemann, 1968; *Come to Cornwall,* Benn, 1969; *Come to Devon,* Benn, 1969; *Come to Somerset,* Benn, 1970; *Dagger and the Flame,* Heinemann, 1970; *Good Dog Dandy,* Collins, 1971; *The Secret of Villa Rosa,* Collins, 1971; *Where's My Girl?,* Collins, 1972; *Diamond in the Sky,* Collins, 1975; *Eat What You Grow* (illustrated by Robert Micklewright), Carousel, 1975; *Portrait of Rye* (adult non-fiction), Henry Goulden, 1976; *Countryside Quiz* (illustrated by R. Micklewright), Carousel, 1978; *Home to Witchend,* Armada, 1978; *Marston-Master Spy,* Heinemann, 1978; *Wonder Why Book of Exploring a Wood* (illustrated by Elsie Wrigley), Carousel, 1978; *Wonder Why Book of Exploring the Seashore* (illustrated by Jenny Heath), Carousel, 1979; *Words for All Seasons* (adult non-fiction), Lutterworth, 1979.

"Susan and Bill" series; published by Thomas Nelson: *Susan and Bill and the Ivy Clad Oak* (illustrated by Ernest Shepard), 1954; *. . . and the Wolf Dog,* 1954; *. . . and the Golden Clock,* 1955; *. . . and the Vanishing Boy,* 1955; *. . . and the Saucy Kate,* 1956; *. . . and the Bright Star Circus,* 1960; *. . . and the Pirates Bold,* 1961.

Also author of *The Roman Treasure Mystery, See How It Grows, Susan and Bill and the Dark Stranger.*

SIDELIGHTS: Saville began writing books for young people in 1942. The son of a bookseller, he was exposed from childhood to books and reading. Consequently, it was no surprise when he pursued a career in publishing, later becoming a full-time writer.

Saville's first book, *Mystery at Witchend,* was written in instalments while he was on war work in London. Each instalment was sent to his wife and children who were staying in Shropshire for the duration of World War II. When *Mystery at Witchend* was finally published, it proved to be extremely successful and was serialized by BBC radio.

Seven White Gates, Saville's second book, included characters from the first story who called themselves "The Lone Pine Club." The adventures of the club grew to include twenty titles, some of which were also broadcast by the BBC, and have sold over two million copies.

The greatest share of Saville's stories are set in England—the locale most familiar to him and his readers—although some tales for older readers are set against backgrounds in Italy, Spain, France, Holland, and Luxemburg. "All fiction is influenced by 'Place.' Consequently, I travel as widely as possible." Saville's appreciation for locale has also lead him to write non-fiction accounts of various British districts and towns, and the Shropshire Hills; most notable are those dealing with his home regions of Rye and Winchelsea.

Saville's fiction is designed to appeal to a wide age range. The adventures of secret agent Marston Baines, for example, appeal to adolescents while the Susan and Bill series is aimed at younger readers.

All in all, Saville has written more than eighty books with the entertainment of young readers being his foremost objective. In addition to fiction, he has written books on nature, travel, and gardening. He receives large quantities of mail from his readers and is noted for answering each letter personally.

FOR MORE INFORMATION SEE: Roger Lancelyn Green, *Tellers of Tales,* F. Watts, 1965; Brian Doyle, *The Who's Who of Children's Literature,* Schocken Books, 1968; *Sussex Life,* September, 1978.

SCOTT, John Anthony 1916-
(Tony Scott)

PERSONAL: Born January 20, 1916, in London, England; became U.S. citizen, 1943; son of Philip and Nora (Mort de Bois) Scott; married Maria Haller (now a teacher), August 28, 1940; children: Elizabeth (Mrs. Preston Waddington), John W., Robert A. *Education:* Attended St. Paul's School, London, England; Trinity College, Oxford, B.A. (first class honors), 1937, M.A., 1945; Columbia University, B.A., 1947, Ph.D., 1950. *Politics:* Reform Democrat. *Home:* 3555 Oxford Ave., New York, N.Y.

CAREER: Columbia University, New York, N.Y., lecturer in European history, 1946-48; Amherst College, Amherst, Mass., instructor in European history, 1948-51; Fieldston School, New York, N.Y., instructor in U.S. history and chairman of department, 1951—. Instructor at Seminar on American Culture, Cooperstown, N.Y., 1963; sometime ballad singer at Old Sturbridge Village. Aided in organization of Prayer Pilgrimage to Washington, 1957, and two youth marches for integrated schools, 1958, 1959; New York metropolitan coordinator for March on Washington for Equal Rights and Jobs, August, 1963. *Military service:* U.S. Army, Armored Forces and Intelligence, 1942-45; served in Europe; became staff sergeant; received Field Citation. *Member:* American Historical Association, National Association of Independent Schools, Association for the Study of Negro

JOHN ANTHONY SCOTT

Life and History, Authors Guild. *Awards, honors:* Fellow, Social Science Research Council.

WRITINGS: (Co-editor) *Introduction to Contemporary Civilization in the West,* Columbia University Press, 1946; *Republican Ideas and the Liberal Tradition in France,* Columbia University Press, 1950; (editor and co-author with Fanny Kemble) *Journal of a Residence on a Georgian Plantation in 1838-39,* Knopf, 1961; (editor) *Living Documents in American History,* Volume I, Washington Square, 1963; (editor and translator) *The Defense of Gracchus Babeuf before the High Court of Vendome,* Gehenna Press, 1964; (editor) Thomas More, *Utopia,* Washington Square, 1965; *The Ballad of America: The History of the United States in Song and Story,* Bantam, 1965, Grosset, 1966; (editor) Frank Moore, *The Diary of the American Revolution,* Washington Square, 1967; *Settlers on the Eastern Shore 1607-1750,* Knopf, 1967; *Trumpet of a Prophecy: Revolutionary America, 1763-1783,* Knopf, 1969; *Teaching for a Change,* Bantam, 1972; *Fanny Kemble's America,* Crowell, 1973; *Hard Trials on My Way: Slavery and the Struggle Against It, 1800-1860,* Knopf, 1974; *Woman Against Slavery: The Life of Harriet Beecher Stowe,* Crowell, 1978.

Recordings for Heirloom Records: (Writer of script and producer) "The New Deal through Its Songs and Ballads," "Irish Immigration through Its Songs and Ballads," and "The Negro People through Their Songs and Ballads"; (writer and performer with Gene Bonyun and Bill Bonyun) "The American Revolution through Its Songs and Ballads"; (writer with Bill Bonyun) "The Civil War through Its Songs and Ballads."

SIDELIGHTS: "I am an historian, I teach history and I write about it for anybody who cares to read. Much of my writing has been prompted by students' questions; they'd ask about things in class for which I had no answer, and that would start me thinking. I rarely start out with the idea that I'm going to write a book: I just keep collecting materials—pamphlets, letters diaries, songs—which are the lifeblood of an historian's craft. Then sooner or later the thought comes to me, 'Gee, it would be exciting to write a book about that.' And so I do.

"Writing I find both difficult and necessary. Necessary, because an historian tries to contribute to what is known about people and about life. Difficult, because writing, the ordering of symbols on paper, is a way of exploring a reality that is not always easy to understand. Then again, writing is a craft. It takes effort and patience to write and to rewrite, to pare away what is not essential, to say what you really mean, and to say it as briefly and as clearly as possible.

"Who do I write for? Basically I'd have to say for young people of all ages from elementary school to the graduate level in our universities. But I also hope that what I write will appeal to many other people too.

"Is writing profitable? It depends upon the sense in which you use that word. I've never made much money out of writing, but I find writing very rewarding. I write about what I please, I say what I please, and I come to my own conclusions. It's a form of freedom, if you like."

Calling textbooks "mere dry husks of facts," Scott insists that his students learn history directly from original sources, and supplies them with mimeographed copies of documents that are ordinarily seen only by scholars. He writes: "Documents are the life blood of history. . . . Historical documentation for me includes national song, the so-called 'folk music' that is a profound embodiment of American historical experience from the beginning to the present. No small part of my researches has been in the digging out of old and forgotten songs dealing with the great events and conflicts of the past." Scott has been known to strum a guitar and sing obscure colonial tunes for his classes.

HOBBIES AND OTHER INTERESTS: Tennis, swimming, bicycle riding, ice skating, and traveling. ("At various times I have travelled on foot or by bike in France, Germany, Greece, Austria, and Yugoslavia. . . . I have been in almost every state of the Union.").

FOR MORE INFORMATION SEE: Time, June 1, 1962; *Horn Book,* April, 1968, August, 1978.

SEED, Sheila Turner 1937(?)-1979 (Sheila R. Turner)

OBITUARY NOTICE: Born about 1937; died June 22, 1979, of a brain aneurysm, in Evanston, Ill. Editor, writer, and photographer. As director of Scholastic's Youth News Services, Seed supplied the company's numerous magazines with stories. World travel provided her with material for stories and photographs, and she was a contributor to the travel section of the *New York Times* under her maiden name, Sheila R. Turner. *Obituaries: New York Times,* June 23, 1979; *Contemporary Authors,* Volume 89-92, Gale, 1980.

The Love of Books, the Golden Key
That opens the Enchanted Door.

—Andrew Lang

SHIPPEN, Katherine B(inney) 1892-1980

OBITUARY NOTICE—See sketch in *SATA* Volume 1: Born April 1, 1892, in Hoboken, N.J.; died February 20, 1980, in Suffern, N.Y. Teacher and writer of books for young people. Before taking up her writing career, Shippen worked as a history teacher and as curator of social studies at the Brooklyn Children's Museum. Among her historical works for young people are *New Found World, Passage to America,* and *Miracle in Motion.* She also produced several biographies, including *Leif Eriksson, Andrew Carnegie and the Age of Steel,* and *Milton S. Hershey.* Shippen's *New Found World* and *Men, Microscopes, and Living Things* were named Newbery Honor Books in 1946 and 1956, respectively. *Men, Microscopes, and Living Things* was also included on the International Board on Books for Young People's honor list in 1956. *For More Information See: Current Biography,* Wilson, 1954; *Contemporary Authors,* Volume 5-8 revised, Gale, 1969; *Anthology of Children's Literature,* Houghton, 1970. *Obituaries: AB Bookman's Weekly,* April 14, 1980; *Contemporary Authors,* Volume 93-96, Gale, 1980.

STEWART, George Rippey 1895-1980

OBITUARY NOTICE—See sketch in *SATA* Volume 3: Born May 31,1895, in Sewickley, Pa.; died August 22, 1980, in San Francisco, Calif. Educator and writer. Stewart was affiliated with the University of California at Berkeley for nearly forty years when he was named professor emeritus in 1962. His fields of study included history, forestry, meteorology, and onomastics. In addition to his well-known novels, *Storm* and *Fire,* Stewart wrote nonfiction books, including *The Year of the Oath, Committee of Vigilance: Revolution in San Francisco,* and *Pickett's Charge.* For children Stewart wrote *To California by Covered Wagon,* based upon an actual journey made during the mid-1800s. *For More Information See: Current Biography,* Wilson, 1942; *The Oxford Companion to American Literature,* 4th edition, Oxford University Press, 1965; *Contemporary Authors,* Volume 1-4, revised, Gale, 1967; *Who's Who in America,* 38th edition, Marquis, 1974; *Atlantic,* February, 1968. *Obituaries: Time,* September 8, 1980; *Publishers Weekly,* September 12, 1980; *AB Bookman's Weekly,* October 6, 1980; *Contemporary Authors,* Volume 101-104, Gale, 1981.

The city of Quebec—with its ramparts, its houses dating from the French regime, its old lamp posts, its town gates and its cellars—remains the symbol of New France. ▪ (From *québec je t'aime: i love you* by Miyuki Tanobe. Illustrated by the author.)

MIYUKI TANOBE

TANOBE, Miyuki 1937-

PERSONAL: Born December 20, 1937, in Japan; came to Canada, 1971; naturalized Canadian citizen, 1976; daughter of Tomizo (an opthamologist and violinist) and Yuki (a singer and koto player; maiden name, Hayase) Tanobe; married Maurice Savignac (a researcher), December 10, 1971. *Education:* University of Tokyo, diploma in arts and license for teaching, 1960; also attended Ecole superieure nationale des Beaux Arts, Paris, 1963-65. *Home:* Saint-Antoine-sur-Richelieu, Vercheres County, Quebec, Canada YOL 1RO.

CAREER: Painter. Has had solo exhibitions at Galerie L'Art Francais, Montreal, Quebec, 1972 and 1974, Japanese Pavillon, Montreal, 1973, and Marlborough-Godard, Montreal, and Toronto, Ontario, 1976. *Awards, honors:* Children's Book Showcase Award, 1976, for *québec je t'aime: i love you.*

EXHIBITIONS—Solo collections: Art Francais, Montreal, 1978, 1979; Nancy Pool, Toronto, 1979. Joint collections: Centre d'Art du Mont-Royal, 1975; Place des Arts, Montreal, 1978; Museum of Fine Arts, Montreal, 1978; Musée d'Art Contemporain, 1978. Permanent collections: Montreal Museum of Fine Arts, Quebec Museum, Joliette Museum (Quebec). Collections: La Laurentienne (Quebec), Saide Bronfman (Montreal), C.I.L.–Shell–Canada Steamship.

WRITINGS—Self-illustrated juveniles: *Miyuke in Quebec,* Scribner, 1976; *québec je t'aime: i love you,* Tundra Books, 1976; *Children of Quebec,* Tundra Books, in press.

WORK IN PROGRESS: "A synthesis on Quebec life, in cities and country, illustrating Gilles Vigneault's poem, 'Les gens de mon pays,' and *Tanobe.*"

SIDELIGHTS: "After studying in Paris and sketching in Greece and Africa, I arrived in Montreal where I caught the French Canadian soul and by painting the lanes and streets of popular districts in Montreal and Quebec cities, I discovered the warmth of the working classes."

Come away, O human child!
To the waters and the wild
With a faery, hand in hand,
For the world's more full of weeping than you can
understand.

—William Butler Yeats

THACKERAY, William Makepeace 1811-1863 (Arthur Pendennis, Esquire; Ikey Solomons, Esquire, Jr.; Michael Angelo Titmarsh)

PERSONAL: Born July 18, 1811, in Calcutta, India; died December 24, 1863, in London, England; buried at Kensal Green; son of Richmond (an officer in the civil service of the East India Company) and Anne (Becher) Thackeray; step-son of Major W. H. Carmichael-Smyth (an officer of the East India Company); married Isabella Gethin Creagh Shawe, August 20, 1836 (separated, 1840; died, 1894); children: Anne Isabella (Mrs. Richmond Thackeray Ritchie), Jane (died in infancy), Harriet Marian. *Education:* Attended the Charterhouse School, 1822-1828; studied at Trinity College, Cambridge, 1829-1830; entered the Middle Temple to read for the Bar, 1831-1832; studied art in Paris, 1834-1835. *Home:* London, England.

CAREER: Author and illustrator. Inherited a large fortune from his father upon reaching the age of majority, 1832; purchased and edited the *National Standard,* a newspaper which failed within the year, 1833; suffered severe monetary losses because of gambling, unsound investments, and the failure of an Indian bank, 1833; impoverished, he moved to Paris to study art, 1834; while there, he became the Paris correspondent for his step-father's newspaper, the *Constitutional,* which soon failed, 1837; settled in Great Coram Street, London, in 1837, turning to journalism to support his family; using various pseudonyms, he became a prolific contributor of sketches and reviews to several magazines and newspapers including *Fraser's Magazine,* beginning 1837, and *Punch,* 1841-1850; travelled in the Mediterranean region, August to October, 1844; the serial publication of *Vanity Fair* (the first work published under his real name), 1847-1848, established Thackeray as one of the foremost English novelists of the day; called to the Bar at Middle Temple, May 26, 1848; delivered a series of lectures in London, 1851; conducted a lecture tour of the United States, 1852-1853, and again, 1855-1856; completed his career as a lecturer with a tour of England and Scotland, 1856; stood unsuccessfully as a member of parliament for the city of Oxford, 1857; founded and edited the *Cornhill Magazine,* November, 1859, to March, 1862.

WILLIAM MAKEPEACE THACKERAY

Of course our young man commenced as a historical painter, deeming that the highest branch of art; and declining (except for preparatory studies) to operate on any but the largest canvasses. ▪ (From *The Newcomes* by William Makepeace Thackeray. Illustrated by Edward Ardizzone.)

WRITINGS—Novels: *Vanity Fair: A Novel without a Hero* (self-illustrated), Bradbury & Evans, monthly issues, 1847-1848, published in two volumes, 1848, Harper & Brothers, circa 1850, new edition, Dutton, 1957 [numerous other editions include those illustrated by Charles Crombie, Dodd, 1924; John Austen, Oxford University Press, 1931; Monica Goddard, Longman, 1957; and those edited by Max J. Herzberg, Macmillan, 1926; Geoffrey and Kathleen Tillotson, Houghton, 1963; Suzanne E. and Roderick A. Jacobs, Harper, 1964; an adaptation for children by Josephine Page, Oxford University Press, 1975]; *The History of Pendennis,*

(From "A Legend of the Rhine" in *The Works of William Makepeace Thackeray.* Illustrated by C. E. Brock.)

His Fortunes and Misfortunes (self-illustrated), Bradbury & Evans, monthly issues, 1848-1850, published in two volumes, 1848-1850, Harper & Brothers, 1850, reissued, Penguin, 1972 [other editions include those edited by Robert Morss Lovett, Scribner's, 1917; M. R. Ridley, Dutton, 1959]; *The History of Samuel Titmarsh and the Great Hoggarty Diamond,* Bradbury & Evans, 1849, reissued as *The Great Hoggarty Diamond* (bound with *The Book of Snobs*), Leypoldt & Holt, 1866.

The History of Henry Esmond, Esquire: A Colonel in the Service of Her Majesty Queen Anne, Smith, Elder, 1852, Leypoldt & Holt, 1866 [later editions include those illustrated by George DuMaurier and others, Houghton, 1900; Curtiss Sprague, Macmillan, 1930; Adolf Hallman, Literary Guild of America, 1950; Edward Ardizzone, Heritage Press, 1966; Janina Ede, Heron Books, 1970; and those edited by William Lyons Phelps, Scott, Foresman, 1902; Hamilton Byron Moore, Ginn, 1924; Walter Graham, Macmillan, 1926; John Sutherland and Michael Greenfield, Penguin, 1970]; *The Luck of Barry Lyndon: A Romance of the Last Century* (first published serially in *Fraser's Magazine*) Appleton, two volumes, 1853, reissued as *The Memoirs of Barry Lyndon,* [London], 1856, reissued, Futura Publications, 1975 [other editions include those edited by Robert L. Morris, University of Nebraska Press, 1962; Martin F. Anisman, New York University Press, 1970]; (under pseudonym Arthur Pendennis, Esquire) *The Newcomes: Memoirs of a Most Respectable Family* (illustrated by Richard Doyle), Bradbury & Evans, monthly issues, 1853-1855, published in two volumes, 1854-1855, Harper & Brothers, two volumes, 1855 [later editions include those with introductions by Angela Thirkell, Heritage Press, circa 1950; M. R. Ridley, Dutton, 1962]; *The Virginians: A Tale of the Last Century* (self-illustrated), Bradbury & Evans, monthly numbers, 1857-1859, published in two volumes, 1858-1859, Leypoldt & Holt, four volumes, 1866, reissued, Dent, 1973.

Lovel the Widower (originally published serially in *Cornhill Magazine;* self-illustrated), Harper & Brothers, 1860; *The*

She looked so haughty that I should have thought her a princess in the very least, with a pedigree reaching as far back as the Deluge. ■ (From *The Rose and the King* by William Makepeace Thackeray. Illustrated by the author.)

Adventures of Philip on His Way through the World, Showing Who Robbed Him, Who Helped Him, and Who Passed Him By, Harper & Brothers, 1862; *Denis Duval* (originally published serially in *Cornhill Magazine*), Harper & Brothers, 1864.

Sketches and stories: (Published anonymously) *The Yellowplush Correspondence* (first published serially in *Fraser's Magazine*), Carey & Hart, 1838, reissued as *The Memoirs of Mr. Charles J. Yellowplush,* J. W. Lovell, 1883; (published anonymously) *The Loving Ballad of Lord Bateman* (illustrated by George Cruikshank; introduction by Charles Dickens), C. Tilt, 1839, reissued, Dent, 1969; *The Book of Snobs* (collected sketches first published in *Punch* as *The Snobs of England by One of Themselves*), [London], 1848, Appleton, 1852, reissued, St. Martin's, 1978; *The Confessions of Fitz-Boodle, and Some Passages in the Life of Major Gahagan* (originally published in *Fraser's Magazine*), Appleton, 1852; *Men's Wives* (originally published in *Fraser's Magazine*), Appleton, 1852; *A Shabby Genteel Story, and Other Tales* (collected from *Fraser's Magazine*), Appleton, 1852, reissued, New York University Press, 1971; *Mr. Brown's Letters to a Young Man about Town* (collected from *Punch*), Appleton, 1853, reprinted, Folcroft, 1974, Norwood Editions, 1978; *Roundabout Papers* (collected from *Cornhill Magazine*), Harper & Brothers, 1863; *Mr. and Mrs. Frank Berry,* G. P. Putnam, 1864; *A Little Dinner at Timmins's,* Leypoldt & Holt, 1866; *The Tremendous Adventures of Major Gahagan,* Leypoldt & Holt, 1866; (under the pseudonym Ikey Solomons, Esquire, Jr.) *Catherine: A Story* (originally published serially in *Fraser's Magazine*), Fields, Osgood, 1869; *The Orphan of Pimlico, and Other Sketches, Fragments, and Drawings* (with notes by Anne Isabella Thackeray), Lippincott, 1876; *A Legend of the Rhine,* G. W. Fitch, 1879; *The Mahogany Tree* (originally published in *Punch;* illustrated by Frank T. Merrill), S. E. Cassino, 1887; *The Cane Bottom'd Chair* (illustrated by F. T. Merrill, H. Hirschauer, and oth-

. . . She procured admission into the place where this saucy hussy was, and drawing from her pocket a dagger and a bowl of poison, she bade her take one or the other. She preferred, it is said, the prussic acid. ■ (From "Miss Tickeetoby's Lectures" in *The Works of William Makepeace Thackeray.* Illustrated by C. E. Brock.)

. . . And away I went, with an army of a hundred and seventy-three thousand eight hundred men at my heels. ■ (From "Phil Fogarty" in *The Works of William Makepeace Thackeray.* Illustrated by C. E. Brock.)

ers), S. E. Cassino, 1891; *Pumpernickel,* [London], 1915; *Fairy Days,* privately printed, 1919; (for children) *The Thackeray Alphabet* (a reproduction of the self-illustrated manuscript of 1883), J. Murray, 1929.

Under the pseudonym Michael Angelo Titmarsh: *The Paris Sketch Book* (self-illustrated), J. Macrone, 1840, Appleton, circa 1855; *Comic Tales and Sketches* (self-illustrated), H. Cunningham, 1841; *The Second Funeral of Napoleon, in Three Letters to Miss Smith of London,* H. Cunningham, 1841, J. W. Lovell, 1883; *The Irish Sketch Book* (self-illustrated), Chapman & Hall, two volumes, 1843, Lippincott, 1872, a later edition including critical reviews and illustrations by the author, George Cruikshank, and others, Lippincott, 1879; *Notes of a Journey from Cornhill to Grand Cairo by Way of Lisbon, Athens, Constantinople, and Jerusalem,* Wiley & Hall, 1846; (for children) *Mrs. Perkin's Ball* (self-illustrated), Chapman & Hall, 1847; (for children) *Our Street,* Chapman & Hall, 1848; (for children) *Doctor Birch and His Young Friends,* Chapman & Hall, 1849, Appleton, 1852; *Rebecca and Rowena: A Romance Upon Romance,* Chapman & Hall, 1850, a later edition illustrated by Lex Metz, Story Classics, 1954; (for children) *The Kickleburys on the Rhine,* Smith, Elder, 1850, Stringer & Townsend, 1851; (for children) *The Rose and the Ring; Or, the History of Prince Giglio and Prince Bulbo,* Harper & Brothers, 1854, reissued, Blackie, 1974 [other editions include those illustrated by Gordon Browne, F. A. Stokes, 1909; Thackeray, John Gilbert, and Paul Hogarth (bound with Charles Dickens's *The Magic Fish Bone*), Dutton, 1959].

Lectures: *The English Humorists of the Eighteenth Century,* Smith, Elder, 1853, Harper & Brothers, 1854; *The Four Georges: Sketches of Manners, Morals, Court, and Town Life,* Harper & Brothers, 1860.

Letters: *The Students' Quarter; Or, Paris Five-and-Thirty Years Since,* J. C. Hotten, 1876; *A Collection of Letters of Thackeray, 1847-1855, with Portraits and Reproductions of Letters and Drawings,* Scribner's, 1887, reprinted, Folcroft, 1974; *The "Old England" Letters,* J. Thomson, 1904; *Thackeray's Letters to an American Family,* Century, 1904; *Some Family Letters of William Makepeace Thackeray,* Houghton, 1911, reprinted, Folcroft, 1974, Norwood Editions, 1976; *The Letters and Private Papers of William Makepeace Thackeray* (collected and edited by Gordon N. Ray), Harvard University Press, 1945-1946.

Collections: *Miscellanies,* Bradbury & Evans, four volumes, 1854-1857, Fields, Osgood, 1869; *Ballads,* Bradbury & Evans, 1855, Ticknor & Fields, 1856; *The Works of William Makepeace Thackeray,* Lippincott, ten volumes, 1868, illustrated edition, 22 volumes, 1869, biographical edition with notes by Anne Isabella Thackeray Ritchie, Harper & Brothers, 1898-1899; *Thackerayana* (compiled by Joseph Grego), Chatto & Windus, 1875, reprinted, Haskell House, 1970; *The Complete Poems of William Makepeace Thackeray,* White, Stokes, 1886; *The Complete Works of William Makepeace Thackeray* (with illustrations by the author), Houghton, 1889; *The Prose Works of William Makepeace Thackeray* (edited by W. Jerrold; illustrated by C. E. Brock), Dent, 1902; *The Thackeray Pocket Book* (compiled by Adelaide Rawnsley Fossard), Scribner's, 1908; *Thackeray* (edited by G. K. Chesterton), G. Bell, 1909, reprinted, R. West, 1978.

(From the movie "Becky Sharp," starring Miriam Hopkins, adapted from the novel *Vanity Fair.* Released by RKO Radio Pictures Corp., 1935.)

Selections: *Jeames's Diary, A Legend of the Rhine,* [*and*] *Rebecca and Rowena,* Appleton, 1853; *Punch's Prize Novelists, The Fat Contributor,* [*and*] *Travels in London,* Appleton, 1853; *The Fatal Boots,* [*and*] *Cox's Diary,* Bradbury & Evans, 1855; *Sketches and Travels in London* (collected from *Punch*), Bradbury & Evans, 1856; *Early and Late Papers Hitherto Uncollected,* Ticknor & Fields, 1867; *Burlesques* (self-illustrated), Lippincott, 1869; *Henry Esmond* [*and*] *Lovel the Widower,* Fields, Osgood, 1869; *Stray Moments with Thackeray: His Humor, Satire, and Characters* (edited by William H. Rideing), Appleton, 1880; *Character Sketches,* J. W. Lovell, 1883; (for children) *The Christmas Books of Mr. M. A. Titmarsh* (self-illustrated), J. W. Lovell, 1883; *Cox's Diary, The Bedford-Row Conspiracy,* [*and*] *A Little Dinner at Timmins's,* J. W. Lovell, 1883; *Novels by Eminent Hands,* J. W. Lovell, 1883; *Chips from Thackeray* (selected by Thomas Mason), Bryce & Son (Glasgow), 1884; *Sultan Stork, and Other Stories and Sketches,* G. Redway, 1887; *Loose Sketches: An Eastern Adventure,* F. T. Sabin, 1894; *Sketch Books,* Harper & Brothers, 1898; *Contributions to "Punch,"* Harper & Brothers, 1898; *Ballads, Critical Reviews, Tales, Various Essays, Letters, Sketches,* Harper & Brothers, 1899; *The Hitherto Unidentified Contributions of W. M. Thackeray to "Punch,"* Harper & Brothers, 1899, reissued, Haskell House, 1971; *Mr. Thackeray's Writings in "The National Standard" and "Constitutional,"* W. T. Spencer, 1899.

Selections from the Book of Snobs, Roundabout Papers, and Balads, Doubleday & McClure, 1901; *Stray Papers: Stories, Reviews, Verses, and Sketches, 1821-1847* (edited by Lewis Melville), Hutchinson, 1901, reprinted, Kraus Reprint, 1971; *The Pocket Thackeray* (compiled by A. H. Hyatt), Chatto & Windus, 1906; *The New Sketch Book,* Alston Rivers, 1906; *The Sense and Sentiment of Thackeray,* Harper & Brothers, 1909; *Boys and Girls from Thackeray* (compiled by Kate Dickinson Sweetser), Harper & Brothers, 1925; *Contributions to the "Morning Chronicle,"* University of Illinois Press, 1955, reprinted, 1966; *The English Humourists, Charity and Humour, and The Four Georges,* Dent, 1968; *Thackeray: The Major Novels,* Manchester, 1971.

Collected illustrations: *Etchings by the Late William Makepeace Thackeray,* H. Sotheran, 1878; *A Book of Drawings by William Makepeace Thackeray,* [Philadelphia], 1925; *The Illustrations of William Makepeace Thackeray,* David & Charles, 1979.

ADAPTATIONS—Movies and filmstrips: "Vanity Fair" (motion pictures), Thomas A. Edison, Inc., 1915, Hugo Ballin Productions, Inc., 1923, Allied Pictures Corporation, 1932; "Vanity Fair" (filmstrip), Educational Record Sales, 1972; "Becky Sharp" (motion picture), an adaptation of *Vanity Fair* and the play entitled "Becky Sharp" by Langdon Mitchell, Pioneer Pictures, Inc., 1935; "Barry Lyndon" (motion picture), staring Ryan O'Neal, Marisa Berenson, Patrick Magee, Marie Kean, and Hardy Kruger, narrated by Michael Hordern, Warner Brothers, 1975.

Plays: Landgon Mitchell, *Becky Sharp* (four-act), H. S. Stone, 1899; "Becky Sharp," produced at the Manhattan Theatre, beginning September 14, 1904, the Lyceum Theatre, beginning March 20, 1911, and the Knickerbocker Theatre, beginning June 3, 1929; Jevan Brandon-Thomas, *Vanity Fair* (three-act), S. French, 1949.

(From the movie "Barry Lyndon," starring Ryan O'Neal and Marisa Berenson. Released by Warner Brothers, 1975.)

Still she held up, in spite of these rebuffs, and tried to make a character for herself, and conquer scandal. She went to church very regularly, and sang louder than anybody there. ■ (From *Vanity Fair* by William Makepeace Thackeray. Illustrated by the author.)

SIDELIGHTS: **July 18, 1811.** Born in Calcutta, India, where his father held a government position.

1817. Sent by widowed mother to England for his education.

"When I first saw England she was in mourning for the young Princess Charlotte, the hope of the Empire. . . .

". . . I remember peeping through the colonnade at Carlton House, and seeing the abode of the great Prince Regent. I can yet see the guards pacing before the gates of the Palace. The palace! What palace? The palace exists no more than the palace of Nebuchadnezzar. It is but a name now." [Lewis Melville, *The Life of William Makepeace Thackeray,* Volume I, Herbert Stone & Co., 1899.[1]]

August, 1822. Mother and stepfather returned to England. Thackeray was sent to Charterhouse School, where he displayed an early inclination towards writing. "I have not yet drawn out a plan for my stories, but certain germs thereof are yet budding in my mind, which I hope by assiduous application will flourish yet and bring forth fruit. I always feel as if I were at home when I am writing."[1]

"Doctor Russell [instructor] is treating me every day with such manifest unkindness and injustice, that I really can scarcely bear it: It is so hard when you endeavour to work hard, to find your attempts nipped in the bud—if ever I get a respectable place in my form, he is sure to bring me down again; to day there was such a flagrant instance of it, that it was the general talk of the school. . . . On every possible occasion he shouts out reproaches against me for leaving his precious school forsooth! He has lost a hundred boys within two years, and is of course very angry about [it]—There are but 370 in the school, I wish there were only 369." [Gordon Ray, *Thackeray—The Uses of Adversity—1811-1846,* McGraw-Hill, 1955.[2]]

February, 1829. Attended Trinity College, Cambridge, for two years. Contributed to *The Snob,* a literary magazine. "I was too young to form opinions but I did form them—& these told me that there was little use in studying what could after a certain point be of no earthly use to me—they told me that subtle reasonings & deep meditations on angles & parallelograms might be much better employed on other subjects—that three years industrious waste of time might obtain for me mediocre honors which I did not value a straw."[2]

1830. Travelled to Germany, where he met the aging author Goethe, an event which he dubbed as one of the most memorable experiences of his life. "My delight in those days was to make caricatures for children. I was touched to find that they were remembered, and some even kept until the present time; and very proud to be told, as a lad, that the great Goethe had looked at some of them."[1]

1831. Entered law, a career ambition abandoned within the year. "I have been taking a little recreation in the fields of Civil-law, & as I expected have not found the Pandects of Justinian much to my taste. I suppose however it must be—a clergyman I cannot be, nor a physician so I must drudge up poor & miserable the first part of my life, & just reach the pinnacle (or somewhere near it I trust, when my eyes will hardly be able to see the prospect I have been striving all my life to arrive at—These are the pleasures of the law—& to these I must I fear dedicate myself—As I have thought a great deal on the profession I *must* take; & the more I think of it the less I like it—However I believe it is the best among the positive professions & as such I must take it, for better or worse. . . ." [Gordon Ray, editor, *The Letters of William Makepeace Thackeray,* Volume I, Harvard University Press, 1945.[3]]

January, 1833. Association with the National Standard and Journal of Literature, Science, Music, Theatricals and the Fine Arts. Thackeray later assumed editorship. "How I long for the sight of a dear green curtain again—after going 3 times a week to the play for a year one misses it so, O the delight of seeing the baize slowly ascending—the spangled shoes which first appear then as it gradually Draws up legs stomachs heads till finally it ends in all the glories of a part of 'musqueteers' drinking—a dance—an inn with an infinity of bells jingling or a couple of gay dogs in cocked hats with pieces of silk dangling out of their pockets for handkerchiefs—Yet another month. & all this paradise will be in my reach—really London is to me only the place where the Theatres are."[2] The newspaper failed within the year.

1834. Attempted a career as an artist in Paris. "I have been thinking very seriously of turning artist. I can draw better than I can do anything else, and certainly I should like it better than any other occupation, as why shouldn't I?"[1]

". . . The streets are filled with picture-shops, the people themselves are pictures walking about; the churches, theatres, eating-houses, concert-rooms, are covered with pictures; Nature itself is inclined more kindly to him, for the sky is a thousand times more bright and beautiful, and the sun shines for the greater part of the year.

"As for myself—I am in a state of despair—I have got enough torn-up pictures to roast an ox by—the sun riseth upon my efforts and goeth down on my failures, and I have become latterly so disgusted with myself and art and everything belonging to it, that for a month past I have been lying on sofas reading novels, and never touching a pencil.

"In these six months, I have not done a thing worth looking at. O God, when will Thy light enable my fingers to work, and my colours to shine—if in another six months, I can do no better, I will arise and go out and hang myself."[2]

1836. Returned to England to establish *The Constitutional,* serving as its Paris correspondent. The venture failed.

August 20, 1836. Married Isabella Shawe. "I am arrived at such a pitch of sentimentality (for a plain girl without a penny in the world) that my whole seyn, être, or being, is boulversé or capsized—I sleep not neither do I eat, only smoke a little and build castles in the clouds; thinking all the day of the propriety of a sixieme, boiled beef and soup for dinner, and the possession of the gal of my art."[2]

1837. Marriage compelled Thackeray into writing for many periodicals in an attempt to earn a living. "I am as poor as a rat, and my spending runs so deucedly close to my earnings that if the payment of these is delayed I and an amiable family run the risk of intermediate starvation. "I remember dining at this table with my wife when a sovereign was all I had in the world, and I spent 17s. of it. I wanted to nerve and excite myself up to writing."[2]

March 14, 1839. Stunned by death of eight and half month-old daughter, Jane. "What shall I say to you about our little darling who is gone? I don't feel sorrow for her, and think of her only as something charming that for a season we were allowed to enjoy . . . and now I would be almost sorry—no that is not true—but I would not ask to have the dear little Jane back again and subject her to the degradation of life and pain."[2]

1840. Sorrow pervaded him as his wife, afflicted with mental illness, was placed away from her family, leaving him to the care of their daughters. "At first she was in a fever and violent, then she was indifferent, now she is melancholy & silent and we are glad of it. She bemoans her condition and that is a great step to cure. She knows everybody and recollects things but in a stunned confused sort of way. She kissed me at first very warmly and with tears in her eyes, then she went away from me, as if she felt she was unworthy of having such a God of a husband. God help her."[2]

"I cannot live without the tenderness of some woman, and expect when I am sixty, I shall be marrying a girl of eleven or twelve, innocent, barley-sugar-loving, in a pinafore.

". . . Though my marriage was a wreck, . . . I would do it again, for behold, Love is the crown and completion of all earthly good."[1]

1841. Commencement of long association with satirical journal *Punch* which he helped to establish. "Poor fellows of the pen and pencil! we must live. The public likes light literature, and we write it. Here am I writing magazine jokes and follies, and why? Because the public likes such, and will purchase no other."[1]

1844. *The Luck of Barry Lyndon* published in *Fraser's Magazine* began a period of high literary output.

January, 1847. *Vanity Fair* emerged to assure his reputation as a novelist, not just as a humorist. "I think I have never had any ambition hitherto, or cared what the world thought my work, good or bad; but now the truth forces itself upon me, if the world will once take to admiring Titmarsh, all his guineas will be multiplied by ten. Guineas are good. I have got children, only ten years more to the fore say, etc.; now is the time, my lad, to make your A when the sun at length has begun to shine. Well, I think if I can make a push at the present minute—if my friends will shout, Titmarsh for ever! hurrah for, etc., etc.,—I may go up with a run to a pretty fair place in my trade, and be allowed to appear before the public among the first fiddles. But my tunes must be heard in the streets, and organs must grind them. . . .

". . . I hope to be able to last six years in the literary world; for though I shall write, I daresay, very badly, yet the public won't find it out for some time, and I shall live on my past reputation. It is a pity to be sure. If I could get a place and rest, I think I could do something better than I have done, and leave a good and lasting book behind me; but Fate is overruling. . . ."[1]

1849. Worked on *Pendennis*. Incapacitated with a near-fatal fever.

1850. Formally resigned from *Punch,* although his contributions continued.

1851. Formulated a series of lectures on English humorists of the eighteenth century. "I have been living in the last century for weeks past—all day that is—going at night as usual into the present age; until I get to fancy myself almost as familiar with one as the other. . . .

"I tried the great room at Willis's yesterday, and recited a part of the multiplication table to a waiter at the opposite end so as to try the voice. He said he could hear perfectly: and I daresay he could but the thoughts somehow swell and amplify with that high-pitched voice and elaborate distinctness—as I perceive how poets become selfish I see how orators become humbugs and selfish in their way too: absorbed in that selfish pursuit and turning of periods." [Gordon Ray, *Thackeray—The Age of Wisdom—1847-1863,* McGraw-Hill, 1958.[4]]

1852. Embarked on lecture tour in America. "The curious thing is that I think I improve in my reading; at certain passages a sort of emotion springs up, and I begin to understand how actors feel affected over and over again at the same passages of the play;—they are affected off the stage too: I hope I shan't be. . . .

April, 1853. Returned to England

1853-1855. Wrote *The Newcomes* while traveling abroad.

1857. Lost a close election for a seat in Parliament.

1859. Edited *Cornhill Magazine,* to which his daughter contributed her first published writings. "I am pressed into the service of this magazine, and engaged to write ever so much more for the next three years. Then, if I last so long, I shall be free of books and publishers, and hope to see friends to whose acquaintance I look back with. . . .

"When I read it, I blubbered like a child; it was so good, so simple, so honest; and my little girl wrote it, every word of it." [Lewis Melville, *The Life of William M. Thackeray,* Volume II, Herbert Stone & Co., 1899.[5]]

1862. Resigned editorship of *Cornhill* due to failing health. Overcome by a deep melancholy and haunted by images of his wife. "Yesterday, in the street, I saw a pair of eyes so like two which used to brighten at my coming once, that the whole past came back as I walked lonely, in the rush of the Strand, and I was young again in the midst of joys and sorrows, alike sweet and sad, alike sacred and fondly remembered."[1]

December 24, 1863. Died in London, England. "Our books are diaries, in which our feelings must of necessity be set down. As we look to the page written last month, or ten years ago, we remember the day and its events; . . . It is not the words I see, but that past day; that bygone page of life's history; that tragedy, comedy it may be, which our little home company was enacting; that merry-making which we shared; that funeral which we followed; that bitter, bitter grief which we buried."[5]

FOR MORE INFORMATION SEE: Theodore Taylor, *Thackeray: The Humourist and the Man of Letters,* J. C. Hotten, 1864, reprinted, Haskell House, 1971; James Hannay, *Studies on Thackeray,* [London], 1869, reprinted, Folcroft, 1972; W. B. Jerrold, *A Day with William Makepeace Thackeray,* [London], 1871; Anthony Trollope, *Thackeray,* Macmillan, 1879, reprinted, Folcroft, 1977; Charles P. Johnson, *Hints to Collectors of Original Editions of the Works of William Makepeace Thackeray,* G. Redway, 1885, reprinted, Folcroft, 1972; C. P. Johnson, *The Early Writings of William Makepeace Thackeray,* E. Stock, 1888, reprinted, Norwood, 1975; H. C. Merivale and E. T. Marzials, *Life of Thackeray,* W. Scott, 1891, reprinted, Folcroft, 1973; Adolphus A. Jack, *Thackeray: A Study,* Macmillan, 1895, reprinted, Kennikat, 1970; Eyre Crowe, *With Thackeray in America,* Scribner's, 1893, reprinted, Norwood, 1976.

Charles Whibley, *William Makepeace Thackeray,* W. Blackwood, 1903, reprinted, Arden Library, 1977; James Grant Wilson, *Thackeray in the United States, 1852 to 1853, 1855 to 1856,* Smith, Elder, 1904, reprinted, R. West, 1973; Isadore G. Mudge and M. Earl Sears, *A Thackeray Dictionary,* G. Routledge & Sons, 1910, reprinted, Humanities, 1962; Lewis Saul Benjamin, *William Makepeace Thackeray: A Biography Including Hitherto Uncollected Letters and Speeches and a Bibliography of 1300 Items,* J. Lane, 1910, reprinted, Scholarly Press, 1968.

Albert S. Canning, *Dickens and Thackeray Studied in Three Novels,* R. West, 1911, reprinted, Kennikat, 1972; L. S. Benjamin, *Some Aspects of Thackeray,* Little, Brown, 1911; Francis Hopkinson Smith, *In Thackeray's London,* Doubleday, Page, 1913; Nathaniel W. Stephenson, *The Spiritual Drama in the Life of Thackeray,* Hodder & Stoughton, 1913, reprinted, Folcroft, 1974; Oliver Elton, *Dickens and Thackeray,* E. Arnold, 1924, reprinted, Porter, 1978.

George E. B. Saintsbury, *A Consideration of Thackeray,* Oxford University Press, 1931, reprinted, Folcroft, 1973; Malcolm Elwin, *Thackeray: A Personality,* J. Cape, 1932, reprinted, Russell, 1966; Harold Strong Gulliver, *Thackeray's Literary Apprenticeship: A Study of the Early Newspaper and Magazine Work of William Makepeace Thackeray,* Southern Stationery & Printing Co., 1934, reprinted, Folcroft, 1979, Geoffrey U. Ellis, *Thackeray,* Duckworth, 1935, reprinted, Folcroft, 1973; Herbert N. Wethered, *On the Art of Thackeray,* Longman, 1938, reprinted, Folcroft, 1974; Margaret M. Goodell, *Three Satirists of Snobbery: Thackeray, Meredith, Proust,* [Hamburg], 1939, reprinted, Folcroft, 1976.

John W. Dodds, *Thackeray: A Critical Portrait,* Oxford University Press, 1941, reprinted, Russell, 1963; Lionel Stevenson, *The Showman of Vanity Fair: The Life of William Makepeace Thackeray,* Scribner's, 1947, reprinted, Russell, 1968; Jean Gould, *Young Thack,* Houghton, 1949.

C. E. Eckersley, *William Makepeace Thackeray: The Writer and His Work,* Longmans, Green, 1950; Lambert Ennis, *Thackeray: The Sentimental Cynic,* Northwestern University Press, 1950, reprinted, AMS Press, 1970; John Y. T. Greig, *Thackeray: A Reconsideration,* Oxford University Press, 1950, reprinted, Shoe String, 1967; Gordon N. Ray, *The Buried Life: A Study of the Relation between Thackeray's Fiction and His Personal History,* Royal Society of Literature of the United Kingdom, 1952, reprinted, Haskell, 1974; G. N. Ray, *Thackeray,* McGraw, 1955-1958; P. R. Krishnasvami, *In Thackeray's Workshop,* privately printed (Madras), 1956, reprinted, Arden Library, 1971; Laurence R. M. Brander, *Thackeray,* Longmans, Green, 1959, revised edition, 1964.

Geoffrey Tillotson, *Thackeray the Novelist,* Methuen, 1963, reissued, 1974; John R. Loofbourow, *Thackeray and the Form of Fiction,* Princeton University Press, 1964, reprinted, Gordian, 1976; Dudley Flamm, *Thackeray's Critics: An Annotated Bibliography of British and American Criticism,* University of North Carolina Press, 1967; Alexander Welsh, *Thackeray: A Collection of Critical Essays,* Prentice-Hall,

(From *The Newcomes* by William Makepeace Thackeray, edited by Arthur Pendennis. Illustrated by Richard Doyle.)

1968; G. Tillotson and Donald Hawes, *Thackeray: The Critical Heritage,* Routledge & Kegan Paul, 1968; James M. Wheatley, *Patterns in Thackeray's Fiction,* M.I.T. Press, 1969; Michael G. Sundell, *Twentieth Century Interpretations of Vanity Fair,* Prentice-Hall, 1969.

Peter Quennell, *Casanova in London,* Stein & Day, 1971; Juliet McMaster, *Thackeray: The Major Novels,* Manchester University Press, 1971; Barbara Hardy, *The Exposure of Luxury: Radical Themes in Thackeray,* Owen, 1972; John A. Sutherland, *Thackeray at Work,* Athlone Press, 1974; Jack P. Rawlins, *Thackeray's Novels: A Fiction That Is True,* University of California Press, 1974; John C. Olmsted, *Thackeray and His Twentieth-Century Critics: An Annotated Bibliography of British and American Criticism, 1900-1975,* Garland Publishing, 1977; John Carey, *Thackeray: Prodigal Genius,* Faber, 1977; Kenneth C. Phillips, *The Language of Thackeray,* Deutsch, 1978; Margaret Foster, *Memoirs of a Victorian Gentleman,* Secker & Warburg, 1978, Morrow, 1979; Arthur Pollard, *Vanity Fair: A Casebook,* 1978; E. F. Harden, *The Emergence of Thackeray's Serial Fiction,* University of Georgia Press, 1979; S. K. Sinha, *Thackeray: A Study in Technique,* Humanities, 1979; R. A. Colby, *Thackeray's Canvass of Humanity,* Ohio State University Press, 1979.

(Movie) "The Portrait of William M. Thackeray" (29 min., sound, black & white, 16 mm.), WHYY-TV (Philadelphia), released by National Educational Television Film Service, 1958.

TOURNIER, Michel 1924-

PERSONAL: Born December 19, 1924, in Paris, France; son of Alphonse and Marie-Madeleine (Fournier) Tournier. *Education:* Studied law and philosophy in Paris, France, and Tuebingen, Germany. *Residence:* Le Presbytère Choisel, 78460 Chevreuse, France. *Office:* Editions Plon, 8 rue Garanciere, Parie 6e, France.

CAREER: Novelist. He has been literary director for Editions Plon, Paris, France, and has also worked in radio and television, and for newspapers. *Member:* Academie Goncourt (1972—). *Awards, honors:* Grand Prix du Roman from Academie Francaise, 1967, for *Vendredi, ou les Limbes du Pacifique;* Prix Goncourt, 1970, for *Le Roi des Aulnes.*

WRITINGS—Novels: *Vendredi, ou les Limbes du Pacifique* (young adult), Gallimard, 1967, revised edition, 1972 translation by Norman Denny published in America as *Friday,* Doubleday, 1969 (translation by Denny published in England as *Friday, or The Other Island,* Collins, 1969), French edition reissued as *Vendredi, ou la vie sauvage,* Flammarion, 1971, translation by Ralph Manheim published as *Friday and Robinson: Life on Esperanza Island,* Knopf, 1972; *Le Roi des Aulnes,* Gallimard, 1970, translation by Barbara Bray published as *The Ogre,* Doubleday, 1972; *Les Météors,* Gallimard, 1976, translation by Anne Carter published as *The Meteors,* Doubleday, 1980; *Le Vent Paraclet,* Gallimard, 1977; *Le Coq de Bruyère,* Gallimard, 1978.

"Come with me," said Robinson. He took the cabin boy by the hand and together they climbed the rocky hill. ▪(From *Friday and Robinson* by Michel Tournier. Translated by Ralph Manheim. Illustrated by David Stone Martin.)

MICHEL TOURNIER

SIDELIGHTS: In *Friday* (once described as the story of Robinson Crusoe "seen through the eyes of Freud, Jung, and Claude Levi-Strauss"), Tournier "has attempted nothing less than an exploration of the soul of modern man." Thomas Fleming continues: "Again and again, he finds fresh and original ways of viewing primary experiences such as time and work and religious faith, the relationship of men to animals and trees and their own shadowy selves, to civilization and the essential earth. The telling is intensely French. The focus is on thinking, and thinking about feeling. There is little or no attempt to build up massive amounts of believable detail or anecdote."

With a similar, predominantly interior emphasis, Tournier's second novel, *The Ogre,* is a blend of myth and mythic symbols with reality. The author, writes R. Z. Sheppard, "proves a clever exploiter of the current enthusiasm for mysticism and mythology." He calls Tournier "a good Hegelian," but also "a good Jungian. Signs, symbols and archetypes are pried from every incident and lifted chaotically into the mythological vacuum of the modern world. . . . [His synthesis] has much to do with his notion that symbols have lives of their own and possess a diabolical potential."

FOR MORE INFORMATION SEE: Horn Book, February, 1973; Margery Fisher, *Who's Who in Children's Books,* Holt, 1975.

TURNGREN, Annette 1902(?)-1980 (A. T. Hopkins)

OBITUARY NOTICE: Born about 1902 in Montrose, Minn.; died May 14, 1980, in Hopkins, Minn. Editor and author. Employed at one time by the *New York Times,* Turngren held editorial positions in the juvenile department of a book publisher and with a number of magazines, including a post as associate editor of a magazine for teen-age girls. Young people were her primary audience in books like *Flaxen Braids, Mystery Plays a Golden Flute,* and *The Mystery of the Hidden Village.* The last title was a Junior Literary Guild selection. *For More Information See: Authors of Books for Young People,* 2nd edition, Scarecrow, 1971; *Contemporary Authors,* Volume 9-12, revised, Gale, 1974. *Obituaries: AB Bookman's Weekly,* July 14-21, 1980; *Contemporary Authors,* Volume 101-104, Gale, 1981.

WEIK, Mary Hays 1898(?)-1979

OBITUARY NOTICE—See sketch in *SATA* Volume 3: Born about 1898 in Greencastle, Ind.; died December 25, 1979, in Manhattan, N.Y. Journalist and writer of books, poetry, short stories, and radio scripts. Weik's book, *The Jazz Man,* was among those chosen as best illustrated children's books of the year by the *New York Times* in 1966, was a runner-up for the Caldecott Medal, and was a John Newbery Honor Book in 1967. Weik began her career as a newspaper reporter in Chicago and Indianapolis; later she moved to New York City where she worked as a staff writer for Street & Smith Publications and as a consultant to social agencies and schools. A political activist, Weik was co-founder and director of the Fellowship of World Citizens after World War II. Her opposition to nuclear power led her to co-found the Committee to End Radiological Hazards and to edit an anti-nuclear newsletter, *Window on the World. For More Information See: More Books by More People,* Citation Press, 1974; *Who's Who in America,* 39th edition, Marquis, 1976; *Contemporary Authors,* Volume 21-24, revised, Gale, 1977. *Obituaries: New York Times,* December 29, 1979; *Contemporary Authors,* Volume 93-96, Gale, 1980.

WENDELIN, Rudolph 1910-

PERSONAL: Born February 27, 1910, in Herndon, Kan.; son of Paul Henry (a mechanic) and Mary (Hauptman) Wendelin; married Carrol Bergman, March 11, 1944; children: Michael, David, Elizabeth. *Education:* Attended University of Kansas, Lawrence, Kan., 1929-1932; Layton Art School, Milwaukee, Wis., 1934-35; Milwaukee Art Institute, Milwaukee, Wis., 1936; Corcoran, Washington, D.C., 1938-40. *Politics:* Democrat. *Religion:* Lutheran. *Home:* 4516 Seventh St., N., Arlington, Va. 22203.

RUDOLPH WENDELIN

Everybody was happy because Christmas was in the air. ■ (From *The City That Forgot About Christmas* by Mary Warren. Illustrated by Rudolph Wendelin.)

CAREER: Illustrator; exhibit designer. United States Department of Agriculture, Forest Service, Washington, D.C., art manager, helped to establish the first campaign and coordinate the art material for Smokey the Bear, worked on Smokey the Bear campaign throughout his entire career with the Forest Service, 1944-73. Designed the three-color Forest Conservation commemorative four-cent stamp, 1958; co-designed Fifth World Forestry Congress Commemorative stamp, 1960; designed the three-color Range Conservation Commemorative stamp, 1961; designed the three-color John Muir Commemorative stamp, 1964. Free-lance art services include National Memorial Park, Maryland Resources Institute, Wilderness society, American Forestry Association, Society of American Foresters, plus many others. Commissioned to do five-foot bronze statue for New Mexico Recreation Division in Smoky Bear State Park, 1978. Arlington County Neighborhood Conservation, 1972-75; Arlington County Historical Commission, 1973; Arlington County Site Plan Review Committee, 1974.

EXHIBITIONS: Landscape Club, Washington, D.C., 1969-76; (one-man show) U.S. Department of Agriculture, Washington, D.C., 1972; (two-man show) Arts Club, Washington, D.C., 1975; numerous paintings in private collections and in government buildings. *Military service:* U.S. Navy, first class, 1942-45. *Member:* Washington Landscape Club (president, 1975), National Lutheran Human Relations Society, Federal Artists and Designers, Western Arts Council. *Awards, honors:* National Competition House Design, area award, 1939; Mostra Internazionale D.'Arte Cinetografica, movie animation, U.S. Department of Agriculture, 1949; Department of Agriculture Superior Service Award, 1960, 1970;

Federal Artist and Designers Awards, design, 1961, sculpture, 1967, illustration, 1969; Horace Hart Award, Graphic Arts Council, 1969; National Forest Fire Prevention Awards, The Silver Smokey, 1969, The Golden Smokey, 1972; Washington Landscape Club, first prize in watercolor, 1975.

ILLUSTRATOR: Mary P. Warren, *City That Forgot About Christmas,* Concordia, 1968; Reginald V. Truitt, *High Winds, High Tide,* National Resource Institute, 1968; Reginald V. Truitt, *Assateague: The Place Across,* National Resource Institute, 1971. Work has appeared in numerous government publications and also in *Timber, Recreation, Fire Prevention, Wildlife Federation Magazine, American Forests, Society of American Foresters Journal, Arlington Daily News* (weekly editorial cartoons), and many others.

SIDELIGHTS: "My first impressions of 'art,' as a small boy, were the simple decorations my mother embroidered on my school bag, designs of teeter-totters and rabbits which I would copy. I began drawing on my own during early elementary school years, first simple stick figures which evolved into more realistic figures of people, animals and barnyard scenes. A short correspondence course in cartooning during eighth grade, which I never finished, introduced me to the use of drawing ink, art gum, pen and brush . . . into caricature and political cartooning which fascinated me.

"Enrolling in the School of Architecture at the University of Kansas in 1929, opened new avenues to explore my creative energies. Courses in history of art and architecture, classes in outdoor sketching and life drawing, exposure to art collections and association with students and teachers in the arts gave new impetus to my dreams. The School of Architecture here at the University was just then breaking away from the old classical system of Beaux Arts indoctrination and students were exploring shapes and designs from three dimensional models. Learning fundamental principles of design, perspective, architectural drafting, rendering and planning construction were invaluable later on in planning and executing art assignments. . . . The work and philosophy of Frank Lloyd Wright greatly influenced my architectural development and works produced.

"The depression of the early 30's halted my studies to obtain a degree and I started to look for a job. . . . Learning the fundamentals of mapping and the use of surveying instruments in college ROTC, enabled me to get a job in my home county in Kansas, to make a map of a proposed recreational lake project. Using my experience in this project together with samples of my other drawing work, a job opened up for me in the Forest Service regional office in Milwaukee in 1933.

"After my discharge from the Navy [after World War II], I returned to my old job in the Forest Service just in time to have a part in the first National Forest Fire Prevention campaigns built around the growing popularity of 'Smokey the Bear.' Assigned to this program as part of my work, I became closely identified with the development of Smokey's image through my work as 'his' art director and graphic caretaker. During, almost thirty years with the program, countless creations to support the work from exhibits, animated movies, advice on many commercial products, cartoons, posters, educational publications, etc., poured from my desk. Retirement in 1973, has not kept me from continuing working under contract for the program—designs for litter bags, monthly cartoons, paintings for calendars, and a 5′ bronze statue to be erected in a New Mexico State Park.

"In 1968 an opportunity came from Concordia Publishing House to create the characters and do final illustrations for a children's book, *The City That Forgot About Christmas.* My interest in painting people of all age groups is reflected in the final illustrations, which were done same size and in acrylics.

FOR MORE INFORMATION SEE: Albuquerque Journal, August 10, 1969; *Junior Scholastic,* February 14, 1969; *Salt Lake Tribune,* January 9, 1969; *The Alexandria Gazette,* April 29, 1969; *Linn's Stamp News,* July 9, 1969; *The Washington Post,* June 12, 1973.

WESTALL, Robert (Atkinson) 1929-

PERSONAL: Born October 7, 1929, in Tynemouth, England; son of Robert and Maggie Alexandra (Leggett) Westall; married Jean Underhill (an administrator), July 26, 1958; children: (Robert) Christopher. *Education:* University of Durham, B.A. (first class honors), 1953; University of London, D.F.A., 1957. *Politics:* "Right-wing socialist." *Religion:* Society of Friends (Quakers). *Residence:* Northwich, England.

CAREER: Sir John Deane's College, Northwich, England, art teacher and head of department, 1960—, head of careers guidance, 1970—. Director of Telephone Samaritans of Mid-Cheshire, 1965-75. *Military service:* British Army, Royal Signals, 1953-55. *Awards, honors:* Carnegie Medal from Library Association of Great Britain, 1976, for *The Machine-Gunners; Devil on the Road* was one of three runners-up for the Carnegie Medal, 1979.

WRITINGS: The Machine-Gunners (*Horn Book* honor list; novel), Macmillan [London], 1975, Greenwillow, 1976; *The Wind Eye* (novel; *Horn Book* honor list), Macmillan [London], 1976, Greenwillow, 1977; *The Watch House* (novel), Macmillan [London], 1977, Greenwillow, 1978; *The Devil on the Road,* Macmillan [London], 1978, Greenwillow, 1979; *Fanthom Five,* Macmillan [London], 1979, *Scarecrows,* Macmillan [London], 1980. Staff writer for *Cheshire Life,* 1968-71. Art and architecture critic for *Cheshire Chronicle,* 1962—; art critic for *Guardian,* 1970.

WORK IN PROGRESS: Futuretrack Five, a novel about the young in a world of idleness brought about by the mini-chip computer; *The Cats of Seroster,* a saga of Tolkienesque proportions involving a race of telepathic cats; *The Sand-Warriors,* a comic novel about 18-year-old conscripts doing army service in the Canal Zone during the troubles of 1954; *The Bird of Dawning,* a 14-year-old cabin-boy on a tugboat enduring the Liverpool Blitz.

SIDELIGHTS: "I'm a Protestant writer, I suppose. My heroes are always alone with their consciences. Only they aren't battling with Sin; they're battling with fear. Fear of Chaos; which is only another word for things that are too big and complicated to understand—*at present.* Sin is only a by-product—take away the fear, and the Sin drops off of its own accord.

"The main thing to avoid is belonging to any big organization whether the Roman Catholic Church or the Communist Party—it's paying someone to do your thinking for you.

"Any man is worth listening to, when he's telling you something he's worked out for himself, something he's noticed himself.

"I like little groups of people who meet because they like each other. I like Hippies—the sort you've got to search for, because they've found something good, and gone off to quietly enjoy it. People who try to ram things down your throat don't really believe what they're ramming. They think if they can convince you, maybe they can convince themselves. If I see a herd on the move, I run the other way, instinctively.

"Big beliefs, big organizations are like junk-car yards. Worth looking at, to see if you can find something useful to pull off, buy and use. I like weird customized cars.

"I hate doing public speaking. It wears the surface of an author's mind away. A half-hour speech can use up a month of writing creativity.

"I like cats, because you have to *earn* their friendship; old wall-clocks; Buddhist statues; birdwatching and people-watching; other people's gardens; ruins and the sea.

"I have recently come to realize that I am really an historical novelist who was actually witnessing as a child the history he is now writing about. Although I am just fifty years old, the world of my childhood now seems a foreign country, strange as ancient China, of which nearly all the customs have passed away.

"No television; the radio used half-an-hour a day, to save batteries which had to be taken to a shop to be charged; batteries which, if carried carelessly, spilled acid which burnt your clothes. No radio news, except the cricket scores. Three rides in a car before I reached the age of fifteen, in tiny cars with windows made of yellow celluloid, at which tiny curtains were draped.

"Saturday evenings with *all* the shops open till nearly midnight; people shopping, meeting friends and talking in the street for hours under the flaring Gothic gaslights. Even small children of five out with their families, playing around, quite safe.

"For all children were the responsibility of all adults. I can remember, miles from home, one day, an old lady telling me off for throwing handfuls of sand in the road; I obeyed her implicitly; if she did not know my mother she would know one of my relations . . . It may sound terribly restrictive; in reality it felt so *safe*.

"Yet those were the years of the Depression; millions out of work; Hitler and the Nazis growing in power. Already some Jews were in the camps. But such things were never discussed in front of the children. Looking back, I'm glad.

"I cannot say I like the way the world is going. There have been advances; more prosperity in the West; a growth of conscience among the Western middle classes; the liberation, still incomplete, of women. But there has been a decay in the way people belonged together, looked after each other, and were proudly determined to stand on their own two feet. So when I found I could go back into history, I didn't see any reason why I shouldn't keep going. You can never turn the clock back; but you can be like a miner, burrowing back into the past to try to rescue some of the good things that we have forgotten in the rush for 'progress.' Each of my books is a separate prospecting-expedition."

HOBBIES AND OTHER INTERESTS: "My main avocational interests are designing, building, and sailing model yachts."

FOR MORE INFORMATION SEE: Publishers Weekly, February 14, 1977; *Times Literary Supplement,* December 2, 1977; *Horn Book,* October, 1977, February and August, 1978.

WHEELER, Opal 1898-

PERSONAL: Born in October, 1898; married John Macrae (then president of E. P. Dutton Publishing Co.), September, 1939 (died February 18, 1944). *Education:* Attended Wisconsin State Normal School; studied at the University of Wisconsin, the University of Washington, and Columbia University; studied piano in France and voice in Italy. *Home:* Belvedere, California.

CAREER: Musician, composer, and author. After completing her education, Opal Wheeler spent many years teaching music; she devoted a great deal of her time to music therapy sessions with emotionally and physically handicapped children; began to write, for children, biographies of famous composers. *Awards, honors:* Runner-up for the Randolph J. Caldecott Medal for *Sing Mother Goose* in 1946, and for *Sing in Praise: A Collection of the Best Loved Hymns* in 1947.

WRITINGS—All co-authored with Sybil Deucher; all published by Dutton; all illustrated by Mary Greenwalt: *Mozart,*

OPAL WHEELER

"Bravo! Bravo!" the cries rang out even before the composition was ended. Bowing many times, Nicolo left the stage. ■(From *Paganini, Master of Strings* by Opal Wheeler. Illustrated by Henry J. Gillette.)

the Wonder Boy, 1934, enlarged edition, 1941, reissued, 1968; *Joseph Haydn, the Merry Little Peasant,* 1936; *Sebastian Bach, The Boy from Thuringia,* 1937; *Curtain Calls for Joseph Haydn and Sebastian Bach: Musical Plays for Children,* 1939; *Franz Schubert and His Merry Friends,* 1939; *Edward MacDowell and His Cabin in the Pines,* 1940; *Curtain Calls for Franz Schubert,* 1941; *Curtain Calls for Wolfgang Mozart: A Musical Play for Children,* 1941.

All published by Dutton, except as indicated: (With Helen de Long) *The Singing Choir,* C. C. Birchard, 1933; *Stephen Foster and His Little Dog Tray* (illustrated by Greenwalt), 1941; *Ludwig Beethoven and the Chiming Tower Bells* (illustrated by Greenwalt), 1942, reissued, 1968; *Sing for Christmas* (illustrated by Gustaf Tenggren), 1943; *Handel at the Court of Kings* (illustrated by Greenwalt), 1943; *Sing for America* (illustrated by Tenggren), 1944; *Sing Mother Goose* (illustrated by Marjorie Torrey), 1945; *Sing in Praise: A Collection of the Best Loved Hymns* (illustrated by Torrey), 1946; *H.M.S. Pinafore* (adapted from story and music by Gilbert and Sullivan; illustrated by Fritz Kredel), 1946; *Robert Schumann and Mascot Ziff* (illustrated by Christine Price), 1947; *Frederic Chopin, Son of Poland* (illustrated by Price), 1948-49.

All published by Dutton: *Paganini, Master of Strings* (illustrated by Henry S. Gillette), 1950; *Hans Andersen, Son of Denmark* (illustrated by Henry C. Pitz), 1951; *Stars over Bethlehem* (illustrated by Price), 1952; *The Story of Peter Tschaikowsky* (illustrated by Price), 1953; *The Miracle Dish* (illustrated by Floyd I. Webb), 1957; *Peter Tschaikowsky and the Nutcracker Ballet,* 1959; *Adventures of Richard Wagner* (illustrated by Webb), 1960; *Moses* (illustrated by Linford Donovan), 1962.

SIDELIGHTS: While teaching music to children, Wheeler discovered that there was very little biographical material on the prominent composers which was suitable for young readers. She found it necessary to provide her students with these biographies herself. Her stories are designed to give young people background information on the great composers while arousing interest in their music through charming anecdotes which accent the human qualities of these men. To this end, she has fictionalized her biographies and screened the textual material in order to make them more appropriate for children. The critics have responded to her work with conditional approval. The *London Times Literary Supplement* has given *Peter Tschaikowsky and the Nutcracker Ballet* qualified praise. "Adult readers in possession of the facts will know that for the young reader more truth has to be suppressed in the story of Tschaikowsky than in that of any other great composer. However, here again, as in her earlier volume, *The Story of Tschaikowsky,* Opal Wheeler has brilliantly transformed a melancholic pervert into a romantic innocent whom 'the kiddies' will love. Yet so much fiction is intermingled with fact that the book, with its charming illustrations and incorporation of simple piano pieces, can really only be recommended for the very, very young."

Hans Andersen, Son of Denmark drew a similar comment from the *New York Herald Tribune.* "One expects that many children under twelve will enjoy this book. And anything that gives them a deeper and longer-lasting interest in Andersen's genius is worthwhile. However, for a really good biography of this strange genius, we must turn to books not slanted for younger children."

The reviewers do agree, however, that not all the facts of the composers' lives would make enjoyable or suitable reading matter for youngsters. As the *New York Herald Tribune* points out regarding *Ludwig Beethoven and the Chiming Tower Bells:* "Nothing quite corresponds in the literature of American childhood to the series of which this is the seventh, and let us say at once, the best. . . . One reason why this is the best of the series is that it had by far the hardest problem to meet: faced with tragedy so stark, blows of fate so staggering, how to present such a career without leaving on the impressionable mind of childhood, a scar sensitive as a wound? The answer is again selection."

FOR MORE INFORMATION SEE: New York Herald Tribune, November 29, 1942; *Horn Book* magazine, January-December, 1947; *New York Herald Tribune,* November 11, 1951; *London Times Literary Supplement,* May 20, 1960; Muriel Fuller, editor, *More Junior Authors,* Wilson, 1963.

Dear little child, this little book
Is less a primer than a key
To sunder gates where wonder waits
Your "Open Sesame!"

—Rupert Hughes

WHITEHOUSE, Arthur George 1895-1979 (Arch Whitehouse)

OBITUARY NOTICE—See sketch in *SATA* Volume 14: Born December 11, 1895, in Northampton, England; died November 15, 1979, in Lincoln Park, N.J. Author, cartoonist, screenwriter, and journalist. Whitehouse drew upon his experiences as an aerial gunner in World War I and as a correspondent in World War II to write more than forty books on warfare and aviation. For children he wrote *Scarlet Streamers, Spies with Wings,* and *The Laughing Falcon.* Before he began writing about the military, Whitehouse had worked as a sports writer and cartoonist on the *Passaic Daily News* and *Elizabeth Daily Journal.* He also was a script writer for Metro-Goldwyn-Mayer in Hollywood. *For More Information See:* Arch Whitehouse, *The Fledgling,* Duell, Sloan & Pearce, 1965; *Contemporary Authors,* Volume 5-8, revised, Gale, 1969; *The Men Behind Boy's Fiction,* Howard Baker, 1970; *Authors of Books for Young People,* 2nd edition, Scarecrow, 1971. *Obituaries: New York Times,* November 16, 1979; *Contemporary Authors,* Volume 89-92, Gale, 1980.

CUMULATIVE INDEX TO ILLUSTRATIONS AND AUTHORS

Illustrations Index

(In the following index, the number of the volume in which an illustrator's work appears is given *before* the colon, and the page on which it appears is given *after* the colon. For example, a drawing by Adams, Adrienne appears in Volume 2 on page 6, another drawing by her appears in Volume 3 on page 80, another drawing in Volume 8 on page 1, and another drawing in Volume 15 on page 107.)

YABC

Index citations including this abbreviation refer to listings appearing in *Yesterday's Authors of Books for Children,* also published by the Gale Research Company, which covers authors who died prior to 1960.

Aas, Ulf, *5:* 174
Abbé, S. van. *See* van Abbé, S., *16:* 142
Abel, Raymond, *6:* 122; *7:* 195; *12:* 3; *21:* 86
Accorsi, William, *11:* 198
Acs, Laszlo, *14:* 156
Adams, Adrienne, *2:* 6; *3:* 80; *8:* 1; *15:* 107; *16:* 180; *20:* 65; *22:* 134-135
Adams, John Wolcott, *17:* 162
Adkins, Alta, *22:* 250
Adkins, Jan, *8:* 3
Adler, Peggy, *22:* 6
Agard, Nadema, *18:* 1
Aichinger, Helga, *4:* 5, 45
Akasaka, Miyoshi, *YABC 2:* 261
Akino, Fuku, *6:* 144
Alajalov, *2:* 226
Albright, Donn, *1:* 91
Alcorn, John, *3:* 159; *7:* 165
Alden, Albert, *11:* 103
Alexander, Martha, *3:* 206; *11:* 103; *13:* 109
Alexeieff, Alexander, *14:* 6
Aliki. *See* Brandenburg, Aliki
Allamand, Pascale, *12:* 9
Alland, Alexander, *16:* 255
Alland, Alexandra, *16:* 255
Allen, Gertrude, *9:* 6
Almquist, Don, *11:* 8; *12:* 128; *17:* 46; *22:* 110
Aloise, Frank, *5:* 38; *10:* 133
Althea. *See* Braithwaite, Althea
Altschuler, Franz, *11:* 185; *23:* 141
Ambrus, Victor G., *1:* 6-7, 194; *3:* 69; *5:* 15; *6:* 44; *7:* 36; *8:* 210; *12:* 227; *14:* 213; *15:* 213; *22:* 209
Ames, Lee J., *3:* 12; *9:* 130; *10:* 69; *17:* 214; *22:* 124
Amon, Aline, *9:* 9
Amoss, Berthe, *5:* 5
Amundsen, Dick, *7:* 77
Amundsen, Richard E., *5:* 10
Ancona, George, *12:* 11
Anderson, Alasdair, *18:* 122
Anderson, C. W., *11:* 10
Anderson, Carl, *7:* 4
Anderson, Erica, *23:* 65
Anderson, Laurie, *12:* 153, 155
Anderson, Wayne, *23:* 119
Andrew, John, *22:* 4
Andrews, Benny, *14:* 251
Angelo, Valenti, *14:* 8; *18:* 100; *20:* 232
Anglund, Joan Walsh, *2:* 7, 250-251
Anno, Mitsumasa, *5:* 7
Antal, Andrew, *1:* 124
Appleyard, Dev, *2:* 192
Archer, Janet, *16:* 69
Ardizzone, Edward, *1:* 11, 12; *2:* 105; *3:* 258; *4:* 78; *7:* 79; *10:* 100; *15:* 232; *20:* 69, 178; *23:* 223; *YABC 2:* 25
Arenella, Roy, *14:* 9
Armer, Austin, *13:* 3
Armer, Laura Adams, *13:* 3
Armer, Sidney, *13:* 3
Armitage, Eileen, *4:* 16
Armstrong, George, *10:* 6; *21:* 72
Arno, Enrico, *1:* 217; *2:* 22, 210; *4:* 9; *5:* 43; *6:* 52
Arnosky, Jim, *22:* 20
Arrowood, Clinton, *12:* 193; *19:* 11
Artzybasheff, Boris, *13:* 143; *14:* 15
Aruego, Ariane, *6:* 4
See also Dewey, Ariane
Aruego, Jose, *4:* 140; *6:* 4; *7:* 64
Asch, Frank, *5:* 9
Ashby, Gail, *11:* 135
Ashley, C. W., *19:* 197
Ashmead, Hal, *8:* 70
Atene, Ann, *12:* 18
Atkinson, J. Priestman, *17:* 275
Atwood, Ann, *7:* 9
Austerman, Miriam, *23:* 107
Austin, Margot, *11:* 16
Austin, Robert, *3:* 44
Averill, Esther, *1:* 17
Axeman, Lois, *2:* 32; *11:* 84; *13:* 165; *22:* 8; *23:* 49
Ayer, Jacqueline, *13:* 7
Ayer, Margaret, *15:* 12

B.T.B. *See* Blackwell, Basil T., *YABC 1:* 68, 69
Babbitt, Natalie, *6:* 6; *8:* 220
Bacon, Bruce, *4:* 74
Bacon, Paul, *7:* 155; *8:* 121
Bacon, Peggy, *2:* 11, 228
Baker, Alan, *22:* 22
Baker, Charlotte, *2:* 12
Baker, Jeannie, *23:* 4
Baker, Jim, *22:* 24
Baldridge, C. LeRoy, *19:* 69
Balet, Jan, *11:* 22
Balian, Lorna, *9:* 16
Ballis, George, *14:* 199
Banik, Yvette Santiago, *21:* 136
Banner, Angela. *See* Maddison, Angela Mary
Bannerman, Helen, *19:* 13, 14
Bannon, Laura, *6:* 10; *23:* 8
Bare, Arnold Edwin, *16:* 31
Bargery, Geoffrey, *14:* 258
Barkley, James, *4:* 13; *6:* 11; *13:* 112
Barling, Tom, *9:* 23
Barnes, Hiram P., *20:* 28
Barnett, Moneta, *16:* 89; *19:* 142
Barney, Maginel Wright, *YABC 2:* 306
Barnum, Jay Hyde, *11:* 224; *20:* 5
Barrer-Russell, Gertrude, *9:* 65
Barrett, Ron, *14:* 24
Barron, John N., *3:* 261; *5:* 101; *14:* 220
Barrows, Walter, *14:* 268
Barry, Ethelred B., *YABC 1:* 229
Barry, James, *14:* 25
Barry, Katharina, *2:* 159; *4:* 22

Barry, Robert E., 6: 12
Barth, Ernest Kurt, 2: 172; 3: 160; 8: 26; 10: 31
Barton, Byron, 8: 207; 9: 18; 23: 66
Bartram, Robert, 10: 42
Bartsch, Jochen, 8: 105
Bate, Norman, 5: 16
Bauernschmidt, Marjorie, 15: 15
Baum, Allyn, 20: 10
Baum, Willi, 4: 24-25; 7: 173
Baumhauer, Hans, 11: 218; 15: 163, 165, 167
Baynes, Pauline, 2: 244; 3: 149; 13: 133, 135, 137-141; 19: 18, 19, 20
Beame, Rona, 12: 40
Beard, Dan, 22: 31, 32
Beard, J. H., YABC 1: 158
Bearden, Romare, 9: 7; 22: 35
Beardsley, Aubrey, 17: 14; 23: 181
Beaucé, J. A., 18: 103
Beck, Charles, 11: 169
Beck, Ruth, 13: 11
Becker, Harriet, 12: 211
Beckhoff, Harry, 1: 78; 5: 163
Bedford, F. D., 20: 118, 122
Bee, Joyce, 19: 62
Beech, Carol, 9: 149
Behr, Joyce, 15: 15; 21: 132; 23: 161
Behrens, Hans, 5: 97
Belden, Charles J., 12: 182
Bell, Corydon, 3: 20
Bemelmans, Ludwig, 15: 19, 21
Benda, W. T., 15: 256
Bendick, Jeanne, 2: 24
Bennett, F. I., YABC 1: 134
Bennett, Rainey, 15: 26; 23: 53
Bennett, Richard, 15: 45; 21: 11, 12, 13
Bennett, Susan, 5: 55
Benton, Thomas Hart, 2: 99
Berelson, Howard, 5: 20; 16: 58
Berenstain, Jan, 12: 47
Berenstain, Stan, 12: 47
Berg, Joan, 1: 115; 3: 156; 6: 26, 58
Berger, William M., 14: 143; YABC 1: 204
Bering, Claus, 13: 14
Berkowitz, Jeanette, 3: 249
Bernadette. See Watts, Bernadette
Bernstein, Zena, 23: 46
Berrill, Jacquelyn, 12: 50
Berry, Erick. See Best, Allena.
Berry, William A., 6: 219
Berry, William D., 14: 29; 19: 48
Berson, Harold, 2: 17-18; 4: 28-29, 220; 9: 10; 12: 19; 17: 45; 18: 193; 22: 85
Bertschmann, Harry, 16: 1
Beskow, Elsa, 20: 13, 14, 15
Best, Allena, 2: 26
Bethers, Ray, 6: 22
Bettina. See Ehrlich, Bettina
Betts, Ethel Franklin, 17: 161, 164-165; YABC 2: 47
Bewick, Thomas, 16: 40-41, 43-45, 47; YABC 1: 107
Bianco, Pamela, 15: 31
Bible, Charles, 13: 15
Bice, Clare, 22: 40
Biggers, John, 2: 123
Bileck, Marvin, 3: 102
Bimen, Levent, 5: 179
Birch, Reginald, 15: 150; 19: 33, 34, 35, 36; YABC 1: 84; YABC 2: 34, 39
Bird, Esther Brock, 1: 36
Birmingham, Lloyd, 12: 51
Biro, Val, 1: 26
Bjorklund, Lorence, 3: 188, 252; 7: 100; 9: 113; 10: 66; 19: 178; YABC 1: 242
Blackwell, Basil T., YABC 1: 68, 69
Blades, Ann, 16: 52
Blaisdell, Elinore, 1: 121; 3: 134
Blake, Quentin, 3: 170; 9: 21; 10: 48; 13: 38; 21: 180
Blass, Jacqueline, 8: 215
Blegvad, Erik, 2: 59; 3: 98; 5: 117; 7: 131; 11: 149; 14: 34, 35; 18: 237; YABC 1: 201
Bloch, Lucienne, 10: 12
Blumenschein, E. L., YABC 1: 113, 115
Boardman, Gwenn, 12: 60
Bock, Vera, 1: 187; 21: 41
Bock, William Sauts, 8: 7; 14: 37; 16: 120; 21: 141
Bodecker, N. M., 8: 13; 14: 2; 17: 55-57
Bohdal, Susi, 22: 44
Bolian, Polly, 3: 270; 4: 30; 13: 77
Bolognese, Don, 2: 147, 231; 4: 176; 7: 146; 17: 43; 23: 192
Bond, Arnold, 18: 116
Bond, Barbara Higgins, 21: 102
Bonsall, Crosby, 23: 6
Booth, Franklin, YABC 2: 76
Bordier, Georgette, 16: 54
Borja, Robert, 22: 48
Bornstein, Ruth, 14: 44
Borten, Helen, 3: 54; 5: 24
Boston, Peter, 19: 42
Bottner, Barbara, 14: 46
Bourke-White, Margaret, 15: 286-287
Bowser, Carolyn Ewing, 22: 253
Bozzo, Frank, 4: 154
Bradford, Ron, 7: 157
Bradley, William, 5: 164
Brady, Irene, 4: 31
Braithwaite, Althea, 23: 12-13
Bramley, Peter, 4: 3
Brandenberg, Aliki, 2: 36-37
Brandon, Brumsic, Jr., 9: 25
Bransom, Paul, 17: 121
Brenner, Fred, 22: 85
Brett, Bernard, 22: 54
Brick, John, 10: 15
Bridwell, Norman, 4: 37
Briggs, Raymond, 10: 168; 23: 20, 21
Brinckloe, Julie, 13: 18
Brisley, Joyce L., 22: 57
Brock, C. E., 15: 97; 19: 247, 249; 23: 224, 225; YABC 1: 194, 196, 203
Brock, Emma, 7: 21
Brock, Henry Matthew, 15: 81; 16: 141; 19: 71
Bromhall, Winifred, 5: 11
Brooke, L. Leslie, 16: 181-183, 186; 17: 15-17; 18: 194
Brooker, Christopher, 15: 251
Brotman, Adolph E., 5: 21
Brown, David, 7: 47
Brown, Denise, 11: 213
Brown, Judith Gwyn, 1: 45; 7: 5; 8: 167; 9: 182, 190; 20: 16, 17, 18; 23: 142
Brown, Marc Tolon, 10: 17, 197; 14: 263
Brown, Marcia, 7: 30; YABC 1: 27
Brown, Margery W., 5: 32-33; 10: 3
Browne, Dik, 8: 212
Browne, Gordon, 16: 97
Browne, Hablot K., 15: 80; 21: 14, 15, 16, 17, 18, 19, 20
Browning, Coleen, 4: 132
Bruce, Robert, 23: 23
Brule, Al, 3: 135
Brundage, Frances, 19: 244
Brychta, Alex, 21: 21
Bryson, Bernarda, 3: 88, 146
Buba, Joy, 12: 83
Buchanan, Lilian, 13: 16
Buck, Margaret Waring, 3: 30
Buehr, Walter, 3: 31
Buff, Conrad, 19: 52, 53, 54
Buff, Mary, 19: 52, 53
Bull, Charles Livingston, 18: 207
Bullen, Anne, 3: 166, 167
Burchard, Peter, 3: 197; 5: 35; 6: 158, 218
Burger, Carl, 3: 33
Burgeson, Marjorie, 19: 31
Burkert, Nancy Ekholm, 18: 186; 22: 140; YABC 1: 46
Burn, Doris, 6: 172
Burningham, John, 9: 68; 16: 60-61
Burns, Howard M., 12: 173
Burns, Raymond, 9: 29
Burr, Dane, 12: 2
Burra, Edward, YABC 2: 68
Burridge, Marge Opitz, 14: 42
Burris, Burmah, 4: 81
Burton, Virginia Lee, 2: 43; YABC 1: 24
Busoni, Rafaello, 1: 186; 3: 224; 6: 126; 14: 5; 16: 62-63
Butterfield, Ned, 1: 153
Buzzell, Russ W., 12: 177
Byfield, Barbara Ninde, 8: 18
Byrd, Robert, 13: 218

Caddy, Alice, *6:* 41
Cady, Harrison, *17:* 21, 23; *19:* 57, 58
Caldecott, Randolph, *16:* 98, 103; *17:* 32-33, 36, 38-39; *YABC 2:* 172
Calder, Alexander, *18:* 168
Caldwell, Doreen, *23:* 77
Callahan, Kevin, *22:* 42
Cameron, Julia Margaret, *19:* 203
Campbell, Ann, *11:* 43
Campbell, Walter M., *YABC 2:* 158
Caraway, James, *3:* 200-201
Carle, Eric, *4:* 42; *11:* 121; *12:* 29
Carrick, Donald, *5:* 194
Carrick, Valery, *21:* 47
Carroll, Lewis. *See* Dodgson, Charles L., *20:* 148; *YABC 2:* 98
Carroll, Ruth, *7:* 41; *10:* 68
Carter, Harry, *22:* 179
Carter, Helene, *15:* 38; *22:* 202, 203; *YABC 2:* 220-221
Carty, Leo, *4:* 196; *7:* 163
Cary, *4:* 133; *9:* 32; *20:* 2; *21:* 143
Cary, Page, *12:* 41
Case, Sandra E., *16:* 2
Cassel, Lili. *See* Wronker, Lili Cassel, *3:* 247; *10:* 204; *21:* 10
Cassels, Jean, *8:* 50
Cassel-Wronker, Lili. *See also* Wronker, Lili Cassel
Castle, Jane, *4:* 80
Cather, Carolyn, *3:* 83; *15:* 203
Cellini, Joseph, *2:* 73; *3:* 35; *16:* 116
Chalmers, Mary, *3:* 145; *13:* 148
Chambers, C. E., *17:* 230
Chambers, Dave, *12:* 151
Chambers, Mary, *4:* 188
Chapman, C. H., *13:* 83, 85, 87
Chapman, Frederick T., *6:* 27
Chappell, Warren, *3:* 172; *21:* 56
Charlip, Remy, *4:* 48
Charlot, Jean, *1:* 137, 138; *8:* 23; *14:* 31
Charmatz, Bill, *7:* 45
Chartier, Normand, *9:* 36
Chase, Lynwood M., *14:* 4
Chastain, Madye Lee, *4:* 50
Chen, Tony, *6:* 45; *19:* 131
Cheney, T. A., *11:* 47
Chess, Victoria, *12:* 6
Chew, Ruth, *7:* 46
Cho, Shinta, *8:* 126
Chorao, Kay, *7:* 200-201; *8:* 25; *11:* 234
Christensen, Gardell Dano, *1:* 57
Christy, Howard Chandler, *17:* 163-165, 168-169; *19:* 186, 187; *21:* 22, 23, 24, 25
Chronister, Robert, *23:* 138
Church, Frederick, *YABC 1:* 155
Chute, Marchette, *1:* 59
Chwast, Jacqueline, *1:* 63; *2:* 275; *6:* 46-47; *11:* 125; *12:* 202; *14:* 235
Chwast, Seymour, *3:* 128-129; *18:* 43
Cirlin, Edgard, *2:* 168
Clarke, Harry, *23:* 172, 173
Clayton, Robert, *9:* 181
Cleaver, Elizabeth, *8:* 204; *23:* 36
Clement, Charles, *20:* 38
Clevin, Jörgen, *7:* 50
Coalson, Glo, *9:* 72, 85
Cober, Alan, *17:* 158
Cochran, Bobbye, *11:* 52
CoConis, Ted, *4:* 41
Coerr, Eleanor, *1:* 64
Coggins, Jack, *2:* 69
Cohen, Alix, *7:* 53
Cohen, Vincent O., *19:* 243
Cohen, Vivien, *11:* 112
Colbert, Anthony, *15:* 41; *20:* 193
Colby, C. B., *3:* 47
Cole, Olivia H. H., *1:* 134; *3:* 223; *9:* 111
Collier, David, *13:* 127
Colonna, Bernard, *21:* 50
Connolly, Jerome P., *4:* 128
Cooke, Donald E., *2:* 77
Coombs, Patricia, *2:* 82; *3:* 52; *22:* 119
Cooney, Barbara, *6:* 16-17, 50; *12:* 42; *13:* 92; *15:* 145; *16:* 74, 111; *18:* 189; *23:* 38, 89, 93; *YABC 2:* 10
Cooper, Marjorie, *7:* 112
Copelman, Evelyn, *8:* 61; *18:* 25
Corbino, John, *19:* 248
Corcos, Lucille, *2:* 223; *10:* 27
Corey, Robert, *9:* 34
Corlass, Heather, *10:* 7
Cornell, Jeff, *11:* 58
Corrigan, Barbara, *8:* 37
Corwin, Judith Hoffman, *10:* 28
Cory, Fanny Y., *20:* 113
Cosgrove, Margaret, *3:* 100
Costello, David F., *23:* 55
Cox, Charles, *8:* 20
Craft, Kinuko, *22:* 182
Crane, Alan H., *1:* 217
Crane, H. M., *13:* 111
Crane, Walter, *18:* 46-49, 53-54, 56-57, 59-61; *22:* 128
Credle, Ellis *1:* 69
Crofut, Susan, *23:* 61
Crowell, Pers, *3:* 125
Cruikshank, George, *15:* 76, 83; *22:* 74, 75, 76, 77, 78, 79, 80, 81, 82, 84, 137
Crump, Fred H., *11:* 62
Cruz, Ray, *6:* 55
Cuffari, Richard, *4:* 75; *5:* 98; *6:* 56; *7:* 13, 84, 153; *8:* 148, 155; *9:* 89; *11:* 19; *12:* 55, 96, 114; *15:* 51, 202; *18:* 5; *20:* 139; *21:* 197; *22:* 14, 192; *23:* 15, 106
Cugat, Xavier, *19:* 120
Cunette, Lou, *20:* 93; *22:* 125
Cunningham, David, *11:* 13
Cunningham, Imogene, *16:* 122, 127
Curry, John Steuart, *2:* 5; *19:* 84
Curtis, Bruce, *23:* 96

D'Amato, Alex, *9:* 48; *20:* 25
D'Amato, Janet, *9:* 48; *20:* 25
Daniel, Alan, *23:* 59
Daniel, Lewis C., *20:* 216
Daniels, Steve, *22:* 16
Danyell, Alice, *20:* 27
Darley, F.O.C., *16:* 145; *19:* 79, 86, 88, 185; *21:* 28, 36; *YABC 2:* 175
Darling, Lois, *3:* 59; *23:* 30, 31
Darling, Louis, *1:* 40-41; *2:* 63; *3:* 59; *23:* 30, 31
Darrow, Whitney, Jr., *13:* 25
Dauber, Liz, *1:* 22; *3:* 266
Daugherty, James, *3:* 66; *8:* 178; *13:* 27-28, 161; *18:* 101; *19:* 72; *YABC 1:* 256; *YABC 2:* 174
d'Aulaire, Edgar, *5:* 51
d'Aulaire, Ingri, *5:* 51
David, Jonathan, *19:* 37
Davis, Allan, *20:* 11; *22:* 45
Davis, Bette J., *15:* 53; *23:* 95
Davis, Marguerite, *YABC 1:* 126, 230
Dean, Bob, *19:* 211
de Angeli, Marguerite, *1:* 77; *YABC 1:* 166
de Bosschère, Jean, *19:* 252; *21:* 4
De Bruyn, M(onica) G., *13:* 30-31
De Cuir, John F., *1:* 28-29
De Grazia, *14:* 59
de Groat, Diane, *9:* 39; *18:* 7; *23:* 123
de Groot, Lee, *6:* 21
Delaney, A., *21:* 78
de Larrea, Victoria, *6:* 119, 204
Delessert, Etienne, *7:* 140; *YABC 2:* 209
Delulio, John, *15:* 54
Denetsosie, Hoke, *13:* 126
Dennis, Morgan, *18:* 68-69
Dennis, Wesley, *2:* 87; *3:* 111; *11:* 132; *18:* 71-74; *22:* 9
Denslow, W. W., *16:* 84-87; *18:* 19-20, 24
de Paola, Tomie, *8:* 95; *9:* 93; *11:* 69
Detmold, Edward J., *22:* 104, 105, 106, 107; *YABC 2:* 203
Detrich, Susan, *20:* 133
DeVelasco, Joseph E., *21:* 51
de Veyrac, Robert, *YABC 2:* 19
DeVille, Edward A., *4:* 235
Devito, Bert, *12:* 164
Devlin, Harry, *11:* 74
Dewey, Ariane, *7:* 64
See also Aruego, Ariane
Diamond, Donna, *21:* 200; *23:* 63
Dick, John Henry, *8:* 181
Dickey, Robert L., *15:* 279
DiFiore, Lawrence, *10:* 51; *12:* 190
Dillard, Annie, *10:* 32

Dillon, Corinne B., *1:* 139
Dillon, Diane, *4:* 104, 167; *6:* 23; *13:* 29; *15:* 99
Dillon, Leo, *4:* 104, 167; *6:* 23; *13:* 29; *15:* 99
Dines, Glen, *7:* 66-67
Dinsdale, Mary, *10:* 65; *11:* 171
Dixon, Maynard, *20:* 165
Doares, Robert G., *20:* 39
Dobias, Frank, *22:* 162
Dobrin, Arnold, *4:* 68
Dodd, Ed, *4:* 69
Dodgson, Charles L., *20:* 148; *YABC 2:* 98
Dodson, Bert, *9:* 138; *14:* 195
Dohanos, Stevan, *16:* 10
Dolson, Hildegarde, *5:* 57
Domanska, Janina, *6:* 66-67; *YABC 1:* 166
Donahue, Vic, *2:* 93; *3:* 190; *9:* 44
Donald, Elizabeth, *4:* 18
Donna, Natalie, *9:* 52
Doré, Gustave, *18:* 169, 172, 175; *19:* 93, 94, 95, 96, 97, 98, 99, 100, 101, 102, 103, 104, 105; *23:* 188
Doremus, Robert, *6:* 62; *13:* 90
Dorfman, Ronald, *11:* 128
Dougherty, Charles, *16:* 204; *18:* 74
Douglas, Goray, *13:* 151
Dowd, Vic, *3:* 244; *10:* 97
Dowden, Anne Ophelia, *7:* 70-71; *13:* 120
Doyle, Richard, *21:* 31, 32, 33; *23:* 231
Drawson, Blair, *17:* 53
Drew, Patricia, *15:* 100
Drummond, V. H., *6:* 70
du Bois, William Pene, *4:* 70; *10:* 122
Duchesne, Janet, *6:* 162
Duke, Chris, *8:* 195
Dulac, Edmund, *19:* 108, 109, 110, 111, 112, 113, 114, 115, 117; *23:* 187; *YABC 1:* 37; *YABC 2:* 147
Dulac, Jean, *13:* 64
Dunn, Phoebe, *5:* 175
Dunn, Tris, *5:* 175
Dunnington, Tom, *3:* 36; *18:* 281
Dutz, *6:* 59
Duvoisin, Roger, *2:* 95; *6:* 76-77; *7:* 197
Dypold, Pat, *15:* 37

Eagle, Michael, *11:* 86; *20:* 9; *23:* 18
Earle, Olive L., *7:* 75
Eaton, Tom, *4:* 62; *6:* 64; *22:* 99
Ebel, Alex, *11:* 89
Ebert, Len, *9:* 191
Edrien, *11:* 53
Edwards, Gunvor, *2:* 71
Edwards, Linda Strauss, *21:* 134
Eggenhofer, Nicholas, *2:* 81
Egielski, Richard, *11:* 90; *16:* 208
Ehrlich, Bettina, *1:* 83
Eichenberg, Fritz, *1:* 79; *9:* 54; *19:* 248; *23:* 170; *YABC 1:* 104-105; *YABC 2:* 213
Einsel, Naiad, *10:* 35
Einsel, Walter, *10:* 37
Einzig, Susan, *3:* 77
Eitzen, Allan, *9:* 56; *12:* 212; *14:* 226; *21:* 194
Elgaard, Greta, *19:* 241
Elgin, Kathleen, *9:* 188
Ellacott, S. E., *19:* 118
Elliott, Sarah M., *14:* 58
Emberley, Ed, *8:* 53
Englebert, Victor, *8:* 54
Enos, Randall, *20:* 183
Enright, Maginel Wright, *19:* 240, 243
Erhard, Walter, *1:* 152
Erickson, Phoebe, *11:* 83
Escourido, Joseph, *4:* 81
Estrada, Ric, *5:* 52, 146; *13:* 174
Ets, Marie Hall, *2:* 102
Eulalie, *YABC 2:* 315
Evans, Katherine, *5:* 64
Ewing, Juliana Horatia, *16:* 92

Falls, C. B., *1:* 19
Faul-Jansen, Regina, *22:* 117
Faulkner, Jack, *6:* 169
Fava, Rita, *2:* 29
Fax, Elton C., *1:* 101; *4:* 2; *12:* 77
Feelings, Tom, *5:* 22; *8:* 56; *12:* 153; *16:* 105
Fehr, Terrence, *21:* 87
Feiffer, Jules, *3:* 91; *8:* 58
Fellows, Muriel H., *10:* 42
Fenton, Carroll Lane, *5:* 66; *21:* 39
Fenton, Mildred Adams, *5:* 66; *21:* 39
Fetz, Ingrid, *11:* 67; *12:* 52; *16:* 205; *17:* 59
Fiammenghi, Gioia, *9:* 66; *11:* 44; *12:* 206; *13:* 57, 59
Field, Rachel, *15:* 113
Fink, Sam, *18:* 119
Finlay, Winifred, *23:* 72
Fiorentino, Al, *3:* 240
Fisher, Leonard Everett, *3:* 6; *4:* 72, 86; *6:* 197; *9:* 59; *16:* 151, 153; *23:* 44; *YABC 2:* 169
Fisher, Lois, *20:* 62; *21:* 7
Fitschen, Marilyn, *2:* 20-21; *20:* 48
Fitzgerald, F. A., *15:* 116
Fitzhugh, Louise, *1:* 94; *9:* 163
Fitzhugh, Susie, *11:* 117
Fitzsimmons, Arthur, *14:* 128
Flack, Marjorie, *21:* 67; *YABC 2:* 122
Flagg, James Montgomery, *17:* 227
Flax, Zeona, *2:* 245
Fleishman, Seymour, *14:* 232
Fleming, Guy, *18:* 41
Floethe, Richard, *3:* 131; *4:* 90
Floherty, John J., Jr., *5:* 68
Flora, James, *1:* 96
Florian, Douglas, *19:* 122
Flory, Jane, *22:* 111
Floyd, Gareth, *1:* 74; *17:* 245
Flynn, Barbara, *7:* 31; *9:* 70
Fogarty, Thomas, *15:* 89
Folger, Joseph, *9:* 100
Folkard, Charles, *22:* 132
Forberg, Ati, *12:* 71, 205; *14:* 1; *22:* 113
Ford, H. J., *16:* 185-186
Foreman, Michael, *2:* 110-111
Fortnum, Peggy, *6:* 29; *20:* 179; *YABC 1:* 148
Foster, Genevieve, *2:* 112
Foster, Gerald, *7:* 78
Foster, Laura Louise, *6:* 79
Foster, Marian Curtis, *23:* 74
Fox, Charles Phillip, *12:* 84
Fox, Jim, *6:* 187
Fracé, Charles, *15:* 118
Frame, Paul, *2:* 45, 145; *9:* 153; *10:* 124; *21:* 71; *23:* 62
Francoise. *See* Seignobosc, Francoise, *21:* 145, 146
Frank, Lola Edick, *2:* 199
Frank, Mary, *4:* 54
Frankenberg, Robert, *22:* 116
Frascino, Edward, *9:* 133
Frasconi, Antonio, *6:* 80
Fraser, Betty, *2:* 212; *6:* 185; *8:* 103
Fraser, F. A., *22:* 234
Freeman, Don, *2:* 15; *13:* 249; *17:* 62-63, 65, 67-68; *18:* 243; *20:* 195; *23:* 213, 217
French, Fiona, *6:* 82-83
Friedman, Marvin, *19:* 59
Frith, Michael K., *15:* 138; *18:* 120
Frost, A. B., *17:* 6-7; *19:* 123, 124, 125, 126, 127, 128, 129, 130; *YABC 1:* 156-157, 160; *YABC 2:* 107
Fry, Guy, *2:* 224
Fry, Rosalie, *3:* 72; *YABC 2:* 180-181
Fry, Rosalind, *21:* 153, 168
Fuchs, Erich, *6:* 84
Fulford, Deborah, *23:* 159
Funk, Tom, *7:* 17, 99

Gaberell, J., *19:* 236
Gackenbach, Dick, *19:* 168
Gaetano, Nicholas, *23:* 209
Gag, Flavia, *17:* 49, 52
Gag, Wanda, *YABC 1:* 135, 137-138, 141, 143
Gagnon, Cécile, *11:* 77
Gal, Laszlo, *14:* 127
Galdone, Paul, *1:* 156, 181, 206; *2:* 40, 241; *3:* 42, 144; *4:* 141; *10:* 109, 158; *11:* 21; *12:* 118, 210; *14:* 12; *16:* 36-37; *17:* 70-74; *18:* 111, 230; *19:* 183; *21:* 154; *22:* 150, 245

Gallagher, Sears, *20:* 112
Galster, Robert, *1:* 66
Gammell, Stephen, *7:* 48; *13:* 149
Gannett, Ruth Chrisman, *3:* 74; *18:* 254
Garbutt, Bernard, *23:* 68
Garnett, Eve, *3:* 75
Garraty, Gail, *4:* 142
Garrett, Edmund H., *20:* 29
Garrison, Barbara, *19:* 133
Gaver, Becky, *20:* 61
Gay, Zhenya, *19:* 135, 136
Geary, Clifford N., *1:* 122; *9:* 104
Geer, Charles, *1:* 91; *3:* 179; *4:* 201; *6:* 168; *7:* 96; *9:* 58; *10:* 72; *12:* 127
Geisel, Theodor Seuss, *1:* 104-105, 106
Geldart, William, *15:* 121; *21:* 202
Genia, *4:* 84
Gentry, Cyrille R., *12:* 66
George, Jean, *2:* 113
Geritz, Franz, *17:* 135
Gervase, *12:* 27
Gibbons, Gail, *23:* 78
Giguère, George, *20:* 111
Gilbert, John, *19:* 184; *YABC 2:* 287
Gill, Margery, *4:* 57; *7:* 7; *22:* 122
Gillette, Henry J., *23:* 237
Gilman, Esther, *15:* 124
Giovanopoulos, Paul, *7:* 104
Githens, Elizabeth M., *5:* 47
Gladstone, Gary, *12:* 89; *13:* 190
Gladstone, Lise, *15:* 273
Glanzman, Louis S., *2:* 177; *3:* 182
Glaser, Milton, *3:* 5; *5:* 156; *11:* 107
Glass, Marvin, *9:* 174
Glattauer, Ned, *5:* 84; *13:* 224; *14:* 26
Glauber, Uta, *17:* 76
Gleeson, J. M., *YABC 2:* 207
Gliewe, Unada, *3:* 78-79; *21:* 73
Glovach, Linda, *7:* 105
Gobbato, Imero, *3:* 180-181; *6:* 213; *7:* 58; *9:* 150; *18:* 39; *21:* 167
Godfrey, Michael, *17:* 279
Goffstein, M. B., *8:* 71
Golbin, Andrée, *15:* 125
Goldfeder, Cheryl, *11:* 191
Goldsborough, June, *5:* 154-155; *8:* 92; *14:* 266; *19:* 139
Goldstein, Leslie, *5:* 8; *6:* 60; *10:* 106
Goldstein, Nathan, *1:* 175; *2:* 79; *11:* 41, 232; *16:* 55
Goodall, John S., *4:* 92-93; *10:* 132; *YABC 1:* 198
Goode, Diane, *15:* 126
Goodwin, Harold, *13:* 74
Goodwin, Philip R., *18:* 206
Gordon, Gwen, *12:* 151
Gordon, Margaret, *4:* 147; *5:* 48-49; *9:* 79
Gorecka-Egan, Erica, *18:* 35
Gorey, Edward, *1:* 60-61; *13:* 169; *18:* 192; *20:* 201
Gorsline, Douglas, *1:* 98; *6:* 13; *11:* 113; *13:* 104; *15:* 14; *YABC 1:* 15
Gosner, Kenneth, *5:* 135
Gotlieb, Jules, *6:* 127
Gough, Philip, *23:* 47
Grabianski, *20:* 144
Graham, A. B., *11:* 61
Graham, L., *7:* 108
Graham, Margaret Bloy, *11:* 120; *18:* 305, 307
Grahame-Johnstone, Anne, *13:* 61
Grahame-Johnstone, Janet, *13:* 61
Gramatky, Hardie, *1:* 107
Grant, Gordon, *17:* 230, 234; *YABC 1:* 164
Grant, (Alice) Leigh, *10:* 52; *15:* 131; *20:* 20
Gray, Reginald, *6:* 69
Green, Eileen, *6:* 97
Greenaway, Kate, *17:* 275; *YABC 1:* 88-89; *YABC 2:* 131, 133, 136, 138-139, 141
Greenwald, Sheila, *1:* 34; *3:* 99; *8:* 72
Greiffenhagen, Maurice, *16:* 137
Greifferhager, Maurice, *YABC 2:* 288
Greiner, Robert, *6:* 86
Gretz, Susanna, *7:* 114
Gretzer, John, *1:* 54; *3:* 26; *4:* 162; *7:* 125; *16:* 247; *18:* 117
Grieder, Walter, *9:* 84
Grifalconi, Ann, *2:* 126; *3:* 248; *11:* 18; *13:* 182
Gringhuis, Dirk, *6:* 98; *9:* 196
Gripe, Harald, *2:* 127
Grisha, *3:* 71
Grose, Helen Mason, *YABC 1:* 260; *YABC 2:* 150
Grossman, Robert, *11:* 124
Groth, John, *15:* 79; *21:* 53, 54
Gschwind, William, *11:* 72
Guggenheim, Hans, *2:* 10; *3:* 37; *8:* 136
Guilbeau, Honoré, *22:* 69
Guthrie, Robin, *20:* 122

Haas, Irene, *17:* 77
Hader, Berta H., *16:* 126
Hader, Elmer S., *16:* 126
Hafner, Marylin, *22:* 196, 216
Haldane, Roger, *13:* 76; *14:* 202
Hale, Kathleen, *17:* 79
Hall, Douglas, *15:* 184
Hall, H. Tom, *1:* 227
Hall, Vicki, *20:* 24
Halpern, Joan, *10:* 25
Hamberger, John, *6:* 8; *8:* 32; *14:* 79
Hamil, Tom, *14:* 80
Hamilton, Helen S., *2:* 238
Hamilton, J., *19:* 83, 85, 87
Hammond, Chris, *21:* 37
Hammond, Elizabeth, *5:* 36, 203
Hampshire, Michael, *5:* 187; *7:* 110-111
Hampson, Denman, *10:* 155; *15:* 130
Handville, Robert, *1:* 89
Hane, Roger, *17:* 239
Hanley, Catherine, *8:* 161
Hann, Jacquie, *19:* 144
Hanson, Joan, *8:* 76; *11:* 139
Hardy, David A., *9:* 96
Hardy, Paul, *YABC 2:* 245
Harlan, Jerry, *3:* 96
Harnischfeger, *18:* 121
Harper, Arthur, *YABC 2:* 121
Harrington, Richard, *5:* 81
Harrison, Florence, *20:* 150, 152
Harrison, Harry, *4:* 103
Hart, William, *13:* 72
Hartelius, Margaret, *10:* 24
Hartshorn, Ruth, *5:* 115; *11:* 129
Harvey, Gerry, *7:* 180
Hassell, Hilton, *YABC 1:* 187
Hasselriis, Else, *18:* 87; *YABC 1:* 96
Hauman, Doris, *2:* 184
Hauman, George, *2:* 184
Hausherr, Rosmarie, *15:* 29
Hawkinson, John, *4:* 109; *7:* 83; *21:* 64
Hawkinson, Lucy, *21:* 64
Haydock, Robert, *4:* 95
Haywood, Carolyn, *1:* 112
Healy, Daty, *12:* 143
Hechtkopf, H., *11:* 110
Heigh, James, *22:* 98
Henneberger, Robert, *1:* 42; *2:* 237
Henry, Thomas, *5:* 102
Henstra, Friso, *8:* 80
Herbert, Wally, *23:* 101
Herbster, Mary Lee, *9:* 33
Hergé. *See* Remi, Georges
Hermanson, Dennis, *10:* 55
Herrington, Roger, *3:* 161
Heustis, Louise L., *20:* 28
Heyduck-Huth, Hilde, *8:* 82
Heyer, Hermann, *20:* 114, 115
Heyman, Ken, *8:* 33
Higginbottom, J. Winslow, *8:* 170
Hildebrandt, Greg, *8:* 191
Hildebrandt, Tim, *8:* 191
Hilder, Rowland, *19:* 207
Himler, Ronald, *6:* 114; *7:* 162; *8:* 17, 84, 125; *14:* 76; *19:* 145
Hirsh, Marilyn, *7:* 126
Hitz, Demi, *11:* 135; *15:* 245
Ho, Kwoncjan, *15:* 132
Hoban, Lillian, *1:* 114; *22:* 157
Hoban, Tana, *22:* 159
Hoberman, Norman, *5:* 82
Hodges, C. Walter, *2:* 139; *11:* 15; *12:* 25; *23:* 34; *YABC 2:* 62-63
Hodges, David, *9:* 98
Hofbauer, Imre, *2:* 162
Hoff, Syd, *9:* 107; *10:* 128
Hoffman, Rosekrans, *15:* 133
Hoffmann, Felix, *9:* 109

Illustrations Index

Hofsinde, Robert, *21:* 70
Hogan, Inez, *2:* 141
Hogarth, Paul, *YABC 1:* 16
Hogenbyl, Jan, *1:* 35
Hogner, Nils, *4:* 122
Hogrogian, Nonny, *3:* 221; *4:* 106-107; *5:* 166; *7:* 129; *15:* 2; *16:* 176; *20:* 154; *22:* 146; *YABC 2:* 84, 94
Holberg, Richard, *2:* 51
Holiday, Henry, *YABC 2:* 107
Holland, Janice, *18:* 118
Holland, Marion, *6:* 116
Holling, Holling C., *15:* 136-137
Hollinger, Deanne, *12:* 116
Holmes, B., *3:* 82
Holmes, Bea, *7:* 74
Holz, Loretta, *17:* 81
Homar, Lorenzo, *6:* 2
Homer, Winslow, *YABC 2:* 87
Honigman, Marian, *3:* 2
Hood, Susan, *12:* 43
Hook, Jeff, *14:* 137
Hoover, Carol A., *21:* 77
Hoover, Russell, *12:* 95; *17:* 2
Horder, Margaret, *2:* 108
Horvat, Laurel, *12:* 201
Hotchkiss, De Wolfe, *20:* 49
Hough, Charlotte, *9:* 112; *13:* 98; *17:* 83
Houlihan, Ray, *11:* 214
Houston, James, *13:* 107
How, W. E., *20:* 47
Howard, Alan, *16:* 80
Howard, J. N., *15:* 234
Howe, Stephen, *1:* 232
Howell, Pat, *15:* 139
Howell, Troy, *23:* 24
Howes, Charles, *22:* 17
Hudnut, Robin, *14:* 62
Huffaker, Sandy, *10:* 56
Huffman, Joan, *13:* 33
Huffman, Tom, *13:* 180; *17:* 212; *21:* 116
Hughes, Arthur, *20:* 148, 149, 150
Hughes, Shirley, *1:* 20, 21; *7:* 3; *12:* 217; *16:* 163
Hülsmann, Eva, *16:* 166
Hummel, Lisl, *YABC 2:* 333-334
Humphrey, Henry, *16:* 167
Hunt, James, *2:* 143
Hurd, Clement, *2:* 148, 149
Hurd, Peter, *YABC 2:* 56
Hustler, Tom, *6:* 105
Hutchins, Pat, *15:* 142
Hutchinson, William M., *6:* 3, 138
Hutchison, Paula, *23:* 10
Hutton, Clarke, *YABC 2:* 335
Hutton, Warwick, *20:* 91
Hyman, Trina Schart, *1:* 204; *2:* 194; *5:* 153; *6:* 106; *7:* 138, 145; *8:* 22; *10:* 196; *13:* 96; *14:* 114; *15:* 204; *16:* 234; *20:* 82; *22:* 133

Ide, Jacqueline, *YABC 1:* 39
Ilsley, Velma, *3:* 1; *7:* 55; *12:* 109
Inga, *1:* 142
Ingraham, Erick, *21:* 177
Innocenti, Roberto, *21:* 123
Ipcar, Dahlov, *1:* 124-125
Irvin, Fred, *13:* 166; *15:* 143-144
Isaac, Joanne, *21:* 76
Ives, Ruth, *15:* 257

Jacobs, Barbara, *9:* 136
Jacobs, Lou, Jr., *9:* 136; *15:* 128
Jacques, Robin, *1:* 70; *2:* 1; *8:* 46; *9:* 20; *15:* 187; *19:* 253; *YABC 1:* 42
Jagr, Miloslav, *13:* 197
Jakubowski, Charles, *14:* 192
Jambor, Louis, *YABC 1:* 11
James, Gilbert, *YABC 1:* 43
James, Harold, *2:* 151; *3:* 62; *8:* 79
James, Will, *19:* 150, 152, 153, 155, 163
Janosch. *See* Eckert, Horst
Jansson, Tove, *3:* 90
Jaques, Faith, *7:* 11, 132-33; *21:* 83, 84
Jauss, Anne Marie, *1:* 139; *3:* 34; *10:* 57, 119; *11:* 205; *23:* 194
Jeffers, Susan, *17:* 86-87
Jefferson, Louise E., *4:* 160
Jeruchim, Simon, *6:* 173; *15:* 250
Jeschke, Susan, *20:* 89
John, Diana, *12:* 209
John, Helen, *1:* 215
Johnson, Bruce, *9:* 47
Johnson, Crockett. *See* Leisk, David
Johnson, D. William, *23:* 104
Johnson, Harper, *1:* 27; *2:* 33; *18:* 302; *19:* 61
Johnson, James David, *12:* 195
Johnson, James Ralph, *1:* 23, 127
Johnson, Milton, *1:* 67; *2:* 71
Johnson, Pamela, *16:* 174
Johnstone, Anne, *8:* 120
Johnstone, Janet Grahame, *8:* 120
Jones, Carol, *5:* 131
Jones, Elizabeth Orton, *18:* 124, 126, 128-129
Jones, Harold, *14:* 88
Jones, Wilfred, *YABC 1:* 163
Jucker, Sita, *5:* 93
Jupo, Frank, *7:* 148-149

Kakimoo, Kozo, *11:* 148
Kalmenoff, Matthew, *22:* 191
Kamen, Gloria, *1:* 41; *9:* 119; *10:* 178
Kane, Henry B., *14:* 90; *18:* 219-220
Kane, Robert, *18:* 131
Karlin, Eugene, *10:* 63; *20:* 131
Katona, Robert, *21:* 85
Kaufman, Angelika, *15:* 156
Kaufman, John, *13:* 158
Kaufmann, John, *1:* 174; *4:* 159; *8:* 43, 192; *10:* 102; *18:* 133-134; *22:* 251
Kaye, Graham, *1:* 9
Keane, Bil, *4:* 135
Keats, Ezra Jack, *3:* 18, 105, 257; *14:* 101, 102
Keegan, Marcia, *9:* 122
Keeping, Charles, *9:* 124, 185; *15:* 28, 134; *18:* 115
Keith, Eros, *4:* 98; *5:* 138
Kelen, Emery, *13:* 115
Kellogg, Steven, *8:* 96; *11:* 207; *14:* 130; *20:* 58; *YABC 1:* 65, 73
Kelly, Walt, *18:* 136-141, 144-146, 148-149
Kemble, E. W., *YABC 2:* 54, 59
Kennedy, Paul Edward, *6:* 190; *8:* 132
Kennedy, Richard, *3:* 93; *12:* 179; *YABC 1:* 57
Kent, Rockwell, *5:* 166; *6:* 129; *20:* 225, 226, 227, 229
Kepes, Juliet, *13:* 119
Kessler, Leonard, *1:* 108; *7:* 139; *14:* 107, 227; *22:* 101
Kettelkamp, Larry, *2:* 164
Key, Alexander, *8:* 99
Kiakshuk, *8:* 59
Kiddell-Monroe, Joan, *19:* 201
Kidder, Harvey, *9:* 105
Kimball, Yeffe, *23:* 116
Kindred, Wendy, *7:* 151
King, Robin, *10:* 164-165
Kingman, Dong, *16:* 287
Kingsley, Charles, *YABC 2:* 182
Kipling, John Lockwood, *YABC 2:* 198
Kipling, Rudyard, *YABC 2:* 196
Kirk, Ruth, *5:* 96
Kirmse, Marguerite, *15:* 283; *18:* 153
Kirschner, Ruth, *22:* 154
Klapholz, Mel, *13:* 35
Knight, Christopher, *13:* 125
Knight, Hilary, *1:* 233; *3:* 21; *15:* 92, 158-159; *16:* 258-260; *18:* 235; *19:* 169; *YABC 1:* 168-169, 172
Knotts, Howard, *20:* 4
Kocsis, J. C. *See* Paul, James
Koering, Ursula, *3:* 28; *4:* 14
Koerner, Henry. *See* Koerner, W.H.D.
Koerner, W. H. D., *14:* 216; *21:* 88, 89, 90, 91; *23:* 211
Komoda, Kiyo *9:* 128; *13:* 214
Konashevicha, V., *YABC 1:* 26
Konigsburg, E. L., *4:* 138
Korach, Mimi, *1:* 128-129; *2:* 52; *4:* 39; *5:* 159; *9:* 129; *10:* 21
Koren, Edward, *5:* 100
Kossin, Sandy, *10:* 71; *23:* 105
Kovacević, Zivojin, *13:* 247
Krahn, Fernando, *2:* 257

Kramer, Frank, *6:* 121
Kraus, Robert, *13:* 217
Kredel, Fritz, *6:* 35; *17:* 93-96; *22:* 147; *YABC 2:* 166, 300
Krementz, Jill, *17:* 98
Kresin, Robert, *23:* 19
Krush, Beth, *1:* 51, 85; *2:* 233; *4:* 115; *9:* 61; *10:* 191; *11:* 196; *18:* 164-165
Krush, Joe, *2:* 233; *4:* 115; *9:* 61; *10:* 191; *11:* 196; *18:* 164-165
Kubinyi, Laszlo, *4:* 116; *6:* 113; *16:* 118; *17:* 100
Kuhn, Bob, *17:* 91
Künstler, Mort, *10:* 73
Kurelek, William, *8:* 107
Kuriloff, Ron, *13:* 19
Kuskin, Karla, *2:* 170
Kutzer, Ernst, *19:* 249

La Croix, *YABC 2:* 4
Laimgruber, Monika, *11:* 153
Laite, Gordon, *1:* 130-131; *8:* 209
Lamb, Jim, *10:* 117
Lambert, Saul, *23:* 112
Lambo, Don, *6:* 156
Landa, Peter, *11:* 95; *13:* 177
Landshoff, Ursula, *13:* 124
Lane, John, *15:* 176-177
Lane, John R., *8:* 145
Lang, Jerry, *18:* 295
Langler, Nola, *8:* 110
Lantz, Paul, *1:* 82, 102
Larsen, Suzanne, *1:* 13
Larsson, Karl, *19:* 177
La Rue, Michael D., *13:* 215
Lasker, Joe, *7:* 186-187; *14:* 55
Laham, Barbara, *16:* 188-189
Lathrop, Dorothy, *14:* 117, 118-119; *15:* 109; *16:* 78-79, 81; *YABC 2:* 301
Lattimore, Eleanor Frances, *7:* 156
Lauden, Claire, *16:* 173
Lauden, George, Jr., *16:* 173
Laune, Paul, *2:* 235
Lawrence, Stephen, *20:* 195
Lawson, Carol, *6:* 38
Lawson, George, *17:* 280
Lawson, Robert, *5:* 26; *6:* 94; *13:* 39; *16:* 11; *20:* 100, 102, 103; *YABC 2:* 222, 224-225, 227-235, 237-241
Lazarevich, Mila, *17:* 118
Lazarus, Keo Felker, *21:* 94
Lazzaro, Victor, *11:* 126
Leacroft, Richard, *6:* 140
Leaf, Munro, *20:* 99
Leander, Patricia, *23:* 27
Lear, Edward, *18:* 183-185
Lebenson, Richard, *6:* 209; *7:* 76; *23:* 145
Le Cain, Errol, *6:* 141; *9:* 3; *22:* 142
Lee, Doris, *13:* 246
Lee, Manning de V., *2:* 200; *17:* 12; *YABC 2:* 304
Lee, Robert J., *3:* 97
Leech, John, *15:* 59
Lees, Harry, *6:* 112
Legrand, Edy, *18:* 89, 93
Lehrman, Rosalie, *2:* 180
Leichman, Seymour, *5:* 107
Leisk, David, *1:* 140-141; *11:* 54
Leloir, Maurice, *18:* 77, 80, 83, 99
Lemke, Horst, *14:* 98
Lemon, David Gwynne, *9:* 1
Lenski, Lois, *1:* 144
Lent, Blair, *1:* 116-117; *2:* 174; *3:* 206-207; *7:* 168-169
Lerner, Sharon, *11:* 157; *22:* 56
Leslie, Cecil, *19:* 244
Levin, Ted, *12:* 148
Levy, Jessica Ann, *19:* 225
Lewin, Ted, *4:* 77; *8:* 168; *20:* 110; *21:* 99, 100
Lewis, Allen, *15:* 112
Leydon, Rita Flodén, *21:* 101
Lieblich, Irene, *22:* 173
Liese, Charles, *4:* 222
Lilly, Charles, *8:* 73; *20:* 127
Lindberg, Howard, *10:* 123; *16:* 190
Linden, Seymour, *18:* 200-201
Linell. *See* Smith, Linell
Lionni, Leo, *8:* 115
Lipinsky, Lino, *2:* 156; *22:* 175
Lippman, Peter, *8:* 31
Lisker, Sonia O., *16:* 274
Lissim, Simon, *17:* 138
Little, Harold, *16:* 72
Livesly, Lorna, *19:* 216
Llerena, Carlos Antonio, *19:* 181
Lloyd, Errol, *11:* 39; *22:* 178
Lo, Koon-chiu, *7:* 134
Lobel, Anita, *6:* 87; *9:* 141; *18:* 248
Lobel, Arnold, *1:* 188-189; *5:* 12; *6:* 147; *7:* 167, 209; *18:* 190-191
Loefgren, Ulf, *3:* 108
Loescher, Ann, *20:* 108
Loescher, Gil, *20:* 108
Lofting, Hugh, *15:* 182-183
Lonette, Reisie, *11:* 211; *12:* 168; *13:* 56
Longtemps, Ken, *17:* 123
Looser, Heinz, *YABC 2:* 208
Lopshire, Robert, *6:* 149; *21:* 117
Lord, John Vernon, *21:* 104; *23:* 25
Lorraine, Walter H., *3:* 110; *4:* 123; *16:* 192
Loss, Joan, *11:* 163
Louderback, Walt, *YABC 1:* 164
Low, Joseph, *14:* 124, 125; *18:* 68; *19:* 194
Lowenheim, Afred, *13:* 65-66
Lowitz, Anson, *17:* 124; *18:* 215
Lowrey, Jo, *8:* 133
Lubell, Winifred, *1:* 207; *3:* 15; *6:* 151
Lubin, Leonard B., *19:* 224; *YABC 2:* 96
Luhrs, Henry, *7:* 123; *11:* 120
Lupo, Dom, *4:* 204
Lydecker, Laura, *21:* 113
Lynch, Charles, *16:* 33
Lyon, Elinor, *6:* 154
Lyon, Fred, *14:* 16
Lyons, Oren, *8:* 193

Maas, Dorothy, *6:* 175
Macdonald, Alister, *21:* 55
MacDonald, Norman, *13:* 99
MacDonald, Roberta, *19:* 237
Macguire, Robert Reid, *18:* 67
MacIntyre, Elisabeth, *17:* 127-128
Mack, Stan, *17:* 129
Mackay, Donald, *17:* 60
Mackinstry, Elizabeth, *15:* 110
Maclise, Daniel, *YABC 2:* 257
Madden, Don, *3:* 112-113; *4:* 33, 108, 155; *7:* 193; *YABC 2:* 211
Maddison, Angela Mary, *10:* 83
Maestro, Giulio, *8:* 124; *12:* 17; *13:* 108
Maik, Henri, *9:* 102
Maitland, Antony, *1:* 100, 176; *8:* 41; *17:* 246
Malvern, Corrine, *2:* 13
Manet, Edouard, *23:* 170
Mangurian, David, *14:* 133
Manning, Samuel F., *5:* 75
Maraja, *15:* 86; *YABC 1:* 28; *YABC 2:* 115
Marcellino, Fred, *20:* 125
Marchiori, Carlos, *14:* 60
Margules, Gabriele, *21:* 120
Mariana. *See* Foster, Marian Curtis
Marino, Dorothy, *6:* 37; *14:* 135
Markham, R. L., *17:* 240
Mars, W. T., *1:* 161; *3:* 115; *4:* 208, 225; *5:* 92, 105, 186; *8:* 214; *9:* 12; *13:* 121
Marsh, Christine, *3:* 164
Marsh, Reginald, *17:* 5; *19:* 89; *22:* 90, 96
Marshall, Anthony D., *18:* 216
Marshall, James, *6:* 160
Martin, David Stone, *23:* 232
Martin, Fletcher, *18:* 213; *23:* 151
Martin, Rene, *7:* 144
Martin, Stefan, *8:* 68
Martinez, John, *6:* 113
Masefield, Judith, *19:* 208, 209
Mason, George F., *14:* 139
Massie, Diane Redfield, *16:* 194
Matsubara, Naoko, *12:* 121
Matsuda, Shizu, *13:* 167
Matte, L'Enc, *22:* 183
Matthews, F. Leslie, *4:* 216
Matthieu, Joseph, *14:* 33
Matulay, Laszlo, *5:* 18
Matus, Greta, *12:* 142
Mawicke, Tran, *9:* 137; *15:* 191
Maxwell, John Alan, *1:* 148
Mayan, Earl, *7:* 193
Mayer, Mercer, *11:* 192; *16:* 195-196; *20:* 55, 57
Mayhew, Richard, *3:* 106

Mays, Victor, *5:* 127; *8:* 45, 153; *14:* 245; *23:* 50
Mazza, Adriana Saviozzi, *19:* 215
McCann, Gerald, *3:* 50; *4:* 94; *7:* 54
McClary, Nelson, *1:* 111
McClintock, Theodore, *14:* 141
McCloskey, Robert, *1:* 184-185; *2:* 186-187; *17:* 209
McClung, Robert, *2:* 189
McCormick, Dell J., *19:* 216
McCrady, Lady, *16:* 198
McCrea, James, *3:* 122
McCrea, Ruth, *3:* 122
McCully, Emily, *2:* 89; *4:* 120-121, 146, 197; *5:* 2, 129; *7:* 191; *11:* 122; *15:* 210
McCurdy, Michael, *13:* 153
McDermott, Beverly Brodsky, *11:* 180
McDermott, Gerald, *16:* 201
McDonald, Jill, *13:* 155
McDonald, Ralph J., *5:* 123, 195
McDonough, Don, *10:* 163
McFall, Christie, *12:* 144
McGee, Barbara, *6:* 165
McGregor, Malcolm, *23:* 27
McHugh, Tom, *23:* 64
McKay, Donald, *2:* 118
McKee, David, *10:* 48; *21:* 9
McKie, Roy, *7:* 44
McLachlan, Edward, *5:* 89
McMillan, Bruce, *22:* 184
McNaught, Harry, *12:* 80
McPhail, David, *14:* 105; *23:* 135
McVay, Tracy, *11:* 68
Meddaugh, Susan, *20:* 42
Melo, John, *16:* 285
Mendelssohn, Felix, *19:* 170
Meng, Heinz, *13:* 158
Merrill, Frank T., *16:* 147; *19:* 71; *YABC 1:* 226, 229, 273
Meryweather, Jack; *10:* 179
Meyer, Herbert, *19:* 189
Meyer, Renate, *6:* 170
Meyers, Bob, *11:* 136
Micale, Albert, *2:* 65; *22:* 185
Middleton-Sandford, Betty, *2:* 125
Mikolaycak, Charles, *9:* 144; *12:* 101; *13:* 212; *21:* 121; *22:* 168
Miles, Jennifer, *17:* 278
Milhous, Katherine, *15:* 193; *17:* 51
Millais, John E., *22:* 230, 231
Millar, H. R., *YABC 1:* 194-195, 203
Miller, Don, *15:* 195; *16:* 71; *20:* 106
Miller, Grambs, *18:* 38; *23:* 16
Miller, Jane, *15:* 196
Miller, Marcia, *13:* 233
Miller, Marilyn, *1:* 87
Miller, Shane, *5:* 140
Mizumura Kazue, *10:* 143; *18:* 223
Mochi, Ugo, *8:* 122
Mohr, Nicholasa, *8:* 139
Montresor, Beni, *2:* 91; *3:* 138
Moon, Eliza, *14:* 40
Moon, Ivan, *22:* 39
Mora, Raul Mina, *20:* 41
Mordvinoff, Nicolas, *15:* 179
Morrill, Leslie, *18:* 218
Morrow, Gray, *2:* 64; *5:* 200; *10:* 103, 114; *14:* 175
Morton, Marian, *3:* 185
Moses, Grandma, *18:* 228
Moss, Donald, *11:* 184
Moyers, William, *21:* 65
Mozley, Charles, *9:* 87; *20:* 176, 192, 193; *22:* 228; *YABC 2:* 89
Mugnaini, Joseph, *11:* 35
Mullins, Edward S., *10:* 101
Munari, Bruno, *15:* 200
Munowitz, Ken, *14:* 148
Munson, Russell, *13:* 9
Murphy, Bill, *5:* 138
Murr, Karl, *20:* 62
Mutchler, Dwight, *1:* 25
Myers, Bernice, *9:* 147
Myers, Lou, *11:* 2

Nakatani, Chiyoko, *12:* 124
Nason, Thomas W., *14:* 68
Nast, Thomas, *21:* 29
Natti, Susanna, *20:* 146
Navarra, Celeste Scala, *8:* 142
Naylor, Penelope, *10:* 104
Neebe, William, *7:* 93
Needler, Jerry, *12:* 93
Negri, Rocco, *3:* 213; *5:* 67; *6:* 91, 108; *12:* 159
Neill, John R., *18:* 8, 10-11, 21, 30
Ness, Evaline, *1:* 164-165; *2:* 39; *3:* 8; *10:* 147; *12:* 53
Neville, Vera, *2:* 182
Newberry, Clare Turlay, *1:* 170
Newfeld, Frank, *14:* 121
Nicholson, William, *15:* 33-34; *16:* 48
Nickless, Will, *16:* 139
Nicolas, *17:* 130, 132-133; *YABC 2:* 215
Niebrugge, Jane, *6:* 118
Nielsen, Jon, *6:* 100
Nielsen, Kay, *15:* 7; *16:* 211-213, 215, 217; *22:* 143; *YABC 1:* 32-33
Ninon, *1:* 5
Nixon, K., *14:* 152
Noonan, Julia, *4:* 163; *7:* 207
Nordenskjold, Birgitta, *2:* 208
Norman, Michael, *12:* 117
Nussbaumer, Paul, *16:* 219
Nyce, Helene, *19:* 219

Oakley, Graham, *8:* 112
Oakley, Thornton, *YABC 2:* 189
Obligado, Lilian, *2:* 28, 66-67; *6:* 30; *14:* 179; *15:* 103
Obrant, Susan, *11:* 186
Oechsli, Kelly, *5:* 144-145; *7:* 115; *8:* 83, 183; *13:* 117; *20:* 94
Ohlsson, Ib, *4:* 152; *7:* 57; *10:* 20; *11:* 90; *19:* 217
Oliver, Jenni, *23:* 121
Olschewski, Alfred, *7:* 172
Olsen, Ib Spang, *6:* 178-179
Olugebefola, Ademola, *15:* 205
O'Neil, Dan IV, *7:* 176
O'Neill, Jean, *22:* 146
O'Neill, Steve, *21:* 118
Ono, Chiyo, *7:* 97
Orbaan, Albert, *2:* 31; *5:* 65, 171; *9:* 8; *14:* 241; *20:* 109
Orbach, Ruth, *21:* 112
Orfe, Joan, *20:* 81
Ormsby, Virginia H., *11:* 187
Orozco, José Clemente, *9:* 177
Orr, Forrest W., *23:* 9
Orr, N., *19:* 70
Osmond, Edward, *10:* 111
O'Sullivan, Tom, *3:* 176; *4:* 55
Otto, Svend, *22:* 130, 141
Oudry, J. B., *18:* 167
Oughton, Taylor, *5:* 23
Overlie, George, *11:* 156
Owens, Carl, *2:* 35; *23:* 52
Owens, Gail, *10:* 170; *12:* 157; *19:* 16; *22:* 70
Oxenbury, Helen, *3:* 150-151

Padgett, Jim, *12:* 165
Page, Homer, *14:* 145
Pak, *12:* 76
Palazzo, Tony, *3:* 152-153
Palladini, David, *4:* 113
Palmer, Heidi, *15:* 207
Palmer, Juliette, *6:* 89; *15:* 208
Palmer, Lemuel, *17:* 25, 29
Panesis, Nicholas, *3:* 127
Papas, William, *11:* 223
Papish, Robin Lloyd, *10:* 80
Paraquin, Charles H., *18:* 166
Park, W. B., *22:* 189
Parker, Lewis, *2:* 179
Parker, Nancy Winslow, *10:* 113; *22:* 164
Parker, Robert, *4:* 161; *5:* 74; *9:* 136
Parker, Robert Andrew, *11:* 81
Parnall, Peter, *5:* 137; *16:* 221
Parrish, Maxfield, *14:* 160, 161, 164, 165; *16:* 109; *18:* 12-13; *YABC 1:* 149, 152, 267; *YABC 2:* 146, 149
Parry, Marian, *13:* 176; *19:* 179
Pascal, David, *14:* 174
Pasquier, J. A., *16:* 91
Paterson, Diane, *13:* 116
Paterson, Helen, *16:* 93
Paton, Jane, *15:* 271
Paul, James, *4:* 130; *23:* 161
Payne, Joan Balfour, *1:* 118
Payson, Dale, *7:* 34; *9:* 151; *20:* 140
Payzant, Charles, *21:* 147
Peake, Mervyn, *22:* 136, 149; *23:* 162, 163, 164; *YABC 2:* 307

Peat, Fern B., *16:* 115
Peck, Anne Merrimann, *18:* 241
Pederson, Sharleen, *12:* 92
Pedersen, Vilhelm, *YABC 1:* 40
Peet, Bill, *2:* 203
Peltier, Leslie C., *13:* 178
Pendle, Alexy, *7:* 159; *13:* 34
Peppe, Rodney, *4:* 164-165
Perl, Susan, *2:* 98; *4:* 231; *5:* 44-45, 118; *6:* 199; *8:* 137; *12:* 88; *22:* 193; *YABC 1:* 176
Pesek, Ludek, *15:* 237
Petersham, Maud, *17:* 108, 147-153
Petersham, Miska, *17:* 108, 147-153
Peterson, R. F., *7:* 101
Peterson, Russell, *7:* 130
Petie, Haris, *2:* 3; *10:* 41, 118; *11:* 227; *12:* 70
Petrides, Heidrun, *19:* 223
Peyton, K. M., *15:* 212
Pfeifer, Herman, *15:* 262
Phillips, Douglas, *1:* 19
Phillips, F. D., *6:* 202
"Phiz." *See* Browne, Hablot K., *15:* 65; *21:* 14, 15, 16, 17, 18, 19, 20
Piatti, Celestino, *16:* 223
Picarella, Joseph, *13:* 147
Pickard, Charles, *12:* 38; *18:* 203
Picken, George A., *23:* 150
Pickens, David, *22:* 156
Pienkowski, Jan, *6:* 183
Pimlott, John, *10:* 205
Pincus, Harriet, *4:* 186; *8:* 179; *22:* 148
Pinkney, Jerry, *8:* 218; *10:* 40; *15:* 276; *20:* 66
Pinkwater, Manus, *8:* 156
Pinto, Ralph, *10:* 131
Pitz, Henry C., *4:* 168; *19:* 165; *YABC 2:* 95, 176
Pogany, Willy, *15:* 46, 49; *19:* 222, 256
Polgreen, John, *21:* 44
Politi, Leo, *1:* 178; *4:* 53; *21:* 48
Polseno, Jo, *1:* 53; *3:* 117; *5:* 114; *17:* 154; *20:* 87
Ponter, James, *5:* 204
Poortvliet, Rien, *6:* 212
Portal, Colette, *6:* 186; *11:* 203
Porter, George, *7:* 181
Potter, Beatrix, *YABC 1:* 208-210, 212, 213
Potter, Miriam Clark, *3:* 162
Powers, Richard M., *1:* 230; *3:* 218; *7:* 194
Pratt, Charles, *23:* 29
Price, Christine, *2:* 247; *3:* 163, 253; *8:* 166
Price, Garrett, *1:* 76; *2:* 42
Price, Hattie Longstreet, *17:* 13
Price, Norman, *YABC 1:* 129
Prince, Leonora E., *7:* 170
Prittie, Edwin J., *YABC 1:* 120
Pudlo, *8:* 59
Purdy, Susan, *8:* 162
Puskas, James, *5:* 141
Pyk, Jan, *7:* 26
Pyle, Howard, *16:* 225-228, 230-232, 235

Quackenbush, Robert, *4:* 190; *6:* 166; *7:* 175, 178; *9:* 86; *11:* 65, 221
Quidor, John, *19:* 82
Quirk, Thomas, *12:* 81

Rackham, Arthur, *15:* 32, 78, 214-227; *17:* 105, 115; *18:* 233; *19:* 254; *20:* 151; *22:* 129, 131, 132, 133; *23:* 175; *YABC 1:* 25, 45, 55, 147; *YABC 2:* 103, 142, 173, 210
Rafilson, Sidney, *11:* 172
Raible, Alton, *1:* 202-203
Ramsey, James, *16:* 41
Ransome, Arthur, *22:* 201
Rand, Paul, *6:* 188
Raphael, Elaine, *23:* 192
Rappaport, Eva, *6:* 190
Raskin, Ellen, *2:* 208-209; *4:* 142; *13:* 183; *22:* 68
Rau, Margaret, *9:* 157
Raverat, Gwen, *YABC 1:* 152
Ravielli, Anthony, *1:* 198; *3:* 168; *11:* 143
Ray, Deborah, *8:* 164
Ray, Ralph, *2:* 239; *5:* 73
Rayner, Mary, *22:* 207
Razzi, James, *10:* 127
Read, Alexander D. "Sandy," *20:* 45
Reid, Stephen, *19:* 213; *22:* 89
Reiss, John J., *23:* 193
Relf, Douglas, *3:* 63
Relyea, C. M., *16:* 29
Remi, Georges, *13:* 184
Remington, Frederic, *19:* 188
Renlie, Frank, *11:* 200
Reschofsky, Jean, *7:* 118
Rethi, Lili, *2:* 153
Reusswig, William, *3:* 267
Rey, H. A., *1:* 182; *YABC 2:* 17
Reynolds, Doris, *5:* 71
Ribbons, Ian, *3:* 10
Rice, Elizabeth, *2:* 53, 214
Rice, James, *22:* 210
Richards, Henry, *YABC 1:* 228, 231
Richardson, Ernest, *2:* 144
Richardson, Frederick, *18:* 27, 31
Rieniets, Judy King, *14:* 28
Riger, Bob, *2:* 166
Riley, Kenneth, *22:* 230
Ringi, Kjell, *12:* 171
Rios, Tere. *See* Versace, Marie
Ripper, Charles L., *3:* 175
Rivkin, Jay, *15:* 230
Roach, Marilynne, *9:* 158
Roberts, Cliff, *4:* 126
Roberts, Doreen, *4:* 230
Roberts, Jim, *22:* 166; *23:* 69
Roberts, W., *22:* 2, 3
Robinson, Charles, *3:* 53; *5:* 14; *6:* 193; *7:* 150; *7:* 183; *8:* 38; *9:* 81; *13:* 188; *14:* 248-249; *23:* 149
Robinson, Charles [1870-1937], *17:* 157, 171-173, 175-176; *YABC 2:* 308-310, 331
Robinson, Jerry, *3:* 262
Robinson, Joan G., *7:* 184
Robinson, T. H., *17:* 179, 181-183
Robinson, W. Heath, *17:* 185, 187, 189, 191, 193, 195, 197, 199, 202; *23:* 167; *YABC 1:* 44; *YABC 2:* 183
Rocker, Fermin, *7:* 34; *13:* 21
Rockwell, Anne, *5:* 147
Rockwell, Gail, *7:* 186
Rockwell, Norman, *23:* 39, 196, 197, 199, 200, 203, 204, 207; *YABC 2:* 60
Rodriguez, Joel, *16:* 65
Roever, J. M., *4:* 119
Rogers, Carol, *2:* 262; *6:* 164
Rogers, Frances, *10:* 130
Rogers, William A., *15:* 151, 153-154
Rojankovsky, Feodor, *6:* 134, 136; *10:* 183; *21:* 128, 129, 130
Rose, Carl, *5:* 62
Rosenblum, Richard, *11:* 202; *18:* 18
Rosier, Lydia, *16:* 236; *20:* 104; *21:* 109; *22:* 125
Ross, Clare, *3:* 123; *21:* 45
Ross, John, *3:* 123; *21:* 45
Ross, Tony, *17:* 204
Rossetti, Dante Gabriel, *20:* 151, 153
Roth, Arnold, *4:* 238; *21:* 133
Rouille, M., *11:* 96
Rounds, Glen, *8:* 173; *9:* 171; *12:* 56; *YABC 1:* 1-3
Rubel, Nicole, *18:* 255; *20:* 59
Rud, Borghild, *6:* 15
Rudolph, Norman Guthrie, *17:* 13
Ruffins, Reynold, *10:* 134-135
Russell, E. B., *18:* 177, 182
Ruth, Rod, *9:* 161
Ryden, Hope, *8:* 176

Sabaka, Donna R., *21:* 172
Sacker, Amy, *16:* 100
Sagsoorian, Paul, *12:* 183; *22:* 154
Saint Exupéry, Antoine de, *20:* 157
Sale, Morton, *YABC 2:* 31
Sambourne, Linley, *YABC 2:* 181
Sampson, Katherine, *9:* 197
Samson, Anne S., *2:* 216
Sandberg, Lasse, *15:* 239, 241
Sanderson, Ruth, *21:* 126
Sandin, Joan, *4:* 36; *6:* 194; *7:* 177; *12:* 145, 185; *20:* 43; *21:* 74

Sapieha, Christine, *1:* 180
Sarg, Tony, *YABC 2:* 236
Sargent, Robert, *2:* 217
Saris, *1:* 33
Sarony, *YABC 2:* 170
Sasek, Miroslav, *16:* 239-242
Sassman, David, *9:* 79
Savage, Steele, *10:* 203; *20:* 77
Savitt, Sam, *8:* 66, 182; *15:* 278; *20:* 96
Scabrini, Janet, *13:* 191
Scarry, Richard, *2:* 220-221; *18:* 20
Schaeffer, Mead, *18:* 81, 94; *21:* 137, 138, 139
Scharl, Josef, *20:* 132; *22:* 128
Scheel, Lita, *11:* 230
Schick, Joel, *16:* 160; *17:* 167; *22:* 12
Schindelman, Joseph, *1:* 74; *4:* 101; *12:* 49
Schindler, Edith, *7:* 22
Schlesinger, Bret, *7:* 77
Schmid, Eleanore, *12:* 188
Schmiderer, Dorothy, *19:* 224
Schmidt, Elizabeth, *15:* 242
Schoenherr, John, *1:* 146-147, 173; *3:* 39, 139; *17:* 75
Schomburg, Alex, *13:* 23
Schongut, Emanuel, *4:* 102; *15:* 186
Schoonover, Frank, *17:* 107; *19:* 81, 190, 233; *22:* 88, 129; *YABC 2:* 282, 316
Schottland, Miriam, *22:* 172
Schramm, Ulrik, *2:* 16; *14:* 112
Schreiber, Elizabeth Anne, *13:* 193
Schreiber, Ralph W., *13:* 193
Schreiter, Rick, *14:* 97; *23:* 171
Schroeder, E. Peter, *12:* 112
Schroeder, Ted, *11:* 160; *15:* 189
Schrotter, Gustav, *22:* 212
Schulz, Charles M., *10:* 137-142
Schwartz, Charles, *8:* 184
Schwartzberg, Joan, *3:* 208
Schweitzer, Iris, *2:* 137; *6:* 207
Scott, Anita Walker, *7:* 38
Scribner, Joanne, *14:* 236
Sebree, Charles, *18:* 65
Sedacca, Joseph M., *11:* 25; *22:* 36
Seignobosc, Francoise, *21:* 145, 146
Sejima, Yoshimasa, *8:* 187
Selig, Sylvie, *13:* 199
Seltzer, Isadore, *6:* 18
Seltzer, Meyer, *17:* 214
Sempé, *YABC 2:* 109
Sendak, Maurice, *1:* 135, 190; *3:* 204; *7:* 142; *15:* 199; *17:* 210; *YABC 1:* 167
Sengler, Johanna, *18:* 256
Seredy, Kate, *1:* 192; *14:* 20-21; *17:* 210
Sergeant, John, *6:* 74
Servello, Joe, *10:* 144
Seton, Ernest Thompson, *18:* 260-269, 271
Seuss, Dr. *See* Geisel, Theodor
Severin, John Powers, *7:* 62
Sewall, Marcia, *15:* 8; *22:* 170
Seward, Prudence, *16:* 243
Sewell, Helen, *3:* 186; *15:* 308
Shanks, Anne Zane, *10:* 149
Sharp, William, *6:* 131; *19:* 241; *20:* 112
Shaw, Charles G., *13:* 200; *21:* 135
Shecter, Ben, *16:* 244
Shekerjian, Haig, *16:* 245
Shekerjian, Regina, *16:* 245
Shenton, Edward, *YABC 1:* 218-219, 221
Shepard, Ernest H., *3:* 193; *4:* 74; *16:* 101; *17:* 109; *YABC 1:* 148, 153, 174, 176, 180-181
Shepard, Mary, *4:* 210; *22:* 205
Sherwan, Earl, *3:* 196
Shields, Charles, *10:* 150
Shields, Leonard, *13:* 83, 85, 87
Shimin, Symeon, *1:* 93; *2:* 128-129; *3:* 202; *7:* 85; *11:* 177; *12:* 139; *13:* 202-203
Shinn, Everett, *16:* 148; *18:* 229; *21:* 149, 150, 151
Shore, Robert, *YABC 2:* 200
Shortall, Leonard, *4:* 144; *8:* 196; *10:* 166; *19:* 227, 228-229, 230
Shulevitz, Uri, *3:* 198-199; *17:* 85; *22:* 204
Sibley, Don, *1:* 39; *12:* 196
Sidjakov, Nicolas, *18:* 274
Siebel, Fritz, *3:* 120; *17:* 145
Siegl, Helen, *12:* 166; *23:* 216
Sills, Joyce, *5:* 199
Silverstein, Alvin, *8:* 189
Silverstein, Virginia, *8:* 189
Simon, Eric M., *7:* 82
Simon, Howard, *2:* 175; *5:* 132; *19:* 199
Simont, Marc, *2:* 119; *4:* 213; *9:* 168; *13:* 238, 240; *14:* 262; *16:* 179; *18:* 221
Singer, Edith G., *2:* 30
Skardinski, Stanley, *23:* 144
Slackman, Charles B., *12:* 201
Sloan, Joseph, *16:* 68
Sloane, Eric, *21:* 3
Slobodkin, Louis, *1:* 200; *3:* 232; *5:* 168; *13:* 251; *15:* 13, 88
Slobodkina, Esphyr, *1:* 201
Smalley, Janet, *1:* 154
Smee, David, *14:* 78
Smith, Alvin, *1:* 31, 229; *13:* 187
Smith, E. Boyd, *19:* 70; *22:* 89; *YABC 1:* 4-5, 240, 248-249
Smith, Edward J., *4:* 224
Smith, Eunice Young, *5:* 170
Smith, Howard, *19:* 196
Smith, Jessie Willcox, *15:* 91; *16:* 95; *18:* 231; *19:* 57, 242; *21:* 29, 156, 157, 158, 159, 160, 161; *YABC 1:* 6; *YABC 2:* 180, 185, 191, 311, 325
Smith, Linell Nash, *2:* 195
Smith, Maggie Kaufman, *13:* 205
Smith, Ralph Crosby, *2:* 267
Smith, Robert D., *5:* 63
Smith, Susan Carlton, *12:* 208
Smith, Terry, *12:* 106
Smith, Virginia, *3:* 157
Smith, William A., *1:* 36; *10:* 154
Smyth, M. Jane, *12:* 15
Snyder, Jerome, *13:* 207
Sofia, *1:* 62; *5:* 90
Solbert, Ronni, *1:* 159; *2:* 232; *5:* 121; *6:* 34; *17:* 249
Solonevich, George, *15:* 246; *17:* 47
Sommer, Robert, *12:* 211
Sorel, Edward, *4:* 61
Sotomayor, Antonio, *11:* 215
Soyer, Moses, *20:* 177
Spaenkuch, August, *16:* 28
Spanfeller, James, *1:* 72, 149; *2:* 183; *19:* 230, 231, 232; *22:* 66
Sparks, Mary Walker, *15:* 247
Spence, Geraldine, *21:* 163
Spier, Jo, *10:* 30
Spier, Peter, *3:* 155; *4:* 200; *7:* 61; *11:* 78
Spilka, Arnold, *5:* 120; *6:* 204; *8:* 131
Spivak, I. Howard, *8:* 10
Spollen, Christopher J., *12:* 214
Sprattler, Rob, *12:* 176
Spring, Bob, *5:* 60
Spring, Ira, *5:* 60
Staffan, Alvin E., *11:* 56; *12:* 187
Stahl, Ben, *5:* 181; *12:* 91
Stamaty, Mark Alan, *12:* 215
Stanley, Diana, *3:* 45
Steig, William, *18:* 275-276
Stein, Harve, *1:* 109
Steinel, William, *23:* 146
Stephens, Charles H., *YABC 2:* 279
Stephens, William M., *21:* 165
Steptoe, John, *8:* 197
Stern, Simon, *15:* 249-250; *17:* 58
Stevens, Mary, *11:* 193; *13:* 129
Stewart, Charles, *2:* 205
Stirnweis, Shannon, *10:* 164
Stobbs, William, *1:* 48-49; *3:* 68; *6:* 20; *17:* 117, 217
Stone, David, *9:* 173
Stone, David K., *4:* 38; *6:* 124; *9:* 180
Stone, Helen V., *6:* 209
Stratton-Porter, Gene, *15:* 254, 259, 263-264, 268-269
Streano, Vince, *20:* 173
Strong, Joseph D., Jr., *YABC 2:* 330
Ströyer, Poul, *13:* 221
Stubis, Talivaldis, *5:* 182, 183; *10:* 45; *11:* 9; *18:* 304; *20:* 127
Stubley, Trevor, *14:* 43; *22:* 219; *23:* 37
Stuecklen, Karl W., *8:* 34, 65; *23:* 103
Stull, Betty, *11:* 46
Suba, Susanne, *4:* 202-203; *14:* 261; *23:* 134
Sugarman, Tracy, *3:* 76; *8:* 199

Sullivan, James F., *19:* 280; *20:* 192
Sumichrast, Jözef, *14:* 253
Summers, Leo, *1:* 177; *2:* 273; *13:* 22
Svolinsky, Karel, *17:* 104
Swain, Su Zan Noguchi, *21:* 170
Swan, Susan, *22:* 220-221
Sweet, Darryl, *1:* 163; *4:* 136
Sweetland, Robert, *12:* 194
Sylvester, Natalie G., *22:* 222
Szasz, Susanne, *13:* 55, 226; *14:* 48
Szekeres, Cyndy, *2:* 218; *5:* 185; *8:* 85; *11:* 166; *14:* 19; *16:* 57, 159

Tait, Douglas, *12:* 220
Takakjian, Portia, *15:* 274
Takashima, Shizuye, *13:* 228
Talarczyk, June, *4:* 173
Tallon, Robert, *2:* 228
Tamburine, Jean, *12:* 222
Tandy, H. R., *13:* 69
Tanobe, Miyuki, *23:* 221
Tarkington, Booth, *17:* 224-225
Teale, Edwin Way, *7:* 196
Teason, James, *1:* 14
Tee-Van, Helen Damrosch, *10:* 176; *11:* 182
Tempest, Margaret, *3:* 237, 238
Templeton, Owen, *11:* 77
Tenggren, Gustaf, *18:* 277-279; *19:* 15; *YABC 2:* 145
Tenniel, John, *YABC 2:* 99
Thackeray, William Makepeace, *23:* 224, 228
Thelwell, Norman, *14:* 201
Thistlethwaite, Miles, *12:* 224
Thollander, Earl, *11:* 47; *18:* 112; *22:* 224
Thomas, Allan, *22:* 13
Thomas, Harold, *20:* 98
Thomas, Martin, *14:* 255
Thompson, George, *22:* 18
Thomson, Arline K., *3:* 264
Thorvall, Kerstin, *13:* 235
Thurber, James, *13:* 239, 242-245, 248-249
Tichenor, Tom, *14:* 207
Tilney, F. C., *22:* 231
Timmins, Harry, *2:* 171
Tinkelman, Murray, *12:* 225
Tolford, Joshua, *1:* 221
Tolkien, J. R. R., *2:* 243
Tolmie, Ken, *15:* 292
Tomes, Jacqueline, *2:* 117; *12:* 139
Tomes, Margot, *1:* 224; *2:* 120-121; *16:* 207; *18:* 250; *20:* 7
Toner, Raymond John, *10:* 179
Toothill, Harry, *6:* 54; *7:* 49
Toothill, Ilse, *6:* 54
Torbert, Floyd James, *22:* 226
Toschik, Larry, *6:* 102
Totten, Bob, *13:* 93
Tremain, Ruthven, *17:* 238
Trez, Alain, *17:* 236
Trier, Walter, *14:* 96
Tripp, Wallace, *2:* 48; *7:* 28; *8:* 94; *10:* 54, 76; *11:* 92
Trnka, Jiri, *22:* 151; *YABC 1:* 30-31
Troyer, Johannes, *3:* 16; *7:* 18
Tsinajinie, Andy, *2:* 62
Tsugami, Kyuzo, *18:* 198-199
Tuckwell, Jennifer, *17:* 205
Tudor, Bethany, *7:* 103
Tudor, Tasha, *18:* 227; *20:* 185, 186, 187; *YABC 2:* 46, 314
Tunis, Edwin, *1:* 218-219
Turkle, Brinton, *1:* 211, 213; *2:* 249; *3:* 226; *11:* 3; *16:* 209; *20:* 22; *YABC 1:* 79
Turska, Krystyna, *12:* 103
Tusan, Stan, *6:* 58; *22:* 236-237
Tzimoulis, Paul, *12:* 104

Uchida, Yoshiko, *1:* 220
Ulm, Robert, *17:* 238
Unada. *See* Gliewe, Unada, *3:* 78-79; *21:* 73
Ungerer, Tomi, *5:* 188; *9:* 40; *18:* 188
Unwin, Nora S., *3:* 65, 234-235; *4:* 237; *YABC 1:* 59; *YABC 2:* 301
Utpatel, Frank, *18:* 114
Utz, Lois, *5:* 190

Van Abbé, S., *16:* 142; *18:* 282; *YABC 2:* 157, 161
Vandivert, William, *21:* 175
Van Everen, Jay, *13:* 160; *YABC 1:* 121
Van Loon, Hendrik Willem, *18:* 285, 289, 291
Van Stockum, Hilda, *5:* 193
Van Wely, Babs, *16:* 50
Vasiliu, Mircea, *2:* 166, 253; *9:* 166; *13:* 58
Vavra, Robert, *8:* 206
Vawter, Will, *17:* 163
Veeder, Larry, *18:* 4
Ver Beck, Frank, *18:* 16-17
Verney, John, *14:* 225
Verrier, Suzanne, *5:* 20; *23:* 212
Versace, Marie, *2:* 255
Vestal, H. B., *9:* 134; *11:* 101
Viereck, Ellen, *3:* 242; *14:* 229
Vigna, Judith, *15:* 293
Vilato, Gaspar E., *5:* 41
Vimnèra, A., *23:* 154
Vo-Dinh, Mai, *16:* 272
Vogel, Ilse-Margret, *14:* 230
von Schmidt, Eric, *8:* 62
Vosburgh, Leonard, *1:* 161; *7:* 32; *15:* 295-296; *23:* 110
Voter, Thomas W., *19:* 3, 9
Vroman, Tom, *10:* 29

Wagner, John, *8:* 200
Wagner, Ken, *2:* 59
Wainwright, Jerry, *14:* 85
Waldman, Bruce, *15:* 297
Walker, Charles, *1:* 46; *4:* 59; *5:* 177; *11:* 115; *19:* 45
Walker, Dugald Stewart, *15:* 47
Walker, Gil, *8:* 49; *23:* 132
Walker, Jim, *10:* 94
Walker, Mort, *8:* 213
Walker, Stephen, *12:* 229; *21:* 174
Wallace, Beverly Dobrin, *19:* 259
Wallner, Alexandra, *15:* 120
Wallner, John C., *9:* 77; *10:* 188; *11:* 28; *14:* 209
Wallower, Lucille, *11:* 226
Walters, Audrey, *18:* 294
Walton, Tony, *11:* 164
Waltrip, Lela, *9:* 195
Waltrip, Mildred, *3:* 209
Waltrip, Rufus, *9:* 195
Wan, *12:* 76
Ward, Keith, *2:* 107
Ward, Lynd, *1:* 99, 132, 133, 150; *2:* 108, 158, 196, 259; *18:* 86
Warner, Peter, *14:* 87
Warren, Betsy, *2:* 101
Warren, Marion Cray, *14:* 215
Washington, Nevin, *20:* 123
Washington, Phyllis, *20:* 123
Waterman, Stan, *11:* 76
Watkins-Pitchford, D. J., *6:* 215, 217
Watson, Aldren, *2:* 267; *5:* 94; *13:* 71; *19:* 253; *YABC 2:* 202
Watson, Gary, *19:* 147
Watson, J. D., *22:* 86
Watson, Karen, *11:* 26
Watson, Wendy, *5:* 197; *13:* 101
Watts, Bernadette, *4:* 227
Webber, Helen, *3:* 141
Webber, Irma E., *14:* 238
Weber, William J., *14:* 239
Webster, Jean, *17:* 241
Wegner, Fritz, *14:* 250; *20:* 189
Weidenear, Reynold H., *21:* 122
Weihs, Erika, *4:* 21; *15:* 299
Weil, Lisl, *7:* 203; *10:* 58; *21:* 95; *22:* 188, 217
Weiner, Sandra, *14:* 240
Weisgard, Leonard, *1:* 65; *2:* 191, 197, 204, 264-265; *5:* 108; *21:* 42; *YABC 2:* 13
Weiss, Emil, *1:* 168; *7:* 60
Weiss, Harvey, *1:* 145, 223
Wells, Frances, *1:* 183
Wells, H. G., *20:* 194, 200
Wells, Rosemary, *6:* 49; *18:* 297
Wells, Susan, *22:* 43
Wendelin, Rudolph, *23:* 234
Werenskiold, Erik, *15:* 6
Werth, Kurt, *7:* 122; *14:* 157; *20:* 214
Wetherbee, Margaret, *5:* 3
Wheatley, Arabelle, *11:* 231; *16:* 276

Wheelright, Rowland, *15:* 81; *YABC 2:* 286
Whistler, Rex, *16:* 75
White, David Omar, *5:* 56; *18:* 6
Whithorne, H. S., *7:* 49
Whitney, George Gillett, *3:* 24
Wiese, Kurt, *3:* 255; *4:* 206; *14:* 17; *17:* 18-19; *19:* 47
Wiesner, William, *4:* 100; *5:* 200, 201; *14:* 262
Wiggins, George, *6:* 133
Wikland, Ilon, *5:* 113; *8:* 150
Wilde, George, *7:* 139
Wildsmith, Brian, *16:* 281-282; *18:* 170-171
Wilkinson, Gerald, *3:* 40
Williams, Ferelith Eccles, *22:* 238
Williams, Garth, *1:* 197; *2:* 49, 270; *4:* 205; *15:* 198, 302-304, 307; *16:* 34; *18:* 283, 298-301; *YABC 2:* 15-16, 19
Williams, Maureen, *12:* 238
Williams, Patrick, *14:* 218
Wilson, Charles Banks, *17:* 92
Wilson, Dagmar, *10:* 47
Wilson, Edward A., *6:* 24; *16:* 149; *20:* 220-221; *22:* 87
Wilson, Jack, *17:* 139
Wilson, John, *22:* 240
Wilson, Peggy, *15:* 4
Wilson, W. N., *22:* 26
Wilwerding, Walter J., *9:* 202
Winchester, Linda, *13:* 231
Windham, Kathryn Tucker, *14:* 260
Winslow, Will, *21:* 124
Winter, Milo, *15:* 97; *19:* 221; *21:* 181, 203, 204, 205; *YABC 2:* 144
Wise, Louis, *13:* 68
Wiseman, B., *4:* 233
Wishnefsky, Phillip, *3:* 14
Wiskur, Darrell, *5:* 72; *10:* 50; *18:* 246
Woehr, Lois, *12:* 5
Wohlberg, Meg, *12:* 100; *14:* 197
Wolf, J., *16:* 91
Wondriska, William, *6:* 220
Wonsetler, John C., *5:* 168
Wood, Grant, *19:* 198
Wood, Myron, *6:* 220
Wood, Owen, *18:* 187
Wood, Ruth, *8:* 11
Woodson, Jack, *10:* 201
Wooten, Vernon, *23:* 70
Worboys, Evelyn, *1:* 166-167
Worth, Wendy, *4:* 133
Wrenn, Charles L., *YABC 1:* 20, 21
Wright, Dare, *21:* 206
Wright, George, *YABC 1:* 268
Wronker, Lili Cassel, *3:* 247; *10:* 204; *21:* 10
Wyeth, Andrew, *13:* 40; *YABC 1:* 133-134
Wyeth, N. C., *13:* 41; *17:* 252-259, 264-268; *18:* 181; *19:* 80, 191, 200; *21:* 57, 183; *22:* 91; *23:* 152; *YABC 1:* 133, 223; *YABC 2:* 53, 75, 171, 187, 317

Yang, Jay, *1:* 8; *12:* 239
Yap, Weda, *6:* 176
Yashima, Taro, *14:* 84
Yohn, F. C., *23:* 128; *YABC 1:* 269
Young, Ed, *7:* 205; *10:* 206; *YABC 2:* 242
Young, Noela, *8:* 221

Zacks, Lewis, *10:* 161
Zalben, Jane Breskin, *7:* 211
Zallinger, Jean, *4:* 192; *8:* 8, 129; *14:* 273
Zallinger, Rudolph F., *3:* 245
Zelinsky, Paul O., *14:* 269
Zemach, Margot, *3:* 270; *8:* 201; *21:* 210-211
Zemsky, Jessica, *10:* 62
Zinkeisen, Anna, *13:* 106
Zonia, Dhimitri, *20:* 234-235
Zweifel, Francis, *14:* 274

Author Index

(In the following index, the number of the volume in which an author's sketch appears is given *before* the colon, and the page on which it appears is given *after* the colon. For example, the sketch of Aardema, Verna, appears in Volume 4 on page 1).

YABC

Index citations including this abbreviation refer to listings appearing in *Yesterday's Authors of Books for Children,* also published by the Gale Research Company, which covers authors who died prior to 1960.

Author Index

Aardema, Verna, *4:* 1
Aaron, Chester, *9:* 1
Abbott, Alice. *See* Borland, Kathryn Kilby, *16:* 54
Abbott, Alice. *See* Speicher, Helen Ross (Smith), *8:* 194
Abbott, Jacob, *22:* 1
Abbott, Manager Henry. *See* Stratemeyer, Edward L., *1:* 208
Abdul, Raoul, *12:* 1
Abel, Raymond, *12:* 2
Abell, Kathleen, *9:* 1
Abercrombie, Barbara (Mattes), *16:* 1
Abernethy, Robert G., *5:* 1
Abisch, Roslyn Kroop, *9:* 3
Abisch, Roz. *See* Abisch, Roslyn Kroop, *9:* 3
Abodaher, David J. (Naiph), *17:* 1
Abrahall, C. H. *See* Hoskyns-Abrahall, Clare, *13:* 105
Abrahall, Clare Hoskyns. *See* Hoskyns-Abrahall, Clare, *13:* 105
Abrahams, Robert D(avid), *4:* 3
Abrams, Joy, *16:* 2
Ackerman, Eugene, *10:* 1
Adair, Margaret Weeks, *10:* 1
Adams, Adrienne, *8:* 1
Adams, Andy, *YABC 1:* 1
Adams, Dale. *See* Quinn, Elisabeth, *22:* 197
Adams, Harriet S(tratemeyer), *1:* 1
Adams, Harrison. *See* Stratemeyer, Edward L., *1:* 208
Adams, Hazard, *6:* 1
Adams, Richard, *7:* 1
Adams, Ruth Joyce, *14:* 1
Adamson, Graham. *See* Groom, Arthur William, *10:* 53
Adamson, Joy, *11:* 1; *22:* 5 (Obituary)
Adamson, Wendy Wriston, *22:* 6
Addona, Angelo F., *14:* 1
Addy, Ted. *See* Winterbotham, R(ussell) R(obert), *10:* 198
Adelberg, Doris. *See* Orgel, Doris, *7:* 173
Adelson, Leone, *11:* 2
Adkins, Jan, *8:* 2
Adler, David A., *14:* 2
Adler, Irene. *See* Storr, Catherine (Cole), *9:* 181
Adler, Irving, *1:* 2
Adler, Peggy, *22:* 6
Adler, Ruth, *1:* 4
Adoff, Arnold, *5:* 1
Adorjan, Carol, *10:* 1
Adshead, Gladys L., *3:* 1
Aesop, Abraham. *See* Newbery, John, *20:* 135
Agapida, Fray Antonio. *See* Irving, Washington, *YABC 2:* 164
Agard, Nadema, *18:* 1
Agle, Nan Hayden, *3:* 2
Agnew, Edith J(osephine), *11:* 3
Ahern, Margaret McCrohan, *10:* 2
Aichinger, Helga, *4:* 4
Aiken, Clarissa (Lorenz), *12:* 4
Aiken, Conrad, *3:* 3
Aiken, Joan, *2:* 1
Ainsworth, Norma, *9:* 4
Ainsworth, Ruth, *7:* 1
Aistrop, Jack, *14:* 3
Aitken, Dorothy, *10:* 2
Akers, Floyd. *See* Baum, L(yman) Frank, *18:* 7
Albert, Burton, Jr., *22:* 7
Alberts, Frances Jacobs, *14:* 4
Albrecht, Lillie (Vanderveer), *12:* 5
Alcott, Louisa May, *YABC 1:* 7
Alden, Isabella (Macdonald), *YABC 2:* 1
Alderman, Clifford Lindsey, *3:* 6
Aldis, Dorothy (Keeley), *2:* 2
Aldon, Adair. *See* Meigs, Cornelia, *6:* 167
Aldrich, Ann. *See* Meaker, Marijane, *20:* 124
Aldrich, Thomas Bailey, *17:* 2
Aldridge, Josephine Haskell, *14:* 5
Alegria, Ricardo E., *6:* 1
Alexander, Anna Cooke, *1:* 4
Alexander, Frances, *4:* 6
Alexander, Jocelyn (Anne) Arundel, *22:* 9
Alexander, Linda, *2:* 3
Alexander, Lloyd, *3:* 7
Alexander, Martha, *11:* 4
Alexander, Rae Pace. *See* Alexander, Raymond Pace, *22:* 10
Alexander, Raymond Pace, *22:* 10
Alexander, Sue, *12:* 5
Alexander, Vincent Arthur, *23:* 1 (Obituary)
Alexeieff, Alexandre A., *14:* 5
Alger, Horatio, Jr., *16:* 3
Alger, Leclaire (Gowans), *15:* 1
Aliki. *See* Brandenberg, Aliki, *2:* 36
Alkema, Chester Jay, *12:* 7
Allamand, Pascale, *12:* 8
Allan, Mabel Esther, *5:* 2
Allee, Marjorie Hill, *17:* 11
Allen, Adam [Joint pseudonym]. *See* Epstein, Beryl and Samuel, *1:* 85
Allen, Allyn. *See* Eberle, Irmengarde, *2:* 97; *23:* 68 (Obituary)
Allen, Betsy. *See* Cavanna, Betty, *1:* 54
Allen, Gertrude E(lizabeth), *9:* 5
Allen, Leroy, *11:* 7
Allen, Marjorie, *22:* 11
Allen, Merritt Parmelee, *22:* 12
Allen, Nina (Strömgren), *22:* 13
Allen, Samuel (Washington), *9:* 6
Allerton, Mary. *See* Govan, Christine Noble, *9:* 80

Alleyn, Ellen. *See* Rossetti, Christina (Georgina), *20:* 147
Allison, Bob, *14:* 7
Allred, Gordon T., *10:* 3
Almedingen, Martha Edith von. *See* Almedingen, E. M., *3:* 9
Allsop, Kenneth, *17:* 13
Almedingen, E. M., *3:* 9
Almquist, Don, *11:* 8
Alsop, Mary O'Hara, *2:* 4
Alter, Robert Edmond, *9:* 8
Althea. *See* Braithwaite, Althea, *23:* 11
Altsheler, Joseph A(lexander), *YABC 1:* 20
Alvarez, Joseph A., *18:* 2
Ambrus, Victor G(tozo), *1:* 6
Amerman, Lockhart, *3:* 11
Ames, Evelyn, *13:* 1
Ames, Gerald, *11:* 9
Ames, Lee J., *3:* 11
Ames, Mildred, *22:* 14
Amon, Aline, *9:* 8
Amoss, Berthe, *5:* 4
Anckarsvard, Karin, *6:* 2
Ancona, George, *12:* 10
Andersen, Hans Christian, *YABC 1:* 23
Andersen, Ted. *See* Boyd, Waldo T., *18:* 35
Anderson, C(larence) W(illiam), *11:* 9
Anderson, Ella. *See* MacLeod, Ellen Jane (Anderson), *14:* 129
Anderson, Eloise Adell, *9:* 9
Anderson, George. *See* Groom, Arthur William, *10:* 53
Anderson, J(ohn) R(ichard) L(ane), *15:* 3
Anderson, Joy, *1:* 8
Anderson, (John) Lonzo, *2:* 6
Anderson, Lucia (Lewis), *10:* 4
Anderson, Mary, *7:* 4
Anderson, Norman D(ean), *22:* 15
Andrews, F(rank) Emerson, *22:* 17
Andrews, J(ames) S(ydney), *4:* 7
Andrews, Julie, *7:* 6
Andrews, Roy Chapman, *19:* 1
Angell, Judie, *22:* 18
Angell, Madeline, *18:* 3
Angelo, Valenti, *14:* 7
Angier, Bradford, *12:* 12
Angle, Paul M(cClelland), *20:* 1 (Obituary)
Anglund, Joan Walsh, *2:* 7
Angrist, Stanley W(olff), *4:* 9
Anita. *See* Daniel, Anita, *23:* 65
Annett, Cora. *See* Scott, Cora Annett, *11:* 207
Annixter, Jane. *See* Sturtzel, Jane Levington, *1:* 212
Annixter, Paul. *See* Sturtzel, Howard A., *1:* 210
Anno, Mitsumasa, *5:* 6
Anrooy, Frans van. *See* Van Anrooy, Francine, *2:* 252
Anthony, C. L. *See* Smith, Dodie, *4:* 194
Anthony, Edward, *21:* 1
Anticaglia, Elizabeth, *12:* 13
Anton, Michael (James), *12:* 13
Appel, Benjamin, *21:* 5 (Obituary)
Appiah, Peggy, *15:* 3
Appleton, Victor [Collective pseudonym], *1:* 9
Appleton, Victor II [Collective pseudonym], *1:* 9
Apsler, Alfred, *10:* 4
Aquillo, Don. *See* Prince, J(ack) H(arvey), *17:* 155
Arbuthnot, May Hill, *2:* 9
Archer, Frank. *See* O'Connor, Richard, *21:* 111
Archer, Jules, *4:* 9
Archer, Marion Fuller, *11:* 12
Archibald, Joseph S. *3:* 12
Arden, Barbie. *See* Stoutenburg, Adrien, *3:* 217
Ardizzone, Edward, *1:* 10; *21:* 5 (Obituary)
Arehart-Treichel, Joan, *22:* 18
Arenella, Roy, *14:* 9
Armer, Alberta (Roller), *9:* 11
Armer, Laura Adams, *13:* 2
Armour, Richard, *14:* 10
Armstrong, George D., *10:* 5
Armstrong, Gerry (Breen), *10:* 6
Armstrong, Richard, *11:* 14
Armstrong, William H., *4:* 11
Arnett, Carolyn. *See* Cole, Lois Dwight, *10:* 26
Arnold, Elliott, *5:* 7; *22:* 19 (Obituary)
Arnold, Oren, *4:* 13
Arnoldy, Julie. *See* Bischoff, Julia Bristol, *12:* 52
Arnosky, Jim, *22:* 19
Arnott, Kathleen, *20:* 1
Arnov, Boris, Jr., *12:* 14
Arnstein, Helene S(olomon), *12:* 15
Arntson, Herbert E(dward), *12:* 16
Arora, Shirley (Lease), *2:* 10
Arquette, Lois S(teinmetz), *1:* 13
Arrowood, (McKendrick Lee) Clinton, *19:* 10
Arthur, Ruth M., *7:* 6
Artis, Vicki Kimmel, *12:* 17
Artzybasheff, Boris (Miklailovich), *14:* 14
Aruego, Ariane. *See* Dewey, Ariane, *7:* 63
Aruego, Jose, *6:* 3
Arundel, Honor, *4:* 15
Arundel, Jocelyn. *See* Alexander, Jocelyn (Anne) Arundel, *22:* 9
Asbjörnsen, Peter Christen, *15:* 5
Asch, Frank, *5:* 9
Ashabranner, Brent (Kenneth), *1:* 14
Ashe, Geoffrey (Thomas), *17:* 14
Ashey, Bella. *See* Breinburg, Petronella, *11:* 36
Ashford, Daisy. *See* Ashford, Margaret Mary, *10:* 6
Ashford, Margaret Mary, *10:* 6
Ashley, Elizabeth. *See* Salmon, Annie Elizabeth, *13:* 188
Asimov, Isaac, *1:* 15
Asinof, Eliot, *6:* 5
Aston, James. *See* White, T(erence) H(anbury), *12:* 229
Atene, Ann. *See* Atene, (Rita) Anna, *12:* 18
Atene, (Rita) Anna, *12:* 18
Atkinson, M. E. *See* Frankau, Mary Evelyn, *4:* 90
Atkinson, Margaret Fleming, *14:* 15
Atticus. *See* Fleming, Ian (Lancaster), *9:* 67
Atwater, Florence (Hasseltine Carroll), *16:* 11
Atwater, Montgomery Meigs, *15:* 10
Atwood, Ann, *7:* 8
Ault, Phillip H., *23:* 1
Aung, (Maung) Htin, *21:* 5
Aung, U. Htin. *See* Aung, (Maung) Htin, *21:* 5
Austin, Elizabeth S., *5:* 10
Austin, Margot, *11:* 15
Austin, Oliver L. Jr., *7:* 10
Austin, Tom. *See* Jacobs, Linda C., *21:* 78
Averill, Esther, *1:* 16
Avery, Al. *See* Montgomery, Rutherford, *3:* 134
Avery, Gillian, *7:* 10
Avery, Kay, *5:* 11
Avery, Lynn. *See* Cole, Lois Dwight, *10:* 26
Avi. *See* Wortis, Avi, *14:* 269
Ayars, James S(terling), *4:* 17
Ayer, Jacqueline, *13:* 7
Ayer, Margaret, *15:* 11
Aylesworth, Thomas G(ibbons), *4:* 18
Aymar, Brandt, *22:* 21

Baastad, Babbis Friis. *See* Friis-Baastad, Babbis, *7:* 95
Babbis, Eleanor. *See* Friis-Baastad, Babbis, *7:* 95
Babbitt, Natalie, *6:* 6
Babcock, Dennis Arthur, *22:* 21
Bach, Richard David, *13:* 7
Bachman, Fred, *12:* 19
Bacmeister, Rhoda W(arner), *11:* 18
Bacon, Elizabeth, *3:* 14
Bacon, Margaret Hope, *6:* 7
Bacon, Martha Sherman, *18:* 4
Bacon, Peggy, *2:* 11
Baden-Powell, Robert (Stephenson Smyth), *16:* 12
Baerg, Harry J(ohn), *12:* 20
Bagnold, Enid, *1:* 17
Bailey, Alice Cooper, *12:* 22

Bailey, Bernadine Freeman, *14:* 16
Bailey, Carolyn Sherwin, *14:* 18
Bailey, Jane H(orton), *12:* 22
Bailey, Maralyn Collins (Harrison), *12:* 24
Bailey, Matilda. *See* Radford, Ruby L., *6:* 186
Bailey, Maurice Charles, *12:* 25
Bailey, Ralph Edgar, *11:* 18
Baity, Elizabeth Chesley, *1:* 18
Bakeless, John (Edwin), *9:* 12
Bakeless, Katherine Little, *9:* 13
Baker, Alan, *22:* 22
Baker, Augusta, *3:* 16
Baker, Betty (Lou), *5:* 12
Baker, Charlotte, *2:* 12
Baker, Elizabeth, *7:* 12
Baker, James W., *22:* 23
Baker, Janice E(dla), *22:* 24
Baker, Jeannie, *23:* 3
Baker, Jeffrey J(ohn) W(heeler), *5:* 13
Baker, Jim. *See* Baker, James W., *22:* 23
Baker, Laura Nelson, *3:* 17
Baker, Margaret, *4:* 19
Baker, Margaret J(oyce), *12:* 25
Baker, Mary Gladys Steel, *12:* 27
Baker, (Robert) Michael, *4:* 20
Baker, Nina (Brown), *15:* 12
Baker, Rachel, *2:* 13
Baker, Samm Sinclair, *12:* 27
Balaam. *See* Lamb, G(eoffrey) F(rederick), *10:* 74
Balch, Glenn, *3:* 18
Balducci, Carolyn Feleppa, *5:* 13
Baldwin, Anne Norris, *5:* 14
Baldwin, Clara, *11:* 20
Baldwin, Gordo. *See* Baldwin, Gordon C., *12:* 30
Baldwin, Gordon C., *12:* 30
Baldwin, James (Arthur), *9:* 15
Balet, Jan (Bernard), *11:* 21
Balian, Lorna, *9:* 16
Ball, Zachary. *See* Masters, Kelly R., *3:* 118
Ballard, Lowell Clyne, *12:* 30
Ballard, (Charles) Martin, *1:* 19
Balogh, Penelope, *1:* 20
Balow, Tom, *12:* 31
Bamfylde, Walter. *See* Bevan, Tom, *YABC 2:* 8
Bamman, Henry A., *12:* 32
Bancroft, Griffing, *6:* 8
Bancroft, Laura. *See* Baum, L(yman) Frank, *18:* 7
Baner, Skulda V(anadis), *10:* 8
Banks, Laura Stockton Voorhees, *23:* 5 (Obituary)
Banner, Angela. *See* Maddison, Angela Mary, *10:* 82
Bannerman, Helen (Brodie Cowan Watson), *19:* 12
Bannon, Laura, *6:* 9
Barbary, James. *See* Baumann, Amy (Brown), *10:* 9
Barbary, James. *See* Beeching, Jack, *14:* 26
Barbour, Ralph Henry, *16:* 27
Barclay, Isabel. *See* Dobell, I.M.B., *11:* 77
Bare, Arnold Edwin, *16:* 31
Barish, Matthew, *12:* 32
Barker, Albert W., *8:* 3
Barker, Melvern, *11:* 23
Barker, S. Omar, *10:* 8
Barker, Will, *8:* 4
Barkley, James Edward, *6:* 12
Barnaby, Ralph S(tanton), *9:* 17
Barnes, (Frank) Eric Wollencott, *22:* 25
Barnstone, Willis, *20:* 3
Barnum, Jay Hyde, *20:* 4
Barnum, Richard [Collective pseudonym], *1:* 20
Barr, Donald, *20:* 5
Barr, George, *2:* 14
Barr, Jene, *16:* 32
Barrett, Ron, *14:* 23
Barrie, J(ames) M(atthew), *YABC 1:* 48
Barry, James P(otvin), *14:* 24
Barry, Katharina (Watjen), *4:* 22
Barry, Robert, *6:* 12
Barth, Edna, *7:* 13
Barthelme, Donald, *7:* 14
Bartlett, Philip A. [Collective pseudonym], *1:* 21
Bartlett, Robert Merill, *12:* 33
Barton, Byron, *9:* 17
Barton, May Hollis [Collective pseudonym], *1:* 21
Bartos-Hoeppner, Barbara, *5:* 15
Baruch, Dorothy W(alter), *21:* 6
Bashevis, Isaac. *See* Singer, Isaac Bashevis, *3:* 203
Bason, Lillian, *20:* 6
Bas, Rutger. *See* Rutgers van der Loeff, An(na) Basenau, *22:* 211
Bassett, John Keith. *See* Keating, Lawrence A, *23:* 107
Bate, Lucy, *18:* 6
Bate, Norman, *5:* 15
Bates, Barbara S(nedeker), *12:* 34
Bates, Betty, *19:* 15
Batten, Mary, *5:* 17
Batterberry, Ariane Ruskin, *13:* 10
Battles, Edith, *7:* 15
Baudouy, Michel-Aime, *7:* 18
Bauer, Helen, *2:* 14
Bauer, Marion Dane, *20:* 8
Bauernschmidt, Marjorie, *15:* 14
Baum, Allyn Z(elton), *20:* 9
Baum, L(yman) Frank, *18:* 7
Baum, Willi, *4:* 23
Baumann, Amy (Brown), *10:* 9
Baumann, Hans, *2:* 16
Baumann, Kurt, *21:* 8
Bawden, Nina. *See* Kark, Nina Mary, *4:* 132
Baylor, Byrd, *16:* 33
Baynes, Pauline (Diana), *19:* 17
BB. *See* Watkins-Pitchford, D. J., *6:* 214
Beach, Charles Amory [Collective pseudonym], *1:* 21
Beach, Edward L(atimer), *12:* 35
Beach, Stewart Taft, *23:* 5
Beachcroft, Nina, *18:* 31
Bealer, Alex W(inkler III), *8:* 6; *22:* 26 (Obituary)
Beals, Carleton, *12:* 36
Beame, Rona, *12:* 39
Beaney, Jan. *See* Udall, Jan Beaney, *10:* 182
Beard, Charles Austin, *18:* 32
Beard, Dan(iel Carter), *22:* 26
Bearden, Romare (Howard), *22:* 34
Beardmore, Cedric. *See* Beardmore, George, *20:* 10
Beardmore, George, *20:* 10
Beatty, Hetty Burlingame, *5:* 18
Beatty, Jerome, Jr., *5:* 19
Beatty, John (Louis), *6:* 13
Beatty, Patricia (Robbins), *1:* 21
Bechtel, Louise Seaman, *4:* 26
Beck, Barbara L., *12:* 41
Becker, Beril, *11:* 23
Becker, John (Leonard), *12:* 41
Beckman, Gunnel, *6:* 14
Bedford, A. N. *See* Watson, Jane Werner, *3:* 244
Bedford, Annie North. *See* Watson, Jane Werner, *3:* 244
Beebe, B(urdetta) F(aye), *1:* 23
Beebe, (Charles) William, *19:* 21
Beech, Webb. *See* Butterworth, W. E., *5:* 40
Beeching, Jack, *14:* 26
Beeler, Nelson F(rederick), *13:* 11
Beers, Dorothy Sands, *9:* 18
Beers, Lorna, *14:* 26
Beers, V(ictor) Gilbert, *9:* 18
Begley, Kathleen A(nne), *21:* 9
Behn, Harry, *2:* 17
Behnke, Frances L., *8:* 7
Behr, Joyce, *15:* 15
Behrens, June York, *19:* 30
Behrman, Carol H(elen), *14:* 27
Beiser, Arthur, *22:* 36
Beiser, Germaine, *11:* 24
Belknap, B. H. *See* Ellis, Edward S(ylvester), *YABC 1:* 116
Bell, Corydon, *3:* 19
Bell, Emily Mary. *See* Cason, Mabel Earp, *10:* 19
Bell, Gertrude (Wood), *12:* 42
Bell, Gina. *See* Iannone, Jeanne, *7:* 139
Bell, Janet. *See* Clymer, Eleanor, *9:* 37
Bell, Margaret E(lizabeth), *2:* 19
Bell, Norman (Edward), *11:* 25
Bell, Raymond Martin, *13:* 13
Bell, Thelma Harrington, *3:* 20
Bellairs, John, *2:* 20
Belloc, (Joseph) Hilaire (Pierre), *YABC 1:* 62

Bell-Zano, Gina. *See* Iannone, Jeanne, *7:* 139
Belpré, Pura, *16:* 35
Belting, Natalie Maree, *6:* 16
Belton, John Raynor, *22:* 37
Belvedere, Lee. *See* Grayland, Valerie, *7:* 111
Bemelmans, Ludwig, *15:* 15
Benary, Margot. *See* Benary-Isbert, Margot, *2:* 21; *21:* 9
Benary-Isbert, Margot, *2:* 21; *21:* 9 (Obituary)
Benasutti, Marion, *6:* 18
Benchley, Nathaniel, *3:* 21
Benchley, Peter, *3:* 22
Bender, Lucy Ellen, *22:* 38
Bendick, Jeanne, *2:* 23
Bendick, Robert L(ouis), *11:* 25
Benedict, Dorothy Potter, *11:* 26; *23:* 5 (Obituary)
Benedict, Lois Trimble, *12:* 44
Benedict, Rex, *8:* 8
Benét, Laura, *3:* 23; *23:* 6 (Obituary)
Benét, Stephen Vincent, *YABC 1:* 75
Benet, Sula, *21:* 10
Benezra, Barbara, *10:* 10
Benj. F. Johnson, of Boone. *See* Riley, James Whitcomb, *17:* 159
Bennett, John, *YABC 1:* 84
Bennett, Rainey, *15:* 27
Bennett, Richard, *21:* 11
Benson, Sally, *1:* 24
Bentley, Phyllis (Eleanor), *6:* 19
Berelson, Howard, *5:* 20
Berenstain, Janice, *12:* 44
Berenstain, Stan(ley), *12:* 45
Berg, Jean Horton, *6:* 21
Bergaust, Erik, *20:* 12
Berger, Melvin H., *5:* 21
Berger, Terry, *8:* 10
Berkowitz, Freda Pastor, *12:* 48
Berliner, Franz, *13:* 13
Berna, Paul, *15:* 27
Bernadette. *See* Watts, Bernadette, *4:* 226
Bernard, Jacqueline (de Sieyes), *8:* 11
Bernstein, Joanne E(ckstein), *15:* 29
Bernstein, Theodore M(enline), *12:* 49
Berrien, Edith Heal. *See* Heal, Edith, *7:* 123
Berrill, Jacquelyn (Batsel), *12:* 50
Berrington, John. *See* Brownjohn, Alan, *6:* 38
Berry, B. J. *See* Berry, Barbara, J., *7:* 19
Berry, Barbara J., *7:* 19
Berry, Erick. *See* Best, Allena Champlin, *2:* 25
Berry, Jane Cobb, *22:* 39 (Obituary)
Berry, William D(avid), *14:* 28
Berson, Harold, *4:* 27
Berwick, Jean. *See* Meyer, Jean Shepherd, *11:* 181
Beskow, Elsa (Maartman), *20:* 13
Best, (Evangel) Allena Champlin, *2:* 25
Best, (Oswald) Herbert, *2:* 27
Beth, Mary. *See* Miller, Mary Beth, *9:* 145
Bethancourt, T. Ernesto, *11:* 27
Bethell, Jean (Frankenberry), *8:* 11
Bethers, Ray, *6:* 22
Bethune, J. G. *See* Ellis, Edward S(ylvester), *YABC 1:* 116
Betteridge, Anne. *See* Potter, Margaret (Newman), *21:* 119
Bettina. *See* Ehrlich, Bettina, *1:* 82
Betz, Eva Kelly, *10:* 10
Bevan, Tom, *YABC 2:* 8
Bewick, Thomas, *16:* 38
Beyer, Audrey White, *9:* 19
Bialk, Elisa, *1:* 25
Bianco, Margery (Williams), *15:* 29
Bible, Charles, *13:* 14
Bice, Clare, *22:* 39
Bickerstaff, Isaac. *See* Swift, Jonathan, *19:* 244
Biegel, Paul, *16:* 49
Biemiller, Carl Ludwig, *21:* 13 (Obituary)
Bierhorst, John, *6:* 23
Billout, Guy René, *10:* 11
Birch, Reginald B(athurst), *19:* 31
Birmingham, Lloyd, *12:* 51
Biro, Val, *1:* 26
Bischoff, Julia Bristol, *12:* 52
Bishop, Claire (Huchet), *14:* 30
Bishop, Curtis, *6:* 24
Bisset, Donald, *7:* 20
Bitter, Gary G(len), *22:* 41
Bixby, William, *6:* 24
Black, Algernon David, *12:* 53
Black, Irma S(imonton), *2:* 28
Blackburn, Claire. *See* Jacobs, Linda C., *21:* 78
Blackburn, John(ny) Brewton, *15:* 35
Blackett, Veronica Heath, *12:* 54
Blades, Ann, *16:* 51
Bladow, Suzanne Wilson, *14:* 32
Blaine, John. *See* Goodwin, Harold Leland, *13:* 73
Blaine, John. *See* Harkins, Philip, *6:* 102
Blaine, Marge. *See* Blaine, Margery Kay, *11:* 28
Blaine, Margery Kay, *11:* 28
Blair, Ruth Van Ness, *12:* 54
Blair, Walter, *12:* 56
Blake, Olive. *See* Supraner, Robyn, *20:* 182
Blake, Quentin, *9:* 20
Blake, Walker E. *See* Butterworth, W. E., *5:* 40
Bland, Edith Nesbit. *See* Nesbit, E(dith), *YABC 1:* 193
Bland, Fabian [Joint pseudonym]. *See* Nesbit, E(dith), *YABC 1:* 193
Blassingame, Wyatt (Rainey), *1:* 27
Bleeker, Sonia, *2:* 30
Blegvad, Erik, *14:* 33
Blegvad, Lenore, *14:* 34
Blishen, Edward, *8:* 12
Bliss, Reginald. *See* Wells, H(erbert) G(eorge), *20:* 190
Bliss, Ronald G(ene), *12:* 57
Bliven, Bruce Jr., *2:* 31
Bloch, Lucienne, *10:* 11
Bloch, Marie Halun, *6:* 25
Bloch, Robert, *12:* 57
Blochman, Lawrence G(oldtree), *22:* 42
Block, Irvin, *12:* 59
Blough, Glenn O(rlando), *1:* 28
Blue, Rose, *5:* 22
Blume, Judy (Sussman), *2:* 31
Blyton, Carey, *9:* 22
Boardman, Fon Wyman, Jr., *6:* 26
Boardman, Gwenn R., *12:* 59
Bobbe, Dorothie, *1:* 30
Bock, Hal. *See* Bock, Harold I., *10:* 13
Bock, Harold I., *10:* 13
Bock, William Sauts Netamux'we, *14:* 36
Bodecker, N. M., *8:* 12
Boden, Hilda. *See* Bodenham, Hilda Esther, *13:* 16
Bodenham, Hilda Esther, *13:* 16
Bodie, Idella F(allaw), *12:* 60
Bodker, Cecil, *14:* 39
Boeckman, Charles, *12:* 61
Boesch, Mark J(oseph), *12:* 62
Boesen, Victor, *16:* 53
Boggs, Ralph Steele, *7:* 21
Bohdal, Susi, *22:* 43
Boles, Paul Darcy, *9:* 23
Bolian, Polly, *4:* 29
Bolliger, Max, *7:* 22
Bolton, Carole, *6:* 27
Bolton, Evelyn. *See* Bunting, Anne Evelyn, *18:* 38
Bond, Gladys Baker, *14:* 41
Bond, J. Harvey. *See* Winterbotham, R(ussell) R(obert), *10:* 198
Bond, Michael, *6:* 28
Bond, Nancy (Barbara), *22:* 44
Bond, Ruskin, *14:* 43
Bonehill, Captain Ralph. *See* Stratemeyer, Edward L., *1:* 208
Bonham, Barbara, *7:* 22
Bonham, Frank, *1:* 30
Bonner, Mary Graham, *19:* 37
Bonsall, Crosby (Barbara Newell), *23:* 6
Bontemps, Arna, *2:* 32
Bonzon, Paul-Jacques, *22:* 46
Boone, Pat, *7:* 23
Bordier, Georgette, *16:* 53

Borja, Corinne, *22:* 47
Borja, Robert, *22:* 47
Borland, Hal, *5:* 22
Borland, Harold Glen. *See* Borland, Hal, *5:* 22
Borland, Kathryn Kilby, *16:* 54
Bornstein, Ruth, *14:* 44
Borski, Lucia Merecka, *18:* 34
Borten, Helen Jacobson, *5:* 24
Borton, Elizabeth. *See* Trevino, Elizabeth B. de, *1:* 216
Bortstein, Larry, *16:* 56
Bosco, Jack. *See* Holliday, Joseph, *11:* 137
Boshell, Gordon, *15:* 36
Boshinski, Blanche, *10:* 13
Boston, Lucy Maria (Wood), *19:* 38
Bosworth, J. Allan, *19:* 45
Bothwell, Jean, *2:* 34
Bottner, Barbara, *14:* 45
Boulle, Pierre (Francois Marie-Louis), *22:* 49
Bourne, Leslie. *See* Marshall, Evelyn, *11:* 172
Bourne, Miriam Anne, *16:* 57
Bova, Ben, *6:* 29
Bowen, Betty Morgan. *See* West, Betty, *11:* 233
Bowen, Catherine Drinker, *7:* 24
Bowen, David. *See* Bowen, Joshua David, *22:* 51
Bowen, Joshua David, *22:* 51
Bowen, Robert Sidney, *21:* 13 (Obituary)
Bowie, Jim. *See* Stratemeyer, Edward L., *1:* 208
Bowman, James Cloyd, *23:* 7
Bowman, John S(tewart), *16:* 57
Boyce, George A(rthur), *19:* 46
Boyd, Waldo T., *18:* 35
Boyer, Robert E(rnst), *22:* 52
Boyle, Ann (Peters), *10:* 13
Boylston, Helen (Dore), *23:* 8
Boz. *See* Dickens, Charles, *15:* 55
Bradbury, Bianca, *3:* 25
Bradbury, Ray (Douglas), *11:* 29
Bradley, Virginia, *23:* 11
Brady, Irene, *4:* 30
Bragdon, Elspeth, *6:* 30
Braithwaite, Althea, *23:* 11
Brancato, Robin F(idler), *23:* 14
Brandenberg, Aliki Liacouras, *2:* 36
Brandenberg, Franz, *8:* 14
Brandhorst, Carl T(heodore), *23:* 16
Brandon, Brumsic, Jr., *9:* 25
Brandon, Curt. *See* Bishop, Curtis, *6:* 24
Branfield, John (Charles), *11:* 36
Branley, Franklyn M(ansfield), *4:* 32
Branscum, Robbie, *23:* 17
Bratton, Helen, *4:* 34
Braude, Michael, *23:* 18
Braymer, Marjorie, *6:* 31
Brecht, Edith, *6:* 32
Breck, Vivian. *See* Breckenfeld, Vivian Gurney, *1:* 33
Breckenfeld, Vivian Gurney, *1:* 33
Breda, Tjalmar. *See* DeJong, David C(ornel), *10:* 29
Breinburg, Petronella, *11:* 36
Breisky, William J(ohn), *22:* 53
Brennan, Joseph L., *6:* 33
Brennan, Tim. *See* Conroy, Jack (Wesley), *19:* 65
Brenner, Barbara (Johnes), *4:* 34
Brent, Stuart, *14:* 47
Brett, Bernard, *22:* 53
Brett, Grace N(eff), *23:* 19
Brewster, Benjamin. *See* Folsom, Franklin, *5:* 67
Brewton, John E(dmund), *5:* 25
Brick, John, *10:* 14
Bridgers, Sue Ellen, *22:* 56
Bridges, William (Andrew) *5:* 27
Bridwell, Norman, *4:* 36
Brier, Howard M(axwell), *8:* 15
Briggs, Raymond (Redvers), *23:* 19
Brimberg, Stanlee, *9:* 25
Brin, Ruth F(irestone), *22:* 56
Brinckloe, Julie (Lorraine), *13:* 17
Brindel, June (Rachuy), *7:* 25
Brindze, Ruth, *23:* 22
Brink, Carol Ryrie *1:* 34
Brinsmead, H(esba) F(ay), *18:* 36
Brisley, Joyce Lankester, *22:* 57
Britt, Dell, *1:* 35
Bro, Margueritte (Harmon), *19:* 46
Brock, Betty, *7:* 27
Brock, Emma L(illian), *8:* 15
Brockett, Eleanor Hall, *10:* 15
Broderick, Dorothy M., *5:* 28
Brokamp, Marilyn, *10:* 15
Brondfield, Jerome, *22:* 55
Brondfield, Jerry. *See* Brondfield, Jerome, *22:* 55
Bronson, Lynn. *See* Lampman, Evelyn Sibley, *4:* 140; *23:* 115 (Obituary)
Brooke, L(eonard) Leslie, *17:* 15
Brooke-Haven, P. *See* Wodehouse, P(elham) G(renville), *22:* 241
Brooks, Anita, *5:* 28
Brooks, Gwendolyn, *6:* 33
Brooks, Jerome, *23:* 23
Brooks, Lester, *7:* 28
Brooks, Polly Schoyer, *12:* 63
Brooks, Walter R(ollin), *17:* 17
Brosnan, James Patrick, *14:* 47
Brosnan, Jim. *See* Brosnan, James Patrick, *14:* 47
Broun, Emily. *See* Sterne, Emma Gelders, *6:* 205
Brower, Millicent, *8:* 16
Brower, Pauline (York), *22:* 59
Browin, Frances Williams, *5:* 30
Brown, Alexis. *See* Baumann, Amy (Brown), *10:* 9
Brown, Bill. *See* Brown, William L., *5:* 34
Brown, Billye Walker. *See* Cutchen, Billye Walker, *15:* 51
Brown, Bob. *See* Brown, Robert Joseph, *14:* 48
Brown, Dee (Alexander), *5:* 30
Brown, Eleanor Frances, *3:* 26
Brown, George Earl, *11:* 40
Brown, Irene Bennett, *3:* 27
Brown, Ivor, *5:* 31
Brown, Judith Gwyn, *20:* 15
Brown, Marc Tolon, *10:* 17
Brown, Marcia, *7:* 29
Brown, Margaret Wise, *YABC 2:* 9
Brown, Margery, *5:* 31
Brown, Marion Marsh, *6:* 35
Brown, Myra Berry, *6:* 36
Brown, Pamela, *5:* 33
Brown, Robert Joseph, *14:* 48
Brown, Rosalie (Gertrude) Moore, *9:* 26
Brown, Vinson, *19:* 48
Brown, Walter R(eed), *19:* 50
Brown, William L(ouis), *5:* 34
Browne, Hablot Knight, *21:* 13
Browne, Matthew. *See* Rands, William Brighty, *17:* 156
Browning, Robert, *YABC 1:* 85
Brownjohn, Alan, *6:* 38
Bruce, Mary, *1:* 36
Bryant, Bernice (Morgan), *11:* 40
Brychta, Alex, *21:* 21
Bryson, Bernarda, *9:* 26
Buchan, John, *YABC 2:* 21
Buchwald, Art(hur), *10:* 18
Buchwald, Emilie, *7:* 31
Buck, Lewis, *18:* 37
Buck, Margaret Waring, *3:* 29
Buck, Pearl S(ydenstricker), *1:* 36
Buckeridge, Anthony, *6:* 38
Buckley, Helen E(lizabeth), *2:* 38
Buckmaster, Henrietta, *6:* 39
Budd, Lillian, *7:* 33
Buehr, Walter, *3:* 30
Buff, Conrad, *19:* 51
Buff, Mary Marsh, *19:* 54
Bulla, Clyde Robert, *2:* 39
Bunting, A. E.. *See* Bunting, Anne Evelyn, *18:* 38
Bunting, Anne Evelyn, *18:* 38
Bunting, Eve. *See* Bunting, Anne Evelyn, *18:* 38
Bunting, Glenn (Davison), *22:* 60
Burch, Robert J(oseph), *1:* 38
Burchard, Peter D(uncan), *5:* 34
Burchard, Sue, *22:* 61
Burchardt, Nellie, *7:* 33
Burdick, Eugene (Leonard), *22:* 61
Burford, Eleanor. *See* Hibbert, Eleanor, *2:* 134
Burger, Carl, *9:* 27
Burgess, Anne Marie. *See* Gerson, Noel B(ertram), *22:* 118
Burgess, Em. *See* Burgess, Mary Wyche, *18:* 39
Burgess, Mary Wyche, *18:* 39

Author Index

Burgess, Michael. *See* Gerson, Noel B(ertram), *22:* 118
Burgess, Robert F(orrest), *4:* 38
Burgess, Thornton W(aldo), *17:* 19
Burgwyn, Mebane H., *7:* 34
Burke, John. *See* O'Connor, Richard, *21:* 111
Burland, C. A. *See* Burland, Cottie A., *5:* 36
Burland, Cottie A., *5:* 36
Burlingame, (William) Roger, *2:* 40
Burman, Ben Lucien, *6:* 40
Burn, Doris, *1:* 39
Burnett, Frances (Eliza) Hodgson, *YABC 2:* 32
Burnford, S. D. *See* Burnford, Sheila, *3:* 32
Burnford, Sheila, *3:* 32
Burningham, John (Mackintosh), *16:* 58
Burns, Paul C., *5:* 37
Burns, Ray. *See* Burns, Raymond (Howard), *9:* 28
Burns, Raymond, *9:* 28
Burns, William A., *5:* 38
Burroughs, Polly, *2:* 41
Burroway, Janet (Gay), *23:* 24
Burt, Jesse Clifton, *20:* 18 (Obituary)
Burt, Olive Woolley, *4:* 39
Burton, Hester, *7:* 35
Burton, Maurice, *23:* 27
Burton, Robert (Wellesley), *22:* 62
Burton, Virginia Lee, *2:* 42
Burton, William H(enry), *11:* 42
Busoni, Rafaello, *16:* 61
Butler, Beverly, *7:* 37
Butters, Dorothy Gilman, *5:* 39
Butterworth, Oliver, *1:* 40
Butterworth, W(illiam) E(dmund III), *5:* 40
Byars, Betsy, *4:* 40
Byfield, Barbara Ninde, *8:* 19

Cable, Mary, *9:* 29
Cadwallader, Sharon, *7:* 38
Cady, (Walter) Harrison, *19:* 56
Cain, Arthur H., *3:* 33
Cain, Christopher. *See* Fleming, Thomas J(ames), *8:* 19
Cairns, Trevor, *14:* 50
Caldecott, Moyra, *22:* 63
Caldecott, Randolph (J.), *17:* 31
Caldwell, John C(ope), *7:* 38
Calhoun, Mary (Huiskamp), *2:* 44
Calkins, Franklin. *See* Stratemeyer, Edward L., *1:* 208
Call, Hughie Florence, *1:* 41
Callen, Larry. *See* Callen, Lawrence Willard, Jr., *19:* 59
Callen, Lawrence Willard, Jr., *19:* 59
Calvert, John. *See* Leaf, (Wilbur) Munro, *20:* 99
Cameron, Edna M., *3:* 34
Cameron, Eleanor (Butler), *1:* 42
Cameron, Elizabeth. *See* Nowell, Elizabeth Cameron, *12:* 160
Cameron, Polly, *2:* 45
Camp, Walter (Chauncey), *YABC 1:* 92
Campbell, Ann R., *11:* 43
Campbell, Bruce. *See* Epstein, Samuel, *1:* 87
Campbell, Hope, *20:* 19
Campbell, Jane. *See* Edwards, Jane Campbell, *10:* 34
Campbell, R. W. *See* Campbell, Rosemae Wells, *1:* 44
Campbell, Rosemae Wells, *1:* 44
Campion, Nardi Reeder, *22:* 64
Canfield, Dorothy. *See* Fisher, Dorothy Canfield, *YABC 1:* 122
Canusi, Jose. *See* Barker, S. Omar, *10:* 8
Caplin, Alfred Gerald, *21:* 22 (Obituary)
Capp, Al. *See* Caplin, Alfred Gerald, *21:* 22
Cappel, Constance, *22:* 65
Capps, Benjamin (Franklin), *9:* 30
Carafoli, Marci. *See* Ridlon, Marci, *22:* 211
Caras, Roger A(ndrew), *12:* 65
Carbonnier, Jeanne, *3:* 34
Carey, Bonnie, *18:* 40
Carey, Ernestine Gilbreth, *2:* 45
Carini, Edward, *9:* 30
Carle, Eric, *4:* 41
Carleton, Captain L. C. *See* Ellis, Edward S(ylvester), *YABC 1:* 116
Carley, V(an Ness) Royal, *20:* 20 (Obituary)
Carlisle, Clark, Jr. *See* Holding, James, *3:* 85
Carlsen, Ruth C(hristoffer), *2:* 47
Carlson, Bernice Wells, *8:* 19
Carlson, Dale Bick, *1:* 44
Carlson, Natalie Savage, *2:* 48
Carlson, Vada F., *16:* 64
Carol, Bill J. *See* Knott, William Cecil, Jr., *3:* 94
Carpelan, Bo (Gustaf Bertelsson), *8:* 20
Carpenter, Allan, *3:* 35
Carpenter, Frances, *3:* 36
Carpenter, Patricia (Healy Evans), *11:* 43
Carr, Glyn. *See* Styles, Frank Showell, *10:* 167
Carr, Harriett Helen, *3:* 37
Carr, Mary Jane, *2:* 50
Carrick, Carol, *7:* 39
Carrick, Donald, *7:* 40
Carroll, Curt. *See* Bishop, Curtis, *6:* 24
Carroll, Latrobe, *7:* 40
Carroll, Laura. *See* Parr, Lucy, *10:* 115
Carroll, Lewis. *See* Dodgson, Charles Lutwidge, *YABC 2:* 297
Carse, Robert, *5:* 41
Carson, Captain James. *See* Stratemeyer, Edward L., *1:* 208
Carson, John F., *1:* 46
Carson, Rachel (Louise), *23:* 28
Carter, Bruce. *See* Hough, Richard (Alexander), *17:* 83
Carter, Dorothy Sharp, *8:* 21
Carter, Helene, *15:* 37
Carter, (William) Hodding, *2:* 51
Carter, Katharine J(ones), *2:* 52
Carter, Phyllis Ann. *See* Eberle, Irmengarde, *2:* 97; *23:* 68 (Obituary)
Carter, William E., *1:* 47
Cartner, William Carruthers, *11:* 44
Cartwright, Sally, *9:* 30
Cary. *See* Cary, Louis F(avreau), *9:* 31
Cary, Louis F(avreau), *9:* 31
Caryl, Jean. *See* Kaplan, Jean Caryl Korn, *10:* 62
Case, Marshal T(aylor), *9:* 33
Case, Michael. *See* Howard, Robert West, *5:* 85
Casewit, Curtis, *4:* 43
Casey, Brigid, *9:* 33
Casey, Winifred Rosen. *See* Rosen, Winifred, *8:* 169
Cason, Mabel Earp, *10:* 19
Cass, Joan E(velyn), *1:* 47
Cassel, Lili. *See* Wronker, Lili Cassell, *10:* 204
Cassel-Wronker, Lili. *See* Wronker, Lili Cassell, *10:* 204
Castellanos, Jane Mollie (Robinson), *9:* 34
Castillo, Edmund L., *1:* 50
Castle, Lee. [Joint pseudonym]. *See* Ogan, George F. and Margaret E. (Nettles), *13:* 171
Caswell, Helen (Rayburn), *12:* 67
Catherall, Arthur, *3:* 38
Catlin, Wynelle, *13:* 19
Catton, (Charles) Bruce, *2:* 54
Catz, Max. *See* Glaser, Milton, *11:* 106
Caudill, Rebecca, *1:* 50
Causley, Charles, *3:* 39
Cavallo, Diana, *7:* 43
Cavanah, Frances, *1:* 52
Cavanna, Betty, *1:* 54
Cawley, Winifred, *13:* 20
Caxton, Pisistratus. *See* Lytton, Edward G(eorge) E(arle) L(ytton) Bulwer-Lytton, Baron, *23:* 125
Cebulash, Mel, *10:* 19
Ceder, Georgiana Dorcas, *10:* 21
Cerf, Bennett, *7:* 43
Cerf, Christopher (Bennett), *2:* 55
Cetin, Frank (Stanley), *2:* 55

Author Index

Chadwick, Lester [Collective pseudonym], *1:* 55
Chaffee, Allen, *3:* 41
Chaffin, Lillie D(orton), *4:* 44
Challans, Mary, *23:* 33
Chalmers, Mary, *6:* 41
Chambers, Aidan, *1:* 55
Chambers, Margaret Ada Eastwood, *2:* 56
Chambers, Peggy. *See* Chambers, Margaret, *2:* 56
Chandler, Caroline A(ugusta), *22:* 66 (Obituary)
Chandler, Edna Walker, *11:* 45
Chandler, Ruth Forbes, *2:* 56
Channel, A. R. *See* Catherall, Arthur, *3:* 38
Chapman, Allen [Collective pseudonym], *1:* 55
Chapman, (Constance) Elizabeth (Mann), *10:* 21
Chapman, Walker. *See* Silverberg, Robert, *13:* 206
Chappell, Warren, *6:* 42
Charles, Louis. *See* Stratemeyer, Edward L., *1:* 208
Charlip, Remy, *4:* 46
Charlot, Jean, *8:* 22
Charmatz, Bill, *7:* 45
Charosh, Mannis, *5:* 42
Chase, Alice. *See* McHargue, Georgess, *4:* 152
Chase, Mary (Coyle), *17:* 39
Chase, Mary Ellen, *10:* 22
Chastain, Madye Lee, *4:* 48
Chauncy, Nan, *6:* 43
Chaundler, Christine, *1:* 56
Chen, Tony *6:* 44
Chenault, Nell. *See* Smith, Linell Nash, *2:* 227
Cheney, Cora, *3:* 41
Cheney, Ted. *See* Cheney, Theodore Albert, *11:* 46
Cheney, Theodore Albert, *11:* 46
Chernoff, Goldie Taub, *10:* 23
Cherryholmes, Anne, *See* Price, Olive, *8:* 157
Chetin, Helen, *6:* 46
Chew, Ruth, *7:* 45
Chidsey, Donald Barr, *3:* 42
Childress, Alice, *7:* 46
Childs, (Halla) Fay (Cochrane), *1:* 56
Chimaera, *See* Farjeon, Eleanor, *2:* 103
Chipperfield, Joseph E(ugene), *2:* 57
Chittenden, Elizabeth F., *9:* 35
Chittum, Ida, *7:* 47
Chorao, (Ann Mc)Kay (Sproat), *8:* 24
Chrisman, Arthur Bowie, *YABC 1:* 94
Christensen, Gardell Dano, *1:* 57
Christgau, Alice Erickson, *13:* 21
Christian, Mary Blount, *9:* 35
Christopher, Matt(hew F.), *2:* 58
Christy, Howard Chandler, *21:* 22
Chu, Daniel, *11:* 47
Chukovsky, Kornei (Ivanovich), *5:* 43
Church, Richard, *3:* 43
Churchill, E. Richard, *11:* 48
Chute, B(eatrice) J(oy), *2:* 59
Chute, Marchette (Gaylord), *1:* 58
Chwast, Jacqueline, *6:* 46
Chwast, Seymour, *18:* 42
Ciardi, John (Anthony), *1:* 59
Clair, Andrée, *19:* 61
Clapp, Patricia, *4:* 50
Clare, Helen, *See* Hunter Blair, Pauline, *3:* 87
Clark, Ann Nolan, *4:* 51
Clark, Frank J(ames), *18:* 43
Clark, Garel [Joint pseudonym]. *See* Garelick, May, *19:* 130
Clark, Margaret Goff, *8:* 26
Clark, Mavis Thorpe, *8:* 27
Clark, Merle. *See* Gessner, Lynne, *16:* 119
Clark, Patricia (Finrow), *11:* 48
Clark, Ronald William, *2:* 60
Clark, Van D(eusen), *2:* 61
Clark, Virginia. *See* Gray, Patricia, *7:* 110
Clark, Walter Van Tilburg, *8:* 28
Clarke, Arthur C(harles), *13:* 22
Clarke, Clorinda, *7:* 48
Clarke, John. *See* Laklan, Carli, *5:* 100
Clarke, Mary Stetson, *5:* 46
Clarke, Michael. *See* Newlon, Clarke, *6:* 174
Clarke, Pauline. *See* Hunter Blair, Pauline, *3:* 87
Clarkson, Ewan, *9:* 36
Cleary, Beverly (Bunn), *2:* 62
Cleaver, Bill, *22:* 66
Cleaver, Carole, *6:* 48
Cleaver, Elizabeth (Mrazik), *23:* 34
Cleaver, Vera, *22:* 67
Cleishbotham, Jebediah. *See* Scott, Sir Walter, *YABC 2:* 280
Cleland, Mabel. *See* Widdemer, Mabel Cleland, *5:* 200
Clemens, Samuel Langhorne, *YABC 2:* 51
Clemons, Elizabeth. *See* Nowell, Elizabeth Cameron, *12:* 160
Clerk, N. W. *See* Lewis, C. S., *13:* 129
Cleven, Cathrine. *See* Cleven, Kathryn Seward, *2:* 64
Cleven, Kathryn Seward, *2:* 64
Clevin, Jörgen, *7:* 49
Clewes, Dorothy (Mary), *1:* 61
Clifford, Eth. *See* Rosenberg, Ethel, *3:* 176
Clifford, Harold B., *10:* 24
Clifford, Margaret Cort, *1:* 63
Clifford, Martin. *See* Hamilton, Charles Harold St. John, *13:* 77
Clifford, Mary Louise (Beneway), *23:* 36
Clifford, Peggy. *See* Clifford, Margaret Cort, *1:* 63
Clifton, Harry. *See* Hamilton, Charles Harold St. John, *13:* 77
Clifton, Lucille, *20:* 20
Clifton, Martin. *See* Hamilton, Charles Harold St. John, *13:* 77
Clinton, Jon. *See* Prince, J(ack) H(arvey), *17:* 155
Clive, Clifford. *See* Hamilton, Charles Harold St. John, *13:* 77
Cloudsley-Thompson, J(ohn) L(eonard), *19:* 61
Clymer, Eleanor, *9:* 37
Coates, Belle, *2:* 64
Coates, Ruth Allison, *11:* 49
Coats, Alice M(argaret), *11:* 50
Coatsworth, Elizabeth, *2:* 65
Cobb, Jane. *See* Berry, Jane Cobb, *22:* 39 (Obituary)
Cobb, Vicki, *8:* 31
Cobbett, Richard. *See* Pluckrose, Henry (Arthur), *13:* 183
Cober, Alan E., *7:* 51
Cobham, Sir Alan. *See* Hamilton, Charles Harold St. John, *13:* 77
Cocagnac, A(ugustin) M(aurice-Jean), *7:* 52
Cochran, Bobbye A., *11:* 51
Cockett, Mary, *3:* 45
Coe, Douglas [Joint pseudonym]. *See* Epstein, Beryl and Samuel, *1:* 87
Coen, Rena Neumann, *20:* 24
Coerr, Eleanor, *1:* 64
Coffin, Geoffrey. *See* Mason, F. van Wyck, *3:* 117
Coffman, Ramon Peyton, *4:* 53
Coggins, Jack (Banham), *2:* 68
Cohen, Barbara, *10:* 24
Cohen, Daniel, *8:* 31
Cohen, Joan Lebold, *4:* 53
Cohen, Peter Zachary, *4:* 54
Cohen, Robert Carl, *8:* 33
Cohn, Angelo, *19:* 63
Coit, Margaret L(ouise), *2:* 70
Colbert, Anthony, *15:* 39
Colby, C. B., *3:* 46
Colby, Jean Poindexter, *23:* 37
Cole, Annette. *See* Steiner, Barbara A(nnette), *13:* 213
Cole, Davis, *See* Elting, Mary, *2:* 100
Cole, Jack. *See* Stewart, John (William), *14:* 189
Cole, Jackson. *See* Schisgall, Oscar, *12:* 187
Cole, Lois Dwight, *10:* 26
Cole, William (Rossa), *9:* 40
Coles, Robert (Martin), *23:* 38
Collier, Christopher, *16:* 66
Collier, Ethel, *22:* 68
Collier, James Lincoln, *8:* 33

Collier, Jane. *See* Collier, Zena, *23:* 41
Collier, Zena, *23:* 41
Collins, David, *7:* 52
Colman, Hila, *1:* 65
Colonius, Lillian, *3:* 48
Colorado (Capella), Antonio J(ulio), *23:* 42
Colt, Martin. *See* Epstein, Samuel, *1:* 87
Colum, Padraic, *15:* 42
Columella. *See* Moore, Clement Clarke, *18:* 224
Colver, Anne, *7:* 54
Colwell, Eileen (Hilda), *2:* 71
Comfort, Jane Levington. *See* Sturtzel, Jane Levington, *1:* 212
Comfort, Mildred Houghton, *3:* 48
Comins, Ethel M(ae), *11:* 53
Commager, Henry Steele, *23:* 43
Cone, Molly (Lamken), *1:* 66
Conford, Ellen, *6:* 48
Conger, Lesley. *See* Suttles, Shirley (Smith), *21:* 166
Conklin, Gladys (Plemon), *2:* 73
Conkling, Hilda, *23:* 45
Conly, Robert Leslie, *23:* 45
Connolly, Jerome P(atrick), *8:* 34
Conquest, Owen. *See* Hamilton, Charles Harold St. John, *13:* 77
Conroy, Jack (Wesley), *19:* 65
Conroy, John. *See* Conroy, Jack (Wesley), *19:* 65
Constant, Alberta Wilson, *22:* 70
Conway, Gordon. *See* Hamilton, Charles Harold St. John, *13:* 77
Cook, Bernadine, *11:* 55
Cook, Fred J(ames), *2:* 74
Cook, Joseph J(ay), *8:* 35
Cook, Lyn. *See* Waddell, Evelyn Margaret, *10:* 186
Cooke, David Coxe, *2:* 75
Cooke, Donald Ewin, *2:* 76
Cookson, Catherine (McMullen), *9:* 42
Coolidge, Olivia E(nsor), *1:* 67
Coombs, Charles, *3:* 49
Coombs, Chick. *See* Coombs, Charles, *3:* 49
Coombs, Patricia, *3:* 51
Cooney, Barbara, *6:* 49
Cooper, Gordon, *23:* 47
Cooper, James Fenimore, *19:* 68
Cooper, James R. *See* Stratemeyer, Edward L., *1:* 208
Cooper, John R. [Collective pseudonym], *1:* 68
Cooper, Kay, *11:* 55
Cooper, Lee (Pelham), *5:* 47
Cooper, Susan, *4:* 57
Copeland, Helen, *4:* 57
Copeland, Paul W., *23:* 48
Coppard, A(lfred) E(dgar), *YABC 1:* 97
Corbett, Scott, *2:* 78
Corbin, Sabra Lee. *See* Malvern, Gladys, *23:* 133
Corbin, William. *See* McGraw, William Corbin, *3:* 124
Corby, Dan. *See* Catherall, Arthur, *3:* 38
Corcoran, Barbara, *3:* 53
Corcos, Lucille, *10:* 27
Cordell, Alexander. *See* Graber, Alexander, *7:* 106
Corey, Dorothy, *23:* 49
Cormack, M(argaret) Grant, *11:* 56
Cormier, Robert Edmund, *10:* 28
Cornell, J. *See* Cornell, Jeffrey, *11:* 57
Cornell, Jean Gay, *23:* 50
Cornell, Jeffrey, *11:* 57
Cornish, Samuel James, *23:* 51
Correy, Lee. *See* Stine, G. Harry, *10:* 161
Corrigan, (Helen) Adeline, *23:* 53
Corrigan, Barbara, *8:* 36
Cort, M. C. *See* Clifford, Margaret Cort, *1:* 63
Corwin, Judith Hoffman, *10:* 28
Cosgrave, John O'Hara II, *21:* 26 (Obituary)
Coskey, Evelyn, *7:* 55
Costello, David F(rancis), *23:* 53
Cott, Jonathan, *23:* 55
Cottler, Joseph, *22:* 71
Courlander, Harold, *6:* 51
Cousins, Margaret, *2:* 79
Cowie, Leonard W(allace), *4:* 60
Cowley, Joy, *4:* 60
Cox, Donald William, *23:* 56
Cox, Jack. *See* Cox, John Roberts, *9:* 42
Cox, John Roberts, *9:* 42
Coy, Harold, *3:* 53
Craig, John Eland. *See* Chipperfield, Joseph, *2:* 57
Craig, John Ernest, *23:* 58
Craig, M. Jean, *17:* 45
Craig, Margaret Maze, *9:* 43
Craig, Mary Francis, *6:* 52
Crane, Caroline, *11:* 59
Crane, Roy. *See* Crane, Royston Campbell, *22:* 72 (Obituary)
Crane, Royston Campbell, *22:* 72 (Obituary)
Crane, Stephen (Townley), *YABC 2:* 94
Crane, Walter, *18:* 44
Crane, William D(wight), *1:* 68
Crary, Margaret (Coleman), *9:* 43
Craven, Thomas, *22:* 72
Crawford, Deborah, *6:* 53
Crawford, John E., *3:* 56
Crawford, Phyllis, *3:* 57
Crayder, Dorothy, *7:* 55
Crayder, Teresa. *See* Colman, Hila, *1:* 65
Crayon, Geoffrey. *See* Irving, Washington, *YABC 2:* 164
Crecy, Jeanne. *See* Williams, Jeanne, *5:* 202
Credle, Ellis, *1:* 68
Cresswell, Helen, *1:* 70
Cretan, Gladys (Yessayan), *2:* 82
Crew, Helen (Cecilia) Coale, *YABC 2:* 95
Crichton, (J.) Michael, *9:* 44
Crofut, Bill. *See* Crofut, William E. III, *23:* 59
Crofut, William E. III, *23:* 59
Cromie, William J(oseph), *4:* 62
Crompton, Anne Eliot, *23:* 61
Crompton, Richmal. *See* Lamburn, Richmal Crompton, *5:* 101
Cronbach, Abraham, *11:* 60
Crone, Ruth, *4:* 63
Crosby, Alexander L., *2:* 83; *23:* 62 (Obituary)
Crosher, G(eoffry) R(obins), *14:* 51
Cross, Wilbur Lucius, III, *2:* 83
Crossley-Holland, Kevin, *5:* 48
Crouch, Marcus, *4:* 63
Crout, George C(lement), *11:* 60
Crowe, Bettina Lum, *6:* 53
Crowell, Pers, *2:* 84
Crowfield, Christopher. *See* Stowe, Harriet (Elizabeth) Beecher, *YABC 1:* 250
Crownfield, Gertrude, *YABC 1:* 103
Crowther, James Gerald, *14:* 52
Cruikshank, George, *22:* 73
Crump, Fred H., Jr., *11:* 62
Crump, J(ames) Irving, *21:* 26 (Obituary)
Cruz, Ray, *6:* 54
Cuffari, Richard, *6:* 55
Cullen, Countee, *18:* 64
Culp, Louanna McNary, *2:* 85
Cummings, Betty Sue, *15:* 51
Cummings, Parke, *2:* 85
Cummins, Maria Susanna, *YABC 1:* 103
Cunliffe, John Arthur, *11:* 62
Cunningham, Captain Frank. *See* Glick, Carl (Cannon), *14:* 72
Cunningham, Cathy. *See* Cunningham, Chet, *23:* 63
Cunningham, Chet, *23:* 63
Cunningham, Dale S(peers), *11:* 63
Cunningham, E. V. *See* Fast, Howard, *7:* 80
Cunningham, Julia W(oolfolk), *1:* 72
Curiae, Amicus. *See* Fuller, Edmund (Maybank), *21:* 45
Curie, Eve, *1:* 73
Curley, Daniel, *23:* 63
Curry, Jane L(ouise), *1:* 73
Curry, Peggy Simson, *8:* 37
Curtis, Patricia, *23:* 64
Curtis, Peter. *See* Lofts, Norah Robinson, *8:* 119
Cushman, Jerome, *2:* 86
Cutchen, Billye Walker, *15:* 51
Cutler, (May) Ebbitt, *9:* 46

Cutler, Samuel. *See* Folsom, Franklin, *5:* 67
Cutt, W(illiam) Towrie, *16:* 67
Cuyler, Stephen. *See* Bates, Barbara S(nedeker), *12:* 34

Dahl, Borghild, *7:* 56
Dahl, Roald, *1:* 74
Dahlstedt, Marden, *8:* 38
Dale, Jack. *See* Holliday, Joseph, *11:* 137
Dalgliesh, Alice, *17:* 47; *21:* 26 (Obituary)
Daly, Jim. *See* Stratemeyer, Edward L., *1:* 208
Daly, Maureen, *2:* 87
D'Amato, Alex, *20:* 24
D'Amato, Janet, *9:* 47
Damrosch, Helen Therese. *See* Tee-Van, Helen Damrosch, *10:* 176
Dana, Barbara, *22:* 84
Danachair, Caoimhin O. *See* Danaher, Kevin, *22:* 85
Danaher, Kevin, *22:* 85
D'Andrea, Kate. *See* Steiner, Barbara A(nnette), *13:* 213
Dangerfield, Balfour. *See* McCloskey, Robert, *2:* 185
Daniel, Anita, *23:* 65
Daniel, Anne. *See* Steiner, Barbara A(nnette), *13:* 213
Daniel, Hawthorne, *8:* 39
Daniels, Guy, *11:* 64
Darby, J. N. *See* Govan, Christine Noble, *9:* 80
Darby, Patricia (Paulsen), *14:* 53
Darby, Ray K., *7:* 59
Daringer, Helen Fern, *1:* 75
Darke, Marjorie, *16:* 68
Darling, Lois M., *3:* 57
Darling, Louis, Jr., *3:* 59; *23:* 66 (Obituary)
Darling, Kathy. *See* Darling, Mary Kathleen, *9:* 48
Darling, Mary Kathleen, *9:* 48
Darrow, Whitney. *See* Darrow, Whitney, Jr., *13:* 24
Darrow, Whitney, Jr., *13:* 24
Dauer, Rosamond, *23:* 66
Daugherty, Charles Michael, *16:* 70
Daugherty, James (Henry), *13:* 26
d'Aulaire, Edgar Parin, *5:* 49
d'Aulaire, Ingri (Maartenson Parin) *5:* 50
Daveluy, Paule Cloutier, *11:* 65
Davenport, Spencer. *See* Stratemeyer, Edward L., *1:* 208
David, Jonathan. *See* Ames, Lee J., *3:* 11
Davidson, Basil, *13:* 30
Davidson, Jessica, *5:* 52
Davidson, Margaret, *5:* 53
Davidson, Marion. *See* Garis, Howard R(oger), *13:* 67
Davidson, Mary R., *9:* 49
Davidson, Rosalie, *23:* 67
Davis, Bette J., *15:* 53
Davis, Burke, *4:* 64
Davis, Christopher, *6:* 57
Davis, Daniel S(heldon), *12:* 68
Davis, Julia, *6:* 58
Davis, Mary L(ee), *9:* 49
Davis, Mary Octavia, *6:* 59
Davis, Paxton, *16:* 71
Davis, Robert, *YABC 1:* 104
Davis, Russell G., *3:* 60
Davis, Verne T., *6:* 60
Dawson, Elmer A. [Collective pseudonym], *1:* 76
Dawson, Mary, *11:* 66
Day, Thomas, *YABC 1:* 106
Dazey, Agnes J(ohnston), *2:* 88
Dazey, Frank M., *2:* 88
Deacon, Richard. *See* McCormick, (George) Donald (King), *14:* 141
Dean, Anabel, *12:* 69
de Angeli, Marguerite, *1:* 76
DeArmand, Frances Ullmann, *10:* 29
deBanke,Cecile, *11:* 67
De Bruyn, Monica, *13:* 30
de Camp, Catherine C(rook), *12:* 70
DeCamp, L(yon) Sprague, *9:* 49
Decker, Duane, *5:* 53
Defoe, Daniel, *22:* 86
DeGering, Etta, *7:* 60
de Grummond, Lena Young, *6:* 61
Deiss, Joseph J., *12:* 72
DeJong, David C(ornel), *10:* 29
de Jong, Dola, *7:* 61
Dc Jong, Meindert, *2:* 89
de Kay, Ormonde, Jr., *7:* 62
de Kiriline, Louise. *See* Lawrence, Louise de Kirilene, *13:* 126
deKruif, Paul (Henry) *5:* 54
De Lage, Ida, *11:* 67
de la Mare, Walter, *16:* 73
Delaney, Harry, *3:* 61
Delano, Hugh, *20:* 25
De La Ramée, (Marie) Louise, *20:* 26
Delaune, Lynne, *7:* 63
DeLaurentis, Louise Budde, *12:* 73
Delderfield, Eric R(aymond), *14:* 53
Delderfield, R(onald) F(rederick), *20:* 34
De Leeuw, Adele Louise, *1:* 77
Delmar, Roy. *See* Wexler, Jerome (LeRoy), *14:* 243
Deloria, Vine (Victor), Jr., *21:* 26
Del Rey, Lester, *22:* 97
Delton, Judy, *14:* 54
Delulio, John, *15:* 54
Delving, Michael. *See* Williams, Jay, *3:* 256
Demarest, Doug. *See* Barker, Will, *8:* 4
Demas, Vida, *9:* 51
Dennis, Morgan, *18:* 68
Dennis, Wesley, *18:* 70
Denslow, W(illiam) W(allace), *16:* 83
de Paola, Thomas Anthony, *11:* 68
de Paola, Tomie. *See* de Paola, Thomas Anthony, *11:* 68
deRegniers, Beatrice Schenk (Freedman), *2:* 90
Derleth, August (William) *5:* 54
Derman, Sarah Audrey, *11:* 71
Derry Down Derry. *See* Lear, Edward, *18:* 182
Derwent, Lavinia, *14:* 56
De Selincourt, Aubrey, *14:* 56
Desmond, Alice Curtis, *8:* 40
Detine, Padre. *See* Olsen, Ib Spang, *6:* 177
Deutsch, Babette, *1:* 79
Devaney, John, *12:* 74
Devereux, Frederick L(eonard), Jr., *9:* 51
Devlin, Harry, *11:* 73
Devlin, (Dorothy) Wende, *11:* 74
DeWaard, E. John, *7:* 63
Dewey, Ariane, *7:* 63
Dick, Trella Lamson, *9:* 51
Dickens, Charles, *15:* 55
Dickens, Monica, *4:* 66
Dickinson, Peter, *5:* 55
Dickinson, Susan, *8:* 41
Dickinson, William Croft, *13:* 32
Dickson, Naida, *8:* 41
Dietz, David H(enry), *10:* 30
Dietz, Lew, *11:* 75
Dillard, Annie, *10:* 31
Dillon, Diane, *15:* 98
Dillon, Eilis, *2:* 92
Dillon, Leo, *15:* 99
Dines, Glen, *7:* 65
Dinsdale, Tim, *11:* 76
DiValentin, Maria, *7:* 68
Dixon, Franklin W. [Collective pseudonym], *1:* 80. *See also* Svenson, Andrew E., *2:* 238; Stratemeyer, Edward, *1:* 208
Dixon, Peter L., *6:* 62
Doane, Pelagie, *7:* 68
Dobell, I(sabel) M(arian) B(arclay), *11:* 77
Dobler, Lavinia G., *6:* 63
Dobrin, Arnold, *4:* 67
"Dr. A." *See* Silverstein, Alvin, *8:* 188
Dodd, Ed(ward) Benton, *4:* 68
Dodge, Bertha S(anford), *8:* 42
Dodge, Mary (Elizabeth) Mapes, *21:* 27
Dodgson, Charles Lutwidge, *YABC 2:* 97
Dodson, Kenneth M(acKenzie), *11:* 77
Doherty, C. H., *6:* 65
Dolson, Hildegarde, *5:* 56

Domanska, Janina, *6:* 65
Donalds, Gordon. *See* Shirreffs, Gordon D., *11:* 207
Donna, Natalie, *9:* 52
Doob, Leonard W(illiam), *8:* 44
Dor, Ana. *See* Ceder, Georgiana Dorcas, *10:* 21
Doré, (Louis Christophe Paul) Gustave, *19:* 92
Dorian, Edith M(cEwen) *5:* 58
Dorian, Harry. *See* Hamilton, Charles Harold St. John, *13:* 77
Dorian, Marguerite, *7:* 68
Dorman, Michael, *7:* 68
Doss, Helen (Grigsby), *20:* 37
Doss, Margot Patterson, *6:* 68
Dougherty, Charles, *18:* 74
Douglas, James McM. *See* Butterworth, W. E., *5:* 40
Douglas, Kathryn. *See* Ewing, Kathryn, *20:* 42
Douglas, Marjory Stoneman, *10:* 33
Douty, Esther M(orris), *8:* 44; *23:* 68 (Obituary)
Dow, Emily R., *10:* 33
Dowdell, Dorothy (Florence) Karns, *12:* 75
Dowden, Anne Ophelia, *7:* 69
Dowdey, Landon Gerald, *11:* 80
Downey, Fairfax, *3:* 61
Downie, Mary Alice, *13:* 32
Doyle, Richard, *21:* 31
Draco, F. *See* Davis, Julia, *6:* 58
Dragonwagon, Crescent, *11:* 81
Drake, Frank. *See* Hamilton, Charles Harold St. John, *13:* 77
Drapier, M. B.. *See* Swift, Jonathan, *19:* 244
Drawson, Blair, *17:* 52
Dresang, Eliza (Carolyn Timberlake), *19:* 106
Drew, Patricia (Mary), *15:* 100
Drewery, Mary, *6:* 69
Drummond, V(iolet) H., *6:* 71
Drummond, Walter. *See* Silverberg, Robert, *13:* 206
Drury, Roger W(olcott), *15:* 101
du Blanc, Daphne. *See* Groom, Arthur William, *10:* 53
du Bois, William Pene, *4:* 69
DuBose, LaRocque (Russ), *2:* 93
Ducornet, Erica, *7:* 72
Dudley, Nancy. *See* Cole, Lois Dwight, *10:* 26
Dudley, Ruth H(ubbell), *11:* 82
Dugan, Michael (Gray), *15:* 101
du Jardin, Rosamond (Neal), *2:* 94
Dulac, Edmund, *19:* 107
Dumas, Alexandre (the elder), *18:* 74
Duncan, Gregory. *See* McClintock, Marshall, *3:* 119
Duncan, Julia K. [Collective pseudonym], *1:* 81
Duncan, Lois. *See* Arquette, Lois S., *1:* 13
Duncan, Norman, *YABC 1:* 108
Dunlop, Agnes M. R., *3:* 62
Dunn, Judy. *See* Spangenberg, Judith Dunn, *5:* 175
Dunn, Mary Lois, *6:* 72
Dunnahoo, Terry, *7:* 73
Dunne, Mary Collins, *11:* 83
Dupuy, T(revor) N(evitt), *4:* 71
Durrell, Gerald (Malcolm), *8:* 46
Du Soe, Robert C., *YABC 2:* 121
Dutz. *See* Davis, Mary Octavia, *6:* 59
Duvall, Evelyn Millis, *9:* 52
Duvoisin, Roger (Antoine), *2:* 95; *23:* 68 (Obituary)
Dwiggins, Don, *4:* 72
Dwight, Allan. *See* Cole, Lois Dwight, *10:* 26

Eagar, Frances, *11:* 85
Eager, Edward (McMaken), *17:* 54
Eagle, Mike, *11:* 86
Earle, Olive L., *7:* 75
Earnshaw, Brian, *17:* 57
Eastman, Charles A(lexander), *YABC 1:* 110
Eastwick, Ivy O., *3:* 64
Eaton, George L. *See* Verral, Charles Spain, *11:* 255
Eaton, Tom, *22:* 99
Ebel, Alex, *11:* 88
Eberle, Irmengarde, *2:* 97; *23:* 68 (Obituary)
Eccles. *See* Williams, Ferelith Eccles, *22:* 237
Eckblad, Edith Berven, *23:* 68
Eckert, Horst, *8:* 47
Edell, Celeste, *12:* 77
Edelman, Lily (Judith), *22:* 100
Edgeworth, Maria, *21:* 33
Edmonds, I(vy) G(ordon), *8:* 48
Edmonds, Walter D(umaux), *1:* 81
Edmund, Sean. *See* Pringle, Laurence, *4:* 171
Edsall, Marian S(tickney), *8:* 50
Edwards, Bertram. *See* Edwards, Herbert Charles, *12:* 77
Edwards, Bronwen Elizabeth. *See* Rose, Wendy, *12:* 180
Edwards, Dorothy, *4:* 73
Edwards, Harvey, *5:* 59
Edwards, Herbert Charles, *12:* 77
Edwards, Jane Campbell, *10:* 34
Edwards, Julie. *See* Andrews, Julie, *7:* 6
Edwards, Julie. *See* Stratemeyer, Edward L., *1:* 208
Edwards, Monica le Doux Newton, *12:* 78
Edwards, Sally, *7:* 75
Edwards, Samuel. *See* Gerson, Noel B(ertram), *22:* 118
Eggenberger, David, *6:* 72
Egielski, Richard, *11:* 89
Egypt, Ophelia Settle, *16:* 88
Ehrlich, Bettina (Bauer), *1:* 82
Eichberg, James Bandman. *See* Garfield, James B., *6:* 85
Eichenberg, Fritz, *9:* 53
Eichner, James A., *4:* 73
Eifert, Virginia S(nider), *2:* 99
Einsel, Naiad, *10:* 34
Einsel, Walter, *10:* 37
Eiseman, Alberta, *15:* 102
Eisenberg, Azriel, *12:* 79
Eitzen, Allan, *9:* 57
Eitzen, Ruth (Carper), *9:* 57
Elam, Richard M(ace, Jr.), *9:* 57
Elfman, Blossom, *8:* 51
Elia. *See* Lamb, Charles, *17:* 101
Eliot, Anne. *See* Cole, Lois Dwight, *10:* 26
Elisofon, Eliot, *21:* 38 (Obituary)
Elkin, Benjamin, *3:* 65
Elkins, Dov Peretz, *5:* 61
Ellacott, S(amuel) E(rnest), *19:* 117
Elliott, Sarah M(cCarn), *14:* 57
Ellis, Edward S(ylvester), *YABC 1:* 116
Ellis, Ella Thorp, *7:* 76
Ellis, Harry Bearse, *9:* 58
Ellis, Mel, *7:* 77
Ellison, Lucile Watkins, *22:* 102 (Obituary)
Ellison, Virginia Howell, *4:* 74
Ellsberg, Edward, *7:* 78
Elspeth. *See* Bragdon, Elspeth, *6:* 30
Elting, Mary, *2:* 100
Elwart, Joan Potter, *2:* 101
Emberley, Barbara A(nne), *8:* 51
Emberley, Ed(ward Randolph), *8:* 52
Embry, Margaret (Jacob), *5:* 61
Emerson, Alice B. [Collective pseudonym], *1:* 84
Emery, Anne (McGuigan), *1:* 84
Emrich, Duncan (Black Macdonald), *11:* 90
Emslie, M. L. *See* Simpson, Myrtle L(illias), *14:* 181
Engdahl, Sylvia Louise, *4:* 75
Engle, Eloise Katherine, *9:* 60
Englebert, Victor, *8:* 54
Enright, Elizabeth, *9:* 61
Epp, Margaret A(gnes), *20:* 38
Epple, Anne Orth, *20:* 40
Epstein, Anne Merrick, *20:* 41
Epstein, Beryl (Williams), *1:* 85
Epstein, Samuel, *1:* 87
Erdman, Loula Grace, *1:* 88
Ericson, Walter. *See* Fast, Howard, *7:* 80
Erlich, Lillian (Feldman), *10:* 38
Ervin, Janet Halliday, *4:* 77
Estep, Irene (Compton), *5:* 62
Estes, Eleanor, *7:* 79
Estoril, Jean. *See* Allan, Mabel Esther, *5:* 2
Ets, Marie Hall, *2:* 102

Eunson, Dale, *5:* 63
Evans, Katherine (Floyd), *5:* 64
Evans, Mari, *10:* 39
Evans, Mark, *19:* 118
Evans, Patricia Healy. *See* Carpenter, Patricia, *11:* 43
Evarts, Hal G. (Jr.), *6:* 72
Evernden, Margery, *5:* 65
Ewen, David, *4:* 78
Ewing, Juliana (Horatia Gatty), *16:* 90
Ewing, Kathryn, *20:* 42
Eyerly, Jeannette Hyde, *4:* 80

Fabe, Maxene, *15:* 103
Faber, Doris, *3:* 67
Faber, Harold, *5:* 65
Fabre, Jean Henri (Casimir), *22:* 102
Facklam, Margery Metz, *20:* 43
Fadiman, Clifton (Paul), *11:* 91
Fair, Sylvia, *13:* 33
Fairfax-Lucy, Brian, *6:* 73
Fairman, Joan A(lexandra), *10:* 41
Faithfull, Gail, *8:* 55
Falconer, James. *See* Kirkup, James, *12:* 120
Falkner, Leonard, *12:* 80
Fall, Thomas. *See* Snow, Donald Clifford, *16:* 246
Fanning, Leonard M(ulliken), *5:* 65
Faralla, Dana, *9:* 62
Faralla, Dorothy W. *See* Faralla, Dana, *9:* 62
Farb, Peter, *12:* 81; *22:* 109 (Obituary)
Farjeon, (Eve) Annabel, *11:* 93
Farjeon, Eleanor, *2:* 103
Farley, Carol, *4:* 81
Farley, Walter, *2:* 106
Farnham, Burt. *See* Clifford, Harold B., *10:* 24
Farquhar, Margaret C(utting), *13:* 35
Farr, Finis (King), *10:* 41
Farrell, Ben. *See* Cebulash, Mel, *10:* 19
Farrington, Benjamin, *20:* 45 (Obituary)
Farrington, Selwyn Kip, Jr., *20:* 45
Fassler, Joan (Grace), *11:* 94
Fast, Howard, *7:* 80
Fatchen, Max, *20:* 45
Father Xavier. *See* Hurwood, Bernhardt J., *12:* 107
Fatio, Louise, *6:* 75
Faulhaber, Martha, *7:* 82
Faulkner, Anne Irvin, *23:* 70
Faulkner, Nancy. *See* Faulkner, Anne Irvin, *23:* 70
Feagles, Anita MacRae, *9:* 63
Feague, Mildred H., *14:* 59
Fecher, Constance, *7:* 83
Feelings, Muriel (Grey), *16:* 104
Feelings, Thomas, *8:* 55
Feelings, Tom. *See* Feelings, Thomas, *8:* 55
Feiffer, Jules, *8:* 57
Feil, Hila, *12:* 81
Feilen, John. *See* May, Julian, *11:* 175
Feldman, Anne (Rodgers), *19:* 121
Fellows, Muriel H., *10:* 41
Felsen, Henry Gregor, *1:* 89
Felton, Harold William, *1:* 90
Felton, Ronald Oliver, *3:* 67
Fenner, Carol, *7:* 84
Fenner, Phyllis R(eid), *1:* 91
Fenten, D. X., *4:* 82
Fenton, Carroll Lane, *5:* 66
Fenton, Edward, *7:* 86
Fenton, Mildred Adams, *21:* 38
Feravolo, Rocco Vincent, *10:* 42
Ferber, Edna, *7:* 87
Ferguson, Bob. *See* Ferguson, Robert Bruce, *13:* 35
Ferguson, Robert Bruce, *13:* 35
Fergusson, Erna, *5:* 67
Fermi, Laura, *6:* 78
Fern, Eugene A., *10:* 43
Ferris, Helen Josephine, *21:* 39
Ferris, James Cody [Collective pseudonym], *1:* 92
Fiammenghi, Gioia, *9:* 64
Fiarotta, Noel, *15:* 104
Fiarotta, Phyllis, *15:* 105
Fichter, George S., *7:* 92
Fidler, Kathleen, *3:* 68
Fiedler, Jean, *4:* 83
Field, Edward, *8:* 58
Field, Eugene, *16:* 105
Field, Rachel (Lyman), *15:* 106
Fife, Dale (Odile), *18:* 110
Fighter Pilot, A. *See* Johnston, H(ugh) A(nthony) S(tephen), *14:* 87
Figueroa, Pablo, *9:* 66
Fijan, Carol, *12:* 82
Fillmore, Parker H(oysted), *YABC 1:* 121
Fink, William B(ertrand), *22:* 109
Finkel, George (Irvine), *8:* 59
Finlay, Winifred, *23:* 71
Finlayson, Ann, *8:* 61
Firmin, Peter, *15:* 113
Fischbach, Julius, *10:* 43
Fisher, Aileen (Lucia), *1:* 92
Fisher, Dorothy Canfield, *YABC 1:* 122
Fisher, John (Oswald Hamilton), *15:* 115
Fisher, Laura Harrison, *5:* 67
Fisher, Leonard Everett, *4:* 84
Fisher, Margery (Turner), *20:* 47
Fitch, Clarke. *See* Sinclair, Upton (Beall), *9:* 168
Fitch, John, IV. *See* Cormier, Robert Edmund, *10:* 28
Fitschen, Dale, *20:* 48
Fitzgerald, Captain Hugh. *See* Baum L(yman) Frank, *18:* 7
Fitzgerald, Edward Earl, *20:* 49
Fitzgerald, F(rancis) A(nthony), *15:* 115
Fitzgerald, John D(ennis), *20:* 50
Fitzhardinge, Joan Margaret, *2:* 107
Fitzhugh, Louise, *1:* 94
Flack, Marjorie, *YABC 2:* 123
Flash Flood. *See* Robinson, Jan M., *6:* 194
Fleischman, (Albert) Sid(ney), *8:* 61
Fleming, Alice Mulcahey, *9:* 67
Fleming, Ian (Lancaster), *9:* 67
Fleming, Thomas J(ames), *8:* 64
Fletcher, Charlie May, *3:* 70
Fletcher, Helen Jill, *13:* 36
Flexner, James Thomas, *9:* 70
Flitner, David P., *7:* 92
Floethe, Louise Lee, *4:* 87
Floethe, Richard, *4:* 89
Flood, Flash. *See* Robinson, Jan M., *6:* 194
Flora, James (Royer), *1:* 95
Florian, Douglas, *19:* 122
Flory, Jane Trescott, *22:* 110
Flynn, Barbara, *9:* 71
Flynn, Jackson. *See* Shirreffs, Gordon D., *11:* 207
Folsom, Franklin (Brewster), *5:* 67
Fooner, Michael, *22:* 112
Forberg, Ati, *22:* 113
Forbes, Esther, *2:* 108
Forbes, Graham B. [Collective pseudonym], *1:* 97
Forbes, Kathryn. *See* McLean, Kathryn (Anderson), *9:* 140
Ford, Albert Lee. *See* Stratemeyer, Edward L., *1:* 208
Ford, Elbur. *See* Hibbert, Eleanor, *2:* 134
Ford, Hildegarde. *See* Morrison, Velma Ford, *21:* 110
Ford, Marcia. *See* Radford, Ruby L., *6:* 186
Foreman, Michael, *2:* 110
Forester, C(ecil) S(cott), *13:* 38
Forman, Brenda, *4:* 90
Forman, James Douglas, *8:* 64
Forrest, Sybil. *See* Markun, Patricia M(aloney), *15:* 189
Forsee, (Frances) Aylesa, *1:* 97
Foster, Doris Van Liew, *10:* 44
Foster, E(lizabeth) C(onnell), *9:* 71
Foster, Elizabeth, *10:* 45
Foster, Elizabeth Vincent, *12:* 82
Foster, F. Blanche, *11:* 95
Foster, Genevieve (Stump), *2:* 111; *23:* 73 (Obituary)
Foster, John T(homas), *8:* 65
Foster, Laura Louise, *6:* 78
Foster, Margaret Lesser, *21:* 43 (Obituary)
Foster, Marian Curtis, *23:* 73
Fourth Brother, The. *See* Aung, (Maung) Htin, *21:* 5

Fowke, Edith (Margaret), *14:* 59
Fowles, John, *22:* 114
Fox, Charles Philip, *12:* 83
Fox, Eleanor. *See* St. John, Wylly Folk, *10:* 132
Fox, Fontaine Talbot, Jr., *23:* 75 (Obituary)
Fox, Freeman. *See* Hamilton, Charles Harold St. John, *13:* 77
Fox, Lorraine, *11:* 96
Fox, Michael Wilson, *15:* 117
Fox, Paula, *17:* 59
Frances, Miss. *See* Horwich, Frances R., *11:* 142
Franchere, Ruth, *18:* 111
Francis, Dorothy Brenner, *10:* 46
Francis, Pamela (Mary), *11:* 97
Francoise. *See* Seignobosc, Francoise, *21:* 145
Frank, Josette, *10:* 47
Frankau, Mary Evelyn, *4:* 90
Frankel, Bernice, *9:* 72
Frankenberg, Robert, *22:* 115
Franklin, Harold, *13:* 53
Franklin, Steve. *See* Stevens, Franklin, *6:* 206
Franzén, Nils-Olof, *10:* 47
Frasconi, Antonio, *6:* 79
Frazier, Neta Lohnes, *7:* 94
Freed, Alvyn M., *22:* 117
Freedman, Russell (Bruce), *16:* 115
Freeman, Don, *17:* 60
Freeman, Ira M(aximilian), *21:* 43
French, Allen, *YABC 1:* 133
French, Dorothy Kayser, *5:* 69
French, Fiona, *6:* 81
French, Paul. *See* Asimov, Isaac, *1:* 15
Frewer, Glyn, *11:* 98
Frick, C. H. *See* Irwin, Constance Frick, *6:* 119
Frick, Constance. *See* Irwin, Constance Frick, *6:* 119
Friedlander, Joanne K(ohn), *9:* 73
Friedman, Estelle, *7:* 95
Friendlich, Dick. *See* Friendlich, Richard, *11:* 99
Friendlich, Richard J., *11:* 99
Friermood, Elisabeth Hamilton, *5:* 69
Friis, Babbis. *See* Friis-Baastad, Babbis, *7:* 95
Friis-Baastad, Babbis, *7:* 95
Friskey, Margaret Richards, *5:* 72
Fritz, Jean (Guttery), *1:* 98
Froman, Elizabeth Hull, *10:* 49
Froman, Robert (Winslow), *8:* 67
Frost, A(rthur) B(urdett), *19:* 122
Frost, Erica. *See* Supraner, Robyn, *20:* 182
Frost, Lesley, *14:* 61
Frost, Robert (Lee), *14:* 63
Fry, Rosalie, *3:* 71
Fuchs, Erich, *6:* 84
Fujita, Tamao, *7:* 98
Fujiwara, Michiko, *15:* 120
Fuller, Catherine L(euthold), *9:* 73
Fuller, Edmund (Maybank), *21:* 45
Fuller, Iola. *See* McCoy, Iola Fuller, *3:* 120
Fuller, Lois Hamilton, *11:* 99
Funk, Thompson. *See* Funk, Tom, *7:* 98
Funk, Tom, *7:* 98
Funke, Lewis, *11:* 100
Fyleman, Rose, *21:* 46

Gaeddert, Lou Ann (Bigge), *20:* 58
Gág, Wanda (Hazel), *YABC 1:* 135
Gage, Wilson. *See* Steele, Mary Q., *3:* 211
Gagliardo, Ruth Garver, *22:* 118 (Obituary)
Galdone, Paul, *17:* 69
Galinsky, Ellen, *23:* 75
Gallant, Roy (Arthur), *4:* 91
Gallico, Paul, *13:* 53
Galt, Thomas Franklin, Jr., *5:* 72
Galt, Tom. *See* Galt, Thomas Franklin, Jr., *5:* 72
Gamerman, Martha, *15:* 121
Gannett, Ruth Stiles, *3:* 73
Gannon, Robert (Haines), *8:* 68
Gantos, Jack. *See* Gantos, John (Bryan), Jr., *20:* 59
Gantos, John (Bryan), Jr., *20:* 59
Gard, Joyce. *See* Reeves, Joyce, *17:* 158
Gard, Robert Edward, *18:* 113
Garden, Nancy, *12:* 85
Gardner, Jeanne LeMonnier, *5:* 73
Gardner, Martin, *16:* 117
Gardner, Richard A., *13:* 64
Garelick, May, *19:* 130
Garfield, James B., *6:* 85
Garfield, Leon, *1:* 99
Garis, Howard R(oger), *13:* 67
Garner, Alan, *18:* 114
Garnett, Eve C. R., *3:* 75
Garraty, John A., *23:* 76
Garrett, Helen, *21:* 48
Garrigue, Sheila, *21:* 49
Garrison, Barbara, *19:* 132
Garrison, Frederick. *See* Sinclair, Upton (Beall), *9:* 168
Garst, Doris Shannon, *1:* 100
Garst, Shannon. *See* Garst, Doris Shannon, *1:* 100
Garthwaite, Marion H., *7:* 100
Gates, Doris, *1:* 102
Gatty, Juliana Horatia. *See* Ewing, Juliana (Horatia Gatty), *16:* 90
Gault, William Campbell, *8:* 69
Gaver, Becky. *See* Gaver, Rebecca, *20:* 60
Gaver, Rebecca, *20:* 60
Gay, Kathlyn, *9:* 74
Gay, Zhenya, *19:* 134
Geis, Darlene, *7:* 101
Geisel, Theodor Seuss, *1:* 104
Geldart, William, *15:* 121
Gelinas, Paul J., *10:* 49
Gelman, Steve, *3:* 75
Gemming, Elizabeth, *11:* 104
Gentleman, David, *7:* 102
George, Jean Craighead, *2:* 112
George, John L(othar), *2:* 114
George, S(idney) C(harles), *11:* 104
Georgiou, Constantine, *7:* 102
Geras, Adele (Daphne), *23:* 76
Gergely, Tibor, *20:* 61 (Obituary)
Gerson, Noel B(ertram), *22:* 118
Gessner, Lynne, *16:* 119
Gibbons, Gail, *23:* 77
Gibbs, Alonzo (Lawrence), *5:* 74
Gibson, Josephine. *See* Joslin, Sesyle, *2:* 158
Gidal, Sonia, *2:* 115
Gidal, Tim N(ahum), *2:* 116
Giegling, John A(llan), *17:* 75
Gilbert, (Agnes) Joan (Sewell), *10:* 50
Gilbert, Nan. *See* Gilbertson, Mildred, *2:* 116
Gilbert, Sara (Dulaney), *11:* 105
Gilbertson, Mildred Geiger, *2:* 116
Gilbreath, Alice (Thompson), *12:* 87
Gilbreth, Frank B., Jr., *2:* 117
Gilfond, Henry, *2:* 118
Gilge, Jeanette, *22:* 121
Gill, Derek L(ewis) T(heodore), *9:* 75
Gill, Margery Jean, *22:* 122
Gillett, Mary, *7:* 103
Gillette, Henry Sampson, *14:* 71
Gilman, Dorothy. *See* Dorothy Gilman Butters, *5:* 39
Gilman, Esther, *15:* 123
Gilmore, Iris, *22:* 123
Gilson, Barbara. *See* Gilson, Charles James Louis, *YABC 2:* 124
Gilson, Charles James Louis, *YABC 2:* 124
Ginsburg, Mirra, *6:* 86
Giovanopoulos, Paul, *7:* 104
Gipson, Frederick B., *2:* 118
Gittings, Jo Manton, *3:* 76
Gittings, Robert, *6:* 88
Gladstone, Gary, *12:* 88
Glaser, Milton, *11:* 106
Glaspell, Susan, *YABC 2:* 125
Glauber, Uta (Heil), *17:* 75
Glazer, Tom, *9:* 76
Gles, Margaret Breitmaier, *22:* 124
Glick, Carl (Cannon), *14:* 72
Glick, Virginia Kirkus, *23:* 78 (Obituary)
Gliewe, Unada, *3:* 77
Glines, Carroll V(ane), Jr., *19:* 137
Glovach, Linda, *7:* 105
Glubok, Shirley, *6:* 89
Glynne-Jones, William, *11:* 107
Godden, Rumer, *3:* 79

Author Index

Gode, Alexander. *See* Gode von Aesch, Alexander (Gottfried Friedrich), *14:* 74
Gode von Aesch, Alexander (Gottfried Friedrich), *14:* 74
Goettel, Elinor, *12:* 89
Goetz, Delia, *22:* 125
Goffstein, M(arilyn) B(rooke), *8:* 70
Golann, Cecil Paige, *11:* 109
Golbin, Andrée, *15:* 124
Gold, Phyllis, *21:* 50
Gold, Sharlya, *9:* 77
Goldfeder, Cheryl. *See* Pahz, Cheryl Suzanne, *11:* 189
Goldfeder, Jim. *See* Pahz, James Alon, *11:* 190
Goldfrank, Helen Colodny, *6:* 89
Goldin, Augusta, *13:* 72
Goldsborough, June, *19:* 138
Goldstein, Philip, *23:* 79
Goldston, Robert (Conroy), *6:* 90
Gonzalez, Gloria, *23:* 80
Goodall, John S(trickland), *4:* 92
Goode, Diane, *15:* 125
Goodman, Elaine, *9:* 78
Goodman, Walter, *9:* 78
Goodrich, Samuel Griswold, *23:* 82
Goodwin, Hal. *See* Goodwin, Harold Leland, *13:* 73
Goodwin, Harold Leland, *13:* 73
Goossen, Agnes. *See* Epp, Margaret A(gnes), *20:* 38
Gordon, Colonel H. R. *See* Ellis, Edward S(ylvester), *YABC 1:* 116
Gordon, Dorothy, *20:* 61
Gordon, Esther S(aranga), *10:* 50
Gordon, Frederick [Collective pseudonym], *1:* 106
Gordon, Hal. *See* Goodwin, Harold Leland, *13:* 73
Gordon, John, *6:* 90
Gordon, Lew. *See* Baldwin, Gordon C., *12:* 30
Gordon, Margaret (Anna), *9:* 79
Gordon, Selma. *See* Lanes, Selma G., *3:* 96
Gordon, Sol, *11:* 111
Gordon, Stewart. *See* Shirreffs, Gordon D., *11:* 207
Gorelick, Molly C., *9:* 80
Gorham, Michael. *See* Folsom, Franklin, *5:* 67
Gorsline, Douglas (Warner), *11:* 112
Goryan, Sirak. *See* Saroyan, William, *23:* 210
Gottlieb, Gerald, *7:* 106
Goudey, Alice E., *20:* 64
Goudge, Elizabeth, *2:* 119
Goulart, Ron, *6:* 92
Gould, Jean R(osalind), *11:* 114
Gould, Lilian, *6:* 92
Gould, Marilyn, *15:* 127
Govan, Christine Noble, *9:* 80
Graber, Alexander, *7:* 106
Graff, Polly Anne. *See* Colver, Anne, *7:* 54
Graff, (S.) Stewart, *9:* 82
Graham, Ada, *11:* 115
Graham, Eleanor, *18:* 116
Graham, Frank, Jr., *11:* 116
Graham, John, *11:* 117
Graham, Lorenz B(ell), *2:* 122
Graham, Margaret Bloy, *11:* 119
Graham, Robin Lee, *7:* 107
Grahame, Kenneth, *YABC 1:* 144
Gramatky, Hardie, *1:* 107; *23:* 89 (Obituary)
Grange, Peter. *See* Nicole, Christopher Robin, *5:* 141
Granstaff, Bill, *10:* 51
Grant, Bruce, *5:* 75
Grant, Eva, *7:* 108
Grant, (Alice) Leigh, *10:* 52
Grant, Matthew C. *See* May, Julian, *11:* 175
Grant, Myrna (Lois), *21:* 51
Grant, Neil, *14:* 75
Gravel, Fern. *See* Hall, James Norman, *21:* 54
Graves, Charles Parlin, *4:* 94
Gray, Elizabeth Janet, *6:* 93
Gray, Genevieve S., *4:* 95
Gray, Jenny. *See* Gray, Genevieve S., *4:* 95
Gray, Nicholas Stuart, *4:* 96
Gray, Patricia, *7:* 110
Gray, Patsey. *See* Gray, Patricia, *7:* 110
Grayland, V. Merle. *See* Grayland, Valerie, *7:* 111
Grayland, Valerie, *7:* 111
Great Comte, The. *See* Hawkesworth, Eric, *13:* 94
Greaves, Margaret, *7:* 113
Green, Adam. *See* Weisgard, Leonard, *2:* 263
Green, D. *See* Casewit, Curtis, *4:* 43
Green, Jane, *9:* 82
Green, Mary Moore, *11:* 120
Green, Morton, *8:* 71
Green, Norma B(erger), *11:* 120
Green, Phyllis, *20:* 65
Green, Roger (Gilbert) Lancelyn, *2:* 123
Green, Sheila Ellen, *8:* 72
Greenaway, Kate, *YABC 2:* 129
Greenberg, Harvey R., *5:* 77
Greene, Bette, *8:* 73
Greene, Carla, *1:* 108
Greene, Constance C(larke), *11:* 121
Greene, Ellin, *23:* 89
Greene, Graham, *20:* 66
Greene, Wade, *11:* 122
Greenfeld, Howard, *19:* 140
Greenfield, Eloise, *19:* 141
Greening, Hamilton. *See* Hamilton, Charles Harold St. John, *13:* 77
Greenleaf, Barbara Kaye, *6:* 95
Greenwald, Sheila. *See* Green, Sheila Ellen, *8:* 72
Gregg, Walter H(arold), *20:* 75
Gregori, Leon, *15:* 129
Grendon, Stephen. *See* Derleth, August (William), *5:* 54
Grenville, Pelham. *See* Wodehouse, P(elham) G(renville), *22:* 241
Gretz, Susanna, *7:* 114
Gretzer, John, *18:* 117
Grey, Jerry, *11:* 123
Grice, Frederick, *6:* 96
Grieder, Walter, *9:* 83
Griese, Arnold A(lfred), *9:* 84
Grifalconi, Ann, *2:* 125
Griffith, Jeannette. *See* Eyerly, Jeanette, *4:* 80
Griffiths, G(ordon) D(ouglas), *20:* 75 (Obituary)
Griffiths, Helen, *5:* 77
Grimm, Jacob Ludwig Karl, *22:* 126
Grimm, Wilhelm Karl, *22:* 126
Grimm, William C(arey), *14:* 75
Grimshaw, Nigel (Gilroy), *23:* 91
Grimsley, Gordon. *See* Groom, Arthur William, *10:* 53
Gringhuis, Dirk. *See* Gringhuis, Richard H. *6:* 97
Gringhuis, Richard H., *6:* 97
Grinnell, George Bird, *16:* 121
Gripe, Maria (Kristina), *2:* 126
Grohskopf, Bernice, *7:* 114
Grol, Lini Richards, *9:* 85
Grollman, Earl A., *22:* 152
Groom, Arthur William, *10:* 53
Gross, Sarah Chokla, *9:* 86
Grossman, Robert, *11:* 124
Groth, John, *21:* 53
Gruenberg, Sidonie M(atsner), *2:* 127
Gugliotta, Bobette, *7:* 116
Guillaume, Jeanette G. (Flierl), *8:* 74
Guillot, Rene, *7:* 117
Gundrey, Elizabeth, *23:* 91
Gunston, Bill. *See* Gunston, William Tudor, *9:* 88
Gunston, William Tudor, *9:* 88
Gunther, John, *2:* 129
Gurko, Leo, *9:* 88
Gurko, Miriam, *9:* 89
Gustafson, Sarah R. *See* Riedman, Sarah R., *1:* 183
Guy, Rosa (Cuthbert), *14:* 77

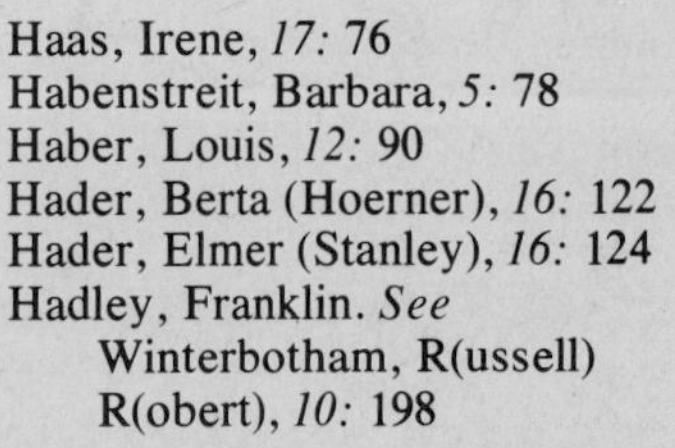

Haas, Irene, *17:* 76
Habenstreit, Barbara, *5:* 78
Haber, Louis, *12:* 90
Hader, Berta (Hoerner), *16:* 122
Hader, Elmer (Stanley), *16:* 124
Hadley, Franklin. *See* Winterbotham, R(ussell) R(obert), *10:* 198

Hafner, Marylin, *7:* 119
Haggard, H(enry) Rider, *16:* 129
Haggerty, James J(oseph) *5:* 78
Hagon, Priscilla. *See* Allan, Mabel Esther, *5:* 2
Hahn, Emily, *3:* 81
Hahn, Hannelore, *8:* 74
Hahn, James (Sage), *9:* 90
Hahn, (Mona) Lynn, *9:* 91
Haig-Brown, Roderick (Langmere), *12:* 90
Haines, Gail Kay, *11:* 124
Haining, Peter, *14:* 77
Haldane, Roger John, *13:* 75
Hale, Edward Everett, *16:* 143
Hale, Helen. *See* Mulcahy, Lucille Burnett, *12:* 155
Hale, Kathleen, *17:* 78
Hale, Linda, *6:* 99
Hall, Adele, *7:* 120
Hall, Anna Gertrude, *8:* 75
Hall, Donald (Andrew, Jr.), *23:* 92
Hall, Elvajean, *6:* 100
Hall, James Norman, *21:* 54
Hall, Jesse. *See* Boesen, Victor, *16:* 53
Hall, Lynn, *2:* 130
Hall, Malcolm, *7:* 121
Hall, Marjory. *See* Yeakley, Marjory Hall, *21:* 207
Hall, Rosalys Haskell, *7:* 121
Hallard, Peter. *See* Catherall, Arthur, *3:* 38
Hallas, Richard. *See* Knight, Eric (Mowbray), *18:* 151
Halliburton, Warren J., *19:* 143
Hallin, Emily Watson, *6:* 101
Hall-Quest, Olga W(ilbourne), *11:* 125
Hallstead, William F(inn) III, *11:* 126
Hallward, Michael, *12:* 91
Halsell, Grace, *13:* 76
Halter, Jon C(harles), *22:* 152
Hamberger, John, *14:* 79
Hamil, Thomas Arthur, *14:* 80
Hamil, Tom. *See* Hamil, Thomas Arthur, *14:* 80
Hamilton, Charles Harold St. John, *13:* 77
Hamilton, Clive. *See* Lewis, C. S., *13:* 129
Hamilton, Dorothy, *12:* 92
Hamilton, Edith, *20:* 75
Hamilton, Elizabeth, *23:* 94
Hamilton, Robert W. *See* Stratemeyer, Edward L., *1:* 208
Hamilton, Virginia, *4:* 97
Hammer, Richard, *6:* 102
Hammerman, Gay M(orenus), *9:* 92
Hammontree, Marie (Gertrude), *13:* 89
Hampson, (Richard) Denman, *15:* 129
Hamre, Leif, *5:* 79
Hancock, Sibyl, *9:* 92
Hane, Roger, *20:* 79 (Obituary)
Haney, Lynn, *23:* 95
Hanff, Helene, *11:* 128
Hanlon, Emily, *15:* 131
Hann, Jacquie, *19:* 144
Hanna, Paul R(obert), *9:* 93
Hano, Arnold, *12:* 93
Hanser, Richard (Frederick), *13:* 90
Hanson, Joan, *8:* 75
Harald, Eric. *See* Boesen, Victor, *16:* 53
Hardwick, Richard Holmes Jr., *12:* 94
Hardy, Alice Dale [Collective pseudonym], *1:* 109
Hardy, David A(ndrews), *9:* 95
Hardy, Stuart. *See* Schisgall, Oscar, *12:* 187
Hark, Mildred. *See* McQueen, Mildred Hark, *12:* 145
Harkaway, Hal. *See* Stratemeyer, Edward L., *1:* 208
Harkins, Philip, *6:* 102
Harlan, Glen. *See* Cebulash, Mel, *10:* 19
Harmelink, Barbara (Mary), *9:* 97
Harmon, Margaret, *20:* 80
Harnan, Terry, *12:* 94
Harnett, Cynthia (Mary), *5:* 79
Harper, Wilhelmina, *4:* 99
Harrington, Lyn, *5:* 80
Harris, Christie, *6:* 103
Harris, Colver. *See* Colver, Anne, *7:* 54
Harris, Dorothy Joan, *13:* 91
Harris, Janet, *4:* 100; *23:* 97 (Obituary)
Harris, Joel Chandler, *YABC 1:* 154
Harris, Leon A., Jr., *4:* 101
Harris, Lorle K(empe), *22:* 153
Harris, Rosemary (Jeanne), *4:* 101
Harrison, Deloris, *9:* 97
Harrison, Harry, *4:* 102
Hartley, Ellen (Raphael), *23:* 97
Hartley, William B(rown), *23:* 98
Hartman, Louis F(rancis), *22:* 154
Hartshorn, Ruth M., *11:* 129
Harwin, Brian. *See* Henderson, LeGrand, *9:* 104
Harwood, Pearl Augusta (Bragdon), *9:* 98
Haskell, Arnold, *6:* 104
Haskins, James, *9:* 100
Haskins, Jim. *See* Haskins, James, *9:* 100
Hassler, Jon (Francis), *19:* 145
Hatlo, Jimmy, *23:* 100 (Obituary)
Haugaard, Erik Christian, *4:* 104
Hauser, Margaret L(ouise), *10:* 54
Hausman, Gerald, *13:* 93
Hausman, Gerry. *See* Hausman, Gerald, *13:* 93
Hautzig, Esther, *4:* 105
Havenhand, John. *See* Cox, John Roberts, *9:* 42
Havighurst, Walter (Edwin), *1:* 109
Haviland, Virginia, *6:* 105
Hawes, Judy, *4:* 107
Hawk, Virginia Driving. *See* Sneve, Virginia Driving Hawk, *8:* 193
Hawkesworth, Eric, *13:* 94
Hawkins, Arthur, *19:* 146
Hawkins, Quail, *6:* 107
Hawkinson, John, *4:* 108
Hawkinson, Lucy (Ozone), *21:* 63
Hawley, Mable C. [Collective pseudonym], *1:* 110
Hawthorne, Captain R. M. *See* Ellis, Edward S(ylvester), *YABC 1:* 116
Hawthorne, Nathaniel, *YABC 2:* 143
Hay, John, *13:* 95
Hay, Timothy. *See* Brown, Margaret Wise, *YABC 2:* 9
Haycraft, Howard, *6:* 108
Haycraft, Molly Costain, *6:* 110
Hayden, Robert E(arl), *19:* 147
Hayes, Carlton J. H., *11:* 129
Hayes, John F., *11:* 129
Hayes, Will, *7:* 122
Hayes, William D(imitt), *8:* 76
Hays, Wilma Pitchford, *1:* 110
Haywood, Carolyn, *1:* 111
Head, Gay. *See* Hauser, Margaret L(ouise), *10:* 54
Headley, Elizabeth. *See* Cavanna, Betty, *1:* 54
Headstrom, Richard, *8:* 77
Heady, Eleanor B(utler), *8:* 78
Heal, Edith, *7:* 123
Healey, Brooks. *See* Albert, Burton, Jr., *22:* 7
Heath, Veronica. *See* Blackett, Veronica Heath, *12:* 54
Heaven, Constance. *See* Fecher, Constance, *7:* 83
Hecht, Henri Joseph, *9:* 101; *22:* 155 (Obituary)
Hechtkopf, Henryk, *17:* 79
Hegarty, Reginald Beaton, *10:* 54
Heiderstadt, Dorothy, *6:* 111
Hein, Lucille Eleanor, *20:* 80
Heinlein, Robert A(nson), *9:* 102
Heins, Paul, *13:* 96
Helfman, Elizabeth S., *3:* 83
Helfman, Harry, *3:* 84
Hellman, Hal. *See* Hellman, Harold, *4:* 109
Hellman, Harold, *4:* 109
Helps, Racey, *2:* 131
Hemming, Roy, *11:* 130
Henderley, Brooks [Collective pseudonym], *1:* 113
Henderson, LeGrand, *9:* 104
Henderson, Nancy Wallace, *22:* 155
Henderson, Zenna (Chlarson) *5:* 81
Hendrickson, Walter Brookfield, Jr., *9:* 104
Henry, Joanne Landers, *6:* 112
Henry, Marguerite, *11:* 131

Henry, O. *See* Porter, William Sydney, *YABC 2:* 259
Henry, Oliver. *See* Porter, William Sydney, *YABC 2:* 259
Henstra, Friso, *8:* 80
Herald, Kathleen. *See* Peyton, Kathleen (Wendy), *15:* 211
Herbert, Cecil. *See* Hamilton, Charles Harold St. John, *13:* 77
Herbert, Don, *2:* 131
Herbert, Frank (Patrick), *9:* 105
Herbert, Wally. *See* Herbert, Walter William, *23:* 101
Herbert, Walter William, *23:* 101
Hergé. *See* Remi, Georges, *13:* 183
Herman, Charlotte, *20:* 81
Hermanson, Dennis (Everett), *10:* 55
Herrmanns, Ralph, *11:* 133
Herron, Edward A(lbert), *4:* 110
Hertz, Grete Janus, *23:* 102
Hess, Lilo, *4:* 111
Heuman, William, *21:* 64
Hewett, Anita, *13:* 97
Hey, Nigel S(tewart), *20:* 83
Heyduck-Huth, Hilde, *8:* 81
Heyerdahl, Thor, *2:* 132
Heyliger, William, *YABC 1:* 163
Heyward, Du Bose, *21:* 66
Hibbert, Christopher, *4:* 112
Hibbert, Eleanor Burford, *2:* 134
Hickman, Janet, *12:* 97
Hickok, Lorena A., *20:* 83
Hicks, Eleanor B. *See* Coerr, Eleanor, *1:* 64
Hicks, Harvey. *See* Stratemeyer, Edward L., *1:* 208
Hieatt, Constance B(artlett), *4:* 113
Hiebert, Ray Eldon, *13:* 98
Higdon, Hal, *4:* 115
Highet, Helen. *See* MacInnes, Helen, *22:* 181
Hightower, Florence, *4:* 115
Hildick, E. W. *See* Hildick, Wallace, *2:* 135
Hildick, (Edmund) Wallace, *2:* 135
Hill, Grace Brooks [Collective pseudonym], *1:* 113
Hill, Grace Livingston, *YABC 2:* 162
Hill, Kathleen Louise, *4:* 116
Hill, Kay. *See* Hill, Kathleen Louise, *4:* 116
Hill, Lorna, *12:* 97
Hill, Monica. *See* Watson, Jane Werner, *3:* 244
Hill, Robert W(hite), *12:* 98
Hill, Ruth A. *See* Viguers, Ruth Hill, *6:* 214
Hill, Ruth Livingston. *See* Munce, Ruth Hill, *12:* 156
Hillerman, Tony, *6:* 113
Hillert, Margaret, *8:* 82
Hilton, Irene (P.), *7:* 124
Hilton, Ralph, *8:* 83
Hilton, Suzanne, *4:* 117
Himler, Ann, *8:* 84
Himler, Ronald, *6:* 114
Hinton, S(usan) E(loise), *19:* 147
Hirsch, S. Carl, *2:* 137
Hirsh, Marilyn, *7:* 126
Hiser, Iona Seibert, *4:* 118
Hitte, Kathryn, *16:* 158
Hitz, Demi, *11:* 134
Ho, Minfong, *15:* 131
Hoban, Lillian, *22:* 157
Hoban, Russell C(onwell), *1:* 113
Hoban, Tana, *22:* 158
Hobart, Lois, *7:* 127
Hoberman, Mary Ann, *5:* 82
Hochschild, Arlie Russell, *11:* 135
Hodge, P(aul) W(illiam), *12:* 99
Hodges, C(yril) Walter, *2:* 138
Hodges, Carl G., *10:* 56
Hodges, Elizabeth Jamison, *1:* 114
Hodges, Margaret Moore, *1:* 116
Hoexter, Corinne K., *6:* 115
Hoff, Carol, *11:* 136
Hoff, Syd(ney), *9:* 106
Hoffman, Phyllis M., *4:* 120
Hoffman, Rosekrans, *15:* 133
Hoffmann, Felix, *9:* 108
Hofsinde, Robert, *21:* 69
Hogan, Inez, *2:* 140
Hogan, Bernice Harris, *12:* 99
Hogarth, Jr. *See* Kent, Rockwell, *6:* 128
Hogg, Garry, *2:* 142
Hogner, Dorothy Childs, *4:* 121
Hogrogian, Nonny, *7:* 128
Hoke, Helen (L.), *15:* 133
Hoke, John, *7:* 129
Holbeach, Henry. *See* Rands, William Brighty, *17:* 156
Holberg, Ruth Langland, *1:* 117
Holbrook, Peter. *See* Glick, Carl (Cannon), *14:* 72
Holbrook, Stewart Hall, *2:* 143
Holding, James, *3:* 85
Holisher, Desider, *6:* 115
Holl, Adelaide (Hinkle), *8:* 84
Holland, Isabelle, *8:* 86
Holland, Janice, *18:* 117
Holland, John L(ewis), *20:* 87
Holland, Marion, *6:* 116
Hollander, John, *13:* 99
Holliday, Joe. *See* Holliday, Joseph, *11:* 137
Holliday, Joseph, *11:* 137
Holling, Holling C(lancy), *15:* 135
Holm, (Else) Anne (Lise), *1:* 118
Holman, Felice, *7:* 131
Holmes, Rick. *See* Hardwick, Richard Holmes Jr., *12:* 94
Holmquist, Eve, *11:* 138
Holt, Margaret, *4:* 122
Holt, Michael (Paul), *13:* 100
Holt, Stephen. *See* Thompson, Harlan H., *10:* 177
Holt, Victoria. *See* Hibbert, Eleanor, *2:* 134
Holton, Leonard. *See* Wibberley, Leonard, *2:* 271
Holyer, Erna Maria, *22:* 159
Holyer, Ernie. *See* Holyer, Erna Maria, *22:* 159
Holz, Loretta (Marie), *17:* 81
Homze, Alma C., *17:* 82
Honig, Donald, *18:* 119
Honness, Elizabeth H., *2:* 145
Hood, Joseph F., *4:* 123
Hood, Robert E., *21:* 70
Hooker, Ruth, *21:* 71
Hooks, William H(arris), *16:* 159
Hoopes, Ned E(dward), *21:* 73
Hoopes, Roy, *11:* 140
Hoover, Helen (Drusilla Blackburn), *12:* 100
Hope, Laura Lee [Collective pseudonym], *1:* 119
Hope Simpson, Jacynth, *12:* 102
Hopf, Alice L(ightner) *5:* 82
Hopkins, A. T.. *See* Turngren, Annette, *23:* 233 (Obituary)
Hopkins, Joseph G(erard) E(dward), *11:* 141
Hopkins, Lee Bennett, *3:* 85
Hopkins, Lyman. *See* Folsom, Franklin, *5:* 67
Hopkins, Marjorie, *9:* 110
Horgan, Paul, *13:* 102
Hornblow, Arthur, (Jr.), *15:* 138
Hornblow, Leonora (Schinasi), *18:* 120
Horner, Dave, *12:* 104
Hornos, Axel, *20:* 88
Horvath, Betty, *4:* 125
Horwich, Frances R(appaport), *11:* 142
Hosford, Dorothy (Grant), *22:* 161
Hosford, Jessie, *5:* 83
Hoskyns-Abrahall, Clare, *13:* 105
Houck, Carter, *22:* 164
Hough, (Helen) Charlotte, *9:* 110
Hough, Richard (Alexander), *17:* 83
Houghton, Eric, *7:* 132
Houlehen, Robert J., *18:* 121
Household, Geoffrey (Edward West), *14:* 81
Houston, James A(rchibald), *13:* 106
Howard, Prosper. *See* Hamilton, Charles Harold St. John, *13:* 77
Howard, Robert West, *5:* 85
Howarth, David, *6:* 117
Howell, Pat, *15:* 139
Howell, S. *See* Styles, Frank Showell, *10:* 167
Howell, Virginia Tier. *See* Ellison, Virginia Howell, *4:* 74
Howes, Barbara, *5:* 87
Hoyle, Geoffrey, *18:* 121
Hoyt, Olga (Gruhzit), *16:* 161
Hubbell, Patricia, *8:* 86
Hudson, Jeffrey. *See* Crichton, (J.) Michael, *9:* 44
Huffaker, Sandy, *10:* 56

Author Index

Hughes, Langston, *4:* 125
Hughes, Monica, *15:* 140
Hughes, Richard (Arthur Warren), *8:* 87
Hughes, Shirley, *16:* 162
Hull, Eleanor (Means), *21:* 74
Hull, Eric Traviss. *See* Harnan, Terry, *12:* 94
Hull, H. Braxton. *See* Jacobs, Helen Hull, *12:* 112
Hull, Katharine, *23:* 103
Hülsmann, Eva, *16:* 165
Hults, Dorothy Niebrugge, *6:* 117
Hume, Lotta Carswell, *7:* 133
Hume, Ruth Fox, *22:* 165 (Obituary)
Humphrey, Henry (III), *16:* 167
Hungerford, Pixie. *See* Brinsmead, H(esba) F(ay), *18:* 36
Hunt, Francis. *See* Stratemeyer, Edward L., *1:* 208
Hunt, Irene, *2:* 146
Hunt, Mabel Leigh, *1:* 120
Hunt, Morton, *22:* 165
Hunter, Dawe. *See* Downie, Mary Alice, *13:* 32
Hunter, Hilda, *7:* 135
Hunter, Kristin (Eggleston), *12:* 105
Hunter, Mollie. *See* McIllwraith, Maureen, *2:* 193
Hunter Blair, Pauline, *3:* 87
Huntington, Harriet E(lizabeth), *1:* 121
Huntsberry, William E(mery), *5:* 87
Hurd, Clement, *2:* 147
Hurd, Edith Thacher, *2:* 150
Hurwitz, Johanna, *20:* 88
Hurwood, Bernhardt J., *12:* 107
Hutchins, Carleen Maley, *9:* 112
Hutchins, Pat, *15:* 141
Hutchins, Ross E(lliott), *4:* 127
Hutchmacher, J. Joseph, *5:* 88
Hutto, Nelson (Allen), *20:* 90
Hutton, Warwick, *20:* 90
Hyde, Dayton O(gden), *9:* 113
Hyde, Hawk. *See* Hyde, Dayton O(gden), *9:* 113
Hyde, Margaret Oldroyd, *1:* 122
Hyde, Wayne F., *7:* 135
Hylander, Clarence J., *7:* 137
Hyman, Robin P(hilip), *12:* 108
Hyman, Trina Schart, *7:* 137
Hymes, Lucia M., *7:* 139
Hyndman, Jane Andrews, *1:* 122; *23:* 103 (Obituary)
Hyndman, Robert Utley, *18:* 123

Iannone, Jeanne, *7:* 139
Ibbotson, Eva, *13:* 108
Ibbotson, M. C(hristine), *5:* 89
Ilsley, Velma (Elizabeth), *12:* 109
Ingham, Colonel Frederic. *See* Hale, Edward Everett, *16:* 143
Ingraham, Leonard W(illiam), *4:* 129
Ingrams, Doreen, *20:* 92
Inyart, Gene, *6:* 119
Ionesco, Eugene, *7:* 140
Ipcar, Dahlov (Zorach), *1:* 125
Irvin, Fred, *15:* 143
Irving, Robert. *See* Adler, Irving, *1:* 2
Irving, Washington, *YABC 2:* 164
Irwin, Constance Frick, *6:* 119
Irwin, Keith Gordon, *11:* 143
Isaac, Joanne, *21:* 75
Isham, Charlotte H(ickox), *21:* 76
Ish-Kishor, Judith, *11:* 144
Ish-Kishor, Sulamith, *17:* 84
Israel, Elaine, *12:* 110
Iwamatsu, Jun Atsushi, *14:* 83

Jackson, C. Paul, *6:* 120
Jackson, Caary. *See* Jackson, C. Paul, *6:* 120
Jackson, Jesse, *2:* 150
Jackson, O. B. *See* Jackson, C. Paul, *6:* 120
Jackson, Robert B(lake), *8:* 89
Jackson, Sally. *See* Kellogg, Jean, *10:* 66
Jackson, Shirley, *2:* 152
Jacob, Helen Pierce, *21:* 77
Jacobs, Flora Gill, *5:* 90
Jacobs, Helen Hull, *12:* 112
Jacobs, Leland Blair, *20:* 93
Jacobs, Linda C., *21:* 78
Jacobs, Lou(is), Jr., *2:* 155
Jacobson, Daniel, *12:* 113
Jacobson, Morris K(arl), *21:* 79
Jacopetti, Alexandra, *14:* 85
Jagendorf, Moritz (Adolf), *2:* 155
James, Andrew. *See* Kirkup, James, *12:* 120
James, Dynely. *See* Mayne, William, *6:* 162
James, Harry Clebourne, *11:* 144
James, Josephine. *See* Sterne, Emma Gelders, *6:* 205
James, T. F. *See* Fleming, Thomas J(ames), *8:* 64
James, Will(iam Roderick), *19:* 148
Jane, Mary Childs, *6:* 122
Janeway, Elizabeth (Hall), *19:* 165
Janosch. *See* Eckert, Horst, *8:* 47
Jansen, Jared. *See* Cebulash, Mel, *10:* 19
Janson, H(orst) W(oldemar), *9:* 114
Jansson, Tove, *3:* 88
Janus, Grete. *See* Hertz, Grete Janus, *23:* 102
Jaques, Faith, *21:* 81
Jarman, Rosemary Hawley, *7:* 141
Jarrell, Randall, *7:* 141
Jauss, Anne Marie, *10:* 57
Jayne, Lieutenant R. H. *See* Ellis, Edward S(ylvester), *YABC 1:* 116
Jeake, Samuel Jr. *See* Aiken, Conrad, *3:* 3
Jefferies, (John) Richard, *16:* 168
Jeffers, Susan, *17:* 86
Jefferson, Sarah. *See* Farjeon, Annabel, *11:* 93
Jeffries, Roderic, *4:* 129
Jenkins, Marie M., *7:* 143
Jenkins, William A(twell), *9:* 115
Jennings, Gary (Gayne), *9:* 115
Jennings, Robert. *See* Hamilton, Charles Harold St. John, *13:* 77
Jennings, S. M. *See* Meyer, Jerome Sydney, *3:* 129
Jennison, C. S. *See* Starbird, Kaye, *6:* 204
Jennison, Keith Warren, *14:* 86
Jensen, Virginia Allen, *8:* 90
Jewett, Eleanore Myers, *5:* 90
Jewett, Sarah Orne, *15:* 144
Johns, Avery. *See* Cousins, Margaret, *2:* 79
Johnson, A. E. [Joint pseudonym] *See* Johnson, Annabell and Edgar, *2:* 156, 157
Johnson, Annabell Jones, *2:* 156
Johnson, Charles R., *11:* 146
Johnson, Chuck. *See* Johnson, Charles R., *11:* 146
Johnson, Crockett. *See* Leisk, David Johnson, *1:* 141
Johnson, D(ana) William, *23:* 103
Johnson, Dorothy M., *6:* 123
Johnson, Edgar Raymond, *2:* 157
Johnson, Elizabeth, *7:* 144
Johnson, Eric W(arner), *8:* 91
Johnson, Evelyne, *20:* 95
Johnson, Gaylord, *7:* 146
Johnson, Gerald White, *19:* 166
Johnson, James Ralph, *1:* 126
Johnson, LaVerne B(ravo), *13:* 108
Johnson, Lois S(mith), *6:* 123
Johnson, Lois W(alfrid), *22:* 165
Johnson, of Boone, Benj. F. *See* Riley, James Whitcomb, *17:* 159
Johnson, (Walter) Ryerson, *10:* 58
Johnson, Shirley K(ing), *10:* 59
Johnson, Siddie Joe, *20:* 95 (Obituary)
Johnson, William Weber, *7:* 147
Johnston, Agnes Christine. *See* Dazey, Agnes J., *2:* 88
Johnston, H(ugh) A(nthony) S(tephen), *14:* 87
Johnston, Johanna, *12:* 115
Johnston, Portia. *See* Takakjian, Portia, *15:* 273
Johnston, Tony, *8:* 94
Jones, Adrienne, *7:* 147
Jones, Diana Wynne, *9:* 116
Jones, Elizabeth Orton, *18:* 123
Jones, Evan, *3:* 90
Jones, Gillingham. *See* Hamilton, Charles Harold St. John, *13:* 77
Jones, Harold, *14:* 87
Jones, Helen L., *22:* 167 (Obituary)
Jones, Hortense P., *9:* 118

Jones, Mary Alice, *6:* 125
Jones, Weyman, *4:* 130
Jonk, Clarence, *10:* 59
Jordan, Hope (Dahle), *15:* 150
Jordan, June, *4:* 131
Jordan, Mildred, *5:* 91
Jorgenson, Ivar. *See* Silverberg, Robert, *13:* 206
Joseph, Joseph M(aron), *22:* 167
Joslin, Sesyle, *2:* 158
Joyce, J(ames) Avery, *11:* 147
Jucker, Sita, *5:* 92
Judd, Frances K. [Collective pseudonym], *1:* 127
Jumpp, Hugo. *See* MacPeek, Walter G., *4:* 148
Jupo, Frank J., *7:* 148
Juster, Norton, *3:* 91
Justus, May, *1:* 127

Kabdebo, Tamas. *See* Kabdebo, Thomas, *10:* 60
Kabdebo, Thomas, *10:* 60
Kakimoto, Kozo, *11:* 147
Kalashnikoff, Nicholas, *16:* 173
Kalb, Jonah, *23:* 105
Kaler, James Otis, *15:* 151
Kalnay, Francis, *7:* 149
Kamen, Gloria, *9:* 118
Kane, Henry Bugbee, *14:* 91
Kane, Robert W., *18:* 131
Kaplan, Bess, *22:* 168
Kaplan, Irma, *10:* 61
Kaplan, Jean Caryl Korn, *10:* 62
Karen, Ruth, *9:* 120
Kark, Nina Mary, *4:* 132
Karlin, Eugene, *10:* 62
Karp, Naomi J., *16:* 174
Kashiwagi, Isami, *10:* 64
Kästner, Erich, *14:* 91
Katchen, Carole, *9:* 122
Kathryn. *See* Searle, Kathryn Adrienne, *10:* 143
Katona, Robert, *21:* 84
Katz, Bobbi, *12:* 116
Katz, Fred, *6:* 126
Katz, William Loren, *13:* 109
Kaufman, Mervyn D., *4:* 133
Kaufmann, Angelika, *15:* 155
Kaufmann, John, *18:* 132
Kaula, Edna Mason, *13:* 110
Kavaler, Lucy, *23:* 106
Kay, Helen. *See* Goldfrank, Helen Colodny, *6:* 89
Kay, Mara, *13:* 111
Kaye, Geraldine, *10:* 64
Keane, Bil, *4:* 134
Keating, Bern. *See* Keating, Leo Bernard, *10:* 65
Keating, Lawrence A., *23:* 107
Keating, Leo Bernard, *10:* 65
Keats, Ezra Jack, *14:* 99
Keegan, Marcia, *9:* 121
Keen, Martin L., *4:* 135
Keene, Carolyn. *See* Adams, Harriet S., *1:* 1
Keeping, Charles (William James), *9:* 123
Keir, Christine. *See* Pullein-Thompson, Christine, *3:* 164
Keith, Carlton. *See* Robertson, Keith, *1:* 184
Keith, Harold (Verne), *2:* 159
Kelen, Emery, *13:* 114
Keller, B(everly) L(ou), *13:* 115
Keller, Charles, *8:* 94
Keller, Gail Faithfull. *See* Faithfull, Gail, *8:* 55
Kellin, Sally Moffet, *9:* 125
Kellogg, Gene. *See* Kellogg, Jean, *10:* 66
Kellogg, Jean, *10:* 66
Kellogg, Steven, *8:* 95
Kellow, Kathleen. *See* Hibbert, Eleanor, *2:* 134
Kelly, Eric P(hilbrook), *YABC 1:* 165
Kelly, Ralph. *See* Geis, Darlene, *7:* 101
Kelly, Regina Z., *5:* 94
Kelly, Walt(er Crawford), *18:* 135
Kelsey, Alice Geer, *1:* 129
Kempner, Mary Jean, *10:* 67
Kempton, Jean Welch, *10:* 67
Kendall, Carol (Seeger), *11:* 148
Kendall, Lace. *See* Stoutenburg, Adrien, *3:* 217
Kennedy, John Fitzgerald, *11:* 150
Kennedy, Joseph, *14:* 104
Kennedy, (Jerome) Richard, *22:* 169
Kennedy, X. J. *See* Kennedy, Joseph, *14:* 104
Kennell, Ruth E., *6:* 127
Kenny, Herbert A(ndrew), *13:* 117
Kent, Margaret, *2:* 161
Kent, Rockwell, *6:* 128
Kent, Sherman, *20:* 96
Kenworthy, Leonard S., *6:* 131
Kenyon, Ley, *6:* 131
Kepes, Juliet A(ppleby), *13:* 118
Kerigan, Florence, *12:* 117
Kerman, Gertrude Lerner, *21:* 85
Kerr, Jessica, *13:* 119
Kerr, M. E. *See* Meaker, Marijane, *20:* 124
Kerry, Frances. *See* Kerigan, Florence, *12:* 117
Kerry, Lois. *See* Arquette, Lois S., *1:* 13
Ker Wilson, Barbara, *20:* 97
Kessler, Leonard P., *14:* 106
Kesteven, G. R. *See* Crosher, G(eoffry) R(obins), *14:* 51
Kettelkamp, Larry, *2:* 163
Kevles, Bettyann, *23:* 107
Key, Alexander (Hill), *8:* 98; *23:* 108 (Obituary)
Khanshendel, Chiron. *See* Rose, Wendy, *12:* 180
Kherdian, David, *16:* 175
Kiddell, John, *3:* 93
Kiefer, Irene, *21:* 87
Killilea, Marie (Lyons), *2:* 165
Kilreon, Beth. *See* Walker, Barbara K., *4:* 219
Kimbrough, Emily, *2:* 166
Kimmel, Eric A., *13:* 120
Kindred, Wendy, *7:* 150
Kines, Pat Decker, *12:* 118
King, Arthur. *See* Cain, Arthur H., *3:* 33
King, Billie Jean, *12:* 119
King, Cynthia, *7:* 152
King, Frank O., *22:* 170 (Obituary)
King, Marian, *23:* 108
King, Martin. *See* Marks, Stan(ley), *14:* 136
King, Martin Luther, Jr., *14:* 108
King, Reefe. *See* Barker, Albert W., *8:* 3
King, Stephen, *9:* 126
Kingman, (Mary) Lee, *1:* 133
Kingsland, Leslie William, *13:* 121
Kingsley, Charles, *YABC 2:* 179
Kinney, C. Cle, *6:* 132
Kinney, Harrison, *13:* 122
Kinney, Jean Stout, *12:* 120
Kinsey, Elizabeth. *See* Clymer, Eleanor, *9:* 37
Kipling, (Joseph) Rudyard, *YABC 2:* 193
Kirk, Ruth (Kratz), *5:* 95
Kirkup, James, *12:* 120
Kirkus, Virginia. *See* Glick, Virginia Kirkus, *23:* 78 (Obituary)
Kirtland, G. B. *See* Joslin, Sesyle, *2:* 158
Kishida, Eriko, *12:* 123
Kisinger, Grace Gelvin, *10:* 68
Kissin, Eva H., *10:* 68
Kjelgaard, James Arthur, *17:* 88
Kjelgaard, Jim. *See* Kjelgaard, James Arthur, *17:* 88
Klass, Morton, *11:* 152
Kleberger, Ilse, *5:* 96
Klein, H. Arthur, *8:* 99
Klein, Leonore, *6:* 132
Klein, Mina C(ooper), *8:* 100
Klein, Norma, *7:* 152
Klimowicz, Barbara, *10:* 69
Knickerbocker, Diedrich. *See* Irving, Washington, *YABC 2:* 164
Knight, Damon, *9:* 126
Knight, David C(arpenter), *14:* 111
Knight, Eric (Mowbray), *18:* 151
Knight, Francis Edgar, *14:* 112
Knight, Frank. *See* Knight, Francis Edgar, *14:* 112
Knight, Hilary, *15:* 157
Knight, Mallory T. *See* Hurwood, Bernhardt J., *12:* 107
Knight, Ruth Adams, *20:* 98 (Obituary)

Knott, Bill. *See* Knott, William Cecil, Jr., *3:* 94
Knott, William Cecil, Jr., *3:* 94
Knowles, John, *8:* 101
Knox, Calvin. *See* Silverberg, Robert, *13:* 206
Knudson, R. R. *See* Knudson, Rozanne, *7:* 154
Knudson, Rozanne, *7:* 154
Koch, Dorothy Clarke, *6:* 133
Kocsis, J. C.. *See* Paul, James, *23:* 161
Koerner, W(illiam) H(enry) D(avid), *21:* 88
Kohler, Julilly H(ouse), *20:* 99 (Obituary)
Kohn, Bernice (Herstein), *4:* 136
Kohner, Frederick, *10:* 70
Kolba, Tamara, *22:* 171
Komisar, Lucy, *9:* 127
Komoda, Kiyo, *9:* 127
Komroff, Manuel, *2:* 168; *20:* 99 (Obituary)
Konigsburg, E(laine) L(obl), *4:* 137
Koning, Hans. *See* Koningsberger, Hans, *5:* 97
Koningsberger, Hans, *5:* 97
Konkle, Janet Everest, *12:* 124
Koob, Theodora (Johanna Foth), *23:* 110
Korach, Mimi, *9:* 128
Koren, Edward, *5:* 98
Korinetz, Yuri (Iosifovich), *9:* 129
Korty, Carol, *15:* 159
Kossin, Sandy (Sanford), *10:* 71
Koutoukas, H. M.. *See* Rivoli, Mario, *10:* 129
Kouts, Anne, *8:* 103
Kramer, George. *See* Heuman, William, *21:* 64
Krantz, Hazel (Newman), *12:* 126
Krasilovsky, Phyllis, *1:* 134
Kraus, Robert, *4:* 139
Krauss, Ruth, *1:* 135
Krautter, Elisa. *See* Bialk, Elisa, *1:* 25
Kredel, Fritz, *17:* 92
Krementz, Jill, *17:* 96
Kristof, Jane, *8:* 104
Kroeber, Theodora (Kracaw), *1:* 136
Kroll, Francis Lynde, *10:* 72
Kroll, Steven, *19:* 168
Krumgold, Joseph, *1:* 136; *23:* 111 (Obituary)
Krush, Beth, *18:* 162
Krush, Joe, *18:* 163
Krüss, James, *8:* 104
Kubinyi, Laszlo, *17:* 99
Kumin, Maxine (Winokur), *12:* 127
Kunhardt, Dorothy Meserve, *22:* 172 (Obituary)
Künstler, Morton, *10:* 73
Kupferberg, Herbert, *19:* 169
Kuratomi, Chizuko, *12:* 128
Kurelek, William, *8:* 106
Kurland, Gerald, *13:* 123
Kuskin, Karla (Seidman), *2:* 169
Kuttner, Paul, *18:* 165
Kvale, Velma R(uth), *8:* 108
Kyle, Elisabeth. *See* Dunlop, Agnes M. R., *3:* 62

Lacy, Leslie Alexander, *6:* 135
Lader, Lawrence, *6:* 135
Lady of Quality, A. *See* Bagnold, Enid, *1:* 17
La Farge, Oliver (Hazard Perry), *19:* 170
La Farge, Phyllis, *14:* 113
La Fontaine, Jean de, *18:* 166
Lagerlöf, Selma (Ottiliana Lovisa), *15:* 160
Laimgruber, Monika, *11:* 153
Laklan, Carli, *5:* 100
la Mare, Walter de. *See* de la Mare, Walter, *16:* 73
Lamb, Beatrice Pitney, *21:* 92
Lamb, Charles, *17:* 101
Lamb, G(eoffrey) F(rederick), *10:* 74
Lamb, Lynton, *10:* 75
Lamb, Mary Ann, *17:* 112
Lamb, Robert (Boyden), *13:* 123
Lambert, Saul, *23:* 111
Lamburn, Richmal Crompton, *5:* 101
Lamorisse, Albert (Emmanuel), *23:* 112
Lamplugh, Lois, *17:* 116
Lampman, Evelyn Sibley, *4:* 140; *23:* 115 (Obituary)
Lamprey, Louise, *YABC 2:* 221
Lancaster, Bruce, *9:* 130
Land, Barbara (Neblett), *16:* 177
Land, Jane [Joint pseudonym]. *See* Borland, Kathryn Kilby, *16:* 54. *See* Speicher, Helen Ross (Smith), *8:* 194
Land, Myrick (Ebben), *15:* 174
Land, Ross [Joint pseudonym]. *See* Borland, Kathryn Kilby, *16:* 54. *See* Speicher, Helen Ross (Smith), *8:* 194
Landau, Elaine, *10:* 75
Landeck, Beatrice, *15:* 175
Landin, Les(lie), *2:* 171
Landshoff, Ursula, *13:* 124
Lane, Carolyn, *10:* 76
Lane, John, *15:* 175
Lanes, Selma G., *3:* 96
Lang, Andrew, *16:* 178
Lange, John. *See* Crichton, (J.) Michael, *9:*
Lange, Suzanne, *5:* 103
Langner, Nola, *8:* 110
Langstaff, John, *6:* 135
Langstaff, Launcelot. *See* Irving, Washington, *YABC 2:* 164
Langton, Jane, *3:* 97
Lanier, Sidney, *18:* 176
Larrick, Nancy G., *4:* 141
Larsen, Egon, *14:* 115
Larson, Eve. *See* St. John, Wylly Folk, *10:* 132
Larson, William H., *10:* 77
Lasell, Elinor H., *19:* 178
Lasell, Fen H. *See* Lasell, Elinor H., *19:* 178
Lasher, Faith B., *12:* 129
Lasker, Joe, *9:* 131
Lasky, Kathryn, *13:* 124
Lassalle, C. E. *See* Ellis, Edward S(ylvester), *YABC 1:* 116
Latham, Barbara, *16:* 187
Latham, Frank B., *6:* 137
Latham, Jean Lee, *2:* 171
Latham, Mavis. *See* Clark, Mavis Thorpe, *8:* 27
Latham, Philip. *See* Richardson, Robert S(hirley), *8:* 164
Lathrop, Dorothy P(ulis), *14:* 116
Lattimore, Eleanor Frances, *7:* 155
Lauber, Patricia (Grace), *1:* 138
Laugesen, Mary E(akin), *5:* 104
Laughbaum, Steve, *12:* 131
Laughlin, Florence, *3:* 98
Laurence, Ester Hauser, *7:* 156
Lauritzen, Jonreed, *13:* 125
Lavine, Sigmund A., *3:* 100
Lawrence, Louise de Kiriline, *13:* 126
Lawrence, Mildred, *3:* 101
Lawson, Don(ald Elmer), *9:* 132
Lawson, Marion Tubbs, *22:* 172
Lawson, Robert, *YABC 2:* 222
Laycock, George (Edwin) *5:* 105
Lazarevich, Mila, *17:* 118
Lazarus, Keo Felker, *21:* 94
Lea, Alec, *19:* 179
Lea, Richard. *See* Lea, Alec, *19:* 179
Leacroft, Helen, *6:* 139
Leacroft, Richard, *6:* 139
Leaf, (Wilbur) Munro, *20:* 99
Lear, Edward, *18:* 182
Leavitt, Jerome E(dward), *23:* 115
LeCain, Errol, *6:* 141
Lee, Carol. *See* Fletcher, Helen Jill, *13:* 36
Lee, Dennis (Beynon), *14:* 120
Lee, (Nelle) Harper, *11:* 154
Lee, Manning de V(illeneuve), *22:* 173 (Obituary)
Lee, Mary Price, *8:* 111
Lee, Mildred, *6:* 142
Lee, Robert C., *20:* 104
Lee, Robert J., *10:* 77
Lee, Tanith, *8:* 112
Leekley, Thomas B(riggs), *23:* 117
Lefler, Irene (Whitney), *12:* 131
Le Gallienne, Eva, *9:* 133
LeGrand. *See* Henderson, LeGrand, *9:* 104
Le Guin, Ursula K(roeber), *4:* 142
Legum, Colin, *10:* 78

Lehr, Delores, *10:* 79
Leichman, Seymour, *5:* 106
Leighton, Margaret, *1:* 140
Leipold, L. Edmond, *16:* 189
Leisk, David Johnson, *1:* 141
Leitch, Patricia, *11:* 155
Lenard, Alexander, *21:* 95 (Obituary)
L'Engle, Madeleine, *1:* 141
Lengyel, Emil, *3:* 102
Lens, Sidney, *13:* 127
Lenski, Lois, *1:* 142
Lent, Blair, *2:* 172
Lent, Henry Bolles, *17:* 119
Leodhas, Sorche Nic. *See* Alger, Leclaire (Gowans), *15:* 1
Leong Gor Yun. *See* Ellison, Virginia Howell, *4:* 74
Lerner, Marguerite Rush, *11:* 156
Lerner, Sharon (Ruth), *11:* 157
LeShan, Eda J(oan), *21:* 95
LeSieg, Theo. *See* Geisel, Theodor Seuss, *1:* 104
Leslie, Robert Franklin, *7:* 158
Lesser, Margaret, *22:* 173 (Obituary)
Lester, Julius B., *12:* 132
Le Sueur, Meridel, *6:* 143
Leutscher, Alfred (George), *23:* 117
Levin, Betty, *19:* 179
Levin, Marcia Obrasky, *13:* 128
Levin, Meyer, *21:* 96
Levine, I(srael) E., *12:* 134
Levine, Joan Goldman, *11:* 157
Levine, Rhoda, *14:* 122
Levitin, Sonia, *4:* 144
Lewin, Ted, *21:* 98
Lewis, C(live) S(taples), *13:* 129
Lewis, Claudia (Louise), *5:* 107
Lewis, E. M., *20:* 105
Lewis, Elizabeth Foreman, *YABC 2:* 243
Lewis, Francine. *See* Wells, Helen, *2:* 266
Lewis, Hilda (Winifred), *20:* 105 (Obituary)
Lewis, Lucia Z. *See* Anderson, Lucia (Lewis), *10:* 4
Lewis, Paul. *See* Gerson, Noel B(ertram), *22:* 118
Lewis, Richard, *3:* 104
Lewiton, Mina, *2:* 174
Lexau, Joan M., *1:* 144
Ley, Willy, *2:* 175
Leydon, Rita (Flodén), *21:* 100
Libby, Bill. *See* Libby, William M., *5:* 109
Libby, William M., *5:* 109
Liberty, Gene, *3:* 106
Liebers, Arthur, *12:* 134
Lieblich, Irene, *22:* 173
Lietz, Gerald S., *11:* 159
Lifton, Betty Jean, *6:* 143
Lightner, A. M. *See* Hopf, Alice L. *5:* 82
Liman, Ellen (Fogelson), *22:* 174
Limburg, Peter R(ichard), *13:* 147
Lincoln, C(harles) Eric, *5:* 111
Linde, Gunnel, *5:* 112
Lindgren, Astrid, *2:* 177
Lindop, Edmund, *5:* 113
Lindquist, Jennie Dorothea, *13:* 148
Lindquist, Willis, *20:* 105
Lingard, Joan, *8:* 113
Lionni, Leo, *8:* 114
Lipinsky de Orlov, Lino S., *22:* 174
Lipkind, William, *15:* 178
Lipman, David, *21:* 101
Lipman, Matthew, *14:* 122
Lippincott, Joseph Wharton, *17:* 120
Lippincott, Sarah Lee, *22:* 177
Lipsyte, Robert, *5:* 114
Lisle, Seward D. *See* Ellis, Edward S(ylvester), *YABC 1:* 116
Liss, Howard, *4:* 145
List, Ilka Katherine, *6:* 145
Liston, Robert A., *5:* 114
Litchfield, Ada B(assett), *5:* 115
Little, (Flora), Jean, *2:* 178
Littledale, Freya (Lota), *2:* 179
Lively, Penelope, *7:* 159
Liversidge, (Henry) Douglas, *8:* 116
Livingston, Myra Cohn, *5:* 116
Livingston, Richard R(oland), *8:* 118
Llerena-Aguirre, Carlos Antonio, *19:* 180
Llewellyn Lloyd, Richard Dafydd Vyvyan, *11:* 160
Llewellyn, Richard. *See* Llewellyn Lloyd, Richard Dafydd Vyvyan, *11:* 160
Llewellyn, T. Harcourt. *See* Hamilton, Charles Harold St. John, *13:* 77
Lloyd, Errol, *22:* 178
Lloyd, Norman, *23:* 118 (Obituary)
Lloyd, (Mary) Norris, *10:* 79
Lobel, Anita, *6:* 146
Lobel, Arnold, *6:* 147
Lobsenz, Amelia, *12:* 135
Lobsenz, Norman M., *6:* 148
Lochlons, Colin. *See* Jackson, C. Paul, *6:* 120
Locke, Clinton W. [Collective pseudonym], *1:* 145
Locke, Lucie, *10:* 81
Loeb, Robert H., Jr., *21:* 102
Loescher, Ann Dull, *20:* 107
Loescher, Gil(burt Damian), *20:* 107
Löfgren, Ulf, *3:* 106
Loeper, John J(oseph), *10:* 81
Lofting, Hugh, *15:* 180
Lofts, Norah (Robinson), *8:* 119
Logue, Christopher, *23:* 119
Lomas, Steve. *See* Brennan, Joseph L., *6:* 33
Lomask, Milton, *20:* 109
London, Jack, *18:* 195
London, Jane. *See* Geis, Darlene, *7:* 101
London, John Griffith. *See* London, Jack, *18:* 195
Lonergan, (Pauline) Joy (Maclean), *10:* 82
Long, Helen Beecher [Collective pseudonym], *1:* 146
Long, Judith Elaine, *20:* 110
Long, Judy. *See* Long, Judith Elaine, *20:* 110
Longfellow, Henry Wadsworth, *19:* 181
Longman, Harold S., *5:* 117
Longtemps, Kenneth, *17:* 123
Longway, A. Hugh. *See* Lang, Andrew, *16:* 178
Loomis, Robert D., *5:* 119
Lopshire, Robert, *6:* 149
Lord, Beman, *5:* 119
Lord, (Doreen Mildred) Douglas, *12:* 136
Lord, John Vernon, *21:* 103
Lord, Nancy. *See* Titus, Eve, *2:* 240
Lord, Walter, *3:* 109
Lorraine, Walter (Henry), *16:* 191
Loss, Joan, *11:* 162
Lot, Parson. *See* Kingsley, Charles, *YABC 2:* 179
Lothrop, Harriet Mulford Stone, *20:* 110
Lourie, Helen. *See* Storr, Catherine (Cole), *9:* 181
Love, Katherine, *3:* 109
Lovelace, Delos Wheeler, *7:* 160
Lovelace, Maud Hart, *2:* 181; *23:* 120 (Obituary)
Lovett, Margaret (Rose), *22:* 179
Low, Alice, *11:* 163
Low, Elizabeth Hammond, *5:* 120
Low, Joseph, *14:* 123
Lowe, Jay, Jr.. *See* Loper, John J(oseph), *10:* 81
Lowenstein, Dyno, *6:* 150
Lowitz, Anson C., *18:* 214
Lowitz, Sadyebeth (Heath), *17:* 125
Lowry, Lois, *23:* 120
Lowry, Peter, *7:* 160
Lubell, Cecil, *6:* 150
Lubell, Winifred, *6:* 151
Lucas, E(dward) V(errall), *20:* 117
Luckhardt, Mildred Corell, *5:* 122
Ludlum, Mabel Cleland. *See* Widdemer, Mabel Cleland, *5:* 200
Lueders, Edward (George), *14:* 125
Lugard, Flora Louisa Shaw, *21:* 104
Luger, Harriett M(andelay), *23:* 122
Luhrmann, Winifred B(ruce), *11:* 165
Luis, Earlene W., *11:* 165
Lum, Peter. *See* Crowe, Bettina Lum, *6:* 53
Lund, Doris (Herold), *12:* 137

Author Index

Lunn, Janet, *4:* 146
Luttrell, Guy L., *22:* 180
Lutzker, Edythe, *5:* 124
Luzzati, Emanuele, *7:* 161
Lydon, Michael, *11:* 165
Lyle, Katie Letcher, *8:* 121
Lynch, Lorenzo, *7:* 161
Lynch, Patricia, *6:* 153
Lynch, Patricia (Nora), *9:* 134
Lynn, Mary. *See* Brokamp, Marilyn, *10:* 15
Lynn, Patricia. *See* Watts, Mabel Pizzey, *11:* 227
Lyon, Elinor, *6:* 154
Lyon, Lyman R. *See* De Camp, L(yon) Sprague, *9:* 49
Lyons, Dorothy, *3:* 110
Lystad, Mary (Hanemann), *11:* 166
Lyttle, Richard B(ard), *23:* 123
Lytton, Edward G(eorge) E(arle) L(ytton) Bulwer-Lytton, Baron, *23:* 125

Maas, Selve, *14:* 127
MacBeth, George, *4:* 146
MacClintock, Dorcas, *8:* 122
MacDonald, Anson. *See* Heinlein, Robert A(nson), *9:* 102
MacDonald, Betty (Campbell Bard), *YABC 1:* 167
Macdonald, Blackie. *See* Emrich, Duncan, *11:* 90
Mac Donald, Golden. *See* Brown, Margaret Wise, *YABC 2:* 9
Macdonald, Marcia. *See* Hill, Grace Livingston, *YABC 2:* 162
Macdonald, Zillah K(atherine), *11:* 167
MacFarlane, Iris, *11:* 170
MacGregor-Hastie, Roy, *3:* 111
MacInnes, Helen, *22:* 181
MacIntyre, Elisabeth, *17:* 125
Mack, Stan(ley), *17:* 128
MacKellar, William, *4:* 148
Mackenzie, Dr. Willard. *See* Stratemeyer, Edward L., *1:* 208
MacLean, Alistair (Stuart), *23:* 131
MacLeod, Beatrice (Beach), *10:* 82
MacLeod, Ellen Jane (Anderson), *14:* 129
MacMillan, Annabelle. *See* Quick, Annabelle, *2:* 207
MacPeek, Walter G., *4:* 148
MacPherson, Margaret, *9:* 135
Macrae, Hawk. *See* Barker, Albert W., *8:* 3
MacRae, Travis. *See* Feagles, Anita (MacRae), *9:* 63
Macumber, Mari. *See* Sandoz, Mari, *5:* 159
Madden, Don, *3:* 112
Maddison, Angela Mary, *10:* 82
Maddock, Reginald, *15:* 184
Madian, Jon, *9:* 136
Madison, Arnold, *6:* 155
Madison, Winifred, *5:* 125
Maestro, Giulio, *8:* 123
Maher, Ramona, *13:* 149
Mahon, Julia C(unha), *11:* 171
Mahony, Elizabeth Winthrop, *8:* 125
Mahy, Margaret, *14:* 129
Maidoff, Ilka List. *See* List, Ilka Katherine, *6:* 145
Maik, Henri. *See* Hecht, Henri Joseph, *9:* 101
Malcolmson, Anne. *See* Storch, Anne B. von, *1:* 221
Malcolmson, David, *6:* 157
Malmberg, Carl, *9:* 136
Malo, John, *4:* 149
Malvern, Gladys, *23:* 133
Manchel, Frank, *10:* 83
Mangione, Jerre, *6:* 157
Mangurian, David, *14:* 131
Maniscalco, Joseph, *10:* 85
Manley, Seon, *15:* 185
Mann, Peggy, *6:* 157
Mannheim, Grete (Salomon), *10:* 85
Manning, Rosemary, *10:* 87
Manning-Sanders, Ruth, *15:* 186
Manton, Jo. *See* Gittings, Jo Manton, *3:* 76
Manushkin, Fran, *7:* 161
Mapes, Mary A. *See* Ellison, Virginia Howell, *4:* 74
Mara, Jeanette. *See* Cebulash, Mel, *10:* 19
Marasmus, Seymour. *See* Rivoli, Mario, *10:* 129
Marcellino. *See* Agnew, Edith J., *11:* 3
Marchant, Bessie, *YABC 2:* 245
Marchant, Catherine. *See* Cookson, Catherine (McMulen), *9:* 42
Marcher, Marion Walden, *10:* 87
Marcus, Rebecca B(rian), *9:* 138
Margolis, Richard J(ules), *4:* 150
Mariana. *See* Foster, Marian Curtis, *23:* 73
Marino, Dorothy Bronson, *14:* 134
Mark, Jan, *22:* 182
Mark, Pauline (Dahlin), *14:* 136
Mark, Polly. *See* Mark, Pauline (Dahlin), *14:* 136
Markins, W. S. *See* Jenkins, Marie M., *7:* 143
Marks, J(ames) M(acdonald), *13:* 150
Marks, Margaret L., *23:* 134 (Obituary)
Marks, Mickey Klar, *12:* 139
Marks, Peter. *See* Smith, Robert Kimmel, *12:* 205
Marks, Stan(ley), *14:* 136
Markun, Patricia M(aloney), *15:* 189
Marlowe, Amy Bell [Collective pseudonym], *1:* 146
Marokvia, Mireille (Journet), *5:* 126
Mars, W. T. *See* Mars, Witold Tadeusz, J., *3:* 114
Mars, Witold Tadeusz, J., *3:* 114
Marsh, J. E. *See* Marshall, Evelyn, *11:* 172
Marsh, Jean. *See* Marshall, Evelyn, *11:* 172
Marshall, Anthony D(ryden), *18:* 215
Marshall, (Sarah) Catherine, *2:* 182
Marshall, Douglas. *See* McClintock, Marshall, *3:* 119
Marshall, Evelyn, *11:* 172
Marshall, James, *6:* 161
Marshall, S(amuel) L(yman) A(twood), *21:* 107
Martin, Eugene [Collective pseudonym], *1:* 146
Martin, Fredric. *See* Christopher, Matt, *2:* 58
Martin, J(ohn) P(ercival), *15:* 190
Martin, Jeremy. *See* Levin, Marcia Obransky, *13:* 128
Martin, Lynne, *21:* 109
Martin, Marcia. *See* Levin, Marcia Obransky, *13:* 128
Martin, Nancy. *See* Salmon, Annie Elizabeth, *13:* 188
Martin, Patricia Miles, *1:* 146
Martin, Peter. *See* Chaundler, Christine, *1:* 56
Martin, Rene, *20:* 123 (Obituary)
Martin, Vicky. *See* Storey, Victoria Carolyn, *16:* 248
Martineau, Harriet, *YABC 2:* 247
Martini, Teri, *3:* 116
Marzani, Carl (Aldo), *12:* 140
Masefield, John, *19:* 204
Mason, F. van Wyck, *3:* 117
Mason, Frank W. *See* Mason, F. van Wyck, *3:* 117
Mason, George Frederick, *14:* 138
Mason, Miriam E(vangeline), *2:* 183
Mason, Tally. *See* Derleth, August (William), *5:* 54
Mason, Van Wyck. *See* Mason, F. van Wyck, *3:* 117
Masselman, George, *19:* 214
Massie, Diane Redfield, *16:* 193
Masters, Kelly R., *3:* 118
Masters, William. *See* Cousins, Margaret, *2:* 79
Mathis, Sharon Bell, *7:* 162
Matson, Emerson N(els), *12:* 141
Matsui, Tadashi, *8:* 126
Matsuno, Masako, *6:* 161
Matte, (Encarnacion) L'Enc, *22:* 182
Matus, Greta, *12:* 142
Maves, Mary Carolyn, *10:* 88
Maves, Paul B(enjamin), *10:* 88
Mawicke, Tran, *15:* 190
Maxon, Anne. *See* Best, Allena Champlin, *2:* 25
Maxwell, Arthur S., *11:* 173

Maxwell, Edith, *7:* 164
May, Charles Paul, *4:* 151
May, Julian, *11:* 175
Mayberry, Florence V(irginia Wilson), *10:* 89
Mayer, Ann M(argaret), *14:* 140
Mayer, Mercer, *16:* 195
Mayne, William, *6:* 162
Mays, (Lewis) Victor, (Jr.), *5:* 126
Mazza, Adriana, *19:* 215
McCaffrey, Anne, *8:* 127
McCain, Murray, *7:* 165
McCall, Edith S., *6:* 163
McCall, Virginia Nielsen, *13:* 151
McCallum, Phyllis, *10:* 90
McCarthy, Agnes, *4:* 152
McCarty, Rega Kramer, *10:* 91
McCaslin, Nellie, *12:* 143
McClintock, Marshall, *3:* 119
McClintock, Mike. *See* McClintock, Marshall, *3:* 119
McClintock, Theodore, *14:* 140
McClinton, Leon, *11:* 178
McCloskey, Robert, *2:* 185
McClung, Robert M., *2:* 188
McCord, David (Thompson Watson), *18:* 217
McCormick, Dell J., *19:* 216
McCormick, (George) Donald (King), *14:* 141
McCoy, Iola Fuller, *3:* 120
McCoy, J(oseph) J(erome), *8:* 127
McCrady, Lady, *16:* 197
McCrea, James, *3:* 121
McCrea, Ruth, *3:* 121
McCullough, Frances Monson, *8:* 129
McCully, Emily Arnold, *5:* 128
McCurdy, Michael, *13:* 153
McDearmon, Kay, *20:* 123
McDermott, Beverly Brodsky, *11:* 179
McDermott, Gerald, *16:* 199
McDole, Carol. *See* Farley, Carol, *4:* 81
McDonald, Gerald D., *3:* 123
McDonald, Jill (Masefield), *13:* 154
McDonald, Lucile Saunders, *10:* 92
McDonnell, Lois Eddy, *10:* 94
McEwen, Robert (Lindley), *23:* 134 (Obituary)
McFall, Christie, *12:* 144
McFarland, Kenton D(ean), *11:* 180
McGaw, Jessie Brewer, *10:* 95
McGee, Barbara, *6:* 165
McGiffin, (Lewis) Lee (Shaffer), *1:* 148
McGill, Marci. *See* Ridlon, Marci, *22:* 211
McGinley, Phyllis, *2:* 190
McGovern, Ann, *8:* 130
McGowen, Thomas E., *2:* 192
McGowen, Tom. *See* McGowen, Thomas, *2:* 192
McGrady, Mike, *6:* 166
McGraw, Eloise Jarvis, *1:* 149
McGraw, William Corbin, *3:* 124
McGregor, Craig, *8:* 131
McGuire, Edna, *13:* 155
McHargue, Georgess, *4:* 152
McIlwraith, Maureen, *2:* 193
McKay, Robert W., *15:* 192
McKown, Robin, *6:* 166
McLean, Kathryn (Anderson), *9:* 140
McLeod, Emilie Warren, *23:* 135
McMeekin, Clark. *See* McMeekin, Isable McLennan, *3:* 126
McMeekin, Clark. *See* McMeekin, Isabel McLennan, *3:* 126
McMeekin, Isabel McLennan, *3:* 126
McMillan, Bruce, *22:* 183
McMullen, Catherine. *See* Cookson, Catherine (McMullen), *9:* 42
McMurtrey, Martin A(loysius), *21:* 110
McNair, Kate, *3:* 127
McNeer, May, *1:* 150
McNeill, Janet, *1:* 151
McNickle, (William) D'Arcy, *22:* 185 (Obituary)
McNulty, Faith, *12:* 144
McPherson, James M., *16:* 202
McQueen, Mildred Hark, *12:* 145
Mead, Margaret, *20:* 123 (Obituary)
Mead, Russell (M., Jr.), *10:* 96
Meade, Ellen (Roddick), *5:* 130
Meade, Marion, *23:* 136
Meader, Stephen W(arren), *1:* 153
Meadow, Charles T(roub), *23:* 136
Meadowcroft, Enid LaMonte. *See* Wright, Enid Meadowcroft, *3:* 267
Meaker, M. J. *See* Meaker, Marijane, *20:* 124
Meaker, Marijane, *20:* 124
Means, Florence Crannell, *1:* 154
Medary, Marjorie, *14:* 143
Medearis, Mary, *5:* 130
Mee, Charles L., Jr., *8:* 132
Meeker, Oden, *14:* 144
Meeks, Esther MacBain, *1:* 155
Mehdevi, Alexander, *7:* 166
Mehdevi, Anne (Marie) Sinclair, *8:* 132
Meigs, Cornelia Lynde, *6:* 167
Melcher, Frederic Gershom, *22:* 185 (Obituary)
Melcher, Marguerite Fellows, *10:* 96
Melin, Grace Hathaway, *10:* 96
Mellersh, H(arold) E(dward) L(eslie), *10:* 97
Meltzer, Milton, *1:* 156
Melville, Anne. *See* Potter, Margaret (Newman), *21:* 119
Melwood, Mary. *See* Lewis, E. M., *20:* 105
Melzack, Ronald, *5:* 130
Memling, Carl, *6:* 169
Mendel, Jo. [House pseudonym]. *See* Bond, Gladys Baker, *14:* 41
Meng, Heinz (Karl), *13:* 157
Mercer, Charles (Edward), *16:* 203
Meredith, David William. *See* Miers, Earl Schenck, *1:* 160
Merriam, Eve, *3:* 128
Merrill, Jean (Fairbanks), *1:* 158
Metcalf, Suzanne. *See* Baum, L(yman) Frank, *18:* 7
Meyer, Carolyn, *9:* 140
Meyer, Edith Patterson, *5:* 131
Meyer, F(ranklyn) E(dward), *9:* 142
Meyer, Jean Shepherd, *11:* 181
Meyer, Jerome Sydney, *3:* 129
Meyer, June. *See* Jordan, June, *4:* 131
Meyer, Louis A(lbert), *12:* 147
Meyer, Renate, *6:* 170
Meyers, Susan, *19:* 216
Meynier, Yvonne (Pollet), *14:* 146
Micale, Albert, *22:* 185
Micklish, Rita, *12:* 147
Miers, Earl Schenck, *1:* 160
Miklowitz, Gloria D., *4:* 154
Mikolaycak, Charles, *9:* 143
Miles, Betty, *8:* 132
Miles, Miska. *See* Martin, Patricia Miles, *1:* 146
Milhous, Katherine, *15:* 192
Militant. *See* Sandburg, Carl (August), *8:* 177
Millar, Barbara F., *12:* 149
Miller, Albert G(riffith), *12:* 150
Miller, Alice P(atricia McCarthy), *22:* 187
Miller, Don, *15:* 194
Miller, Eddie. *See* Miller, Edward, *8:* 134
Miller, Edward, *8:* 134
Miller, Helen M(arkley), *5:* 133
Miller, Jane (Judith), *15:* 196
Miller, John. *See* Samachson, Joseph, *3:* 182
Miller, Mary Beth, *9:* 145
Milne, A(lan) A(lexander), *YABC 1:* 174
Milne, Lorus J., *5:* 133
Milne, Margery, *5:* 134
Milotte, Alfred G(eorge), *11:* 181
Milton, Hilary (Herbert), *23:* 137
Minarik, Else Holmelund, *15:* 197
Miner, Lewis S., *11:* 183
Minier, Nelson. *See* Stoutenburg, Adrien, *3:* 217
Mintonye, Grace, *4:* 156
Mirsky, Jeannette, *8:* 135
Mirsky, Reba Paeff, *1:* 161
Miskovits, Christine, *10:* 98
Miss Francis. *See* Horwich, Francis R., *11:* 142
Miss Read. *See* Saint, Dora Jessie, *10:* 132
Mitchell, (Sibyl) Elyne (Keith), *10:* 98

Mizumura, Kazue, *18:* 222
Moe, Barbara, *20:* 126
Moffett, Martha (Leatherwood), *8:* 136
Mohn, Viola Kohl, *8:* 138
Mohr, Nicholasa, *8:* 138
Molarsky, Osmond, *16:* 204
Molloy, Paul, *5:* 135
Moncure, Jane Belk, *23:* 139
Monjo, F(erdinand) N., *16:* 206
Monroe, Lyle. *See* Heinlein, Robert A(nson), *9:* 102
Montana, Bob, *21:* 110(Obituary)
Montgomery, Constance. *See* Cappell, Constance, *22:* 65
Montgomery, Elizabeth Rider, *3:* 132
Montgomery, L(ucy) M(aud), *YABC 1:* 182
Montgomery, Rutherford George, *3:* 134
Montresor, Beni, *3:* 136
Moody, Ralph Owen, *1:* 162
Moon, Sheila (Elizabeth), *5:* 136
Moore, Anne Carroll, *13:* 158
Moore, Clement Clarke, *18:* 224
Moore, Eva, *20:* 127
Moore, Fenworth. *See* Stratemeyer, Edward L., *1:* 208
Moore, Janet Gaylord, *18:* 236
Moore, John Travers, *12:* 151
Moore, Margaret Rumberger, *12:* 154
Moore, Marianne (Craig), *20:* 128
Moore, Regina. *See* Dunne, Mary Collins, *11:* 83
Moore, Rosalie. *See* Brown, Rosalie (Gertrude) Moore, *9:* 26
Moore, Ruth, *23:* 142
Moore, S. E., *23:* 142
Mordvinoff, Nicolas, *17:* 129
More, Caroline. *See* Cone, Molly Lamken, *1:* 66
More, Caroline. *See* Strachan, Margaret Pitcairn, *14:* 193
Morey, Charles. *See* Fletcher, Helen Jill, *13:* 36
Morey, Walt. *3:* 139
Morgan, Jane. *See* Cooper, James Fenimore, *19:* 68
Morgan, Lenore, *8:* 139
Morgan, Shirley, *10:* 99
Morrah, Dave. *See* Morrah, David Wardlaw, Jr., *10:* 100
Morrah, David Wardlaw, Jr., *10:* 100
Morressy, John, *23:* 143
Morris, Desmond (John), *14:* 146
Morris, Robert A., *7:* 166
Morrison, Gert W. *See* Stratemeyer, Edward L., *1:* 208
Morrison, Lillian, *3:* 140
Morrison, Lucile Phillips, *17:* 134
Morrison, Velma Ford, *21:* 110
Morrison, William. *See* Samachson, Joseph, *3:* 182
Morriss, James E(dward), *8:* 139
Morrow, Betty. *See* Bacon, Elizabeth, *3:* 14
Morse, Carol. *See* Yeakley, Marjory Hall, *21:* 207
Morton, Miriam, *9:* 145
Moscow, Alvin, *3:* 142
Mosel, Arlene, *7:* 167
Moskin, Marietta D(unston), *23:* 144
Moss, Don(ald), *11:* 183
Motz, Lloyd, *20:* 133
Mountfield, David. *See* Grant, Neil, *14:* 75
Mowat, Farley, *3:* 142
Mulcahy, Lucille Burnett, *12:* 155
Muller, Billex. *See* Ellis, Edward S(ylvester), *YABC 1:* 116
Mullins, Edward S(wift), *10:* 101
Mulvihill, William Patrick, *8:* 140
Mun. *See* Leaf, (Wilbur) Munro, *20:* 99
Munari, Bruno, *15:* 199
Munce, Ruth Hill, *12:* 156
Munowitz, Ken, *14:* 149
Munson(-Benson), Tunie, *15:* 201
Munzer, Martha E., *4:* 157
Murphy, Barbara Beasley, *5:* 137
Murphy, E(mmett) Jefferson, *4:* 159
Murphy, Pat. *See* Murphy, E(mmett) Jefferson, *4:* 159
Murphy, Robert (William), *10:* 102
Murray, Marian, *5:* 138
Murray, Michele, *7:* 170
Musgrave, Florence, *3:* 144
Mussey, Virginia T. H. *See* Ellison, Virginia Howell, *4:* 74
Mutz. *See* Kunstler, Morton, *10:* 73
Myers, Bernice, *9:* 146
Myers, Hortense (Powner), *10:* 102
Myrus, Donald (Richard), *23:* 147

Nash, Linell. *See* Smith, Linell Nash, *2:* 227
Nash, (Fredric) Ogden, *2:* 194
Nast, Elsa Ruth. *See* Watson, Jane Werner, *3:* 244
Nathan, Dorothy (Goldeen), *15:* 202
Nathan, Robert, *6:* 171
Navarra, John Gabriel, *8:* 141
Naylor, Penelope, *10:* 104
Naylor, Phyllis Reynolds, *12:* 156
Nazaroff, Alexander I., *4:* 160
Neal, Harry Edward, *5:* 139
Nee, Kay Bonner, *10:* 104
Needleman, Jacob, *6:* 172
Negri, Rocco, *12:* 157
Neigoff, Anne, *13:* 165
Neigoff, Mike, *13:* 166
Neilson, Frances Fullerton (Jones), *14:* 149
Neimark, Anne E., *4:* 160
Nelson, Esther L., *13:* 167
Nelson, Mary Carroll, *23:* 147
Nesbit, E(dith), *YABC 1:* 193
Nesbit, Troy. *See* Folsom, Franklin, *5:* 67
Nespojohn, Katherine V., *7:* 170
Ness, Evaline (Michelow), *1:* 165
Neufeld, John, *6:* 173
Neumeyer, Peter F(lorian), *13:* 168
Neurath, Marie (Reidemeister), *1:* 166
Neville, Emily Cheney, *1:* 169
Neville, Mary. *See* Woodrich, Mary Neville, *2:* 274
Nevins, Albert J., *20:* 134
Newberry, Clare Turlay, *1:* 170
Newbery, John, *20:* 135
Newell, Crosby. *See* Bonsall, Crosby (Barbara Newell), *23:* 6
Newell, Edythe W., *11:* 185
Newlon, Clarke, *6:* 174
Newman, Robert (Howard), *4:* 161
Newman, Shirlee Petkin, *10:* 105
Newton, James R(obert), *23:* 149
Newton, Suzanne, *5:* 140
Nic Leodhas, Sorche. *See* Alger, Leclaire (Gowans), *15:* 1
Nichols, Cecilia Fawn, *12:* 159
Nichols, (Joanna) Ruth, *15:* 204
Nickelsburg, Janet, *11:* 185
Nickerson, Betty. *See* Nickerson, Elizabeth, *14:* 150
Nickerson, Elizabeth, *14:* 150
Nicol, Ann. *See* Turnbull, Ann (Christine), *18:* 281
Nicolas. *See* Mordvinoff, Nicolas, *17:* 129
Nicolay, Helen, *YABC 1:* 204
Nicole, Christopher Robin, *5:* 141
Nielsen, Kay (Rasmus), *16:* 210
Nielsen, Virginia. *See* McCall, Virginia Nielsen, *13:* 151
Nixon, Joan Lowery, *8:* 143
Nixon, K. *See* Nixon, Kathleen Irene (Blundell), *14:* 152
Nixon, Kathleen Irene (Blundell), *14:* 152
Noble, Iris, *5:* 142
Nodset, Joan M. *See* Lexau, Joan M., *1:* 144
Nolan, Jeannette Covert, *2:* 196
Noonan, Julia, *4:* 163
Norcross, John. *See* Conroy, Jack (Wesley), *19:* 65
Nordhoff, Charles (Bernard), *23:* 150
Nordstrom, Ursula, *3:* 144
Norman, James. *See* Schmidt, James Norman, *21:* 141
Norris, Gunilla B(rodde), *20:* 139
North, Andrew. *See* Norton, Alice Mary, *1:* 173
North, Captain George. *See* Stevenson, Robert Louis, *YABC 2:* 307

North, Joan, *16:* 218
North, Robert. *See* Withers, Carl A., *14:* 261
North, Sterling, *1:* 171
Norton, Alice Mary, *1:* 173
Norton, Andre. *See* Norton, Alice Mary, *1:* 173
Norton, Browning. *See* Norton, Frank R(owland) B(rowning), *10:* 107
Norton, Frank R(owland) B(rowning), *10:* 107
Norton, Mary, *18:* 236
Nowell, Elizabeth Cameron, *12:* 160
Nussbaumer, Paul (Edmond), *16:* 218
Nyce, (Nellie) Helene von Strecker, *19:* 218
Nyce, Vera, *19:* 219
Nye, Robert, *6:* 174

Oakes, Vanya, *6:* 175
Oakley, Don(ald G.), *8:* 144
Oakley, Helen, *10:* 107
Obrant, Susan, *11:* 186
O'Brien, Robert C.. *See* Conly, Robert Leslie, *23:* 45
O'Carroll, Ryan. *See* Markun, Patricia M(aloney), *15:* 189
O'Connell, Peg. *See* Ahern, Margaret McCrohan, *10:* 2
O'Connor, Patrick. *See* Wibberley, Leonard, *2:* 271
O'Connor, Richard, *21:* 111 (Obituary)
O'Dell, Scott, *12:* 161
Odenwald, Robert P(aul), *11:* 187
Oechsli, Kelly, *5:* 143
Offit, Sidney, *10:* 108
Ofosu-Appiah, L(awrence) H(enry), *13:* 170
Ogan, George F., *13:* 171
Ogan, M. G. [Joint pseudonym]. *See* Ogan, George F. and Margaret E. (Nettles), *13:* 171
Ogan, Margaret E. (Nettles), *13:* 171
Ogburn, Charlton, Jr., *3:* 145
O'Hara, Mary. *See* Alsop, Mary O'Hara, *2:* 4
Ohlsson, Ib, *7:* 171
Olcott, Frances Jenkins, *19:* 220
Olds, Elizabeth, *3:* 146
Olds, Helen Diehl, *9:* 148
Oldstyle, Jonathan. *See* Irving, Washington, *YABC 2:* 164
O'Leary, Brian, *6:* 176
Oliver, John Edward, *21:* 112
Olmstead, Lorena Ann, *13:* 172
Olney, Ross R., *13:* 173
Olschewski, Alfred, *7:* 172
Olsen, Ib Spang, *6:* 177
Olugebefola, Ademole, *15:* 204
Ommanney, F(rancis) D(ownes), *23:* 159
O'Neill, Mary L(e Duc), *2:* 197
Opie, Iona, *3:* 148
Opie, Peter, *3:* 149
Oppenheim, Joanne, *5:* 146
Orbach, Ruth Gary, *21:* 112
Orgel, Doris, *7:* 173
Orleans, Ilo, *10:* 110
Ormondroyd, Edward, *14:* 153
Ormsby, Virginia H(aire), *11:* 187
Osborne, Chester G., *11:* 188
Osborne, David. *See* Silverberg, Robert, *13:* 206
Osborne, Leone Neal, *2:* 198
Osmond, Edward, *10:* 110
Otis, James. *See* Kaler, James Otis, *15:* 151
Ouida. *See* De La Ramée, (Marie) Louise, *20:* 26
Ousley, Odille, *10:* 111
Owen, Caroline Dale. *See* Snedecker, Caroline Dale (Parke), *YABC 2:* 296
Owen, Clifford. *See* Hamilton, Charles Harold St. John, *13:* 77
Oxenbury, Helen, *3:* 151

Packer, Vin. *See* Meaker, Marijane, *20:* 124
Page, Eileen. *See* Heal, Edith, *7:* 123
Page, Eleanor. *See* Coerr, Eleanor, *1:* 64
Pahz, (Anne) Cheryl Suzanne, *11:* 189
Pahz, James Alon, *11:* 190
Paice, Margaret, *10:* 111
Paine, Roberta M., *13:* 174
Paisley, Tom. *See* Bethancourt, T. Ernesto, *11:* 27
Palazzo, Anthony D., *3:* 152
Palazzo, Tony. *See* Palazzo, Anthony D., *3:* 152
Palder, Edward L., *5:* 146
Pallas, Norvin, *23:* 160
Palmer, C(yril) Everard, *14:* 153
Palmer, (Ruth) Candida, *11:* 191
Palmer, Heidi, *15:* 206
Palmer, Juliette, *15:* 208
Panetta, George, *15:* 210
Pansy. *See* Alden, Isabella (Macdonald), *YABC 2:* 1
Panter, Carol, *9:* 150
Papashvily, George, *17:* 135
Papashvily, Helen (Waite), *17:* 141
Pape, D(onna) L(ugg), *2:* 198
Paradis, Adrian A(lexis), *1:* 175
Paradis, Marjorie (Bartholomew), *17:* 143
Parish, Peggy, *17:* 144
Park, Bill. *See* Park, W(illiam) B(ryan), *22:* 188
Park, W(illiam) B(ryan), *22:* 188
Parker, Elinor, *3:* 155
Parker, Nancy Winslow, *10:* 113
Parker, Richard, *14:* 156
Parker, Robert. *See* Boyd, Waldo T., *18:* 35
Parkinson, Ethelyn M(inerva), *11:* 192
Parks, Edd Winfield, *10:* 114
Parks, Gordon (Alexander Buchanan), *8:* 145
Parley, Peter. *See* Goodrich, Samuel Griswold, *23:* 82
Parlin, John. *See* Graves, Charles Parlin, *4:* 94
Parnall, Peter, *16:* 220
Parr, Lucy, *10:* 115
Parrish, Mary. *See* Cousins, Margaret, *2:* 79
Parrish, (Frederick) Maxfield, *14:* 158
Parry, Marian, *13:* 175
Pascal, David, *14:* 174
Paschal, Nancy. *See* Trotter, Grace V(iolet), *10:* 180
Patent, Dorothy Hinshaw, *22:* 190
Paterson, Katherine (Womeldorf), *13:* 176
Paton, Alan (Stewart), *11:* 194
Paton Walsh, Gillian, *4:* 164
Patterson, Lillie G., *14:* 174
Paul, Aileen, *12:* 164
Paul, James, *23:* 161
Pauli, Hertha, *3:* 155
Paulsen, Gary, *22:* 192
Paulson, Jack. *See* Jackson, C. Paul, *6:* 120
Pavel, Frances, *10:* 116
Payson, Dale, *9:* 150
Payzant, Charles, *18:* 239
Payzant, Jessie Mercer Knechtel. *See* Shannon, Terry, *21:* 147
Paz, A. *See* Pahz, James Alon, *11:* 190
Paz, Zan. *See* Pahz, Cheryl Suzanne, *11:* 189
Peake, Mervyn, *23:* 162
Peale, Norman Vincent, *20:* 140
Pearce, (Ann) Philippa, *1:* 176
Peare, Catherine Owens, *9:* 152
Pease, Howard, *2:* 199
Peck, Anne Merriman, *18:* 240
Peck, Richard, *18:* 242
Peck, Robert Newton III, *21:* 113
Peeples, Edwin A., *6:* 181
Peet, Bill. *See* Peet, William B., *2:* 201
Peet, William Bartlett, *2:* 201
Pelaez, Jill, *12:* 165
Pellowski, Anne, *20:* 145
Pelta, Kathy, *18:* 245
Peltier, Leslie C(opus), *13:* 177
Pembury, Bill. *See* Groom, Arthur William, *10:* 53
Pendennis, Arthur, Esquire. *See* Thackeray, William Makepeace, *23:* 223

Author Index

Pender, Lydia, *3:* 157
Pendery, Rosemary, *7:* 174
Penn, Ruth Bonn. *See* Rosenberg, Ethel, *3:* 176
Pennage, E. M. *See* Finkel, George (Irvine), *8:* 59
Penrose, Margaret. *See* Stratemeyer, Edward L., *1:* 208
Pepe, Phil(ip), *20:* 145
Peppe, Rodney, *4:* 164
Percy, Charles Henry. *See* Smith, Dodie, *4:* 194
Perera, Thomas Biddle, *13:* 179
Perkins, Marlin, *21:* 114
Perl, Lila, *6:* 182
Perl, Susan, *22:* 193
Perlmutter, O(scar) William, *8:* 149
Perrine, Mary, *2:* 203
Pershing, Marie. *See* Schultz, Pearle Henriksen, *21:* 142
Peters, Caroline. *See* Betz, Eva Kelly, *10:* 10
Peters, S. H. *See* Porter, William Sydney, *YABC 2:* 259
Petersham, Maud (Fuller), *17:* 146
Petersham, Miska, *17:* 149
Peterson, Hans, *8:* 149
Peterson, Harold L(eslie), *8:* 151
Peterson, Helen Stone, *8:* 152
Petie, Haris, *10:* 118
Petrides, Heidrun, *19:* 222
Petrovskaya, Kyra. *See* Wayne, Kyra Petrovskaya, *8:* 213
Petry, Ann (Lane), *5:* 148
Pevsner, Stella, *8:* 154
Peyton, K. M. *See* Peyton, Kathleen (Wendy), *15:* 211
Peyton, Kathleen (Wendy), *15:* 211
Pfeffer, Susan Beth, *4:* 166
Phelan, Mary Kay, *3:* 158
Phillips, Irv. *See* Phillips, Irving W., *11:* 196
Phillips, Irving W., *11:* 196
Phillips, Jack. *See* Sandburg, Carl (August), *8:* 177
Phillips, Leon. *See* Gerson, Noel B(ertram), *22:* 118
Phillips, Loretta (Hosey), *10:* 119
Phillips, Louis, *8:* 155
Phillips, Mary Geisler, *10:* 119
Phillips, Prentice, *10:* 119
Phipson, Joan. *See* Fitzhardinge, Joan M., *2:* 107
Phiz. *See* Browne, Hablot Knight, *21:* 13
Phleger, Marjorie Temple, *1:* 176
Piaget, Jean, *23:* 166 (Obituary)
Piatti, Celestino, *16:* 222
Picard, Barbara Leonie, *2:* 205
Pienkowski, Jan, *6:* 182
Pierce, Katherine. *See* St. John, Wylly Folk, *10:* 132
Pierce, Ruth (Ireland), *5:* 148
Pierik, Robert, *13:* 180
Pike, E(dgar) Royston, *22:* 194
Pilarski, Laura, *13:* 181
Pilgrim, Anne. *See* Allan, Mabel Esther, *5:* 2
Pilkington, Francis Meredyth, *4:* 166
Pilkington, Roger (Windle), *10:* 120
Pine, Tillie S(chloss), *13:* 182
Pinkwater, Manus, *8:* 156
Piper, Roger. *See* Fisher, John (Oswald Hamilton), *15:* 115
Piro, Richard, *7:* 176
Pitrone, Jean Maddern, *4:* 167
Pitz, Henry C., *4:* 167
Pizer, Vernon, *21:* 116
Place, Marian T., *3:* 160
Plaidy, Jean. *See* Hibbert, Eleanor, *2:* 134
Platt, Kin, *21:* 117
Plimpton, George (Ames), *10:* 121
Plowman, Stephanie, *6:* 184
Pluckrose, Henry (Arthur), *13:* 183
Plum, J. *See* Wodehouse, P(elham) G(renville), *22:* 241
Plummer, Margaret, *2:* 206
Podendorf, Illa E., *18:* 247
Poe, Edgar Allan, *23:* 167
Pohlmann, Lillian (Grenfell), *11:* 196
Pointon, Robert. *See* Rooke, Daphne (Marie), *12:* 178
Pola. *See* Watson, Pauline, *14:* 235
Polatnick, Florence T., *5:* 149
Polder, Markus. *See* Krüss, James, *8:* 104
Polhamus, Jean Burt, *21:* 118
Politi, Leo, *1:* 177
Polking, Kirk, *5:* 149
Polland, Madeleine A., *6:* 185
Polseno, Jo, *17:* 153
Pomerantz, Charlotte, *20:* 146
Pond, Alonzo W(illiam), *5:* 150
Poole, Gray Johnson, *1:* 179
Poole, Josephine, *5:* 152
Poole, Lynn, *1:* 179
Portal, Colette, *6:* 186
Porter, Katherine Anne, *23:* 192 (Obituary)
Porter, William Sydney, *YABC 2:* 259
Posell, Elsa Z., *3:* 160
Posten, Margaret L(ois), *10:* 123
Potter, (Helen) Beatrix, *YABC 1:* 205
Potter, Margaret (Newman), *21:* 119
Potter, Marian, *9:* 153
Potter, Miriam Clark, *3:* 161
Powell, Richard Stillman. *See* Barbour, Ralph Henry, *16:* 27
Powers, Anne. *See* Schwartz, Anne Powers, *10:* 142
Powers, Margaret. *See* Heal, Edith, *7:* 123
Prelutsky, Jack, *22:* 195
Price, Christine, *3:* 162; *23:* 192 (Obituary)
Price, Garrett, *22:* 197 (Obituary)
Price, Jennifer. *See* Hoover, Helen (Drusilla Blackburn), *12:* 100
Price, Lucie Locke. *See* Locke, Lucie, *10:* 81
Price, Olive, *8:* 157
Prieto, Mariana B(eeching), *8:* 160
Prince, J(ack) H(arvey), *17:* 155
Pringle, Laurence, *4:* 171
Proctor, Everitt. *See* Montgomery, Rutherford, *3:* 134
Provensen, Alice, *9:* 154
Provensen, Martin, *9:* 155
Pryor, Helen Brenton, *4:* 172
Pugh, Ellen T., *7:* 176
Pullein-Thompson, Christine, *3:* 164
Pullein-Thompson, Diana, *3:* 165
Pullein-Thompson, Josephine, *3:* 166
Purdy, Susan Gold, *8:* 161
Purscell, Phyllis, *7:* 177
Putnam, Arthur Lee. *See* Alger, Horatio, Jr., *16:* 3
Pyle, Howard, *16:* 224
Pyne, Mable Mandeville, *9:* 155

Quackenbush, Robert M., *7:* 177
Quammen, David, *7:* 179
Quarles, Benjamin, *12:* 166
Queen, Ellery, Jr. *See* Holding, James, *3:* 85
Quick, Annabelle, *2:* 207
Quin-Harkin, Janet, *18:* 247
Quinn, Elisabeth, *22:* 197
Quinn, Vernon. *See* Quinn, Elisabeth, *22:* 197

Rabe, Berniece, *7:* 179
Rabe, Olive H(anson), *13:* 183
Rackham, Arthur, *15:* 213
Radford, Ruby L(orraine), *6:* 186
Radlauer, Edward, *15:* 227
Radlauer, Ruth (Shaw), *15:* 229
Raebeck, Lois, *5:* 153
Raftery, Gerald (Bransfield), *11:* 197
Raiff, Stan, *11:* 197
Ralston, Jan. *See* Dunlop, Agnes M. R., *3:* 62
Ramal, Walter. *See* de la Mare, Walter, *16:* 73
Ranadive, Gail, *10:* 123
Rand, Paul, *6:* 188
Randall, Florence Engel, *5:* 154
Randall, Janet. *See* Young, Janet & Robert, *3:* 268-269
Randall, Robert. *See* Silverberg, Robert, *13:* 206
Randall, Ruth Painter, *3:* 167
Randolph, Lieutenant J. H. *See* Ellis, Edward S(ylvester), *YABC 1:* 116

Author Index

Rands, William Brighty, *17:* 156
Ranney, Agnes V., *6:* 189
Ransome, Arthur (Michell), *22:* 198
Rapaport, Stella F(read), *10:* 126
Raphael, Elaine (Chionchio), *23:* 192
Rappaport, Eva, *6:* 189
Raskin, Edith (Lefkowitz), *9:* 156
Raskin, Ellen, *2:* 209
Raskin, Joseph, *12:* 166
Rathjen, Carl H(enry), *11:* 198
Rau, Margaret, *9:* 157
Raucher, Herman, *8:* 162
Ravielli, Anthony, *3:* 169
Rawlings, Marjorie Kinnan, *YABC 1:* 218
Rawls, (Woodrow) Wilson, *22:* 205
Ray, Deborah, *8:* 163
Ray, Irene. *See* Sutton, Margaret Beebe, *1:* 213
Ray, JoAnne, *9:* 157
Ray, Mary (Eva Pedder), *2:* 210
Raymond, Robert. *See* Alter, Robert Edmond, *9:* 8
Rayner, Mary, *22:* 207
Razzell, Arthur (George), *11:* 199
Razzi, James, *10:* 126
Read, Elfreida, *2:* 211
Read, Piers Paul, *21:* 119
Redding, Robert Hull, *2:* 212
Redway, Ralph. *See* Hamilton, Charles Harold St. John, *13:* 77
Redway, Ridley. *See* Hamilton, Charles Harold St. John, *13:* 77
Reed, Betty Jane, *4:* 172
Reed, Gwendolyn E(lizabeth), *21:* 120
Reed, William Maxwell, *15:* 230
Reeder, Colonel Red. *See* Reeder, Russell P., Jr., *4:* 174
Reeder, Russell P., Jr., *4:* 174
Rees, Ennis, *3:* 169
Reeves, James, *15:* 231
Reeves, Joyce, *17:* 158
Reeves, Ruth Ellen. *See* Ranney, Agnes V., *6:* 189
Reggiani, Renée, *18:* 248
Reid, Barbara, *21:* 121
Reid, Eugenie Chazal, *12:* 167
Reid, John Calvin, *21:* 122
Reid Banks, Lynne, *22:* 208
Reinfeld, Fred, *3:* 170
Reiss, Johanna de Leeuw, *18:* 250
Reiss, John J., *23:* 193
Reit, Seymour, *21:* 123
Reit, Sy. *See* Reit, Seymour, *21:* 123
Remi, Georges, *13:* 183
Renault, Mary. *See* Challans, Mary, *23:* 33
Rendina, Laura Cooper, *10:* 127
Renick, Marion (Lewis), *1:* 180
Renlie, Frank H., *11:* 200
Renvoize, Jean, *5:* 157
Resnick, Seymour, *23:* 193
Retla, Robert. *See* Alter, Robert Edmond, *9:* 8
Reuter, Carol (Joan), *2:* 213
Rey, H(ans) A(ugusto), *1:* 181
Reyher, Becky. *See* Reyher, Rebecca Hourwich, *18:* 253
Reyher, Rebecca Hourwich, *18:* 253
Rhys, Megan. *See* Williams, Jeanne, *5:* 202
Ricciuti, Edward R(aphael), *10:* 110
Rice, Elizabeth, *2:* 213
Rice, Inez, *13:* 186
Rice, James, *22:* 210
Rich, Elaine Sommers, *6:* 190
Rich, Josephine , *10:* 129
Richard, Adrienne, *5:* 157
Richards, Frank. *See* Hamilton, Charles Howard St. John, *13:* 77
Richards, Hilda. *See* Hamilton, Charles Howard St. John, *13:* 77
Richards, Laura E(lizabeth Howe), *YABC 1:* 224
Richardson, Grace Lee. *See* Dickson, Naida, *8:* 41
Richardson, Robert S(hirley), *8:* 164
Richoux, Pat, *7:* 180
Richter, Conrad, *3:* 171
Richter, Hans Peter, *6:* 191
Ridge, Antonia, *7:* 181
Ridley, Nat, Jr. *See* Stratemeyer, Edward L., *1:* 208
Ridlon, Marci, *22:* 211
Riedman, Sarah R(egal), *1:* 183
Riesenberg, Felix, Jr., *23:* 194
Rikhoff, Jean, *9:* 158
Riley, James Whitcomb, *17:* 159
Ringi, Kjell. *See* Ringi, Kjell Arne Sörensen, *12:* 168
Ringi, Kjell Arne Sörensen, *12:* 168
Rinkoff, Barbara (Jean), *4:* 174
Rios, Tere. *See* Versace, Marie Teresa, *2:* 254
Ripley, Elizabeth Blake, *5:* 158
Ripper, Charles L., *3:* 174
Ritchie, Barbara (Gibbons), *14:* 176
Riverside, John. *See* Heinlein, Robert A(nson), *9:* 102
Rivoli, Mario, *10:* 129
Roach, Marilynne K(athleen), *9:* 158
Roach, Portia. *See* Takakjian, Portia, *15:* 273
Robbins, Raleigh. *See* Hamilton, Charles Harold St. John, *13:* 77
Robbins, Ruth, *14:* 177
Roberts, David. *See* Cox, John Roberts, *9:* 42
Roberts, Jim. *See* Bates, Barbara S(nedeker), *12:* 34
Roberts, Terence. *See* Sanderson, Ivan T., *6:* 195
Roberts, Willo Davis, *21:* 125
Robertson, Barbara (Anne), *12:* 172
Robertson, Don, *8:* 165
Robertson, Dorothy Lewis, *12:* 173
Robertson, Jennifer (Sinclair), *12:* 174
Robertson, Keith, *1:* 184
Robins, Seelin. *See* Ellis, Edward S(ylvester), *YABC 1:* 116
Robinson, Adjai, *8:* 165
Robinson, Barbara (Webb), *8:* 166
Robinson, Charles, *6:* 192
Robinson, Charles [1870-1937], *17:* 171
Robinson, Jan M., *6:* 194
Robinson, Jean O., *7:* 182
Robinson, Joan (Mary) G(ale Thomas), *7:* 183
Robinson, Maudie (Millian Oller), *11:* 200
Robinson, Ray(mond Kenneth), *23:* 194
Robinson, T(homas) H(eath), *17:* 178
Robinson, W(illiam) Heath, *17:* 184
Robison, Bonnie, *12:* 175
Robottom, John, *7:* 185
Roche, A. K. [Joint pseudonym with Boche Kaplan]. *See* Abisch, Roslyn Kroop, *9:* 3
Rockwell, Norman (Percevel), *23:* 195
Rockwell, Thomas, *7:* 185
Rockwood, Roy [Collective pseudonym], *1:* 185
Rodgers, Mary, *8:* 167
Rodman, Emerson. *See* Ellis, Edward S(ylvester), *YABC 1:* 116
Rodman, Maia. *See* Wojciechowska, Maia, *1:* 228
Rodman, Selden, *9:* 159
Rodowsky, Colby, *21:* 126
Roe, Harry Mason. *See* Stratemeyer, Edward L., *1:* 208
Rogers, (Thomas) Alan (Stinchcombe), *2:* 215
Rogers, Frances, *10:* 130
Rogers, Matilda, *5:* 158
Rogers, Pamela, *9:* 160
Rogers, Robert. *See* Hamilton, Charles Harold St. John, *13:* 77
Rogers, W(illiam) G(arland), *23:* 208
Rojan. *See* Rojankovsky, Feodor (Stepanovich), *21:* 127
Rojankovsky, Feodor (Stepanovich), *21:* 127
Rokeby-Thomas, Anna E(lma), *15:* 233
Roland, Albert, *11:* 201
Rolerson, Darrell A(llen), *8:* 168
Roll, Winifred, *6:* 194
Rollins, Charlemae Hill, *3:* 175
Rongen, Björn, *10:* 131
Rood, Ronald (N.), *12:* 177

Rooke, Daphne (Marie), *12:* 178
Rose, Anne, *8:* 168
Rose, Florella. *See* Carlson, Vada F., *16:* 64
Rose, Wendy, *12:* 180
Rosen, Sidney, *1:* 185
Rosen, Winifred, *8:* 169
Rosenbaum, Maurice, *6:* 195
Rosenberg, Ethel, *3:* 176
Rosenberg, Nancy Sherman, *4:* 177
Rosenberg, Sharon, *8:* 171
Rosenbloom, Joseph, *21:* 131
Rosenblum, Richard, *11:* 202
Rosenburg, John M., *6:* 195
Ross, David, *20:* 147 (Obituary)
Ross, Tony, *17:* 203
Rossetti, Christiana (Georgina), *20:* 147
Roth, Arnold, *21:* 133
Rothkopf, Carol Z., *4:* 177
Rothman, Joel, *7:* 186
Rounds, Glen (Harold), *8:* 171
Rourke, Constance (Mayfield), *YABC 1:* 232
Rowland, Florence Wightman, *8:* 173
Roy, Liam. *See* Scarry, Patricia, *2:* 218
Rubel, Nicole, *18:* 255
Ruchlis, Hy, *3:* 177
Rudolph, Marguerita, *21:* 133
Rudomin, Esther. *See* Hautzig, Esther, *4:* 105
Ruedi, Norma Paul. *See* Ainsworth, Norma, *9:* 4
Ruhen, Olaf, *17:* 204
Rukeyser, Muriel, *22:* 211 (Obituary)
Rumsey, Marian (Barritt), *16:* 236
Rushmore, Helen, *3:* 178
Rushmore, Robert (William), *8:* 174
Ruskin, Ariane, *7:* 187
Russell, Charlotte. *See* Rathjen, Carl H(enry), *11:* 198
Russell, Franklin, *11:* 203
Russell, Helen Ross, *8:* 175
Russell, Patrick. *See* Sammis, John, *4:* 178
Russell, Solveig Paulson, *3:* 179
Ruth, Rod, *9:* 160
Ruthin, Margaret, *4:* 178
Rutgers van der Loeff, An(na) Basenau, *22:* 211
Rutz, Viola Larkin, *12:* 181
Ryan, Cheli Durán, *20:* 154
Ryan, John (Gerald Christopher), *22:* 214
Ryan, Peter (Charles), *15:* 235
Rydberg, Ernest E(mil), *21:* 135
Rydell, Wendell. *See* Rydell, Wendy, *4:* 178
Rydell, Wendy, *4:* 178
Ryden, Hope, *8:* 176
Sabin, Edwin Legrand, *YABC 2:* 277
Sabuso. *See* Phillips, Irving W., *11:* 196
Sachs, Marilyn, *3:* 180
Sackett, S(amuel) J(ohn), *12:* 181
Sackson, Sid, *16:* 237
Sadie, Stanley (John), *14:* 177
Sage, Juniper [Joint pseudonym]. *See* Brown, Margaret Wise, *YABC 2:* 9
Sage, Juniper. *See* Hurd, Edith, *2:* 150
Sagsoorian, Paul, *12:* 183
Saint, Dora Jessie, *10:* 132
St. Briavels, James. *See* Wood, James Playsted, *1:* 229
Saint Exupéry, Antoine de, *20:* 154
St. George, Judith, *13:* 187
St. John, Philip. *See* Del Rey, Lester, *22:* 97
St. John, Wylly Folk, *10:* 132
St. Meyer, Ned. *See* Stratemeyer, Edward L., *1:* 208
St. Tamara. *See* Kolba, Tamara, *22:* 171
Saito, Michiko. *See* Fujiwara, Michiko, *15:* 120
Salmon, Annie Elizabeth, *13:* 188
Salter, Cedric. *See* Knight, Francis Edgar, *14:* 112
Samachson, Dorothy, *3:* 182
Samachson, Joseph, *3:* 182
Sammis, John, *4:* 178
Samson, Anne S(tringer), *2:* 216
Samson, Joan, *13:* 189
Samuels, Charles, *12:* 183
Samuels, Gertrude, *17:* 206
Sanchez, Sonia, *22:* 214
Sanchez-Silva, Jose Maria, *16:* 237
Sandberg, (Karin) Inger, *15:* 238
Sandberg, Lasse (E. M.), *15:* 239
Sandburg, Carl (August), *8:* 177
Sandburg, Charles A. *See* Sandburg, Carl (August), *8:* 177
Sandburg, Helga, *3:* 184
Sanderlin, George, *4:* 180
Sanderlin, Owenita (Harrah), *11:* 204
Sanderson, Ivan T., *6:* 195
Sandin, Joan, *12:* 185
Sandoz, Mari (Susette), *5:* 159
Sanger, Marjory Bartlett, *8:* 181
Sarac, Roger. *See* Caras, Roger A(ndrew), *12:* 65
Sarg, Anthony Fredrick. *See* Sarg, Tony, *YABC 1:* 233
Sarg, Tony, *YABC 1:* 233
Sargent, Robert, *2:* 216
Sargent, Shirley, *11:* 205
Sarnoff, Jane, *10:* 133
Saroyan, William, *23:* 210
Sasek, Miroslav, *16:* 239; *23:* 218 (Obituary)
Sattler, Helen Roney, *4:* 181
Saunders, Caleb. *See* Heinlein, Robert A(nson), *9:* 102
Saunders, Keith, *12:* 186
Saunders, Rubie (Agnes), *21:* 136
Savage, Blake. *See* Goodwin, Harold Leland, *13:* 73
Savery, Constance (Winifred), *1:* 186
Saville, (Leonard) Malcolm, *23:* 218
Saviozzi, Adriana. *See* Mazza, Adriana, *19:* 215
Savitt, Sam, *8:* 181
Savitz, Harriet May, *5:* 161
Sawyer, Ruth, *17:* 207
Sayers, Frances Clarke, *3:* 185
Sazer, Nina, *13:* 191
Scabrini, Janet, *13:* 191
Scagnetti, Jack, *7:* 188
Scanlon, Marion Stephany, *11:* 206
Scarf, Maggi. *See* Scarf, Maggie, *5:* 162
Scarf, Maggie, *5:* 162
Scarry, Patricia (Murphy), *2:* 218
Scarry, Patsy. *See* Scarry, Patricia, *2:* 218
Scarry, Richard (McClure), *2:* 218
Schaefer, Jack, *3:* 186
Schaeffer, Mead, *21:* 137
Schechter, Betty (Goodstein), *5:* 163
Scheer, Julian (Weisel), *8:* 183
Scheffer, Victor B., *6:* 197
Schell, Orville H., *10:* 136
Schemm, Mildred Walker, *21:* 139
Scherf, Margaret, *10:* 136
Schick, Eleanor, *9:* 161
Schiff, Ken, *7:* 189
Schiller, Andrew, *21:* 139
Schiller, Barbara (Heyman), *21:* 140
Schisgall, Oscar, *12:* 187
Schlein, Miriam, *2:* 222
Schloat, G. Warren, Jr., *4:* 181
Schmid, Eleonore, *12:* 188
Schmiderer, Dorothy, *19:* 223
Schmidt, Elizabeth, *15:* 242
Schmidt, James Norman, *21:* 141
Schneider, Herman, *7:* 189
Schneider, Nina, *2:* 222
Schnirel, James R(einhold), *14:* 178
Schoen, Barbara, *13:* 192
Scholastica, Sister Mary. *See* Jenkins, Marie M., *7:* 143
Scholefield, Edmund O. *See* Butterworth, W. E., *5:* 40
Schone, Virginia, *22:* 215
Schoor, Gene, *3:* 188
Schreiber, Elizabeth Anne (Ferguson), *13:* 192
Schreiber, Ralph W(alter), *13:* 194
Schroeder, Ted, *20:* 163 (Obituary)
Schulman, Janet, *22:* 216
Schulman, L(ester) M(artin), *13:* 194
Schultz, Gwendolyn, *21:* 142
Schultz, James Willard, *YABC 1:* 238

Schultz, Pearle Henriksen, *21:* 142
Schulz, Charles M(onroe), *10:* 137
Schurfranz, Vivian, *13:* 194
Schutzer, A. I., *13:* 195
Schwartz, Alvin, *4:* 183
Schwartz, Anne Powers, *10:* 142
Schwartz, Charles W(alsh), *8:* 184
Schwartz, Elizabeth Reeder, *8:* 184
Schwartz, Stephen (Lawrence), *19:* 224
Scoppettone, Sandra, *9:* 162
Scott, Cora Annett (Pipitone), *11:* 207
Scott, Dan [House pseudonym]. *See* Barker, S. Omar, *10:* 8
Scott, Dan. *See* Stratemeyer, Edward L., *1:* 208
Scott, John, *14:* 178
Scott, John Anthony, *23:* 219
Scott, John M(artin), *12:* 188
Scott, Tony. *See* Scott, John Anthony, *23:* 219
Scott, Sir Walter, *YABC 2:* 280
Scribner, Charles Jr., *13:* 195
Scuro, Vincent, *21:* 144
Seamands, Ruth (Childers), *9:* 163
Searight, Mary W(illiams), *17:* 211
Searle, Kathryn Adrienne, *10:* 143
Sears, Stephen W., *4:* 184
Sebastian, Lee. *See* Silverberg, Robert, *13:* 206
Sechrist, Elizabeth Hough, *2:* 224
Sedges, John. *See* Buck, Pearl S., *1:* 36
Seed, Jenny, *8:* 186
Seed, Sheila Turner, *23:* 220 (Obituary)
Seeger, Elizabeth, *20:* 163 (Obituary)
Seeger, Pete(r), *13:* 196
Segal, Lore, *4:* 186
Seidelman, James Edward, *6:* 197
Seidman, Laurence (Ivan), *15:* 244
Seigal, Kalman, *12:* 190
Seignobosc, Francoise, *21:* 145
Seixas, Judith S., *17:* 212
Sejima, Yoshimasa, *8:* 186
Selden, George. *See* Thompson, George Selden, *4:* 204
Selig, Sylvie, *13:* 199
Selsam, Millicent E(llis), *1:* 188
Seltzer, Meyer, *17:* 213
Sendak, Maurice (Bernard), *1:* 190
Sengler, Johanna, *18:* 255
Serage, Nancy, *10:* 143
Seredy, Kate, *1:* 193
Seroff, Victor I(lyitch), *12:* 190
Serraillier, Ian (Lucien), *1:* 193
Servello, Joe, *10:* 143
Service, Robert W(illiam), *20:* 163
Serwer, Blanche L., *10:* 144
Seton, Anya, *3:* 188
Seton, Ernest Thompson, *18:* 257
Seuling, Barbara, *10:* 145
Seuss, Dr. *See* Geisel, Theodor Seuss, *1:* 104
Severn, Bill. *See* Severn, William Irving, *1:* 195
Severn, David. *See* Unwin, David S(torr), *14:* 217
Severn, William Irving, *1:* 195
Seward, Prudence, *16:* 242
Sexton, Anne (Harvey), *10:* 146
Seymour, Alta Halverson, *10:* 147
Shafer, Robert E(ugene), *9:* 164
Shahn, Ben(jamin), *21:* 146 (Obituary)
Shahn, Bernarda Bryson. *See* Bryson, Bernarda, *9:* 26
Shanks, Ann Zane (Kushner), *10:* 148
Shannon, Terry, *21:* 147
Shapp, Martha, *3:* 189
Sharfman, Amalie, *14:* 179
Sharma, Partap, *15:* 244
Sharmat, Marjorie Weinman, *4:* 187
Sharp, Margery, *1:* 196
Sharpe, Mitchell R(aymond), *12:* 191
Shaw, Arnold, *4:* 189
Shaw, Charles (Green), *13:* 200
Shaw, Flora Louisa. *See* Lugard, Flora Louisa Shaw, *21:* 104
Shaw, Ray, *7:* 190
Shaw, Richard, *12:* 192
Shay, Arthur, *4:* 189
Shecter, Ben, *16:* 243
Sheedy, Alexandra Elizabeth, *19:* 225
Sheehan, Ethna, *9:* 165
Shekerjian, Regina Tor, *16:* 244
Sheldon, Ann [Collective pseudonym], *1:* 198
Sheldon, Aure, *12:* 194
Shelton, William Roy, *5:* 164
Shemin, Margaretha, *4:* 190
Shepard, Ernest Howard, *3:* 191
Shephard, Esther, *5:* 165
Shepherd, Elizabeth, *4:* 191
Sherburne, Zoa, *3:* 194
Sherman, Diane (Finn), *12:* 194
Sherman, Elizabeth. *See* Friskey, Margaret Richards, *5:* 72
Sherman, Nancy. *See* Rosenberg, Nancy Sherman, *4:* 177
Sherrod, Jane. *See* Singer, Jane Sherrod, *4:* 192
Sherry, (Dulcie) Sylvia, *8:* 187
Sherwan, Earl, *3:* 195
Shiefman, Vicky, *22:* 217
Shields, Charles, *10:* 149
Shimin, Symeon, *13:* 201
Shinn, Everett, *21:* 148
Shippen, Katherine B(inney), *1:* 198; *23:* 221 (Obituary)
Shipton, Eric, *10:* 151
Shirreffs, Gordon D(onald), *11:* 207
Shortall, Leonard W., *19:* 226
Shotwell, Louisa R., *3:* 196
Showalter, Jean B(reckinridge), *12:* 195
Showers, Paul C., *21:* 152
Shub, Elizabeth, *5:* 166
Shulevitz, Uri, *3:* 197
Shulman, Alix Kates, *7:* 191
Shulman, Irving, *13:* 204
Shumsky, Zena. *See* Collier, Zena, *23:* 41
Shura, Mary Francis. *See* Craig, Mary Francis, *6:* 52
Shuttlesworth, Dorothy, *3:* 200
Shyer, Marlene Fanta, *13:* 205
Sibley, Don, *12:* 195
Siculan, Daniel, *12:* 197
Sidjakov, Nicolas, *18:* 272
Sidney, Margaret. *See* Lothrop, Harriet Mulford Stone, *20:* 110
Silcock, Sara Lesley, *12:* 199
Silver, Ruth. *See* Chew, Ruth, *7:* 45
Silverberg, Robert, *13:* 206
Silverman, Mel(vin Frank), *9:* 166
Silverstein, Alvin, *8:* 188
Silverstein, Virginia B(arbara Opshelor), *8:* 190
Simon, Charlie May. *See* Fletcher, Charlie May, *3:* 70
Simon, Howard, *21:* 154 (Obituary)
Simon, Joe. *See* Simon, Joseph H., *7:* 192
Simon, Joseph H., *7:* 192
Simon, Martin P(aul William), *12:* 200
Simon, Mina Lewiton. *See* Lewiton, Mina, *2:* 174
Simon, Norma, *3:* 201
Simon, Seymour, *4:* 191
Simon, Shirley (Schwartz), *11:* 210
Simonetta, Linda, *14:* 179
Simonetta, Sam, *14:* 180
Simont, Marc, *9:* 167
Simpson, Colin, *14:* 181
Simpson, Myrtle L(illias), *14:* 181
Sinclair, Upton (Beall), *9:* 168
Singer, Isaac. *See* Singer, Isaac Bashevis, *3:* 203
Singer, Isaac Bashevis, *3:* 203
Singer, Jane Sherrod, *4:* 192
Singer, Susan (Mahler), *9:* 170
Sisson, Rosemary Anne, *11:* 211
Sivulich, Sandra (Jeanne) Stroner, *9:* 171
Skelly, James R(ichard), *17:* 215
Skinner, Constance Lindsay, *YABC 1:* 247
Skinner, Cornelia Otis, *2:* 225
Skorpen, Liesel Moak, *3:* 206
Skurzynski, Gloria (Joan), *8:* 190
Slackman, Charles B., *12:* 200
Slade, Richard, *9:* 171
Sleator, William, *3:* 207
Sleigh, Barbara, *3:* 208
Slicer, Margaret O., *4:* 193
Slobodkin, Florence (Gersh), *5:* 167
Slobodkin, Louis, *1:* 199
Slobodkina, Esphyr, *1:* 201
Slote, Alfred, *8:* 192
Small, Ernest. *See* Lent, Blair, *2:* 172

Smaridge, Norah, *6:* 198
Smiley, Virginia Kester, *2:* 227
Smith, Beatrice S(chillinger), *12:* 201
Smith, Betty, *6:* 199
Smith, Bradford, *5:* 168
Smith, Datus C(lifford) Jr., *13:* 208
Smith, Dodie, *4:* 194
Smith, Dorothy Stafford, *6:* 201
Smith, E(lmer) Boyd, *YABC 1:* 248
Smith, Eunice Young, *5:* 169
Smith, Frances C., *3:* 209
Smith, Gary R(ichard), *14:* 182
Smith, George Harmon, *5:* 171
Smith, H(arry) Allen, *20:* 171 (Obituary)
Smith, Howard Everett Jr., *12:* 201
Smith, Hugh L(etcher), *5:* 172
Smith, Imogene Henderson, *12:* 203
Smith, Jean. *See* Smith, Frances C., *3:* 209
Smith, Jean Pajot, *10:* 151
Smith, Jessie Willcox, *21:* 155
Smith, Johnston. *See* Crane, Stephen (Townley), *YABC 2:* 84
Smith, Lafayette. *See* Higdon, Hal, *4:* 115
Smith, Linell Nash, *2:* 227
Smith, Marion Hagens, *12:* 204
Smith, Marion Jaques, *13:* 209
Smith, Mary Ellen, *10:* 152
Smith, Mike. *See* Smith, Mary Ellen, *10:* 152
Smith, Nancy Covert, *12:* 204
Smith, Norman F., *5:* 172
Smith, Robert Kimmel, *12:* 205
Smith, Ruth Leslie, *2:* 228
Smith, Sarah Stafford. *See* Smith, Dorothy Stafford, *6:* 201
Smith, Susan Carlton, *12:* 207
Smith, Vian (Crocker), *11:* 213
Smith, William A., *10:* 153
Smith, William Jay, *2:* 229
Smith, Z. Z. *See* Westheimer, David, *14:* 242
Snedeker, Caroline Dale (Parke), *YABC 2:* 296
Sneve, Virginia Driving Hawk, *8:* 193
Sniff, Mr. *See* Abisch, Roslyn Kroop, *9:* 3
Snodgrass, Thomas Jefferson. *See* Clemens, Samuel Langhorne, *YABC 2:* 51
Snow, Donald Clifford, *16:* 246
Snow, Dorothea J(ohnston), *9:* 172
Snyder, Anne, *4:* 195
Snyder, Jerome, *20:* 171 (Obituary)
Snyder, Zilpha Keatley, *1:* 202
Snyderman, Reuven K., *5:* 173
Sobol, Donald J., *1:* 203
Soderlind, Arthur E(dwin), *14:* 183
Softly, Barbara (Frewin), *12:* 209
Sohl, Frederic J(ohn), *10:* 154
Solbert, Romaine G., *2:* 232
Solbert, Ronni. *See* Solbert, Romaine G., *2:* 232
Solomons, Ikey, Esquire, Jr.. *See* Thackeray, William Makepeace, *23:* 223
Solonevich, George, *15:* 245
Solot, Mary Lynn, *12:* 210
Sommer, Elyse, *7:* 192
Sommer, Robert, *12:* 211
Sommerfelt, Aimee, *5:* 173
Sonneborn, Ruth, *4:* 196
Sorche, Nic Leodhas. *See* Alger, Leclaire (Gowans), *15:* 1
Sorensen, Virginia, *2:* 233
Sorrentino, Joseph N., *6:* 203
Sortor, June Elizabeth, *12:* 212
Sortor, Toni. *See* Sortor, June Elizabeth, *12:* 212
Soskin, V. H. *See* Ellison, Virginia Howell, *4:* 74
Sotomayor, Antonio, *11:* 214
Soudley, Henry. *See* Wood, James Playsted, *1:* 229
Soule, Gardner (Bosworth), *14:* 183
Soule, Jean Conder, *10:* 154
Southall, Ivan, *3:* 210
Spanfeller, James J(ohn), *19:* 230
Spangenberg, Judith Dunn, *5:* 175
Spar, Jerome, *10:* 156
Sparks, Mary W., *15:* 247
Spaulding, Leonard. *See* Bradbury, Ray, *11:* 29
Speare, Elizabeth George, *5:* 176
Spearing, Judith (Mary Harlow), *9:* 173
Specking, Inez, *11:* 217
Speicher, Helen Ross (Smith), *8:* 194
Spellman, John W(illard), *14:* 186
Spence, Eleanor (Rachel), *21:* 163
Spencer, Ann, *10:* 156
Spencer, Cornelia. *See* Yaukey, Grace S. *5:* 203
Spencer, Elizabeth, *14:* 186
Spencer, William, *9:* 175
Sperry, Armstrong W., *1:* 204
Sperry, Raymond, Jr. [Collective pseudonym], *1:* 205
Spiegelman, Judith M., *5:* 179
Spier, Peter (Edward), *4:* 198
Spilhaus, Athelstan, *13:* 209
Spilka, Arnold, *6:* 203
Spink, Reginald (William), *11:* 217
Spinossimus. *See* White, William, *16:* 276
Spollen, Christopher, *12:* 213
Sprigge, Elizabeth, *10:* 157
Spykman, E(lizabeth) C., *10:* 157
Spyri, Johanna (Heusser), *19:* 232
Squire, Miriam. *See* Sprigge, Elizabeth, *10:* 157
Squires, Phil. *See* Barker, S. Omar, *10:* 8
S-Ringi, Kjell. *See* Ringi, Kjell, *12:* 168
Stadtler, Bea, *17:* 215
Stafford, Jean, *22:* 218 (Obituary)
Stahl, Ben(jamin), *5:* 179
Stamaty, Mark Alan, *12:* 214
Stambler, Irwin, *5:* 181
Stanhope, Eric. *See* Hamilton, Charles Harold St. John, *13:* 77
Stankevich, Boris, *2:* 234
Stanley, Robert. *See* Hamilton, Charles Harold St. John, *13:* 77
Stanstead, John. *See* Groom, Arthur William, *10:* 53
Stapp, Arthur D(onald), *4:* 201
Starbird, Kaye, *6:* 204
Stark, James. *See* Goldston, Robert, *6:* 90
Starkey, Marion L., *13:* 211
Starret, William. *See* McClintock, Marshall, *3:* 119
Staunton, Schuyler. *See* Baum, L(yman) Frank, *18:* 7
Stearns, Monroe (Mather), *5:* 182
Steele, Chester K. *See* Stratemeyer, Edward L., *1:* 208
Steele, Mary Q., *3:* 211
Steele, (Henry) Max(well), *10:* 159
Steele, William O(wen), *1:* 205
Steig, William, *18:* 275
Stein, M(eyer) L(ewis), *6:* 205
Stein, Mini, *2:* 234
Steinbeck, John (Ernst), *9:* 176
Steinberg, Alfred, *9:* 178
Steinberg, Fred J., *4:* 201
Steiner, Barbara A(nnette), *13:* 213
Steiner, Stan(ley), *14:* 187
Stephens, Mary Jo, *8:* 196
Stephens, William M(cLain), *21:* 165
Steptoe, John (Lewis), *8:* 198
Sterling, Dorothy, *1:* 206
Sterling, Helen. *See* Hoke, Helen (L.), *15:* 133
Sterling, Philip, *8:* 198
Stern, Madeleine B(ettina), *14:* 188
Stern, Philip Van Doren, *13:* 215
Stern, Simon, *15:* 248
Sterne, Emma Gelders, *6:* 205
Steurt, Marjorie Rankin, *10:* 159
Stevens, Carla M(cBride), *13:* 217
Stevens, Franklin, *6:* 206
Stevens, Peter. *See* Geis, Darlene, *7:* 101
Stevenson, Anna (M.), *12:* 216
Stevenson, Augusta, *2:* 235
Stevenson, Janet, *8:* 199
Stevenson, Robert Louis, *YABC 2:* 307
Stewart, A(gnes) C(harlotte), *15:* 250
Stewart, Charles. *See* Zurhorst, Charles (Stewart, Jr.), *12:* 240
Stewart, Elizabeth Laing, *6:* 206
Stewart, John (William), *14:* 189
Stewart, George Rippey, *3:* 213; *23:* 221 (Obituary)

Author Index

Stewart, Mary (Florence Elinor), *12:* 217
Stewart, Robert Neil, *7:* 192
Stiles, Martha Bennett, *6:* 207
Stillerman, Robbie, *12:* 219
Stine, G(eorge) Harry, *10:* 161
Stinetorf, Louise, *10:* 162
Stirling, Arthur. *See* Sinclair, Upton (Beall), *9:* 168
Stirling, Nora B., *3:* 214
Stirnweis, Shannon, *10:* 163
Stobbs, William, *17:* 216
Stoddard, Edward G., *10:* 164
Stoddard, Hope, *6:* 207
Stoddard, Sandol. *See* Warburg, Sandol Stoddard, *14:* 234
Stoiko, Michael, *14:* 190
Stokes, Cedric. *See* Beardmore, George, *20:* 10
Stokes, Jack (Tilden), *13:* 218
Stolz, Mary (Slattery), *10:* 165
Stone, Alan [Collective pseudonym], *1:* 208. *See also* Svenson, Andrew E., *2:* 238
Stone, D(avid) K(arl), *9:* 179
Stone, Eugenia, *7:* 193
Stone, Gene. *See* Stone, Eugenia, *7:* 193
Stone, Helen V., *6:* 208
Stone, Irving, *3:* 215
Stone, Raymond [Collective pseudonym], *1:* 208
Stone, Richard A. *See* Stratemeyer, Edward L., *1:* 208
Stonehouse, Bernard, *13:* 219
Storch, Anne B. von. *See* von Storch, Anne B., *1:* 221
Storey, (Elizabeth) Margaret (Carlton), *9:* 180
Storey, Victoria Carolyn, *16:* 248
Storme, Peter. *See* Stern, Philip Van Doren, *13:* 215
Storr, Catherine (Cole), *9:* 181
Stoutenburg, Adrien, *3:* 217
Stover, Allan C(arl), *14:* 191
Stover, Marjorie Filley, *9:* 182
Stowe, Harriet (Elizabeth) Beecher, *YABC 1:* 250
Strachan, Margaret Pitcairn, *14:* 193
Stranger, Joyce. *See* Wilson, Joyce M(uriel Judson), *21:* 201
Stratemeyer, Edward L., *1:* 208
Stratton-Porter, Gene, *15:* 251
Strayer, E. Ward. *See* Stratemeyer, Edward L., *1:* 208
Streano, Vince(nt Catello), *20:* 172
Streatfeild, Noel, *20:* 173
Street, Julia Montgomery, *11:* 218
Strong, Charles. *See* Epstein, Samuel, *1:* 87
Ströyer, Poul, *13:* 221
Stuart, Forbes, *13:* 222
Stuart, Ian, *See* MacLean, Alistair (Stuart), *23:* 131
Stuart, (Hilton) Jesse, *2:* 236
Stuart, Sheila. *See* Baker, Mary Gladys Steel, *12:* 27
Stubis, Talivaldis, *5:* 183
Stubley, Trevor (Hugh), *22:* 218
Sture-Vasa, Mary. *See* Alsop, Mary, *2:* 4
Sturton, Hugh. *See* Johnston, H(ugh) A(nthony) S(tephen), *14:* 87
Sturtzel, Howard A(llison), *1:* 210
Sturtzel, Jane Levington, *1:* 212
Styles, Frank Showell, *10:* 167
Suba, Susanne, *4:* 202
Subond, Valerie. *See* Grayland, Valerie, *7:* 111
Suhl, Yuri, *8:* 200
Sullivan, George E(dward), *4:* 202
Sullivan, Mary W(ilson), *13:* 224
Sullivan, Thomas Joseph, Jr., *16:* 248
Sullivan, Tom. *See* Sullivan, Thomas Joseph, Jr., *16:* 248
Supraner, Robyn, *20:* 182
Surge, Frank, *13:* 225
Susac, Andrew, *5:* 184
Sutcliff, Rosemary, *6:* 209
Sutherland, Margaret, *15:* 271
Suttles, Shirley (Smith), *21:* 166
Sutton, Margaret (Beebe), *1:* 213
Svenson, Andrew E., *2:* 238
Swain, Su Zan (Noguchi), *21:* 169
Swan, Susan, *22:* 219
Swarthout, Kathryn, *7:* 194
Sweeney, James B(artholomew), *21:* 170
Swenson, Allan A(rmstrong), *21:* 172
Swenson, May, *15:* 271
Swift, David. *See* Kaufmann, John, *18:* 132
Swift, Hildegarde Hoyt, *20:* 184 (Obituary)
Swift, Jonathan, *19:* 244
Swiger, Elinor Porter, *8:* 202
Swinburne, Laurence, *9:* 183
Sylvester, Natalie G(abry), *22:* 222
Syme, (Neville) Ronald, *2:* 239
Synge, (Phyllis) Ursula, *9:* 184
Sypher, Lucy Johnston, *7:* 195
Szasz, Suzanne Shorr, *13:* 226
Szekeres, Cyndy, *5:* 184

Taber, Gladys (Bagg), *22:* 223 (Obituary)
Tabrah, Ruth Milander, *14:* 194
Tait, Douglas, *12:* 220
Takakjian, Portia, *15:* 273
Takashima, Shizuye, *13:* 227
Talbot, Charlene Joy, *10:* 169
Talbot, Toby, *14:* 195
Talker, T. *See* Rands, William Brighty, *17:* 156
Tallcott, Emogene, *10:* 170
Talmadge, Marian, *14:* 196
Tamarin, Alfred, *13:* 229
Tamburine, Jean, *12:* 221
Tannenbaum, Beulah, *3:* 219
Tanner, Louise S(tickney), *9:* 185
Tanobe, Miyuki, *23:* 222
Tapio, Pat Decker. *See* Kines, Pat Decker, *12:* 118
Tarkington, (Newton) Booth, *17:* 218
Tarry, Ellen, *16:* 250
Tarshis, Jerome, *9:* 186
Tashjian, Virginia A., *3:* 220
Tasker, James, *9:* 187
Tate, Ellalice. *See* Hibbert, Eleanor, *2:* 134
Tate, Joan, *9:* 188
Tatham, Campbell. *See* Elting, Mary, *2:* 100
Taylor, Barbara J., *10:* 171
Taylor, Carl, *14:* 196
Taylor, David, *10:* 172
Taylor, Elizabeth, *13:* 230
Taylor, Florance Walton, *9:* 190
Taylor, Florence M(arion Tompkins), *9:* 191
Taylor, Herb(ert Norman, Jr.), *22:* 223
Taylor, Mildred D., *15:* 275
Taylor, Robert Lewis, *10:* 172
Taylor, Sydney (Brenner), *1:* 214
Taylor, Theodore, *5:* 185
Teal, Val, *10:* 174
Teale, Edwin Way, *7:* 196
Tee-Van, Helen Damrosch, *10:* 176
Telescope, Tom. *See* Newbery, John, *20:* 135
Temko, Florence, *13:* 231
Templar, Maurice. *See* Groom, Arthur William, *10:* 53
Tenggren, Gustaf, *18:* 277
Tennant, Kylie, *6:* 210
ter Haar, Jaap, *6:* 211
Terhune, Albert Payson, *15:* 277
Terris, Susan, *3:* 221
Terry, Luther L(eonidas), *11:* 220
Terry, Walter, *14:* 198
Terzian, James P., *14:* 199
Thacher, Mary McGrath, *9:* 192
Thackeray, William Makepeace, *23:* 223
Tharp, Louise Hall, *3:* 223
Thayer, Jane. *See* Woolley, Catherine, *3:* 265
Thayer, Peter. *See* Wyler, Rose, *18:* 303
Thelwell, Norman, *14:* 200
Thieda, Shirley Ann, *13:* 233
Thiele, Colin (Milton), *14:* 201
Thistlethwaite, Miles, *12:* 223
Thollander, Earl, *22:* 224
Thomas, H. C.. *See* Keating, Lawrence A., *23:* 107
Thomas, J. F. *See* Fleming, Thomas J(ames), *8:* 64
Thomas, Joan Gale. *See* Robinson, Joan G., *7:* 183

Thomas, Lowell (Jackson), Jr., *15:* 290
Thompson, Christine Pullein. *See* Pullein-Thompson, Christine, *3:* 164
Thompson, David H(ugh), *17:* 236
Thompson, Diana Pullein. *See* Pullein-Thompson, Diana, *3:* 165
Thompson, George Selden, *4:* 204
Thompson, Harlan H., *10:* 177
Thompson, Josephine Pullein. *See* Pullein-Thompson, Josephine, *3:* 166
Thompson, Kay, *16:* 257
Thompson, Stith, *20:* 184 (Obituary)
Thompson, Vivian L., *3:* 224
Thorndyke, Helen Louise [Collective pseudonym], *1:* 216
Thorne, Ian. *See* May, Julian, *11:* 175
Thornton, W. B. *See* Burgess, Thornton Waldo, *17:* 19
Thorpe, E(ustace) G(eorge), *21:* 173
Thorvall, Kerstin, *13:* 233
Thum, Marcella, *3:* 226
Thundercloud, Katherine. *See* Witt, Shirley Hill, *17:* 247
Thurber, James (Grover), *13:* 235
Thwaite, Ann (Barbara Harrop), *14:* 206
Tichenor, Tom, *14:* 206
Timmins, William F., *10:* 177
Tinkelman, Murray, *12:* 224
Titmarsh, Michael Angelo. *See* Thackeray, William Makepeace, *23:* 223
Titus, Eve, *2:* 240
Tobias, Tobi, *5:* 187
Todd, Anne Ophelia. *See* Dowden, Anne Ophelia, *7:* 69
Todd, Barbara K., *10:* 178
Todd, H(erbert) E(atton), *11:* 221
Tolkien, J(ohn) R(onald) R(euel), *2:* 242
Tolles, Martha, *8:* 203
Tolmie, Ken(neth Donald), *15:* 291
Tomfool. *See* Farjeon, Eleanor, *2:* 103
Tomlinson, Jill, *3:* 227
Tompert, Ann, *14:* 208
Toner, Raymond John, *10:* 179
Toonder, Martin. *See* Groom, Arthur William, *10:* 53
Toothaker, Roy Eugene, *18:* 280
Tooze, Ruth, *4:* 205
Topping, Audrey R(onning), *14:* 209
Tor, Regina. *See* Shekerjian, Regina Tor, *16:* 244
Torbert, Floyd James, *22:* 226
Totham, Mary. *See* Breinburg, Petronella, *11:* 36
Tournier, Michel, *23:* 232
Townsend, John Rowe, *4:* 206
Toye, William E(ldred), *8:* 203
Traherne, Michael. *See* Watkins-Pitchford, D. J., *6:* 214
Trapp, Maria (Augusta) von, *16:* 260
Travers, P(amela) L(yndon), *4:* 208
Trease, (Robert) Geoffrey, *2:* 244
Tredez, Alain, *17:* 236
Treece, Henry, *2:* 246
Tregaskis, Richard, *3:* 228
Trell, Max, *14:* 211
Tremain, Ruthven, *17:* 237
Trent, Timothy. *See* Malmberg, Carl, *9:* 136
Tresselt, Alvin, *7:* 197
Trevino, Elizabeth B(orton) de, *1:* 216
Trevor, (Lucy) Meriol, *10:* 180
Trez, Alain. *See* Tredez, Alain, *17:* 236
Tripp, Eleanor B., *4:* 210
Tripp, Paul, *8:* 204
Trivett, Daphne (Harwood), *22:* 227
Trollope, Anthony, *22:* 229
Trost, Lucille Wood, *12:* 226
Trotter, Grace V(iolet), *10:* 180
Tucker, Caroline. *See* Nolan, Jeannette, *2:* 196
Tudor, Tasha, *20:* 184
Tully, John (Kimberley), *14:* 212
Tunis, Edwin (Burdett), *1:* 217
Turkle, Brinton, *2:* 248
Turlington, Bayly, *5:* 187
Turnbull, Agnes Sligh, *14:* 213
Turnbull, Ann (Christine), *18:* 281
Turner, Alice K., *10:* 181
Turner, Ann W(arren), *14:* 214
Turner, Elizabeth, *YABC 2:* 332
Turner, Josie. *See* Crawford, Phyllis, *3:* 57
Turner, Philip, *11:* 222
Turner, Sheila R.. *See* Seed, Sheila Turner, *23:* 220 (Obituary)
Turngren, Annette, *23:* 233 (Obituary)
Turngren, Ellen, *3:* 230
Tusan, Stan, *22:* 236
Twain, Mark. *See* Clemens, Samuel Langhorne, *YABC 2:* 51
Tweedsmuir, Baron. *See* Buchan, John, *YABC 2:* 21
Tyler, Anne, *7:* 198

Ubell, Earl, *4:* 210
Uchida, Yoshiko, *1:* 219
Udall, Jan Beaney, *10:* 182
Udry, Janice May, *4:* 212
Ullman, James Ramsey, *7:* 199
Ulm, Robert, *17:* 238
Ulyatt, Kenneth, *14:* 216
Unada. *See* Gliewe, Unada, *3:* 77
Uncle Gus. *See* Rey, H. A., *1:* 181
Uncle Ray. *See* Coffman, Ramon Peyton, *4:* 53
Underhill, Alice Mertie, *10:* 182
Ungerer, Jean Thomas, *5:* 187
Ungerer, Tomi. *See* Ungerer, Jean Thomas, *5:* 187
Unkelbach, Kurt, *4:* 213
Unnerstad, Edith, *3:* 230
Unrau, Ruth, *9:* 192
Unstead R(obert) J(ohn), *12:* 226
Unsworth, Walt, *4:* 215
Untermeyer, Louis, *2:* 250
Unwin, David S(torr), *14:* 217
Unwin, Nora S., *3:* 233
Usher, Margo Scegge. *See* McHargue, Georgess, *4:* 152
Uttley, Alice Jane, *3:* 235
Uttley, Alison. *See* Uttley, Alice Jane, *3:* 235
Utz, Lois, *5:* 189

Vaeth, J(oseph) Gordon, *17:* 239
Valen, Nanine, *21:* 173
Valens, Evans G., Jr., *1:* 220
Van Abbé, Salaman, *18:* 282
Van Anrooy, Francine, *2:* 252
Van Anrooy, Frans. *See* Van Anrooy, Francine, *2:* 252
Vance, Eleanor Graham, *11:* 223
Vandenburg, Mary Lou, *17:* 240
Vander Boom, Mae M., *14:* 219
Van der Veer, Judy, *4:* 216
Vandivert, Rita (Andre), *21:* 174
Van Duyn, Janet, *18:* 283
Van Dyne, Edith. *See* Baum, L(yman) Frank, *18:* 7
Van Leeuwen, Jean, *6:* 212
Van Lhin, Erik. *See* Del Rey, Lester, *22:* 97
Van Loon, Hendrik Willem, *18:* 284
Van Orden, M(erton) D(ick), *4:* 218
Van Rensselaer, Alexander (Taylor Mason), *14:* 219
Van Riper, Guernsey, Jr., *3:* 239
Van Stockum, Hilda, *5:* 191
Van Tuyl, Barbara, *11:* 224
Van Vogt, A(lfred) E(lton), *14:* 220
Van Woerkom, Dorothy (O'Brien), *21:* 176
Van Wyck Mason. *See* Mason, F. van Wyck, *3:* 117
Van-Wyck Mason, F. *See* Mason, F. van Wyck, *3:* 117
Varley, Dimitry V., *10:* 183
Vasiliu, Mircea, *2:* 254
Vaughan, Carter A. *See* Gerson, Noel B(ertram), *22:* 118
Vaughan, Harold Cecil, *14:* 221
Vaughan, Sam(uel) S., *14:* 222
Vaughn, Ruth, *14:* 223
Vavra, Robert James, *8:* 206
Vecsey, George, *9:* 192
Veglahn, Nancy (Crary), *5:* 194
Venable, Alan (Hudson), *8:* 206
Vequin, Capini. *See* Quinn, Elisabeth, *22:* 197
Verne, Jules, *21:* 178

Verney, John, *14:* 224
Vernon, (Elda) Louise A(nderson), *14:* 225
Vernor, D. *See* Casewit, Curtis, *4:* 43
Verral, Charles Spain, *11:* 225
Versace, Marie Teresa Rios, *2:* 254
Vesey, Paul. *See* Allen, Samuel (Washington), *9:* 6
Vestly, Anne-Cath(arina), *14:* 228
Vicarion, Count Palmiro. *See* Logue, Christopher, *23:* 119
Vicker, Angus. *See* Felsen, Henry Gregor, *1:* 89
Victor, Edward, *3:* 240
Viereck, Ellen K., *14:* 229
Viereck, Phillip, *3:* 241
Viertel, Janet, *10:* 183
Vigna, Judith, *15:* 292
Viguers, Ruth Hill, *6:* 214
Villiard, Paul, *20:* 188 (Obituary)
Villiers, Alan (John), *10:* 184
Vincent, Mary Keith. *See* St. John, Wylly Folk, *10:* 132
Vining, Elizabeth Gray. *See* Gray, Elizabeth Janet, *6:* 93
Vinson, Kathryn, *21:* 193
Viorst, Judith, *7:* 200
Visser, W(illiam) F(rederick) H(endrik), *10:* 186
Vo-Dinh, Mai, *16:* 271
Vogel, Ilse-Margret, *14:* 231
Vogel, John H(ollister), Jr., *18:* 292
Vogt, Esther Loewen, *14:* 231
Voight, Virginia Frances, *8:* 208
von Almedingen, Martha Edith. *See* Almedingen, E. M., *3:* 9
von Klopp, Vahrah. *See* Malvern, Gladys, *23:* 133
von Storch, Anne B., *1:* 221
Vosburgh, Leonard (W.), *15:* 294
Voyle, Mary. *See* Manning, Rosemary, *10:* 87

Waddell, Evelyn Margaret, *10:* 186
Wagenheim, Kal, *21:* 196
Wagner, Sharon B., *4:* 218
Wagoner, David (Russell), *14:* 232
Wahl, Jan, *2:* 256
Walden, Amelia Elizabeth, *3:* 242
Waldman, Bruce, *15:* 297
Waldron, Ann Wood, *16:* 273
Walker, Barbara K., *4:* 219
Walker, David Harry, *8:* 210
Walker, Diana, *9:* 193
Walker, Holly Beth. *See* Bond, Gladys Baker, *14:* 41
Walker, Mildred. *See* Schemm, Mildred Walker, *21:* 139
Walker, (Addison) Mort, *8:* 211
Walker, Stephen J., *12:* 228
Wallace, Barbara Brooks, *4:* 221
Wallace, Beverly Dobrin, *19:* 258
Wallace, John A., *3:* 243
Wallace, Nigel. *See* Hamilton, Charles Harold St. John, *13:* 77
Waller, Leslie, *20:* 188
Wallis, G. McDonald. *See* Campbell, Hope, *20:* 19
Wallner, John C., *10:* 189
Wallower, Lucille, *11:* 226
Walsh, Jill Paton. *See* Paton Walsh, Gillian, *4:* 164
Walter, Villiam Christian. *See* Andersen, Hans Christian, *YABC 1:* 23
Walters, Audrey, *18:* 293
Walton, Richard J., *4:* 223
Waltrip, Lela (Kingston), *9:* 194
Waltrip, Rufus (Charles), *9:* 195
Walworth, Nancy Zinsser, *14:* 233
Wannamaker, Bruce. *See* Moncure, Jane Belk, *23:* 139
Warbler, J. M. *See* Cocagnac, A. M., *7:* 52
Warburg, Sandol Stoddard, *14:* 234
Ward, Lynd (Kendall), *2:* 257
Ward, Martha (Eads), *5:* 195
Wardell, Dean. *See* Prince, J(ack) H(arvey), *17:* 155
Ware, Leon (Vernon), *4:* 224
Warner, Frank A. [Collective pseudonym], *1:* 222
Warner, Gertrude Chandler, *9:* 195
Warren, Billy. *See* Warren, William Stephen, *9:* 196
Warren, Elizabeth. *See* Supraner, Robyn, *20:* 182
Warren, Joyce W(illiams), *18:* 294
Warren, Mary Phraner, *10:* 190
Warren, William Stephen, *9:* 196
Warshofsky, Isaac. *See* Singer, Isaac Bashevis, *3:* 203
Washburne, Heluiz Chandler, *10:* 192
Waters, John F(rederick), *4:* 225
Watkins-Pitchford, D. J., *6:* 214
Watson, Clyde, *5:* 196
Watson, James, *10:* 192
Watson, Jane Werner, *3:* 244
Watson, Pauline, *14:* 235
Watson, Sally, *3:* 245
Watson, Wendy (McLeod), *5:* 198
Watt, Thomas, *4:* 226
Watts, Bernadette, *4:* 226
Watts, Franklin (Mowry), *21:* 196 (Obituary)
Watts, Mabel Pizzey, *11:* 227
Waugh, Dorothy, *11:* 228
Wayland, Patrick. *See* O'Connor, Richard, *21:* 111
Wayne, Kyra Petrovskaya, *8:* 213
Wayne, Richard. *See* Decker, Duane, *5:* 53
Waystaff, Simon. *See* Swift, Jonathan, *19:* 244
Weales, Gerald (Clifford), *11:* 229
Weaver, Ward. *See* Mason, F. van Wyck, *3:* 117
Webb, Christopher. *See* Wibberley, Leonard, *2:* 271
Webber, Irma E(leanor Schmidt), *14:* 237
Weber, Alfons, *8:* 215
Weber, Lenora Mattingly, *2:* 260
Weber, William John, *14:* 239
Webster, Alice (Jane Chandler), *17:* 241
Webster, David, *11:* 230
Webster, Frank V. [Collective pseudonym], *1:* 222
Webster, James, *17:* 242
Webster, Jean. *See* Webster, Alice (Jane Chandler), *17:* 241
Wechsler, Herman, *20:* 189 (Obituary)
Weddle, Ethel H(arshbarger), *11:* 231
Wegner, Fritz, *20:* 189
Weihs, Erika, *15:* 297
Weik, Mary Hays, *3:* 247; *23:* 233 (Obituary)
Weil, Ann Yezner, *9:* 197
Weil, Lisl, *7:* 202
Weilerstein, Sadie Rose, *3:* 248
Weiner, Sandra, *14:* 240
Weingarten, Violet, *3:* 250
Weingartner, Charles, *5:* 199
Weir, LaVada, *2:* 261
Weir, Rosemary (Green), *21:* 196
Weisberger, Bernard A(llen), *21:* 198
Weisgard, Leonard (Joseph), *2:* 263
Weiss, Adelle, *18:* 296
Weiss, Harvey, *1:* 222
Weiss, Malcolm E., *3:* 251
Weiss, Miriam. *See* Schlein, Miriam, *2:* 222
Weiss, Renee Karol, *5:* 199
Welch, Jean-Louise. *See* Kempton, Jean Welch, *10:* 67
Welch, Pauline. *See* Bodenham, Hilda Esther, *13:* 16
Welch, Ronald. *See* Felton, Ronald Oliver, *3:* 67
Wellman, Manly Wade, *6:* 217
Wellman, Paul I., *3:* 251
Wells, H(erbert) G(eorge), *20:* 190
Wells, Helen, *2:* 266
Wells, J. Wellington. *See* DeCamp, L(yon) Sprague, *9:* 49
Wells, Rosemary, *18:* 296
Wels, Byron G(erald), *9:* 197
Welty, S. F. *See* Welty, Susan F., *9:* 198
Welty, Susan F., *9:* 198
Wendelin, Rudolph, *23:* 233
Werner, Jane. *See* Watson, Jane Werner, *3:* 244
Werner, K. *See* Casewit, Curtis, *4:* 43
Wersba, Barbara, *1:* 224
Werstein, Irving, *14:* 240
Werth, Kurt, *20:* 213

West, Barbara. *See* Price, Olive, *8:* 157
West, Betty, *11:* 233
West, C. P. *See* Wodehouse, P(elham) G(renville), *22:* 241
West, James. *See* Withers, Carl A., *14:* 261
West, Jerry. *See* Stratemeyer, Edward L., *1:* 208
West, Jerry. *See* Svenson, Andrew E., *2:* 238
West, Ward. *See* Borland, Hal, *5:* 22
Westall, Robert (Atkinson), *23:* 235
Westervelt, Virginia (Veeder), *10:* 193
Westheimer, David, *14:* 242
Weston, John (Harrison), *21:* 199
Westwood, Jennifer, *10:* 194
Wexler, Jerome (LeRoy), *14:* 243
Wheatley, Arabelle, *16:* 275
Wheeler, Captain. *See* Ellis, Edward S(ylvester), *YABC 1:* 116
Wheeler, Janet D. [Collective pseudonym], *1:* 225
Wheeler, Opal, *23:* 236
Whelan, Elizabeth M(urphy), *14:* 244
Whitcomb, Jon, *10:* 195
White, Anne Terry, *2:* 267
White, Dale. *See* Place, Marian T., *3:* 160
White, Dori, *10:* 195
White, E(lwyn) B(rooks), *2:* 268
White, Eliza Orne, *YABC 2:* 333
White, Florence M(eiman), *14:* 244
White, Laurence B., Jr., *10:* 196
White, Ramy Allison [Collective pseudonym], *1:* 225
White, Robb, *1:* 225
White, T(erence) H(anbury), *12:* 229
White, William, Jr., *16:* 276
Whitehead, Don(ald) F., *4:* 227
Whitehouse, Arch. *See* Whitehouse, Arthur George, *14:* 246; *23:* 238 (Obituary)
Whitehouse, Arthur George, *14:* 246; *23:* 238 (Obituary)
Whitinger, R. D. *See* Place, Marian T., *3:* 160
Whitman, Walt(er), *20:* 215
Whitney, Alex(andra), *14:* 249
Whitney, Phyllis A(yame), *1:* 226
Wibberley, Leonard, *2:* 271
Widdemer, Mabel Cleland, *5:* 200
Widenberg, Siv, *10:* 197
Wier, Ester, *3:* 252
Wiese, Kurt, *3:* 254
Wiesner, Portia. *See* Takakjian, Portia, *15:* 273
Wiesner, William, *5:* 200
Wiggin, Kate Douglas (Smith), *YABC 1:* 258
Wilbur, Richard (Purdy), *9:* 200
Wilde, Gunther. *See* Hurwood, Bernhardt, J., *12:* 107
Wilder, Laura Ingalls, *15:* 300
Wildsmith, Brian, *16:* 277
Wilkins, Frances, *14:* 249
Wilkinson, Brenda, *14:* 250
Wilkinson, Burke, *4:* 229
Will. *See* Lipkind, William, *15:* 178
Willard, Barbara (Mary), *17:* 243
Willard, Mildred Wilds, *14:* 252
Willey, Robert. *See* Ley, Willy, *2:* 175
Williams, Barbara, *11:* 233
Williams, Beryl. *See* Epstein, Beryl, *1:* 85
Williams, Charles. *See* Collier, James Lincoln, *8:* 33
Williams, Clyde C., *8:* 216
Williams, Eric (Ernest), *14:* 253
Williams, Ferelith Eccles, *22:* 237
Williams, Frances B. *See* Browin, Frances Williams, *5:* 30
Williams, Garth (Montgomery), *18:* 298
Williams, Guy R., *11:* 235
Williams, Hawley. *See* Heyliger, William, *YABC 1:* 163
Williams, J. R. *See* Williams, Jeanne, *5:* 202
Williams, J. Walker. *See* Wodehouse, P(elham) G(renville), *22:* 241
Williams, Jay, *3:* 256
Williams, Jeanne, *5:* 202
Williams, Maureen, *12:* 238
Williams, Michael. *See* St. John, Wylly Folk, *10:* 132
Williams, Patrick J. *See* Butterworth, W. E., *5:* 40
Williams, Selma R(uth), *14:* 256
Williams, Slim. *See* Williams, Clyde C., *8:* 216
Williams, Ursula Moray, *3:* 257
Williamson, Joanne Small, *3:* 259
Wilma, Dana. *See* Faralla, Dana, *9:* 62
Wilson, Beth P(ierre), *8:* 218
Wilson, Carter, *6:* 218
Wilson, Dorothy Clarke, *16:* 283
Wilson, Ellen (Janet Cameron), *9:* 200
Wilson, (Leslie) Granville, *14:* 257
Wilson, Hazel, *3:* 260
Wilson, John, *22:* 239
Wilson, Joyce M(uriel Judson), *21:* 201
Wilson, Walt(er N.), *14:* 258
Wilton, Elizabeth, *14:* 259
Wilwerding, Walter Joseph, *9:* 201
Winders, Gertrude Hecker, *3:* 261
Windham, Basil. *See* Wodehouse, P(elham) G(renville), *22:* 241
Windham, Kathryn T(ucker), *14:* 259
Winfield, Arthur M. *See* Stratemeyer, Edward L., *1:* 208
Winfield, Edna. *See* Stratemeyer, Edward L., *1:* 208
Winter, Milo (Kendall), *21:* 202
Winter, R. R.. *See* Winterbotham, R(ussell) R(obert), *10:* 198
Winterbotham, R(ussell) R(obert), *10:* 198
Winthrop, Elizabeth. *See* Mahony, Elizabeth Winthrop, *8:* 125
Wirtenberg, Patricia Z., *10:* 199
Wise, William, *4:* 230
Wise, Winifred E., *2:* 273
Wiseman, B(ernard), *4:* 232
Withers, Carl A., *14:* 261
Witt, Shirley Hill, *17:* 247
Wizard, Mr. *See* Herbert, Don, *2:* 131
Wodehouse, P(elham) G(renville), *22:* 241
Wohlrabe, Raymond A., *4:* 234
Wojciechowska, Maia, *1:* 228
Wolcott, Patty, *14:* 264
Wolfe, Burton H., *5:* 202
Wolfe, Louis, *8:* 219
Wolfenden, George. *See* Beardmore, George, *20:* 10
Wolff, Robert Jay, *10:* 199
Wolkstein, Diane, *7:* 204
Wondriska, William, *6:* 219
Wood, Edgar A(llardyce), *14:* 264
Wood, James Playsted, *1:* 229
Wood, Kerry. *See* Wood, Edgar A(llardyce), *14:* 264
Wood, Nancy, *6:* 220
Woodard, Carol, *14:* 266
Woodburn, John Henry, *11:* 236
Woodrich, Mary Neville, *2:* 274
Woods, Margaret, *2:* 275
Woods, Nat. *See* Stratemeyer, Edward L., *1:* 208
Woodson, Jack. *See* Woodson, John Waddie, Jr., *10:* 200
Woodson, John Waddie, Jr., *10:* 200
Woodward, Cleveland, *10:* 201
Woody, Regina Jones, *3:* 263
Wooldridge, Rhoda, *22:* 249
Woolley, Catherine, *3:* 265
Woolsey, Janette, *3:* 266
Worcester, Donald Emmet, *18:* 301
Worline, Bonnie Bess, *14:* 267
Wormser, Sophie, *22:* 250
Worth, Valerie, *8:* 220
Wortis, Avi, *14:* 269
Wriggins, Sally Hovey, *17:* 248
Wright, Dare, *21:* 206
Wright, Enid Meadowcroft, *3:* 267
Wright, Esmond, *10:* 202
Wright, Frances Fitzpatrick, *10:* 202
Wright, Judith, *14:* 270
Wright, Kenneth. *See* Del Rey, Lester, *22:* 97

Wright, R(obert) H., *6:* 220
Wrightson, Patricia, *8:* 220
Wronker, Lili Cassel, *10:* 204
Wyeth, N(ewell) C(onvers), *17:* 249
Wyler, Rose, *18:* 303
Wyndham, Lee. *See* Hyndman, Jane Andrews, *1:* 122; *23:* 103 (Obituary)
Wyndham, Robert. *See* Hyndman, Robert Utley, *18:* 123
Wynter, Edward (John), *14:* 271
Wynyard, Talbot. *See* Hamilton, Charles Harold St. John, *13:* 77
Wyss, Thelma Hatch, *10:* 205

Yamaguchi, Marianne, *7:* 205
Yang, Jay, *12:* 239
Yashima, Taro. *See* Iwamatsu, Jun Atsushi, *14:* 83
Yates, Elizabeth, *4:* 235
Yaukey, Grace S(ydenstricker), *5:* 203
Yeakley, Marjory Hall, *21:* 207
Yep, Laurence M., *7:* 206
Yerian, Cameron John, *21:* 208
Yerian, Margaret A., *21:* 209
Yolen, Jane H., *4:* 237
York, Andrew. *See* Nicole, Christopher Robin, *5:* 141
Yonge, Charlotte Mary, *17:* 272
York, Carol Beach, *6:* 221
Young, Bob. *See* Young, Robert W., *3:* 269
Young, Clarence [Collective pseudonym], *1:* 231
Young, Ed, *10:* 205
Young, Edward. *See* Reinfeld, Fred, *3:* 170
Young, Jan. *See* Young, Janet Randall, *3:* 268
Young, Janet Randall, *3:* 268
Young, Margaret B(uckner), *2:* 275
Young, Miriam, *7:* 208
Young, (Rodney Lee) Patrick (Jr.), *22:* 251
Young, Robert W., *3:* 269
Young, Scott A(lexander), *5:* 204

Zalben, Jane Breskin, *7:* 211
Zallinger, Jean (Day), *14:* 272
Zappler, Lisbeth, *10:* 206
Zellan, Audrey Penn, *22:* 252
Zemach, Harve, *3:* 270
Zemach, Margot, *21:* 209
Ziemienski, Dennis, *10:* 206
Zillah. *See* Macdonald, Zillah K., *11:* 167
Zim, Herbert S(pencer), *1:* 231
Zimmerman, Naoma, *10:* 207
Zindel, Paul, *16:* 283
Ziner, (Florence) Feenie, *5:* 204
Zion, (Eu)Gene, *18:* 305
Zolotow, Charlotte S., *1:* 233
Zonia, Dhimitri, *20:* 233
Zurhorst, Charles (Stewart, Jr.), *12:* 240
Zweifel, Frances, *14:* 273